A TIME TO BUILD

A TIME TO

BUILD

Michael Novak

THE MACMILLAN COMPANY, NEW YORK

230
N935

ACKNOWLEDGMENTS

The author wishes to thank the following for permission to reproduce copy-righted material: *Daedalus* for "Christianity: Renewed or Slowly Abandoned?" (Winter 1967), copyright © 1966 by the American Academy of Arts and Sciences; *Christianity and Crisis* for "The Christian and the Atheist" (March 21, 1966) Copyright © 1966 by Christianity and Crisis, Inc.; *Ararat* for "The Odd Logic of Theism and Non-theism" (1967), copyright © 1967 by the Armenian General Benevolent Union of America, Inc.; *Continuum* for "Lonergan's Starting Place: The Performance of Asking Questions," copyright © 1964 by Frederick E. Crowe, S.J.; *The Critic* for "An American in Rome" (Dec. 1964-Jan. 1965) and for "Dietrich Bonhoeffer" (June 1967), copyright © 1964 and 1967 by The Thomas More Association; *The National Catholic Reporter* for "Reasons for Chastity" Dec. 16, 1964), "New Morality and Total War" (September 1, 1965), "Our Terrorism, Our Brutality" (August 18, 1965), "Niebuhr on Man and Society: Equanimity After Polemics" (Feb. 23, 1966), "Novak Calls War Immoral" (Jan. 4, 1967), "From Romanità to Catholicity" (Sept. 11, 1964); *Commentary* for "American Catholicism After the Council" (August 1965) and for "Paulus Tillich: In Memoriam" (April 1967) copyright © 1965 and 1967 by the American Jewish Committee; *Concilium* for "Diversity of Structures and Freedom Within Structures of the Church," copyright © 1965 by Paulist

Fathers, Inc. and Stichting Concilium; *Commonweal* "The Timidity Crisis," (Sept. 24, 1965), for "Schleiermacher on Christ and Religion" (April 2, 1965), and "The Absolute Future" (Jan. 13, 1967); *Marriage Magazine* for "Adult Obedience" (1967); *The Christian Century* for "The Ecclesiology of Birth Control" (April, 14, 1965), "Where is Theology Going?" (Nov. 3, 1965), and "The Case for Catholic Humility" (Nov. 17, 1965), copyright © 1965 by Christian Century Foundation; *Philosophy and Phenomenological Research* for "A Key to Aristotle's 'Substance'" (Sept. 1963); John Knox Press for "The Free Churches and the Roman Church" from *Voluntary Associations,* ed. by D. B. Robertson, © M. E. Bratcher 1966; *Perspectives* for "Facing the Protestant Reality" (Oct.–Nov. 1959); *Religious Education* for "Religion and Revolution" (March–April 1966); *Journal of Ecumenical Studies* for "The Free Churches and the Roman Church" (Summer 1965), "Authority in Ecumenical Perspective" (Summer 1966), "The Philosophical Roots of Religious Unity" (Winter 1966), and "The Traditional Pragmatism" (1967), copyright © 1965, 1966, 1967 by Duquesne University; Duquesne University Press for "Moral Society and Immoral Man" from *Church-State Relations in Ecumenical Perspective,* ed. by Elwyn A. Smith, copyright © 1966 Duquesne University; New American Library for "Toward a Positive Sexual Morality" from *What Modern Catholics Think About Birth Control,* ed. by William Birmingham, copyright © 1964 New American Library; the *Saturday Evening Post* for "The New Nuns" (July 30, 1966) copyright © 1966 The Curtis Publishing Company; *Book Week/World Journal Tribune* for some paragraphs from "Bonhoeffer's Way," (Feb. 19, 1967).

The author would also like to express his gratitude to Miss Sandra Grady for her secretarial assistance, and Miss Kathy McHale for her assistance in reading the proofs.

FOR RICHARD

(who, at thirteen months, threatened more than once

the safety of this manuscript)

and his time

Contents

A Prefatory Note   xiii

Introduction: Kairos   1

PART ONE:
CHRISTIANITY RENEWED OR SLOWLY ABANDONED? 15

ONE: Christianity: Renewed or Slowly Abandoned?   17
    I. Something is Dead   19
    II. The Inadequacy of American Christianity   27
    III. The Required Transformation and Its
        Risks   31
    IV. Beginning the Task   34
    V. The Relationship of Christian Faith
        to Atheism   37
    VI. A Renewed Creativity   45

TWO: The Christian and the Atheist   51

THREE: The Odd Logic of Theism and Nontheism   60

FOUR: The Nonbeliever and the New Liturgical   70
    Movement

FIVE: Lonergan's Starting Place: The Performance
    of Asking Questions   79

I. Pragmatism and Ordinary Language   81
II. Lonergan's Starting Place   85
III. Concluding Remarks   93

PART TWO:
BEYOND CHILDHOOD: BEYOND ADOLESCENCE   97

SIX: Romanità Has Seen Its Lovely Days   99
I. A Reporter's Journal   102
II. From Romanità to Catholicity   105

SEVEN: American Catholicism After the Council   112

EIGHT: Diversity of Structures and Freedom Within
Structures   134
I. Diversity of Structures and Freedom Within
Structures in the Church   135
II. Domani   143

NINE: Adult Obedience   148
I. Think Concretely   149
II. The Ecclesiology of Birth Control   152
III. Adult Obedience   155
IV. A New View of Infallibility   159

TEN: The Substance of Transubstantiation   165

PART THREE:
DIVERSELY ONE   189

ELEVEN: The Free Churches and the Roman Church   191
I. A New Judgment Required   193
II. The Anabaptist Idea of the Church   197
III. Anabaptism and the World   204
IV. The Free Churches and Roman Catholicism 208

TWELVE: Beginning the Encounter   215
I. The Religion After The "Post-Religious"
Age   217

II. Facing The Protestant Reality 220
III. The Most Influential Voice 229
THIRTEEN: Paulus Tillich: In Memoriam 232
I. Tillich and Empiricism 237
II. Where Does Tillich Begin? 247
III. Paul Tillich and the Future 255

FOURTEEN: Dietrich Bonhoeffer 266

FIFTEEN: The Emergence of Hope 285
I. Where is Theology Going? 288
II. Religion and Revolution 291
III. The God Who Will Be 294

SIXTEEN: The Philosophical Roots of Religious Unity 301
I. The Experience of Intentionality 302
II. One Drive, Two Phases 307
III. The Source of Objectivity 309
IV. Autonomy and Community 313
V. Ecumenism 315

PART FOUR:
AN ETHIC FOR A NEW AGE 321

SEVENTEEN: The Traditional Pragmatism 323
I. The State of Current Scholarship 328
II. The Aristotelian Revolution 331
III. Aquinas on Charity 335
IV. Conclusion 343

EIGHTEEN: Moral Society and Immoral Man 354
I. The Meaning of Love 356
II. Where is Love Learned? 357
III. The Role of Society in Morals 360
IV. The Open Society and the Open Church 363
V. Conclusion 368

NINETEEN: Reasons for Chastity 373

TWENTY: Toward a Positive Sexual Morality 382

TWENTY-ONE: Our Terrorism, Our Brutality   403
            I. The Abstractions of National Interest   405
            II. Three Levels of Interpretation   412
            III. The Plague is in Us, Too   423
            IV. Conclusion   427

TWENTY-TWO: The New Nuns   429
            Index   479

A Prefatory Note

A SERIES of objections can be raised against any new collection of essays. There are already too many books published every day. A collection is a nonbook; it does not advance consecutive dialectic, but is strung together like beads upon an inexpensive string. Moreover, some of the essays in almost any collection do not deserve to live; few things that have been written do.

I have read enough book reviews not to entertain false hopes for the present collection. Let it be said from the outset that the collection is my idea, and that I have put together pieces that I like. There are things I wish to say to an audience that only a book reaches, and there are things I would like to have at hand in one place. Moreover, as one whose chosen and almost daily exercised form is the essay, I do not think that to write a book is *ipso facto* to perform more artistically than to labor at essays and to collect one's fruits. Again, as one whose scholarly interests move upon a broad front, and who delights in the exercise of many different varieties of prose, I know of no other forum except a collection for allowing my concerns to clash, hoping that one investigation may illuminate another. Finally, since the task to which the present generation seems called is that of imagining a new civilization in its full range of possibilities, the weaknesses inherent in moving upon a broad front seem to me a danger that must be braved.

Stanford, California
January, 1967   MICHAEL NOVAK

A TIME TO BUILD

Introduction: Kairos

I

THIS book is a collection of essays. It is also an argument. It takes for granted that the images and values by which men once coped with their experience have been shattered. Great numbers of men are without roots, without sure purposes, without the cultural support of the past. This book assumes that the situation of the restless, rootless ones is to be emulated, not avoided; theirs is the authentic situation in our culture.

The argument is that it is not enough to be restless and rootless. Hard work is required, the hard work of seeking, defining, and establishing what are authentic human values in our time. What is a man? How ought he to live? What may he hope for? We are not, now, certain of these things.

We do not know, for example, as Camus showed, when, and under what circumstances, murder is forbidden. Each free and responsible citizen of the interlocking viper's nest of our civilization is guilty of the bloodshed carried out in his name through revolutions, brushfire wars, and unnecessary famines.* Moreover, the pressure of modern communications and the terror of urban life require us to help more speedily than ever before the lonely ones, the psychotic ones, like Lee Oswald, Perry Smith, Dick Hickock, Richard Speck,

---

* Paul Hanly Furfey, *The Respectable Murderers* (Herder and Herder, New York, 1966).

1

Charles Whitman. When such men appear in our peaceful neighborhoods, do their actions tell us that poisons are suffusing American life? Do they reveal a plague that has also infected nuns, lawyers, housewives, engineers, waitresses, and students? Are we all guilty of increasing domestic and international violence? Perhaps civilization without murder is impossible. Hitler argued that democracies kill the poor and the sick slowly; he would be direct and kill them quickly. Perhaps there must always be a lowest class, subject to thinking meanly of themselves and, finally, to self-destruction. Perhaps the peace of civilization is built, necessarily, on countervailing violence. Hegel's phrase, that history is a butcher's bench, seems descriptive of our time.

But, if so, we need to redefine our explicit moral values. For we do not *say* that, in certain circumstances, we approve of murder—if it is far away in Asia, for example. We speak of our peaceful aims, never of our murderous means, of democracy not napalm. But is it in a general sense murder to enjoy outdoor barbecues while other human beings, even in our own country, do not eat? Is it murder in another sense to kill a man's pride by not renting him a house, because his ancestors were African and slaves? Is it murder—although perhaps necessary murder—to pay taxes for CIA agents and international intrigue? We no longer know what to count as murder, though we commit violence through our agents every day and try not to think of what we do.

The discovery of basic human values is the only achievement that can redeem the turmoil and the bloodshed of our century. We do not have solid values. The old values, traditions, and conventions permitted too much evil—permitted an intolerable weight of evil which can no longer be endured. Those who speak for law and order no longer always speak for genuine morality. Not so long ago, there was nothing one could do about starvation and disease in Africa, Latin America, Asia—or in the United States for that matter. In those days law and order protected whatever enclaves of safety were possible. But it is sometimes criminal, now, to insist on law and order which defend the old law and the old order—which defend the white Christian in particular. The moral struggle is no longer a class struggle. It is, perhaps accidentally, a racial struggle, a struggle between the favored few and the once desperate, now barely hopeful, majority.

There is a sudden choking thirst for hope among those who have been wandering for centuries in the deserts of poverty.

The argument of this book, in short, is that hard work must be begun, the hard work of discovering which are genuine and which are spurious human values among those we inherit. It is not enough to shout that God is dead, or that the urban style now succeeds the style of the town. Description is not enough. The time for construction is already overdue. One man alone cannot hope to succeed; only that a line or two thrown out into the dark might catch and hold, until stronger are made ready.

II

A time to build: we have a civilization to build. A time to build: *now* is the time to build. A time to build: the point of life is that it is a time to build. Man is a creator and it is his responsibility to fill and possess the earth. He has accomplished that first responsibility; the earth is or soon will be filled. But to possess the earth—to possess it in freedom, truth, justice, and love—that further task has yet to be accomplished. We seem to stand on the threshold of a new era of civilization. We have come out from a dark tunnel—the light, as Camus saw, is up ahead:

We are at the extremity now. At the end of this tunnel of darkness, however, there is inevitably a light, which we already divine and for which we have only to fight to insure its coming. All of us, among the ruins, are preparing a renaissance beyond the limits of nihilism. But few of us know it.*

There is "inevitably" a light, as both atheists and theists recognize. Human life on earth is in many ways *as if* there were a God. There is something about ourselves and about our experience of life which convinces us, despite onrushes of doubt, that we have had to fight, have but to take up responsibility, in order to step forward. Whether our science gives us grounds or not, men believe in the directedness of evolution; they believe in the possibility—more, in the fact—of human progress. They do not believe, if they are wise, in the in-

* *The Rebel* (Vintage Books, New York, 1953), p. 305.

evitability of progress apart from human care and effort; evolution is not to be written with a capital "E." For in our lifetime we have seen Hitler, though we have not yet been able to face, let alone to digest, the outrage and the terror he inflicted upon twenty million victims. Barbarism is our secret name, and as airplanes of the United States drop flaming, sticky napalm upon concentrations of human beings we dare not let ourselves forget that name. Yet though we daily flirt with barbarism, each worshiping his own local God, we continue to rise in the morning, continue to study and to plan, continue to labor, continue to hope. Hope is the fact on which the coming civilization is built. Hope is the excellence that unites theist and atheist. Hope is the one bond among contemporary men.

The world we desire is one in which wolf lies down with lamb. The Russian poet Yevtushenko expresses it, as well as the diaries of the American marine and the North Vietnamese soldier who are seeking one another out for destruction. Hope is the saddest virtue, for where it unites there also it encounters division. A better world—free, truthful, just, brotherly—but where? according to whose idea? under what system?

A time to create: an open civilization to imagine and to labor for. There must be, one day, an alliance between cultures describing themselves as "capitalist" and as "communist," for there is increasingly only one world and there must one day be one culture. Such a culture must be rich in diversity, not homogeneous. It must be open to alternatives and possibilities, not closed. It must be a culture of many philosophies, many theologies, many varieties of economic and political theory and practice. There is no need for all human beings to be the same. The chief vice of historical peoples is to wish to make all others what they themselves are, to forge themselves into the procrustean bed of civilization. By contrast, the genuine avant-garde of humanity is composed of those—they seem to be so few—who are men of dialogue. Conversation is the chief good of civilized human society. In conversation, each partner is what he is, although he takes the risk of being influenced by the other; conversation is a dangerous life. Truthfulness, respect, difference, a capacity to listen—these are the modes by which human dignity expresses itself. Short of them, there is no dignity.

A time to create: it is too easy to criticize and to lament, too facile to destroy. Nihilism is infantile. To enter into nihilism and to earn one's way out of it is the task to which civilization calls us. The values, beliefs, and traditions of the past no longer support us automatically; we must test them anew, select and purify them, and in many cases supplant them. It is wearying to hear, over and over, about the crisis of our civilization, about anxiety, about the collapse of authority, about the loss of faith. Where are those imagining the future, and ready to work today? "Real generosity toward the future," Camus saw, "lies in giving all to the present." * Philosophers tell us that now is not the time for grandiose schemes but for soundings. But soundings are easy; it is sustained thinking that is difficult. Forays left and forays right are, after all, a simple matter for a man of middling intelligence; to some matters everyone has given a little thought. But where there is no vision, the people perish; we are in desperate danger of perishing.

Our age is one of transition, from familiar cultural forms to a culture whose shape is not yet clear. The state of transition accounts for the fact that some persons do not notice anything amiss, and others seem to know only the language of crisis and loss. The first are nourished by the old forms; the second are suspended between the old and the new, unable to retreat to the old, unable to imagine and to advance toward the new. A great number of sensitive persons are ground between the stones of advancing history. In a more stable culture, they might have endured or even thrived; today, desire is crushed from them.

What will happen to Christianity in this vast transition? It is not impertinent to reply: Who cares! Christianity was made for man, not man for Christianity. It is important that man survive—that freedom, truth, justice, and love advance. If these advance, then Christianity will in some fashion advance. For it is useful to have popes, bishops, priests, church buildings, and all the rest; but such things may perish and Christianity yet survive. The priority of values in Christianity must be re-established. What is indispensable is that the civilization announced by Jesus remain our goal, and that participation in his life—through secular, effective love for one another—continue among men. The rest falls into the category of means, and under the judgment of a severe pragmatic test: Does it help?

"In the beginning," St. John tells us, "was the Word. And the Word was with God . . . and in Him were made all things that were

* *Ibid.*, p. 304.

made." (Jn: 1.1) The Christian tradition has identified this Logos
with the historical Jesus. Jesus was the pattern through whom and
by whom and with whom all things were made. We have, then, two
sources of knowledge about Jesus: the historical Jesus, and the things
that were made. All places, persons, and events in history have been
made through him. One does not have to be a Christian, then, in
order to obtain insight into the genuine source and meaning of human
life. Even when he is not named, Jesus is present in every historical
and cultural movement. He is known by Marxists and Buddhists,
Hindus and Mohammedans: he is known in the value men place
upon understanding and upon loving, and in the trust which men
repose in life. For what do Christians *mean* by Jesus as Logos but
the principle of life, love, and truth? Nothing in history escapes the
force of this principle, this Pantokrator. Even torture, death, and destruction are not unexpected. When God revealed himself in the historical Jesus Christ, he spoke a word which did not promise life, love,
or truth except through suffering and death. The symbol for Jesus is
a surd, a cross, a sign of the irrational, in which nevertheless hope is
found.

I do not mean to reduce Jesus to a syncretic gnosis. On the contrary, the revelation of God in the historical Jesus Christ is a privileged revelation, clearer, sharper, more complete than in any other
place. In Jesus, historical forces were launched that have brought us
to the present. In Jesus, the hidden God has spoken in history more
clearly than anywhere else. But the Christ is not his only revelation.
"To some he spoke through Moses and the prophets; to others,
through the things that were made." St. Paul writes:

For it is not the hearers of the law who are righteous before God, but the
doers of the law who will be justified. When Gentiles who have not the
law do by nature what the law requires, they are a law to themselves,
even though they do not have the law. They show that what the law
requires is written on their hearts, while their conscience also bears witness and their conflicting thoughts accuse or perhaps excuse them on that
day when, according to my gospel, God judges the secrets of men by
Jesus Christ. (Rom. 2:13-16)

In Jesus, as we are told by means of the metaphor "son," God
has sent his only son. Is Jesus God? Hans Küng has noted that perhaps the best metaphor for expressing their relationship may be

borrowed from modern astronomy. Is the star which we see today the same as the one whose light left its point of origin billions of light years ago? God reveals himself in Jesus. He is the true light.

But men who are not Christians are not ignorant about the values of living, understanding, and loving. For so many generations men have tried to distinguish themselves from one another, as if to assert their own advantages and the disadvantages of others, that they have grown unaccustomed—sometimes even unable—to see how much the same they are in spirit. Among Christians, it was as if grace were not everywhere, as if all of creation had not been redeemed. Among enlightened nonbelievers, it was as if intelligence and love were to be found only among the enlightened. But it is difficult enough to be faithful for a lifetime to the demands of living, of understanding, and of loving. No one who has discovered even a little of his own egotism, flights from understanding, resentments, and fears, will be inclined to think that others are less faithful than he. And it is surely not by crying "Lord, Lord," that one enters the kingdom of heaven; one cannot hide behind the grace of Jesus, for there are stringent tests for discerning in whom that grace is at work. "How can you love the God whom you do not see, if you do not love your neighbor whom you do see?" (1 Jn. 4:20)

Christianity has changed often in the past. It is undergoing a cultural change again. The point is that no one yet knows what Christianity is, only what it has been in the hands, mainly, of the white people of Europe and America over the past thirty generations. But *all* things are made in his image; Jesus is further to be revealed in future history. What will Christianity be like, mediated through the consciousness of a technical, secular, international culture? What will it be like, mediated through the consciousness of Asia and Africa? We do not yet know. There is a Christianity still to be built.

III

The present problems of Judaism and Christianity are worth the pain and sweat expended on their solution, because Judaism and Christianity are in some sense of the word true: they tell us more about man's nature and his destiny than any alternative view, and they are open-ended. Both Judaism and Christianity have a memory;

they keep us in contact with the bloodshed and the elation, the long sorrows and the struggles, of our predecessors. On the other hand, both Judaism and Christianity look for a new age to come, both are oriented toward the future, and both insist upon man's responsibility to, and need to learn from, the present. In the wisdom of both Judaism and Christianity, God counts man's historical, secular actions as precious; God cares about what men do in history. In brief, both Judaism and Christianity are capable of changing with the needs of history, since they recognize the same Lord speaking in the covenant and in daily history. Moreover, for centuries, both Judaism and Christianity have been able to tell their stories of compassion, quest, honesty, and covenant; in our culture no better way of instructing the young in key human values has been found, no way richer in the truth of symbol, myth, and imagery.

Nevertheless, the main problem of Jews and Christians is not a religious problem; it is the problem of making the world more human. The chief problems of our time are those of hunger, national aspiration, and racial mistrust; consequently our wars are frequent, bitter, and difficult to resolve. In America, these problems take one concrete form: how to awaken the white middle classes to reality. For college students, this problem is acute. Even if not all these students come from middle-class homes, still, economic, social, and political power in our society resides in the middle class. It does little good for protest marchers in Berkeley to demonstrate on Telegraph Avenue where a majority already accepts their point; the task of the middle-class student lies in the middle-class suburbs. The universities ill prepare students for this task.

The best universities teach students to be critical of the complacency of middle-class America; but, after graduation, the young are swallowed by that complacency. Where else will they work, teach, or live except in middle-class surroundings? In every city of this land there are young couples of taste, sensitivity, seriousness, and discrimination who are overwhelmed with isolation and loneliness, far removed from the books, theater, and discussions that made their college days critical and creative. Now they are condemned to that meaningless ritual of kaffee klatches, office parties, and outdoor barbecues which characterize suburban neighborliness. They have had to learn to sheathe their intellects, to hide their cynicisms and enthusiasms, and perhaps even to pretend that they don't read books, lest they embarrass their associates. Good manners stifle dissent in the living room; loyalty to the mother organization stifles it at the office; pro football stifles it on the commuter train.

And the lesser universities? They are finishing schools for middle-class life. They are founded in, by, and for middle-class values. They are supervised by, censured by, and subordinated to middle-class directors and trustees. Young people go to such universities—are sent to such universities—in order to get ahead, to meet the right people, to make useful contacts, to open up a road to a prosperous future in the suburb of their choice. No criticism, no prophetic judgment, not even a Beatle haircut, ripples the huge vat of complacency into which they are thrown, mollified, and slowly stirred. Apathetic is not the apt word: homogenized is better.

Thirty years ago, the parents of many college-age Americans went to college. It was possible, then, to carry a "gentlemanly C," to work one's way through night school, to climb the ladder of social prestige painfully, to sow one's wild oats, and even to experience a taste of rebellion against parents and home. But thirty years ago there was a depression, and then there was a war. Life was hard, and there was not much room for dissent. (Biographies like Eric Sevareid's *Not So Wild a Dream* indicate that some students in the 1930's experienced a ferment like that of the present.) The American success story was still being written. Consequently, we experience today the frightfulness of the annual alumni reunions, when once critical and creative students return as bankers, lawyers, rising young corporation men, doctors, real estate brokers and merchants. They drive station wagons, wear beanies, and now claim to understand what's real and what isn't. "What the hell happened to this university since we left?"

On parents' day, one gains the distinct impression that the new students are more mature than their parents—more open, more sure of who they are, more flexible and yet more committed to their values; more international in outlook, less confined to the biases of their class, and also more articulate. Their parents give the impression of having been so busy they never had the chance to think out what they might like to become. They took whatever path lay open; they postponed "the better things" until later and now it is too late. Nowhere is nihilism more clearly manifested than in the middle-aged people of America. Cold fear marks them. They experience a world they never were prepared to face, a world they did not make and do not understand.

The story may best be told through a concrete profile. The banker who inherited his father's bank in what was once a small town, his future secure, is now threatened by rapid urban growth, by the influx of national banks, and the techniques of modern bright young competitors. He hardly recognizes the city of his birth. His father's great house is now part of a slum. The government over a period of thirty years has changed the rules of wealth, income, taxes—ever more changes, nothing stable. The places that dominate the headlines are places he never studied about in school; the same Saigon whose misfortunes brought about a twenty-five percent decline in his investments in 1966 might have been, so far as he knew in 1956, in Siam. He is awed by computers and men who walk in outer space; he doesn't understand the principles of jet propulsion, or the new math. In school, he never read the books his children read; he is shocked by the theater they enjoy. The long hair worn by his son offends every sensibility he has patiently acquired; the music the boy listens to brings the new barbarity that seems to engulf his world within the precincts of his sacred home. A quiet fury whose source he does not recognize sometimes leaps to his lips. He constantly adds up his net worth in money and real estate and thinks his family will one day be grateful he left it to them—his evanescent mark upon the world. He is a stranger, acquainted with meaninglessness, yet obliged by his upbringing to insist that he is happy and that things are looking up. In company, he always wears a smile.

His youngest boy, a senior at the best university in the area, has declared himself, though an atheist, a conscientious objector; the son has announced that he will go to jail rather than serve. Neither of his older brothers, who graduated from the same school eight and five years ago respectively, were like that; the elder served, with distinction, in Korea. The middle son is a churchgoer and insurance broker, an upstanding citizen with his eye on an eventual political career. Whence, then (his father asks), came this ill-clad atheist and coward, this *jailbird?* And the boy is happy! Decisiveness is plain in his eyes—*bullheaded, stubborn, his mind completely "twisted."*

Yes, the young man is decisive. He has faced a moral test of great proportions. He anticipated his father's rejection and lack of understanding. He expects no better of his draft board—men like his father. But he will not serve in a war he thinks immoral; he will not kill.

What will have happened to America when this youngest son is forty-five, a young man whose future opened with so brave and desolate a choice? Have we produced something new? Have we reared at last, in the children of affluence and the children with a thousand open opportunities in front of them, men with a taste for profound moral development? They are perhaps the first who, having bread, are free to take for certain that they cannot live by bread alone.

I V

There are two values cherished by the young: identity and community. If the ancient myth, the myth even of their fathers and older brothers, was to find a niche in the world, the myth by which the young live is to find themselves. Who am I? Where do I wish to go? The pressures of success do not weigh heavily upon them; success, as their fathers and their older brothers construe it, seems too easy. Lockheed, IBM, and Raytheon bid for their services; even as college professors they face a seller's market. To succeed, they have only to drift, to work within their present capabilities. Man was not made to keep machines running, or even to speed up the pace of the machines. Technological progress has come so far that the question no longer is: Can we do it? The human challenge is: Ought we to do it? Technologically, we can destroy the entire globe; we are able now—or soon will be—to do a great many fearful things. Should we? Who do we think we are, and what do we wish to become?

There are, we have painfully learned, no absolutes. The young have correctly discovered that every law is a law from a standpoint, for a given purpose, assuming a certain view of the world. But the world is ever calling earlier views into question; purposes are manifold; and standpoints are many. In the search for moral authenticity, the young are thrown back upon themselves. Thus they are unafraid of sexual experimentation, of drugs, of raising difficult and painful questions about themselves, of departing for all continents and every danger spot. To be authentic in our era is to recognize that every valid virtue arises out of human experience and has a limited scope.

To be authentic is to have appropriated the profound truth of relativity. Validity is relative to a standpoint.

But to be morally objective in our age is to be open to a community of standpoints; it is to recognize, in the phrase of John S.
Dunne, the relativity of relativity. Inquiry does not end when one
discovers that standpoints are relative. It is necessary to ask further
in each case: Which standpoint is most adequate for the matter at
hand? In a community in which there is free and open participation,
one may hope that one's own mistakes and biases will be challenged;
one may hope to grow; and one may hope to become more supple
and effective in dealing with things as they are. No one is born
objective, nor does objectivity come wrapped in silver on a platter
marked "Thomism," "Marxism," or "Scientific Humanism." All
standpoints are relative. But even this conviction is relative, and hence
one must play standpoint against standpoint in the hope that the richness and variety of human experience will faithfully be served and
none of it neglected.

Consequently, the search for personal identity speedily becomes
the search for community. Like all quests, this one, too, can de-
generate into the search for a like-minded circle, a flight into premature closure. But at its heart the search for community is a search,
formally, for greater openness and, materially, for more accurate
responsiveness to the real world as it is. Community is the bearer of
the sense of reality; alone, the human being loses his bearings. Even
the hermit must stand in the presence of the saints and employ the
writings of the sages. But only that community bears reality which
encourages dissent. Without the practice of dissent the people perish.
For the real world changes, and unless the common wisdom is challenged to change with it, reality passes the community by and disaster
overtakes it.

Community exists to foster free and independent persons. Free
and independent persons exist to create community. We have here a
paradox, a beneficent circle, whose deterioration is also circular. If
community fails, individual persons suffer distortion; if individual
persons fail, the community becomes distorted. The bell tolls for each
and tolls for all.

Identity and community: the young are not far from the secrets
of the highest wisdom our civilization has attained. If they persevere,
they will create a civilization fairer than that of Camelot, fairer than

the America of the past. Identity and community: better pillars for a new world are scarcely to be found.

V

It is, moreover, the vision of this new world to come which demands our attention. There has been too much energy expended destroying, criticizing, jabbing the illusions of the past. The young are tired of eight studies of hate to two of love; nine monographs on perversion, only one on achievement; seventeen books on pathology to one on creativity. Enough has been said about the decline of the West. Now is the time for visions of a world civilization. Now is the time for imagination, hope, and creativity.

Christianity need not suffer in the new age of hope. For already a new Christianity is taking shape outside of, and alongside of, and partly within the old Christianity. Groups of persons meet to discover and to invent their own identity and to create community with one another. When they meet, in a seminar room or in a living room, they take food and drink together—impossible to celebrate community without eating and drinking together. It may be coffee instead of wine, cookies instead of unleavened bread. But it is a eucharist of joy, of gratitude, of hope, of pilgrimage. Perhaps it is not, institutionally, a sacrament; it is, nonetheless, a living symbol. "Stokely," a friend asked of Stokely Carmichael late in the morning hours at such a meeting, "when the world is as you wish it to be, what will it be like?" There was not much silence before the answer came: "Men will love one another."

There is no direct assault upon love, of course, except by the path of justice; and there is no direct assault upon justice except by the acquisition and the exercise of power. The young know that. Perhaps they have yet to learn that there is no human continuity except through institutions, no division of labor freeing each man for himself except through institutions. But, presently, they are so saddened by the ways in which institutions become ends instead of means that it is difficult for them to open themselves to the reality of institutions, and to create institutions in their own beautiful and daring image. Such an effort is yet to come.

In any case, a new church is already taking shape in the universities, in discussion groups, in movements for justice and brotherhood. It has its hymns, its communal liturgy, its shared values, its aspirations, and its essential fidelity to the covenant of God with his people— though God is scarcely mentioned, and is recognized only in the protecting of an open place, a silence, in the heart. Perhaps one day such parachurches will replace the cumbersome, awkward, preposterous churches which at present seem dedicated each to its local patriotism and its local God. They are, in any case, leaven in the loaf. How the transformation will take place, how the continuity of the ancient people of God with his present people will be established, it is neither easy nor proper to foresee. For men who are free are accustomed to labor in darkness. In the darkness, a man is required only to build, not to succeed. It is often others who inherit what an earlier generation hardly dared to imagine. Besides, in the darkness it is the Lord who builds; and, unless he builds, the builders labor in vain.

Part One

❖

CHRISTIANITY:

RENEWED

OR SLOWLY

ABANDONED?

I

Christianity:
Renewed or Slowly Abandoned?

Perhaps this book is addressed more to the "good religious folk" of America than to the rootless and the restless; the latter will take most of what I say for granted. They have already peered into the abyss.

What accounts, then, for the compliance of the churchgoers of the world, who live by the values and traditions of the past? They try to heap up dikes around themselves in modern life. They try to keep the terror out. They do not like to be unhappy; they want movies and books and paintings to be pleasing. The lawyer who deals all day with infidelity, greed, dishonesty, inconsistency, cowardice, does not wish to go home to watch the theater of the absurd on television. Because life is not like that? It is too like that, and the lawyer wishes, for a time, to forget. In the Bible belt, in the towns and suburbs from Bangor to Bakersfield, a myth of decency, love, happiness, and affability is cultivated; the successful American is required by the myth to smile often and repeat aloud that things are looking up. American get-up-and-go has been built on self-deception; the naive good are self-deceivers.

The following essay was commissioned in August 1965 by the American Academy of Arts and Sciences. Over the next ten months it grew through at least eight drafts, and was among the papers criticized in two two-day conferences at the Academy's hilltop mansion in Brookline, Massachusetts. Echoing in some of its sentences are objections voiced in these conferences by other conferees. The intellectual weakness of Christianity and Judaism, manifested through countless attitudes and arguments at the conference, struck me forcibly. What does the Christian have that he can say intelligibly to an academic community of the highest standards? A great deal, my heart felt; but my head could not make strong words come. As the deadline for the final draft neared, I threw away typed page after typed page. Even in the end I was dissatisfied. How can one voice hopes for the future which do not sound like self-deception?

On the day I completed the manuscript, in a New York weightily oppressed by one-hundred-degree heat, I stopped by Fifty-third Street to talk with Norman Podhoretz. "Do you know any clergymen who believe in immortality?" he asked me. "I get the impression listening to them that no one believes it any more. In God, yes. Everybody today believes in God, some kind of God. But I think I hear in the way they speak, read in the way they write, 'I don't believe what I am saying; encourage me!' "

Is ritual belief, inherited belief, easy belief, to be abandoned? What, then, will there be left?

PROFOUND changes have become apparent in the field of religion in the latter half of the twentieth century. This paper attempts to analyze these changes, as they are occurring among younger Americans. The title of a sober pastoral of Emmanuel Cardinal Suhard of Paris, issued at the conclusion of World War II, states rather well the fundamental question: "The Church Today: Growth or Decline?" [1]

The transformation that Christianity, in particular, is now experiencing is unique in its rapidity, profundity, and intensity, although it is not without partial historical analogues. Our task will be to sort out the ambiguities that arise from these changes: Is Christianity slowly exercising its perennial powers of assimilation over yet another culture, or is it dying the death of a thousand qualifications? Our procedure will be to report other statements and interpretations of the present religious situation, and then to offer an analysis of our town.

I. *Something is Dead*

The evidence that a profound ambiguity has stolen into contemporary Christian consciousness is so overwhelming that one hardly knows where to point. Perhaps the testimony of a conservative Anglican divine will be most telling. Professor E. L. Mascall takes as a leitmotif for his book *The Secularization of Christianity* the following quotation:

There is no longer a Christian mind. It is a commonplace that the mind of modern man has been secularized. For instance, it has been deprived of any orientation towards the supernatural. Tragic as this fact is, it would not be so desperately tragic had the Christian mind held out against the secular drift. But unfortunately the Christian mind has succumbed to the secular drift with a degree of weakness and nervelessness unmatched in Christian history. It is difficult to do justice in words to the complete loss of intellectual morale in the twentieth-century Church.[2]

Ever since the appearance in England and the United States of Bishop John A. T. Robinson's *Honest to God*,[3] the literate public has become aware of the themes of "a religionless Christianity," a "secular Christianity," and, finally, a "death-of-God theology." The young German minister, Dietrich Bonhoeffer, who was executed by the Nazis at the age of thirty-nine and whose enigmatic reflections in *Letters and Papers from Prison*[4] largely inspired the present interpretations of what is happening to Christianity, has been featured in *Life* and *Time*. Bonhoeffer, writing within an orthodox, world-despising Lutheran context, discovered in prison that the world had "come of age," that it was in its "adulthood." In order to drive men to their knees, the traditional Christian apologetic sometimes attempted to humiliate them or to point to something "beyond" that they lacked. It must now give way to a "worldly Christianity," an optimistic full-hearted engagement of Christians in secular tasks. Christ, "the man for others," is found in worldly service. Christians should appeal not to a transcendent but to an immanent God, "the Divine in the midst of things." They should live "as if God does not exist," since God as *deux ex machina* is no longer needed by men.[5]

The excitement that such reflections generated among those Protestants who had been trying to live with the Barthian, neo-orthodox,
transcendent God, the "wholly Other," is not difficult to imagine.
The long years of "crisis theology" had begun to weigh too heavily.[6]
Bonhoeffer's optimism regarding the world came as a great release,
especially for younger men [7] too long dominated by the unchallenged
views of Barth, Tillich, Reinhold Niebuhr, and Bultmann. Concomitantly, the entrance of many Christians into the civil rights
movement and into the struggles of the "inner city" seemed to corroborate Bonhoeffer's vision. Christians who were involved in "religion" often had little sympathy for the necessary social and political
reforms. Christians involved in living "for others" dreamed dreams
of a new kind of society in the United States. They felt all too keenly
the "irrelevance" not only of the religious establishment but also
of the religion of the past. The project of working out a new "radical
theology," without reference to the traditional transcendent God of
Christianity, seemed quite plausible precisely to some who were most
motivated by Christian impulses to "love their neighbor."

A classic story in the literature of our culture, told over and over
again in the works of such writers as Dreiser, Farrell, Anderson,
Roth, Updike, concerns an odyssey from a religious upbringing to
"enlightenment." Observers who do not believe in God scarcely share
the excitement of Christians regarding the new age of religionless
Christianity. Miss Marghanita Laski wrote: "Religionless Christianity, though often profoundly exciting to those who have hitherto
taken an organized church for granted, seems to the unbeliever a
natural response to the often noted fact that the vitality of impulses
atrophy as they become institutionalized." She was not impressed by
the attempt, as she saw it, to invent "a mishmash of apparently less
controversial religion." [8] Alasdair MacIntyre opened his review of
Honest to God with one memorable sentence, "What is striking about
Dr. Robinson's book is first and foremost that he is an atheist," and
closed it with another, "The creed of the English is that there is no
God and that it is wise to pray to him from time to time." [9] W. W.
Bartley III, himself a former Protestant become enlightened, reviewed
some of the Bonhoeffer literature and wondered whether, had he not
been executed, Bonhoeffer might not later have quite simply "for-
saken Protestant theology." Bartley registered a characteristic Anglo-
American philosophical complaint about the "shallow and woolly

eclectic thinking, as well as the occasional downright incompetence and self-deception" of the earlier giants of American Protestant theology, Paul Tillich and Reinhold Niebuhr. Then he concentrated on Bonhoeffer:

It becomes rather urgent for a person holding a view like Bonhoeffer's— that there is literally no need for Christianity or for God in an adult world—to explain what if anything does distinguish a Christian from others and why, indeed, anyone should in such circumstances remain a Christian. It is precisely at this point that Bonhoeffer, who is rarely profound but usually clear, becomes as vague as any conventional German theologian. The role of the Christian is conceived now as a fundamentally ethical one of total engagement in social and personal life in full collaboration with like-minded liberal secularists.[10]

There is, in these comments by nonbelievers, a little of the *a priori* confidence enunciated some years ago by Sigmund Freud. "I think," Freud calmly addressed an imaginary believer, "you are defending a lost cause." He continued:

Our God *Logos* will fulfill whichever of these wishes nature outside us allows, but he will do it very gradually, only in the unforeseeable future, and for a new generation of men. . . . On the way to this distant goal your religious doctrines will have to be discarded. . . . You know why: in the long run nothing can withstand reason and experience, and the contradiction which religion offers to both is all too palpable. Even purified religious ideas cannot escape this fate, so long as they try to preserve anything of the consolation of religion. No doubt if they confine themselves to a belief in a higher spiritual being, whose qualities are indefinable and whose purposes cannot be discerned, they will be proof against the challenge of science; but then they will also lose their hold on human interest.[11]

Religious thinkers, thus, seem to be impaled on the horns of a dilemma. If they do not come to a more sophisticated understanding of their faith, tutored by reason and experience, they will be bypassed by the religion of *Logos*; if they do come to a more sophisticated understanding, they will lose all interest in religion, or at least their less educated constituency will. In fact, Freud interprets religious interests as the expression of a need for consolation felt among the less educated and the less mature. If this interpretation is correct, religious people cannot learn from reason and experience, religious thought cannot progress beyond infantile or adolescent defenses, and religion as a cultural force is essentially fixed and static. "My illusions," Freud writes, "are not, like religious ones, incapable of correction." [12] It seems to be a necessary tactic for the nonbeliever to think that religion is closed to further development, incorrigible under the pressures of inquiry and experience. A story is current about a distinguished American positivist who, on hearing Paul Tillich deliver a highly intelligent funeral sermon for a mutual colleague, sputtered angrily: "Why, Tillich isn't a Christian at all!"

A second factor, besides their own opposite commitments, makes it difficult for nonbelievers to understand developments in religious life and thought. The inhibitions of the Victorian era, as Gordon Allport relates,[13] have been reversed. In polite public conversation it is no longer embarrassing to speak openly of sex, but it is embarrassing to speak of religion. Academic writers about religion commonly begin with apologies. "Among modern intellectuals—especially in the universities—the subject of religion seems to have gone into hiding. . . . The persistence of religion in the modern world appears as an embarrassment to the scholars of today." [14] Surveying possibilities for inquiry in his own field, a political scientist writes:

Religions appear to be virtually untouched. Certainly no American political scientist has provided a noteworthy analysis of the idea-system (or idea-systems) that characterizes religions in general. Neither has an American political scientist carefully explored the significance for legal government of the belief-system, organizations, and rituals we call Christianity.[15]

It is difficult to see how political scientists can understand political events in Vietnam, or even the different political styles of such American politicians as Goldwater, Johnson, Stevenson, and Kennedy, without a knowledge of the alternative experiences of religion.

The cautious observer, consequently, will not wish to assent too quickly to the proposition that the transformations being undergone by Christianity in our time are all in the direction of capitulation to atheistic or agnostic secularism. Contemporary atheistic secularism, particularly in America, carries so great a weight of Christian conviction that it does not confront a sophisticated Christianity so much with an antithesis as with a sympathetic stimulus. In our society there are real differences between the world view of the agnostic and that of the Christian. These differences must be located with care; conclusions about their practical consequences ought not to be rashly and ideologically assumed.

In the first place, American atheists or agnostics are not often tempted by nihilism. Dostoevsky once wrote that if there is no God, everything is permitted. But nontheistic humanists in the United States do not appear to be less moral, less critical, less concerned with values, than theistic Americans. On the contrary, nontheists in America appear to retain a profound conviction concerning the possibilities of intelligence in history, a fundamental and hopeful orientation toward a better future for men, a marked capacity to accept responsibility and to act, and a profound respect for the human person and his freedom. These are startling values, on the face of it; but we take them so for granted that we do not wonder about them.

Moreover, because the Christian churches, as institutions, have often set their faces against the advance of science, philosophy, and social reconstruction, the extent to which theist and nontheist alike share many basic values has been masked. Men are commonly blind to the presuppositions that motivate them. Their conscious arguments pivot upon too superficial a plane. No doubt the nontheist wishes to carry his reconstruction of the beliefs and motives of our civilization through to the end. "Atheism is a long-range affair," Jean-Paul Sartre writes.[16] But the point to be doubted is that this reconstruction has yet to be completed. "The Middle Ages," wrote Alfred North Whitehead, "formed one long training of the intellect of Western Europe in the sense of order. . . . The habit of definite exact thought was implanted in the European mind by the long dominance of scholastic logic and scholastic divinity."[17] Whitehead spoke then of the "instinctive conviction" of our culture, "the instinctive tone of thought and not a mere creed of words . . . the inexpugnable belief that every detailed occurrence can be correlated with its antecedents . . .—that there is a secret, a secret which can be unveiled." He added:

When we compare this tone of thought in Europe with the attitude of other civilizations when left to themselves, there seems but one source for its origin. It must come from the medieval insistence on the rationality of God, conceived as with the personal energy of Jehovah and with the rationality of a Greek philosopher. Every detail was supervised and ordered: the search into nature could only result in the vindication of the faith in rationality. Remember that I am not talking of the explicit beliefs of a few individuals. What I mean is the impress on the European mind arising from the unquestioned faith of centuries.[18]

Because he is a Catholic, Christopher Dawson's view is often taken with less than neutral credence, but his remark on this point seems sound: "Nowhere is the dynamism of Western religion more strikingly manifested than in the indirect and unconscious influence it has exercised on social and intellectual movements which are avowedly secular." [19] After wryly confessing his belief in "our God *Logos*" and the primacy of intellect, Sigmund Freud observed: "The primacy of the intellect . . . will presumably set itself the same aims as those whose realization you expect from your God . . . namely the love of man and the decrease of suffering." [20] "Take our moral philosophers, for instance," Albert Camus wrote, "so serious, loving their neighbor and all the rest—nothing distinguishes them from Christians, except that they don't preach in churches." [21] Bertrand Russell points out that his own views on individual and secular ethics are "in close harmony with Christian ethics." The impulsion toward creativity and moral exaltation is "the basis of what the Gospels call duty to God." But this impulsion is, of course, "separable from theological belief." [22] One may agree with Russell that human values are, in principle, separable from theological belief. But one may wonder whether the theoretical separation, however estimable, has been carried out in our society even among practicing nontheists. To step outside Christian institutions is not *ipso facto* to step outside Christian values. The virtues that Walter Kaufmann commends in *Faith of a Heretic* are perfectly compatible with various orthodox understandings of Christion faith. From a Christian point of view, they are superior to many poor but popular statements of that faith.[23] The mien does not make the atheist any more than it does the monk.

Nevertheless, it must be granted that the world view of Judaism and Christianity by which the Enlightenment and secular optimism lived, even while nontheists renounced specific religious beliefs and eschewed religious organizations, has altered swiftly during the past generations. The twin shocks of the Nazi barbarism in Europe and of the new technology in the United States have constituted a turning point in the spiritual history of the West. "The central fact of modern history in the West—by which we mean the long period from the end of the Middle Ages to the present," William Barrett writes, "is unquestionably the decline of religion." This decline means:

that religion is no longer the uncontested center and ruler of man's life, and that the Church is no longer the final and unquestioned home and asylum of his being. . . . The waning of religion is a much more concrete and complex fact than a mere change in conscious outlook; it penetrates the deepest strata of man's total psychic life. . . . The loss of the Church was the loss of a whole system of symbols, images, dogmas, and rites which had the psychological validity of immediate experience, and within which hitherto the whole psychic life of Western man had been safely contained. . . . Western man has spent more than five hundred years— half a millennium—in stripping nature of these projections and turning it into a realm of neutral objects which his science may control.[24]

Thrown into the horrors of Nazi occupation, during which torture was a commonplace and death no mere unpleasant accident to be avoided but a daily instructor, many European thinkers came to reject the cosmic world view of the Enlightenment—to reject the inter-mingling of religious and secular assurances by which Europe had long lived. "We were never more free," Jean-Paul Sartre has written,

than during the German occupation. We had lost all our rights, begin-ning with the right to talk. Every day we were insulted to our faces and had to take it in silence. Under one pretext or another, as workers, Jews, or political prisoners, we were deported *en masse*. Everywhere, on bill-boards, in the newspapers, on the screen, we encountered the revolting and insipid picture of ourselves that our suppressors wanted us to accept. And because of all this we were free. Because the Nazi venom seeped into our thoughts, every accurate thought was a conquest . . . exile, cap-tivity, and especially death (which we usually shrink from facing at all in happier days) became for us the habitual objects of our concern. We learned that they were neither inevitable accidents, nor even constant and inevitable dangers, but they must be considered as our lot itself, our destiny, the profound source of our reality as men.[25]

Yet even existentialism seems to be derivative from Christian faith. Sartre's own language is full of re-interpreted Christian symbols, and Christian theologians have speedily absorbed existentialism.

In the United States, as in England, religion appears to be struggling not so much with doubt or unbelief as with irrelevance. Technology, rather than *blitzkrieg* and brutality, seems to call for a new view of human experience. Alasdair MacIntyre writes:

Christianity provided pre-industrial England with a common frame of reference, with a sense of over-all meaning and with a pattern which gave form to life. . . . But industrial society has never been able to accommodate a religious interpretation of its own activities. The founders of atheist humanism hoped for and predicted secularization not merely in the sense of abandonment of religious belief and practice, but in the sense of a transformation of human goals and hopes from other-worldly into this-worldly. The present was to be judged and transcended, not by looking to the justice of heaven but by looking to that of the future. The hope of glory was to be, and in some important measure was, replaced by the hope of Utopia. But we have neither glory nor Utopia to hope for. The hope that a secular Utopian tradition, whether Liberal or Marxist, sought to provide was never realized. The routine of working-class life, the competitive ladders of the middle classes, absorb us into immediacy. We are dominated by a present to which the idea of a radically different future is alien. What conventional politics promises us is always a brighter version of what we have now. . . . In this situation the substance of religious belief is no longer with us, but in our ordinary secular vocabulary we have no language to express common needs, hopes, and fears that go beyond the immediacies of technique and social structure.[26]

Professor MacIntyre does not agree that the secularization of the modern world is "an accomplished and recognized fact." He detects no "sense of triumph in secular writers." Instead he finds among them "the same uneasiness" that he discovers in theologians.

Between the ten per cent or so of clear and convinced Christians at one end of the scale and the ten per cent or so of convinced sceptics at the other, there is the vast mass of the population, most superstitious to some degree, using the churches and especially the Church of England to celebrate birth, marriage and death, and to a lesser degree Christmas. This use or misuse of the churches is rooted in a set of vague, half-formulated and inconsistent beliefs.[27]

The relationship between Christianity and Western culture is, it appears, ambiguous. In order to understand what is transpiring within American Christianity today, we will need a few more specifics and, more than that, a new set of interpretive tools.

II. *The Inadequacy of American Christianity*

"Jesus, I love that car," an American father exclaims on his death bed, in a story by John Updike. Does any symbol touch contemporary Americans so closely as their own cars? The dying man's son reflects later in the closing lines of the story:

Any day now we will trade it in; we are just waiting for the phone to ring. I know how it will be. My father traded in many cars. It happens so cleanly, before you expect it. He would drive off in the old car up the dirt road exactly as usual and when he returned the car would be new, and the old was gone, gone, utterly dissolved back into the mineral world from which it was conjured, dismissed without a blessing, a kiss, a testament, or any ceremony of farewell. We in America need ceremonies is I suppose . . . the point of what I have written.[28]

The American imagination sometimes seems impoverished, governed by machines, the human subject driven out. "We in America have from the beginning been cleaving and baring the earth, attacking, reforming the enormity of nature we were given, which we took to be hostile. We have explored, on behalf of all mankind, this paradox; the more matter is outwardly mastered, the more it overwhelms us in our hearts." [29] The basic experiences of human life in which religious life is renewed—finitude, suffering, evil, compassion, wonder, freedom, joy—are not widely celebrated in our culture. Homogeneity is our mark. We do not so much live as undergo processing. John Updike describes a young hitchhiking sailor:

He had the full body, the frank and fresh blue-eyed face of the docile Titans—guileless, competent, mildly earnest—that we have fattened, an ocean removed from the slimming Latin passions and Nordic anxieties of Europe, on our unprecedented abundance of milk and honey, vitamins and proteins. He had that instinctive optimism of the young animal that in America is the only generatrix of hope we have allowed ourselves; until recently, it seemed enough.[30]

The analytical, technical, verbal mind, moreover, is pre-eminent in the academies and the journals. Everywhere the living sources of religion are rendered arid. Of a rural Pennsylvania church Updike writes: "The nave was dimly lit, the congregation small, the sermon short, and the wind howled a nihilistic counterpoint beyond the black windows blotted with garbled apostles. . . . There was a strong sepia flavor of early Christianity: a minority flock furtively gathered within the hostile enormity of a dying, sobbing empire." [31] All the more is this true in Manhattan: "The churches of the Village had [a] Second Century quality. In Manhattan, Christianity is so feeble its future seems before it. . . . One hastens homeward afterward, head down, hurrying to assume the disguise—sweaters and suntans—of a non-churchgoer." [32] Even in private conversation, the atheist is a threat to the believer:

I feared [the astronomer's] visit. I was twenty-four, and the religious revival within myself was at its height. Earlier that summer, I had discovered Kierkegaard. . . .

[The astronomer] had an air of seeing beyond me, of seeing into the interstellar structure of things, of having transcended, except perhaps in the niggling matter of lust, the clouds of human subjectivity—vaporous hopes supported by immaterial rationalizations. It was his vigorous, clear vision that I feared. . . .

"My Lord, Walter," Bela said, "why are you reading [Plato]? Is this the one where he proves two and two equals four?" And thus quickly, at a mere wink from this atheist, Platonism and all its attendant cathedrals came tumbling down.[33]

The educated believer, aware of the decline of the Judaeo-Christian world view in his own psychic life and in that of the educated public, cannot escape facing the possibility that Christianity has reached the end of the line. He may meet this question by distinguishing between the Judaeo-Christian world view and the actual Christian faith. Is the ancient Judaeo-Christian world view, constituted by confidence in the final rationality of history and in the ultimate importance of individual personality, required for the life of faith? Supposing that the bases of a technical, secular, international culture are significantly different from the bases of the Hebraic-Greek-Roman world in which Christianity took root, can Christianity survive?

The evidence that the end of the line has been reached is impressive. In the United States, the theological content of Christian belief appears to be minimal. The vast majority of American Christians do not seem to be concerned about the problems involved in attempting to straddle two so widely different world views as those of the traditional Judaeo-Christian world and the recent technical world. "An observer of the American church scene of today," writes Wilhelm Pauck, "can hardly fail to note that theology is not in the center of concern among Protestants. In the main the laity of the churches is unconcerned about theological questions, and few ministers appear compelled to orient their work to clear theological principles." Ministers, he goes on, "cannot but be aware of the fact that today Christian truth goes nowhere unchallenged, indeed, that Christianity is actively being opposed by rival 'secular faiths' of scientism, humanism, nationalism, socialism, and even the democratic faith." Moreover, ministers do not appear to be "guided by a theological awareness of the specific nature of Christianity." [34]

Yet precisely here emerges the nub of the question. The rapid strides made in science, communications, and technology since World War II have suddenly made the "specific nature of Christianity" problematic even for theologians. The transplantation of primitive Christianity into the Greek categories of the third and fourth centuries, or the transformation of Platonic Christianity into Aristotelian categories by Aquinas in the thirteenth century, or the upheaval that separated post-Reformation from pre-Reformation Christianity might possibly offer historical parallels for the profound adaptations required of Christianity today. But each of these preceding stages had more in common with one another than any one of them has with the situation today. The elements to be emphasized, moreover, are not only the vast complexity but also the suddenness of the transformation Christianity faces today.

By "Judaeo-Christian world view," I only in part refer to an actual historical view of persons in generations preceding our own, generations which lacked historical consciousness and extensive knowledge of alternatives different from their own. Aquinas, for example, took as obvious the implicit medieval form of life, a form which saw the universe in (as it were) spatial terms: every event, every object, every person had a proper place in a cosmic scheme. Things might be in motion, but there were ascertainable hierarchies of order and place. To identify something was to be able to assign it its proper place in its proper order. Our own life-form today is not this medieval form; that does not mean that our form is better or worse, or that Aquinas believed the medieval form ought to be insisted upon as final and absolute—he merely took it for granted. Thus, I do not wish to saddle Aquinas, or Luther, or any other historical figure with an explicit affirmation of what I say about "the Judaeo-Christian world view," a concept which is in any case too comprehensive and abstract to suggest the variety and differences in the views of actual historical thinkers. But what I do assert is that a form of life has been operative in the past, a set of assumptions or symbols or models which are no longer our own. To be able to become conscious of such a form is, *ipso facto,* to subject it to criticism in the light of other alternatives. Modern science and modern experience have made us conscious in this way. Thus, what characterizes our age is the ability to step back from what seemed earlier to be an intimate part of the structure of human consciousness.

I have tried to avoid giving this life form the pejorative name, "Christendom," with its associations of feudalism, Machiavellian politics, and the alliance of throne and altar. I have called it by an honorable name, the "Judaeo-Christian world view," in order to suggest that even our reformers, even our revolutionaries, even our present civil religion, have taken it for granted. "The core of culture is cult." Christopher Dawson, T. S. Eliot, and other defenders of "Christian culture" have been urging us to try to maintain the core values of the past in the name of our civilization itself. What I am suggesting is that we are on the threshold of a *new* civilization, and that we are witnessing the birth of a *new* form of life. A new set of core values will not spring forth full-blown, like Venus from the sea, but neither will it be serenely continuous with the past. Not all the hard-won gains of the past will be lost, nor will everything new be true or good. At the very least, a transformation of values is in store. We are living through a change in implicit assumptions, in guiding models, in symbols, in values. Such a change does not, *a priori* or necessarily, mean the dissolution of Judaism and Christianity, but it does call for their transformation—perhaps as a butterfly comes from a cocoon. Judaism and Christianity have helped to launch the historical forces which now call for this traumatic transformation. If they are meant for all ages, they have the resources to meet it. If not, they will perish.

III. *The Required Transformation and Its Risks*

To what extent can Christianity be separated from the world view that once so thoroughly dominated Western culture, the world view implicit, for example, in the Declaration of Independence and even in the Preamble and Bill of Rights of the Constitution? Let us suppose that there is no pattern of logical rationality to human history, no Creator who granted "inalienable rights" to individual human beings, no intervening Providence watching over the affairs of men and ultimately making Liberty and Justice prosper. Let us suppose that there is no integrated, interrelated cosmos, in which the individual has a "place," "a station," or even a "stewardship." Let us suppose that the ideal of the "whole man," of the "integrated personality" who is "reconciled to his lot" and "realizes his talents," of the man who receives "a vocation" from God, is not sufficiently open-ended. Let us suppose that human life in a technical world is bound to be fragmented, a little frantic, often impersonal, and scarcely dependent upon "God" for control of storms and rain, famine, illness, and poverty. Let us suppose that, since the strategy of concentrating upon soluble problems proves much more immediately productive, man's sense of mystery should atrophy. Let us further suppose that most human beings define as the measure of their personal value the contribution they can make toward the worldly welfare of this and future generations. Do such suppositions establish a context in which "the specific nature of Christianity" has evaporated? Is a Christianity that accepts such presuppositions unfaithful to itself? Can there be a "secular" Christianity, just as valid as a "Platonic" Christianity, an "Aristotelian" Christianity, or a "Deistic" Christianity?

Such questions have come to exercise Christian theologians in this decade; but they have arisen during a moment of embarrassment. On the one hand, there are countless Christians living quite obliviously and contentedly (and often productively, in their fashion) according to half-understood and contradictory symbols inherited from the past: symbols of a manipulating Providence, a Creator immanent within Evolution, a cosmic Policeman [35] who guarantees the importance of the individual in "the scheme of things." Competitive life in a pragmatic, technical, pluralistic society has, of course, blunted the edge of many Sunday-morning symbols. During weekdays the force of such symbols may not be much in evidence. But, on the other hand, even the educated Christian elite has recently borrowed most of its cherished language from Kierkegaard, from Buber, from Heidegger; from European, and largely Germanic, existentialism and personalism. In the United States, Paul Tillich and Reinhold Niebuhr have been, for an elite, the prime molders of religious language. Tillich has attempted to stand "on the boundary" between classical ontology and continental existentialism, and to mediate these to the more pragmatic, concrete American temper.[36] Reinhold Niebuhr has attempted to return to the mythical language of the ancient Hebrews, the language of "the self and the dramas of history." Neither Tillich nor Niebuhr speaks the spare, technical, secular language of the non-religious intellectual elite in this country. Their tone of voice, their key concepts, and their symbols derive largely from the European context of Schleiermacher, Schelling, Barth, and Bultmann.

So long as America remained a Protestant country, the insularity of Protestant theological life (it goes without saying that American Catholic theological life has been far more insular) could exist without being noticed. But recently American Protestants have been discovering that the American university is dominated philosophically by Anglo-American language analysis and more generally by the pragmatic methods and categories of physical science, the social sciences, and technology. In today's workaday world, moreover, American culture is not rural and Protestant but urban, utilitarian, and secular. In the world of politics, questions of power and pragmatism—often weak points in Protestant thought—loom large, and the captivating style is that of John F. Kennedy. In the field of social reform, the Negro is the moral hero. In the world of letters, music, and painting, and only somewhat less so in the worlds of psychology and sociology, where the *lingua franca* of American intellectual life is now forged, the Jewish community provides far more than its share of leaders. The cultural hegemony of the white Anglo-Saxon Protestant has been shattered; he must now take seriously interpretations of human life other than his own. Thus only now, a century later, is he experiencing Nietzsche's perception that God is dead, only now is he facing the accumulated secularization of daily life in America.

Many of the younger Christian theologians wish to break more decisively than Niebuhr and Tillich have from the thought patterns of the past. Some of them are attempting to speak the language of contemporary secular fiction and drama; [37] others the language of sociology;[38] still others the austere language of Anglo-American language analysis.[39] It is not yet clear whether "the specific nature of Christianity" can be articulated in these special languages. But one reason for this uncertainty is the prior uncertainty concerning what constitutes the "specific nature of Christianity." To what propositions, to what style of life, to what symbols, to what method of resolving issues is a Christian specifically committed? How *in fact* does a Christian differ from an atheist? The cultural transition forced upon Christians by the shape of the emerging technical civilization has posed questions of the most radical, most fundamental sort.

Moreover, the new technological, secular society that is rapidly sweeping the world has its center of maximum intensity in the United States. It is America that one half of the world, at least, now imitates. It is a serious question whether American theologians, renouncing the only theological languages they presently have, German ontology and German existentialism, have the resources to carry through an intellectual transformation of Christianity. The bias of American theology, left to itself, is toward ethics and activism. Whether, for example, American theologians of the past accepted the immanent God of European liberal theology, or the transcendent God of European neo-orthodoxy, the result tended to be the same: social action. Can there be an intellectual transformation of Christianity if Christianity is reduced to an effort at social relevance? Christians would then have nothing to say to one another that nonbelievers could not say to them.

Critics both inside and outside the churches warn about the dangers of attempting to relate Judaism or Christianity too easily to the patterns of thought and predilections of any cultural epoch. Judaism and Christianity are for the ages, not for this epoch merely. No bias is more seductive than the bias of the present, the bias of identification with an avant-garde to whom the future belongs. A young Jewish rabbi recently warned me, as I prepared this article, not to ignore the potential overt conflict between religious and secular values. He wrote: "I think that liberal Catholics are mistaken when they believe that their recent absorption into the intellectual, social, and political establishment removes all sources of tension. Indeed it may, but only at the expense of their religious integrity. This has already been evidenced among the Jews."

H. Stuart Hughes doubts whether the great changes prompted by
the Johannine revolution within Catholicism

can take place within the framework of the Church as it has been traditionally understood. I find the conservatives in the Italian and Spanish
hierarchies not wholly in the wrong when they warn of the perils ahead.
I do not believe that Catholicism will cease to exist. But I think it quite
possible that the post-Johannine Church—at least the Church of the educated—will become so private, so personal, so enmeshed in the vocabulary
and concepts of the secular world as to be almost unrecognizable as the
Catholicism of the past. Whether this will be a loss or a gain is for the
members of the faith alone to decide.[40]

The stakes, then, are high. Few are unaware of the risk involved.
Certain astute observers, in fact, think that some of those engaged
in the *aggiornamento* of Christianity, whether Protestant or Catholic,
are undergoing a fundamental crisis, not of renewal but of belief:
They have lost heart, but disguise this fact from themselves by
frenetic efforts to reform the institutions in which they no longer
feel at home.[41] Again, Christianity is a historical community whose
pilgrimage across the centuries is made through the medium of a
clumsy, inefficient, steadily evolving but indispensable set of institutions. Yet many Christians seem to think of the church as a collection
of individuals who must forever be recalled to a noninstitutional, interior, spiritual renewal. Such critics are apt to be ready to abandon
the traditional symbols and institutions of Christianity in order to
establish new institutions that might preserve their own fervor into
the future. Others seem to accept, without a sense of historical ambiguity, the slogans of "secular" Christianity and the program of social
and political "relevance." They seem to forget that what to one
generation appears to be "relevant" to secular culture may to a later
generation of prophets appear to have been a betrayal of the faith.
They forget that the scars left by the relevance of some past forms
of Christianity have not yet healed.

IV. *Beginning the Task*

The Christian community is, and ought to be, pluralistic. It is not
likely that all Christians will accept any one theory of how the needed
transformation is to be accomplished. The age cries for experimenta-

tion and for diverse initiatives even in contrary directions. The advantage of belonging to such a community is that each member helps to correct the mistakes of the other. Out of the finite insights of many individuals and many churches comes a rounder wisdom than could be achieved by one man or one church alone. The Christian community extends temporally as well as spatially. In the testimony of the past there is leverage against the biases of the present, which are, especially in a culture boasting of rapid change and swift obsolescence, the most compelling of all. The danger of belonging to such a historical community is to fail to meet the new on its own terms, when the hour is ripe. The advantage is to learn to demand evidence concerning an identification of the new with the true, particularly where human values are at stake. In recent Western history, the church seems to have erred most frequently, often grievously, on the side of conservatism.

My quiet conviction is that Christianity is now entering upon one of the most creative periods of its history. Dissatisfaction with the present and a longing for renewal have been generated in the almost universal anguish of two world wars. I believe that Christianity is true; it offers in the round, and in connection with other beliefs from other sources, the most adequate interpretation of human nature and destiny that we have. Certainly many of the themes that it prominently asserts seem as if they are true. Russell, Freud, Camus, and many others borrow from them to some depth. In any case, no argument for Christianity is of serious interest unless such claims to truth are made. Every human group in our time faces the radical transformation of beliefs and values that Christianity faces. As Alasdair MacIntyre has pointed out, few secular men today speak triumphantly. No one holds the keys to human destiny in his hands. We live with large areas of gray and with still larger areas of black. Our brightest light illuminates best only immediate things. Some human beings will prefer the security of clarity, but others are bound to venture into the area of mystery.

At this point Christianity and Judaism become "relevant." Because the world view that supported Christianity for so long has fallen away, the inner life of many Christians is bound to be shaken. We may expect to see larger and larger defections from the churches in the next two or three decades. Sociologists may tell us that more people are going to church than ever before, and even that this churchgoing is part of a more general and authentic search for values in American society.[42] But if some of these churchgoers are seeking a tidy cosmic picture in which they will find their place and learn what is expected of them, Christianity—if it is faithful to itself—will increasingly disappoint them, for Christian theologians are increasingly detaching themselves from the Judaeo-Christian world view of the past. They are prepared to be much more modest in the clarity and sense of structure they claim to attain. They are trying to devise a Christian style for living in the gray and blackness, for employing the pragmatic techniques of the small area of brightness. In the latter task, they are often at one with secular social reformers. In the former task, they keep alive the human sense of mystery, of wonder, of awe, of finitude, of longing, of courage and adventure, that is proper to those who explore the reaches of the human spirit in solitude and in community.

To be sure, there are many persons in our culture whose sense of mystery has atrophied. They are busy men, technical, humane, but practical. The freedom and diversity of a technical civilization offers them many avenues of preoccupation, apart from reflection upon the mysteries of human destiny. But to others such a life seems less than human. Christianity becomes relevant for these people precisely when it draws them into reflection upon who they are and how they relate to one another. Freed from the Judaeo-Christian world view, Christianity does not try to escape the real obscurity of human destiny. Evil men prosper; rain falls on just and unjust alike; God does not coddle those who accept his covenant. The world seems as if the atheist could be right. Hence the psalmist's plea: "Let not my enemies rejoice, O Lord; let me not blush and be confounded." Dachau and Belsen symbolize vividly the power of evil and the silent patience of God, who does not intervene. Life is not a morality play.

But is not appeal to a hidden God only a play on words? How does a completely hidden God differ from no God at all? The Christian believes himself always in the presence of One who understands and wills all the contingencies, even the crippling ones, of human life. For the Christian, events are not flat, mechanical, literal; other persons, events, and things are what they are, but they are also "alive" and symbolic. They are part of a conversation with God. The Christian does not visualize human life as part of a great, stable cosmic picture. He affirms that life, though often as unpredictable and contingent and erratic as a tale told by an idiot, signifies something. But what it signifies is not entirely clear; the mystery is not dispelled. The Christianity of the present has, of necessity, shed the securities promised by the Judaeo-Christian world view of the past. The Christian today knows how profound is the darkness in which he has been left. A greater modesty, a greater sense of contingency and darkness, a greater sense of comradeship with non-Christians do not ill become Christians. What is being abandoned is not Christianity but the cultural world view that was its first matrix, its cocoon, for the first two millennia of its existence.

V. *The Relationship of Christian Faith to Atheism*

The task of re-interpreting basic Christian symbols in the open-ended scientific context of the new era will not be accomplished swiftly. But if the Judaeo-Christian world view is now adjudged inadequate, it was always inadequate. Only our ignorance prevented us from seeing its inadequacies earlier. Assuming that Christian faith is true, not only must its disengagement from the Judaeo-Christian world view be possible, but there must have already been signs of strain in the past. Were not medieval Christians too smug in their Ptolemaic world, thinking themselves the center of the universe? Were not Reformation Christians too dogmatic and too pessimistic? Were not liberal Christians too sanguine, thinking that knowledge is powerful and power innocent? When one looks back at "ages of faith," or "golden eras," one is not always certain that there were then better Christians, only a different style of Christian. It has always been a struggle to be a good Christian; no age mass-produces them. When the Son of Man returns, Jesus asked, will he find one in ten thousand faithful to his Word? Now that the illusions of Judaeo-Christian culture are passing away, Christians will again become accustomed to being a few, a tiny remnant, among the multitudes of men.

In this new context, one pressing inquiry is how the Christian differs from the atheist. No one way of working out this question has found universal acceptance,[43] but public discussion seems, at least, to be identifying the area in which the answer lies. Two basic propositions underlie my own proposal. The first conviction is that man is a question-asking animal; the second is that he is a symbol-making animal. Appeal is not made to a special "religious experience," nor to a personal "encounter with the Transcendent." Rather, each man is asked to reflect upon the experience of human life that he already has. Each man decides for himself who he is, and so works out his own destiny. From this point of view, Christianity is not conceived as "filling a need," in the sense in which food and water fill human needs. Men are obviously able to live, and to live well, apart from Christianity.

Under the tutelage of other world religions, men have been taught in other, but often similar, ways about the mysteries of human life.[44] Among Western atheists and agnostics, important convictions nourished by Christianity have been widely diffused. The historical dynamism of liberalism, confidence in the preciousness of human life, trust in the intelligibility of the contingent and the empirical, compassion, a thirst for justice and equality, an assumption that progress in history, though ambiguous, is possible—such beliefs, even if they are now separable from Christian institutions and symbols, do not contradict, but rather express, the basic imperatives of Christian life.

Two historical tragedies of vast dimensions prevent some observers from reading the relationship of Christianity to contemporary culture in this way. First, Christian institutions and symbols have often been used in opposition to those efforts at philosophical, scientific, and social reconstruction that have built the modern age. Many Christians now wish to say that, far from being normative for the Christianity of the future, the Christianity of the preceding era was defective in its openness and wisdom; it should have joined more thoroughly than it did in the social and intellectual revolutions of the last four centuries. As a Jewish rabbi and philosopher has asked:

Why has the modern Church on the whole been lukewarm, indifferent or downright hostile to liberal drives when it might well have wholeheartedly embraced or spearheaded them? . . . Why has the liberalism of the modern age been allowed to be shot through with a thoroughgoing secularist bias, when it might conceivably have been given a religious and Christian impetus? . . . How could [Christian or Jew] ever have been indifferent, lukewarm, or hostile to the liberal ideal—and this in the name of their faith! . . . when that ideal is the most authentic modern secular expression of their faith? How could they have ever feared the free scientific exploration of the world when, long freed of idolatrous worship of the world, they should have been the first of all scientific explorers? Why afraid of technology, when they were the first to believe that the earth is handed over to human rule? Above all else, how could any Jew or Christian who ever believed in one Father of all men have failed to rally to the modern struggle on behalf of man's common humanity, or have sabotaged secularists who led this struggle? [45]

Secondly, missionaries, exporting to other cultures not only Christianity but the Judaeo-Christian culture as well, stifled a native response and an original testimony. We have thus been deprived of learning what an indigenous Asian or African Christianity would have been like. If Christianity is for all men, we are impoverished by its limitation to Western forms. Why could not other cultures have been as free as the Greeks and the Romans, the Goths and the Huns, to develop their own style of Christian life? [46] We suffer now for the historic power and the arrogance of Western Judaeo-Christian culture.

Nevertheless, it seems sensible to envisage an anthropology, a sociology, a psychology of man that will be flexible enough to relate in one view all the types of human culture, all the varieties of men. One strand of such a hope is the prosaic fact that men ask questions. Men have a capacity to raise ever further questions, to question their own presuppositions, to alter their lines of inquiry and routines of behavior, and to turn in ever new directions. In this capacity is rooted the possibility of human development in history, the variety of human life, and the sense of self-transcendence that arises in human consciousness. This drive to ask questions is of itself unrestricted and unstructured; it is prior to and more fertile than the presuppositions and concrete determination of any particular line of inquiry. It is open-ended, capable of coping with new and unexpected experiences, and able to revise its methods and its conclusions. Some men detect in man's continuing questioning of human existence a sign of the presence of God. Hardly a writer concerned with the search for God does not point to this capacity as the basic evidence for, and guide to the meaning of, a transcendent principle in human experience.

To be sure, this evidence is ambiguous. Some men interpret the evidence in a materialistic sense; others see no signs of God in the drive to understand, to question. Those who believe in God, however, seem both to become aware of his presence and to govern their language about him through the kind of self-transcendence experienced in exercising their drive to understand, their capacity to wonder, and their inability to regard any finite system as adequate to human aspiration. The atheist seems to take the drive to understand as a matter of plain fact; the believer reflects upon it, is led to wonder, and then silently to adore.

Perhaps, however, a generation ago it was easier to take the basic drive to inquire as a matter of plain fact. Many thinkers seemed to assume that there was an obvious and "objective" method of inquiry, which spared them the perils of subjectivity and mystery; there was, for example, scientific method, Freud's "reason and experience" whose symbol was *Logos*. To assume, with Sidney Hook and Bertrand Russell, that "All knowledge that we have is *scientific knowledge*"[47] was to take a short cut to a sense of security and self-esteem. Those who took such a short cut were *tout court* rational and objective. This was due to no merit of their own, but merely a consequence of adopting the scientific method. But in our generation it is not so obvious why one should adopt the scientific method. If the world in which we live is absurd—and by *world* I do not mean some vast metaphysical cosmos, but the immediate crises and issues facing human society, like domestic social reform, environmental control, and political conflict—then it is not obvious that fidelity to scientific method will assuage our ills. On the contrary, if human existence is, in fact, impervious to intelligence, then the attempt to be intelligent may only heighten our peril. Perhaps the examined life is not worth living. Moreover, there is no necessary connection between science and liberalism.

I am not arguing against fidelity to scientific method or against a commitment to the employment of intelligence in human affairs. I am only trying to expose the presuppositions that are prior to such fidelity and such commitment. Even if one does not reflect upon these presuppositions, they are operative in the decision to commit oneself to science and intelligence, for other options—nihilism, irrationality, escape—are available. Thus, a commitment to science and to intelligence requires a justification. It does not merely "happen." The swiftest justification, of course, is that to raise the issue of justification is already to appeal to intelligence. Moreover, in practice, men cannot help justifying their choices. One may choose to live as a sheep; what one cannot do, once that choice is made, is to justify one's choice.

Still, men can, astonishingly enough, successfully employ science and intelligence in understanding and taking responsibility for their environment. What kind of world is this, in which such a situation is true? There is no short cut to an interpretation of human life, by way of an incantation of phrases like "science," "scientific method," and "our God *Logos.*" Even less so is there a short cut by way of the argument that "contemporary philosophers say. . . ." Why should anyone accept, without inquiry into basic presuppositions, what contemporary philosophers happen to think?

In short, it seems apparent to many younger thinkers that atheists and agnostics, particularly those who are committed to scientific method and intelligent analysis, are—from a formal point of view—as much involved in fundamental interpretations, decisions, and commitments as is a man of religious faith. Insofar as science is a method, it is as available to theists as to nontheists. Insofar as it is a way of life, it must justify itself by meeting the tests of human living, just as a religious faith must justify itself.

At this point, the second proposition, that man is a symbol-making animal, enters the discussion. Human actions have not only a pragmatic, literal, immediate meaning. They also reveal the character, self-image, intentions, and purposes of their agents. Men do not act only according to verbal, analytical statements of abstract principle; they also act according to imaginative models, symbols, or styles of human behavior. For some men, it appears, a human being is to be understood as an especially complicated machine; for others, as an instrument in the betterment of the lot of future generations; for still others, as an end in himself. There are those for whom the style of human action is best symbolized by Sisyphus, or Prometheus, or a rhinoceros, or outcasts waiting for perhaps nothing at all, or an expert in the white coat, or a careful and detached observer, or a calculator who thinks of life as an instance of game theory, or a crisp but affable executive. Men who perform the same actions, which achieve roughly the same pragmatic effects, operate under different core symbols. A rebel may rebel out of Promethean defiance or out of a humble passion for justice. Democracy succeeds because it recognizes the freedom available to individuals and communities on the level of basic symbols, even when common pragmatic purposes are to be achieved.

But it would be a mistake to believe that symbols are unimportant.

The relationship between motivating symbol and concrete action is not so clear and direct as the relationship between a verbal premise and its implications. What one surrenders in changing basic symbols may not become apparent immediately in one's actions. But it would be very surprising to anthropologists, sociologists, and psychologists alike if, after a change in social or personal symbols, changes in action did not follow. Christian faith, it must be apparent, has traditionally employed cultural symbols of various sorts—one time one set of symbols; another time another set—as vivid interpretations of human existence and as motives of action. The strain put upon the symbols used in the preceding cultural epoch has reached a point of maximum intensity; this strain is also apparent among human beings generally.

But there are several reasons why there is hope that Christian symbols will regain their vigor, in a fresh style and an authentic interpretation. Already some Christians have lived according to a new style even though a theory of what they were doing was not yet available; such diverse Christians, for example, as John F. Kennedy and Pope John XXIII. Kennedy articulated a realism, a pragmatism, a modest hopefulness that once again makes political action in the name of freedom and compassion possible. He transplanted the ideals of Christian life in the world from the Judaeo-Christian context into the technical, fluid, secular context of a new era. Pope John XXIII began a renewal so thorough in one of the most ancient of Western institutions that the shape of world politics and world cultural forces has been radically altered, for any change in Roman Catholicism powerfully affects the self-definition of many other institutions, religious or secular.

Secondly, one of the first fruits of Pope John's revolution is a renewed ecumenical movement—a movement of cooperation, mutual criticism, and mutual support that is beginning to touch not only Protestants and Catholics but Christians and Jews. Ultimately, it will reach all men of all religious faiths and of none. Religious people are beginning to think of themselves less as separate sects than as brothers, whose differences, however important and mutually enriching, do not outweigh their common sense of mystery and humanity. In particular, the ecumenical movement has brought enormous mutual stimulation to the various Christian bodies that lived for so long in intellectual isolation from one another. During the period of isolation, differences of social status, temperament, and personality were often institutional-ized. Belonging to a sect, a man was content to be in some ways less than fully human; he adhered to a limited style or pattern of life. There was a "Protestant principle," a "Catholic principle," and many subtypes of complacent differentiation. Now each of the Christian communities is putting pressure on the others. Admiration is leading to emulation. Certain Catholics are closer in spirit to some Presbyte-rians, than either are to many members in their own religious com-munities. Moreover, in each communion traits usually associated with other communions are beginning to emerge—Protestants learn Cath-olic attitudes toward worldly things like food and drink, Catholics learn prophetic criticism of institutional idolatry. Christianity is ceas-ing to be sectarian; it is becoming more roundly human.

A third factor for hope is that a profound spiritual change is occur-ring in the academy. The serious study of religion is moving outside the seminaries and into the universities. Fred M. Hechinger has reported in *The New York Times* [48] that at universities around the country, "students have been enrolling in courses on religion in record numbers. Some institutions," he continues, "find it difficult to re-cruit enough faculty members to fill the demand." According to Mr. Hechinger's survey, the interest in courses in religion is largely intellectual. He concludes: "Many students who are volunteering for the Peace Corps were identified as those most interested in courses in religion." Now that philosophy has become analytical, and literature courses are often technical, courses in religion offer a privileged neutral opportunity for studies in the comparative interpretation of basic human values like freedom, love, justice, and openness. It should be added that theology is becoming the province of laymen; applications to the few university graduate schools in theology in the country are extremely high. Moreover, since the Second Vatican Council, newspapers and journals like *Commentary, Harper's,* and *The New Republic* have given an increasing proportion of space both to reporting and to analyzing events and trends in contemporary theology. *The New York Times* made a major addition to its staff in 1965 in assigning John Cogley as religion editor. The most pertinent and complete account of theological development is now often to be found in the "secular" press. Frequent international consultation among theologians assures the continued flow of ideas. In these ways, religion is ceasing to be sectarian and parochial.

More important, there are signs of a new type of inquiry within the academy. "The trend seems to be," Mr. Hechinger reports from comments of one academic spokesman, "that the faculty is not afraid of religion any more and does not feel a threat to it—does not feel that it's a form of superstition left over from the Middle Ages."[49] It seems plain to many students, if not to members of an older generation, that in a pluralistic society there are many interpretations of human life, only one of which is represented by the pragmatist who is confident that mankind can make progress, can find some degree of happiness, can be assured that the success of science is no illusion. If I read some members of the younger generation correctly, their marked commitments in ethics are leading them to reopen metaphysical questions. They have not started with an ontology, on which they then "base" their ethics. They are driven to metaphysics not by crisis and despair, but by reflection upon their own hope. Their metaphysics is not one of sickly reflection apart from action, but of action illumined by reflection and of reflection prompted by, required by, and terminating in action. The young are healing the philosophical breach between thought and action.

It would, of course, be a mistake to estimate that there is a widespread religious revival among the young. Those who identify Christianity with the obsolete Judaeo-Christian world view continue to leave the churches in great numbers. For many God is irrelevant. He figures in nothing that they do, or understand, or hope. But many thoughtful students, particularly those, believers or not, who are concerned about questions of values, recognize that people who are serious about their Christian faith or their atheism have much in common. Neither group has seen God, and both are passionately concerned about the fate of human beings. Our ecumenical age has perhaps discovered that the debates of even a generation ago between theists and anti-theists were, on both sides, insufficiently modest. Many Christians are discovering that the Judaeo-Christian world view was an illusory support of their faith, while many atheists are discovering that their own convictions have the structure of a faith.

Thus, in particular, some serious atheists discover that, from a purely formal point of view, they live by three basic principles. With or without intellectual justifications, they believe that to pursue intelligence, to try to make our social order (in Mississippi, for example) more intelligent, is to live fruitfully and well. They have a principle of vision: to create out of chaos a more intelligent, if fitful, center of light. Secondly, they do not expect to be totally successful in history. Their hopes are modest. We cannot eliminate suffering from the world, Camus tells us, but we can diminish by a little the amount of suffering; and this suffices for a human life. Many live by such a principle of resignation. Thirdly, many find that they experience deep compassion regarding any human being who is suffering, and they think that such compassion is good. Despite appearances that tempt them to indifference, they care about human beings as they care about no other phenomenon in the universe. And they are glad to care.

How, then, speaking formally, do these principles of vision, of resignation, and of compassion differ from the faith, hope, and charity of the believer? The believer does not see God. The only proof he has that he loves God, whom he does not see, is that he loves those human beings whom he does see (I Jn: 5). If they are serious, believer and unbeliever live by love for men. Yet those who love human beings are not many but few. Those few who are serious about their atheism or their belief require one another. For the battle against the hucksters, who daily increase and multiply, striving to possess the earth, is desperate. In the churches as in the buildings of our cities, there are countless petty men for whom persons are not ends but means: fodder for organizations, functions of society, useful citizens, faithful followers.

VI. *A Renewed Creativity*

Religion, then, appears to some young people as a function of the question-asking and the symbol-making man. Who am I? What may I hope? What should I do? These questions put them in the midst of the mysteries of human destiny. Such young people are not pleased

with what they have seen in the churches. They do not often find
satisfaction there for the question-asking or the symbol-making impulse. Nevertheless, even the most unrelieved and oppressive of the
institutional churches convey (sometimes despite themselves) a sense
of history, a sense of community, a sense of mystery. But, ironically,
while the symbol-making impulse is encountering new sympathy and
serious inquiry in the universities, the symbols and sentiments prominent in the institutional churches repel by their dishonesty and irrelevance many who would be prepared to respond to what the
churches are supposed to be. Although some of the young, motivated
perhaps by their work among the poor, are prepared to accept the
style and limitations of the religion of the uneducated, the religion of
the middle classes shocks them by its pettiness.

The key religious symbols of Judaism and Christianity speak of freedom, love, justice, openness to events, to others, and to the world;
they speak of the mystery and tragedy of human life, of the kind of
hope that leads to action without sentimental illusions. Emil L.
Fackenheim writes:

Here it is at long last time to bear direct witness to Him who has been the
God of Israel for more than three millennia, and the God of the Christian
Church since its inception. *He is the One who is infinite, yet relates Himself to finite men; who in His power does not need man, yet in His love
chooses to need him; who in His self-sufficiency does not require the world
yet wishes to require it—and bids man do His will in it.*

Such a God does not require demythologizing. He already *is* demythologized, and has been so ever since He first revealed Himself in an infinity
destructive of all finite idols. (Only the images man forms of Him require
demythologizing, but even these are *recognized* as being mere images.)

The infinite value of the human person, always part of both Jewish and
Christian faith, must now by faith be accepted as . . . a goal demanding
secular realization—by and on behalf of all men. And in accepting this
demand, modern Jew and Christian must descend into this secular world,
from what has often been, and still is, a remote Heaven.[50]

Such a testimony is necessary, because it is a temptation for the believer today to state publicly only what a secular thinker might affirm;
there is a seductive absolutism in the widespread ignorance and indifference regarding religion. On the other hand, the believer is

becoming increasingly aware of the nontheistic alternative. Religion is becoming self-critical; the first condition of renewed creativity is therefore present. Because of the advance of secular intelligence, human capacities, and alternative viewpoints, it has become increasingly difficult for the man of religious faith to take for granted the world view that he receives from his parents. No one can be born a Christian. Being born into a Christian family usually involves inheriting patterns of thought, images, and sentiments that must be replaced by other more authentic patterns. But the nontheist must also grope for a set of imaginative symbols, a moral style, and appropriate attitudes by which to live humanly in the technical world we are building. There is no *a priori* argument for deciding whether theism, or nontheism, is a more adequate interpretation of human life. Although proportionally the numbers of Christians continue to grow less, those who remain Christian are working toward a clearer view of what their interpretation of human life entails. In living this interpretation they will test its empirical and pragmatic justification.

Perhaps a statement of the character of Christianity, however fragmentary and incomplete, is called for at this point. Christianity offers a community of inquiry in which to pursue one's concern for human values and the mystery of human life. Its eucharistic liturgy has an intimate, audacious power. Christianity is not merely an instrument of social relevance nor does it honor mere meditation, apart from responsibility for the survival and the welfare of the human race. Christianity is not a form of activism. In a culture of increasing leisure, it can teach men how to contemplate and how to explore important depths of the human spirit. It recognizes that social action comes to fruition in the free personal development of each man.

Moreover, human actions have, like liturgy, a social context. In the world in which we are coming to live, this context embraces all men: one's neighbor is the Viet-Cong, the Russian, the Harlemite, or the Nobb Hill matron. Christianity offers no escape from the complexities and ambiguities of the new world culture; nor does it offer (as Judaeo-Christian culture often did) a complacent satisfaction that one has all, or even any, complete answers. Rather, it offers a historical community of inadequate human beings, who are trying to be faithful to the good news that God, despite appearances, loves the world and asks men to take responsibility for building up a human community of freedom and truth, justice and compassion. It offers a rich history of reflection upon the crushing difficulties involved in such a task. But it does not allow us to think ourselves innocent, as mere victims of a pathetic fate. It does not rescue us, as President Kennedy said one spring and then experienced one autumn before our eyes, from the inequalities of fate. It demands that we take ourselves as we are, assuming responsibility for those deeds of ours that increase the common suffering. It teaches that God is present everywhere. It does not offer security, but reconciliation: a wellspring of creative, painfully growing brotherhood.

NOTES

1. Emmanuel Célestin Suhard, *The Church Today* (Chicago, 1953).
2. E. L. Mascall, *The Secularization of Christianity* (New York, 1966) quoting from Harry Blamires, *The Christian Mind* (New York, 1963), p. 3.
3. John A. T. Robinson, *Honest to God* (London, 1963; Philadelphia, 1963).
4. Dietrich Bonhoeffer, *Letters and Papers from Prison* (New York, 1953).
5. The passages most commented upon are *ibid.*, pp. 208-15; 217-20; 222-27; 236-44.
6. In a passage popular with the new theologians, Saul Bellow deplores talk of human suffering "in the mouths of safe, comfortable people playing at crisis, alienation, apocalypse and desperation. . . . We must get it out of our heads that this is a doomed time, that we are waiting for the end, and the rest of it, mere junk from fashionable magazines. Things are grim enough without these shivery games. People frightening one another—a poor sort of moral exercise." *Herzog* (New York, 1965), pp. 385-86.
7. The most widely discussed theological book of 1965 was Harvey Cox's *The Secular City* (New York), with the jacket inscription: "The Secular City: A celebration of its liberties and an invitation to its discipline." William Hamilton and Thomas J. J. Altizer, in *Radical Theology and the Death of God* (New York, 1966) also announce a new optimism. See, e.g., p. 113, for the way in which Hamilton chooses Bonhoeffer over Niebuhr and Tillich.
8. *Punch*, June 23, 1965, quoted in *New Theology*, No. 3, eds. Martin E. Marty and Dean G. Peerman (New York, 1966), p. 17.
9. Alasdair MacIntyre, "God and the Theologians," *Encounter* (Vol. 21, No. 3), reprinted in part in *The Honest to God Debate*, ed. David L. Edwards (Philadelphia, 1963), pp. 215-28.
10. W. W. Bartley III, "The Bonhoeffer Revival," *The New York Review of Books* (Vol. 2, August 26, 1965), p. 16.
11. Sigmund Freud, *The Future of an Illusion* (New York, 1964), pp. 87-89.
12. *Ibid.*, p. 86.
13. Gordon Allport, *The Individual and His Religion* (New York, 1950), p. 1,

14. *Ibid.*
15. Charles S. Hyneman, *The Study of Politics* (Urbana, Illinois, 1959), pp. 62-63.
16. Jean-Paul Sartre, *The Words* (New York, 1964), p. 253.
17. Alfred North Whitehead, *Science and the Modern World* (New York, 1948), pp. 12-13.
18. *Ibid.*, p. 13.
19. Christopher Dawson, *Religion and the Rise of Western Culture* (London, 1950), p. 22.
20. Freud, *op. cit.*, p. 88.
21. Albert Camus, *The Fall* (New York, 1961), p. 133.
22. Bertrand Russell, *Authority and the Individual* (Boston, 1960), pp. 70-71.
23. Walter Kaufmann, *Faith of a Heretic* (New York, 1961), see especially pp. 291-342.
24. William Barrett, *Irrational Man* (Doubleday & Co., Inc.: New York, 1962), pp. 24-25, Copyright © 1958 by William Barrett.
25. *Ibid.*, pp. 239-40, quoting from Jean-Paul Sartre, *The Republic of Silence.*
26. MacIntyre, *op. cit.*, pp, 225-26.
27. *Ibid.*, p. 223.
28. John Updike, *Pigeon Feathers and Other Stories* (Alfred A. Knopf, Inc.: New York, 1962), p. 279.
29. *Ibid.*, p. 248.
30. *Ibid.*, p. 263.
31. *Ibid.*, p. 250.
32. *Ibid.*, pp. 251-52.
33. *Ibid.*, pp. 179, 181-82.
34. Wilhelm Pauck, "Theology in the Life of Contemporary American Protestantism," *Religion and Culture: Essays in Honor of Paul Tillich,* ed. Walter Leibrecht (New York, 1959), p. 270.
35. See J. B. Phillips, *Your God Is Too Small* (New York, 1961), p. 8, for a brief popular exposition of some dozen or more "inadequate conceptions of God which still linger unconsciously in many minds."
36. See Paul Tillich, "The Conquest of Intellectual Provincialism: Europe and America," *Theology and Culture,* ed. Robert C. Kimball (New York, 1959), pp. ᾿59-76; a remarkable essay in which Tillich reflects on what it meant for him, as a German, to rethink his theology in an American context.
37. Gabriel Vahanian, *The Death of God: The Culture of Our Post Christian Era* (New York, 1961); Thomas J. J. Altizer and William Hamilton, *op. cit.*
38. Harvey Cox, *op. cit.*
39. Paul M. Van Buren, The *Secular Meaning of the Gospel* (New York, 1963).
40. H. Stuart Hughes, "Pope John's Revolution: Secular or Religious?" *Commonweal,* Vol. 83, No. 10 (December 10, 1965), p. 303.
41. Daniel Callahan, *Honesty in the Church* (New York, 1965).
42. Talcott Parsons, "The Pattern of Religious Organization in the United

States," *Symbolism in Religion and Literature,* ed. Rollo May (New York, 1960), pp. 152-77, esp. pp. 173-76.

43. I have attempted to deal with this problem in *Belief and Unbelief* (New York, 1965), and in "The Christian and the Atheist," *Christianity and Crisis* (March 21, 1966). The reader might also consult Daniel Callahan, "Freud Saw It Coming," *Commonweal* (June 3, 1966), pp. 312-13, and the exchange of letters in *ibid.* (July 1, 1966), pp. 405, 423-25. See also, Justus George Lawler, "Theology and Its Uses of History," *Continuum* (Spring, 1966), pp. 92-101; and Eugene Fontinell, "Reflections on Faith and Metaphysics," *Cross Currents* (Winter, 1966), pp. 15-40; Raymond J. Nogar, O.P., *Lord of the Absurd* (New York, 1966) and Leslie Dewart, *The Future of Belief* (New York, 1966).

44. The young Roman Catholic theologian Hans Küng contends that, from a Christian point of view, other world religions are the ordinary sufficient human means of salvation; Christianity is an extraordinary means. See Hans Küng, *Freedom Today* (New York, 1966).

45. Emil L. Fackenheim, "A Jew Looks at Christianity and Secularist Liberalism," *The Restless Church,* ed. William Kilbourn (Philadelphia, 1966), pp. 87, 98. Professor Fackenheim urges Jews and Christians to address the secular liberal "so as to embrace his liberalism and repudiate his secularism." *Ibid.,* p. 97.

46. Paul Tillich, *Christianity and the Encounter with World Religions* (New York, 1963) and *The Future of Religions* (Chicago, 1966).

47. Sidney Hook, citing Russell, in *The Quest for Being* (New York, 1961), p. 214.

48. *The New York Times,* May 8, 1966.

49. *Ibid.*

50. Fackenheim, *op. cit.* p. 97.

2

The Christian and the Atheist

The word "existential" displeases three types of thinkers in America. Those given to the clarity of Anglo-American language analysis find words like "being," "nothingness," "nausea," "ultimate concern," and "commitment" foggy and evasive. Hardy Thomists in their isolated lairs—analysts of medieval language and logic—distrust "subjectivism" and "situation ethics." Protestant theologians of the optimistic avant-garde have been impressed by the Marxist critique of existentialism; for them existentialism is the last gasp of the corrupt West, it is immature, it is too centered in the brooding of the impotent subject, and its theory of eyeball-to-eyeball encounter is a naive analysis of social relations.

So let us avoid the word "existentialism" and speak instead of style. A man's style is not reducible to the list of propositions to which he gives assent; it is not defined by his theories, his code of behavior, or the deliverances of self-analysis. Style is not what he says (or thinks) about himself in words; nor even what others say (or think) about him in words. A style of life cannot be adequately described in words, for living involves more than speaking or thinking. A style of life is concrete—how John F. Kennedy spoke, answered questions, chose his battles, kept his nerve, played. Style is to role as existence to essence. Yet style does not derive from individual actions in their discreteness but in their connection; style does not emerge from a single frame of film but from a kinetic series; style is dynamic. It is an elucence of men in motion. It flashes forth from actions. It is the concrete form of action. It is the manner, mode, quality, and aim of action. It is the haecceitas *beloved of Scotus and Hopkins. It springs from the vital principles of personality, from drive and courage and imagination and intelligence. It is always sexual in overtones, since human emotion and energy are entangled with sexual potency and impotency. The style is the man.*

One cannot speak adequately of ethics without speaking of style. More important than laws, imperatives, codes, precepts, rules, premises, and propositions are human models. Human beings have style. Men do not so much obey laws as imitate other men. Without models morals die. Camus and Sartre are more influential by their living than by their writing; and their writing is influential because it manages to communicate their way of living. (Not idly did they write novels and plays to accompany their philosophical essays.) The man is the style. Student existentialists are imitators even more than they are memorizers of arguments. In proportion as they have the words but not the way of life they are "inauthentic." Moreover, the imitation itself must be of a special kind: to imitate a way of life is not to copy another's life but to do as well in handling one's own unique life as the model did in his. Since each human life is unique, it is always startling to see how similar men are, how few live authentically according to their own unique possibilities.

The style of self-discovery—the style of being oneself—is in some ways unique for each man who seeks to learn it. It is achieved and it is distinguished from other styles (1) when a man refuses to accept words, propositions, codes, or laws as the final criteria of ethical action, and (2) when a man refuses to understand imitation as mere copying. The style of self-discovery is the one style which many men can share in common while each develops it uniquely. It respects both a man's commonness and his uniqueness.

In a later section I would like to say more about the question of style in ethics, by way of a study of the use Aristotle made of "the man of practical wisdom." At present, I want to use the notion of style to illuminate an increasingly sticky issue: how the atheist differs from the Christian. For a long time Christians tried very hard to show how favored they were. If other men received through creation a "general revelation," Christians were given a "special revelation." If other men lived by "nature," Christians lived by "grace." But in the concrete, what are the differences to be observed between Christians and atheists in a classroom at a pluralistic university? Who can pick out the Christians in a dormitory? At the present time, those who call themselves radical theologians are falling over themselves to show how similar Christians are to atheists. Nevertheless, theological pursuit of the secular is presently much encumbered by biblical justifications and appeals to the contagion and magnetism of Jesus. It seems much cleaner simply to be secular.

The present essay, written late in 1965, attempts to suggest that contemporary ethical thinking is much too verbal; the symbolic character of human action has been overlooked. Without a new understanding of the symbolic, without a new awareness of the importance of style or way of life, Christianity is rendered mute in ethics.

WHAT is the difference between a man who is a Christian and a wholly secular man? In the last two generations we have experienced, on a large scale, the positive values involved in atheism. This striking development has unsettled our theories. It is not true that, as Dostoevsky asserted, "if there is no God, everything is permitted." A modest, concerned, effective atheism is now recognized as a viable way of life, not only for individuals but for the whole human community.

"Religion," one might say, has been so successful that even atheists have adopted many of its basic values as their own. Camus has chosen honesty, Walter Kaufmann nobility and creativity, Bertrand Russell compassion, and Alfred North Whitehead scientific conscience, with explicit dependence upon Christian history. There is nothing in a merely scientific view of the world to justify the choice of such values; historically speaking, religion sponsored or nourished them until they ripened sufficiently to be chosen apart from religion.

Quite clearly, Christians *do* certain things that nonbelievers do not —worship, pray, etc. But today few serious Christians are prepared to say that "grace" is operative only in such professedly "religious" acts. Participation in church and sacraments distinguishes Christians in an objective way; but what discernible difference is there inwardly and in action? For most of the moments of every day, believers and nonbelievers perform similar acts. We lack a theory to express how, if at all, they differ.

Consequently, the radical problem concerns those human actions that both believers and nonbelievers alike perform: plain, ordinary, nonecclesiastical—in a word, secular—actions. In such actions how does a man of faith in Jesus Christ differ from a man without such faith? Two young men find themselves walking side by side in a march for racial justice in Mississippi; both are equally prepared to accept death as one of the possible consequences of their acts; both are equally willing to lay down their lives for their brothers. Yet one is a Christian, the other an atheist. In what respect do they differ?

One common solution is to point to their different motivations. The Christian acts in imitation of Jesus Christ, but the atheist acts because he believes in justice and equality, and because he has compassion upon those who suffer. However, this solution breaks down. For the Christian may also share the motivations of the atheist; and the atheist may frankly admit that he sees in Christ a model, without accepting "all the other things" about Christ.

Moreover, a "religious" motivation is in itself not discriminating; alone, it seriously weakens the believer's capacity for realistic judgment. Those whose chief motive for action is "the will of God," or the "imitation of Jesus Christ" or even *"agape"* soon find that almost any type of action can be performed, and historically has been performed, in its name. Their version of Christianity will appear to be softheaded and sentimental. The motivations of the nonbeliever will, by comparison, appear to be hardheaded, critical and discerning. A specifically "Christian" motivation, in this view, is mere icing on a cake. Accordingly, only in proportion as the Christian shares the pragmatism and secular discernment of the atheist will he share in the substance of authentic moral action. (In Mississippi Christian segregationist and freedom worker alike may appeal to the same "Christian" motivation.)

Ineluctably then the realistic Christian appears to be drawn toward the appropriation of hard, profane values and critical, pragmatic methods. Why be a Christian at all?

Our present theoretical impasse appears to have arisen because we do not have adequate conceptual tools for the analysis of human action. Into this vacuum more adequate pragmatic theories rush, but are such theories themselves adequate? Human actions must meet a certain pragmatic standard, it is true; but individual men are not merely instruments of the common good, nor grist for the wheels of progress, nor are they merely problem-solvers.

Thus, the quality of action is not adequately measured by pragmatic standards. Not all the technical adjustments that society still needs will suffice to constitute the moral health or beauty of the human community. To see this, one does not need to minimize the role of pragmatism, technical planning or social reform, but only to note that even the classical exponents of such roles call their theory "instrumentalism." Man does not seem to be merely an instrument. Instrumentalism alone, as Henry David Aiken has been arguing, does not exhaust the capacities of vision, action and development.

In addition to the pragmatic standard, human action must meet other criteria. As we set out to plan the cities in which ninety per cent of the nation will shortly be living, what qualities of human action do we wish most to promote? Having mastered the techniques toward which instrumentalism has so brilliantly directed our attention, and having through these techniques achieved the preconditions of the good life for each and every man, what then shall we do? What kind of life shall we lead? We may wish to live mature, healthy, beautiful lives; and we may wish to know how that is to be done, for the alternatives are many and the time allotted to each of us is brief.

No doubt, each man must answer this question for himself. Each man chooses his own way of life amid the contingencies in which he finds himself. In fact, many do not choose, or do so only imperceptibly; many merely drift. Of our generation, Camus said it would be written, "They fornicated, and they read the papers." There is always, however, an option for each man: to seize some responsibility for the activities of his life. Some men in fact develop their capacities to a higher excellence than others. Consequently a theory of action must account for the differences proper to each individual agent.

But such action is also symbolic. Two men reading the same paper may acquire a similar fund of information, so far as their replies to factual questions may reveal and even so far as their ability to compare and analyze and systematize that information may be tested. But does what they read *mean* the same thing to each? Are their judgments similarly affected, their imaginations stimulated, the trajectories of their subsequent actions altered?

For some persons life is an instance of game theory; it is an endless crossword puzzle, a series of "challenges," delightful so long as boredom is kept at bay. Human action is symbolic, and to many the ultimate symbol is *divertissement*; the ultimate anxiety is tedium.

Thus no single act means only what its pragmatic effect achieves (its "cash value"). Every action also means what the agent intends it to mean, i.e., what he is symbolizing by it. Two men riding the same subway car, working in the same office on similar tasks, may be creating through their lives two entirely different symbolic patterns. Action is like speech: each life utters a unique word.

Thus men strive not only to be effective, to be useful to one another, but also to communicate. Before it is too late they want to make sure their word is heard, their burden expressed, despite their inarticulateness. (When God acted to reveal himself, he spoke a Word.)

Each individual agent is unique, because the symbolic value of his actions is his own. Perhaps we may make a common metaphor into a technical term: each action is unique because the "horizon" of each individual is unique. Commonly, a horizon is the limit of what can be seen from a given point. A horizon has two poles, the subject and the range of what the subject can observe. But as I am now using the word, a horizon also indicates a dynamic orientation, for the human subject is not stationary. He moves through many and varied experiences, gains new insights, sometimes is led by experience to shift those criteria of relevance and evidence that guide his judgment, and regularly "tries to do" projects that carry his view into the future.

He is distinctive because he develops in time; his horizon constantly changes both in its subjective pole and in its objective context. His acts of knowing encompass more than enlarged bodies of information. One insight leads to a change in his capacity to understand, and sometimes a whole field of prior insights is rearranged by an overriding insight that throws a new light upon what he knew before. Again, the swiftness and sureness of his judgment in assessing the evidence for his ideas develop as he becomes a master in any given field of inquiry. Finally, what he is "trying to do" with his life undergoes regular revision.

The dynamic concept of horizon has a threefold function.

It calls attention to the symbolic dimension of human action (including inquiry). Different men discern different significance in a given action or invest the same acts with different significance.

It highlights the fact that the subject and all the objects or persons to whom he is related fall within the same symbolic framework. The dualism of the subject and the object is finally untenable, for objects are known by subjects only insofar as they fall within the horizon of the subject.

It emphasizes that knowing and acting are not exhaustively analyzed into the categories either of classical rationalism or of naturalistic pragmatism. The horizon of a subject is influenced by all the experiences, emotions, memories, tendencies, interests, desires, insights, and judgments of the subject. There is no pure isolated ego, no atom of consciousness confronting pure objects "objectively out there now." Nor is the dualism of the emotive and the cognitive tenable.

Finally, the concept of horizon is not Husserlian. It does not attempt to picture two objective spheres "out there," one subsumed within the other. Husserl is Platonist in his epistemology, and consequently his metaphysics includes this world and another world.

But the concept of horizon here adumbrated is not Platonic; it derives from a suggestion by Bernard Lonergan, and its intellectual lineage is anti-Platonic. Its purpose is not to project a metaphysical world out beyond the immediate, tangible world; it denies that there is any metaphysical world out there. Its purpose is to articulate the fact that human deeds in this present concrete, historical world are symbolic of human intentions and not exhaustively translatable into the categories of instrumentalism. Such action does not merely solve problems, control the environment or predict and manipulate effects. It also intends to say something about the character of life; it expresses vision, or lack of it. Action follows from being; what you are speaks through what you do. Your model is reflected in your style.

Now a Christian who is conscious of what he is (and no one of us fully is, we are only trying to be) is a "new being." He is, according to his belief, sharing in the life of God. But what is God's life? God is not believed to be passive, and hence the best of our inadequate supply of words for speaking of him will surely be gerunds rather than nouns.

God is not truth and love but knowing and loving. To share in God's living is to share in God's knowing and loving. To become a Christian is to begin to "put on the mind of Christ," to begin to enter into a new horizon. It is to start to understand the world, life, history, others, oneself as God understands; and to begin to love as God loves.

Grace is, then, conceived to be a new way of knowing, a new way of loving. For this reason it is said to "build upon" nature; even before the advent of grace men understand and love. It does not destroy intelligence or the capacity to love; it enlarges them beyond limits men could hope to achieve without it. Grace alters the standards of human understanding and loving, and in this sense it "contradicts" nature.

But no one who lives in grace has carte blanche to condemn intelligence or to denigrate the capacity of men to love. For to do so is to destroy the very operations through which grace acts. If we stifle our drive of inquiry, how can we come to investigate ever more fully the ways of God? If we repress our capacity for love, how can we become agents of the love of God? The capital sin of "the religious age" and of all fundamentalism, is to neglect human intelligence and love, and to construct an artificial, magical world in which "grace" is to operate as if in a vacuum, like some *deus ex machina*.

Nevertheless, a withering critique of "the religious age" can be launched effectively without abandoning the claim that to be a Christian is to be different from a nonbeliever. The differences need not be obvious to every man in the street: a Christian and an atheist sitting in the subway or marching in Mississippi may look alike; they may even be blood brothers. What changed empirically, psychologically, when one became a Christian, or an atheist, was the symbolic meaning of his life. Even if both still take Christ as a model for certain of their actions—sacrificing themselves for others, for example—the way in which they understand this model and relate to it is different.

For the atheist, Christ is a historical figure like Socrates whose life taught a lesson. For the knowledgeable Christian, he is also God who lives yet in the understanding and the knowing of his people.

Christians do not merely *imitate* him; in some further way (how?) he lives in them. Their actions are now not only theirs but his. The significance of what they do may or may not be rewarded with historical, pragmatic efficacy; but because it is also Christ's, their action rescues some of the beauty and the pain of history from going unnoticed and unthanked. Christians are not called to succeed in history, only to labor for success and to care about it. The further standard they hope to meet, beyond pragmatic efficacy, is that of human meaningfulness.

Christians believe that Christ has spoken most adequately of the symbolic content of life in history. A man who consciously lives in Christ and Christ in him seems to live as fully as he can in a given historical context. He experiences its triviality, dignity, joy, emptiness, cruelty, loveliness. God's disclosure of himself in Christ is not yet complete; each Christian discloses something new in new historical contexts.

No doubt there are many men who fail to see in Christ what Christians see, who find in him a narrow, restricting, even degrading view of life. Such men try to symbolize in what they do some other quality of life. What distinguishes Christians is that their actions occur within the unlimited horizon of Christ's understanding and loving. Within that horizon their own present horizon is ever "under judgment." Their judge lives within them, calmly disclosing their insufficiencies. They must gradually "grow up into the stature of Christ."

The Christian in Mississippi or on the subway is conscious that God lives within him, presses upon him, drives him on—not magically but by stimulating his intelligence and discriminating love until they are exercised to their utmost. Grace acts through the secular; there is no other world. But God—through events in our lives, Scripture, life in the church, conscious response to the sacraments—illuminates our understanding of this world and enlarges our capacity to love it, so that we, too, pierced by its beauty, might be willing to die for it.

The atheist, through other events, books, communities, is pierced by the earth's beauty and dies for it without recognizing the significance Christians give it: that it is man's, and we are Christ's and Christ is God's. The difference is not in the external act or in its historical effect but in its symbolic content. Believers and nonbelievers *do* the same things; they interpret their lives differently. Perhaps (as Daniel Callahan has noted) after two or three generations of widespread atheism, the difference between Christian and atheistic symbols will lead to increasingly divergent courses of action.

In any case, to determine which set of symbols is correct is a further question. No one has seen God. Both believer and nonbeliever are in a darkness, searching out what it is to be a man.

3

The Odd Logic of Theism and Nontheism

Pluralism forces upon each of us the realization that our own interpretation of human life may not, in fact, be correct. For other men of good will and integrity, our friends, interpret life differently than we do. Yet no one can avoid interpreting human life. For one must act, and every human action casts a symbolic shadow; in every action, a man is trying to do something and of necessity has an image, however unverbalized, of himself, his situation, and the world in which he is acting. We accuse one another of not being sufficiently realistic. What we mean by such accusations is that the accused imagines the world incorrectly; we point to experiences or insights or evidences that he has overlooked. Life may, in the end, be a tale told by an idiot; but each human action signifies something to its agent, each is part of a tale. Human beings love stories because each lives out a story of his own creation.

Theism is a story or, rather, it is a basic pattern (as the triangle is a pattern in a novel) on which a limitless variety of stories may be spun. Nontheism is another such pattern. According to theism, certain human experiences (like friendship, creativity, understanding, compassion, honesty) are more than merely human experiences; they are also a participation in the life of God, a God hidden and not otherwise perceived. According to the various forms of nontheism, such experiences are purely and simply human experiences, the more poignant for their fragility. Neither the theist nor the nontheist sees God; for both there are the same evidences, the same fragile experiences. Theism and nontheism are rival stories. Judaism and Christianity, to name but two, are historical traditions in which the story of theism is given shape, color, and historical rootage: the God of Judaism and Christianity has made his presence felt at concrete places at specific times.

It is, then, no accident that in the civilization most affected by Judaism and Christianity concrete history should be deemed important. Again, according to the Jewish and Christian stories, each human being (regardless of race or sex) is precious in God's sight, and each human being is held responsible for his actions in history, particularly for his secular actions: how he treats his neighbor, cares for the poor, helps to establish a kingdom of justice, freedom, and love. Again, according to the Jewish and Christian stories, every person, place, and event in history springs from the creative understanding of one source; consequently, if men try hard enough they are assured that every detail of history, no matter how negligible it appears, is related in some way to every other and hence rewards persistent inquiry. It is not surprising that in a civilization in which these stories have taken root for thousands of years, empirical science should have arisen, and an unparalleled dynamism of social reform and political revolution should have been generated.

What we are witnessing in our century is an effort to disengage the values which have shaped our civilization from the stories which inspired them. Perhaps that disengagement can be effectively established; it would be idle and mean-spirited to insist in advance that it cannot. Yet the irony remains that those who remain faithful to the stories of Judaism and Christianity and consider them, in some difficult sense, to be true, now share the values inculcated by those stories with those who reject the stories and yet retain the values. It is this coincidence in basic values that makes the logic of theism and of nontheism, in our culture at least, so odd. There are, of course, nontheists who are nihilists, for whom love is no better than hate, dishonesty than honesty, destruction than creativity; and there are theists who think they can actually talk to God, as if he were a Person or a Force or a thing "out there" somewhere in the inventory of things separate from themselves. But those nontheists who are

humanists and those theists who do not see God share a similar secular
faith. For both, the measure of human value consists in personal integrity,
human community, and creativity. For the theist, such values are signs of
God's presence; for a nontheist, they are not signs but simple, plain hu-
man values. The difference is almost like that between black-and-white
and technicolor; both theist and nontheist experience the same world, but
their experience has a different quality, a different resonance, a different
ring. One may, perhaps, only be imagining things; and the other may be
blind to certain things. Presumably, one of them is correct and the other
not. The test comes in living. But it is just possible that nontheists in our
society have appropriated the point of the Jewish and Christian stories
better than theists. On the supposition that deeds speak louder than words,
and that telling stories is not enough, sorting out which is which and who
is who will require the astuteness and the fairness of a judge very like
what Jews and Christians seem to mean by God, if there is one.

I WRITE about belief in God as a Christian; specifically, as a Roman
Catholic. And the problem that preoccupies me is how my experience
of human life differs from that of an atheist or an agnostic. Put another way: what evidence in experience leads me to think that being
a Catholic is a more correct response to life than being an atheist or
an agnostic? Let me wrestle with the problem in general terms; it is
not the questions of Catholicism versus Protestantism, Orthodoxy, or
Judaism, etc., which preoccupy me, but the issue of theism vs. nontheism.

The position of the agnostic—to be expeditious—seems to me
untenable as a way of life. For a way of life, like a drama onstage, is
already in action when the question arises. Life is already, to use
Heidegger's phrase, thrown. One lives either as a theist or as a nontheist; actions speak louder than theories, and if one cannot make
up one's mind, still one's actions define one's identity. At the end, the
trajectory will have been clear. One will have lost the opportunity to
take conscious responsibility for the movement; one will have let slip
the opportunity to choose. Agnosticism is possible in thinking but not
in living.

Yet it is perhaps too pat merely to reject agnosticism. An accurate
rendering of the inner spirit of many of us seems to suggest that we

both believe in God (whatever he is) and disbelieve in him. On Mondays, Wednesdays, and Fridays, we believe; on the other days, the implausibility, the irrelevance, the remoteness, the vagueness of such belief assails us and we relapse again into that attention to immediate detail which constitutes unbelief. We forget. And then we are reminded—but perhaps by an illusion, a wish, a failure of nerve. Still, if agnosticism means indecision, we are not merely indecisive; it is rather that both sides of the decision call to us. Rare is the undivided man. We are not agnostics, then, in a complacent sense—one does not announce that one is an agnostic as one would say "I'm an American." We are, despite ourselves, divided inwardly.

It is here that a piece of evidence suggests itself. The theory that belief in God springs from a fount of illusion in our hearts, and draws impulsion from centuries upon centuries of religious conditioning, supposes in effect that we live in a century of transition. On one side of the watershed, the vast majority of men, even educated men, once believed in God; ahead, the vast majority of educated men, at least, will not. Those who come between are divided; for them neither belief nor unbelief has been reduced to a routine.

Perhaps our question, then, should be revised. Two or three generations hence, what difference will it have made to the human race if we decide today upon hypothesis A (unbelief) or hypothesis B (belief)? More exactly, what difference will it make to his children, and his grandchildren, if a believer ceases to believe, or a nontheist involves himself in an historical community of belief? Such an important decision (why do I say "important"?) ought to make an experienceable difference in the concrete stream of life. There may well be reasons why such a difference might easily be overlooked within the span of one's own lifetime (both belief and unbelief are long-term projects, not merely a matter of affirming or denying a set of words). But in two generations, or three, surely differences ought to be observable.

We have, then, a vague, imprecise, and perhaps untestable hypothesis. But we have at least begun to formulate our basic questions in a meaningful fashion. Belief in God—what difference does it make? What is the "cash value" of unbelief? The perspective required is that of a cycle of generations. We are social animals, whose society spans more time than our individual lives. We are historical animals. Our decisions affect posterity as well.

A young man I have never met tells me by telephone: "I was brought up in the Orthodox Church. I have no use for it now—the ones who speak to me are people like Camus. But what do we teach our children? That's what we can't decide."

How shall we communicate values in a nonreligious age? Nowadays there is no popular liturgy; there are no processions, feast days, paintings, morality plays. The local, parochial culture of home and parish has been dissolved by the automobile, television, and the move from suburb to suburb. "We in America lack ceremonies," John Updike tells us. The languages of love, of birth, and of death more and more elude us; basic experiences embarrass us. The socially acceptable language about sexual love is clinical. Technese is our mother tongue.

The universities have come to replace the churches at the moral center of our society. The culture of the university is so much stronger than the culture of the American home and most forms of American religion that students frequently experience an "identity crisis" not long after their exposure to it. Having once been committed to religious values, many of them now grow afraid to be caught red-handed defending a commitment. (They make them, but resist speaking of them in intellectual company.) Having, once, too easily accepted a popular language about human values (love, human dignity, brotherhood, patriotism), they now hesitate to admit to having values—hesitate to define them, hesitate even to inquire seriously about them unless a wide range of alternatives allows escape. To survive in America, flexibility is indispensable. Skepticism saves. Principles are too gross for actual, changing life. (Is there anything the flexible American cannot be drawn into doing?)

In such a civilization, human values float free like chunks of grease in acid; they cling who can. Yet folk singers tie bonds philosophers unloose: millions sing of justice, freedom, brotherhood, human dignity, who cannot define or analyze concepts that move their hearts. The liturgy of peace parades, campus Reformations led by bearded prophets protesting hierarchical complacency, the voices of young men dreaming visions in the land where their fathers sinned, suggest that basic impulses have been redirected, not overcome. Is the burden of reason too oppressive? Or, faced with the tasks of life, irrelevant? Old Left gives way to New. Nietzsche is cherished in halls that once heard the voice of Emerson. Through mass murders in Chicago, Texas, Cincinnati, Kansas and Boston, the violence that built this nation

surfaces: murder is an American way of life. For an optimistic continent, President Kennedy's assassination compresses the philosophy of
the absurd into a single, swift spasm.

As I interpret the human situation in America, the easy optimism
of the atheist of a former generation has disappeared. The scientist
has lost his innocence. Technology brings hell along with paradise:
napalm and A-bomb are no harder to accept than fire falling on
Sodom and Gomorrah. After Hitler, we require no horned and fork-
tailed satans. What need do we have for biblical myths, now that
there are secular analogues? To be a man is no different now, only
more sophisticated. Intelligence, compassion, courage, resignation
have not lost their poignant beauty, nor urgency, nor infrequency.
"There are not," Pascal said, "four honest men in a century." The
population explosion has not raised, but lowered, that proportion:
falsehood seems indispensable to current international, political, and
economic affairs, and we are each involved in one another's lies.
(When, with a lamp, you discover an honest professor, flatter him a
little. Or watch him open a new book to the index and run his finger
down the column for his name.)

God, on the other hand, seems more remote than ever. When we
desire rain, the weatherman is consulted before the priest, and the
rain-sowing airplane makes mere prayer presumptuous. When we do
for ourselves what we can, increasingly little is left for God. The *deus
ex machina* is obsolete, victim among others of automation. The Russian spacemen testify that they have been in heaven and Our Father
is not there. Where then? Even churchmen today criticize the
churches. Even ministers preach atheism. In a post-religious age even
saints, apparently, desire above all to be secular.

The logic of theism, then, like the logic of nontheism, has become
increasingly odd. The world we live in seems less tame, wilder, less
malleable than it has ever seemed before. Human experience shows it
to be a bundle of loose ends.

We cannot change the ultimate character of the world; we accept
it—whether in rebellion or in resignation or in gratitude. It remains
what it is; the most we can do is alter it a little. The chief task is to
keep ourselves alive: to preserve the race. Even that we may not
have the sanity, the wisdom or the strength to do. And then we must
alter ourselves: no one of us has achieved the understanding, or the
love, that are still possible for us. Nor is the human race a brother-

hood. "I should like," Albert Camus wrote, "to be able to love my country and still love justice." Which of us fulfills that wish today?

The tasks incumbent upon us are huge. Beside them, the question of theism fades into insignificance. But does it? What did Judaism teach us to expect from life? What did Christianity tell us to look for? Is the world, after all, so different from what the best of our ancestors were led to believe? Even in the caves, a man was able to lay down his life for a brother, or to slay him.

What we cannot accept is the scientific world view of the Judaeo-Christian period. The ancient picture of the cosmos has been fragmented. The harmony and unity and certainty are gone. Yet the need for self-knowledge and the urgency of brotherhood have not disappeared. Where our ancestors once found God in the harmonious cosmic picture (but did they, the serious ones?), we find the poignancy of human aspirations. Are we, then, less theistic than formerly? A wholly altered science alters the conditions of self-knowledge and brotherhood; it does not abrogate their primacy.

To many persons, the traditional communities of faith, cluttered with the residue of a wholly different scientific, cultural viewpoint, no longer speak sense. To others, the essence of these traditional communities has been discerned: that self-knowledge and brotherhood indicate that men, despite appearances, participate in the source of understanding and love. That human persons, despite appearances, are not aliens in an uncomprehending space, but are beloved of one who is called "God." The world known to human experience, these traditional communities of faith dare to propose, is a world in which self-knowledge and brotherhood are basic, constitutional laws. These laws are subject to pragmatic testing. Live by them and see. Taste and see that the Lord is sweet.

Moreover, one may observe the behavior of those who violate these laws: those who flee self-knowledge, or treat other men as means to their own ends. Such men often prosper. But what are the human possibilities they realize? Again, one may observe the behavior of those who are faithful to the examined life, and architects of human brotherhood, who, nevertheless, do not interpret these basic values as signs of God's presence among men. One may observe the secular saints: Socrates, David Hume, Camus, and an increasing legion of others. What kind of world is it in which self-knowledge and brotherhood are not only possible, and not only creative, but also freely chosen by intelligent men who criticize their own presuppositions? It is not a very different world from what Judaism or Christianity (cultural residues aside) would lead me to expect. To the theist, the admirable behavior of the nontheist is one more sign that the constitution of the world has been conceived in intelligence and love. Nontheists live as if there were a God; reflective theists live as if God did nothing, never interfered, never interrupted.

To the nontheist, the intelligent Jew or Christian, when he is at his best, meets secular and humanistic standards of behavior; in *The Plague,* Rieux says of Father Paneloux, "He is one of us." From an empirical point of view, Judaism and Christianity seem to encourage behavior that is indistinguishable from that of representative secular, humanistic heroes. Why not, then, drop all language about "God" and turn churches and synagogues into art museums and centers for remedial reading?

In fact, the theist replies, churches and synagogues have in the past been both. Why not?

God is in man. Grace is everywhere. Nothing is merely secular— the logic of theism and the logic of nontheism are, in our time, becoming blessedly similar. God is not conceived of as the Designer of a thousand-year-plan for the world, nor as a Manipulator, nor Policeman, nor Ticket-taker, nor Supervisor of the status quo. He is thought of, not as a person or a thing, but as the source of understanding and love in human beings. Not as though the prosaic workings of biochemistry were disrupted, but as though faced with the marvels of biochemistry a man shifts from the role of observer to that of participant: conscious, inquiring, seeking to love, he finds himself taking part in a conversation. Faith in God is not a leap, unless breaking a silence and risking rejection is a leap: ordinary courage is required.

For the nontheist, too much poetry, fantasy, illusion are required to make such a risk reasonable. A fact is a fact, not a symbol. Men sometimes understand and sometimes love: that's a fact, signifying nothing.

In argument, theist and nontheist rarely make statements that may be placed in contradiction; they shout past one another. They have been so intent on showing how they differ that each seldom reaches the other's point of view; and converts seldom do justice to the "illusions" of their past. Here we go round a prickly pear.

The test of living: (1) Act in the name of human dignity, and then analyze what beliefs about the world you have taken for granted. (2) Answer a sophomore's questions: "But why should I be good? Why be honest? Why be compassionate?" (3) Reflect: If a commitment to asking questions requires an examined life, that is, actions consistent with my understanding, and if it makes a man pass judgment upon himself, then the drive to ask questions is a central drive in the repertoire of human abilities. The evolutionary process in which it emerges is astonishing. (4) On a quiet winter evening, under a lamp, ask: Why is there anything at all?

The theist and the nontheist continually test their interpretations of human life under the pressures of daily living. The question of theism vs. nontheism is not a scientific question, in the sense that a single experiment can be devised at one moment to test which interpretation of human life is true. Moreover, since nontheists in our society have appropriated so many Jewish and Christian values—the dignity of each person, the importance of community, the significance of historical responsibility and action, compassion, fidelity to understanding, and the like—and since theists recognize that God is not an object, thing, or person, the theoretical difference between believer and unbeliever has become almost impossible to state. No one has seen God. Theist as well as nontheist stand in a darkness, hearing no voices, seeing no visions, feeling no revelatory feelings.

The theist, however, believes that the stories told in his community of faith—of genesis, exodus, promised land; of expectation, contradiction, death and resurrection—illuminate the truth of human life. The theist finds human experience symbolic as well as secular; significant as well as pragmatic. He believes history to be a conversation, a dialogue: responsibility is response to a hidden lover. The stories are not merely stories; their point is real.

The nontheist is much more literal and much more level-headed. He is much more skeptical, pragmatic and stringent. The risk he runs is that of meaninglessness; deprived of symbols, he lives in a desert. He overcomes the risk by "making his own meanings": by choosing to be creative rather than destructive, by preferring friendship to hatred, by valuing human beings as ends rather than as means, by trying to diminish the number of human beings who suffer from poverty, disease, and ignorance. It is precisely in these ways that the theist, who does not see God, believes men to be acting in a way consistent with God's own nature, and, even to be participating in

God's own life. The danger of the theist is to attach the name and sanctions of God to his own small vision of the world; his danger is idolatry. The danger of the nontheist is cynicism.

Nontheist and theist, in our society, need one another. The theist tells the stories in whose light the values by which even the nontheist lives are dramatically illuminated. The nontheist chastens with his skepticism the luxuriant proclivities of the theist for obscurantism, idolatry, and dogmatism.

Three generations hence, our children's children will be poorer if either the symbols or the skepticism are lost. Each of us chooses how much of both he will labor to transmit.

4

The Nonbeliever
and the New Liturgical Movement

There is, without a doubt, a crisis of faith among many American Catholics. In Massachusetts, a fourteen-year-old girl attended a Newman Club meeting, after which she was overheard to say plaintively: "They're talking about new biblical studies and new liturgy, and I came here to find out whether there's a God." In California, a junior in a Catholic girls' high school raised her hand quizzically: "But, sister, what did Christ die to redeem us from?" In a major theological seminary, where three years ago the seminarians thrilled to the new liturgy and the replacement of canned Thomistic theology with lively new biblical theology, the incoming freshmen are reading Sartre and Camus; bible and liturgy mean nothing to them unless they can be sure there is a God.

Moreover, in an affluent, pluralistic, mobile society, a hundred directions lie open before the young; a thousand activities compete for their attention. God is dying not by denial but by inattention. Listen to the average sermon in the average Catholic church: very little of the beauty of the gospels comes through. The moral code is Irish Jansenist. The preacher's experience with modern living is fragmentary, one-sided, jaundiced. His attempts at satire are usually puerile. What is such a man saying to the young? That he has a stake in saying certain boring things; that his style is ugly in comparison with that of folk singers, athletes, young and pragmatic politicians, peace corpsmen, spacemen, playboys and bunnies. The beauty and joy and discipline of modern life lie elsewhere than in the American Catholic clergy.

"What do you think of the new pope?" a friend asked another Catholic at Berkeley. "To be truthful," came the reply, "I never think of him." Organized religion is not saying much to the young. It is not needed. After the anxieties of very early adolescence, when its solace is feverishly sought, it has nothing to contribute. Some American priests are impossible to talk to; they are conformists, boosters who speak clichés. Too many are organization men. The young among them—young in spirit or young in age—are risking reputation, life, and limb in the move for social justice, in the attempt to create genuine community and the development of free consciences among their people; but the new priests, who are our hope, are still too few and subject to too many crippling pressures from behind their backs—from an authoritarian pastor, from organizationally prudent chancery officials, or from timid bishops. (It should be plain that some pastors, chancery officials, and bishops are among the new priests; may their numbers multiply.)

The following paper was read in Kiel Auditorium in St. Louis in 1964 before the convention of the national liturgical conference, which for more years than my lifetime has been fighting for the liturgical reforms finally achieved at the Second Vatican Council. The preceding autumn, in Rome, an old priest of seventy had approached me and introduced himself. "I'm on my vacation," he said. "I was a charter member of the liturgical conference back in the beginning. One of the 'nuts,' they called us then." His eyes were shining. "I just wanted to come here and see the final voting." John Cogley overheard and said to me: "These are the people who bore the day and the heat. We owe it all to them. They were the heroes."

In the stifling August of 1964 in St. Louis, it was now safe to attend liturgical conferences. There were sixteen thousand people in the hall. I sat almost alone on a vast expanse of stage raised six feet above the convention floor, waiting forty minutes before it was my turn to speak. I remember the occasion vividly: my stomach was riotously sick and every long-drawn moment seemed to bring me closer to disaster. I pressed my nails into my palms until they almost broke the skin. At the microphone

I spoke nervously and quickly, longing to get away; but then the crisis passed.

At certain parts of my talk, several prominently placed monsignori and priests walked out, some of them in protest. It amazes me still that Catholics do not see themselves as others see them. Some actually think Catholics are, morally and in the life of the spirit, a superior people. They attribute less inflated evaluations to prejudice or bitterness.

IN the century in which we live, since the year 1900, almost fifty million persons in Europe alone have died by violence. Hundreds of thousands of men and women, men and women like ourselves, have died under nighttime bombing raids; fallen under the onslaught of strafing airplanes as they fled down open roads; or died, hungry, chased as refugees by hostile armies from their homes. Moreover, this century of bloodshed is not yet at an end. Even as we sit here, guns are still being fired, tanks are moving, and men of flesh and blood are being killed. Even as we sit here, whether we think of it or not, the same social, moral, political, and economic forces which led to the destruction of so many innocent lives are still operative around us. No one of us knows if we ourselves will live out the length of our days without violence. No one of us knows whether economic or political forces over which we have no control might not suddenly and radically interrupt our lives, move us to a different place on this continent, or take away our own lives or the lives of those we love.

It was in this century of bloodshed that the Second Vatican Council was convened. Pope John said it was done "to let fresh air into the Church" and to "bring the Church up to today." For in the flames and the ruins in which the Europe of 1945 was engulfed, many saw the end of the Middle Ages. A new era of human history was beginning. Beliefs that everyone held secure had been eroded. Old certainties had collapsed. Far more than half the world no longer believed in God. What has the Church, in fact, to say to the new world being born?

In the eyes of many well-educated men, perhaps of most educated men, the Church has almost nothing of value to say to men in this new age. When such men look at questions of social justice, of the rights of minorities like the Negroes, they do not find that the Church has shown much heroic leadership. In their eyes, it seems as though the Church has simply drifted with the crowd. When Hitler assumed power in Europe, the Church condemned him, to be sure, in an obscure encyclical; but meanwhile, the Catholics of Germany were allowed with undisturbed conscience to fight in his armies and to take part in his crimes. In our country, except for some few instances of heroic and early action, the Church has for the most part waited for the Supreme Court and for Negro leaders themselves, before it committed itself to the cause of racial justice. In fact, it is still plain to most nonbelievers in most regions of this country, that Catholics are noticeably lacking among those who support, with actions, the rights of Negroes to their full place in the family, the friendship, and the activities of first-class citizenship.

When the nonbeliever in this country, not only at such places as on the secular campuses, but also in the great business concerns, in the fields of culture and the arts, and in political or professional life, looks out upon the life of religious organizations in this country, including the Roman Catholic Church, he is very seldom struck with admiration. On the contrary, he usually turns away from organized religion with revulsion. To many such men, it seems immoral to be religious in this country. To belong to a church seems to be a betrayal of justice and of truth. To belong to a religious organization in this country seems to mean that one must cease being honest, cease being humble, cease being willing to admit the mistakes of one's own group, cease being open to the consciences of others.

Moreover, most educated men of good will in the nonbelieving community feel that in joining a religious organization, one must cease being faithful even to one's own conscience. They note, for example, that priests cannot speak out according to their own conscience, but must follow the policy of the organization to which they belong, under penalty of serious rebuke. They find that laymen, too, must say what they are told is true, rather than what they might think is true, not only in matters of doctrine, but often even in matters of policy.

They find that religious people are often more eager for apologetics, and more defensive about the image of their organization, than eager to be truthful and honest. They believe that most religious people turn, not to the living God, who judges all men's works and finds them wanting, but to a sentimental God, who gives comfort and peace of mind. They think that religious people are fundamentally selfish and clannish, and rely upon God only as a crutch in the face of their loneliness and the confusions of life on earth. They do not think that religion is a source of moral strength, but rather of moral weakness. They believe that religion dulls the critical faculty and the sensitive conscience. They believe that they can be more conscientious, more honest, more compassionate to the sufferings of others, if they keep themselves free of religious organizations, than if they would join them.

Thus many educated Americans of good will watch the proceedings of the Vatican Council with interest and condescension. They observe that the Council approved the ruling that people can begin to pray in their own language, four hundred years after the Protestants grasped the importance of the vernacular. They watch the Council Fathers argue about the retirement age of bishops, years after ordinary business firms and universities have seen the necessity of laws about retirement. They take Pope John literally when he said that the Church needs to be "brought up to today." They find the Church incredibly backward and they wait for it to tell them a single bit of good news which they have not heard before, and can accept honestly and meaningfully.

It is almost impossible to exaggerate the moral irrelevance of the Church in the eyes of well-educated and well-intentioned persons in our own land. Such persons often believe that the Church is a power bloc, first intent on self-preservation, on announcing its own rights, on defending its own interests; and interested in helping others only when there is something in it for the Church. They find very few Catholics, and certainly not the whole organization, willing to sacrifice themselves for the sake of conscience, for the sake of justice, for the sake of truth. They see very few signs that the Church is even close to being as divine as she claims to be.

There is, then, much that Catholics who are engaged in the liturgical renewal can learn from the judgment passed upon the Church by the nonbeliever. If we look around at our American Catholic Church, we find that so many of its energies are drained off into materialistic interests: into money-raising campaigns, into putting up buildings, into the sponsoring of large rallies. The Church seems so much engaged in externals, so terribly interested in institutional forms, that the life of the Gospels appears to be by comparison neglected. In how many sermons, in how many parishes, is far more heard of the need for money than about the thirst after justice and the life of honesty which the Gospels enjoin?

It seems that the liturgical movement must now begin to set new goals for itself. Thirty years ago, twenty years ago, ten years ago, five years ago, it took some courage to belong to the liturgical movement. Even some in authority looked upon liturgists as "crackpots." Now look at the crowds which a liturgical meeting can gather. We can each ask ourselves, "Where was I ten years ago when the going was rough?" Now that everyone is on the bandwagon, now that it is the law, it is easy to belong. It is time again, then, to begin a new pioneer movement. It is time again to make it necessary to have honesty and courage if one wants to belong to the liturgical movement. It is time to pick up our baggage and march off again on a new adventure.

Pope Paul announced at the beginning of the second session that the fourth aim of the Council was to begin a dialogue with the modern world. If we are willing to listen and to learn from what the men of good will, who do not believe in God, have to tell us about ourselves, then perhaps we shall be ready for this dialogue. They tell us that we lack courage and honesty, that we are conformists, that we are afraid of conscience. They tell us that we have forgotten the Gospels and prefer institutional peace, institutional order, institutional security, to the claims of conscience, the claims of justice, the claims of honesty. And I think that we must say that those accusations, however painful, are rather true.

How can we recover the spirit of the Gospels? I think that we must begin to remember that we are the people of God, not because we have large buildings, not because we are wealthy, not because we have an extensive Canon Law, but because we are humble people among whom the Word of God is being spoken. We must begin to recapture the ideals of those small groups of Christians who met together informally in living rooms, who celebrated the sacraments in small groups in which the experience of community and oneness was very clear. We must begin, as much as we can, to move out of our churches, to abandon the great institutional structure which weighs us down on our pilgrimage. We must be aware of the dangers of our wealth, we must be aware of the betrayal of the Gospels possible because of the largeness of our institution.

To be specific, I think we must begin to encourage the decentralization of our parishes. In some places, and at some times, it would seem good if we could create a more informal liturgy, a liturgy capable of being celebrated in more humble surroundings than that of our great European-style churches. It would be good if our curates could be celebrating Mass in different parts of the parish, in homes where there are special troubles, or in neighborhoods where there are special social problems. It would be good for our priests, and it would be good for our people. Sometimes, of course, it is good to have the whole Christian community gathered in a very large parish, where all social classes, all nationalities, men of all races, can meet. (But we must confess that that happens less and less in our parishes, which are located in neighborhoods rather homogeneous in social structure and social class.) It would be good if the priest could carry the Christian mysteries out of the church buildings and into the homes, stores, gymnasiums, and meeting places where we laymen live out our daily lives.

The liturgy is the prayer of the people of God. It is a realistic prayer. It is in this prayer that most of what the Church has to say to the world is said. It is in the liturgy that the Word is preached. The nonbeliever who comes to the large institutional church can hardly hear that Word. It is not the believing community that he most often finds there; it is a crowd of individuals. It is rare that the sense of community can be experienced in so large a crowd. Moreover, in such a large crowd the preacher must water down the Word of God to the least common denominator. He does not know his people; his people do not know him.

Ways need to be found to break down our large crowds into small communities of believers. There are enough priests for this task, in America at least, if they are used wisely. There are seven days in a week. Where there are four curates in a parish, on six days of the week Mass may be said in different places. In twenty-four places in the parish, during the week, small groups of believers might then meet around the mysteries of God, meditating for a while on God's Word, speaking for a while on the situation of the Gospels in their neighborhood, and then bowing their heads together as God comes into their midst in the Sacrament.

This kind of witness, I think, the nonbeliever could begin to understand. In small groups where there is discussion, it soon becomes possible for individuals to become honest. In small groups where there is common reflection on the Word of God, it soon becomes possible for the individual conscience to awaken and take responsibility for understanding what God is trying to say to him in his particular environment. In such small groups it becomes possible to experience what it is like for two, three, or even twenty to be gathered together in the Lord's name. In such small groups, apart from the riches and burdens of a huge and wealthy institution, it becomes possible to understand what the Gospels are trying to say to men. Such small groups, moreover, would nourish persons of honesty and courage, of responsibility and initiative, who would for the first time in their lives, perhaps, begin to understand what it is to be a Christian. And when Christians begin to understand what it is to be Christian, then perhaps nonbelievers will also begin to understand. For the tragedy is: The consciences of most of us have been asleep. We have indeed been out of date. We have not felt a sense of community, one with another. We have not shown much sign of that thirst after justice which would have before now given us many American martyrs in the cause of justice, in a country which in so many ways lacks, in practice, the justice on whose theory it prides itself so much.

We can have full sympathy with the nonbeliever who, in our presence, in our behavior, observing our attitudes, does not see Christ. It is difficult sometimes to find him in our midst ourselves. The nonbeliever functions, in part, as our conscience. And we, if ever we awaken to what the Gospels really mean to us in our generation, will begin again to function as the conscience of the nonbeliever.

Now that the first, early, heroic liturgical movement has seen the fruition of its sacrifices, the new Constitution on the Liturgy, let those who are hardy and who love the Gospels set off for a new horizon: a liturgy close to the Gospels, small communities alive to the Gospels, informal and experimental liturgical forms in which the spirit of the Gospels has room to breathe again. As a witness to the Gospels, our vast institution is not credible. The new liturgical movement must set its sights on replacing the power bloc with the praying community, on making the Word of God as important as fund-raising, on making worship more important than buildings. The new liturgical movement has a more spiritual task than the old; and it must beware of settling down. We have barely begun to "come up to today." If we are to preach the Gospels so that they can be understood by the men among whom we live, and whom we love, we must set off on another, and equally arduous, equally unpopular, equally suspect journey. The history of the people of God has always been the history of a journey. On this pilgrimage, there is no final stopping place. Let us begin again, then, for our own sake, and for that of our nonbelieving friends.

5

Lonergan's Starting Place: The Performance of Asking Questions

Fifty years ago, one of the movements that gave greatest hope of a Catholic reform in the twentieth century was led by Jacques Maritain and Étienne Gilson, the one a historian of medieval philosophy, the other a recoverer of medieval philosophical themes. Today neo-Thomism is already dimming in memory, and it is fashionable to be condescending toward it. Nevertheless, neo-Thomism played a significant role in contemporary intellectual history. Among Catholics, in particular, it served to provide historical leverage against the Catholic style of the eighteenth and nineteenth centuries—the nonhistorical, static, immobile ideal established by Bossuet and, granted the cultural isolation of Spain, Italy, and Ireland and the ultramontanism dominant in France, still solidly regnant. As soon as one began to study history, even medieval history, easy certitudes and illusory permanencies began to disintegrate.

Neo-Thomism was the first stage in the construction of a new Catholic contribution to modern intellectual life. A second stage has also been reached, a stage hardly known to the American public. This stage was initiated by Maurice Blondel and Joseph Maréchal, and was constituted by an effort to rethink certain key suggestions derived from a study of ancient and medieval philosophy: the analysis of action and intentionality, in particular. If it can be said that modern philosophy since Descartes shows certain key assumptions which serve to characterize it as modern, the study of the thought of other eras was bound to uncover other assumptions and other starting places. Such discoveries could not help having a salutary and creative effect on the current philosophical scene. Through Bolzano in fact, a predecessor of Blondel and Maréchal, the importance of an analysis of intentionality had already struck Husserl and Heidegger. The meaning of action, symbol, intentionality—these, it seems, are key elements in the building of a new human ethic.

The most thorough and profound laborer in this second stage of the Catholic intellectual revival has been a little-known philosopher and theologian, Bernard Lonergan. In a Festschrift *for his sixtieth birthday in 1965, published in* Continuum, *I prepared an introduction to the starting place and basic data in the thinking of Bernard Lonergan. The introduction was aimed at linking the thought of Lonergan to some main currents in American philosophy.*

For it is at this point, in actual work in contemporary secular philosophy, that the third stage of the Catholic intellectual revival comes into its own. Many younger Catholic intellectuals owe their intellectual orientation entirely to modern fields like anthropology, sociology, psychology, or secular philosophy. The generations of isolation—the seven centuries of laziness, Maritain called them—are at an end.

If I were asked to locate my own work, I would say that it is moving between the second and third stages. I owe the greatest stimulation of my undergraduate years to Maritain. I read everything of his I could get my hands on, and formed the ambition of reading everything of his he had ever written (which I have not fulfilled). There were three things, especially, he taught me. First, that the main intellectual task was to speak to our own time: to its poetry, its painting, its politics, its social revolutions, its epistemology, its psychology. Second, that intellectual activity is not wholly expressed in, nor exhausted by, concepts and words; his analysis of creative intuition in the arts liberated me from the vice of words. Third, that liberty is the only air the human personality can breathe, and that contingency and unrepeatable circumstance characterize the texture in which human beings act.

Yet, when all is said and done, Maritain—the gentlest and most charitable of philosophers (after his first two books, at least)—is too much

committed to a language impossible to make fully resonant today. Con-
sequently, my delight in encountering Bernard Lonergan's Insight *was*
intense. Two things struck me about that book. First, I had long thought
that the work of Aristotle and Aquinas must have some relatively simple
starting place. What was it? What lay behind all the many maxims, prin-
ciples, and convictions that recurred in their most important arguments?
It must be possible, I thought, to climb up on their shoulders and begin
as they began; it must be possible to attain the central point from which
the dialectic of their work became intelligible. Lonergan, it seems to me,
has laboriously occupied that position with more intelligence than any
other thinker. Secondly, Lonergan thinks and writes in his native English;
the Anglo-Saxon sense of the concrete, the contingent, the empirical has
reinforced him countless times in his efforts to track down the method
of his chosen guides. Lonergan has made it possible to liberate his chosen
tradition from the dead, bracken waters of static Latin scholasticism, and
to make an ancient stream of thought flow into our more congenial
empirical and pragmatic contemporary currents.

I am far from imagining that the task of working out a profound
empiricism, a profound pragmatism, joining old with new currents, has
been accomplished. Lonergan's contribution from the remote side of the
chasm has been herculean. To join that work with the near side of con-
temporary thought remains a further arduous task. It is but one of the
many kinds of effort which must go into the third stage of contemporary
Catholic intellectual development. That third stage has hardly been
begun: creative insight and criticism applied according to the highest
secular standards to the secular issues of a world of violence and hope.

I. *Pragmatism and Ordinary Language*

SIDNEY HOOK has described his vision of an admirable faith for
the man of the future as a "commitment to the processes and methods
of critical intelligence." [1] It is noteworthy that Professor Hook does
not look for some proposition, some truth, on which to base his
philosophic faith. Instead, he points to a performance, or, rather, to
the moving principle by which particular successful performances are
favored: to critical intelligence and its ability to select successful

processes and methods. Moreover, the performance to which he points is not restricted to philosophers. "All human beings in their everyday experience are guided by the conception of knowledge as scientific knowledge. To deny this is palpably insincere." [2] "The naturalist believes that his assumptions are reasonable because they express, in a more general way, no more than what is expressed by any nonphilosopher, as well as by all philosophers, whatever their school, in their successful working practice. . . ." [3]

Mr. Hook's faith, admittedly, is based on a decision. "But the decision is not arbitrary: one can give good reasons for it or can point to the historical evidence that makes it a reasonable decision, show that in the past generalizations supported merely by hunches, guesses, visions, revelations, *a priori* reasoning have turned out to be unreliable and have failed to predict the occurrences with which they were concerned. In short, the justification for asserting that all knowledge is scientific is not a matter of definition, but is, rather, pragmatic: such a view enables us to achieve our ends in the world, whatever they are, more effectively." [4]

In these few sentences, Mr. Hook has provided us with a suitable way of entering into the philosophy of Bernard Lonergan. There are three mainsprings to Mr. Hook's views, here so briefly cited. (1) His starting place is the dynamism of critical intelligence, i.e., commitment to the processes and methods of science. (2) This critical intelligence is conceived as operative throughout the whole range of human knowing. (3) The choice of critical intelligence as the starting place of philosophy is conceived as a rational choice, for which compelling reasons can be given. Thus, in principle, Mr. Hook's philosophy is self-authenticating; the procedure by which he justifies his choice of his philosophy is the very procedure which is the heart of his philosophy. Critical intelligence offers him both his method and his justification for choosing that method.

We may, of course, choose to quarrel with the way Mr. Hook has formulated human cognitional experience. But the underlying experiences to which he points are indisputable. Men do ask questions; ultimately, this asking of questions springs from the active, restless demands of critical intelligence. In action, this intelligence develops, criticizes, and authenticates methods which meet its own standards. The choice of critical intelligence as the starting place for philosophy is indeed rational and self-authenticating.

Thus we may say that basic, common cognitional experiences are available to every man: wonder, inquiry, understanding, reflection, reasonable choice. But when each man reflects upon these experiences he is apt to interpret them differently than his fellows. It is on this second, mediate level that metaphysics occurs; metaphysics is the articulation of basic experience, the mediation (through reflection) of the immediate.[5] Lonergan's genius is to have seen that metaphysics has its ground in immediate cognitional experience, and that various metaphysical systems are overt or covert attempts to articulate this experience. Thus he has carried Kant's revolution, a "halfway house," [6] to its term. He has returned metaphysics to its place of origin in human experience, where its assertions can be systematically and singly verified. By beginning and ending in common, ordinary experience, he has exorcised from the Western tradition that gnosticism which pretends, from above, to encompass experience and history in the grasp of necessity and logical system. As Mr. Henry David Aiken has written: "Reason, it cannot be too often said, is not a *Logos,* but an activity of the human mind. . . . We cannot possibly rehabilitate the gnostic cult of reason which dominated Western philosophy till the end of the eighteenth century. And we cannot do so because, since Kant, the devastating criticism of that cult has undermined the spurious mystique upon which it rests." [7] Lonergan has done a more thorough job on that mystique than Kant. And he has also been more faithful to the experience of critical intelligence.

Mr. Aiken has further written of reason as an activity: "In the course of history it has taken many different forms and its standards have been constantly subject to change in accordance with man's changing conception of himself." [8] That is why Lonergan's emphasis on the correct articulation of cognitional experience is so insistent: "Every statement in philosophy and metaphysics can be shown to imply statements regarding cognitional fact." [9] He centers philosophical discussion upon that cognitional experience which, as Mr. Hook testifies, all men share. He invites Mr. Hook and Mr. Aiken and all who might be similarly concerned to measure their accounts of this cognitional experience against his own. As a man conceives his knowing to be, so he conceives himself to be. Thus Mr. Aiken writes: "Philosophical analysis is, at bottom, nothing but the device by means of which we attempt to discover, or uncover, what we really are." [10]

But Mr. Aiken believes that one key to cognitional experience lies in an analysis of a given ordinary language. Thus he is caught in a web not of his own making. "I do not choose what I mean, or intend, by truth or by justice; nor do I decide what principle of knowledge or of justice I will live by. I find myself talking and thinking in a certain way, just as I find, sometimes with great difficulty, those ideals and procedures by which I live." [11] "The philosophers of ordinary language, as I envisage them, are classicists and traditionalists, who, without illusions of perfection, seek to understand and through that understanding to keep alive, the forms of language and of life which, partly by instinct, partly by conviction, determine what we are." [12]

Lonergan does not choose to restrict his analysis of cognitional experience to the analysis of ordinary language. His break with gnosticism is sufficiently deep and secure for him not to need the added caution of confining himself to the cultural, possibly mythic consciousness in which he finds himself. Why should he escape one flight from critical intelligence, only to enmesh himself in what quite probably is another? Mr. Aiken appears to be faithful to critical intelligence, but cautiously: "Wise men, wherever they are, always live ambiguously in the middle way between tradition and revolution. The part of intelligence is to conserve and reform the old patterns when we can and to fashion new ones, gradually, as we must, creating but also re-creating our spiritual destiny, piecemeal, as we go along." [13] Mr. Aiken's wise man seems more politic than philosophical; in politics, Lonergan might approve such wisdom but in philosophy he demands a more searching fidelity. By our critical intelligence, we can criticize the world view implied in the present usages of ordinary language; surely that view is not sacrosanct, nor need we be afraid of intelligence which is faithful to experience.

The difference in the beginning between Lonergan and Aiken in their articulation of cognitional experience, however, comes out, too, in the end. Mr. Aiken dreams of a society "of emancipated, civilized men, who, through reticence, tact, and self-control, are able to redeem the time through consecutive acts of creation, intelligence, and love. . . ." [14] His citizens "would refuse to be overborne by the thought of death. . . . On the contrary, they would find in the amenities and in the work of civilized life an honest alternative to the morbid and self-destructive preoccupation with 'ultimate concern,' whose objectless ends they cannot, finally, fathom." [15] But the openness Lonergan demands is not so easily lulled by amenities and activity; the drive to which day by day he insists on being faithful raises ever further questions about man, his history and his destiny. More radically faithful to critical intelligence than Mr. Aiken, he has a more radical view of the significance and power of critical intelligence in the universe in which we live. Without being morbid, and without trying to "fathom" ends not revealed to man, he, nevertheless, is faithful to the questions intelligence raises about matters of 'ultimate concern.'

II. *Lonergan's Starting Place*

Where does Lonergan start? Like Mr. Hook, he begins not from a statement, a proposition, a truth, but from a performance.[16] He chooses a performance which begins in childhood, that of asking questions. No doubt can be entertained about the fact of the performance. "To doubt questioning is to ask whether questions occur. The condition of the possibility of doubting is the occurrence of questioning." [17] In the performance of asking questions, he hits upon a clearly known, universally accessible, indubitable occurrence. In this occurrence, he anchors a presuppositionless, self-correcting, nondeductive metaphysics. "No doubt the proper place to begin is at the beginning, but some say one issue and others say another is the proper beginning. So there is a question about the beginning and, indeed, no matter where one starts, one starts from some question." [18] For Lonergan, questioning itself is the beginning.

What is found in every question "to constitute it, not as a question about this rather than about that, but simply as questioning? . . . The condition of the possibility of any and all questions is an awareness. . . . What is the awareness of? . . . the questionable is unrestricted: to propose a limit to questioning is to raise the question of the legitimacy of asking questions beyond the limit; and raising this question is already beyond the limit." [19] Men can question anything, and seek methods for answering any question, or for showing that it cannot be answered. But to ask any particular question is to presuppose answers to prior questions. If one drives back particular questions far enough, one catches oneself presupposing the unformed, unstructured "Why?" which is at the heart of human intelligence. Because this radical "Why?" is unstructured, critical intelligence can inspect and revise its own procedures, questioning its own methods of inquiry. This is why Mr. Aiken could note that reason in the course of history has taken many forms and often revised its standards, and it is also why Mr. Hook could appeal to critical intelligence in justifying his allegiance to critical intelligence. The pure, unstructured, unlimited drive to understand is the self-authenticating root of human cognition.

This pure, unlimited drive to understand is a fact and also an achievement.[20] It is a fact, but it is not always operative. It is, when functioning, immediately given. But we become aware of it through the mediation of reflection: it is presupposed in the asking of particular questions, and in the ability to criticize, to revise, and to shift our line of inquiry. Let us try to get at it from another direction, by a more descriptive appeal to cognitional experience.

As a particular question emerges in our awareness, we sometimes feel a psychological tension, which has its release in the joy of discovery. "It is that tension, that drive, that desire to understand, that constitutes the primordial 'Why?' Name it what you please, alertness of mind, intellectual curiosity, the spirit of inquiry, active intelligence, the drive to know. . . . It is prior to any insights, any concepts, any words, for insights, concepts, words have to do with answers; and before we look for answers, we want them; such wanting is the pure question." [21] On the other hand, the pure question presupposes experiences and images; it is about the concretely given or imagined. "No one just wonders. We wonder about something." [22]

In shorthand, we may name this pure question "openness." Obviously, it does not, as fact, dominate human consciousness. "It is a fact to which man has to advert, which he has to acknowledge and accept, whose implications for all his thinking and acting have to be worked out and successfully applied to actual thinking and actual acting." [23] The history of religion, of the sciences, of philosophy is the record, not always favorable, of this achievement. If we limit ourselves for the moment to its achievement in the person of the trained scientific observer, we can see how this openness both enriches and makes demands upon a man's attention, perceptual consciousness, interests, desires, fears, memories, imagination:

For the guiding orientation of the scientist is the orientation of inquiring intelligence, the orientation that of its nature is a pure, detached, disinterested desire simply to know. For there is an intellectual desire, an

Eros of the mind. Without it, there would arise no questioning, no inquiry, no wonder. Without it, there would be no real meaning for such phrases as scientific disinterestedness, scientific detachment, scientific impartiality. Inasmuch as this intellectual drive is dominant, inasmuch as the reinforcing or inhibiting tendencies of other drives are successfully excluded, in that measure the scientific observer becomes an incarnation of inquiring intelligence and his percepts move into coincidence with what are named the data of sense. Accordingly, it is not by sinking into some inert passivity but by positive effort and rigorous training that a man becomes a master of the difficult art of scientific observation.[24]

There is a latent metaphysics in all our knowing; [25] it is immediate and unverbalized. "But it has to be thematized and made explicit, to be brought out into the open in accurately defined concepts and certain judgments. The main task of the metaphysician is not to reveal or prove what is new and unknown; it is to give scientific expression to what already is implicitly acknowledged without being explicitly recognized." [26] Presuppositionless metaphysics begins from questioning: not from the appearance of it, nor from the concept of it, nor from judgments about it, but from the performance.[27] But questioning has two sides, an objective pole and a subjective pole. Lonergan supplies a technical metaphor, horizon,[28] to express how these two poles operate together.

Literally, a horizon is a maximum field of vision from a determinate standpoint; it is specified by two poles, one objective and one subjective, with each pole conditioning the other. The subjective pole is the questioner; more precisely it is his pure, unrestricted drive to know. The objective pole is all that can be questioned. As the subjective pole is unlimited, since man can ask questions about anything, so is the objective pole unlimited. As the subjective pole is one, so is the objective pole one. The subjective pole—the unrestricted drive—is a principle of possible achievement. In actual history, enlargements of man's horizon occur as the subjective pole sweeps more freely into the realm of the objective pole. The primordial unrestrictedness of the subjective pole defines the ultimate horizon that is to be reached only through successive enlargement of the actual horizon.

This pincers movement between subjective pole and objective pole gives Lonergan a tool for defining, flexibly and without imposing a scheme *a priori* or from above, a projection of all that is to be known.

He does not define this field objectively, through its contents, which are as yet unknown. He defines it subjectively, according to the un-restrictedness of the subjective pole. "Thoroughly understand what it is to understand, and not only will you understand the broad lines of all there is to be understood but also you will possess a fixed base, an invariant pattern, opening upon all further developments of under-standing." [29]

What is this "fixed base"? The word 'fixed' can be misleading. Lonergan does not mean that there are a certain number of *propositions* that are invariant. He means that a certain pattern of operations is invariant. He means, it seems, what Mr. Hook means when he sides with John Dewey and Bertrand Russell in defending the thesis that "All knowledge that men have is scientific knowledge." [30] The reason why Mr. Hook finds it "palpably insincere" to deny this thesis is that certain successful intellectual operations are, in some respects, in-variant. Lonergan differs significantly from Mr. Hook, as well as from Dewey and Russell, in his articulation of what these invariant features are. But the issue between Lonergan, Hook, Dewey, and Russell is experimentally decidable. We each have available the immediate cog-nitional experiences which are in question. We each have experienced what it is to know, and hence the invariant features of knowing. We may study the articulation given these experiences by each of these men and choose which most adequately expresses the evidence. We must each perform this test for ourselves; there is no short-cut to self-appropriation in our approach to knowing.

Lonergan is quite clear on the fact that even in this process of deciding between rival interpretations of the activity of understanding we must employ understanding. That is why he believes that the starting place he has chosen for his philosophy is the pivotal one. Even if one were to disagree with Lonergan's articulation of what happens when one understands, one would merely be articulating dif-ferently than Lonergan the central experiences in question. Were a rival articulation better than Lonergan's, Lonergan would have no other choice—if he is to be faithful to understanding—than to accept the better view. In any case, his point about the centrality of a correct understanding of understanding has nothing to lose, but everything to gain, from such challenges.

Lonergan's articulation of what it is to understand rests on three basic terms, two correlations, and a basic orientation.[31] *The basic terms* refer to three cognitional experiences: (1) The experience of becoming aware of data, in such a way that these data provoke questions; and this experience he calls empirical consciousness. (2) The experience of getting the point, hitting on the solution, having insight into data, which issues in a concept unifying the data, i.e., offering an answer to the question posed by the data; and this experience of joyful discovery or rational ordering he calls intellectual consciousness. (3) The experience of reflection, in which one questions whether the answer proposed by intelligent consciousness in fact meets the conditions posed by empirical consciousness; and this experience of self-appropriation and verification is called rational consciousness.

The first two experiences—name them as one pleases—are easier to identify in one's own experience; the third is more complex, but equally accessible. Mr. Hook, for example, was adverting to the third experience when he gave an account of the reasons which led him to declare that his identification of human knowledge with scientific knowledge was reasonable. He had in his possession the data about the two terms "scientific knowledge" and "human knowledge" (empirical consciousness), had the insight into their identity (intelligent consciousness), and finally assured himself that the identification was reasonable (rational consciousness). Long overlooked in the desire to find a short-cut to certainty through immediate sense-experience or immediate insight (Berkeley's "naked, undisguised ideas"), this experience of reflection is being recovered in contemporary Anglo-American investigations into the objectivity or reasonableness of ethical judgments.

If the basic terms in Lonergan's articulation of what it is to understand are empirical consciousness, intellectual consciousness, and rational consciousness (other names would do as well), *the basic correlations* are the relations of (1) to (2), and of (1) *and* (2) to (3). Awakened to empirical consciousness, we may have questions, but we do not progress to understanding until we are made intelligently conscious by insight; until we achieve intelligent consciousness, we are merely searching and puzzled. But even when we are conscious empirically and intelligently, we do not yet know whether we *know* the answer we are looking for. We have *an* answer, but is it a good answer? Not all bright ideas are sound ideas. So empirical and intellectual consciousness must be assessed in the light of rational consciousness. What are our criteria of relevance and evidence? Is the question posed correctly, and does the answer meet it? . . . One important use of the word "to know" in ordinary English, J. L. Austin points out, involves the claim to have answered just such questions.[32] It is when we use the word in this sense that we have, Lonergan would say, rationally appropriated our own knowing: authenticated for ourselves the claim that we in fact know what we say we know.

The basic orientation of Lonergan's articulation of what it is to understand is the pure, detached, disinterested drive to know. As an immediate fact, which can be brought to consciousness through the mediation of reflection, this drive—as we have seen—constitutes one pole of the horizon of human knowing. It is important to emphasize the fact that Lonergan's articulation lays great stress on this subjective pole. For it is the flexibility, self-revision, self-correction, and unrestricted sweep of which this pole is capable that differentiates Lonergan's metaphysics from the gnostic, rationalistic systems of the past. There is here no conceptual system in which the subject is already or is to become enmeshed. There are here no logical categories (Aristotle) nor psychological categories (Kant) to which facts must be made to conform. The detached, disinterested drive to understand criticizes and revises itself, so as to respect and to adapt itself to those things it questions. It is supple and free.

On the other hand, it would be a serious misconception of his task if the knower were to rest satisfied with the claims made, so to speak, in the name of this subjective pole alone. For the knower may claim to know and be mistaken; the subjective feeling of satisfaction is the same whether his knowing is correct or incorrect. If the knower is to be faithful to the drive to know, he will want to attend to the *contents* of the knowing act as much as to his subjective satisfaction. We do not wonder for the sake of wondering but for the sake of correct understanding. It would likewise be a mistake, common in times of romanticism, to glorify the process of inquiry, at the expense of the acquired and verified achievements of inquiry, however tentative and incomplete. It is by means of gradual enlargements of our present horizon that we proceed toward the ultimate horizon toward which, whether we entirely wish it or not, the Eros of understanding propels us. Our progress is by means of a rhythm of restlessness and rest,[33] and both moments are to be respected.

Lonergan's entire effort is directed against the many flights from understanding to which he and we are prey. He tries to expose the incoherence into which misapprehensions about understanding lead us. Such incoherence is not necessarily verbal or propositional. We sometimes misunderstand our own capacities, and this infidelity to ourselves shows up, sooner or later, in our inability to do all that we might do—and, usually, have given signs of hoping to do. Thus Sidney Hook early commits himself to "scientific knowledge," only to end up proposing a philosophy of "speculative audacity": a philosophy which "must be consistent with the findings of science, but outruns and outreaches at any given moment what we strictly know. It is an informed commitment and an intelligent guide to action on behalf of moral ideals." [34] Mr. Hook's commitment to critical intelligence therefore, seems to be broader than a strict construction of "scientific" or even "pragmatic" warrants. His practice is richer than his theory; his earlier position is belied by his later.

A philosophy cannot be proved deductively.[35] Neither can one choose between rival philosophies deductively, by matching them side-by-side and proving one to be logically inconsistent as against the other. To measure realism against the standards of idealism, or idealism against those of realism, is to understand neither the one nor the other. To impose on existentialism the methods of ordinary language analysis, or on ordinary language analysis the concerns of existentialism, is to misrepresent the aims and genius of each. "The reason is that horizon is prior to the meaning of statements—problems and solutions are what they are only in virtue of the horizon in which they arise; they cannot be transported intact into a different horizon." [36] Nor is there a conceptual over-system, a philosophy of philosophies, in which differences of opinion can proposition by proposition be mapped and reconciled.

But there is an unlimited, unrestricted drive to understand, which can adapt itself for particular purposes to any method of inquiry, within any framework, and so adapt itself to any horizon. Absolutely, at least, whether or not anywhere there is a man with sufficient empathy to carry out so vast a project, there is the possibility that each philosophical system can be entered from within, and its differences from other systems sympathetically articulated. For in every system of philosophy there is a latent cognitional theory. And the cognitional experiences of which such theories are attempted articulations, implicitly or explicitly, are immediately and universally accessible. In each system, there is the performance of asking questions. And that is the starting place of cognitional inquiry.

Once having decided on his starting place, Lonergan's program [37] is to discriminate between the two basic relations to which we earlier referred: between the relation of empirical consciousness to intellectual consciousness, and the relation of empirical and intellectual consciousness to rational consciousness. For to discriminate in our own consciousness between these two basic relations is to discriminate between two stages of knowing which we experience: between intuition and knowing that we know. Next, he tries to articulate the experience of knowing—not on the objective side, in all the details of the known, but on the subjective side, in the knowing. He is not interested in cataloguing the experience of knowing in a table of abstract properties; he aims at appropriating the experience articulately and reflectively in his own consciousness. He encourages us to understand knowing not from "outside" as something that occurs in other people, but consciously, in ourselves. His aim is not that we make some sudden leap to a new theory about ourselves, but that painstakingly and carefully we grow into a secure understanding of our own understanding. Finally, he does not appeal to the logic of a goal as yet unknown to ourselves, nor to a presupposed and already structured system of metaphysics foreign to us, but to a personal development of which any cultured consciousness is capable, a development driven by the dynamics of our own consciousness, heading through understanding of ourselves to an understanding of all that we can understand.

The program sounds vaguely familiar. Did not Descartes' *Discourse on Method,* Locke's *Essay on Human Understanding,* Hume's *Inquiry* and *Treatise,* Kant's *Critique* take up the same challenge? The reader cannot help noting, however, that Lonergan's effort is significantly more supple, nuanced, and experiential than that of his predecessors. Moreover, the duality in human knowing which they tried to heal has been set in rounder, fuller light by a full century and a half of scientific experience since the last of them laid down his pen. More experientially than they, Lonergan has got his hands on the indubitable, liberating starting place. His discrimination between the two stages of knowing—in intelligent consciousness and in rational consciousness— is more sophisticated than any of them attained. Finally, it is easier to verify his statements than theirs, because he is more explicit in pointing to the evidence. Grappling with Lonergan's articulation of one's own cognitional experiences, and comparing his articulation with one's own, is a philosophic adventure of the highest order.

III. Concluding Remarks

There are three final remarks to be made about Lonergan's relationship to contemporary Anglo-American philosophy. In the first place, Lonergan is a magnetic thinker. It is impossible to read other philosophers, after undergoing Lonergan's therapeutic, without driving them back to their own articulation of cognitional experience. New and powerful light is shed on both the pre- and the post-critical philosophies by the use of Lonergan's method. Moreover, his device of translating metaphysical statements into cognitional statements rather than into ordinary language statements casts a startling light upon the enterprise of metaphysics. No one in the English-speaking world has a right to claim that metaphysics has no function, until he has grappled with Lonergan.

From a historical point of view, again, no one can any longer pretend to speak for or against the "perennial philosophy" of Aristotle or Aquinas until he has mastered Lonergan. Lonergan shows that his basic correlations between the three levels of consciousness are isomorphic with the metaphysical terms potency, form and act of that tradition; in his hands that whole tradition becomes subject to empirical decision. Lonergan's analysis [38] of the scholasticism of Étienne Gilson, moreover, indicates that it no longer suffices to rely on the previously accepted authorities in reporting that tradition.

Secondly, Lonergan roots the religious impulse in the detached, disinterested drive to know which gives the orientation to his entire philosophy. He frequently refers to man's "natural desire to see God" which Aquinas speaks of in *S.T.* I-II, q. 3, a. 8, and has used as the mainspring of the entire *Summa contra Gentiles*. This move is highly significant for contemporary problems in philosophical theology. Once achieving it, Lonergan has destroyed the apparatus of the necessitarian, rationalist God of the eighteenth-century metaphysicians without destroying an intelligent, decidable approach to God.

Lonergan finds it inconsistent to be faithful to the unrestricted drive to understand and yet to deny that the world is ultimately intelligible, if not to us at least to an intelligent, radical principle. For that would be to say that to pursue intelligence is to go counter to the fundamental character of the universe. Men may try to live rationally in an irrational world, and Mr. Aiken has given us an explicit statement about the wisdom of remaining content amid the amenities and the work of civilized life. But such an attempt is, in the end, an absurdity. It is radically incoherent to assert fidelity to critical intelligence, in the act of asserting that the world does not answer to critical intelligence.

Thirdly, it would not be honest to conclude this introduction to Lonergan's thought without voicing several reservations. In the first place, Lonergan's many duties have prevented him from coming to immediate grips with contemporary Anglo-American philosophy. As a consequence, it is difficult—given, especially, the insularity of Anglo-American philosophy—to construct a dialogue between Lonergan and his national confreres. In Anglo-American circles, as 'Enry 'Iggins in *My Fair Lady* says of France, it does not so much matter what you do in philosophy so long as you pronounce it correctly; and Lonergan often does not have the right accent, even when he is doing something at the heart of contemporary Anglo-American debates.

This remoteness in language and accent is compounded by the excessively rational way in which Lonergan puts his points. To many readers, he appears to be too rationalistic. He sounds like Hegel, when the fashion is for Kierkegaard; or like Kant, when the fashion is for the later Wittgenstein. In fact, the central point in Lonergan's philosophy is experiential, existential, empirical, personalist, Socratic: it is the need that each of us has to come to terms with himself, in his own experience. The key to Lonergan's philosophy is self-appropriation. In reading Lonergan, for example, it is more important to reflect upon one's own cognitional experiences than merely to study the grammar of Lonergan's words in order to "behave well" with them, using them, i.e., in the correct logical order. To concentrate upon the words on the page is to miss those directions buried in the text which instruct the reader to attend to the cognitional data in his personal experience. It is to miss the whole point.

On the other hand, the introspection to which Lonergan invites us is not that of Wundt and nineteenth-century psychologism. For their introspection was intuitive and immediate—in the pattern only of intelligent consciousness—but that of Lonergan is reflective and requires evidence; it is in the pattern of rational consciousness. His is not a philosophy of "intuitionism."

Students of Lonergan should do as he does: begin to reflect upon their own performance as they ask questions, so as to come to know when they know. What in each case, are their own criteria of relevance and evidence? Mr. Richard B. Brandt recommends in his *Ethical Theory* [39] that we learn to place ourselves in a "Qualified Attitude" before reaching an ethical judgment. And Mr. Aiken [40] writes that to say that a moral judgment is true is simply: "(a) to reaffirm it and (b) to avow that it meets whatever tests of objectivity are deemed proper by the moral judge himself." Both Brandt and Aiken, therefore, appeal to what Lonergan calls rational consciousness. It is through recent studies in ethics, then, that Anglo-American philosophers might best approach the thought of Bernard Lonergan. If more philosophers take up the task, we may indeed move, through ethical studies, toward a greater reunion in philosophy than Morton V. White [41] dared to foresee.

NOTES

1. *The Quest for Being,* St Martin's Press, New York, 1961, p. 207.
2. *Ibid.,* p. 217.
3. *Ibid.,* pp. 194-95.
4. *Ibid.,* p. 216.
5. Lonergan, "Metaphysics as Horizon," a review of Emerich Coreth's *Metaphysik,* in *Gregorianum* 44 (1963), 308.
6. Cf. *Insight,* p. xxviii.
7. *Reason and Conduct,* Alfred A. Knopf, New York, 1962, p. 372.
8. *Ibid.*
9. *Insight,* p. xi.
10. *Op. cit.,* p. 368.
11. *Ibid.*
12. *Ibid.,* p. 370.
13. *Ibid.,* pp. 372-73.
14. *Ibid.,* p. 373.
15. *Ibid.*
16. "Metaphysics as Horizon," p. 314.
17. *Ibid.,* p. 315.
18. *Ibid.,* p. 308.

19. *Ibid.*, pp. 308-09.
20. "Openness and Religious Experience," in *Il Problema dell' esperienza religiosa* (Atti del XV Convegno del Centro di Studi Filosofici . . . Gallarate, 1960). Brescia, 1961, p. 460.
21. *Insight*, p. 9.
22. *Ibid.*
23. "Openness . . . ," p. 461.
24. *Insight*, p. 74.
25. "Metaphysics as Horizon," p. 308.
26. *Ibid.*
27. *Ibid.*
28. *Ibid.*, p. 314.
29. *Insight*, p. xxviii.
30. Hook, *op. cit.*, p. 214.
31. "Openness . . . ," p. 461.
32. "Other Minds," in Flew (ed.), *Essays on Language and Logic* (second series), Blackwell, Oxford, 1959, pp. 123-58, cf. esp. 125-35.
33. Cf. F. E. Crowe, "Complacency and Concern in the Thought of St. Thomas," *Theological Studies* 20 (1959) 1-39, 198-230, 343-95.
34. *Op. cit.*, p. 228.
35. "Metaphysics as Horizon," p. 314.
36. *Ibid.*
37. *Insight*, p. xxviii.
38. "Metaphysics as Horizon," pp. 310 f.
39. Prentice-Hall, 1959, pp. 241-70.
40. *Op. cit.*, p. 169.
41. *Toward Reunion in Philosophy*, Harvard University Press, 1956. The concluding part of Prof. White's book, Part IV, concentrates on the relation between ethics, science, and logic, and points to the centrality of the question of justification in each of these disciplines. I read his book as a removing of obstacles, from a logical point of view, for attention to what Lonergan calls, from a cognitional point of view, rational consciousness. "Having concentrated in great measure on removing some of the obstacles in their way, I hope that the master describers, the master builders, and the master moralists in philosophy will be able to work with fewer hindrances and with a greater understanding of each other. More than that, I hope that these occupational barriers will disappear and that we shall once more realize that philosophy can be as varied and full as life itself." (Concluding sentences, p. 299.) Lonergan's achievement is to have begun the hard work of realizing that hope, and to have chosen for philosophy the fullest and most flexible starting place for fulfilling it.

Part Two

BEYOND CHILDHOOD;

BEYOND ADOLESCENCE

Smaller problems now come to our attention; parochial concerns momentarily occupy center stage. So all-encompassing is American Catholicism, protective as a vinyl raincoat, that some Catholics discover only tardily how large and beautiful is the world outside. Still, changes in Catholic life entail changes in the way Protestants, Jews, and humanists identify themselves; Catholicism is part of the cultural memory of every Western man.

The following chapters attempt to identify exactly the causes and conditions that rock Catholicism. Those who think that Catholicism is ever the same (*semper eadem* is their guide) imagine that the barque of Peter is being buffeted entirely from without, or possibly misdirected by members of her crew, or even enduring mutiny. But there are others who think the barque of Peter is being taken apart and renewed plank by plank, so that in the end there awaits the paradox of Theseus: the same barque will be completely new. The risk in such a transformation is great. Unless a community be willing to lose its life it shall not gain it. Catholicism the conservative, the hedger of historical bets, has finally dared to gamble. In boldness there is hope, however slim, of life.

There are, learned psychologists say, three stages in the life of man: paternalism, when the father is obeyed; rebellion, when the son says no and makes it stick; wisdom, when the son forgives his father, is able to listen with respect, yet makes his own decisions. Catholicism has lingered as long as it dared, centuries too long, in childhood. The awakening, heralded by Kant's famous essay on autonomy, has led to a great many Promethean poses and nourished the cult of the adolescent. It requires courage to rebel, and rebellion is indispensable to growth. Autonomy cannot be surrendered as part of the human ideal. Nevertheless, men are members of historical communities and are influenced to the depth of their judgments by the communities in which they stand. The human choice does not lie between autonomy and heteronomy; it lies between integrity and mere belonging. Unavoidably, men belong to groups. The issue is: how far do their communities contribute to the fostering of personal freedom and self-development, and how far do individual persons grow up into the heritage of their community and enlarge it with creative achievements of their own.

Catholicism has long been weighted on the side of community and authority; in her ranks, individual persons and personal autonomy have often suffered grievously; the end of such suffering has not yet come. No word, consequently, excites the contemporary imagination of Catholics so much as "freedom." What kind of freedom? In how many ways, in how many places, must it be achieved? There is not so much freedom in the modern world that anyone can afford to be condescending regarding a struggle in its name. Seldom in history has there been such acute consciousness of the various establishments, power structures, and social systems which everywhere poison the sharp clean taste of freedom. No one gives freedom freely; it must be seized. Catholics will err if they wait for freedom to be handed them from above; and non-Catholics will err if they view the struggle in Catholicism condescendingly, without looking to themselves.

6

Romanità Has Seen Its Lovely Days

The Catholic people of twenty years from now will not be as the Catholic people of today. Even now, the young do not share the sentiments, fears, hesitations of the old; the only church they know is the Church of the Council. The older generation of laymen, priests, bishops—and of the Pope himself—were educated for a different style of Catholic life. Meanwhile, since 1962, the Church has come from very far back. It has not yet caught up to the pacesetters of contemporary life, or even to the ordinary practices of plain, uneducated people. It is by no means exerting intellectual leadership for the future. It has, however, covered an enormous stretch of ground psychologically; the theological and cultural horizon of the Church is no longer what it was in 1962.

Organizational timidity is the besetting sin of the Catholic hierarchy, as many bishops at the Council have confessed. How could it be otherwise in a system that works by appointment from above? To be sure, many individuals among the bishops are personally strong-minded, informed, and modern men; but within the organization they do not always have a chance to speak about basic matters. Many others, plainly, are devoted organization men, who do not relish the confusion that comes with creativity, who do not like to take risks, who venture few new experiments, who are not known for the originality of their ideas or the prophetic depth of their faith.

The problem begins in the seminaries, of course, and it extends also to the role of the curate in the parish, who sometimes cannot even leave *the rectory without the permission of his pastor. The problem extends also to the role of the bishops vis-à-vis the Roman Curia. Authority, obedience, and loyalty are required in every living institution, especially in those which transcend the lifetime of any one generation. But prophecy, originality, and challenging, independent judgment are also required. What differs in history is the way in which these complementary sets of values are coordinated. What characterizes Romanità is the excessive, abnormal preponderance given the first set. Romanità stifles the spirit.*

The men of the Roman Curia act by standards perfectly acceptable in their culture; they often fail even to understand their critics who, they think, must be "disloyal." They also exaggerate the criticism—no one accuses them, as some of them have claimed, of concubinage or simony. The Curia merely has much power, thick complacency, and great narrowness of view.

The bishops of the world have now had a chance to live in Rome for four autumns and to see for themselves how the Church lives in Italy, how the liturgy is carried out, how parishes are run, how much contact there is between clergy and people, what the sentiments of the people are, how the Roman Curia is related to the individual dioceses. But have the bishops gained more courage than they have had hitherto? Have they enough practical sense to organize and get their best sentiments expressed in law, as well as in the press?

There has never been a humble declaration on the part of the Church, confessing its sins, inadequacies, and mistakes in modern times, as the moral leadership of world culture has gradually been passing into other hands. One virtue the official Church lacks almost entirely is humility. The document on the Church in the modern world offers an opportunity for a brief recognition of the truth, opening a vein of thought dear to the Gospels for the Church as a whole.

The New York Times *reported that Pope Paul VI is concerned about some American critics who say that the doctrine of religious liberty must also be applied within the Church. (Who precisely and how many are the persons from whom, in fact, the Pope learns about "American writers"? It is saddening that in this critical moment in American Catholic history we cannot rely upon our Apostolic Delegate for understanding of American ways and sympathy with American purposes.) Surely what Cardinal*

Newman wrote about real assent *is to be applied to the doctrines of the Church, as well as to any other matter of conscience. One does not really assent to belief in the Eucharist simply because one understands the grammatical, notional meaning of the words. The articles of faith must be appropriated by the individual conscience, slowly and steadily, by dint of meditation and action. It is not enough merely to say the words.*

Thus, believing in the doctrines of Christianity is not like believing in an ideological system, or reciting propaganda. The doctrines of Christianity express primarily a life to be lived, only secondarily a set of words to be notionally related. Christianity must become part of the fiber of intelligence and will. Consequently, free acts of conscience must constantly be performed. One cannot pretend to believe what one does not; one must grow gradually into all the teachings of the Church. None of us is fully Catholic; none of us believes fully as he ought. "I believe, Lord; help Thou my unbelief," is a prayer even bishops can say. Moreover, every single doctrine has depths no one has fully penetrated. Without religious liberty within the Church, in the sense required for this task of personal appropriation, there can be no real growth in faith, no free maturation, but only the dry repetition of formulae. We do not fully believe in the Eucharist, in the Trinity, in the divinity of Christ, in the Assumption until by many free, searching acts we make these doctrines flesh of our flesh, blood of our blood; until they affect our thinking, feeling, acting. Religious liberty within the Church is essential if faith is supposed to be gradually, steadily appropriated by each person.

It may be feared that too many Catholics believe only notionally; such was Cardinal Newman's fear less than a century ago. Even notional believers, however, may continue to frequent the sacraments and to contribute to the Church. There is a temptation to allow such Catholics to be the main concern of the Church, and to neglect all those millions of persons too perceptive and too concerned to tolerate the notional faith they encounter in organized religion, who have streamed away from the churches. The reform and renewal required to begin to speak to the indifferent and the hostile is vaster by far than the Council envisaged.

The following chapter is adapted from a script I prepared for the British Broadcasting Company during the summer of 1964, just before the third session of the Council convened. As in the autumn of 1963, when I began The Open Church, *my wife and I were privileged to find ourselves sharing the excitement of Rome for those creative and unforgettable days, perhaps the most exhilarating in Roman Catholic history. I have prefixed parts of "A Council Reporter's Personal Journal" which appeared in* The Critic *in December 1964, in order to help convey the ambiance of the city during those days. The "Journal" makes easy allusion to two facts: that although at the second session of the Council I was free-lancing, at the third session (for three weeks) I was working for* Time; *and also that my book* A New Generation, *which arbitrarily took 1930 as a watershed year, was by then the occasion of much needling from my friends.*

I. *A Reporter's Journal*

IT WAS good to get back to the city again: the sights, the sounds, the many smells of Rome. The same heavy buses roar down the streets, their fumes acrid in the September heat. Fruit crates, coffee bars, and damp, dark doorways give off familiar odors. And, in the evenings, the warm, quiet winds from the hills bring a dusk of the same peace and suspense that I had remembered, and forgotten, from before—a time when all the city seems to hang by a slender thread of happiness, when swallows swoop low over the roof tops and men are indoors waiting for their dinner.

Old, grisly men beg in the streets. They may never see another autumn come to Rome. But the tiled, yellowed roofs will endure: the city immutable while her inhabitants change.

Reporting for a weekly news magazine does not offer the best perspective for capturing the mellowness of Rome. Such a magazine lives by news, by what happens, not by moods or currents of thought. Who did what? When? Why?

But *Time* offered compensatory advantages: the excitement of a bustling office connected to every capital of the world, with every alleyway and mountain hideaway, wherever things are happening. And money to spend to get a story, rivers of money. I was amazed at the amount of material that goes into the files, in support of the few words that appear in print.

Time provided, too, the chance to get to Rome before my classes began again at Harvard. Karen (my wife) arrived in Rome four days before I did and was there to meet my bus as it pulled into the terminal from the airport on September 11, in time for the Council's opening on the fourteenth. A quick visit to the *Time* office before we changed and went to dinner at a favorite restaurant near the Via Veneto, where Karen filled me in on all she had managed to find out.

From then on a round of interviews, lunches, press conferences, briefings, dinners, discussions—a dizzying pace. After a summer indoors, mainly writing and studying, it was exhilarating to dive into all that activity like a swimmer into cold water. Dinner (with other journalists, *periti,* friends), usually kept us quite late and left us light-headed from Valpolicella or Verdicchio. Mornings we slept until eight or nine. John Cogley joined us soon at our special "Pensione Baldoni," with its wide rooms and clear view of Castel Sant'Angelo.

Over our rolls and coffee (Signorina Baldoni always gave Karen an egg, since she thought she looked thin), John kept trying to show me how well things were going under Pope Paul and he brought me up to date on Los Angeles and New York. We teased about the "generation" business, and about his promotion to "grand old man" at forty-eight—the prime of life.

At ten or ten-thirty, Karen and I crossed town in a taxi, up the Muro Torto—I to the *Time* office, Karen to her studio, where she was working hard to complete her etchings on T. S. Eliot's "Ash Wednesday."

At the office, telex queries from New York waited. These were mostly concerned with earlier reports that had been filed. My role was that of "consultant." A veteran reporter, Israel Shenker, newly arrived in Rome from Moscow, took amazingly competent care of the day-to-day reporting. I was free to supply background material, analysis, suggestions for future stories—and to follow my imagination. I sent material to New York almost daily.

About noon "Shenk" and I would hurry by cab over to Father Heston's English-language press briefing. Some years ago Father Heston was my superior in the seminary for two years; the sound of his voice and his efficient reporting brought back memories.

After the half-hour briefing (with Father Robert Trisco of Catholic University, another old friend, filling in details and answering questions), we had lunch in a nearby trattoria or at the American Bar. Which we chose depended partly on how our stomachs were reacting to Italian cooking (you can tell by your breath, a problem in Rome not only for adjusting strangers but also for the Romans). At the American Bar one can find surcease from oil and tomatoes and starch with scrambled eggs, toast, apple pie, and coffee.

On one special occasion several persons from French lay groups, including Mademoiselle Monnet, the first woman auditor, invited me to lunch. Two of them had attended my brother Dick's ordination at Le Mans three years ago, had met my parents, and remembered the day well. This week, in Rome, they had heard of Dick's death in Pakistan. They spoke of meeting him on the *"Mission de France"* before his ordination—tall, thin and full of humor. They promised to write to my parents.

Just after lunch—we had always to hurry—the American Bishop's press panel met in the basement of the USO building. In all honesty, one would have to say that the panel was not as lively as it was the year before. It was not a question of "managing" the news; in some ways, this more "balanced" panel was more interesting to observe. The newcomers made a welcome contribution, but how does one replace the wit of Father Gustave Weigel? Moreover, the frequency of lighter, brighter, sparkling moments—so common with last year's group—was less. New rules for this year forbade "interpretation." It seemed that prudence and moderation (the eighth and ninth capital vices) had again subdued daring and imagination, incisive illumination and ironic repartee. Information was not suppressed, but brilliance was.

At four, there was time for coffee or a Coke, and quick conversations with the dozen people one wanted to see while they were all present in one room. (A reporter spends many hours on the phone in Rome simply trying to locate someone. Six tries for one completed call, leaving a welter of messages in garbled Italian, is the usual ratio.) Then off, practically on the run, to the Dutch Documentation Center (across the river in Piazza Navona, this year) for a lecture by Father Yves Congar, or to the C.C.C.C. for a press conference by Archbishop Heenan, or to the African Bishops' conference for Cardinal Suenens on the subject of seminaries, or Bishop Wright on the laity.

Barely time, then, to buy the Italian and French papers, read them and get dressed for dinner. Dusk, the warm and quiet air. Very tired feet. Flop down on the bed for a little while, then up because you're already late for dinner. Karen is finished at the sink. I ask fearfully, "Do I need to shave?" "Yes."

Getting a cab at this hour is often difficult. After five calls, I find one at a distant stand. He barks into the phone that I should call someone nearer. "But no one answers there." "It will cost more." "That's all right!" and—mentally—*"Time's* paying for it." And cabs in Rome are cheap, by Boston standards.

Dinner often lasts from eight until eleven, sometimes until one. There may be time for a walk in the ancient streets, under an almost full September moon. So many things have been learned in the day's conversation that one is eager to begin writing. But the wine, and especially the liqueur, which one should have refused, has made one drowsy and slow.

The giant-size key wobbles its way into the massive door of 15 Piazza Adriana (the buildings of Rome, to withstand Roman emotions and Roman violence, are built like fortresses). We climb slowly to the second floor. Another lock is negotiated and we're into our familiar hallway, moving on tiptoe not to awaken those who had the good sense to retire earlier.

Tomorrow? A hundred possibilities. But one thing is sure, I ruminate, remembering a dozen images and the baleful liturgy in the Roman churches, Rome is a much more beautiful city than its clergy seem to know. It is like two different worlds which exist side-by-side but never meet: the world of Fellini and the world of Ruffini. It is as if there were two different species of men. An American in Rome feels at home in both worlds. They belong together. What is it that the Roman clergy are afraid of? The old "Christian civilization" they speak about is gone. But such a marvel, this modern city of man, its sounds and smells, its poverty and people, and its bitter hopes. So complex and tangled. So beautiful.

II. *From Romanità to Catholicity*

A Council of the Church, more so than a parliament, has an essentially conservative function to perform. Its task is to reflect upon the Word of God entrusted to the Church, and to speak that Word through decrees and constitutions which will embody it in the sermons, teachings, organizations, institutions by which the Church will henceforth live its daily, concrete life. Ideally, a council is called when the time is ripe, when a set of mature decisions can be expected. Ideally, it does not close off unresolved issues, but answers "Yes" or "No" to questions which have long been ripening on the vine. The perspective in which a council works is not that of years, or even decades, but of generations and indeed centuries.

What makes the Second Vatican Council so unique in history, however, is that it comes at a time when most of the world is secular, when religion carries very little intellectual weight among those who make the world's decisions. Whereas the First Vatican Council in 1869 was content to act as if the secular world did not exist, and to declare itself in propositions quite removed from the language, methods and concerns of the rest of the intellectual world of its time, Pope John XXIII declared in his opening address to the Second Vatican Council in 1962 that the main task of the new Council would be "pastoral." That is to say, the Council would begin to struggle for words which men of the world could understand.

This germinal directive of Pope John struck "the barque of Peter" with shuddering impact. For what it implied was the opening of that major conflict within the Roman Church which many have come to see as the basic meaning of Vatican II. Hardly a Roman Catholic anywhere in the world has not been touched to the depths of his conscience by that conflict. What is the Church? Is it the unchanging, eternal, always right and triumphant "mother of the Truth," or is it a humble community of people on a pilgrimage through dark and uncertain history? Is it humble or proud? Aloof from all others or a partner with all men of good will?

Many Catholics the world around admit their present confusion about the nature of the Church. The conflict in the Church is not, then, between two parties of men, but rather between two parts in the heart of nearly all Catholics.

To understand the consolidation that will be taking place during the third session, it is necessary to have a clear picture of these two conceptions of the Church which are at war in so many hearts. Pope Paul VI made it clear in his opening address at the second session of the Council in 1963 that the main concern of the Council was the Church's conception of itself. Church of Christ, what in mid-twentieth century, do you have to say of yourself? What do you believe yourself to be?

What to many is most striking about Vatican II is that this question should even be asked. For there are many in the Roman Church and outside of it who thought the answer was all-too-clear, all-too-fixed. In the popular consciousness of the West probably no institution had become such a symbol of eternity, clarity, immobility—qualities which attracted some minds, and repelled others, but which were rather generally accepted as accurate by all. There is no doubt that those Catholics who remained Catholics just because of those qualities now feel threatened, and that those once repelled now feel intrigued.

What has occasioned the surprise, however, is the sudden discovery that a Church which for nearly four centuries has remained largely immobile in her official language and style has, preceding those four centuries, a forgotten history of fifteen centuries of the most striking variety, diversity and mobility. The Roman Church has become identified with one moment in her history, one style, one manner. Moreover, that particular style nourished illusions of being unchanging, universal, normative for all times. Now that the moment of truth has come, those affected by that illusion are struggling in their confusion to find something to take its place.

Let us adopt words for this conflict, in order to give it a tentative shape. The conflict in the Church is a conflict between *Romanità* and catholicity—between being Roman and being catholic. That the head of the Church lives in Rome is only an historical fact; to make an abstraction, a system, a method of that fact constitutes *Romanità*. The Roman method these past 400 years has been to insist upon uniformity, to insist that Rome itself is the universal, eternal norm of the faith given men by Christ. Roman language, Roman philosophy, Roman polity, Roman law, these were the ways to Christ, and no others were fully accepted, though some few concessions were made. Missionaries in the Orient in the seventeenth century found their great successes blotted out by Roman insistence upon Roman methods. Churches of the East in communion with Rome have protested sadly and ineffectively as, step by step this last century, their traditions, institutions, and privileges have been forced closer and closer into the Roman mold.

Romanità—that imperial assurance that Rome is the mother city of us all, abetted only too well by the beauty and nostalgia of a great ancient city. *Romanità*—that theological preference for the methods of Descartes, Leibniz and Spinoza: logical, timeless, geometrical. *Romanità*—that approach to law and mortality which begins with the peremptory enunciation of general principles, absolute and universally binding, without respect for history or contingency, only to turn then to niggling lawyers to find ways to bring this vast intellectual construct into touch with the real earth. *Romanità*—that pride and splendor and triumphalism which owe more to Caesar than to Christ, and which look upon the modern age as vulgar, confusing and too much in a hurry.

Indeed, this *Romanità,* exquisite dream of several generations, encounters the rude realities of our time with distaste and consternation. Incense and absolutes, clear imperatives and unchanging Latin words, the image in the mind's eye of an Eternal City tucked in the Alban Mountains, where wise and crafty cardinals refuse to be seduced by the slogans of the marching world—no wonder that nostalgia lingers in many hearts, together with a mystic touch of certainty that somewhere, somehow, there is an eternal base under things, in the light of which passing history is paltry.

Since the time of the French Revolution, it must be remembered, Catholic intellectual life in Europe has been struggling for a rebirth. At the beginning of the nineteenth century, nearly every major institution of Catholic learning in northern Europe had been closed. Nearly everywhere, even in Spain and Italy, links with the first fifteen centuries of Christian history had been forgotten. The Roman schools did not value historical methods or historical studies. From the year 1800 onward, the intellectual wing of the Roman Church has had almost to begin all over again. "We have come from very far back," one of them said in Rome in 1963.

The renaissance of Catholic learning, then, is the most important factor in the conflict at Vatican II. In France and Germany, in the Lowlands and in England, and to a lesser extent in other places, the tasks of scholarship and the creative arts have been begun again, slowly, fitfully. "Every time one of us succeeds in stirring a little flame from the ashes," François Mauriac once said many years ago, "curial Rome steps in and crushes it." Thus the struggle so evident at Vatican II is not new; it is only, now, apparent. Until Vatican II, those in love with *Romanità* had succeeded in keeping their imprint, unchallenged, upon the Church: immobile, triumphant, disdainful of passing history. At Vatican II, other and more catholic voices began to prevail: voices from the Eastern Churches, from the Scripture scholars, from the pastors of a dozen diverse and admirable cultures, from historians, from those who love contemporary civilization as much as any Christians ever loved *Romanità*. In his encyclical, *Pacem in Terris,* Pope John XXIII paid explicit homage to the intellectual laborers, laymen and clerics, whose efforts during the preceding century made this "Easter present to mankind" possible.

The issue at Vatican II, therefore, is the transition from *Romanità* to catholicity. Shall the Church be Latin, or shall it be for all men? Shall it have taken on the form and style of a culture of four centuries ago, and refuse to enter the history of today? Pope John opted for *aggiornamento*. Would the rest of the Church?

The answer has already been given. Were the Vatican Council to adjourn today, its main task would be complete: those in the Church who are struggling for renewal and reform have had their effort legitimized. The process of transition may be lengthy. But the days of *Romanità* have passed. The Church, which has undergone so many major cultural transformations in the past, has begun to enter into the tissue of the civilization which, all around us, is coming into existence upon the ruins of worldwide wars.

Seen from this angle, the encyclical *Ecclesiam Suam,* the first of Pope Paul VI, is a remarkable testimony both to the *Romanità* of the past and to the style of the future. Parts I and II of the encyclical are redolent with phrases, citations from documents, and sentiments dear to the Roman mind. The modern age seems like "an ocean" churning with "confusion" and "bizarre ideas." The Pope's grasp of modern philosophy is quite tenuous and, in the case of philosophy in England and America, practically nonexistent. But in Part III of that encyclical, Pope Paul tries to spell out in his own terms the new style of communication between the Church and the world, a style which he sees differs from the styles of the past. The Pope tries to listen to complaints of Protestants about the papacy, the desire for recognition on the part of other religions than Christians and Jews, the motives which nonbelievers offer for their nonbelief. Rarely has a papal document so revealed a pope's eagerness to learn, and his willingness to commit to paper his own fears and hesitations.

As the time for the third session of the Council nears, therefore, it is fully apparent that the Roman Church is still groping for its new identity. There are many in the Church, in England as in every other

place, who still love the forms of *Romanità* and the beauty that has
been, who still respect the harsh clarity and supposed eternality of
certain propositions, the rigor of a certain logic and the bite of a
style of law. They see the Church in pyramids—both in the logic of
its doctrines and in the structure of its offices. And they fear the
partisans of renewal and reform as modernists under a new name, as
the ghosts of all those heretical lovers of history of the nineteenth and
early twentieth centuries. For they identify orthodoxy with the certainties of *Romanità,* and good order with the policies of *Romanità.*
They do not want to lose the style they love.

It was an English writer who expressed in advance of the Second
Vatican Council, "A Layman's Hopes of the Vatican Council: More
of the Same, Please." And it was another English Catholic who has
recently written in America that the new spirit among Catholics has
dulled ancient animosities, and thus deprived many English Catholics
of the combativeness which, in his eyes, has been their reason for
being. Still a third English Catholic has tried to dissociate religion
from history, to confine the Christian message to questions of individual piety. "The New Testament," he tells us, "is not full of judgments and teachings on the concrete, historical situation, political and
economic and military. . . . It is markedly not so, but concerned with
individual sanctification and salvation: 'What must I do to be saved?'
not, 'Is the present order unjust?' "

There is, then, much debate among Catholics about what the
Church is and what the Church should do. At the coming third session,
the string of several previous debates will be picked up again: the
documents on the Church, on the relation of Scripture and tradition,
on Christian unity, and on bishops and the government of dioceses
have undergone revisions and now must be put in final form. Reports
from those who have seen the new documents indicate that in every
case the documents are open to the new approaches to methodology
and language important to the party of renewal and reform. It is not
surprising, however, that no single document is as good as contemporary scholarship could make it; no single one says all that could
be said or might be preferred by some. The important point is that
every document makes a beginning in turning the Church toward the
best that contemporary study and reflection can offer. From such
beginnings, renewal and reform can proceed.

What will the Council have to say to the men of the world? The

Church cannot present political or social programs for solving the ills of the poor, the oppressed, and indeed of the wealthy. But the Church can awaken consciences about such matters. The Church can encourage the building up of a generation of young men and women who *care* whether "the present order is unjust." It would not be wise to expect shattering statements in this document, *On the Church and the World,* which was inspired by a famous talk of Cardinal Suenens in 1962. But it will no doubt be correct to expect the inculcation of a new *attitude* among Catholics: that it is a part of the Gospel message, not only to save one's own soul, but also to care about one's brothers who do not eat and about the social arrangements which help to determine who shall eat what. To love God is to love what is real and today the reality of human life includes political and social issues which no man of conscience can avoid, however much he differs from his fellows in his response to them.

The coming third session, to conclude, will see the consolidation in a succession of documents of the new catholic attitudes of the Church. In some places, those documents will still have a Roman ring. In some places, those documents will show signs of having been written from more than one point of view, more than one perspective. In every case, those documents will reflect the determination of the Roman Catholic Church to re-enter the intellectual texture and history of our world civilization: endorsing a diversity of practice, a system of checks and balances in ecclesiastical government, a pluralism of cultural traditions, the sovereignty of personal conscience, the humility of the Gospels.

There are certain to be faults and inadequacies in the documents finally accepted at the third session. One or two issues may spark a dramatic advance or reversal. But, generally, the prospect is for the hard, steady work of expediting the transition from *Romanità* to catholicity, from one style of Catholic life to another. The younger students in our schools and colleges already feel the effects of this change of style. Their children and their children's children will see it more completely realized than we.

7

American Catholicism
After the Council

A major marvel of the Second Vatican Council was the attention given it by the general press. Catholics who had long taken their faith for granted, unquestioningly, suddenly saw the Church cut down to human size as stories about its major figures and institutions appeared in their daily papers (often on page one) alongside stories about governors and city councils, premiers and movie stars.

The invitation from Norman Podhoretz of Commentary *in 1965 to produce a fairly lengthy study of the probable effect of the Council on American Catholicism suited one of my key interests. It was an opportunity to think through what was happening to Catholicism because of America, and to American Catholicism because of the Council—and to attempt to state my views to an audience which could reasonably be imagined to be indifferent to intramural Catholicism. Many special Roman Catholic words are almost unintelligible in contemporary intellectual contexts; most of the troublesome words are Latin words, abstract, remote, created for their usefulness to a conceptual system no longer part of the living tissue of intellectual discourse. Catholics do not literally mean that Mary was "assumed" (taken up) into "heaven" (up there); they mean that Mary now shares that state which all Christians hope to attain. Catholics do not literally mean that the "substance" of the bread changes in the Eucharist, in the way in which scientists use the word "substance" (chemical composition), nor in the way ordinary men use the word "sub-stance" (meaning the stuff you can feel, weigh, look at, touch, examine). Sometimes it seems that if Catholics were to deliberately set out to confuse everybody about what they genuinely believe, they could not without great effort do better than they presently do. Latin scholasticism is not nowadays a good language for saying what you mean or, perhaps, even meaning what you say. (It is a common though unspoken conviction of large numbers of people that many priests are merely repeating, with sincerity but not authenticity, words they have worked hard to learn. Why else would they always use the same examples, straight from seminary lectures and texts?)*

I do not wish to make light of the difficulties of working out an Ameri-can language for the Catholic faith. The Latin Redemptor, after all, is a different concept, with vastly different connotations, from the Greek Soter; each culture, through the peculiar resources and limitations of its own language, works out a different style of Christian faith. There may remain "one Lord, one faith, one baptism," but the way of understanding man's relationship to them varies from nation to nation, era to era. I do not wish to make light of the difficulties; but I ardently wish more persons whose task it is to preach the Gospel were aware of the difficulty. Six or eight or twelve years of isolation in the seminary (and sometimes merely in the Catholic school system) in too many cases seems to dull the mind, not only to nuances, but even to fundamental differences in the way men think. Some whose profession would require them to know better do not seem to recognize the peculiarities of a scholastically trained mind; they count themselves "objectively" right and attribute all differences to the prejudices, biases, and inadequacies of others. Confidence in "possessing" —as if it could be possessed—the "one true faith" wreaks deeper psychic harm, in more people, than anyone in the Catholic world has yet diag-nosed. "We have the truth," the sister superior said in her inaugural address as president of a small college; "our task is to carry it to others." What can one do, listening, but cry?

THE CITY of Rome rests placidly in the crystalline Italian sun, century by century, and generations of men appear within her walls and disappear. There are men today, on all continents, who shed tears

when they confront her beauty and her seeming eternality. But today
the city is the symbol of crisis, not of peace.

Countless Roman Catholics of the present generation are challenging, not the essential truths of the Catholic faith, and not even
the role of the bishop of Rome, but the mystical hold which the limited traditions of the City of Rome have long exercised upon the
Catholic world. It is inevitable that a church be secular. How else
could a church live in history, except by entering into the historical
forms of its time and place? But if a church must in any case be secular, many Catholics in the middle of the twentieth century are asking: why must its secularism be Roman and of the baroque Italian
period?

Hardly a conflict at the Second Vatican Council has not been
colored by this fundamental issue: whether the Church shall be
Latin or Catholic. The fundamental opposition is between a party of
nostalgia on the one hand, and a party of the present and the real on
the other. Yet it would be a serious mistake to underestimate the
intelligence, seriousness, conviction, and past successes of the party
of nostalgia. The Church over which that party has presided has for
generations captured the imagination and the intellectual allegiance of
legions of talented men. Through most difficult and disturbing times,
defended and guided by the party of nostalgia, the Church has come
to the threshold of a new age intact and robust.

It is a remarkable fact that although anti-Catholicism has long
been the anti-Semitism of the intellectuals, and although the atheist
has appropriated to himself all the moral pro-words which attract
the young—honesty, courage, integrity, and the rest—the Catholic
Church is at the present moment more intellectually fit than she has
been for centuries. There have seldom been so many first-rate artists,
writers, theologians, philosophers, and men of affairs who are also
Catholic. It is true that countless young people of sensitivity and
intelligence have left the Church in these centuries, and continue to
do so at a high rate. But her present health is a direct result of the
imagination and intelligence and energy of those many who have
remained within.

For some ninety years and longer, an intellectual underground has
been building up in Roman Catholicism. Small at first, centering in
groups of writers, theologians, and philosophers, now in Paris, now
in Tübingen, now at Munich, London, Louvain, Milan, or even

Rome, this underground has self-consciously labored for the renewal and reform of Roman Catholicism from within.

Since early in the last century, young theologians like Johann Möhler of Tübingen (d. 1838) have been working for the reunion of the churches, and writers in France and Germany have strained every nerve to draw Catholicism out of her isolation from the contemporary world. A curious phenomenon all these years is that outsiders writing or speaking of Catholicism have often been as Roman, hierarchical, and monolithic in their view of the Church as the most conservative Catholics. Such outsiders called "Catholic" only those manifestations which bore the stamp of curial and official Rome; perhaps 95 per cent of their utterances about Catholicism had the curial hierarchical pyramid, not the living underground, in mind. Hence the great sense of surprise, shock, and at first hesitant pleasure which nearly everywhere greeted the "new" attitudes of Pope John and the Council.

To be sure, this preoccupation with the outward appearance of pre-Johannine Catholicism was in large measure justified. No Catholic can deny that years of emphasis upon party loyalty and internal discipline, and years of investing the clerical caste with a mythical nimbus of authority, gave the Church an organizational rather than a charismatic stamp. Nevertheless, the unpreparedness of most professional commentators on Catholicism (H. Stuart Hughes is one notable exception) for what has come to the surface since 1962 is the symptom of a sickness in contemporary intellectual life. The antipathy and prejudice which have in the main prevented sympathetic studies of the role of Catholicism in Western civilization are something of a scandal. All too often, especially in the United States, intelligent Catholics, under questioning, have stated what they believe their faith to involve, only to be faced with the rejoinder: "But you can't be in good standing and hold that, can you?" The stereotype is a burden, and the Catholic, like the Negro and the Jew, would like to be taken for what he is, not for what Cardinal Spellman, Graham Greene, Charles de Gaulle, and other assorted Catholics are.

The present crisis in the Church has been occasioned by the official recognition at the Vatican Council of the fact that there are in the Church countless styles of Catholic life, many competing theologies, many philosophies of man, and many conceptions of freedom and law. Italian Catholics and Irish Catholics live in quite different emotional worlds. When the French say *liberté* they do not mean what Americans mean by freedom; Englishmen and Spaniards speaking of law have different concrete experiences in mind; a German and a Latin American mean different things by order; some Catholics in Africa understand spontaneously the notion "people of God," since they are still living a tribal life which is more like that of biblical peoples than is Western life today. "Catholic" does not mean universal and the same, but universal and diverse.

Moreover, it is impossible to make sense out of the current restlessness among Roman Catholics without recalling that, after 1789, nearly every major Catholic institution of learning in northern Europe—and often in the South as well—was seized by the state. Originality and imagination in Catholic studies were at a low ebb in the eighteenth century; but in the nineteenth, Catholic studies were virtually wiped out. Moral theology, for example (as a recent book by John T. Noonan, Jr.,[1] intimates), endured a gap in scholarship for almost the entire first two generations of the nineteenth century. Only toward mid-century were libraries reassembled, eclectic surveys of previous scholarship organized, seminary manuals hastily put together. Too early to benefit by the fruits of historical scholarship just being organized, but cut off by two generations from a living tradition, nineteenth-century Catholic moral theology had virtually to be begun from scraps. Into the vacuum rushed the canon lawyers; about fourfifths of the material in standard textbooks on moral theology used in Catholic seminaries (Regatillo-Zalba, for example) is borrowed from canon law. Here lie the roots of the present Catholic dilemma on birth control.

In 1870, the First Vatican Council articulated the faith of Catholics in the infallibility of the Church, in which the pope shares; marching armies drove the Council from Rome before the complementary role of the bishops could be discussed. Theologically, the chief effect of what the Council did was to establish stringent conditions upon papal teaching, so that the line between the pope's personal opinions and his articulation of the faith of all is now clearly marked. Nevertheless, the chief psychological effect was a heightening of the baroque monarchical view of the papacy dear to certain Roman hearts.

Worse still, modern means of communication were shortly to change the impact and universality of papal teaching; the stage was set for the most pyramidal period in the history of the Church. The pope would be seen at the peak of the pyramid, the papal curia as an intermediary between him and the bishops; below the bishops would come priests and religious, and, like an iceberg nine-tenths of which is under water, laymen would be left by canon law with hardly a mention. (Even now when laymen speak about the Church, they speak of "they." "When will the Church do something about birth control?" means "When will *they*. . . .")

This same period marked the Celtic ascendancy in the Church: not only did Ireland gain political independence from England and ecclesiastical subservience at home, but Irish bishops multiplied in the United States, in Australia, in England, and throughout the mission lands of the British Empire. The Celtic bishops have maintained a theological tradition largely isolated from the life of our times, unfertilized by dissent or pluralism, greatly inclined to viewing the Church as a pyramid and seriously vulnerable to establishing a personality cult around the pope. On the other side of the ledger, the Celtic bishops are in the main excellent organization men, whose primary virtue is loyalty.[2]

In an era of radio, teletype, and television, meanwhile, papal teaching suddenly became not merely the theology of the bishop of Rome, distant and localized, but the ordinary teaching of the Church spread through the world—particularly wherever the nonintellectual Irish were in charge. The whole system of checks and balances in Roman Catholicism was upset. Now, because of radio and the daily press, and a heretofore unheard-of deference to Rome, the "ordinary teaching" of the bishops had lost its crucial theological role. *Whatever* the pope said was now known everywhere, on the instant, and was much more gravely discussed than hitherto. It has become a serious, novel, and yet common misconception among some Catholics to accept all papal opinions as if they were gospel truth.

Three amusing ironies are at work here. The first is that the hyperpapalists often try to comfort non-Catholics by noting that the exercise of papal infallibility is, necessarily, a most rare occurrence. But before their own people, they endow nearly every papal instruction with some subtle measure of infallibility: "near to being infallible" or the like. (Their opponents retort that infallibility, like pregnancy, is or isn't; there's no in-between.)

The second irony is that most of the hyperpapalists, in practice, are selective in their attitude toward Rome; they discount the instructions they don't like—Pius XI on social reconstruction and the sins of capitalism, for example, or Pius XII on liturgical reform.

The third irony is that since 1878 and the pontificate of Leo XIII most of the popes, skipping over the heads of the bishops, have been in alliance with the intellectual underground. The popes have been "liberal," the bishops in the main have not. Leo's *Rerum Novarum,* for example, was a belated effort to awaken the baroque apathies of Roman Catholics to the magnitude of the social reconstruction required in our time; it was a response to the challenge of socialism. Even Leo's choice of Thomas Aquinas as special teacher of the Church was an appeal to historical studies—Leo well knew the low estate of Catholic scholarship in the nineteenth century, and Thomas Aquinas was infinitely better than the manuals then so recently scraped together (and misleadingly purporting to be "Thomistic").

The popes since Leo XIII have been an extraordinary series of leaders. Fr. Gustave Weigel, S.J., said once, not long before his death: "We've had good popes for too long; nothing would be better for the faith than a bad one." Fr. Weigel had a horror of Christians who put their faith not in God but in men; and he seemed to believe that overemphasis on the pope was a characteristic vice of the Catholicism of our time. Others, less gentle than Fr. Weigel, call this vice the Celtic heresy.

Yet every heresy contains a portion of truth, and its error is usually by exaggeration. The Second Vatican Council has set in motion the elaboration of a more authentic view of the role of the bishop of Rome. The distinguishing mark of God's covenanted people is its service to others, and the relationships which unite that people are also relations of service. Bishops and priests are chosen from among the people to represent them before God, to minister to their needs, to preside at their worship, to teach, to govern. They are clearly warned not to rule as the rulers of the gentiles, but by service. And the servant of these servants of God, the center of unity among them, is the bishop of Rome.

The pope has two special services to offer the Catholic people. In the first place, he is a focal point of unity—one of the college of bishops, and yet not merely one among equals, because also the central focus of the others. (The relations between pope and college are not yet thoroughly worked out in history; a great deal remains to be learned through future developments.) In the second place, he offers a single clear voice by which in time of need, the conscience of the Church can be articulated—in exceptional cases, even without consulting the bishops. Hochhuth's play testifies to the usefulness of such a ministry in Christianity; he does not single out the World Council of Churches or the Catholic bishops for equal blame with Pius XII.

Just before the opening of the Second Vatican Council, one of the outstanding theologians of the Catholic underground, later to become the chief light of the Council, voiced his pessimism. "The Council is coming fifty years too soon; if only we had more time!" Everywhere the men working for renewal and reform were hitching their belts for another long siege; they knew renewal would win in the end, but a retrogressive Council might postpone the day. They feared that the many hundreds of Italian bishops, the Spanish and Latin American bishops, and the Celtic bishops would rubber-stamp the seminary theology of the last three generations. "We thought we would come in October, say yes, and be home for good by Christmas," one American bishop later confessed.

Pope John's opening address to the Council on October 11, 1962, was the beginning of the end of the Roman style in the Church. The Pope called for a *pastoral* Council—a realistic Council, a Council attending to the needs of men. No condemnations. No definitions. No subtleties. Traditional *Romanità* could not thrive on that sort of ground.

There is no need to recapitulate here the story of the Council thus far.[3] As to its repercussions in America, however, from 1962 on, pioneering ecumenical gatherings in city after city, attracting thousands, have been electric in their impact. In 1964, Cardinal Cushing urged Boston Catholics for their spiritual profit to listen to Billy Graham. Nuns from St. Louis marched in Selma, Alabama, in 1965; and in quiet defiance of orders from the chancery (while Cardinal Cushing was ill and in the hospital) hundreds of priests and seminarians then marched with the Catholic Interracial Council in the South Boston St. Patrick's Day parade. All of a sudden, things which long ago should have happened are happening. The distance covered between 1962 and 1965 is little short of amazing.

But the distance covered is only, let us say, from 1789 to 1945. Pope John wanted an *aggiornamento* that would bring the Church "up to today." The Council has, in the end, let him down. The Council has hardly begun to cope with the world of the coming era on which we have already embarked. Looking backward, the Council is an astonishing success. But looking forward, the Council is in many ways a failure. Perhaps a Council—an unwieldy organ of more than two thousand men—must inevitably work twenty years or so behind the time, dealing with issues that are ripe for institutional resolution. Perhaps it is enough that the Council has established the *principle* of renewal and reform, and that the old Roman will to eternity and changelessness appears to be broken. The Church is an historical, ever-changing institution, as the Council has recognized; that very fact liberates the energies of the Church to meet the future on its own terms, to enter the coming secular culture as enthusiastically, though in an entirely new manner, as she entered the secular culture of ancient Greece, or Rome, or the early northern countries of Europe.

But a vision of the secular civilization of the future hardly seems to have entered the minds of many of the bishops. Too many of them are more concerned about the "confusions" which the recent changes are causing among their previously undisturbed flocks. Some of the bishops are of an appallingly rigid and frightened cast of mind: Bishop Hannon of Scranton has forbidden his people to take part in Bible vigils (a danger to their faith); Bishop Topel of Spokane has called 1964 "a year of shame" because the newly awakened Catholic press has been calling spades spades, and naming bishops by name for what they do or don't do. Unaccustomed to being held to account for their actions like other men, some bishops may be forgiven for sighing after the good old days.

Nevertheless, the world in which we live is a serious world, not a toy for timid bishops. Between thirty and fifty million people in Europe have been killed by violence since this century began, and the same moral, political, social, and economic factors which contributed to this bloodshed are still operative. A new civilization, as Albert Camus saw in *The Rebel,* is rising on the rubble heap left by the Second World War, a civilization technical beyond any ever known, international in scope, and secularist in attitude. The Church has no time to worry about how deeply a bishop's feelings may be hurt. The question for her is whether the yeast of religious faith will be able to penetrate this technical world at all.

Pope John XXIII was sufficiently sensitive to feel the malaise which after the Second World War gripped Europe and the world: old traditions have been discredited, old beliefs are mere words on the lips even to many who hold them, and for values like justice, human dignity, and liberty it is very difficult to give an intellectual justification. From a coldly scientific point of view, the planet Earth is insignificant; among men, the species is of more significance than the individual; the natural course of history treats men cruelly. It is difficult, as Albert Camus found, to argue one's way out of the nihilism which facts seem to force upon us.

In the United States, few saw dramatized in fire and pain the depths of modern nihilism; besides, the more limited illusions of the pragmatist live longer. Anglo-American life has always maintained amenities of fair play, liberty, and law, for which no creditable account is to be found in Anglo-American philosophy. Such amenities are a part of the Anglo-American inheritance, part of our acquired fund of sentiment which David Hume extolled and which is not yet bankrupt. So long as this inheritance lasts, many philosophers will be able to continue their games with words. But one day they will have to resume the hard work of articulating why we value individual persons more than things, why persons are valuable beyond their usefulness or beyond the contributions they make to the economy, and what, in short, a man is.

These are questions in which believers and nonbelievers have an equal stake, and which are absolutely fundamental for the future. The Council convened by Pope John has barely touched these questions, having become deeply involved in ecclesiastical problems. Thus, as Cardinal Lercaro of Bologna recently warned in Rome, there is a grave danger that the Council will not have lived up to the vision of Pope John. In no case are the documents approved by the Council representative of the best that Catholic theology has to offer. In every case, compromise with the men of *Romanità* or with the bishops who lacked theological sophistication was required. The Council was, under the leadership of Roman minds, badly prepared. It was snatched from disaster only by the ardent hopes and example of Pope John, assisted by the energy, intelligence, and determination of a score of leaders among the cardinals and bishops of the world.

It seems that the bishops, particularly those of the United States, have hardly grasped the extent to which not only the Middle Ages but also the modern age are at an end; a new, technical, secular, urban, pluralistic age has begun. Language appropriate for an agricultural society no longer conveys meaning; even the word "father" means something different for the human spirit after Freud, not to mention what it means in "broken" homes or in those millions of families whose lives center not on parents but on teen-agers.

"Secularism" for many of the American bishops is a dirty word; they blame on it virtually every ill that plagues society, from racial discrimination to lurid advertising. The bishops hardly ever recognize their own complicity in the evils of modern life; one seldom hears them, as a group, confess their own sins. There are, after all, bishops who have in the name of prudence compromised their professed moral code in the matter of race (but who even in the name of the same prudence brook no compromise in the matter of birth control). But most of all, the bishops have yet to come to grips with the fact that atheism and agnosticism represent a noble way of life, a way of life which is more attractive than Celtic folk religion to many young, educated Catholics.

The Catholic people have changed in character under the system of universal education the atheists of the Enlightenment saw fit to pioneer, and under the system of parochial schools the German and Irish bishops of the United States insisted on providing for them. Catholics in the United States constitute the largest body of college-educated Catholics in the history of the Church.

In the last few years, partly under the release granted them by Kennedy's election, partly under the impact of the Council, partly by the ripeness of time, Catholics in the United States have "aged" remarkably. In the schools and universities, in the Catholic and secular press, and in Church meeting rooms, the atmosphere is charged with questions, criticism, and initiatives. The drive to understand, the drive of inquiry and personal appropriation, has clearly been awakened, and pupils from the schools the bishops took such pains to build are, as it were, turning around to bite the bishops' hands. Teachers of the old style hardly know how to cope. The defensive speak of a "breakdown in the spirit of obedience." But in reality nothing has broken down but the image of the pyramid; the questioners and the doers are obeying the Council's directives and following the Council's example.

It is in this sense that the Council has had its greatest success. Catholics now want the whole Church, every day and everywhere, to be one large Council: full of free speech, argument, dissent, respect for diversity, and the slow search for consensus. Not all the bishops are like Pope John; not all like this kind of Church. But who, then, are the better Catholics, those of the Church of silence, conformity and comfort, or those of the Church of freedom and dissent?

In fact, the spirit of faith and obedience among Catholics has seldom been more alert; but this faith is directed toward the whole Church rather than toward the local pastor or diocesan bishop. Catholics listen now with two ears: one for the local voice, one for the voice of renewal and reform which is stirring in many other places, including the Council, if not locally. It is difficult for some pastors to be reminded, perhaps for the first time, that they are stewards and not masters of the faith. In the old days, the great ideal of many a pastor was to let nothing disturb the waters; now such a man hesitates, for fear the disturbance might be the Holy Spirit.

But if the newer Catholics have two ears, they also have three eyes. That, at least, is the claim of Daniel J. Callahan's collection, *The Generation of the Third Eye*.[4] The title is taken from a phrase of John Courtney Murray's, about the introspective, analytic temper of the times, and the contributors are writers, artists, and scholars who are under forty. John Cogley, who at forty-eight finds himself untimely placed in an older generation, adds an "afterword" which shows, if anything can, that there is a difference between the generations.

Two points emerge from this collection. One is that for nearly every contributor the ordinary parish life of the Church in America has been virtually bankrupt. The sermons are abominable, both in theology and in culture; the churches are run as "parish plants" rather than as praying and believing communities. The financial strain of building and maintaining parochial schools seems to have made practical materialists out of the Catholic community.

Secondly, nearly every one of the writers represented has found his nourishment as a Catholic not from the ecclesiastical structure but from the intellectual Catholic underground. Years ago, this one discovered Bernanos and Bloy, or that one Simone Weil. Through a friendship here, a prophetic book there, they developed against the stream of unintellectual Catholicism. It seems likely that the next generation of such Catholics, now in the colleges, will number in the scores of thousands; for the Council has made the underground official.

To be sure, some members of the underground are reacting as if the war were still on; everyone is anticipating a backlash among the bishops. It is perfectly plain that the bishops of the United States, especially those along the Eastern seaboard (Cardinal Spellman and the two recent Apostolic Delegates purportedly share a large responsibility for their nomination) were unprepared for the Council. Many of them for years strenuously opposed liturgical reform, did little to publish the social encyclicals of the popes, treated the new theology of Rahner, Congar, Danièlou, and others as vaguely heretical, and knew almost nothing of the intellectual revolution in contemporary biblical studies. It would be too much to expect that all these bishops, after a brief "graduate school" exposure at the Council to what has been going on in Catholicism these last ninety years, will be able to relay their discoveries to the often unread, firmly set monsignori and pastors who preside over the daily life of their dioceses.

Still, most of the bishops of the United States appear not only to have benefited immeasurably by the Council, but also to have begun to win over their clergy and their Waugh-like laymen. One of the touching aspects of the Council was the sight of old men changing the ideas of a lifetime, and voting—for the good of the Church— for ideas they had many long years opposed. "If you had told me last week that I would vote yes this morning, I'd have said you were crazy," one archbishop from the Midwest told a reporter at the Council, "but I did."

What, then, of the future? The fact that the underground is now official has temporarily brought a wavering in the sense of direction. Since their inception, journals like the *Commonweal* and *Cross Currents* had been saying that reform and renewal are required; suddenly Pope John and the Council have concurred. Now what?

There are enormous institutional problems to be dealt with in Roman Catholicism. There are too few places in which the insight, experience, and concern of the laymen are made institutionally effective. Laymen are given no responsibility; in the business world and in government they are treated as adults, but in the Church as children. The extreme spiritual poverty of parish and diocesan community life seems to be due chiefly to this enforced childlikeness.

One of the brightest spots is the fact that the nearly two hundred thousand nuns in the United States, especially those from the Midwest and the West, are moving swiftly into twentieth-century and secular American life; the example of the six from St. Louis who marched at Selma was a shot heard round the country: even in Boston.

Serious sectional problems are also involved. The Catholic cities of the Eastern seaboard are depressingly dead; the Celtic heresy has killed them. Sister Marie Augusta Neal's thesis for Harvard, *Values and Interests in Social Change,*[5] a study of the Boston clergy, indicates that the future in Boston, at least, is hopeful. But the Boston Catholic paper, *The Pilot,* often has to be ecclesiastically careful, and, when the Cardinal is out of the office, the chancery can be as narrow, complacent, and restrictive as any in the country. Let us not speak of Providence, New York, the major sees of New Jersey, or Philadelphia.

Wherever one visits in America, one finds again and again that the fundamental problem of American Catholicism lies in the bureaucratic minds who hover like flies around many of the bishops, the nervous Nellies of the chancery offices who censor books, discourage talks with Protestants, fear that the Council has caused "confusion" among the faithful, and build (as in one diocese) $400,000 and (in another) $90,000 rectories for the use of no more than four priests. Such men may be loyal administrators and genial golf companions and they may often think of themselves as the most select group in the world; but many of them should recognize that they are among the most unenlightened, mediocre, and complacent men who ever represented the Gospels of Jesus Christ.

This problem is formally like that which afflicts civil government and even universities: how can a living institution make effective in its midst not only bureaucrats but also prophets? How do you get, and keep, open minds and free spirits in administrative posts?

The problem is only exacerbated by the tradition of authoritarianism in the Church and by the tradition of celibacy. The fact is commonly discussed among Catholics that too many of those who advance in the hierarchy seem attracted to these traditions because of their own emotional disturbances. It is probable that some manifestations

of ecclesiastical power reveal deep personal insecurity. There are
very few checks-and-balances in Church structure to minimize the
potential dangers of such disequilibrium.

St. Augustine, that great bishop, once wrote in self-reflection that
bishops are the enemies of the Church, and surely it is true that every
blindness of the local bishop injures the life of the diocese he serves.
The Catholic people, and the clergy, need institutional safeguards
against abuses. The monsignori in Chicago who resisted Cardinal
Meyer's every effort to integrate the parochial schools—for fear those
who form the economic base of their huge, brick parish plants would
move away—and some among the clique who form a purple guard
around Cardinal Spellman are by their impenetrable complacency
scandals to every alert man who encounters them.

Connected with this issue are several others. The ordinary parish
priests, particularly the assistant pastor, are at the present time the
least free members of the Church. In canon law, they have almost no
protection for what may be called in imitation of Thoreau "evangelical
disobedience." How can the Gospels be preached when those of
sensitive conscience are forbidden by administrative prudence to avoid
disturbing the present order? Many a priest finds himself saying
one thing in private, another in public. What is the use of giving one's
life to the service of the Gospels if one is made to serve, instead, the
timidity of those who, with whatever good intentions, flatter the rich,
the powerful, the secure?

Besides, the Catholic people have, until recently, been unwilling
to let a priest speak in his own name; he is taken much too seriously
as speaking for the entire Church. Consequently, many priests do not
speak their own minds; they mouth accepted conventions which will
"disturb" no one. Their acquiescence has entangled them in spider-
webs of their own weaving, and only their own courage will free them
and the Gospels to which they are dedicated.

Thirdly, the descendants of Europe's peasants are only now beginning to lift their eyes from the vulgar and aggressive search for dollars
which they found to be the obvious requirement for coping with the
Protestant Establishment of the United States. No one is deceived into
thinking that "the emerging laymen" (a descriptive phrase for the
religiously and intellectually alert) in this country number more than
a few score thousand, perhaps a few hundred thousand. Apathy, indifference to religion except as a vague and ultimate comfort, and

docility in early assimilating the pyramidal view of the Church mark the vast majority of American Catholics. Here, again, the situation faced by Catholicism in the United States is formally similar to that of the life of general culture and the intellect: the vast majority of the people belong spiritually to the hucksters of Hollywood, Madison Avenue, and the thoughtless pulpit.

But these are largely intramural issues. The internal political structure of the Church as it exists at present inhibits spiritual and intellectual development and it is the business of laymen, nuns, priests, and bishops who care about such things to reform the structure and practices of the institution they love.

On a wider front, there are a whole host of issues of concern to all Americans in which the Church is more or less "officially" involved: education, for example. An increasing number of educated Catholics are critical of the parochial schools not so much because these are intellectually inferior to the public schools (often they aren't), but because their graduates do not seem noticeably different in behavior and attitudes from those who go to the public schools. Why put millions of dollars into a program of such meager religious fruitfulness?

The younger Catholic intellectuals—often products of the Catholic schools—are the most vociferous critics of the schools. But in many new suburbs, the people of the parish rather than the clergy insist on the building of a Catholic school. Many parents seem to feel incompetent to educate their own children in religious matters; they seem to need the feeling of security which comes from placing their children under the moral protection of priests and nuns. Meanwhile, those who teach in the schools, trying valiantly to reach new standards both in secular disciplines and in the "new theology" of Vatican II, become increasingly sensitive to criticism, whose truth they are often willing to admit but whose practicality they sometimes question.

Three relatively modest propositions appear to be developing as a feasible and widespread attitude toward this question: (1) At some period in their education, Catholic children ought to have *some* formal Catholic education; otherwise, their theological education will fall below their general education. But they should spend part of their career also in public and secular schools; (2) At least one important part of religious education can best be given in the home, through public prayer in church, and through personal reading and organized discussion groups; (3) The maintenance of an independent Catholic school system, for part of the education of at least part of the Catholic population, contributes to the diversity and richness of American education.

On a second important public issue, racial justice, only a year ago the inactivity of Catholics threatened to dissipate the trust and good feeling of the then just budding ecumenical movement. For the very Jews and Protestants who were most apt to be open to new dialogue with Catholics were among the first to become sensitive to the moral demands of the racial revolution; and they were scandalized by Catholic inactivity. But gradually, through the lonely witness of such men as the Berrigan brothers (one a Jesuit, one a Josephite), and through the pressure of other active spirits who increasingly allowed themselves to be diverted from the work of Vatican II and other intramural matters, more and more Catholic consciences were touched. An institutional mark of sorts was reached when the well-known Paulist Center on Boston Common threw open its doors, in May 1965, to an ecumenically sponsored teach-in on the emotionally charged issue of racial imbalance in the Boston public schools.

Several important traits of the American Catholic community came to light in these developments; and these traits illuminate Catholic attitudes on other problems. In America more than in Europe, many Catholics are victims of the serious flaws in late scholastic philosophy and theology; many interpret reality through eyes blinded to certain important features. For example, American Catholics commonly interpret a generalization as a normative statement; they register the descriptive mode only with difficulty. If a psychologist or a sociologist describes what frequently happens, they take him to be recommending a course of action; detached analysis is seldom credited. "Is" (in the tradition of the Aristotelian final cause) is taken as an "ought."

Again, many American Catholics are fond of verbal solutions to concrete problems. If the American bishops *said* in 1957 that racial discrimination is immoral, and said it solemnly in their annual proclamation, many Catholics feel the problem has been solved.

Again, if the essential position of the Church is once enunciated, then many American Catholics believe it is illegitimate to blame the Church for the concrete, individual actions or attitudes of the Catholic clergy or people. Thus, if Pius XII in (as Albert Camus sadly noted) an obscure encyclical condemned Nazism, then the *Church* was not involved in Hitler's wars, only errant individuals were. In fact, even if Pius XII had not spoken, the *Church* would have "spoken," silently. For the *Church* is a pure, immaculate, spotless Platonic ideal, not to be confused with the sinners who give her flesh in history. The Church, for example, has always believed in religious liberty, never persecuted Jews or Protestants, always fostered truth and scientific inquiry, ever championed the rights of man, never approved racial discrimination.

Again, the upper blade of Platonic unreality in late scholasticism makes necessary a lower blade of Machiavellian "prudence" in dealing with actual complexities in history. The very bishop who believes most in the sinlessness of the Platonic Church is apt to have a finger in many deals involving local real estate; another is warning the local newspaper not to print a certain story; another is pressuring politicians in this direction or in that. Italian and Irish bishops, in particular, seem to have mastered the regular swing of the pendulum from the rhetoric of sermons on the sinless beauty of the Church to the vigorous use of power for the worldly needs of the Church.

Finally, many American Catholics still seem to prefer group loyalty to truth; self-congratulation to honesty. There is at present a vogue of criticism and self-accusation, to be sure; but many are still untouched by it, and many who voice it seem surprised at the new possibility of speaking out.

This group loyalty has largely blinded American Catholics to the needs of other groups. The oscillation between idealism and cynical prudence has led American Catholics to believe in racial justice while tolerating racial injustice. The emphasis on essential definition rather than on personal appropriation and responsibility, and the confusion of the normative with the descriptive, have enabled American Catholics to be blind to concrete realities in the name of "unchanging principles."

These same traits of mind characterize the usual American Catholic foray into American social or political life, on the censorship of movies, on birth control clinics, on aid to parochial schools, etc. Often the values which Catholics wish to uphold in these matters are commendable in themselves; but the political and social techniques for defending them smack of Italian or Irish scholasticism.

Essentialistic, nonhistorical, and abstract ideals are voiced on the one hand, and ecclesiastical prestige is wielded as political power on the other.

Increasingly, this mental scholasticism is yielding to the sunshine of American liberties and the brisk winds of American realities. Cardinal Cushing has recently recognized that the Catholic conscience need not be articulated in public law, and tentatively approved the amendment of the birth control laws of Massachusetts so that they would be more in conformity with the general public conscience. Catholics can maintain their stricter views in private; the domain of public law is distinguishable from the domain of personal conscience.

Pope John XXIII, Cardinal Cushing's closest ecclesiastical model, made another important distinction in *Mater et Magistra,* concerning communism: the original ideology is one thing, the reality which has evolved under historical pressures is another. Late scholasticism pure and simple was unable to make such a distinction; in its purview, only logic and essential definitions mattered.

In proportion as American Catholics learn to distinguish essences from existents, norms from descriptions, logic from history, their political and social actions will become increasingly more nuanced, reasoned, and appropriate to a democratic society. Catholics will ever have a moral code more strict in certain matters than many other Americans, but their way of defending the values they cherish can become both more effective from their own point of view and less repugnant to others. A more historically minded and concrete philosophy and theology, already gaining in acceptance, will gradually make this transition in intellectual style possible.

Many of the younger Catholic intellectuals, however, are involved neither in the intramural problems of the Church nor in the problems of the "official" Church and American culture. They are getting their degrees or are teaching in the whole spectrum of academic studies, are entering political life or the professions, are active in urban renewal or journalism or the arts. They have little or no interest in ecclesiastical matters; they often resent the ecclesiastical establishment as vaguely stupid, or narrow, or merely professional. They have never had a conversation with a bishop and, except with a personal friend or relative, rarely with a priest. They often remain practicing Catholics, faithful to the sacraments. But the world of the spirit in which they live is that of the general secular world rather than that of the Catholic community at large.

They are concerned about the fact that automobiles are choking our cities; that the very poor continue to suffer gravely in our society; that our complex democracy requires the replacement of venal-minded and unintelligent politicians with men of talent, of some vision, and of suitably thick skin. They are worried about the in-equalities suffered by women in our society. They are disturbed to the depths of their consciences by the risks of wider warfare the U.S. is courting. As Christians, they may feel they have a special stake in these problems, and special emphases in defining and attacking them. But they receive little enlightenment in church on Sunday morning in how they might cope with such problems.

Thus the great irony of American Catholicism is that, after decades of ecclesiastical warnings about the dangers of "secularism," the most sensitive and inquiring young Catholics are presently finding the spiritual values represented by American secularism more compelling than the spiritual attitudes of the Catholic clerical establishment. The secular world has little to say, of course, about God, about ultimate questions of hope, destiny, and conscience; for such matters, and for the Eucharist which is their communal symbol, many young Cath-olics maintain their ties with the historic Church and its spiritual tradition. But they find a broadly conceived pragmatism to be a more adequate philosophical language for dealing with reality than late scholasticism. And they find contemporary political, economic, and social theory more morally relevant than most of the sermons they suffer through on Sunday mornings.

The future of American Catholicism will probably manifest an in-creasing secularization of the thought patterns of clergy and people, to the benefit of the religious faith they cherish. For though most varieties of American secularism appear to be agnostic, few appear to be absolutely closed to religious values. Consequently, many more Catholics will probably adopt some version of pragmatism, with an existentialist emphasis upon self-appropriation and self-criticism, as their basic philosophical and theological language. Given this lan-guage, they will add to the pluralistic values usually championed by secular philosophers, special religious values of their own. And their fundamental ethical and political decisions will involve balancing one of these values against another, in establishing what is best to do here and now on each occasion.

If this prediction is correct, American Catholics will in a sense be recovering the Aristotelian tradition of *phronesis* and the short-lived Thomistic tradition of concrete *prudentia* and *caritas,* which were swallowed up in the abstract, essentialistic "Reason" of late scholasticism. Neither Aristotle nor Thomas Aquinas, however, shared what would today be called "historical consciousness." Thus, the contribution of modern secularism to the wisdom which can be assimilated by the Church is above all an acute awareness of the historical and contingent factors which characterize human history and the development of human intelligence.

American Catholics have little to fear, and much to gain, from the critical assimilation of secular wisdom in their attempt to understand the meanings of their faith at this moment in human history. In so doing, from their own treasury they also bring their own special contribution to the general wisdom of our culture. Their tradition of contemplative life will have much to say to a world of greater leisure; their tradition of emptiness and abandonment in prayer will have much to say to those, like the Anglican Bishop J. A. T. Robinson, who suddenly discover that God cannot be imagined nor, strictly, conceived.

American culture and American Catholicism benefit by the mutual criticism and guarded but respectful cooperation they lend to one another. American Catholicism is becoming, and ought to become, different from any other form of Catholicism in history, because it is *American.* And America, without its minority groups and their special values, is homogenized and vulgar.

Each man who cherishes the needs of the human spirit is a precious asset in a land of buyers and sellers. Every analysis of the life of the spirit in the United States leads to the same conclusion: the real war, the bitter war which lies ahead, is for the soul of the American people. Who will get there first, the huckster and the demagogues, or men of reality and statesmen? On every corner there are barkers who desire, for a fee, to cover up the realities of the world of bloodshed in which we live. There are too few who speak with honesty, with compassion for the weak, with restraining intelligence for the strong, with realism in action. Secular intellectuals and religious men who value such things need each other—and that is why American Catholicism needs soon to be making its intellectual and artistic contributions to American culture.

NOTES

1. *Contraception,* Harvard University Press, 561 pp.
2. A splendid example of Celtic loyalty appeared as an unsigned article in *Herder Correspondence* (vol. 3, no. 11, November 1966) pp. 323-27, entitled "The Myth of the Irish: A Failure of American Catholic Scholarship." It confirms the myth it describes.
3. See, e.g., the reports by the pseudonymous Xavier Rynne, published by Farrar, Straus & Giroux, and my own *The Open Church,* Macmillan: New York.
4. Sheed & Ward, 256 pp.
5. Prentice-Hall, 192 pp.

8

Diversity of Structures
and Freedom Within Structures

*Laymen were at a premium in Rome during the Council. Late in 1963
some sixty of the most prominent Council theologians met in a small
heavily beamed room of the Hotel Columbus (a bomb set off in that room
would have set Roman Catholic theology back fifty years) to plan a new
international periodical to be published simultaneously in nine languages.
In the age of the laity, laymen had to be found somewhere. I had been
sent a printed invitation, and hurried to what I thought would be a re-
ception for several hundred people. As virtually the only layman there,
apart from those serving sherry, I thought the group wished an American
writer to be present. However, awaiting me in January when I returned
to the United States was a letter, much delayed in the mails, asking me to
prepare an article for the first issue of* Concilium, *as the new journal was
to be called. Since the deadline was then but ten days away, in accepting
I walked where angels would have feared to fly. From the description
given in the letter, I understood that footnotes were not desired; in com-
pleting my article, I omitted them.*

*When the first issue of the much-trumpeted journal appeared, I was
flanked by such top theologians as would make a cardinal blush. Moreover, Europeans as they were, their articles referred (it seemed) to every
small journal, dictionary, and remote French, Dutch, or Belgian mono-
graph in print. I was naked in a snow of footnotes. Later, I tried to ignore*

the stiletto allusions of reviewers or, worse, their too charitable silence. Still, I think the essay is of some constructive use. Footnotes, if purists require to be appeased, would not be difficult to supply; and one is certainly owed to a then unpublished paper by Professor Robert N. Bellah of the Department of Social Relations at Harvard with whom, as I wrote this paper, I was taking a seminar in the sociology of religion, and whose broad, imaginative periodization of history gave me the frame which is the best thing in it.

Following the Concilium *essay, I append a related letter which appeared in the* Commonweal *(January 26, 1965) and which was written in response to a request from Bishop Stephen A. Leven of San Antonio.*

I. *Diversity of Structure and Freedom Within Structures in the Church*

TOWARD what new structures should the evolution of the Church be directed in order to enter into the mainstream of the life of men? The present structure of the Catholic Church seems too univocal, particular and uniform. In order to be more human, the Church must be more catholic. Catholics must learn to stress the importance of the concrete, the particular, the different, in a word, the diversity within the Church. Given modern communications, unity of spirit is more easily attained; the maintenance of spiritual diversity, even within the same faith, requires intelligence and care.

Of course, there already exists much diversity among Catholics. We cannot talk about "new structures in the Church" unless we recognize that the human race is seriously and blessedly diverse. Even fundamental words like *structure* itself call to mind different images, different relationships and different attitudes in the different languages of the world. Each of us—and the regional culture of each—is concrete, finite, special. There is not now—and, let us hope, never will be—a universal standardized "man." The ideal of a universal abstract type, of a form which all are to strive to fit, of a uniform structure for all, is a seriously mistaken and dangerous ideal.

In every discussion of "new structures" there is implied a periodization of history: of what has been, is becoming and will be. Perhaps it will be useful to make the hidden theory of this article explicit. In the past, the structure of social action derived its strength from the community, from the *Gemeinschaft*. There are many who interpret the modern age as a crisis of community, a crisis of fragmented society in which individuals are adrift in painful isolation. To such commentators, the fact that questions of moral choice and moral destiny have been differentiated down to the level of the individual person, without a "sense of community" to give these individuals moral support, is the deep tragedy of modern life. I would argue, on the other hand, that it is precisely this differentiation that is the glory of modern life, because it opens out before each of us the radical human trial.

However we interpret the value of modern life, surely the fact is plain enough. Social and communal pressures (whether from family, state, church, economic order or cultural traditions) are less and less important in the actual decisions made by individuals about the content of their lives and their actions. Everywhere we hear talk about "the break-up of the old order," the "lack of respect for old values and traditions," and the rest. Moreover, this process appears to be carried to its farthest extremes precisely in those countries that are generally regarded as "most advanced." It is for this reason that this process seems to be the fruitful key to the interpretation of cultural evolution; the process has many stages analogous to each other. In the new countries of Africa, in the restless nations of Latin America, in the Soviet Union of 1918, in present-day Germany or Sweden, the breakdown of the old order is always different according as the old order is different. At each successive change, more choices are left to the individual.

There are many complaints today, of course, about the "mass man." I think the critics of the new mass man are deceived by external appearances—the sameness of urban buildings, the ubiquity of the same radio broadcasts, newspapers and television images. To be sure, in every age there are many men who refuse to act decisively, who drift with the current of their community. The peasants and townsmen of yesterday (and they are living still in enclaves all around us) appear to produce as many such men as our modern cities. Nevertheless, in too many quarters there lingers a nostalgia for the old forms of "community," for the old pressures of a group in which the individual knows what is expected of him and what benefits are due him. Instead, today's individual must choose his own associations, his own affiliations, his own allegiances.

Is it not the point of critics that the life of the masses seems "formless," and that they are thus susceptible of being roused by demagogues? A truer view, at least in more stable countries, is that individuals are grouped in many voluntary associations, pressure groups, clubs, churches, etc. A system of free associations is complex, but it is not formless. Such a system represents a spiritual victory of great importance for the human race; it maximizes the range of choices within which the individual works out his destiny. Our short-sightedness or our nostalgia can lead us to turn this victory into an ancient defeat.

Two versions of such an ancient defeat should be mentioned. First, in the name of the deficiencies of the old order (surely obvious to all), Marxism replaces the evolution towards the differentiation of individuals with a new set of group pressures, sometimes of the most violent sort. Secondly, "Americanization" (such as it is understood in Gaullist France and among European intellectuals generally) would likewise mean the end of the differentiation of individual moral destiny, unless it is only a myth, generated by a misunderstanding of American life.

In the countries generally thought of as "more advanced," it is precisely the degree of differentiation allowed to individuals—and not industrial superiority—which is the most profound measure of their development. Never in history have young people had so many avenues of differentiation as are now open to them. Where they will live, where they will work, how often they will change jobs, what they will believe, with whom they will associate, how involved they become in issues (and in *which* issues)—neither family, nor church, nor employer, nor party, nor tradition can determine. The *malaise* felt among the young in such countries is not that of having their future predetermined by society or by some organization to which they are bound; it is that of having an "open" future, of not having enough guidance, of having too many possibilities. They must choose even their personal standard of values, their own measure of what constitutes a human life. Faced by so many choices, no one of which compels assent, they are afflicted with *ennui* and powerlessness.

The roots of this *malaise,* however, are fundamentally healthy, sound and praiseworthy. The sickness arises from the too-sudden advent of the very freedom for which the human race has been striving. Freedom, as Dostoevsky forewarned, is so terrifying a burden that few can tolerate it. The young are burdened by a freedom their elders cannot teach them how to use. All attempts to restore a "sense of values," to restore a "community," are only steps backward into the very social pressures from which the young feel liberated. The fact that liberty is terrifying has surprised us. But then such liberty, on so large a scale, is new on the face of the earth, and few generations have ever known what it is to be born with it. It is no wonder that in many places the younger generation seems already older than its years.

If this periodization is correct—and much evidence seems to support it—then any assumption that the "new structures" in the Church must try to re-create the community of the past, in whatever new styles or by whatever new methods, is seriously in error. The search for community is reversion to a lesser value, to an earlier stage of cultural development. What I mean by this needs to be made clear.

To argue for ever-increasing room for differentiation is not to argue for "rugged individualism," economic, personal or spiritual. It is not to argue that "the soul is alone before God," or that men should live "each for himself." It is not to support nineteenth-century Anglo-Saxon individualism, *laissez-faire* or utilitarianism. It is not to support cultural or individual relativism. It is, on the other hand, to allow an *environment,* in which such aberrations can exist, for the sake of a deeper kind of freedom. It is to allow the individual person "to sink or swim" and it is to encourage individuals to become persons, to show individuals *how* "to swim." It is, above all, to emphasize that each individual must become a person by himself; no one can force him to do so; no one else can do it for him. There is no way of mass-producing persons. There is no "new structure" that will automatically reform and renew persons. Individuals (merely) can be "formed" by structures; persons develop chiefly from within, often against the pressures of social structures.

To become a person is to become faithful to one's own insights, and to be faithful to all the claims of one's own unrestricted drive to understand.[1] To be psychotic or neurotic is to have blocked the claims of understanding; it is to have become caught in counterrational patterns that prevent one from acting according to all the claims of the situation in which one finds oneself. Perhaps analogously, to sin is to "turn against the light"; sin is the deliberate choice of what does not make sense, but is desired anyway. The root of a man's thirst for God is his fidelity to understanding; for, though they are not commensurate, the human activity of understanding is a participation in the life of the unseen, unknown God. To follow the claims of understanding with integrity and fidelity is to be on the path toward God. When St. Augustine sought everywhere for God, he found him not outside but within.

The ordinary structures of Catholic life in our time do not seem to show sufficient confidence in the human person. Unity is preferred to differentiation. Attention to the abstract statement is preferred to attention to the different ways in which concrete individuals understand and appropriate that statement. Community of sentiment is more cherished than a community of respect for each other's differences. In short, community is sought on too shallow a level. Confidence is lacking in the ability of men to differ profoundly and yet to be at one in respect for each other's fidelity to understanding.

There is in this matter a gap between the rhetoric of Catholics and the actual facts, between ecclesiastical structure and concrete fact. Pius XII and John XXIII were both Catholics—consecutive popes even—but such different personifications of the faith! Charles de Gaulle and Graham Greene are both Catholics: but such diversity of understanding, ideal and action! A centralized Roman structure, a comparatively uniform liturgy, a predilection for nonhistorical and abstract formulations of the creed, and a lack of organs of honest speech and plainly apparent differences within the Church have masked this rich diversity from the world and from Catholics themselves.

For such reasons, "ecclesiastical" has become a petty term, and even "Catholic" has come to mean its very opposite: not rich in diversity but more narrow and constricted than any moral force except communism. Many laymen in the world (perhaps especially in Anglo-Saxon countries) do not wish to be drawn within the orbit of this narrowness; they do not wish to get caught up in "Catholic" movements or to be identified with "Catholic" causes. Attempts to restore Catholic community—even through the liturgy—do not appeal to all of them. It would be a mistake to think that their resistance is due only to a residue of misguided individualism. They are suspicious of new forms of ecclesiastical uniformity. They wish to be

Catholic, but not ecclesiastical. They wish to retain their own personal response to faith and the integrity of their position in the secular world.

As Simone Weil once wrote, it is a mistake to think that God is interested only in religion. Likewise, it is a mistake to identify the Church with ecclesiastical structures: with the Vatican, with dioceses, with parishes. The Church is the consciousness of the Son of God—insight and love—taking root in the consciousness of men, sacramentally and otherwise. Because he is infinite, their diversity and number do not exhaust his life. Because each of them is finite, they cannot know him without their diversity—without each other. Their fundamental community does not arise from adherence to external structures, however important such structures be for incarnate men. Their fundamental community lies in his conscious life: he is the center toward whom they are all diversely drawn. When each man is most faithful to himself, most faithful to the unique faith which is in him, he is a source of harmony and assistance to the community. When he is unfaithful to himself, the community is deprived of his contribution.

The traditional structures of the Church that have been handed down to us do not, however, take advantage of the gifts given each individual. There do not exist forums of dialogue and communication among those who share the faith. Each of us learns so little from the other. Only the priest speaks, and he often speaks not from his own gifts but with formulae that may or may not be appropriate. It is as though we had contrived structures that could seal up all entrances against the Spirit. It is as though we had hoped that if we succeeded in fixing upon abstract formulae equally distant from all, no one of us might have the terror of encountering God face to face.

But if we are to propose new structures that will not keep us both from the world and from God—and that is what old ecclesiastical structures appear to do now—we must confine ourselves to concrete conditions of only one time and place. Perhaps it will be permissible, then, to discuss the situation in the United States.

Although few American clergy or laymen speak of it, some are convinced that young people in the United States are undergoing a profound crisis of faith. This crisis is often hidden from sight because of a peculiarly American phenomenon. In Latin countries, at least, although many persons unquestioningly believe in God, they nevertheless do not often go to church; in the United States, on the contrary, it seems customary for many persons who are not sure whether they believe in God, or what he is like, nevertheless to go faithfully to church. It is "un-American" not to go to church.

Moreover, nearly one-half of American Catholic children and young people are in Catholic schools—some of them for all the years of their education, from grammar school through university. They early learn the habit of "frequent attendance" at the sacraments. But the early national Catholic communities are breaking up: the Irish no longer all live together, and the Slav, German, and Italian sections of the big cities are beginning to yield to newer immigrant groups. In education and in occupation, American Catholics are increasingly entering into the wider American environment. It is precisely at this point that many young Catholics are beginning to doubt their faith and their own identity.

Most often they have learned their faith "by the book." Intellectually, they have lived in sheltered environments. Their faith has most often been supported by the faith of the community into which they were born. Now that in this generation large numbers of them are moving out of their native communities—many of them physically, others only spiritually—the cultural props of their faith are being left behind. The first impulse of those concerned with this situation is to create *new* Catholic communities—Newman Clubs on the state university campuses, Catholic societies for lawyers, the Catholic Sociology Society, etc. Increasingly, such props appear to be artificial. Can't Catholics simply be human beings? Can't they simply take their place in the secular world? (John F. Kennedy represented an increasingly encountered type of the nonecclesiastical, nonghetto Catholic; he did not, for example, attend Catholic schools.)

Many young Catholics find it possible to suppress their doubts. They continue to go through the motions of belief for a long time. Such metaphysical casualness may seem strange to Europeans, but it is an important trait of the American character. In Europe there seems to be much more insistence on theoretical rigor. Every action appears to have an elaborate justification. One must be wholly convinced of the importance of *l'équipe* and "the community"; one must also be wholly committed to one's own well-developed personal creed. The American insists neither on so much "community" nor on so much "individuality." In a certain sense, the American neither *gives* so much of himself to the team, nor does he *hold back* so much of himself for a personal creed. He seems more "easygoing," less "rigid" —in a word, more "free," if also more colorless—than his European confrère. Metaphysically the American lives, to a great extent, in suspension. The demands which his many roles in society make on him and the vast range of choices open to him require him to maintain great personal flexibility.

Integrity, however, sooner or later draws its line. A choice must be made. The young American Catholic finds little in his background to prepare him for this confusion and sudden loneliness. Moreover, the moral and human development of the many nonbelievers he meets often strikes him as superior to the moral and human level of his sheltered Catholic environment. The American atheist does not seem to show the restlessness of the European atheist; atheism (or agnosticism) seems very much the sensible and admirable way of life. Many of the most intelligent young people are choosing that way, with their first real moral choice.

Not only in the United States but almost everywhere else in the world it seems increasingly that the crisis of belief and unbelief is the fundamental Christian problem of our time. It is a matter of common experience that a calm agnosticism is an attractive, admirable, liveable way of life. There are two ways in which the old structures of ecclesiastical life make the agnostic choice more credible:

1. The ordinary pattern of Catholic life has too little place for open and public honesty, criticism and questioning; a sacrosanct ecclesiastical sphere has been erected in which the probing intelligence of the layman—none too delicate or gracious, perhaps—does not appear to be welcome. The ecclesiastical sphere seems a milieu of falsehood and unreality.

2. On the personal level, the old structures of Catholic preaching and practice pay too little attention to the individual's unrestricted drive to understand, that drive to destroy all false idols and to be content only with the living God. It is assumed too easily that the individual truly has appropriated his faith; belief is taken for granted, and the ways of unbelief are not cherished. But early belief is almost always belief in an idol, and the ways of unbelief are often the purifying ways to God.

These are daily realities which "new structures" in the Church must take into account. The faith of the Catholic of today cannot be supported by the props of a Catholic cultural community. To a great extent we must embrace "the Protestant principle": reliance on the fidelity of the individual conscience, assisted by the Holy Spirit, for the ability of Catholics to take their due places in the secular world. We must develop means of discussion and consensus within the Catholic body, perhaps in the service of worship, after the example of the Quakers and the other Free Churches. Through some such voluntary associations, we must obtain the witness of diverse insight in the one community. We must teach our young people to emulate the honesty and fidelity of "the secular saints"; for to believe is to be only one step more honest, one step more faithful than they, by seeing that the momentum of honesty we feel in our hearts is the attraction of God's life within us.

II. *Domani*

No doubt countless laymen these days are being invited out to lunch by bishops, or stopped on the street and asked: "But what can we bishops *do* to bring laymen into cooperation with us? What practical steps can we take?" Well, it happened once in Rome under the impulsion of the Council. John Cogley and I were invited to lunch by Bishop Leven and the questions were sprung.

. . . It proved surprisingly hard to give workable, pragmatic answers. For years, the efforts of theologians, intellectuals, workers in social action, and journalists have been geared to awakening the Church at large—and the bishops in particular—to the wider dimensions of the preaching of the gospel, outside the traditional diocesan and parish organizations. Now a number of bishops are themselves alert to these dimensions. So it is not enough to go on insisting on *aggiornamento;* the problem is already that of tomorrow: the *domanimento*.

What experiments shall we try, to bring laymen into the official structure of the American Church? One of the American bishops asked me to write out some suggestions for him; perhaps he will count this letter as a redemption of my promise.

In the first place, I have been struck in recent years by conversations with businessmen and professional men who are far from being "liberal" or "progressive," either in politics or in the Church. Most of them—bankers, insurance men, merchants, lawyers, etc.—appear to

be the kind of laymen who would be known around a parish as more
or less "devout Catholics": faithful to weekly Mass, good contributors
to the Church, and a soft touch when the sisters need a ride into town
or a new refrigerator for the convent. Otherwise, they more or less
resist dialogue Mass, show little social and sometimes even little civic
responsibility.

I suppose that in the light of the *aggiornamento* they would be
thought of as "apathetic" laymen, neither knowing nor caring much
about the Council and its work. They are mildly surprised at the
changes which come to their attention, and not sure whether they like
them. They once invested a certain amount of energy in reconciling
themselves to the way the Church did things, and perhaps in defending it against objections. To frank criticisms of the Church, they react
with loyal defense or at least discomfort.

On the other hand, if one can keep a conversation with them going
long enough and establish an atmosphere in which criticism is not
taken as disloyalty, they gradually begin to unwind. Years of being
treated as children, years of suggestions long since suppressed, years
of having blunted their critical and inventive faculties in anything
having to do with the Church, come rushing, fitfully at first, to the
surface. Once they get the idea that they can speak about the Church
as openly as they speak about their businesses, or city politics, or any
other serious part of their lives, their observations become surprisingly
acute. There is often a residual bitterness, because the suppression has
been in effect so long. But mainly there is a sudden ecclesiastical
adulthood; they no longer wish to be children in this one part of their
lives.

It is important to emphasize that the men I am describing are not
"ecclesiastical types." They may take their part in various ecclesiastical organizations, but they avoid fawning over the local monsignor or
pastor, or getting too deeply involved in parish activities. They are not
naturally docile and uncritical. On the other hand, they have poured
so much money into the building of the parish churches and schools
of their locality that they have a natural interest in how that money
is spent and, in general, in the usefulness or uselessness of various
church activities. And, quite clearly, they speak of the clergy as
"they," with some disdain, even if in the presence of the clergy they
are extraordinarily courteous and friendly, and even if members of

the family, or close friends, are priests and give them a certain sympathy with the clergy.

Suppose that a lay synod were set up in a parish, or in a diocese, and that these men were invited to attend. I am fairly confident about the following predictions: (1) The laymen will expect, somewhere along the line, to be asked for money or to help in money-raising. (2) They will not say to their pastor or bishop what they will say to one another concerning their image of the Church, nor their estimate of its presence in their locality; what they say in their cars driving to and from the meeting will not be said at the meeting. (3) They will watch the presiding monsignor or bishop to see if he means what he says when he calls for frankness and candor; and they will, in any case, feel somewhat tongue-tied because the theological or ecclesiastical tone set by the opening remarks lets them know that they are on foreign territory, guests in a house not their own. They do not appreciate theological distinctions, and do not look at the world from the point of view of a bishop or monsignor. In a business conference or a professional meeting, they know just what can be said and what can't be said; in a church meeting, they lack professional ease. (4) They will expect the new synod to be a more sophisticated model of clerical superiority; every decision of consequence will be left to the bishop or pastor, or subject to his veto. (5) Many, at least, will be suspicious that the new idea isn't going to work, for the above reasons, and will resume their activities in secular organizations, where they are more at home, if their suspicions are borne out.

If this rough description of the present disposition of the ordinary layman in the parish or diocese is correct, then the problems of any new official organs to channel lay inventiveness and originality into the American Church are profound. The American Church is structurally clerical, and its attitudes are correspondingly clerical; bishop or pastor makes all decisions of consequence. Such decisions are, of course, made from a clerical point of view, with clerical ideas of what the Church is or should be in mind. Laymen are taught to respect this point of view, to defend it, and to acquiesce in it. Their own development as men of initiative, character, and achievement must come under secular auspices.

The Church is thus a primary instrument in the secularization of lay attitudes; it forces creativity elsewhere. As Martin Marty points out in *Varieties of Unbelief,* the Church even has a role in generating unbelief.

Nevertheless, some priests and some bishops will want to try to oppose the present stream and find some way of making parish and diocesan synods work. No plan thought up in a study will solve the serious problems facing such attempts. For one thing, the major factor in each experiment is the quality of the persons involved. To what extent can the local priest or bishop understand an argument voiced in unfamiliar modes and unfamiliar jargon, especially such as are offensive to ears trained to piety? How soon will he jump into a discussion to give it the "proper" ecclesiastical or theological twist? How well will the laymen involved be able to envisage the Church, not merely as a corporation, but as the people of God, with many responsibilities to the world? In how many cases will laymen be so involved in temporalities—race prejudice, let us say—that they will inhibit the preaching of the gospels? (I know of a priest who preached against the rackets in his locality, accusing those who took part in sin; parishioners, made both wealthy and generous to the Church by the same, telephoned the bishop and he, in turn, that very afternoon, advised the priest to give no more such sermons.)

The Church in America is deeply enmeshed in the politics, economics, real estate, and social structures of our culture. Among both clergy and laity, it is difficult to see where secularism ends and faith begins, or even if they are separable. It is a mistake, then, to think that the priest or bishop represents the faith and the layman the world; both secularism and grace affect both. The struggle to make grace prevail belongs to both.

But if laymen are to be drawn officially into the struggle on behalf of the institutional Church, some significant decisions will have to be left in their hands. Which ones? My suggestion is that each parish synod, or each diocesan synod, work out this matter for itself. The first tentative project, in advance of the first meetings, could be a request by bishop or priest that a group of lawyers, teachers, businessmen, and other laymen draw up a charter for the synod, suggesting which decision-making roles would truly make those particular laymen partly responsible for the Church in their locality. Bishop and pastor, naturally, will want to safeguard the freedom of the preacher of the Gospel. Also, both laymen and clerics will want a system of checks-and-balances, which will help to remedy the weaknesses of individuals. Thus the bishop or pastor should have some means of correcting failures of lay members to meet their responsibility; and the laity in certain matters will wish to have means of redressing wrongs done by a pastor or bishop.

Laymen do not seek power, only responsibility. Indeed, the widely remarked apathy of most laymen is, it seems, a fruit of having placed no responsibility in their hands. For many, the Church is mainly a clerical affair; "the Church" in most lay conversations refers to "they." They only way to change "they" to "we" is to distribute responsibilities. Instead of trying to decide these things abstractly, why not ask several competent men in a given parish, or a given diocese, to suggest ways in which they would be prepared to assume some of the responsibilities of the Church in their locality? Let them prepare the first report. That in itself will be a responsibility. Pastor or bishop can then study the report. A compromise can be worked out. And, in good American fashion, trial-and-error will lead to modifications. Each diocese, each parish, is different; even each group of men is different. Lay responsibility should grow organically, respecting such differences.

Let me close by suggesting that the most valuable men to draw into a diocesan or parish synod are probably not those who are already heads of parish organizations; they are possibly too used to an older system. The new blood to seek is among those lawyers, doctors, businessmen who heretofore have not been seen too often around the Church. They will be surprised by the invitation, and perhaps intrigued.

NOTES

1. Cf. Bernard J. F. Lonergan, S.J., *Insight: A Study of Human Understanding* (London and New York: 1957, 2nd ed. 1958).

9

Adult Obedience

Put ten Protestants and ten Catholics together in a room. Assign them any theological topic for consideration—the authorship of Matthew, natural law, the Eucharist. Return in twenty minutes: they will be discussing the meaning of authority in the church.

In a brace of short essays in various journals (one of them, because of administrative "prudence" has, though paid for, still not been published), I examine the issue from various vantage points, but always in an ecumenical context. Between Catholics and Protestants there are terminological problems, problems of traditional polemics, emotional problems, problems of point of view—and there remain theological differences. But place them exactly: that is the challenge. We do not wish to go round and round the mulberry bush forever; we wish to get things settled, one by one, as we approach a pluralistic, free unity.

Not surprisingly, a key problem running through these essays is the current argument about birth control. Here two traditional Catholic weaknesses coalesce: a negative Augustinian attitude toward sexual intercourse ("if you have the fun you pay the price"); and too great a reliance upon higher authority in matters which can be settled adequately on a lower institutional level. In the immediately following essays, the second weak point will be addressed; in Part Four there will be occasion to address the first.

I. *Think Concretely*

ECUMENICAL discussions about authority usually try to cover all the ground, without sufficient care to touch it. Authority in the church cannot be understood abstractly. There is not an abstract "authority," there are concrete authorities. Authority must be understood sociologically, through a comparison of alternative concrete structures and functions. Every historic institution is a solution to the problems of making decisions regarding recurring, contingent situations. Methodists as well as Catholics must solve these problems.

Secondly, especially among Roman Catholics, authority needs to be demythologized. The sole fundamental authority in the Church is the Holy Spirit. All persons in all roles and all offices are subject to the Spirit. If roles, offices, and persons are accepted uncritically, idolatry is likely to result; Christians will relax their efforts to discern the Spirit and will attribute to roles, offices, and persons a wholesale divinity in which they cannot share.

Much Protestant theological discourse is also systematically misleading upon the question of authority, however. Most Protestants favor theories of freedom, dissent, and a finally unstructured "justification by faith" which leaps over the problems of concrete power and institutional decision-making. Correspondingly, many Protestant theories do not deal adequately with the procedures, pressures, and compromises which characterize the life of their own institutions. (Nowadays many Protestant writers are realists regarding civil institutions, but disillusioned idealists regarding the church). American Baptists favor liberty and deplore authoritarianism, but whether a Baptist convention is any more, or less, free and open than the Second Vatican Council is a fact to be discerned, not by reading apologetics books, but by observing events.

Theology, at its best, imitates the Incarnation. It does not deal with abstract possibilities, or even abstract imperatives, but with actual history. Correspondingly, a theology of authority needs to employ accurate historical, sociological, and political analyses of the concrete structures and methods of authority in the various ages and cultures of Christian history. How many kinds of authority are there? Under what precise circumstances were various roles differentiated? What

similarities to, and dissimilarities from, the evolution of civil structures, methods, and roles may be detected? We badly need an ecumenical history of authority in the Christian church.

Such a history would have the effect of freeing us both from
immobilism and from primitivism. There can be, in the twentieth
century, no real possibility of merely returning to the simpler forms
of authority in the primitive church. The anonymity of great numbers
and distances, the interaction of cultures, and needs that are international in scope, present organic claims that cannot be neglected. Attempts must be made to re-create the small, informal communities of
the primitive church; but we must also meet needs that are technical
and worldwide. Secondly, if our structures and methods of authority
need to be more sophisticated, they cannot, *a fortiori,* be immobile.
The structures and methods by which decisions in the churches are
made are inevitably influenced by the structures and methods of
secular society. There is no reason why the structures and methods
of the churches, since they must in any case be partly secular in style,
should not be learned from the secular achievements of the twentieth
century rather than from the secular achievements of the sixteenth or
the nineteenth century.

The papacy, above all, needs to be demythologized. How far might
Protestants go in recognizing in the church the ministry of a servant
pope, whose task was conceived in different sociological terms than
at present? What are the minimum concrete conditions that they would
place upon such a ministry? For surely it is useful, if also dangerous,
to have within the Church one whose services are twofold: first, to be
the focal point of unity; and, secondly, to speak in a single, clear
voice, when need arises, the conscience of the community.

Can steps be taken to overcome the dangers inherent in the confid-
ing of important services to a single man, in whom original sin is also
at work? (Catholics neglect in their theories the ravages that original
sin wreaks in authority—the crotchetiness of character, the laziness,
the indifference, the ignorance, the pride, the emotional disturbance,
the physical illness that are common. Catholics are as naive regarding the vices of authority, as Protestants regarding its inevitable presence.) Can a system of checks and balances be worked out, a "bill of
rights" set forth for the institutional Church? No doubt the ministry
of the papacy is, in certain circumstances, highly useful. Are there
ways in which the Church might be protected against the weaknesses

to which Peter is, as a man, often prone? Must the Church be more presumptuous here than elsewhere in expecting the regular miraculous interventions of the Holy Spirit? The pope must be free to perform his ministries and to exercise his charisms; but the Church must also be safeguarded against his human weaknesses.

Suppose, for example, that the magisterial deliberations of the pope were open, and subject to the scrutiny and public criticism of the faithful. Suppose that all major decisions intended for the whole Church were, when the world situation allowed, submitted to public consultation, argument, and deepening, at the very least among the college of bishops, and perhaps indirectly among the educated public at large. Suppose that the pope did not see himself as a father, but as a brother. Suppose that the title "vicar of Peter"—for so many centuries the pope's title—were to be restored, and the title "vicar of Christ" applied more properly, to the whole Church; since the whole Church is "a sign lifted up before the peoples," and since the whole Church, not the pope, is Christ's body. Suppose that the balance of evangelical witness between the pope and the ordinary magisterium of the bishops, so badly disturbed by the advent of mass communications which focus on the pope, could be corrected. Suppose that infallibility is seen as a gift to the whole Church, in which the pope merely shares; and that infallibility is conceived, not as a property of propositions, but as a characteristic of God's never-failing mercy toward his people in history. Suppose that the pope did not feel called upon to decide questions of conscience in the general case, but to enunciate values not to be overlooked by men who struggle to make their own decisions. Suppose that the role of the papal teaching office is to provide one more check-and-balance, one more evidence, which the theologian must account for before reaching a decision.

At which of these points is the sociology of *Romanità* violated? At which points is the gospel, or the authentic reflection of the Church upon the gospel, violated?

It is indispensable in the years ahead to think concretely about the various ministries of the Church. What concrete socio-political alternatives are open to men? Which of these most adequately, for our time, give witness to and protect the revelation of Jesus Christ? All sound growth will be organic, continuous with the past. But we ought not to be surprised by sudden, sharpen permutations, of enormous profundity and scope, which characterize the development of living things.

II. *The Ecclesiology of Birth Control*

A saying going the rounds among certain of the American Catholic clergy—"If the Church changes her teaching on birth control I will leave the Church [or the priesthood]"—reveals overtly something that has long been apparent: what is at stake among many American Catholics in the present debate about the anovulant pill and contraceptives is not moral theology but ecclesiology.

For many American Catholics the very center of their image of the Church and its authority is threatened. Even the possibility that the Church might change her recent, not solidly established but heavily emphasized teaching on this point sends shudders through those whose faith is built upon the image of an unchanging Church. To such Catholics it is more important that the Church never alter her teaching than that her teaching should bear up under ever renewed scrutiny.

I would not in any way presume to predict what will be the outcome—say, ten years from now—of the present debate going on in the bosom of the Church about birth control. But it is striking that while the faith of some Catholics will not be shaken at all if the Church changes her recent views on contraception, that of others is deeply troubled even by the possibility of such a change.

The faith of many Catholics is fundamentalist. Over the years the Irish, Bavarian, and Italian traditions in American Catholicism have done little to emphasize the importance of doctrinal development. On the contrary, they have permitted the growth, virtually unchallenged, of an abstract and unrealistic view of the Church as propounding a geometrical, unchanging system of doctrines. That view is very powerful in the spiritual and emotional life even of otherwise progressive Catholics and it is, of course, deeper still in the hearts of the conservatives. "How can the Church have been wrong in a matter of faith and morals?" the latter ask. They do not seriously inquire how long, how solidly, how totally and for what reasons the Church has been committed to a certain view. Whatever they have regularly heard, they accept. More basic still, they see the Church as primarily the articulator and defender of certain unchanging propositions and of certain unchanging do's and don'ts. And if the Church's basic task, to say nothing of the basic claim even of the doctrine of infallibility, is not as they suppose it to be, their extraordinarily firm security is extra-ordinarily shaken.

To be sure, the Church, under the Holy Spirit, teaches with infalli-bility; that is to say, the Holy Spirit is ever with her, and those who live according to her teaching will, by God's grace, ever be able to find salvation. But in accepting the infallible teaching authority of the Church one does not believe that any particular historical articulation of her doctrine is final and complete. One does not believe any one doctrine to be defensible from *every* point of view. If you change the meaning of the basic terms or if you look at them in a different per-spective, the doctrine no longer maintains its guarantee of infallibility; one must understand its terms correctly, with historical rigor. Human language is elusive, is itself subject to the changes of history, and human words, even in a dead language, are less susceptible of being fixed in one meaning than rationalists of the nineteenth century imag-ined. So far as verbal security goes, the grace of infallibility is virtually useless; what saves those who are not experts in the history of doctrine is the love and mercy of Jesus Christ, ever present in the Church.

Thus statements of the teaching authority of the Church are not "frozen footprints." They are a Yes or a No—suitably qualified by their theological context—to certain historical questions. They are stages in an ongoing dialectic, which does not unfold like geometry; the understanding of faith grows as a man grows, by growth in in-sight, wisdom, and grace. Later statements of the Church's teaching can so modify earlier ones as seemingly to reverse them. For theology is not like geometry. The logic of a developing understanding—*fides quaerens intellectum*—is not the logic of premises and conclusions. It is precisely the premises of the argument which are subject to more thorough understanding, as history reveals the partial views and un-refined assumptions in earlier statements. The development of the Church's teaching proceeds not primarily by the drawing out of further implications from fixed premises but by a keener penetration of prem-ises and by the uncovering of weaknesses and limitations in earlier generalizations. One must penetrate as well as extend the statements of one's faith. It is this penetration and revision of premises that is at stake in the matter of birth control, as Cardinal Léger told the Vatican Council.

Another striking factor in the present debate among Catholics is that the conservative argument against contraceptives is very like the conservative argument against religious liberty. In both cases the conservatives pride themselves upon their *logic;* they accuse those who disagree with them of being carried away by "heat rather than light." In both cases those who disagree with the conservatives see quite clearly the point of the conservative logic, but they consider the premises of the conservative argument oversimplified, hence mistaken.

As John Courtney Murray, S.J., has put it, those opposed to religious liberty simply cannot find their way around the logic of the premise "error has no rights." Similarly, those opposed to the anovulant pills and contraceptives simply cannot find their way around the logic of "nature intends intercourse for procreation; and interference with the intentions of nature is evil." As Protestants have long since been aware, neither of these premises is free of difficulties: both oversimplify, and any conclusions drawn from them, however logically, are irrelevant to the realities of sexuality in marriage.

Almost every couple desires to have children, and many desire many children. Still, marriage is not a romantic game and, as Aquinas makes perfectly clear, men share in the natural law insofar as they are provident for themselves and theirs. It is not enough, therefore, to ask married people to seek "romance, adventure and risk"—as one American bishop, afraid of a technical, dehumanized "contraceptive mentality," is wont to do. There is already plenty of romance, adventure and risk in marriage. Husband and wife must be provident; even those who desire twelve children may wish to use contraceptives, not because they are technocrats but because they are responsible human beings.

For the good of human bodies, surgeons will sometimes slice through human skin which "nature intends" to be whole. For the good of their marriages, couples will sometimes use artificial means to direct both the infertility and the fertility which "nature intends" (and it is crucial to see that infertility is as natural as fertility). It is hard to believe that a contraceptive is more artificial than a suture.

Finally, however, what is at stake is neither a "contraceptive" nor a "conservative" mentality but the honesty and humility of the Church. If the opposition to contraceptives by Pius XI and Pius XII was too general and too unrefined, has the Church the courage to admit it? From 1864 to 1964 papal teaching and the ordinary teaching of the bishops of the world changed significantly in the matter of religious liberty, chiefly because the political experience of the democracies introduced the need for further distinctions in a basic premise. The experience of marriage in the twentieth century seems to be crying out for similar distinctions.

Those of us who are Catholic wait with humility for a mature, conscientious judgment on the part of those whose office it is to decide the authentic teaching of the Church. We pray that they will speak with honesty, fullness and humility—and not merely in order to conserve the appearance of always having taught the same thing. It is the motive so to conserve that will be a special temptation for those whose subjective view of the Church requires her to be "objective," apart from history, and unchanging.

III. *Adult Obedience*

One thing is certain about the question of birth control: the next generation of Catholics will not face the problems of conscience faced by the present generation. For there are two aspects to the problem of the present generation, and the next generation will not be confused about either of them.

The first aspect concerns the meaning of marital sexuality. The next generation of young people will understand more consciously than their predecessors that a full sexual love is a full human love; they will not divide the "physical" from the "spiritual," nor speak of "merely sexual" love. Sexual love is a sign, a symbol. It is also a moral imperative. For it commits two married partners to a unity of life which they must try to live up to. Sexual love tells them that they are now two lives in one. To be truthful, each must then be other-centered in attitude and action. Sexual love draws them out of themselves, and makes it illegitimate for them to think of human relationships in terms either of selfishness or of unselfishness. Sexual love invites them to be other-centered, rather than self-centered; those who are worried about how unselfish they are continue to be self-centered.

Marital sexual morality is not primarily a morality of self-control, but primarily a morality of other-centeredness. It is a mistake to approach marital sexual morality from the point of view of the sexual problems of single adolescents. In marriage, the partners are primarily obliged to be concerned about each other; it is wise for them to be playful and free, delighting in each other's delight, opening their hearts to mutual love and mutual joy. Given the priority of other-centeredness, self-control takes care of itself; of course it is required, but it is required because of the presence and the needs of the other.

The morality of marital sexual love is basically the morality of truth-telling: it demands that the couple live up to the unity which their intercourse symbolizes. Marital intercourse is the teacher of all the virtues of human relationships: openness, genuineness, playfulness, dignity, joy, patience, charity, kindness. It establishes the context into which children are happily born.

Not troubled by negative attitudes regarding sexuality, nor by the distorted lenses of adolescent insecurity, the married couples of the future will approach marital intercourse with a freshness of mind not so easy to attain in more fearful generations.

The second aspect of this problem, however, concerns the problems of conscience and authority. Many in the present generation of Catholics do not practice responsible freedom; do not take the risks of freedom; do not mature beyond heteronomy to theonomy. There seem to be many Catholics who are unable to make their own responsible moral decisions. Their attitude seems to be: "Tell me what to do and I'll do it." Such an attitude does not manifest adult obedience; it manifests heteronomy. In many matters it would constitute an illicit surrender of one's adult responsibility to another. It would represent a refusal to take one's moral responsibility into one's own hands. The example of many Germans under Hitler has taught us that obeying orders does not constitute morality.

Heteronomy is an heretical system; it is an ugly and legalistic system; it is a materialistic system: for through it a man sells his freedom, his responsibility, for a few ounces of comfort. He yields his liberty, as Dostoevsky portrayed, to a Grand Inquisitor who modifies Christ's law of freedom in the name of security: "Nothing so terrifies a man as freedom."

Some Catholics even boast of the supposed advantages of a paternalistic, heteronomous system: it brings security, stability, and simple rules, and it puts to sleep the need to ask questions. How many Catholics are there, who even when they discover in their consciences what they ought to do, cannot do it unless they obtain the permission of a priest? How many are there who live under constant heteronomy?

The chief argument which has served to reinforce heteronomy in the minds of many Catholics is fallacious. That argument runs thus: "If you do not obey authority, then what will prevent you from making arbitrary, selfish, purely subjective decisions?" The issue is drawn as though between paternalism and egoism there was no alternative. But, in fact, the Church is a community of friends. In such a community, individual persons rub against one another, criticize one another, bring up questions that the other is prone to forget, extend one another's horizons, and force one another to outgrow their personal bias and to develop in objectivity and in freedom from arbitrariness. Between paternalism and egoism there is community, and it is the main role of the community to help its individual members to grow beyond their subjective prejudices and whims. Community liberates individuals from their own shells, so that they might attain to a fuller, richer humanity, a wider, more objective view of life.

The Church is a community of friends. These friends are mature, responsible each for himself, and yet concerned about one another. They each seek God, and the Holy Spirit resides in each of them. It is through living in such a community, listening to the wisdom of tradition, consulting those whose gift is to preach the Gospel, inquiring of one another, that the consciences of Catholics mature. Catholics are not called to surrender their consciences, but to develop their consciences. The advantage of being a Catholic is to have a long, living tradition and the teaching of those in specially gifted institutional offices to consult, before committing oneself to action. A Catholic has several more sources to take seriously before he can call his own judgment "objective."

But no man can merely surrender his conscience to another. It is psychologically impossible for any authority to "inform" a conscience merely by uttering a command. The human conscience is "informed" only by participating in the light, directly or indirectly, whence the command comes. An adult can act with an informed conscience only when his conscience is illuminated by the form, the intelligence, the love, which motivates the command. Mere submission is not Christian but pagan. Merely to submit is not to act from an informed conscience, but to act as an automaton, or perhaps as an unintelligent soldier.

In the matter of birth control, the faithful Catholic informs his conscience through living in the Catholic community. He raises questions, discusses, listens, argues, prays. In the end, he must do as his conscience, thus broadened, directs. He is not entitled to act merely upon whim, or according to prejudice. But neither is he entitled merely to do what friends, or pastor, or theologians, or bishop, or pope command. He must take all these voices into account. He must bring his conscience to participate in all the light which he can attain. In many cases, even if he cannot attain all the light he would like, he will heed the advice or commands of others, according to the principle that in many matters their judgment may be more reliable than his. But in some serious personal matters, he will be unable merely to follow advice or merely to accept commands. He will have to understand what he is doing, as best he can, and take responsibility for his own actions. He will be willing to face God with his decision.

Such decisions, fashioned through the interchange of mutual criticism of a genuine, open community, and made in the presence of God, *sub specie aeternitatis,* are not heteronomous but theonomous. In them, Catholic maturity reaches its fullest flower. Against the current, if necessary, accepting the risks inherent in responsible choice, morally serious, the theonomous Catholic tastes the joy of the free man. He enters the community of those whose faith has ceased to be a reflected light, and has become a flame in the center of the self. His own informed conscience is his primary source of responsibility; he chooses his own identity and destiny.

Thus, no matter what the papal decision upon the issue of birth control may be, the Catholic community will continue to reflect upon the issue in order to appropriate all the light possible: the Church seeks the whole truth, not momentary unanimity. The teaching office of the pope has a most important role to play in the formation of consciences; but there are also other important roles in the Catholic community. The mature Catholic will meditate upon the pope's decision, if one is forthcoming, attempt to understand it, and absorb its purposes into his conscience. He will try to understand what the pope means by his decision, and to appropriate the light which guided it. Then the Catholic will face the other elements in the decision, his own circumstances, other moral imperatives, and then, in the sight of God, decide to do as he must. A papal decision does not end inquiry; since its purpose is to inform consciences, it prods inquiry. A Catholic meets his Judge—the same Who put a head upon his shoulders—without the pope at his side. He will not be able to excuse his decisions by saying: "Well, the pope decided. . . ." But he will be expected to say:

"Yes, I reflected upon what the pope said and I took account of it in my actions in this way. . . ."

Thus the Catholics of the next generation will have outgrown heteronomy, and will obey their pastors as adults obey their parents: with respect, with openness and docility, but also with full personal responsibility. They will think of the Church, not as a simplified paternalistic chain of command, but as a theonomous community in which there are many gifts of the Spirit, many offices, many questions to face, many checks-and-balances. In such a community, they find liberation from the twin tyrannies of arbitrary paternalism and arbitrary selfishness.

(God speaks:)

But what kind of salvation would a salvation be that was not free?
What would you call it?
We want that salvation to be acquired by himself,
Himself, man. To be procured by himself.
To come, in a sense, from himself. Such is the secret,
Such is the mystery of man's freedom.
Such is the price we set on man's freedom. . . .
All the prostrations in the world
Are not worth the beautiful upright attitude of a free man as
    he kneels. All the submission, all the dejection in the world
Are not equal in value to the soaring up of one single invocation
From a love that is free.

—Charles Péguy

IV. *A New View of Infallibility*

In a recent article in the *Commonweal,* Robert McAfee Brown suggested that Reformation Sunday could become an ecumenical observance in which Roman Catholics might take part. Specifically, he suggested that Roman Catholics might increasingly turn to the problem of admitting the fact of sin, error, and serious change within their own communion. Catholics of the *aggiornamento* readily admit that the Church does change and always needs to be reformed. But at present even very "progressive" spokesmen, like Fr. John Courtney Murray, S.J., are inclined to speak of changes and reforms within

Roman Catholicism as instances of mere "development," not as instances of the Church seriously changing its mind.

One striking feature of Catholic theological discourse, in fact, is the haste with which Catholic theologians attempt to show that even their original ideas and formulations are traditional: "The Church has *always* taught X, 'implicitly' or 'unconsciously.' " Protestant discourse, on the contrary, is distinguished by the haste with which Protestant theologians stress that a "new age" has arrived, or a "new beginning" is necessary, or a "unique" instant is at hand—even when their recommendation is, in fact, traditional or at least analogous to other recommendations in history. Catholics tend to stress what is traditional; Protestants to stress what is original.

But even when this difference in rhetoric is taken into account, other differences in intellectual style remain to be noted. One virtue the Roman Catholic Church has lacked almost entirely in its official outlook these last several generations is humility. That is why the merest suggestion by Pope Paul VI at the second session of the Vatican Council that Catholics repented their own complicity in the division of Christianity was so touching, despite the conditional tense in which it was phrased: *"If* Catholics have been guilty . . ." Humility is a new style, cautiously accepted.

How far can Roman Catholic humility go? Can the Church admit that she has erred, whether in doctrine or in practice? Christ promised that the church would endure through all time, that the gates of hell would not prevail against her, and that those who trust in the mercies God shows men through her will not be disappointed. In the mood of the age of rationalism, whose basic quest was a quest for certainty, post-Tridentine theology has construed these promises as a promise of "inerrancy." Those whose main motive for belief in Roman Catholicism is security—freedom from serious intellectual error—are shaken by the thought that some formulation of doctrine, or some disciplinary practice, could in fact have been mistaken. For some Catholics seem to believe that the one advantage to being Roman Catholic is certitude about statements and practices.

This quest for certainty is a peculiar historical development. Not by accident, it arose at a time when philosophers attempted to "reconstruct" human knowledge in order to establish philosophy upon an absolutely certain basis. In philosophy, this pursuit has proved to be chimerical. Philosophers now seek, not certainty, but understanding.

It is more important to shed as much light as possible upon the whole complex panorama of human life and destiny, however tentatively and modestly, than to narrow down one's focus to find some point which promises utter certainty. The more ardently certitude is sought, the narrower one's focus must become—and, even then, proposed absolutes have the habit of evaporating under a thousand qualifications. When applied to actual life, they are uncertain; when certain, they are irrelevant.

If certitude is chimerical in philosophy, why should it be sought in theology? What is the supposed advantage of certitude? It seems enough to be human, to seek to understand correctly, and to be free. A mind open to facts, wherever they may lead, is a healthier and freer mind than the mind which is afraid to lose its certitudes. Christ came to make us free, not to make us certain.

A church prepared to follow its best present insights, wherever they may lead, seems at least as admirable as one which clings to its past formulae in an effort to be "consistent." A man who admits a mistake is consistent in his fidelity to truth, rather than to his previous utterances; he is no less admirable for that.

But if it is difficult to see why propositional inerrancy is so highly prized, it is also difficult to see what it *means*. Is inerrancy a characteristic of propositions, or of sentences? Does it attach to the *intention* of a formula, or to the *words* of the formula? If it attaches to the latter, then difficulties arise when in common speech the words change their basic meaning. Only historians can then tell us what the original words intended. But if inerrancy attaches to the intention rather than the words, then (a) inerrancy must be exercised primarily by exegetes; (b) inerrancy is threatened by all the possible interpretations and ambiguities which inhere in verbal discourse; and (c) how does any listener know that he understands without error the exegesis of the inerrant exegete? It is obviously not enough merely to repeat the words of the exegete, like an incantation. Verbal discourse is a most unlikely matrix for inerrancy.

It may be that inerrancy and infallibility have been unwisely conceived of as properties of propositions, under the influence of a recent, rationalistic philosophy of language. It does not seem that any form of words can be the subject of such properties. For the meanings and uses of words change with human habits of speech; the intentions expressed through words are subject to human understanding and such understanding is reached only through subjective inquiry and attainment. Language, in short, is not timeless, unambiguous, or in the required way "objective"; it cannot be frozen—like frozen footprints. For the same words keep being used in new ways, new words are invented for old ideas, and new questions are put to former, looser interpretations.

The Roman Catholic Church will not be less credible when she admits that past formulations are often, in present contexts, unintelligible and if taken literally fraught with error; nor even that past formulations were, though made in good faith, erroneous. One does not become a Catholic in order to use words inerrantly, but in order to find God's gracious mercy through fidelity to understanding, wherever inquiry may lead.

Human inquiry, however, takes place in the context of a community; no one person can "go it alone." It is not necessary to put one's total confidence in one's own uncriticized personal judgment; one is required to criticize one's own judgment by the faith of the entire community. "Individual judgment" is no more reliable a guide than "infallible propositions" are. In harking to the teaching of popes and councils, the Catholic has one more institutionalized source of criticism of his own views than the Protestant. But no less than the Protestant, the Catholic must take the risk of discerning what is the intention of Christian faith, even when its expression has been officially attempted.

Ten years ago, who was more correct in the articulation of authentic Catholic faith in the matter of religious liberty—curia and bishops who denied it, or John Courtney Murray who affirmed it? Both could not have been correct. The individual Catholic had to discern which was mistaken, which faithful to the then unresolved intention of the faith.

Inerrancy is primarily a property of the Church, not of propositions; it guarantees the possibility of salvation, not escape from the idiosyncrasies of human language and the contingencies of human understanding. The word which "shall never pass away" was not a set of Aramaic propositions, which most of us have never heard nor read, but "spirit and life," into which all of us have been baptized as one community. The Church can err in language and in understanding; but God is faithful to his promises and lives within her even so.

Nevertheless, if inerrancy is primarily an attribute of the Church, where will it be manifested in her life? It will be manifested partly in the courage which the Church shows in meeting difficult intellectual and linguistic questions put to her by the development of human understanding in history. At times, even though speaking is fraught with hermeneutical risks, the Church must speak. Thus, *secondarily,* inerrancy attaches to propositions of certain limited kinds voiced ordinarily by the solemn testimony of councils and, extraordinarily, by the pope, speaking for the entire Church. But such propositions (a) do not manifest the *content* of the faith of all (only the entire body of revelation does that); rather they enunciate *criteria* for understanding the common faith correctly in *technical theological discourse* and *within a given historical context.* Thus the declarations of Chalcedon bear witness to specific, technical criteria for a correct understanding of the common faith in the context of certain hotly contested theological disputes of their time. Such declarations must be reinterpreted in order to be understood correctly in other contexts.

And such propositions (b) do not exhaust the modes of understanding of the content of the common faith available within the bosom of the Church; for humble and simple persons, the preachers of the kerygma, the liturgical prayer of the Church, and the action of Christians in the world will express this same common faith in other ways than through the use of the technical language of councils and popes.

Again, among the propositions enunciated by councils and popes, various kinds are to be distinguished: the teaching of Chalcedon on Christ, of Trent on virginity and celibacy, of the Syllabus of Errors on religious liberty, of Pius XI on birth control, and of Pius XII on the Assumption, are each of a different kind. Each must be understood in its context. Each is subject to anachronistic and foolish uses. Each operates in a different context and with a different purpose, scope, and cogency. To interpret councils and popes is at least as difficult a task as to interpret Holy Scripture. The ways in which error can surround "inerrancy" are so many that the ordinary meaning of the word "inerrancy" buckles, and it becomes obvious that it is being used in an odd, technical, and often misleading way.

The Catholic, in short, must show good sense, and follow the guidance of the Church somewhat in the way a mature young man follows the guidance of a father: taking what the Church says in context, mulling it over, sifting it, and employing all that he knows of history in trying to decide what it is that constitutes the fidelity of the community of believers. Solemnly enunciated propositions are risks that an historically articulate community must take; the community should not try to duck the task of saying "Yea" and "Nay" when necessary. Yet such propositions are only a part of a much larger ongoing communal life, and they may easily be outgrown or even falsified by changes of the context in which they once made sense. In the ordinary English meaning of the word, there are dozens of ways in which the Church may err in matters of doctrine. Only in an unusual sense of the word is the community of the faithful preserved by the Holy Spirit from "error." That sense requires much fuller and more ecumenical investigation than has yet been given it.

One last word. The First Vatican Council said that the pope shares in that infallibility which the Church possesses. Who else in the Church shares in it? The bishops? The whole covenanted community? We need a rapid "development of doctrine" on the whole question of "development of doctrine," of which the function of the papacy and councils is but one part.

IO

The Substance of Transubstantiation

There is a marked tendency among progressive thinkers to scorn the past as if it were simply in error. But if one accepts the relativity of all human standpoints, then one ought also to recognize the relativity of the contemporary standpoint. Such recognition is liberating; it allows one to enter into the standpoint of a past age with sympathy, and perhaps to learn from it.

When modern people employ the word "substance," they mean something that can be touched or at least weighed, something that occupies space, "a thing," "stuff" susceptible of chemical analysis. Thus anyone who shares the modern notion of substance and who also claims to believe in transubstantiation in the Eucharist, is badly mistaken scientifically and involved in a gross error theologically. A chemical analysis of the substance of bread and wine after the consecration of the Mass reveals that the substance is still bread and wine; there has been no substantial change. The modern word "substance" is, therefore, misleading as a description of the Catholic faith.

It is instructive to notice, however, that for Aristotle and for Aquinas (I do not vouch for any of the followers of either) substance is understood in a very different sense than is common at present. In making his list of Categories, Aristotle made an empirical survey of major interrogative words in Greek and produced a list of the ten major types of questions that the Greeks might have about their experience. Each of the categories, *then, is an heuristic category; each specifies a type of question natural to the Greek language. Of these ten questions the most fundamental one, it appeared to Aristotle, is a question seeking a unity, identity, whole, in the flux of a range of experience: the question, "What-IS-it?" Whatever the most proper answer to this question, it was denoted "substance." Substance, then, is the most adequate answer obtainable to the question "What-IS-it?"*

Applied to the Eucharist in a period of intellectual vigor and questioning, the heuristic category of substance was helpful to Aquinas. If you ask the question "What-IS-it?" of the bread and wine before the consecration, the proper answer is "bread and wine." If you ask the same question after the consecration, the proper answer (for faith) is "the body and blood of Jesus Christ." In a modern sense, no change has occurred in the substance; chemical analysis reveals no differences before or after. But, for faith, the proper answer to the question "What-IS-it?" has changed. In the Aristotelian sense, the substance has changed when the proper answer to that question has changed.

This medieval theory of transubstantiation does not explain how the proper answer to the question shifts from "bread and wine" to "the body and blood of Jesus." It only states that it does. The mystery remains intact. Jesus said, "This is my body; this is my blood." Who knows how? His word suffices. A chemical analysis of the bread and wine does not discover flesh and blood; the change is not a chemical change. From a scientific point of view, those who partake are not partaking of molecules of flesh and blood; cannibalism is not being indulged. Thus, in a scientific age, the word "transubstantiation" is misleading and, if accepted uncritically, is theologically false.

From a contemporary standpoint, the question "What-IS-it?" regarding the Eucharist is not of first importance to love of God or love of neighbor. We have seen Nazis and segregationists employ holy things for evil causes. From a contemporary standpoint, it is much more important to raise the question: "What are we committing ourselves to by this action? What does this celebration mean to the way we live? What difference does it make?" From a contemporary standpoint, it is important to re-create the sense of community, which in a simpler, medieval community Christians took for granted. Meanwhile, contemporary Christians take for granted the actual presence of Jesus, which seemed so marvelous to medieval Christians. Whereas in the bitter, harsh life of the Middle Ages (when the average mortality age was far below our own, and when a high percentage of children died in childbirth or before the age of one), it seemed a miracle that God could take up a special presence under the sign of bread and wine; in our impersonal era the miracle is that God can effect community and reconciliation through the action of the Eucharistic meal. In "this vale of tears," medieval people were deeply touched and much assured by God's wondrous presence in humble bread and wine. In huge urban centers, modern people are deeply touched by the experience of community deriving from God's wondrous ability to unit diverse and separate men through the meal eaten in memory of Jesus. For both medievals and moderns, Jesus is really present in the Eucharist. But the formality under which they become aware of him is different. The modern chemical understanding of substance, together with the modern lack of spontaneous, cultural community, contrast with the medieval heuristic notion of substance and medieval cultural solidarity.

The Eucharist meets the symbolic needs of both ages; it expresses perfectly the brotherhood of men, their gratitude, their historical memory, their courage and resolution regarding the responsibilities of the present and the future. The brotherhood of the Eucharist is a symbol of what the whole world must become. Each man retains his own unique identity, and yet participates in the love and the sorrows of every other. As often as the Eucharist is celebrated, a revolutionary secular act is performed: a forecast of how the world must change is acted out.

Because the Eucharist is so central to revolutionary religion, I have included the following essay on the meaning of "substance" in Aristotle. Once it is widely grasped that Aristotle employed substance as an heuristic or question-asking category, then the historical meaning of "transubstantiation" can be stripped of its modern connotations. When the proper answer to the question "What-IS-it?" shifts from "bread and wine" to "body and blood of Jesus," it is faith in the word of Jesus that motivates the shift. No "hocus pocus" has taken place. The same experiences of taste, touch, smell, sight, and hearing are now—because of the word of Jesus— interpreted in a different way. Since the word of Jesus is reliable, the new interpretation, despite appearances, is the true one. Still, the important

modern question arises: What difference does it make? What experience-
able difference may we expect from participation in this meal?

Consequently, contemporary Christians might state the Christian faith
more accurately from their own standpoint if they spoke of "real com-
munity" rather than of "real presence." Instead of "transubstantiation,"
they might understand the prefix "trans-" to mean "passing beyond" and
use the more accurate phrase, the "transalienation" of the Eucharist. For
a passage from isolation and alienation to a community of autonomous,
responsible persons is really effected, at least as a pledge, by participation
in the Eucharist. Yet in employing more accurate statements of their own
standpoint, contemporary Christians ought not to deny the accuracy of
the phrases "real presence" and "transubstantiation" for those who have
assumed an earlier standpoint.

The following article confines itself simply to the prior task of working
out the meaning of "substance" in Aristotle; it appeared in Philosophy
and Phenomenological Research *in 1963.*

A Key to Aristotle's "Substance"

A SAMPLING of the literature on the subject [1] shows that if Aristotle
assembled the materials for a critical doctrine of substance, he did not
exploit them with clarity. It seems easy to show that Aristotle wavered
on several points; [2] if so, it seems then that Aristotle himself was not
master of his material. I should like to sort out in this paper the
material Aristotle has brought together, to see if there lies within it
the makings of a consistent plausible doctrine. My concern will be
especially with Books Z, H, θ, and Λ of the *Metaphysics,* but with
reference elsewhere and especially to the *Categories.* The primary
question to which I address myself, for it seems to be the crucial one,
is how Aristotle could identify essence with substance; for isn't essence universal? And must not substance be a "this"? If we could
grasp the relationship between essence and universal, and between
essence and individual, we would seem to have in our hands the
crux of the problem of knowing. We could look both ways—toward
knowing the universals of science and toward knowing concrete particulars. Substance is this crux.

I

One way to begin a study of Aristotelian substance is to be quite clear in cutting oneself free from post-Cartesian "substance." Most objections to Aristotelian substance have their roots in a failure here. Aristotle's substance is not an "underlying somewhat," a "something-I-know-not-what," a queer entity inferred "behind" or "beneath" the appearances or characteristics, a residue discovered by the process of "stripping off" as Descartes discovered the "substance" of wax,[3] or a postulated and unseen thing-in-itself behind the veil of phenomena. Aristotle's doctrine is open to misinterpretation in these directions: the language, imagery, and method he uses do suggest "underlying," "unseen," "beyond the appearances," "inferred from the necessities of prediction," and "stripping off." The familiar modern critiques of Aristotle's notion thus seem to have a *prima facie* relevance. But there is a complexity and fullness to Aristotle's notion that modern critiques do not have tools to reach. The gap between Aristotle and the moderns is wider than we are sometimes accustomed to think, and a careful thinker experiences a certain helplessness in trying to move from Aristotle to the present or vice versa.[4]

Aristotle sets certain demands for substance. (In line with the way I have posed the problem, I take "substance simpliciter" and "the substance of so-and-so" as the two sides of the one same sense of "substance." Their union in one sense makes "substance" the crux it is.) For Aristotle, (1) substance must not be present in a subject.[5] (2) It must not be predicable of a subject.[6] (3) It must be a "this." [7] (4) It must be one in number.[8] (5) It must be one by a process of nature.[9] (6) It may be material or immaterial.[10] (7) It must be a living thing, indeed a whole living thing, and not a part.[11] (8) It is primarily essence or form.[12] (9) It has many senses, of which one is primary.[13] (10) It is partly discoverable through linguistic considerations [14] and categorical or logical considerations.[15] (11) It is mainly discoverable through knowledge of reality or "the facts." [16] (12) It is what is most knowable.[17] (13) It is a cause.[17a]

What presuppositions, method, or orientation toward knowledge can be discovered in these varied demands? In the first place, it is clear that the extension of "substance" is not the extension of "body."

Substance is *not* what is discoverable by sense knowledge; it is not the "already out there now real." [18] For substance can be immaterial. Also, matter is of itself unknowable [19] and sensible things are in themselves knowable in a lesser degree than immaterial things.[20] This is surely strange to an empiricist of the British type; it makes different the sense in which Aristotle might be called an empiricist. *His* substance can't be reduced to sense experience; yet: *"Nihil in intellectu nisi primo in sensu."* Demands (3), (5), (6), (7), and (11) make it impossible to take Aristotle's substance as arrived at apart from sense experience. Demands (2) and (10), and perhaps (8) after a fashion, make it tempting to take substance as a mere requisite of language or of logic; Pepper, for example, dismisses substance as flowing from "the fallacy of attribution," and Russell and others think that the modern shift to relative terms has neutralized misleading subject-predicate language.[21] Quine and White object specifically to demand (9) in all its many forms.[22] And so, what on earth can Aristotle be driving at?

Clearly, from demands (12), (11), and (10), to name no others, Aristotle's notion of substance is bound up with his notion of knowledge. For Aristotle, the essence is what we know when we know things.[23] Because essence is in things, things are knowable; because essence is universal, science is possible.[24] We are thus at the heart of the problem we set ourselves in this paper: how is essence related to individuals, and how to universals? Apparently, essence stands at the crossroads: it is what constitutes the "this" or individual, and makes it most real; it is also what makes the individual knowable and capable of science.

But how do we go about discovering substance? How would we verify its presence? What should we look for—what difference does it make? This is where Aristotle fails us. He has not made clear to us his "critical philosophy," the critical explication and justification of his method of discovery and verification. His many gestures in this direction [25] are but inchoate and vague to modern scrutiny; his *ex professo* treatments are at the crucial points [26] too brief and now outdated. Re-creating Aristotle's view on the present question is like piecing together a jigsaw puzzle of which not only are many pieces missing but also the original drawing (which would be guiding reconstruction) was never painted on.

In this situation, prompted by the work of Lonergan,[27] I should like to propose what the original drawing might have been had Aristotle fully completed it. Then, to test the proposal, we may try to put the pieces we now have into place; if these cohere, and if blank spaces occur at plausible openings for the pieces we do not have, the proposal may have been of service. In the first place, then, suppose that Aristotle so far saw the problem of substance as a problem of knowledge, that he came upon the notion of substance because of the demands of the process of discovery. Suppose that he saw the process of discovery (heuristics) as having these steps: gathering information or having experiences,[28] inquiry,[29] and judgment of affirmation or denial.[30] Suppose that the results of these activities are, respectively: data, insights, and truth or falsity (i.e., reality or not).[31] Next, suppose that for Aristotle the knowing which comes at the term of this process is, in Ryle's words, an "achievement verb." [32] Suppose that *instrumental* to this heuristic process and to its terminal achievement there is a linguistic process, extraordinarily helpful but secondary.[33] Suppose that the problem to which Aristotle was addressing himself was to answer Plato's dilemma (echoed by Kant, in a way): viz., how we can have science about the world of our experience and, if we cannot, how the world of our experience can be real.[34] The trick is to avoid appeal to "forms laid up in heaven," to universals, to a queer world duplicating somehow the one of our experience. Finally, suppose that Aristotle solved this dilemma by a peculiar kind of knowing, which subsequent philosophers have almost totally over-looked: a knowing characterized (1) by the fact that it never occurs except in conjunction with an image of the concrete and particular, and yet (2) by the fact that it is an act of intelligence, seeing the point, grasping the correlation or unity, etc. Suppose that this particular kind of knowing was what was constantly and consistently operating in his discussions of substance; but that because he himself did not pay sufficient attention to the peculiarity of this knowing he could not exploit it in clarifying his starting point, criteria, and method of studying substance.[35] In the fourth (and in my theory the most important) of Aristotle's senses of being, to be is to be truly affirmed in judgment.[36] It is obvious then that to be is not to appear; i.e., that to be is not limited to sense-data, and that even sensible things are said to be not inasmuch as they confront the senses but inasmuch as they can be truthfully affirmed in judgment.[37] The real is not "the already out there now"; the real is what is affirmed at the end of an intelligent process moving from data through insight to affirmation. If enough evidence can be accumulated so that immaterial things can be affirmed as existing, there are immaterial substances,[38] whether seen, touched, heard or not. The empiricism of Aristotle is *not* founded on the basis of Humean ideas, but on the basis of data plus insight plus affirmation; so that while for Aristotle all knowing *begins* in the senses he does not *reduce* knowledge to sense-experience. Thus his empiricism tries to tackle both material and immaterial things, making them *both* subject to data, inquiry, affirmation. Again, although Aristotle sees that it is pedagogically easier to begin discussing substance by discussing sensible substances,[39] he obviously thinks sensible substances are inferior to immaterial substances in knowability. Of course: for besides the insights they yield to science and the affirmation of their existence to which they give rise, sensible substances are burdened with a residue of particular time, particular place, and undetermined changeability (i.e., potency, matter) that is useless to science;[40] moreover, sensible substances hold the attention of the senses and offer "cash value" for pragmatic living; they are more congenial *to us,* but they are not what is most knowable.[41] The real is not what we sense but what we affirm; the real is not then what is congenial to us but what can be affirmed, however untouchable or unseeable. In speaking about substance, Aristotle is not speaking about "body" which confronts our senses, but about what can be reached at the term of an intelligent process beginning in sense-observation, proceeding through intelligent inquiry, and terminating in critical affirmation or denial.

This is why Aristotle hits upon essence as that which is primarily substance.[42] Essence is what is known by intelligent inquiry asking 'what-IS-it?'[43] Essence is at one and the same time that which makes an individual what it is and that which makes an individual knowable. As to be is to be truly affirmed in judgment, so what-IS-it is what-is-affirmable in judgment. Essence mediates between being and knowing, and guarantees that what is known does not differ from what is.[44] Aristotle is talking about knowing, not about imagining; unlike the decadent Aristotelians, then,[45] we must not imagine essence as a mysterious duplicate of sense knowledge, only not sensed, i.e., we must not imagine essence as some shining inner core in things, to be reached by spiritual insight or a penetrating look. We must not imagine a Platonic "meaning," "grasped by understanding." Essence is rather what modern science, for example, knows about what a thing is.[46] If science does not know the whole "what," if science is still in the state of development concerning the precise "what-IS-it" of uranium, or the human appendix, or life, and does not yet know; nevertheless, the what-IS-it is the goal which science pursues. The what-IS-it guarantees that discoveries of a later age can be an advance, because the more accurate observations and more critical explanations are related to earlier stages.[47] The exigencies of scientific discovery and progress are the primary reasons for affirming substance. The exigencies of our language (as in predication) only secondarily and ambiguously are such reasons. Substance is implicit in every act of judgment, because every judgment includes hypotheses about what-IS-it. Substance is implicit as a goal, a working aim; Aristotle names it as if it were an entity "within" the thing or "underlying" it, whereas it *is* the thing, as wholly known or known in hope. Substance (more or less perfectly known) is affirmed in every judgment; hence substance is.

As primarily the what-IS-it, substance is not known by confrontation, as a brick wall is known by the eye or hand. Neither is it known only by the insight that grasps laws, relations, universals; [48] for substance is also individual. Substance is known in two ways. In the general case, substance is known indirectly, by making explicit what is taken for granted in every judgment and in the progress of science. Something is taken for granted in the knowing subject, and something in the known object: that something unites knower and known. On the side of the subject, it is the same identical knower who affirms, who has insight, who has considered the data; what he affirms must be what he has understood from what he has experienced: the what-IS-it is the unity uniting the knowing of the knower. On the side of the object, it is the what-IS-it that is latent in the data, that is discovered by inquiry, that is affirmed of the data in judgment; the what-IS-it is the unity uniting the elements of the known. Furthermore, in both knower and known, it is the same identical what-IS-it that perdures through ever more thorough collections of data and more penetrating inquiry. Without a what-IS-it, at least implicit, knowing cannot occur.

In the special case of sensible substances, substance is known in a second way. Whereas in the first case substance is not "seen" or intuited or inferred, but grasped indirectly, made explicit, and affirmed; in the second case substance is grasped by the peculiar kind of intellectual knowing Aristotle speaks of as always conjoined with a concrete image.[49] It is insight into particulars; it is a grasp of the universal *in* the particular. It is an insight into the "necessary" [50] unity or relationship in the data. It is *like* seeing the point of a joke, or the necessity by which a radius pivoting fully on a point must describe a circle; but here it is seeing the what-IS-it within the presented data: as seeing the constitution of oxygen and hydrogen that makes this a specimen of water. The what-IS-it achieved within the presented data of a sensible substance is at one and the same time a "this" and the "necessary, universal formula." ("*This* is H_2O.") Here is the core of Aristotle's philosophy. The universal has no extension beyond its particulars. Both universal and particular are known through the same act. (The particular is not *known* through *sense* knowledge, only sensed thereby.) Both *can* be known only through this one same act. There is not a separate act of knowing universals, and another for knowing the singular. Men know the "this" by reflection on the concrete image in which the insight occurs. Men discover the formula by observing the correlations in the "this" of the concrete image.[51]

Thus Aristotle has broken through the Platonic dualism. He has solved the dilemma. He has kept science, as well as the reality of singulars. His achievement rests on the peculiar kind of knowing that is always conjoined with a concrete image; and, with Lonergan, I am inclined to call 431a 14-16 and 432a 5-8 of *De Anima,* in which Aristotle barely notes this achievement, the most important passages in the Aristotelian corpus. But if it is true as Whitehead says that "All of western philosophy is but a footnote to Plato," we shall have to exert ourselves to return and see the revolution in Aristotle that we missed. On this return, we shall find it easier, perhaps, to see the relation between particular and universal in an example from geometry. To understand the universal necessity with which the figure of a circle results from the pivoting of a radius on a point, it suffices to fix a radius and a point and pivot the radius. Independent of the concrete example, the circle is understood *through* the concrete example; only so.[52] We cannot understand except *through* a concrete example, but *what* is understood is a necessity, an intelligible, nonsensible content. The issue here between Aristotle and Hume is as crucial as that between Aristotle and Plato; one cannot understand Aristotle without seeing how he affirms knowing as empirically controlled insight rather than sensory and imaginative association, and yet does not yield to Platonic "meanings" or extra entities.

II

Let us begin putting together the pieces of Aristotle's puzzle. We can enter the discussion at chapter 13 of Book Z of the *Metaphysics,* in which Aristotle is eliminating universals as candidates for the role of substance. This elimination corresponds well with the two aspects we have distinguished in insight into particulars: the aspect in which the what-IS-it is grasped as particular, and the aspect in which the what-IS-it is grasped as a unity, necessity, universal. The universal cannot be primary substance, for substance is individual.[53] Yet essence can be substance.[54] So there must be a way in which essence is not universal, but individual. Nevertheless, essence will have to be *closely related* to the universal; for substance is a cause of being, and to be is to be affirmed in judgment, so substance is likewise a cause of knowing. Aristotle's peculiar way of knowing the essence *in* the concrete meets these requirements. Now it is precisely this way that Aristotle makes a "fresh start" on his argument in chapter 17. Ross sums up the argument thus far:

Of the four claimants to the title of substance (1028b 33) Aristotle has now discussed substratum, and shown that in its most obvious sense (viz., matter) it is not substance (chapter 3). He has discussed essence from many points of view, but without reaching any very definite conclusion as to whether it is substance (chapters 4-12). He has discussed the universal (and implicitly the fourth claimant, the genus), and shown that it is not substance, and has shown further that substance cannot contain actual substances as its parts (chapters 13-16). He now makes a fresh start and essays to show that essence is substance, using as his guide the principle that substance must be causal, something that answers the question "Why?" [55]

Aristotle's approach is explicitly heuristic. Substance is what answers to the question "Why?" Substance is involved in the very structure of inquiry. Aristotle even notes that some forms of inquiry mask the basic structure; we should not ask "What is man?" but "Why are these bones, sinews, flesh, etc. a man?" [56] That is, we need the *concrete data* to begin intelligent inquiry; we seek the unity-identity-whole in which all the data are accounted for: we seek essence, form, the formal cause in the concrete data. We seek the what-IS-it, and this is substance.

In the first aspect, the what-IS-it is achieved in the particularity of sense-perceptions; it is a "this"; and yet it is not a "this" as a "body". It is not a "this" as sensible or imaginable, for then a kitten too could know substance. It is a "this" as *knowable:* the what-IS-it grasped in concrete data and able to be affirmed in true judgment; but *still as concrete.* In the second aspect, however, the what-IS-it is conceptualized apart from its concrete instantiations; it is universalized. When we gain an insight in the concrete we express it in a concept, in order to fit it into a rational conceptual system. Insight is prior; concept is secondary. The man who knows completely, master of both the first and second aspects, finds it easy to go between the abstract relations of which science speaks and concrete examples. The first aspect enables him to keep close to the world of ordinary experience; the second aspect enables him to conceptualize precisely, to relate, to systematize, to exercise logic through inference and implication.

The what-IS-it of substance is a crux. It is first known in the concrete instance, and it is then brought into conceptual system as a universal. Science and experience meet in it. The dynamic structure of man's knowing requires such a crux. For knowing begins in the wonder provoked by sense presentations,[57] proceeds by inquiry seeking "Why?",[58] and thus seeks the unities-identities-wholes *in experience.*

The unity-identity-whole is a "this," a "what-IS-it, a substance; it is, as answering "Why?", a cause. The unity-identity-whole is not *at first* universal; it is not common to many; it is not a predicate. Thus it cannot be predicated of anything else. Furthermore, the unity-identity-whole is a "this" complete in itself; thus it cannot be "present in another," for it exists "apart." [59] If a "this" were to exist in another as a part, the "this" would not be whole in itself, it would not have in itself a principle of unity or self-cause but would be merely one datum among others for some other unity.[60] Inasmuch as the "this" is a sensible substance, it is subject to destruction; observation pointing to the contrary (of whose inadequacy he was aware) led Aristotle into the blunder that the heavenly bodies might be *im*perishable sensible substances.[61] As thus contingent and also as individual, the "this" is incapable of definition.[62] It is incapable of demonstration and of science. Aristotle sees this as a difficulty, and knows that it will clear up.[63] But inasmuch as he has not made clear the method by which he shifts from this first aspect of the what-IS-it to the second, his doctrine is only vaguely satisfying.

Still, it is this shift from the first aspect to the second that accounts for the other characteristics of substance. Substance has a secondary sense, inasmuch as the what-IS-it of primary substance can be expressed as a concept, abstracted, in order to be the what-IS-it of scientific definition and demonstration, the finished product with which logic has to deal.[64] Because substance has this second aspect, that it yields the universal, abstract concepts of theories, substance assures men of the knowability of things and thus the possibility of science. Because this same substance has the first aspect, as a "this," substance assures men that their science is of things.

III

We must still try to account for demands (4), (5), and (7): substance must be one in number, one by a process of nature, a living thing whole and not as a part. Whereas for modern logicians, the problem of ontology is approached by reducing "is" to univocity (an approach which is of course essential for a logical system) and by passing judgment upon what may be pronominally introduced into the system (as a "value of a variable"); for Aristotle, who is not concerned with reducing philosophy to logic on the model of mathematics, "is" is allowed many senses, but judgment is passed upon what may stand as subject in the primary sense of substance. For we may place "fire" (as one of the four chemical elements), "hand" (detached from the body), and "white" in the subject place of a sentence; but none of them are primary substance.[65] Substance is a (first aspect) what-IS-it, an essence as a "this." "White" cannot be a "this"; as a sensible quality it can occur only in sensible space-time, i.e., instantiated (its reality is the sum of its occurrences [66]), and its occurrence can never be pointed out without pointing out at the same time a surface; so "white" has not the independence of a "this." The best sign of an independent "this" is that it is the subject of contraries; [67] i.e., if pointed to, the "this" would come to mind first, for the contraries change.

But inasmuch as primary substance is essence, formal unity, what-IS-it, its parts cannot themselves be substances.[68] The formal unity in question is the unity of a "this." There cannot be two formal unities in one "this." Formal unity *means* one what-IS-it. In living things, what-IS-it is conferred by self-movement or life.[69] There are several levels of life.[70] When the organizing principle of one level collapses, the organism falls back to the lower level: without the control of understanding, men are like other animals; impressed by skepticism about understanding and about the ability to move, men are like vegetables. When all principle of self-movement leaves an organism, only the chemical organization of matter is left; biological laws cease to operate; the what-IS-it has changed, and this change is by definition substantial. Similarly with parts of an organism. To ask the what-IS-it of the hand is to find that, as living, it is a functional part of the what-IS-it of a man and therefore without a primary what-IS-it of its own; as cut off and no longer living, the hand no longer obeys biological laws, and is chemical matter, without function, without organizing formal principle. It may be recognizable in virtue of its former unity, but that unity is gone and decomposition is steadily destroying even its vestiges. The what-IS-it of living things thus gives Aristotle a dynamic, empirically observable exemplar of the formal unity which a primary "this" exercises over its parts.[71]

Concerning artificial unities, Aristotle wavers.[72] We might ask, what difference is there between the what-IS-it of a clock and the what-IS-it of a man? The unity and what-IS-it of the clock are conferred on it by men, and the moving principle operates by mechanical laws, the laws of inorganic matter. Now the moving principle in men is not only according to mechanical, organic (chemical), biological, and psychological laws but also is self-originating.[73] Natural unities do not depend upon the intelligence and technique of men for their what-IS-it; artificial unities do. Yet since artificial unities are made in imitation of natural unities—not representationally, but in inner organization— there is a great inclination to call them at least para-substances. But as they depend upon human intelligence for their coming to be, so they depend upon it for the decision as to when they are no longer useful. Is a chair still a chair if it has lost three legs? That depends upon those who established its what-IS-it. Is a dog still a dog if it has lost three legs? That depends not on men but on whether sensitive-biological laws cease to operate. Often Aristotle does assimilate artificial substance to natural substances; his strongest statement comes as a "perhaps":

Perhaps, indeed, neither these things themselves, e.g., house or utensil nor any of the other things which are not formed by nature, are substances at

all; for one might say that the nature in natural objects is the only substance to be found in destructible things. (1043b 22f)

IV

We may conclude. Aristotle has not given critical attention, after
the modern fashion, to his doctrine of knowing. Nevertheless, that
doctrine is the starting point of his very investigation. His notion of
human knowing involves a movement from observation through inquiry to affirmation. Whereas the world of sense experience is data
for observation, reality is not observable. For reality is reached only
in affirmation, and affirmation affirms the results of inquiry—which
are intelligible, but not sensible or imaginable. Thus for Aristotle substance is not reached in the first heuristic moment, observation of
"bodies." It is reached as a result of nonsensible intelligent inquiry, and
is affirmed as inescapable. For inasmuch as there can be sensible observation of things, there can be data to provoke men to wonder and
to give them starting points that are "better known" to themselves.
But inasmuch as there can be intelligent inquiry into things, there can
be unities and correlations found in the data. And, further, inasmuch
as these unities can be only wishful thinking and these correlations
might not occur, there can be critical judgment to affirm or to deny
them according as evidence warrants. For the affirmations of science
or of common sense to occur, the notion of substance is at least implicitly present. Substance is the unities and correlations science and
common sense anticipate in data. Substance is the what-IS-it to which
science and common sense refer in the data, about which better and
better explanatory statements aim. Substance is primarily the what-
IS-it as "this," and secondarily the what-IS-it of science's generalized
correlations and theories. While science is developing, substance is
the what-IS-it which the various stages of discovery close in upon.
When science is at term, substance is what-IS-it as fully known: the
"this" of concrete daily life as understood and explained.

Substance is not a new "entity." It is not an "extra" besides the
beds, trees, chemical samples, human beings we live among. It is simply that which is most proper to each of these things; it is these things
themselves, insofar as they can be known in true judgment. Philosophy

is a battle against bewitchment by our imagination. And so we must not imagine substance as an underlying something, as a queer entity neither physical nor mental, etc. The use of a noun-form, "substance," as if naming some such extra entity is misleading to the imagination. We cannot picture substance, nor visualize it; for substance is not an object of our senses or of our imagination. Neither does our intelligence have entities, objects, at which it "looks." Rather, substance is the name for the heuristic goal implied in all intelligent activity: the what-IS-it of each thing. Substance is thus a what-IS-it as a "this" (each thing) and secondarily a what-IS-it as universal (what the thing is). The substance of this large plant, of such trunk, branches, leaves, (what-IS-it?) is an oak; and secondarily it is that conceptual conjunction of characteristics (the unity-identity-whole) which systematically leads us to identify particular oaks. Thus "being an oak" has two aspects: that of essence and that of instance; that of universality and that of individuality; that of a kind and that of a this. For Aristotle, sense experience looks to the instance and the individual, conceptual unification and ordering *(episteme)* looks to the essential and the universal. But the notion of substance bridges both these other ways of knowing; it joins their contents. This old, high oak outside my window is to my senses a "this" and to my generalizing intelligence a "genus: oak" (a type, or class, or kind); but to my judgment both "this" and "genus: oak" are present in one same event of knowing. It is substance, and the act of judgment which is our way of knowing substance, that unite our sense knowledge to our intelligent knowledge. It does not add to, it unites. Substance is no extra entity. Then why talk about it? To fasten our attention on the *intelligibility* of things rather than on their *sensible* presentations. The *data* about an oak that meet our senses are sensible; the intelligent inquiry that discovers the unity-identity-whole in these data leads us to discover that these data are an oak, and what an oak is. Substance gives us the middle term between data of sense and universals of science; substance is the what-IS-it discovered in data, and expressed in a technical concept abstracted *from* particular data. (An abstract, technical concept is, for example: "An oak is any of a genus *Quercus* of hardwood fagaceous trees and shrub, etc.") Substance is the crux between experience and science. It is what individual things are known to be, and adds nothing "extra" to individual things. As the what-IS-it of each concrete thing, substance assures that each thing can be known by science and that science is about things.

But what is this mysterious act of judgment to which our analysis has repeatedly had to refer? It is because we have lost Aristotle's notion of judgment that we have lost his notion of substance. It is because we have lost these two notions that we have, as Henry Aiken suggests we have in his paper on Sidney Hook in *Commentary* February, 1962, p. 146), left the subject, the knower, out of our Anglo-American account of the world. For the act of judgment is not the act of sensing (perceiving) nor the act of intuiting—nor inferring. Common to these other acts of knowing is the root analogy of "seeing," the subtle suggestion that seer and seen are two separate objects. Judging is a much more complex act, in which "seeing" (sensory, imaginative, or intuitive) is only one element. And it intimately involves the knower with the known. It would be too long to study judging and its ground here; I can only say that the best treatments I have encountered for understanding Aristotle are John Henry Newman's *Grammar of Assent* (Image Books), a very English, empirical, concrete phenomenology of judging; and Bernard Lonergan's *Insight,* an exceedingly ambitious, systematic, and powerful critique of judging. I find that recent attention to the notion of justification, especially in ethics, is a rediscovery of the act of judging, its concreteness and complexity. (The dichotomy "objective-subjective" becomes meaningless as this discovery proceeds.) Morton White's tentative efforts at the end of *Toward Reunion in Philosophy* (pp. 278, 284) to isolate a notion of scientific "conscience," and Rawls' and Firth's attempts to spell out in their journal articles the conditions of a justified ethical judgment seem to be moves in a similar direction.

The act of judging, in short, does not add a new datum nor a new predicate to the known, as do the acts of perceiving or intuiting. In a rational scrutiny of its own operating procedures and conditions, and theirs, the act of judging "authenticates"—approves—the other acts of knowing. It joins the acts of sense to those of intelligence, and correspondingly joins their contents; it affirms that the old tree outside my window *is* "genus: oak." And this affirmed unity of the instance and the essence, the particular and the universal, the many and the one, is what we mean by substance: not a new datum, not a new predicate, but a unity reached in a complex act that has no parallel in other acts of knowing.[73a]

One last note ought to be added. Since Aristotle quite clearly intends his inquiry into substance as a propaedeutic to philosophical theology,[74] it might be remarked that he has a different notion of "the real" than that to which we are accustomed. For him, knowing clearly moves from the data of experience to the inquiries of intelligence, and it does not confer reality on the former nor on the latter. "The real" and "existence" are not coextensive with the data of experience immediately, but only mediately, through intelligent inquiry. The real and existence are reached not by sense experience but by inquiry and critical reflection, affirming evidence. What we "sense" or "perceive" may or may not be "real." Aristotle does not hold that sense experience, direct or "naked and undisguised" (Berkeley), is the only evidence; he only presumes that it is the best pedagogical evidence and, against the Platonists, that it is required in every human act of understanding.[75] While the sensible substances with which we are familiar are ranked as primary substances, and as indeed our best pedagogical path to the knowledge of other substances, Aristotle clearly thinks that the First Mover and the other heavenly movers (as distinct from the heavenly bodies, which are material) are immaterial substances, and, as immaterial, primary substances more properly still. Why is this? Because for Aristotle human knowing, too, is more immaterial than material; matter, in fact, is the unknowable.[76] Sense knowledge is needed as the starting point, but only after sense knowledge does intelligent inquiry begin, and the real is reached not in sense knowledge but after intelligent inquiry, in affirmation. What is most real about sensible substance is not its *sensible* side, but its what-IS-it, which can be grasped by intelligence and affirmed.[77] What is real in our present world is not matter, but what is known by intelligent inquiry and true affirmation. Since man is capable of immaterial operation, albeit through a material brain and in necessary conjunction with sense knowledge and imagination, Aristotle believes this immaterial capacity is most properly man's organizing peak, most properly man's what-IS-it, and immortal.[78] Aristotle's notions of material and immaterial, of knowing and of the real, are more fully nuanced and more totally different from Plato's on the one hand and from Hume's on the other, than we are often led to suspect. His position is not at all the one Locke and Hume attribute to him, Platonizing him as did the medieval Arabs. His is the overlooked revolution in our philosophical history.

NOTES

1. Irving Copi, "Essence and Accident," *Journal of Philosophy,* 51 (1954), 706-19; Wilfred Sellars, "Substance and Form in Aristotle," *ibid.,* 54 (1957), 688-99; Rogers Albritton, "Forms of Particular Substances in Aristotle's *Metaphysics,*" *ibid.,* 699-708; E. S. Haring, "Aristotle's Doctrine of Substance," *Review of Metaphysics,* 10 (1957); N. L. Wilson, "Space, Time, and Individuals," *Journal of Philosophy,* 52 (1955), 589-98; D. C. Williams, "Form and Matter," *Philosophical Review,* 67 (1958), 291-312, 499-521.

2. On the question of essence as substance (for essence is a "such," not a "this"), 1033b 18f; on the question of artificial substances, v.g., 1070b 14.1 where house is listed as a substance—or at least as one of three kinds of substance (1070b 9.2); on the question of parts of substances (1040b).

3. *Meditations on First Philosophy,* II, *The Philosophical Works of Descartes,* vol. one, Dover, 1955, 154-55.

4. In the articles cited above, Sellars thinks certain the one thing that Albritton thinks clearly uncertain (cf., opening lines of Albritton); Williams believes a clear account of Aristotle has not been given. G.E.M. Anscombe remarks a sense of "necessary" operative in Aristotle which has been lost sight of in modern philosophy: "Aristotle and the Sea-Battle," *Mind,* 65 (1956), p. 14.

5. 2a 11-13.

6. *Ibid.*

7. 3b 10.

8. *Ibid.*

9. 1041b 28-31; 1042b 15-32 for other kinds of unity.

10. 1074a 36; Books N and M.

11. 1040b 5-16; 1070b 36-1071a 4.

12. Bk. Z, ch. 17.

13. 2a 11-15; 1070b 9.2.

14. 1029b 13.

15 *The Categories,* chs. 1-5.

16. 1030a 29 f.

17. 1028a 37 f.

17a. 1014Ia 9.

18. "To begin from a clear-cut instance, in which there is no need to suppose either intelligence or reasonableness, let us consider a kitten. It is awake and its stream of consciousness flows in the biological pattern. Such consciousness is a higher technique for attaining biological ends. It may be described as orientated toward such ends and as anticipating means to the ends. Moreover, the means lie in external situations, and so anticipation is

extroverted. The kitten's consciousness is directed outwards towards possible opportunities to satisfy appetites. This extroversion is spatial: as it is by the spatial manoeuvres of moving its head and limbs that the kitten deals with means to its end, so the means must also be spatial, for otherwise spatial manoeuvres would be inept and useless. The extroversion is also temporal: present data are distinct from the memories that enrich them; they are no less distinct from the imagined courses of future action to which they lead. Finally, the extroversion is concerned with the 'real': a realistic painting of a saucer of milk might attract a kitten's attention, make it investigate, sniff, perhaps try to lap; but it could not lead to lapping and, still less, to feeling replete; for the kitten, painted milk is not real.

"Let us now characterize a 'body' as an 'already out there now real.' 'Already' refers to the orientation and dynamic anticipation of biological consciousness; such consciousness does not create but finds its environment; it finds it as already constituted, already offering opportunities, already issuing challenges. 'Out' refers to the extroversion of a consciousness that is aware, not of its own ground, but of objects distinct from itself. 'There' and 'now' indicate the spatial and temporal determinations of extroverted consciousness. 'Real,' finally, is a subdivision within the field of the 'already out there now': part of that is mere appearance; but part is real; and its reality consists in its relevance to biological success or failure, pleasure or pain." Bernard Lonergan, *Insight: A Study of Human Understanding,* Philosophical Library, 1957, p. 251.

19. 1036a 9.
20. 1029a 35-b 14.
21. S. C. Pepper, "The Fiction of Attribution," University of California Publications in Philosophy, 9 (1927), 91-121; P. Marhenke and D. S. McKay on "Relations," *ibid.,* 13 (1930), 3-34, 167-87; Bertrand Russell, *Our Knowledge of the External World,* Mentor (1960), ch. 2, esp. 42-48.
22. W. V. Quine, *Word and Object,* M. I. T. Press, 1960, p. 131; M. V. White, *Toward Reunion in Philosophy,* Harvard U. Press, 1956, 61 ff.
23. 1028a 37-38; 1031a 12-14; and 1031a 18.
24. 1031b 3-5. This passage is the more impressive because in it Aristotle takes the hardest possible example, the Platonic Forms; cf., W. D. Ross. *Aristotle's* Metaphysics, commentary, vol. II, p. 177, entry on 1031a 29.
25. The introduction to nearly every treatise begins with methodological comment; at decisive turns in the argument, new methodological comments are given.
26. Of the most crucial point, the link between the intelligible and the sensible, Aristotle writes: "To the thinking soul images serve as if they were contents of perception . . . the soul never thinks without an image." 431a 14-16. ". . . the objects of thought are in the sensible forms. . . . Hence (1) no one can learn or understand anything in the absence of sense, and (2) when the mind is actively aware of anything it is necessarily aware of it along with an image. . . ." With these passages from the *De Anima,* there must be grasped those from the *Post. Anal. I,* ch. 31, about the inadequacy of perception for scientific knowledge, the example of the eclipse;

ch. 33 about necessary connections (in Aristotle's sense, not that of decadent Aristotelians); the "quick wit" described at 89b 10f; and II, chs. 1-3
concerning general heuristics; also the final summary, ch. 19. Implicit in
these passages is a kind of knowing that is not *a priori,* that is dependent
on sense knowledge and imagination, that involves an intuitive factor, that
is not reducible to sense experience although subject to critical analysis
and reflection. An example of this knowing by way of an image is given at
1051a 23-34. Refer back to 431b 24-26.

27. *Op. cit.,* n. 18. For Lonergan's earlier work, see *ibid.,* p. xv.

28. 1029b 3 f; 87b 29-30; 100a 15 ff; etc.

29. 89b 21 ff; 194b 16 f; etc.

30. 1027b 19-28.

31. It is important to note that for Aristotle the real is not reached in sense
data or the immediate gestalt of the senses, but only after affirmation closes
inquiry; the real is an intellectual, not a sensory, content. Other passages
are 1051b 34.1 ff and 1017a 32-35. Because the real "existence" is reached
not by any sense datum or concept but only by those that can be truthfully affirmed, existence is not for Aristotle a predicate or conceptual content, but that which is added by a truthful judgment—a new kind of
content.

32. *The Concept of Mind,* Barnes and Noble, 1960, 149-153.

33. "And first let us make some linguistic remarks about it . . ." 1029b 13.

34. See n. 24.

35. The passages listed in n. 26 are hard to reconcile with post-Cartesian
epistemologies; but Aristotle did not develop these notions with modern
epistemologies in view, nor with his primary interest centered on the critical
problem. Nevertheless, he systematically appealed to different kinds of
knowing, causes, heuristic categories in developing his key notions: matter
is what is unknowable in itself; form is the what-IS-it; act is the completely knowable; the causes are what answer different types of questions,
etc.

36. 1027b 19-28; 1051b 34.1 ff; 1017a 32-35.

37. Contrast the view of Protagoras, that what seems to each man also as-
suredly is, given at 1062b 14 ff., with the passages of the preceding note.
The "sense-datum analysis" of 1063a 7 ff is amusing.

38. J. Owens consistently calls attention to Aristotle's program, as expressed in
the opening chapters of the *Metaphysics* and throughout, of reaching the
eternal, unmoved, purely actual cause of being, by way of the "more knowable to us." *The Doctrine of Being in the Aristotelian Metaphysics,* Pon-
tifical Institute of Medieval Studies, Toronto, 1957, 261, 251, 246.

39. 1029a 34.2 ff.

40. Aristotle had no experience of statistical methods.

41. This distinction between what is most knowable to us and what is most
knowable in itself or in nature, might be of use in distinguishing common
sense knowledge from the theoretical constructs of modern science.

42. Bk. Z, ch. 17.

43. I have taken J. Owens' 'what-IS-being' (as translation for τὸ τί ἦν εἶναι)

where the capitalized IS represents timeless being, and rendered it 'what-IS-it' in order to suggest the other two formulae, what-is and what-it-is, which Aristotle also uses; and also to bring out the interrogative form more clearly. See Owens, 93 ff.

44. 1031b 3-5.

45. Cf., Lonergan's remarks, *op. cit.,* 252, 269.

46. 1031a 20-21; 88a 5 read with 90a 5-6 etc.

47. "For one reaches explanatory conjugates by considering data as similar to other data; but the data, which are similar, also are concrete and individual; and as concrete and individual, they are understood inasmuch as one grasps in them a concrete and intelligible unity, identity, whole (i.e., substance). Nor can one dispense with this grasp or transcend it. For science advances through the interaction of increasingly accurate descriptions and ever more satisfactory explanations of the same objects. Unless the objects are the same, there is no relation between the descriptions and the explanation and so no reason why explanation should modify description or description lead to better explanation. But the only object that is the same is the concrete and intelligible unity, identity, whole; for the explanatory conjugates change; and the descriptive or experiential terms undergo modifications and rearrangements." Lonergan, *op. cit.,* 436.

48. Ross notes that the Aristotelian account states both the individual and the universal side of substance (vol. II, 159-60); and Aristotle will say: "Since substance is of two kinds, the concrete thing and the formula (I mean that one kind of substance is the formula taken with the matter, while another kind is the formula in its generality) . . ." 1039b 20-23. The key to this duality is found in the *De Anima,* 431a 14-16 and 432a 5-8, in which it is made plain that all knowledge arises from an insight into the concrete image. It is this first moment of insight that provides the   ; the subsequent moment of conceptualization provides the universal. The two moments are inextricably related, and generally not separate in *time,* but in analysis.

49. See note 26.

50. "Necessary" not in the sense of *a priori,* but in the sense *"Iⲫτοδε τί, then always . . ."* which is quite similar to Hume's constant conjunction; except that Aristotle would allow that after some recurrences—or even after but one experience—we could catch on (by quick wit) to the inescapability of the case: as when from the moon we could see the earth cutting out the light of the sun and thus understand why, given these factors, an eclipse *must* ensue. Cf., *Post. Anal.,* 87b 39.1—88a 4.1, 89b 10-20, 90a 27-31, 93a 30—b 9.

51. 100a 15—b; 432a 5-8.

52. 1051a 23-33; 432a 5-8; 88b 30-33.

53. 2a 11-15; 3b 10-18; 1038b—1039a 23.

54. Bk. Z, ch. 17.

55. *Op. cit.,* 222.

56. Cf. Ross, *op. cit.,* 224.

57. 981a 23; 982b 12; 100a 15—b 5.

58. 94a 20-23; 89b 21-35.

59. 1a 23-24.1. Since substance is being in the primary sense (1003a 33—b 24), and since substance is primarily essence (1041b 27-31), the concrete thing is not substance inasmuch as it is matter but inasmuch as it is grasped as essence. For matter is unknowable (1036a 9.1) and there is a certain "intuitive thinking or perception" which knows the concrete thing (6-7) and which is relatable to the universal formula by which the concrete thing is stated and recognized (8-9). From these points it becomes possible to envisage a substance "apart from" matter, "not in" matter, "separable from" matter; i.e., nonmaterial substance. Since to be is to be affirmed in judgment, rather than to be sensed or reduced to sense experience, immaterial substances could be affirmed if there were reasons to affirm them. But there is another sense of "apart" operative in the question of substance, as in the categories. Here "apart" seems to mean independence, "thisness," completeness in itself, not common to many, uniqueness; it means ability to exist as a concrete individual with a formal principle of unity of its own. The secondary substance of the Categories cannot meet this criterion, for it is common to many; again, the Metaphysics uses this criterion to rule out substances as parts of substances, for such parts are involved in the formal unity of the whole and thus are not independent. On universal and "this," see all of 1038b, esp. 9-10, 24.1-7, 34.1-36.

60. 1040b 5-10; 1041a 5-6; 1037b 2-4; or 1036a 33 f: ". . . as a circle may exist in bronze or stone wood, it seems plain that these, the bronze or the stone, are not part of the essence of the circle, since it is found apart from them." Again in b 30 f, the living essence is seen as the criterion of unity: "For it is not a hand in any and every state that is a part of man, but only when it can fulfill its work, and therefore only when it is alive; if it is not alive it is not a part."

61. v.g., 1040b 31—1041a 4; in his listing of an "imperishable substance existing apart from the individual and sensible substances" he mentions the stars. But his changeless Mover of chs. 6-7, Bk. Λ, is not confused with the sensible heavenly bodies. See Ross, op. cit., 220, for the distinction of the transcendent intelligibles and, by implication, from the transcendent sensibles (the stars).

62. 1039b 27-31; 1040a 29 f.

63. 1039a 15-23.

64. Ryle has emphasized the difference between achieving an insight and using it in a built theory, op. cit., 317-18.

65. Even "a certain grammatical knowledge" is noted in the categories as a kind of "this"; but whether as habit or act it is a quality of substance. 1b 7-9. One must discriminate among "thises," for they vary just as do the senses of "is" and occur in any of the categories; see 1030a 18-28; 1031a 1-14.

66. Quine's space-time worm gives an image of the total aggregate of a thing's extensions as its reality; Aristotle merely notes that its reality is in its instantiations and not in its intension or universal, but he does not try to visualize its reality. For Aristotle, reality cannot be visualized for it is not

sensible; it is rather the content of intelligent inquiry that is affirmed in judgment, and that content consists of intelligibility in data and not merely of sense stimuli. See Quine, "Identity, Ostension, Hypostasis," *From a Logical Point of View*, Harvard, 1953, 65-79.

67. 4a 10 ff.

68. 1037b 2-4; 1041a 5-6.

69. 412a 20-23, 29-30; b 9.1-14; 413a 20-22.

70. 413a 22 ff.

71. The levels of life seem to accord with the ascending points of view of the sciences: physics, chemistry organic and inorganic, biology, sensitive and rational psychology. What is random and inexplicable on one level finds organization from a "higher" point of view. See Lonergan, *op. cit.*, 13-19, 233-34, 257, 374, 439.

72. 1043b 22-24.2 denies that they are substances; but often he uses them as examples of substances—"house" at 1043a 14 ff.

73. See n. 69.

73a. The act of judging is also the key to the problem of existence; existence is not a predicate—is it not reached as a datum of sense nor as a character or property isolated by intelligence. As a noun-form, as an object (concept, predicate) like other objects, it is misleading. It is reached in the complex act of judging, expressed in the affirmation: "It is the case that . . ." Existence is known in judgment.

74. 983a 6-11; 1096b 1-2.

75. See n. 26; the effect of the doctrine of the *De Anima* is to deny that man's knowledge is either *a priori* or limited to sense experience; since understanding *must* proceed through insight into a concrete presentation, Plato's "consulting of the eternal Forms" is disavowed; since knowledge proceeds from the intelligent inquiry by which "quick wit" achieves insight into the data presented by the senses, and then reflects upon the evidence for affirmation or denial. Protagorean sense knowledge and relativism are disavowed (Bk K, ch. 6).

76. 1036a 9.1.

77. See n. 59.

78. 408b 19.2-29.

Part Three

DIVERSELY ONE

The last few years have taught me how little I know about Protestantism and, despite my efforts to learn, how many prejudices regarding it I share. Again and again I have reacted to manifestations of faith, hope, and love in Protestants with the delight of discovery, as if grace did not have a permanent dwelling among them. I used to discount Protestant concern for social justice as mere humanitarianism and activism; I used to regard the Lutherans as too rigid, the Calvinists as starch-collared and capitalistic, the Methodists and Baptists as quaint and full of regional prejudices, the Unitarians as liberals of little theological weight. The left-wing Protestants were gullible regarding communism, the right-wing Protestants were America Firsters and even racist. The whole Protestant spectrum, I once thought, gave Christianity a bad name.

Catholics I thought, to be sure, had their problems; but the springs of renewal were running strongest there and, if only the world had eyes to see, would become obvious to all. Still, I wished to be charitable, compassionate, and docile regarding Protestant life; I wished to learn. But, to be truthful, I didn't expect to learn too much. I didn't wish to get involved in Protestantism at all; Catholicism was a jungle, and there was no need to add quicksand when there lay ahead a whole secular world to investigate.

Quite generously, in my first theological conversations with Protestants I recognized signs of the Holy Spirit: charity, joy, peace, and the rest. The fact that I hadn't read Barth or Bultmann, wasn't sure who Brunner was, and had never heard of Bonhoeffer, troubled me only a little; my friends hardly knew Rahner, Congar, or Guardini. Still their firm convictions about Schleiermacher and Troeltsch began to unsettle me; how had I remained totally ignorant of what was so basic to others? Surely, I should at least read Reinhold Niebuhr and Paul Tillich with some thoroughness, not so much to change my mind as to be abreast of modern classics. My first cautious readings served only to awaken recognition of how many important discoveries of the Roman Catholic renewal were being voiced by Protestants: they were beginning to recognize Catholic ideas. Moreover, Protestant descriptions of Roman Catholic reality annoyed me immeasurably. Protestant writers objected to matters many Catholics, too, objected to, but Protestants often stated matters incorrectly or in the worst possible light. They seemed to count anything living and vital within Catholicism—the new theology, for example—as marginal and doomed to condemnation. I was sure I had no anti-Protestant animus, and was shocked to discover the depth of the anti-Catholic animus in gentle, scholarly, humane Protestants.

A poor pilgrim's progress. I am ashamed, not so much of my ignorance and clannishness, as of the conviction that I was open-minded. . . . It seems a great mistake to think oneself objective and fair. The only certainty is that one cannot see one's own present biases; the only hope is that reality disconcerts, and that some of its twists and turns may expose one's past biases. Our best honesty is hindsight.

The following chapters cover a longer time span than the other chapters in this book; the earliest dates from 1959. Perhaps for a few readers some of the prejudices I have shared, and some of the growth, will awaken glimpses of recognition.

I I

The Free Churches
and the Roman Church

The most neglected Christians ecumenically are the churches of the American Bible Belt, the Free Churches, the churches of the restless people of the frontier: the Baptists, Disciples of Christ, Seventh-Day Adventists, and less so the Methodists. To many believers from such denominations, the ecumenical movement is the devil's work. A student at Stanford, for example, wrote dozens of letters to leading Free Churchmen asking them about their hopes for the ecumenical movement; the replies were, for the most part, encouraging only for the fact that the respondents seemed slightly embarrassed about their resistance to the movement.

Yet the Free Churches are extremely important in American life. Moreover, their heritage invites emulation. Those Protestants who belong to the classical traditions of the Reformation, Lutherans and more "established" Calvinists, are themselves often condescending toward the Free Churches. There often seems to be as little dialogue between fundamentalist and other Protestants as between Protestants in general and Catholics. There are not lacking classical Protestant historians who regard the Free Church movement and its revivals as the disgraceful side of the Reformation, just as there are not lacking Free Churchmen who regard classical Reformers like Luther and Calvin as halfway Reformers. The mutual suspicion arises from social and political reasons as well as from theological disagreement.

I owe my introduction to the Free Churches to Professor James Luther Adams and so it is fitting that the following essay found its way into a Festschrift *in his honor,* Voluntary Associations *(John Knox Press: Richmond, 1966), although it also appeared in the* Journal of Ecumenical Studies *(vol. 2, no. 3, 1965). Developments among modern Roman Catholic sisters (chapter 22) bear careful comparison with the problems of the Free Churches.*

IT is surely fruitful for Roman Catholics to reflect upon the lessons of doctrine and practice to be learned from the traditions of the Anabaptist, Free Church movement. To this end, one must begin by noting the original and long-lived misjudgment which Catholic historians have passed upon that tradition, especially in its sixteenth-century beginnings. And one must next note similarities between the Anabaptist conception of the Church and the Roman Catholic conception of the professed religious community. This paper, then, discusses the great Anabaptist contribution to Christian—and world—history: the break from the Constantinian order. It concludes by noting how, in our day, the Free Churches have become less like Catholic religious orders and more like "a church"; and how the Roman Catholic Church is at last following the Free Churches in the rejection of the Constantinian order. For Catholics increasingly appeal to the vision of the Church as the covenanted people of God, and employ the methods of open discussion, lay participation, and consensus as important in the daily life of the Church.

The goal of this paper is not a facile ecumenism; its purpose is to draw attention to inner demands and trends in Roman Catholicism and in Anabaptism from which each might learn from the other. The paper is based on the assumption that one fundamental problem of the Christian churches is not theological but philosophical. And that problem seems to be: *which choices of human polity for the structure of a community and for individual life* contribute most, over the long run, to fidelity to the revelation of Jesus Christ?

I. *A New Judgment Required*

The Anabaptists of the sixteenth century are probably best known to Roman Catholics in America through their portrait by Ronald Knox in *Enthusiasm*. Knox portrays the Anabaptists as eccentric people, immature and unwise—swept up by an undercurrent of wild and fantastic emotion beneath the mainstream of European culture. Yet Msgr. Knox has been fascinated by "these enthusiasts." On the last page of his book, he confesses that all through its writing he had been haunted by a refrain from *La Princesse Lointaine*:

> *Frère Trophime*: Inertia is the only vice, Master Erasmus;
> And the only virtue is . . .
> *Erasmus*:   Which?
> *Frère Trophime*:   Enthusiasm!

Earlier, Msgr. Knox confesses a more tangible fear: "More than all the other Christianities, the Catholic Church is institutional. Her enemies too easily conclude that she is thereby incapacitated from all spiritual initiative. . . ." [1] Surely readers of the fiction of Evelyn Waugh would guess that a deep spiritual malaise gripped the Roman Catholic Church, and that spiritual initiative had long ago been lost. Perhaps there is a general longing, then, among Roman Catholics for what the Free Churches of the Anabaptist movement have to teach. Perhaps, in this era of the Second Vatican Council, such lessons are being learned.

Catholics are often inwardly constrained from learning from the Anabaptists, however, first by prejudice, next by ignorance, and thirdly by condescension. Prejudice has arisen against the Free Churches because of their supposed reliance upon the emotions and subjective experience. The Catholic distrusts such reliance for both good motives and bad: good because, narrowly construed, the emotions do not suffice for self-criticism or for perseverance; bad because the Catholic receives little instruction in personal, spiritual initiative, usually taking his cues from the institutions to which he belongs— Catholic piety is much objectified, and the "excesses" of private devotion are looked upon with much suspicion. Ignorance is operative, because Catholics ordinarily know little of the tradition of the Free Churches, their theology, their heroes, their favored doctrines; the proliferation of sects, and above all emphasis on the emotions, suffices to dissuade the Catholic from taking the sects with seriousness. Condescension arises from the Roman Catholic belief that Roman Catholicism is "the one true Church" and that this Church alone truly knows who Christ is and what he wills.[2] The sects do themselves little justice (in the eyes of Catholics) by stressing in their own rhetoric the elements of feeling, experience, and subjectivity. Such rhetoric seems unfortunate, since it is clear from their doctrine and their lives that intelligence and persevering will are also involved in their living of the gospels, and to these qualities Catholics are more inclined to pay respect.

Who were the Anabaptists? They were the "full-way" reformers, the radical reformers.[3] Their characters, their intentions, and their doctrines have long been misunderstood. They aroused the fears, hatred, and wrath of Luther and Calvin. Catholic authorities joined the classical reformers in putting them to death: by the sword, by fire, by torture with heated tongs, and—in parody of their own belief in adult baptism—by drowning. Hunted and imprisoned in life, they were blackened also in death by historians among their enemies. Only in recent years [4] have their writings and deeds come to be taken without ulterior purpose, by neutral scholars, by scholars of their own, or by scholars of antipathetic beliefs who are able, now, to be objective. Thus confronted, on their own merits, the men and women of the radical reformation command respect. The theory and practice of religious liberty so much cherished by Christians today is largely of their earnings. Their standards of belief, practice, and prayer encourage emulation. The courage and calmness with which they went to death, and their long-meditated, explicit doctrine of martyrdom and the cross challenge all who think of themselves as representatives of the Gospels. The missionary impulse which has motivated and sustained their worldwide efforts for many generations proves the depth of their convictions.

The Anabaptist movement is difficult to characterize. It did not emerge behind one leader solely, nor according to a program worked out in advance. It emerged from dissatisfaction with the "compromises" of the classical Reformation, and from other conditions of the time as well. First of all, the movement was widespread: it arose in Spain and Italy in the south, and in England and Scandinavia in the north, but its most vital center appears to have been in Switzerland and Southern Germany, in Moravia, Holland, and the northern

Rhineland.[5] The movement was not primarily theoretical; it seems to have grown according to various pressures of time and place and only gradually to have become conscious of itself.[6] Social and political factors were of high importance in the original impetus of the movement; socialists and Marxists claim it as an early version of their revolution.[7] At certain places and times, the movement erupted into violent revolution, as in the Peasants' Revolt and at Muenster; for the most part, it was peaceable and even pacifist. Fears and social scars held over from preceding generations—fears from the frequent, terrifying plagues, from ignorance, from a changing legal and social order—contributed to the credibility of wild eschatological expectations among the peoples.[8] In many respects, the times seem in restrospect like a nightmare, whose dislocations the paintings of Hieronymus Bosch suggest only too vividly.

In their conception of the church, the radical reformers struck to the heart of the crisis of their times. An older social order, and an older relationship of church and state, were giving way. Where Luther and Calvin tried to carry out their reformation as nearly as possible on theological and ecclesiastical grounds, leaving intact the relationship of church and world, the radical reformers labored for a new cultural order. Important elements in the future of world history lay in their hands. Catholic, Lutheran, and Calvinist authorities were not wrong to see in them a threat to the social order inherited from the time of Constantine; the radical reformers thought of that order as a "fall" and labored for the "restitution" of an older conception of the church and a new order of the world. In view of the subsequent desacralization of the state, the emerging value of religious liberty, and the future pluralism of nearly all world civilizations, we may see in the labors of the radical reformers one of the decisive moments of modern history.

These labors were not accidental, but deliberate; they were not generated by the mood of a moment, but sufficed to inspire men to endure years of persecution and flight before the authorities; and they very often cost blood. One of the most vivid images that remains after studies in this area is of martyrdoms like that of Michael Sattler. Sattler was thirty-seven in 1527, the year of his execution; he had been a Benedictine for many years, and had risen to the rank of prior. He became a Lutheran and, in 1525, an Anabaptist. Forced to flee from city to city with his wife, Sattler was arrested and tried in Ensisheim, where he was executed on a beautiful May 20, 1527. There in the marketplace, a piece was cut from his tongue. Twice, pieces of flesh were torn from his body with hot tongs. He was forged to a cart. Five times on the way to the stake the tongs were again applied to his body. Sattler was then bound with ropes to a ladder; a sack of powder was mercifully tied to his neck to hasten his death; he was thrust into a fire. "Almighty, eternal God," he prayed aloud before he died, "Thou art the way and the truth; because I have not been shown to be in error, I will with Thy help this day testify to the truth and seal it with my blood." When the ropes on his hands had burned through, he raised his two forefingers and repeated Christ's words: "Father, into Thy hands I commend my spirit." [9]

The idea that such martyrs were fanatics was made to take root in historiography; the new order to which they gave witness was in fact disorder in the eyes of Constantinian Catholics and classical reformers. The times were unsettled enough, and some from among the Anabaptists were indeed Maccabean revolutionaries who preached fire and the sword. But even in vilifying the main stream of the Anabaptists, which was by no means Maccabean, an early Catholic historian tells us between the lines what peaceable, devoted lives they led—as their Moravian, Mennonite, and Hutterite descendants have continued to exemplify. In a history called *Of the Cursed Beginnings of the Anabaptists,* about the year 1600, the Jesuit Fischer wrote:

Among all the heresies and sects which have their origin from Luther, . . . not a one has a better appearance and greater external holiness than the Anabaptists. Other sects are for the most part riotous, bloodthirsty and given over to carnal lusts; not so the Anabaptists. They call each other brothers and sisters; they use no profanity nor unkind language; they use no weapons of defense. . . . They own nothing in private but have everything in common. They do not go to law before judicial courts but bear everything patiently, as they say, in the Holy Spirit. Who should suppose that under this sheep's clothing only ravening wolves are hidden? [10]

The heart of Anabaptist witness is their notion of the church. That notion, capable of inspiring great Christians, deserves study. Moreover, if it is true that the Roman Catholic Church now embraces the doctrine of religious liberty, gradually instructed in this doctrine by history, then face-to-face with the Free Churches, Roman Catholicism can no longer be seen as the Constantinian Church. It is no longer accurate, in most countries, to refer to Roman Catholicism as one of Troeltsch's "church type." [11]

What do the Free Churches mean by the idea of the church, and what do Roman Catholics mean? When old prejudices have fallen by their own invalidity, what separates the Roman Church from the Free Church?

II. *The Anabaptist Idea of the Church*

"It was a great step forward," Robert Friedmann tells us, "when Ernst Troeltsch first so clearly distinguished church and sect—although primarily from a sociological point of view. Church is the institution of salvation for all baptized members; sect is the brotherhood of the regenerate, the congregation of saints, a gathered church of true Christians either for the celebration of the Lord's Supper alone or for a collective life according to the Sermon on the Mount." [12] Disappointed because the classical Reformers did not sufficiently preach the Sermon on the Mount, the evangelical Anabaptists necessarily broke with them as with Catholicism. Friedmann continues his resumé of Troeltsch's findings: "While the Middle Ages had monasteries for those who strove toward a pure and holy life, the modern times engendered the Protestant sect, with discipline, aloofness from the world, general priesthood of believers, separation from the state— a congregation of volunteers on the basis of a strong biblicism." [13] Friedmann criticizes Troeltsch's division of church and sect as too broad; not all Protestant sects pursue the highly moral course Troeltsch describes. "Nevertheless, it was a great advance to recognize Pietism as the sect-type within the Church. . . . It is a very significant fact that as soon as Anabaptism became settled or established, it changed from the sect type to the church type. But as it continued to cherish its old heritage, this little church developed a pietistic pattern." [14]

Later in his study, Friedmann reinforces these points by citing the work of Ritschl: "Surprisingly, he found a striking likeness between the Franciscan tertiaries, the [evangelical] Anabaptists, and the Pietists of the seventeenth century. He starts with a glimpse of what he calls the Franciscan idea of church reform: restitution of the early form of Christianity by renunciation of the world, personal purity, poverty, and, finally, expectation of the Kingdom of God. Asceticism within the world and a prevailing religious emotionalism in practicing brotherly love are said to be the main features of this group." [15] Anabaptism, in short, appears to Ritschl as "a revival of the Franciscan reformation, a worldly monasticism." [16] Friedmann offers two criticisms: the Anabaptists are more related to the Spiritual Franciscans than to the third orders; the Pietists are more related to the mystical or spiritual Anabaptists like Casper Schwenckfeld than to the Anabaptists proper.[17]

It is this analogy between the evangelical Anabaptists and the Franciscans which is, initially, most interesting to observe. If, for a moment, we conceive of "the Roman Catholic Church" only as a generic name like "the Protestant Church," and look upon the different modes of Catholic life as sects or denominations within the larger whole, the relationships between evangelical Anabaptist piety and Franciscan piety seem more striking. If, for example, one were to visit a Franciscan or Capuchin monastery in Pennsylvania, and to observe the sandaled friars in their traditional robes, and to see the brothers working on the farm, and then to visit a Mennonite community nearby and observe the traditional clothing and the men working in the fields, one would wonder about the relationship between the books of piety which animate the lives of both groups. One would wonder also about their mutual doctrines on the relationship of Christianity to the world: about retreat, about the Sermon on the Mount, about community of goods, about the relationship between those committed to this special life and others not of the brethren. (It might well be discernible that the Franciscans had more adaptation to the twentieth century than the Mennonites had, at least in externals; but not so much as the American Quakers, who are, as H. Richard Niebuhr has said, "the Anglo-Saxon parallel to Anabaptism." [18])

Friedmann's discussion of Anabaptist spirituality leads back in many ways to the spirituality of Catholic religious orders. He notes that the Anabaptist ordinance of baptism—the rite, after all, from which their name was drawn—was not looked upon so much as a sacrament, a bringing of grace, as the seal of a free, personal commitment to a new life. "In character such baptism might perhaps best be compared with a monastic vow." [19] Let us pursue this comparison.

Roland H. Bainton made current the name "Left-Wing Protestantism" for the Anabaptist movement.[20] His principle of division was separation of church and state; the right wing accepted the land church, the left wing insisted upon separation, tolerance, religious liberty.[21] Franklin H. Littell—in studies to which we must return—goes farther; he finds the heart of the Anabaptist movement in its conception of the church.[22] Harold S. Bender and after him Robert Friedmann object: the idea of the church is important, but derivative; it is not of the essence. "We have not yet arrived at the heart of the matter when we stop with the idea of the 'church'; at the heart we discover one idea only, and that is the idea of faithful and free voluntary discipleship which the Anabaptist is resolved to accept without faltering." [23] "Such discipleship means that the commandment of Jesus Christ, 'Take up thy cross and follow me,' be taken absolutely seriously. That it implies separation from the world, nonconformity and consequently the narrow path which might end in martyrdom, is only too obvious." [24]

The new brotherhood will not admit members who are only nominally or partially Christian; it is a state of perfection, to borrow the technical phrase used of Catholic religious communities. While Luther decided for a *Volkskirche* to include both saints and sinners, the Anabaptists decided for the opposite way, "for the 'church holy' rather than for the 'church universal.' " [25] "That such a 'church holy' is not only a distant ideal but a distinct possibility for man was demonstrated by the Anabaptists, at least in their first period (to 1560), with much dedication and vigor. It meant, of course, complete separation from the world and nonconformity to it. . . ." [26] The Anabaptists will make the counsels of the Gospels the rule of their lives.

Because Anabaptism is a lay movement, of course, it cannot well include celibacy among the defining features of its life; but the number of its early and greatest leaders who were originally priests, and even monks, is, very high: Sattler, Menno Simons, etc. That the spirituality of the monastery should have continued through their sermons and writings to influence their flocks is hardly surprising; neither is it surprising that those most zealous for a life of perfection should have been among those protesting abuses in the monasteries, and been among those reacting most strongly against the practice of celibacy. Again and again among these early priest converts one notes their marriage occurring within the year, and most often, it appears, to a wife devout enough to share the hunted life, and perhaps martyr's life, of her husband. One is forced to conclude that the discipline of celibacy, both because of the otherwise nonexistent scandals which made it possible, and because of the emotional burden it placed upon an already turbulent age, played a larger role in the Reformation than is usually discussed.

But the other two cornerstones of Catholic religious life, particularly obedience, are central in the Anabaptist view of Christian life. Discipleship is the core of the Anabaptist view. "Obedience . . . is the Anabaptist term for 'discipleship.' " [27] "Repentance, rebirth, baptism on faith, and a full dedication to a life of discipleship and obedience— this sequence will be experienced henceforth in innumerable cases throughout the sixteenth century." [28] It is important to note that this experience of regeneration is not merely emotional; it is based on resolution, a willingness to endure a lifetime of hardship, routine, or martyrdom. Friedmann is careful to draw the distinction between evangelical Anabaptism and later pietism. "Pietism" is principally characterized by the subjective experience of the fact that the sinner, though incapable of doing anything good, is yet saved through the atoning death of Christ, and the subsequent joy which goes with such an experience. The pietist "knows of his sinfulness, but in a struggle of repentance he overcomes it and now rejoices in his feeling of being saved and accepted by the Lord." [29] "With the Anabaptist things seem quite different. The rebirth is a radical one, and with it the resolution to a new way in obedience to the 'law of Christ.' " [30]

The Anabaptists appear to spend little reflection on the fact of salvation; they do not seem to meditate long on their own inherent sinfulness. Their theology seems much more hardy and straightforward; they seem simply to take the Lord at his Word, and begin to try to do his will as they perceive it. "It was only about one century later, when the basic attitude of the Brethren became weakened or almost lost, that pietistic emotionalism took the place of the former *Nachfolge* or discipleship motive, and with this change (hardly ever noticed) the genuine Anabaptist spirit faded away." [31]

At this point, Friedmann is willing even to raise the question whether Anabaptism can be considered as a part of "the great Protestant family" at all. "Anabaptism represents a new type of Christianity, different from the traditional patterns of Protestantism in general. It is certainly not a credal (i.e., theological) church in which the idea of salvation takes the center of concern, nor is it a pietistic church in which the fruits of salvation may be enjoyed." [32] What Friedmann does not suggest, and what seems very fruitful as a hypothesis, is that Anabaptism represents a laicizing of the Catholic monastic spirituality; it is a transferral of the focus of the "state of perfection" from a monastic brotherhood, bound by vow and cloistered by walls, to a lay, married brotherhood bound by believers' baptism and separated from the world by the ban. Its root is not a sense of sin, trust in personal justification, and aggressive social reform (classical Reformers); its root is the desire to follow God completely, to withdraw from the world, and to respond to a call to a new and higher form of Christian life (Catholic religious vocation).

Friedmann borrows a contemporary term in trying to elucidate his interpretation of Anabaptism; the connotations of the term are not felicitous, but what he is getting at is clear. He calls Anabaptism an "outstanding example of *existential* Christianity. . . . The term 'existential' means here above all an extreme concreteness of the Christian experience. Such an experience is neither of an intellectual nature (doctrinal understanding) nor is it emotional. For lack of a better description we will call it 'total,' something most typical with all conversion experiences. In this total or concrete Christianity the distinctions between doctrine and ethics, belief and practice, no longer exist. Life becomes here a great 'yes' to the call, something which goes far beyond both mere speculation and mere moralism. Spirituality and obedience become one and the same in such a Christian existence, an unreserved surrender and dedication to the divine will. That such Christian existence has also very little in common with emotionalism becomes likewise clear by now and should make us alert. . . ." [33] This passage asserts quite clearly the sense of vocation, response, and total, concrete giving which characterize the life of the professed Catholic religious, though it does not, of course, specify the three traditional vows. Moreover, it emphasizes the individualistic sense of reality, neglecting the "existential" in social life—which Catholic religious are sometimes led to do.

However, the Anabaptist view, like the view of Roman Catholic religious, does imply the common life. "Brotherly love is the most conspicuous sign of such an existential type of Christianity: where it is practiced we might also speak of a work at the Kingdom of God. It is obvious, moreover, that the Kingdom cannot exist for the 'single one' in his isolation but only for those who have united in the *Koinonia,* the *Gemeinschaft* or *Gemeinde.* Earlier we called it the fellowship of committed disciples." [34]

Even the eschatology that arises among the Anabaptists recalls the eschatology of the cloister. "The brethren are deeply aware of the co-existence of two worlds: this world and the world of the Kingdom . . . . Absolute separation from the world and nonconformity to it easily follow as corollaries. Occasionally we read in Anabaptist tracts phrases like this, 'In these latter and dangerous days . . .' but almost nowhere do we find apocalyptical speculations. Their eschatology is strictly evangelical: the Christian has 'to fight the good fight' (I Tim. 6:12). . . he has to resist sin with all his strength." [35] The postulant who, after due inquiry, finally asked and received baptism in faith "will no longer deviate from his new path"; he will "resist sin in all its subtle temptations." It is presupposed that he will have a "genuinely felt self-surrender unto God (In German, *Gelassenheit,* i.e., self-abandoning, yieldedness)." [36] In short, the Anabaptist, much like the Catholic professed religious, does not live a life like others in the world, but sets for his norm the teachings of the Gospels, binding himself under communal discipline to live according to them. He lives now "as if the world were not."

One crucial difference between the Catholic religious and the Anabaptist, of course, is that the former sees himself as living a special form of life within a larger religious community; the latter sees the church as bounded by his own brotherhood. For the former, the kingdom of God is like a net, gathering in good fish and bad; or like a field in which tares grow together with the wheat. His temptation, of course, and that of the Catholic people, is to think that the "really committed" Catholic is, or ought to be, a religious, while those who do not offer themselves so totally or concretely remain in the lay state. (Theoretically, all agree, a layman can be just as holy as a monk, or holier; but, psychologically, both monk and layman tend to believe that the monk has a better chance at it.) The temptation of the Anabaptist is somewhat similar; it is to mark off "the world" as "out there," as sinful. It must be said that there does not seem to be much spiritual pride in the early Anabaptist communities; the reader of their sermons and tracts [37] is aware rather of their personal seriousness, humility, and dedication, than of vain comparisons with others. Nevertheless, separation from "the others" is the other side of the emphasis upon discipleship.

The Catholic religious cannot by right believe that he is a member of a true, pure community, over against the vast numbers of Catholics; his community is only part of the larger church, all of whom are called to salvation, though many be as tares, bad fish, or goats among those who will in fact be saved. The dynamism of living faithful to a freely taken religious vow, however, appears to be very like the dynamism of living faithful to believers' baptism. Like religious orders, so also the Anabaptist movement seems to have cycles of fervor and relaxation; but perhaps the more elaborate organizational pattern of the religious order, and its more extensive attention to theology, offer more footholds for later reformers within the order than would be possible if entire reliance were placed upon fellowship of spirit maintained from generation to generation. That is to say, the structure of religious orders appears to favor a fruitful as well as a possibly obstructionist conservatism, with institutionally accessible forces of renewal. Moreover, new candidates for the religious community must come from without, by free choice; the Anabaptist communions face the difficulty of having their children growing up habituated to the community and unable quite so strikingly to "choose" it as its original founders had.

Finally, it should be noted that the ordinary lay Catholic is not merely "born into" Catholicism. In countries like the United States, it has become increasingly easy socially and psychologically to leave the church or to change one's church; it must correspondingly be presumed that ordinarily those who remain Catholic choose to do so. Moreover, at the Easter Vigil ceremony, the liturgy leads the people to reaffirm, and thus to appropriate, the baptismal vows made in their name during infancy by their sponsors. The *Mennonite Encyclopedia* quotes with approval the following reflections by a Catholic writer: ". . . The church wants to make up for the missing experience [of baptism]. So on Saturday before Easter she places us around the baptismal font, fills it with water, consecrates it as a sacred source of supernatural life, sprinkles us with it in memory of our first washing, gives us some to take home, that we may use it in the morning and evening. Do you think of this when the priest carries it through the church every Sunday before High Mass, when you bless yourself upon entering and leaving the church, upon leaving and returning to your home?" [38]

To sum up: the Anabaptist view of the church is rooted in the conception of discipleship. And this conception of discipleship seems very similar to the conception of a professed religious life among Catholics, in at least a few important respects. Such a life is a free, voluntary commitment; it forms a band of the "more perfect"; it has discipline; it encourages the piety of abandonment to God's will; it offers itself as a living martyrdom, founded on renunciation of the world and the doctrine of the cross. As a program for Christians living in the world, however, the Anabaptist movement is special; it is for the few; and its most serious internal problem seems to be that of maintaining its early levels of fervor. Meanwhile, the many, too, have to hear the Gospels. What has Anabaptism to say to the world?

III. *Anabaptism and the World*

Ironically, it is the manner in which Anabaptism separated itself from the world that has had the greatest effect upon the world. For the Anabaptist separation, as Littell points out, was not physical so much as spiritual.[39] For this separation, the Anabaptist communities relied not upon a cloister wall, but upon internal social discipline within their midst. This discipline was accepted as a free choice; the Anabaptist churches are Free Churches, in the sense that one cannot be born into them but must choose to enter them. As a consequence, the radical significance of Anabaptism was its sundering of the Constantinian order of Christian society. For many of the Anabaptists, the era of Constantine marked the fall of the Christian church (for others, the fall came earlier).[40] Anabaptism recovered the sense of faith as a free act; it restored the sense of personal seriousness and commitment, even to the point of martyrdom, involved in choosing to become a Christian. Specifically, it recovered the sense of faith as a free act, not metaphysically (which had never been denied) but also *socially*. It denied that the church ought to be coterminous with profane society, to "baptize" profane society, to turn Christianity into Christendom.

The protest of the Free Churches against the established churches did not, in the sixteenth century, succeed in the lands where it arose. The Constantinian era was to be prolonged in the established churches of continental Europe. In England and in America, however, the conception of religious liberty was able to take root in the institutional structure of society.

But if the first contribution of the Free Churches to world history is the break with the Constantinian social order, the second is the method of internal polity adopted in these churches. The first struggle waged by the evangelical Anabaptists was against the landed churches of Roman Catholicism and the classical Reformation. The second was against the Maccabean revolutionaries like Thomas Münzer on the one hand, who would bind the church to the world in new and terrible ways, and against the spiritualizers like Casper Schwenkfeld and Sebastian Franck on the other, who would deprive the church of any community discipline whatever.[41] The original complaint of the Anabaptists, against both Roman Catholics and classical Reformers, was the lack of discipline within the established churches; sinners and virtual pagans were included indiscriminately in the community.[42] The Anabaptists saw the main task of the true church as that of maintaining discipline over its members. Littell defines that task in contemporary terms: "The basic task before the churches is precisely one of Christian discipline: to create within the congregation of new Christians that quality of consecrated thinking and obedience which is appropriate to a Biblical people." [43] The Free Churches, therefore, are not internally free: not, that is, free from their own stringent form of discipline. Their originality lies in the method by which they exercise this discipline.

In the classical Christian communities of the sixteenth century, discipline was exercised pastorally, from above, hierarchically. "The locus of authority in Free Churches is different. It is not, as sometimes argued, in the individual conscience apart, which has a constant tendency to warp along the line of individual self-interest. The locus is in the authority of the Holy Spirit in the midst of the covenantal people." [44] The important elements here are threefold: the covenant; belief in the Holy Spirit who teaches through consensus; and the discipline of the discussion which leads to consensus. "The early Free Churchmen did not favor internal freedom in the Church. Every member was not only free but obligated to participate in the 'talking up'

of discipline; and the discipline was binding." [45] Let us examine these
elements in turn.

In attempting to restore the pure church of the New Testament,
the Anabaptists aimed first of all to restore "a vigorous congrega-
tional life." [46] They desired personal and communal seriousness, and
therefore insisted on an explicit *covenant* or pledge. As Christ was
baptized at the age of thirty, so they thought that all who would
"walk by His way of submission and martyrdom might thereby know
that the Christian life requires mature dedication and discipline." [47]
It requires a "degree of understanding (*Vernunft*) which only mature
persons can possess." [48] Such dedication begins "in a thorough going
repentance," [49] and issues in the decision "to make personal absolu-
tion and to covenant a new life with God and the community of
believers." [50] "In Anabaptist teaching, the new birth has Christ alone
as foundation and must occur radically in the history of both the individual believer and the True Church." [51] In Littell's view, then—
perhaps somewhat overstated at this point—the idea of the covenant,
individual and communal, became the constitutive idea of the Free
Churches, the foundation of Free Church life.

Secondly, the idea of *the Holy Spirit who teaches through consensus*—i.e., through the conscience of the individual *and* of the community—follows upon the idea of the covenant. The "responsibility
of a good conscience toward God" requires "brotherly admonition
and exhortation, the practice of intentional fellowship." [52] "By baptism the believer came under the discipline of a Biblical people—a
discipline which he himself helped make and enforce." [53] "Group consciousness became a dominant force in baptized life." [54] To unlock the
meaning of Scriptures (by "the Key of David"), the individual had
the obligation to test his findings against those of others in the fellowship.[55] To have his sins forgiven (by "the Keys of Peter"), the
individual again had to have recourse to the community.[56] The center
of authority in the movement shifted from the protesting individual
conscience—even from the inspired, charismatic leader—"to the
newly gathered congregations governed by the Holy Spirit in the
midst." [57] Quite strictly, the Anabaptists opposed a salaried hierarchy.[58] They believed the Holy Spirit could teach through a responsible community as well as through a professional clergy. "In the

matter of spiritual government in its various forms the presence and sovereignty of the Holy Spirit was accepted." [59] Two quotations may help us understand this faith. First, from Menno Simons, probably the greatest leader of the early Anabaptists:

Then if I err in some things, which by the grace of God I hope is not the case, I pray everyone for the Lord's sake, lest I be put to shame, that if anyone has stronger and more convincing truth he through brotherly exhortation and instruction might assist me. I desire with my heart to accept it if he is right. Deal with me according to the intention of the Spirit and Word of Christ. [60]

The second is from Karl Barth:

Against the papal, but also against the episcopal and presbyterian/synodal concept stands the fundamental fact that they do not serve but actually hinder the readiness, the openness, the freedom of the congregation for the Word of God and the reformation of the Church. [61]

The third element, then, in the fundamental principle of authority in the Anabaptist communions, is *the discipline of free and honest discussion*. Each member is obligated to take part. Any member may feel free to contradict any other, even an elder. "This highlights the essential point: not personal prestige, but the achievement of a consensus under the guidance of the Holy Spirit." [62] The apparatus of parliamentary procedure may be very simple. "Sometimes the decision takes years of discussion and seeking for guidance. . . ." [63] "The preparation is more important than the actual vote." [64] "The Free Churches are not, it is clear, 'free' in structure or opinion; theirs is a real discipline and order which emerges among the members, ·and is not dictated from above either by prince or by hierarchy." [65] This method of consensus is only a method; but it is founded upon a deep faith. "Our fathers, who were not too struck with their own genius to admit dependence upon One far greater and wiser, were accustomed to refer to Him matters of political import as readily as ecclesiastical. They believed that if a people call on His name with abandon, he would not leave them without guidance. The answer would not be an absolute one—i.e., sufficient for all times and places—but it would be enough to live by." [66]

IV. *The Free Churches and Roman Catholicism*

In the first three sections of this paper, we have wished to make three points. First, from the point of view of the Roman Catholic, the Anabaptist or Free Church tradition is eminently worthy of study, doubly so because prejudged in the past. Secondly, the thirst for Christian perfection in the Anabaptist community is very like the motivating force of Catholic religious communities. Thirdly, Anabaptist emphasis upon the free act of faith, the covenant, and the consensus introduce into Christian polity an admirable way of living out the freedom of the Gospels under communal discipline. It is time to draw pointed lessons from both the Roman Catholic and the Free Church traditions, in the light of the contemporary situation.

In the first place, such lessons must be concrete rather than ideological; we do well not to argue from what Free Churchmen or Catholics are "supposed to be," but from what they are. Good and admirable men live in both communities. Both communities have learned much in the many generations of history which have been lived since the Reformation. Without suggesting a larger body of shared experience than yet exists, we may then point out several ways in which the two traditions are closer to each other now, and will be more so in the future, than they have been since the sixteenth century.

Our first remarks about the Free Church tradition as it is living at present will be critical, but no more so than those of one of its own spokesmen. "Candor compels the admission that, by classical standards, our American churches have taken on the character of establishments. They may still flatter themselves that they have escaped any large measure of political control (the *negative* phase of Free Churchmanship), but in terms of theological and ethical discipline (i.e., the disciplined community witness to working of the Holy Spirit —the *positive* phase of Free Church life), the larger denominations, at least, are establishments. . . . In the long view, acceptance of status as *social* establishments can be as fatal as *political* establishments." [67] The Free Church tradition, in other words, has so far been better able to cope with the Constantinian establishment than with the secular, democratic establishment.

Secondly, it seems to the observer that the original Free Church idea depended more than it knew upon smallness of numbers and perhaps upon persecution from without. So long as the communities were small, the method of consensus was manageable. So long as persecution endured, the tension of fervor had to be high. As the numbers of members grew, as the churches became prosperous, older methods did not seem to work as well. As decisions about when to adapt to the changing times resulted sometimes in surrender to worldly values and sometimes to fixation in cultural or technological primitivism,[68] new instruments of renewal and reform seemed called for. As missionary effort expanded, a larger organization of moneys and personnel at home was required. Thus, gradually, the Anabaptist communities appear to have become increasingly indistinguishable from other Christian communities. Seminaries have been founded, pastors are paid salaries, theology becomes more complex, involvement in social ethics demands ever more expertise, national and international church organizations are founded, moneys need to be raised, and many subtle forms of authority other than consensus in the Holy Spirit begin, in actual fact, to be operative both in individual and in communal faith and practice. The original Free Church insight, it seems, useful, admirable, and historically as significant as it is, does not move upon a wide enough base to support the weight of a religious community of men in history. Many complementary insights, practices, and methods must in actual fact be brought into operation to maintain the historical life of the Free Church. "The issue between Protestantism and Roman Catholicism is not, therefore, individualism vs. discipline: *the issue is how that discipline is to be attained."* [69] As the Free Churches, of human necessity, become more professional and bureaucratic, the question of method becomes wider in base, more sophisticated, and more complex.

From the other direction, Roman Catholicism is shedding many of the impedimenta of the Constantinian era. If we are to look at Roman Catholicism as historical development presents it, we must conclude that it is beginning to appropriate Free Church ideals. Those in the Free Church tradition may, of course, look on this progress with skepticism, with condescension, or with hope, as they choose; just as many Catholics look askance on the polity and practice of the Free Churches. But what will be significant for the future of Christianity will be the degree to which all the Christian churches come to grips with the exigencies of communal and individual fidelity to the revelation of Christ—and that may well require learning from each other's strengths and weaknesses.

It would be irksome, in a paper already so long, to go into great detail about the tentative, gradual movement of Roman Catholicism toward some Free Church ideals. Let us content ourselves with listing several of these developments. (1) The Second Vatican Council has at long last produced a strong statement of religious liberty, consonant with the understanding of religious liberty in the Anabaptist tradition. We may therefore project that, increasingly, moral pressure will be brought upon Constantinian arrangements like those of Spain. (2) The first and second chapters in the constitution on the nature of the church discuss the church, not as a bureaucratic organization but as a mystery and as the people of God, a covenanted community.[70] The traditional hierarchical principle of Roman Catholicism will be retained, but the role of the pastors will be understood primarily as a service to the gathered people and only secondarily as an administrative, juridical rule. Emphasis is laid upon the importance of lay participation in ecclesiastical decisions. (3) According to the widely hailed discourse of Cardinal Suenens at the second session,[71] the constitution will also reflect concern with the doctrine of the Holy Spirit speaking through all members of the church. (4) Although laymen did not at first speak in the Council—except on one occasion [72] the method of consensus was used regularly at the Council. (5) In preparation for the Council, and in the wake of its first two sessions, many "little councils" were held in individual dioceses or parishes, in which laymen participated. The idea of discussion and consensus appears to be taking root.

Roman Catholic theologians are working in each of these directions. Bishops and Cardinals at the Council supported such directions. Many Catholics already believe and attempt to practice them. That such developments are painstaking and slow is not to be despised; solid historical progress is often slow. In any case, the Constantinian, monarchical, juridical conception of polity which has characterized Roman Catholicism for many centuries is not necessary to her life; and the evolution away from this conception has been well begun. We may employ the maxim that a Council of the Church works behind its times by a generation or two, and suggest that theological and programmatic developments among Roman Catholics are already far in advance of the Second Vatican Council. The Council has clearly approved the general orientation.

How far the evolution will go in dissolving the excessive *Romanità* of Roman Catholic polity is not yet clear. Nor is it clear to what extent the Free Churches will come to grips with their own problems of renewal and reform, particularly in the question of discipline. The Free Churches appear to be no longer small, disciplined, and fervent, but complex, embracing both "saints" and "sinners," and ambiguous about questions of authority and decision; they cherish, however, their admirable traditions.

Perhaps God foresees—men do not—how these separate traditions, moving from opposite directions as it were, may one day make one fold.

N O T E S

1. Oxford University Press, 1950, pp. 590-91.
2. Cf. the lead article in the London *Tablet,* March 28, 1964.
3. The most thorough study is George Hunston Williams, *The Radical Reformation* (Philadelphia: Westminster Press, 1962).
4. Cf. Franklin H. Littell, *The Anabaptist View of the Church* (Beacon Hill, Mass.: Starr King Press, 1958, 2nd edition), ch. 5, "The Changing Reputation of the Anabaptists."
5. Cf. Williams.
6. Cf. Littell, introduction: "A Working Definition of Anabaptist."
7. Cf. e.g., *The Rise and Fall of the Anabaptists,* by Belford Bax (London: Swan Sonnenschein & Company, 1903).
8. Cf. Norman Cohn, *The Pursuit of the Millennium* (New York: Harper Torchbooks, 1961).
9. Cf. George Hunston Williams, *Spiritual and Anabaptist Writers,* vol. xxv of Library of Christian Classics (Philadelphia: Westminster Press, 1957).
10. Cf. William R. Estep, *The Anabaptist Story* (Nashville, Tennessee: Broadman Press, 1963), p. 99, quoting from John Horsch, *The Hutterian Brethren* (Goshen, Indiana: Mennonite Historical Society, 1931).
11. Not long before Troeltsch published *The Social Teaching of the Christian Churches,* Leo XIII was asking for a renewal of Thomistic studies, on the grounds that the historical understanding of St. Thomas was of a very low level. In choosing Thomism as representative of a basic type of Christian society, Troeltsch seems (a) to have overrated the influence of Thomism as compared with other elements (such as the Latin jurists) in late medieval society and (b) to have given a very inadequate presentation of such funda-

mental matters as the relation of nature and grace in Aquinas. In twentieth-century Catholicism, Thomistic studies have, on the one hand, proceeded far beyond the Thomism sketched by Troeltsch, and other approaches to philosophy and to theology, on the other hand, have increased in importance. Troeltsch's first description of the "church type" (Harper's Torchbook edition, 1960, vol. 2, p. 461) does not appear to fit either medieval Catholicism or contemporary Catholicism (especially not the latter) with much success.

12. Robert Friedmann, *Hutterite Studies,* (Goshen, Indiana: Mennonite Press, 1961), p. 6.
13. *Ibid.*
14. *Ibid.,* p. 7.
15. *Ibid.,* p. 9.
16. *Ibid.*
17. *Ibid.,* p. 10.
18. *Ibid.,* p. 12.
19. *Ibid.,* p. 38.
20. *Ibid.,* p. 7, quoting from an unpublished paper of Roland H. Bainton. Although Professor Bainton is often credited with inventing the term, John T. McNeill used it publicly two months before Bainton's article appeared. In a telephone conversation on June 21, 1964, a typescript of which Prof. D. B. Robertson has been kind enough to furnish me, Prof. Bainton added: "But now there is somebody in the *Mennonite Quarterly Review* who pointed out that neither of us created it, and that he had run into it in earlier works; and I am sure I did not get it out of McNeill; I got it from somebody else who had invented it. As a matter of fact, Luther uses the expression, except that he inverts the direction—the Catholics on the left and the 'Schwärmer' on the right. But he said that he took the middle of the road, between these other two. . . . The term 'left-wing' I saw somewhere else before I used it or McNeill used it; I don't remember where, and, as I say, I got the idea out of Luther."
21. "The Left Wing of the Reformation," *Journal of Religion,* XXI (1941), pp. 124-34.
22. Cf. Littell, *op. cit.,* and *The Free Church* (Beacon Hill, Mass.: Starr King Press, 1957).
23. Friedman, p. 30.
24. *Ibid.*
25. *Ibid.,* p. 31.
26. *Ibid.,* p. 31.
27. *Ibid.,* p. 38.
28. *Ibid.,* p. 32.
29. *Ibid.,* p. 33.
30. *Ibid.,* p. 34.
31. *Ibid.,* p. 34.
32. *Ibid.,* p. 34.
33. *Ibid.,* p. 35.

34. *Ibid.*, p. 36.
35. *Ibid.*, p. 37.
36. *Ibid.*, p. 38.
37. Cf., v.g., *Spiritual and Anabaptist Writers.*
38. *Mennonite Encyclopedia* (1955) I, 534, quoting from "The Catholic Periodical for the St. Bernard Pastorate of Frankfurt," VI, 1932, no. 3. This encyclopedia article gives a quite narrow, legalistic view of Roman Catholicism, and errs in describing the Catholic teaching on the sacraments. Unhappily, the article in the *Catholic Encyclopedia* (1907) I, 445-46, is even less adequate; it links the Anabaptists by association with the Donatists, overlooks the doctrines of religious liberty or discipleship, and gives disproportionate attention to Thomas Münzer and the Münster revolt —a seriously misleading article.
39. Littell, *The Free Church*, p. 131.
40. Littell, *Anabaptist View of the Church*, pp. 62-64.
41. *The Free Church*, p. 74. Littell also quotes Troeltsch, *Social Teaching* I, (New York: Macmillan, 1931), p. 445, on the stultifying effect of the spiritualizers of Christianity, whose champions "desire the spiritual interpretation of the Gospel, and the universality of the Christianity of the people, without the compromises of the Church and without concealing the purely Divine element in the institutional character of the Church. Its champions desire the ethical radicalism of a Society which is built upon the ideal of the Gospel, without the narrowness and pettiness of the sect. It is, however, impossible to carry the 'spirit of the Gospel' into practice without some opportunistic restriction to that which is practically possible, and without the resolve not to allow the best to be the enemy of the good." Littell, p. 80.
42. *Ibid.*, p. 116.
43. *Ibid.*, p. 118.
44. *Ibid.*, pp. 125-26.
45. *Ibid.*, p. 114.
46. *Anabaptist View* . . . , p. 85.
47. *Ibid.*, p. 84.
48. *Ibid.*
49. *Ibid.*
50. *Ibid.*
51. *Ibid.*, p. 85.
52. *Ibid.*, p. 85.
53. *Ibid.*, p. 86.
54. *Ibid.*, p. 86.
55. *Ibid.*, pp. 85-6.
56. *Ibid.*
57. *Ibid.*, p. 92.
58. *Ibid.*, p. 93.
59. *Ibid.*
60. Preface to *Meditation on the Twenty-fifth Psalm; ibid.*, p. 94.

61. *The Free Church*, p. 130.
62. *Ibid.*, p. 127.
63. *Ibid.*
64. *Ibid.*
65. *Ibid.*
66. *Ibid.*, p. 149.
67. *Ibid.*, p. 150.
68. *Ibid.*, chs. 5 and 6: "The Free Church and 'American Religion' " and "The Free Church and Its Discipline."
69. *Ibid.*, p. 93.
70. *The Documents of Vatican II*, Walter M. Abbot, S.J. (ed.), (New York: Guild Press, 1966) pp. 14-37.
71. Cf. *The Open Church* (New York: Macmillan, 1964), chs. 10-11.
72. *Ibid.*, ch. 20, for the first such occasion.

12

Beginning the Encounter

Only with some trepidation do I include in this chapter three book re-
views, two short and one rather long. Book reviews do not often deserve
to be snatched from the flames of swiftly disappearing periodical litera-
ture; and these reviews have no definitive or permanent value. They are
included because they reveal a Catholic attempting to reinterpret his own
tradition under the pressure of stimulating reading; for me they mark
stages upon a way of thought. The books involved benefited me and re-
reading the reviews helped me to recall those benefits.

The first review considers a book by one of the most promising young
theologians on either side of the Atlantic, a diffident, kind, gentle man
whose lectures are a joy to attend, Prof. Richard R. Niebuhr of Harvard
Divinity School. To bear the name of a famous father and a famous uncle
is no small burden; the young Niebuhr, however, quietly and steadily
pursues his own path. His study of Schleiermacher is, in its implications,
revolutionary. For even now in the late afternoon of neo-orthodoxy hardly
any association is more damning than one with the founder of liberal
theology. Moreover, to be as interested as Professor Niebuhr is in the
religious affections flies in the face of current interest in secularity and
the "post-religious" age. A theologian of stature treads his own path.
Professor Niebuhr is already a theologian of stature.

The other two reviews concern the elder Niebuhr, uncle to Richard R.,
Reinhold Niebuhr. When I wrote the first of these, in the summer of 1959,
I had read only one other book by Niebuhr, Beyond Tragedy. *I felt in that*
book deep resonance with the tradition of Greek tragedy, in which I had
been sympathetically educated. Moreover, I felt in Niebuhr, ironically, a
kinship with the Aristotelian tradition which he has not always recognized:
an emphasis upon contingency, chance, the brokenness, and fragility of
things. I had never been seriously tempted by modern liberal optimism;
Professor Niebuhr was the modern non-Catholic writer with whom, along
with Albert Camus, I could most closely identify. On reading Essays in
Applied Christianity, *and working hard over a review which at that time*
represented a large step for me, I embarked upon an affair of esteem and
eager learning which has not ended. It will be plain that for me Reinhold
Niebuhr is one of the great Christian models in our time. And some read-
ers, perhaps, will smile at the signs in this essay of the determination of
a seminarian—as I was at that time—to commit himself to a course of
protestant Catholicism in the name of catholicity itself.

By the time I came to write the third and shortest review included here,
I had read every book that Reinhold Niebuhr had ever written and had
begun the first tentative drafts of a book of my own about his ethical
thought. Two months before, I had tried to visit Professor Niebuhr in
New York. It was during the subway strike, and the drive by taxi from
the airport was interminably slow. When I finally telephoned the Niebuhr
apartment, Mrs. Niebuhr was obliged to tell me—as she had warned me
might be the case when I called from Boston the evening before—that
Reinhold was too ill to receive me and was indeed going to the hospital.
I had never met him; I was saddened to have to miss him again. But other
reasons for sadness oppressed me that day, and perhaps it was as well that
the first time we were to meet was to be during the subsequent summer,
on a hot and gusty day, at his summer home in Stockbridge. His health
and spirits had taken a turn for the better. He was taller than I had ex-
pected; his eyes were bluer. The vigor and the power of the man had not
been belied by his books. It was a joy to see him. The bond forged by his
books between his life and mine did not need to be spoken of.

I. The Religion After the "Post-Religious" Age

"SCHLEIERMACHER, the Church Father of the nineteenth century," Karl Barth once exclaimed, approvingly, after having testified: "The first place in a history of theology of the most recent times belongs and always will belong to Schleiermacher, and he has no rival." But in the same essay, Barth went on to damn Schleiermacher to oblivion. To reverse this trend of twentieth-century Protestant orthodoxy—to call for a serious re-examination of the spirit, methods, and goals of Protestant theology—Richard R. Niebuhr has written an excellent introduction* to a forgotten theologian, against whom the Protestant theology of our century has, without always saying so, defined itself.

Catholics should be grateful. Although the current fashion among Catholics runs in an opposite direction, Schleiermacher is of all Protestant thinkers most concerned with issues the Catholic humanistic tradition takes seriously. If Catholics are close to Barth on the meaning of faith, as Hans Küng has shown, they are also close to Schleiermacher in his concern for the incarnation of faith in the tissue of secular culture and for the personal appropriation of faith in affective, ethical, and intellectual life.

What most masks the affinity of an important Catholic tradition with Schleiermacher, however, is a basic difference in method and conceptual articulation. Protestants influenced by Barth would no doubt be quick to see important similarities between Schleiermacher's concern about human culture and the "Christian humanism" of one part at least of the Thomistic tradition. But Schleiermacher—and Niebuhr—would hardly be happy to be linked in this way with scholasticism in any of its forms.

Nevertheless, the profound similarities are there. Schleiermacher, it is true, employs a dialectical, an acoustic, method: he is deeply concerned about the way in which the faith is personally heard, personally appropriated, and the preaching of the Word in the community consequently has singular significance in his view of the role of theology. What does not affect *us*, what is not relevant to our *experience* of the

---

* *Schleiermacher on Christ and Religion: A New Introduction* (New York, 1964).

Christ-life objectively given us, appears to him to be merely verbal and unreal. On this score, he rejects a great deal of the Christian intellectual tradition, including not only scholasticism (for which he has a special form of non comprehension) but also many classical theological achievements in Christology and trinitarian theory.

Thomas Aquinas, on the other hand, gives far wider rein to the drive to understand whatever can be understood in the data of faith, even if such understanding seems to be detached and disinterested and not, in the first instance, aimed at its effect upon the religious piety of the inquirer. His preferred method is formal, seeking an understanding of the data as they are related among themselves. Though he was as fully engaged in the cultural and intellectual struggles of Paris in his time as Schleiermacher was in Berlin in his, Thomas seldom allows his own personality to obtrude in his prose, seldom appeals to the involvement or commitment of his student. Yet for him, too, the primary reality was acoustic, and in comparison with it he saw that what he had written was as straw.

As Professor Niebuhr points out, against those (like Brunner) who have long interpreted Schleiermacher as a "subjectivist," Schleiermacher was convinced that the Christ-life was objective and operative yesterday, today, and forever. The task of theology, as Schleiermacher conceived it, is to articulate what is real about that life *today, for us, in this moment of history.* What Schleiermacher did not seem to see, and Aquinas did, is that such a project also involves, at least implicitly, a formal method too. For how can one be sure that the Christ whom one experiences today in all one's own particularity is the same Christ as that testified to by, for example, St. Paul, unless one also has available a transcultural and transtemporal principle of interpretation?

On the other hand, what Schleiermacher saw and many scholastics, particularly after Descartes, did not, is that an effective and truly Christian principle of interpretation must also be historical. For the people of God are on a pilgrimage, and historical contexts and historical cultural communities change; words take on new meanings; discoveries are made, which raise totally new questions; and so in countless ways the authentic Christian consciousness is, and must be, modified and developed and newly articulated. For this task, a Cartesian construction of *"raison"* is of little theological use.

In the context of German idealism and romanticism, Schleiermacher had to set out to construct an epistemology, or at least a theory of interpretation, that would serve the purpose he saw so clearly. His task was made simpler because he could neglect the problems of the formal level, which he despised.

At this stage in his development, the situation of Schleiermacher is very much like that of those Catholic theologians whose orientation is also, like his, pastoral. Their own resources are scriptural, liturgical, patristic, catechetical; like him they are in reaction against scholasticism, and like him they emphasize the centrality of the preaching of the Word. Against merely verbal speculations, Scheiermacher urged the importance of "feeling" and personal appropriation. Citing Newman, these Catholics distinguish between "notional assent" and "real assent," between doctrine conceptually and technically understood, and doctrine "made flesh" in one's own experience, imagination, affections, and actions.

Professor Niebuhr makes clear that the famous *Gefühl* or "feeling" on which the epistemology of Schleiermacher is based is not what would today be called emotive, but rather an abiding sense of personal identity, a radical sort of awareness of being oneself which is presupposed by all thinking and doing. The basic notion bears close comparison with the indirect reflexive knowledge of the self which Lonergan points out was basic for Aquinas. And the whole conception of "the feeling of absolute dependence" as the basis of religion deserves scrutiny, neither as a sense of contingency nor as the search for an emotional prop, but as what Aquinas refers to as the "natural desire to know God." For it is the self becoming reflectively aware of its own dynamism which is in question.

Professor Niebuhr does not, of course, draw such comparisons. He confines himself to making a solid, basically nonpolemical, well-focused study of Schleiermacher at four important moments of intellectual development. If there is a flaw in the study, it lies in (as it appears) Professor Niebuhr's own involvement in the German philosophical tradition; the asides he makes concerning other intellectual traditions, sometimes in his own and sometimes in Schleiermacher's name, reveal the color and the preoccupations of his own conceptual interests.

Robert B. Scharlemann in his masterful *Thomas Aquinas and John*

Gerhard (Yale University Press, 1964), has made a valuable contribution to the task of translation between the acoustic and the formal traditions. Professor Niebuhr's sympathetic and penetrating recovery of Schleiermacher now makes possible the "translation" of the rich and often moving insights of yet another figure crucial to ecumenical understanding into a vocabulary and a conceptual framework more accessible to most Catholics.

II. *Facing the Protestant Reality*

Reinhold Niebuhr comes through his *Essays in Applied Christianity* as a man of upright and pure spirit; his reverence for the Word of God and his sense for the majesty of God are apparent on every page. Further, Dr. Niebuhr's reflections on the Word of God and on the modern world, on the various problems of the Protestant churches, and on Catholicism, mark a step, designedly so or not, in the direction pointed by Pope John XXIII's convocation of an ecumenical council.

The theological-military wars of the sixteenth century are gone. The willful choosing of sides, the acrimony and, finally, the cultural isolation of both Protestant and Catholic, are gone or going. Centuries of cultural strife have complicated religious issues. Consciences are forced to intense effort in an attempt to hear the authentic voice of Christian revelation amid vast turmoil and the bias of history, in a life that is far too short and beset on all sides by grave concerns. "Willful heresy" no longer adequately describes the Protestant position; the Protestant is conscious of doing the best he can to conform himself to the Christian revelation as he has providentially received it. Cultural history has so confused emotional and intellectual issues that only the most foolhardy would enter another man's conscience and accuse him there. The call to unity does not, then, urge that Catholics water down or abandon their own convictions; but it does urge that they cherish non-Catholic Christians with the utmost respect, attention, and brotherly honor. It urges that Catholics clear the unused attic-spaces of their minds of the connotations of cultural and ecclesiastical treason, pride, and rebellion, which their ancestors once attached to Protestantism—connotations whose continued existence in their minds would be grave wrong. The present essays of Dr.

Niebuhr make an excellent start for the Catholic in coming to grips with Protestant reality, testing his own conceptions of it and of himself.

The first set of essays in the volume deals with the liturgy of American Protestantism. Dr. Niebuhr distinguishes the sects from the churches. The churches prefer stability and regulation; their vice is formalism. The sects react against formalism; they cherish vital encounter with God and the responsibility of the individual conscience; their vice lies in soon stereotyping their liberties. Ironically then, Dr. Niebuhr notes, the sects tend to become churches, as the Baptists and the Methodists seem to do; and the churches tend to grant ever more sectarian liberties. At any rate, for the Catholic reader, the problems of Protestant liturgy, viewed over-all, are curiously reminiscent of the problems of Catholic liturgy. Human nature seems to be such that it needs forms in order to give it historic continuity, but creative renewal of forms in order to give it vitality and authenticity. Pius XII's encyclical *Mediator Dei* wrestled with the objective and subjective elements of liturgy; the problem, after all, is insoluble by fiat. It is rooted in the free acts of each attendant at worship, and no legislation guarantees holy accomplishment. Dr. Niebuhr's sympathies are divided between the sects and the churches; both tendencies are necessary, and mutually fruitful.

The second set of essays deals with the current political-social impasse of the modern world, and the demand of many that the churches provide a "moral lead." Dr. Niebuhr's political-social thinking is marked by a discriminating realism. He knows secular liberalism thoroughly, and is one of its most telling critics. He does not reject, however, the providential achievements of secular liberalism: a sharpened historical-literary critical sense, the achievement of political and social freedoms made necessary against the decay, abuses, and injustices of a feudal and then *laissez-faire* civilization. Perhaps the three key convictions of Dr. Niebuhr's political-social thinking are these: (1) the transcendence of God, the Judge of history, moving all forces to his own ends, achieving good not only through the righteous but also through the unrighteous and the stiff-necked; (2) the ambiguity and incompleteness of all human virtue, so that every man can profoundly call himself sinner and so that no unchecked human power is ever really trustworthy; (3) the perplexity and opaqueness of history, whose key is held not by men but by God, and whose clarity will not be within history but at the end of history—so that naive complacency in interpretation, or naive hysteria in times of calamity, are truly naive and certainly not Christian.

The third series of essays, on Karl Barth, reveal in a little more detail Dr. Niebuhr's thinking on Christianity and political-social reality. He is able to criticize Barth searchingly for the ambiguities in the latter's sometimes wholly eschatalogical, at other times challengingly courageous and engaged attitude towards human culture and history. Theoretically, says Dr. Niebuhr, Barth has drawn up an impossible, too-narrow, position; he preaches a Christianity whose goal is wholly supra-temporal, above all human culture and all human crises. In practice, as for example in his brave leadership of anti-Nazi resistance, leadership that has won him stature as the great witness of continental Protestantism, Barth has had to depart from his own theory. Dr. Niebuhr sees Barth's war experience as a type of European Protestantism as a whole. The war taught Europe that eschatalogy and piety are not enough. The social indifference and quietism of the churches (and the hesitating compromises of Catholics) made Nazism possible. Individualistic piety was socially a colossal failure. In the rubble, the churches found release from individualism and pietism. Christian witness, they saw, obviously had much to accomplish in economic institutions, political positions, the whole social order. The statements of social-political policy of the World Council of Churches have since become remarkably acute—and incidentally, roughly parallel, as Dr. Niebuhr remarks, to *Rerum Novarum* and other Roman Catholic pronouncements, save chiefly for differences of emphasis on natural law.

In the fifth section of essays, Dr. Niebuhr deals with the Protestant ecumenical movement. His reflections on the ever deeper level of unity of spirit among Protestants are instructive. Church meets sect, and each is forced to find ways of understanding the values of the other. Europe's emphasis on eschatalogy meets the American "Social Gospel." The post-war European churches, now socially vigorous, are in turn sharp in their critique of American capitalism. The Asian Christians desire still stronger Christian opposition to capitalism and less intransigence towards communism; communism represents in their countries a great force against historic inertia and injustice, a much more effective force than "Christian imperialism" has been. Dr.

Niebuhr is sharply critical of the European-Asian tendency to condemn capitalism and communism in the same breath; he discriminates between the blind idealism of communism, which involves an inhuman, murderous self-righteousness, and the blind idealism of capitalism, also very self-righteousness but increasingly subject to checks and blocks on economic power. His reflections on love rather than on hope as the adequate note of a world-wide Christian consciousness are profound in their Scriptural, theological, and day-to-day awareness.

Finally, Dr. Niebuhr lays his finger on the irreducible element in efforts towards Christian unity: the pride and exclusivism of the churches on the one hand, and the suspicion and fear of exclusivism among the sects on the other. The churches each conceive unity as an embracing by others of *their* polity, hierarchy, dogma, liturgy. The sects conceive unity as fellowship in holiness and desire. World Protestantism, then, including churches like the Anglican and Greek Orthodox and sects like those of the Baptists and Quakers, represent a vast range of tendencies within Christian consciousness, and struggle under great new pressures, because of ecumenicism. As long as denominations were separate, many problems of human nature and Christian Revelation could be overlooked by each church or sect; each simply stuck to its own limited point of view. Laying point of view against point of view in world congresses is showing up the vastness of the Christian consciousness, and the paradoxes and seeming contradictions for human nature that it entails. Eschatalogy clashes with the need for present obedience, liturgy with individual need, theology with creative freedom, order with spontaneity of conscience, eternal truth with contingent growth, engagement in culture with detachment from it. A cast of mind able to handle all these opposing tendencies at once is the critical problem of modern Protestantism, as it is the perennial problem of all Christianity.

And it *is* the critical problem. The realities of human nature and of Christian Revelation do violence to positivism and to idealism, to cynicism and to utopianism. The great merit of the ecumenical movement is that, in laying point of view against point of view, it is beginning the search for an adequate philosophy. Dr. Niebuhr feels that the two points of view represented by the sects and the churches are irreducible. It seems to me that they are so in the same way that positivism and idealism are irreducible: each stresses a value on a different level from that of the other. Both treat the same problems, but on different planes, and hence never meet intellectually. A critical philosophy must be able to distinguish these separate planes and safeguard each. Failing this philosophy, the spirit of love that dominates the movement is so far preventing dissolution and keeping the confrontation creative.

Where does Catholicism fit into Dr. Niebuhr's thinking? The fourth group of essays, which I have saved until last, deals with "The Catholic Heresy." The Catholic reader is forced to wrestle with his own conception of himself if he takes Dr. Niebuhr's thought seriously. Dr. Niebuhr's remarks, kindly and motivated by a love of the Gospel, are penetrating and direct. It is difficult to express the accuracies of his analysis and yet capture the note he misses. He probes the present-day Catholic weaknesses with splendid delicacy; Catholic critics themselves do no better, and his probing gains by coming from without. He lays bare the exact point of difference between the Catholic and the Protestant, although I believe he misunderstands the Catholic side of this point. He catches the emphases of the Catholic imagination in our day which most belie the Gospel—the attitudes of Catholic spirituality and comment which the best Catholic critics, from the times of the Fathers on, have been forced to point out as weeds thriving with the wheat. He detects the habitual lapses in Catholic practice, ecclesiastical and lay, which most betray the Gospel (for which, after all, the Church prays sincerely in the *Confiteor* and *Nobis quoque peccatoribus* at every Mass); and beyond this, he points to the Catholic theological-speculative lacunae which do not yet express adequately the fullness of the Catholic faith (and to fill which, after all, the theological drive of *fides quaerens intellectum* always has more to do on earth.)

What, then, has Dr. Niebuhr to say about "The Catholic Heresy"? In the first place, Catholicism *is,* to Dr. Niebuhr, a heresy; to a Catholic, obviously, Catholicism is the one orthodoxy. What is it, then, in a sincere and searching thinker like Dr. Niebuhr that can make the Church seem sinful and a betrayal of the Gospel? "For the Catholic the Church is an unqualifiedly divine institution. It is Christ on earth and in history, as the pope is the vicar of Christ. Any attack upon the Church is therefore unqualifiedly evil because it is an attack upon

Christ. . . . We recognize in [this tendency] the very quintessence of sin, the tendency of man to make himself God."

Dr. Niebuhr's critique has a weak side. A Catholic would not use the word *unqualifiedly*. For the Catholic the Church is a divine institution, but on the pattern of the Incarnation itself. Christ was both human and divine, and on his human side "ugly and, as it were, despised . . . the most abject of men." (Is. 53.). In a somewhat similar way, and according to the parables of the fish and of the cockle, the Church is on her temporal side often ugly and all too little divine. The Catholic of our era, it is true, tends to avoid facing this side, for he has been under severe attack; the Catholic of our era concentrates on the divinity of the Church, of itself to be believed more than seen, and on those bright moments of history or of her habitual practice which seem to corroborate his belief. In the saints, this belief in the divinity of the Church takes on a marvelous luster, and a depth that can bear martyrdom with joy; in them it is, however, a far purer and less falsified belief than what the ordinary cleric or layman may hold on to.

Furthermore, on Dr. Niebuhr's part, there seems quite an ambiguity in his own use of *"unqualifiedly."* One would like to ask him in what sense does he believe the Church is divine? One would like to hear how far he would interpret such words as: "He who hears you, hears me"; "You in me and I in you"; "My church"; "Saul, Saul, why do you persecute *Me*?" "A holy people . . . without spot or wrinkle." It seems that some sort of theology of the Church must be worked out, to account for both a divine and a human element, not scandalized at the overgrowth of weeds and certain of a spotless part hidden in God. It seems necessary that a steady and objective element be considered, as well as a part rooted deeply in the personal conscience and individuality of each. It seems that in some way the *personal* piety of each must be *communal*: having a social consciousness; and in some way the social forms must not disfigure the personality of any of "the little ones."

The difficulty is that Dr. Niebuhr's analysis catches Catholics at the very moment when their own theology of the Church is undergoing a fuller formulation than hitherto. The last fifty years have seen great efforts to revitalize among Catholics the sense of the Mystical Body, of the interior sanctity and unity that is theirs not through their own merits but through their being lifted from the waters of Baptism into a community of grace. Under the leadership of *Mediator Dei, Mystici Corporis, Humani Generis,* and other papal directives; and under the spur of such works as Msgr. Journet's recent work on the Church (admittedly imperfect and stumbling in itself, but a pioneer and thorough working-out of a new emphasis), this renewed sense of the Church is only showing its first fruits. The liturgical and Scriptural revivals are restoring to ecclesiology the fullness of the notions of "the people of God," and of the historic dialogue, with its successes and recalcitrances, that occurs between the children and the Lord. In short, Dr. Niebuhr's critique is saying, in part, what Catholics are only too embarrassed about themselves. The Catholic idea of the Church is being purged of a too-narrow rationalism and logicism— seen too often, say, in a *De Ecclesia* tract whose orientation is almost wholly apologetic, and whose use of Scripture and of history is both unfeeling and intolerably security-minded.

Dr. Niebuhr's accusation is, then, extremely accurate insofar as Catholics in recent generations have rarely stressed the fallibility, the errors, the sins of the human organization of the Church, while stressing rather the stringently limited infallibility and the divinely promised guidance of the Holy Spirit—divinely promised precisely because it is not a matter of human success or impeccability or uncriticizable human judgment. And if we think of the matter critically, we may find that Catholics do err in blinking at the sins and ambiguities of their public representatives and temporal policies as if these, too, were divine. The reasons for this silence are usually "prudence" and dislike of causing scandal. No doubt these reasons, and the maintenance of a solid front, do have weight. Silence in face of wrongs or errors is itself, however, sometimes a scandal. Certainly a partly human organization is going to carry with it wrongs and errors; for the sake of witness to the divine part, love would sometimes demand speaking out.

Here, since Dr. Niebuhr's essays touch upon these sore points, it might be well to be particular, even at the risk of being controversial— for in the field of human policies there are many points of view. In 1922, the Vatican preferred Mussolini to Don Sturzo, and sent the latter off to asylum in another land, only to change her mind on his party in 1945. Similarly, the Vatican tried compromise with the Nazis at first, and only later jumped clearly to the other side. Only in the last years has the Vatican begun to disassociate itself from Franco's government in Spain. Is each of these changes of mind divine? Is each equally above human criticism? (However true it may be that the Holy Spirit works even through men's mistakes, as well as through their foresight.) Again: the need for liturgical reform and Scriptural revival, and renewal of Thomistic theology, seem to indicate that the past and present showing of the human Church has had its ups and downs. The common attitude and teaching of the theologians seem sometimes in need of criticism and revival; the common piety of the majority of the Church's people seems, by the very fact of liturgical and spiritual revival, in need of constant scrutiny and effort. In short, the scope of human criticism and human reform in the Church is very great, even though rarely defined and talked about expressly. The divinity of the Church is *not* unqualified; each Catholic, looking into his own conscience, knows this all too well. Dr. Niebuhr's inherited fear of uncriticized power leads him to suspect that an authoritarian Church cannot help being pharisaic; perhaps only humility and openness can dispel the charge.

Dr. Niebuhr mentions especially two areas in which the front presented by Catholics causes unnecessarily great friction among Protestants; on the Catholic side, adequate self-criticism would surely help ease part of the friction. The first of these areas is the unnecessary polemic exaggeration of the doctrine of "earning" heaven by merits. In Catholic dogma manuals, needless to say, the doctrine is properly defined to safeguard the doctrine of St. Paul, although it probably is true that the Scriptural and liturgical revivals will help future manuals be much more nuanced and relaxed than in their present apologetic form. But in cultural practice (in sermons and private expressions of piety), the typical understanding of the doctrine seems far too legal and hardly Pauline. There seems more often a *quid pro quo* attitude with God, and merit sounds more like a bank account than the other and primary half of Scriptural emphasis would warrant. Catholics, in short, seem to have the ordinary human capacity for defining an argument correctly, but then use images and express sentiments that prefer one side of the paradox to the exclusion of the other. If Dr. Niebuhr is merely chastising a prevalent Catholic failing on this matter of merit, he can cite Teresa of Avila on his side. I am not sure of Dr. Niebuhr's own position on merit and gratuity. I suspect that if he left aside Catholic exaggerations, and Catholics left aside Protestant exaggerations, both could find in the common-sense interpretation of the many-sided Scriptural statements on merit and gratuity a much more solid background for grasping both sides of the paradox involved.

The second area of friction is loose thinking on "natural law." Dr. Niebuhr is quite resistant to ideas of "natural law" drawn down to fine details and uttered in rigid rationalistic patterns. Thus far he is right. If a law is natural, it is learned by observation of facts and consequent and adequate interpretation of them. The natural law is methodically verifiable, or it is better not to speak of it as natural. Just so, in many areas it is unclear and debatable. Those who toss the phrase "natural law" around freely are frequently conjuring up images of a Newtonian universe, in which they find a complete casuistry as clear and simple as the workings of a computer. Many of the arguments used to expound this "natural law" are developed quite without an adequate philosophy; their formal statement may be flawless but their metaphysical content has been lost en route; they do not prove what they set out to prove. Thus, for example, some of the presentations of the "natural law" on birth control which argue from teleology are not adequate for any but an uncritical audience. Serious challenge soon sends their proponents scurrying for refuge in authority; they have been preaching under guise of "natural law" what they really never have themselves derived from nature. A more personalist, realist, and less rationalistic philosophy would have spared them such ignominy, and the notion of "natural law" such corruption.

Essays in Applied Christianity challenges Catholics to come to grips with an honest, dignified, even loving critique of Catholic failures. The essays do miss the note of breadth, freedom, nonconformity, reform, and renewal within the Roman Church. The essays interpret Catholicism by some frequent external characteristics; self-righteousness, over-organization, lack of humility and self-criticism, and political-social backwardness which may strike outsiders more quickly than Catholics themselves.

On the Protestant side, the essays highlight the tensions which are developing between the many various extremes within Protestantism: the human and Christian paradoxes which insist on accounting for both eternity and time, organization and freedom, divine grace and human culture, liturgy and personal sincerity. These are the very tensions that are both the trial and the spur of authentic Catholicism as well. *Essays in Applied Christianity* leads the Catholic to feel deeply the loss by the Protestant Revolution of so many noble and critical spirits from the bosom of the Church. It would be good to hear more from Dr. Niebuhr on Catholicism.

III. *The Most Influential Voice*

For some thirty years the single most influential Christian voice in the United States has been that of Reinhold Niebuhr. He has stood head and shoulders over other Christian moralists, Protestant and Catholic. The esteem in which he is held by political theorists and men of action is unparalleled. "He helped accomplish in a single generation," Arthur J. Schlesinger, Jr., has said of him, "a revolution in the basis of American political thought." "He is," writes George Kennan, "the father of us all." John F. Kennedy was in many ways his son.

Consequently, in an era in which hundreds of thousands of Christians are suddenly concerned about the "relevance" of the Church, or about the mission of Christians to the world, the life work of Reinhold Niebuhr is of the highest fruitfulness. Every Christian working in the world, every priest and sister concerned about the inner city, will find in Reinhold Niebuhr as in no other American Christian guidance for biblical and realistic action. *Moral Man and Immoral Society, The Irony of American History, The Self and the Dramas of History* and above all *The Nature and Destiny of Man* supply more nourishment of spirit than all those spiritual books, taken together which gave Therese of Lisieux—and countless other Christians— headaches.

Though he retired in 1960 from the Chair in Christian Ethics at Union Theological Seminary which he made famous, Niebuhr still maintains an effective witness concerning ethical matters of national importance—the sorrows of Vietnam have evoked his genius at cold analysis and deep compassion. Moreover, at seventy-four, under the pressure of recurrent strokes and the pain and suffering of their aftermath, Niebuhr has given us a further Christian witness, more private but no less significant: of dignity, courage, forbearance, gentleness and renewed creativity. Reinhold Niebuhr is a great human being, whose teaching is authenticated by his living.

In his latest book, (*Man's Nature and His Communities,* New York, 1965), completed with the aid of his brilliant wife, Professor Niebuhr casts his reflective eye over the basic principles and orientations of his life's work. He now sees human beings, not so much as atomic individuals, as social animals to whom community is as important as individuality. After a lifelong polemic, through which his own views emerged almost universally victorious in American thought, Niebuhr's present views have the equanimity of wisdom, the moderation of long experience. In no other book does Niebuhr write so clearly as the *phronimos,* the voice of sanity.

In the autobiographical introduction to this slender volume, Niebuhr recounts how his horizon has been broadened over the years. From a deeply Protestant—partly Lutheran, partly Social Gospel— starting point, Niebuhr has come to share in the horizon of secular pragmatism, the horizon of the Jewish prophetic tradition concerning social justice, the horizon of the Catholic sense of organic community and, perhaps (since so few Catholics share it), of that *phronesis* which Newman found so important in Aristotle, and which Latin Scholasticism has never comprehended. Through such fidelity and openness and integrity, Niebuhr blazed a trail which anyone who would teach ethics in our pluralistic, ecumenical world must, in his own fashion and with his own originality, traverse. We are, in our time, beginning to think not as Protestants, or Catholics, or Jews, or Humanists, but as human beings; Niebuhr has preceded us.

The goal of Niebuhr's ethical thinking was to develop a realism that would not be cynical and would not lead to acquiescence in the *status quo.* Whereas for many Latin Scholastics, realism and maturity mean mere resignation, for Niebuhr they have meant the pursuit of an impossible possibility, a goal of perfect love and its historical approximation in social justice which is never to be reached within history, but never to be renounced as irrelevant to the harsh realities of sin and egoism. Thus Niebuhr has with iron nerves navigated between the whirlpools of cynicism and the jagged rocks of too much vision. He has developed a flexible, pragmatic conception of a natural law with variable content.

In a variety of ways, Niebuhr has created an ethical position more nearly akin to the practical wisdom of Aristotle and the charity and sense of contingency in Aquinas than any modern Catholic thinker. No other book of his highlights such an interpretation of his thought as this one does. Moreover, in one especially valuable passage, Niebuhr indicates, against Professor Morgenthau, the resources of his own resistance to cynicism, and of his own realistic, limited, final trust. Thus Niebuhr's full spiral of dialectic is completed. A sense of community has balanced his earlier individualism; a sense of hope has balanced his earlier assault on liberalism; a tentative appreciation of dialectical intelligence has balanced his earlier polemic against "Reason." Even when he temporarily overlooks important matters, or for various reasons overemphasizes one point or another, Niebuhr has such a profound sense of balance, and such a self-corrective method, that his students are forearmed.

There is no better way for a young American Catholic to approach the historical tradition of Aristotle and Aquinas, and to avoid the grievous misunderstandings of Latin Scholasticism and a legalistic moral theology, than through the concrete, pragmatic, experimental, biblical wisdom of Reinhold Niebuhr. This most recent book will provide a wise, delightful, reflective overview for those who for years have been nourished by Niebuhr.

13

Paulus Tillich: In Memoriam

It has become fashionable among younger theologians to disdain the work of Paul Tillich, in favor of the "religionless Christianity" of Dietrich Bonhoeffer. But the irony is that, of the two thinkers, Tillich was much more concerned with art and technology, social revolution and secular culture, than Bonhoeffer (whose life, of course, was cut short). Bonhoeffer stands much closer to neo-orthodoxy than Tillich does; Bonhoeffer remained far closer to his German Lutheran heritage than Tillich did. Moreover, as a teacher I have noted that The Courage To Be *speaks more directly and more powerfully to the secular experience of most of the students, especially those who do not believe in God, than does* Letters and Papers from Prison. *The latter book sounds a little too much like sleight-of-hand: God is not needed, and yet one prays; a man who is "religionless" continually quotes from the Bible, and speaks in the accents of an extraordinary piety.*

An accurate assessment of the central difference between Tillich and Bonhoeffer, it seems, must include the fact that the two men belonged to different generations and had a different task. Both sprang from the tradition of German pietism. A reading of Tillich's autobiographical On The Boundary *(New York, 1966) and of the personal reminiscences collected in* I Knew Dietrich Bonhoeffer *(New York, 1967) indicates many similarities in the cultural and familial background of the two thinkers. Temperamentally, Tillich appears to have been much more romantic and*

232

even sentimental, Bonhoeffer much more disciplined and willful. Bonhoeffer appears to have prayed with an intensity and determination, whereas Tillich appears to have responded to God more freely and joyously in painting, music, natural beauty, and the clash of personalities. Of the two, Tillich gives every appearance of being by far the more "worldly" and, indeed, much better company for a night on the town.

Tillich's great intellectual opponents were, on the one hand, the forces which had precipitated the collapse of Western institutions and culture and, on the other hand, the complacency and shallow optimism of many academic positivists and pragmatists in the United States. The one reality which confronted Christians on both these fronts was the "crisis," social and personal, in which our civilization was then absorbed. In analyzing that crisis, Tillich hoped to expose the barbarism of fascism on the one hand and, on the other hand, the inadequate assumptions of the thick-skinned positivists and pragmatists. But by employing the category of "crisis" and by appealing to "boundary situations" like death, suffering, and exile, Tillich did appear to place himself in the position of trying to frighten or to embarrass men into admitting their need for God. It seems quite plain that that was not Tillich's intention; and it also seems that for many temperaments and many styles of mind Tillich succeeded masterfully in describing the human condition in his lifetime.

Bonhoeffer, by contrast, appears always to have been preoccupied with his own projects and to have been eager to make every moment count. Called to regard a flaming sunset, he looks up only for a moment and then returns to his book. No doubt, he is sensitive, companionable, and capable of appreciating beauty. But his main concern is much more serious: the attempt to halt a "drunken driver" who is guiding Germany to ruin. In this serious business, while spending almost two years in prison, Bonhoeffer is not dealing with shallow or complacent men, but with fellow prisoners whose ultimate concern is life, sanity, the rudiments of human community, and hope. Bonhoeffer is in the position of Langdon Gilkey during the latter's imprisonment under the Japanese, as recounted in Shantung Compound *(New York, 1966). The young Gilkey was at that time a nonbeliever, but he was later to find Tillich's analysis of the secular situation in such conditions utterly compelling. Perhaps the chief difference, in this light, is that Tillich and Gilkey had a fundamental conviction about the goodness, freedom, and joy of life, and that they were led to see the "transcendent in the midst of things" by their encounter with ultimate seriousness. By contrast, Bonhoeffer was a person so consumed with ultimate seriousness that he found "the transcendent in the midst of things" by beginning to notice, in a sense for the first time, the simple joys of secular living. A sign of human courage, a letter from a friend, a gift of writing paper from a jailer, the amiable stoicism of prisoners who did not believe in God—these simple graces of earthly life became for Bonhoeffer epiphanies of the presence of the unseen and "unneeded" God. The Bonhoeffer who is in " a boundary situation," and who so takes for granted the strength of his "ultimate concern" that he never needs to mention it, discovers in daily life joys that Tillich and Gilkey never doubted.*

In brief, it seems to me that historians of a future generation will find in Tillich and Bonhoeffer complementary personalities. I cannot mask the fact that Tillich (whom I several times met) awakens in me sentiments of warm affection, while Bonhoeffer (whom I know only through his writing and the testimony of his friends) awakens in me only admiration.

> I want to know you, Unknown One,
> You who are reaching deep into my soul
> And ravaging my life, a savage gale.
> You inconceivable yet related one!
> I want to know you —even serve.
> —Friedrich Nietzsche

PAUL TILLICH (1886–1965) was a human being of immense wisdom. It is, then, according to script that as he walked toward death he should have heard a rumbling chorus of criticism. On the theological front, Bishop Stephen Neill and Kenneth Hamilton were asking, and answering to Tillich's disadvantage: "Is this great construction that Tillich has given gospel or is it not? . . . Is this a gospel of redemption, or when all is said and done a Gnosis, a doctrine of deliverance through illumination?" [1] On the philosophical front, Professor Paul Edwards of Columbia described once more, in the tone of voice which Anglo-American professional philosophers regularly used when discussing him, "Professor Tillich's Confusions." [2] At the end, harsh words against him were added by younger theologians whose mentor he had been.[3] Will Tillich's reputation decline or grow? In what terms should his labors be assessed?

The labors were arduous. Professor James Luther Adams [4] lists some twelve German titles between 1910 and 1933 when Tillich, at the age of forty-seven, finally escaped Hitler by coming to America. After having learned a new language and begun a new way of thinking,[5] Tillich added more than a dozen new titles, including the three volumes of his *Systematic Theology* (1951, 1957, 1963), and scores of articles. Tillich devoured human life—he experienced, questioned, read, visited, conversed, with an appetite unequaled among twentieth-century philosophers and theologians. Yet he seldom missed a scheduled class; and he wrote incessantly.

Tillich loved to eat well and drink well. He loved new inventions, and new problems in all fields of human activity. He loved to walk— to walk and to talk—and the sight of sunlight making spring leaves translucent would make him halt breathless at their beauty. Women, encountering him, sensed his power and vitality and energy; and Tillich himself reacted deeply to women. He loved beauty, he loved joy, he loved creativity; he was also vulnerable and sensitive. A theologian who studied under him and lived with Tillich for many years chose one word to apply to him: "vitality." Audiences found him charismatic; wherever he taught in later years, the largest auditoriums or lecture halls were needed. Students who took part in a discussion with him even once, or took a class from him, often came alive in a new way. It was common to hear from students in his last years at Harvard (even while one observed the ways he was slighted by professionals), that Tillich stood as one of the two most creative teachers they had encountered in their Harvard careers. Aristotle long ago pointed out that the man of wisdom cannot render his wisdom in words; it can be communicated only in subtle ways, through presence and emulation and imitation. Paul Tillich taught by being what he was, more than by saying or by writing.

Still, Tillich the speculative thinker will be judged in the future, not by the memories of those whose lives he enriched, though they are many, but by what he said in print. The vast public record is heaped naked now and vulnerable; the flame of time and criticism must be applied, so that in the burning we may learn how much was tinder, how much substance.

Tillich—to change the figure—wished his work to connect many presently separated shores. He was fond of saying that he stood "on the boundary"—on many boundaries [6]—but particularly on the boundary between theology and philosophy. Yet the one boundary that Tillich bridged most significantly was that between the grand German idealist tradition of the nineteenth century and the alienation and anxiety of twentieth-century experience. In a peculiarly haunting, improbable fusion, it was Tillich's genius to wed his beloved Schelling to Kierkegaard; or again, to rescue the damsel "being" from the jaws of oblivion, and make her handmaiden to existential decision and self-creation; he brought cosmic being from "out there" into the human heart.

It is for this reason that *The Courage To Be,* his Terry Lectures at Yale in 1950,[7] may be his most representative, enduring masterpiece. Tillich was the major, perhaps the only, existentialist to thrive in the new world of America, where the crises of life were not war, pogroms, bloodshed, treason, marching boots, but newspaper strikes, power failures, premature ejaculations, and nervous, clock-driven, neurotic personal relationships. It is unlikely that the dialogue between theology-philosophy and existential psychoanalysis to which Tillich contributed will soon lose its relevance. The souls of Americans are irretrievably fashioned by the past in whose traditions Tillich was thoroughly studied.

His major essays on "The Protestant Principle," [8] on "Kairos," [9] on Christianity and the world religions,[10] and other topics have so influenced theological discourse that ripples from their entry will not soon be lost to sight. Many persons, otherwise not theologically oriented, find his collections of sermons, *The Shaking of the Foundations* (1948) and *The New Being* (1955),[11] worth regular, leisurely, reflective reading. His brief *Dynamics of Faith* (1957)[12] will stand as a classic analysis of the complexity of faith in God, an analysis which does not slight the motive, nor volitional, nor intellectual components of such faith, and which captures the comprehensiveness and driving power of so centered an act.

Consequently, Tillich will stand before historians as a figure to be tangled with, whether or not his own systematic ambitions manifest, as he hoped, creative power. However, there is no doubt that Tillich himself rested his hopes upon the three volumes of his *Systematic*

Theology; it is as a systematic thinker that he invited the judgment of posterity. In accepting this further dare, Tillich draws down upon himself a different standard of criticism. As a versatile, stimulating, ranging mind, he was long ago assured of having, in the retrospective glance of history, few peers upon the American academic scene. But as a clear, systematic, compelling thinker, his claims rightly encounter stubborn resistance; he must prove himself.

In a single essay, it is impossible to take up all the strands of the *Systematic Theology.* Moreover, since Tillich's overriding claim was that he stood "on the boundary," it does not seem correct to center this essay upon the theological content of his work, for such a discussion would mainly be of interest to Christians. The fulcrum point at which Tillich hoped to converse with others besides Christians was his doctrine of God; and his doctrine of God is so basic to the *Systematic Theology* that, if it falls, the seamless garment disintegrates. Unless Tillich is correct about God, he is not (however many good things he has to say) fully correct about Christ, about human society, or about the personal self. For Tillich God is "the answer to the question implied in being"; he is known when man is "in the state of ultimate concern." [13] By Tillich's own testimony, if that concern is wrongly placed philosophy and theology become destructive. The test of Tillich's profoundest claim is his *Systematic Theology;* the test of his *Systematic Theology,* not the only test but for our purposes the fundamental test, is his doctrine of God.

I. *Tillich and Empiricism*

A generation ago, it was fashionable for philosophers of a certain kind not only to become atheists but also to expand considerable energy refuting the arguments of theists. The new generation of philosophers is either a little less certain of its atheism, or a little embarrassed by Promethean postures; in general, younger men are indifferent to the issue or inclined to a very marked modesty regarding pronouncements one way or the other. In this atmosphere, it is possible to read Tillich with a considerable neutrality; one does not from the outset insist that Tillich speak with the accents of A. J. Ayer; one concedes that such a subject matter may need to be approached in many diverse, odd, subtle ways. Nevertheless, the best way to understand Tillich may be by the route of his older antagonists; the aforementioned essay by Professor Paul Edwards, despite its echoes from a more distant time, was published in the year of Tillich's death and will serve our purpose admirably.

Professor Edwards uses the following predicates interchangeably: "meaningless," "unintelligible," "devoid of cognitive content," "failing to make an assertion," "saying nothing at all," and "lacking referential meaning." He writes: ". . . I would be willing to argue that Tillich's theology is all of the things mentioned—meaningless, unintelligible, and all the rest." [14] (By "theology," Edwards seems to mean Tillich's philosophical notion of God rather than his interpretation of Christ, Holy Spirit, Trinity, and other Christian data.) Edwards concedes that logical positivism was immodest in its reach: "There can be no doubt that metaphysical systems are much more complex than some of the enemies of metaphysics believed—frequently they have all kinds of interesting and curious 'links' to experience and they are only on the rarest occasions purely 'transcendent.' " [15] Just at this point, Edwards overlooks the choice he is about to make. He could have followed this lead and, recognizing that Tillich's tradition is not his own, nevertheless have tried fresh ways to get at what Tillich was trying to say. Instead Edwards decides, despite hesitations, to make Tillich's sentences meet the criteria for meaningfulness set forth by logical positivists. It is this choice which characterizes Edwards' work as of an older generation. Tillich himself tells how he once asked a logical positivist to listen to him lecture and stick up a finger every time he heard something he could not understand; the logical positivist replied that he would have to hold his finger up from beginning to end.[16] It will prove illuminating to follow Edwards' attempts, with his limited equipment, to understand Tillich.

No doubt, Tillich's greatest failure in America was his refusal to take logical positivism, pragmatic naturalism, and Anglo-American empiricism with primary seriousness.[17] Tillich was content to co-exist; he was conscious of countless criticisms, assaults, and even insults, and near the end, at least, he had little stomach for the battle. Perhaps he was a victim of the general neglect which Christian theologians in the United States afforded Anglo-American philosophy. Although Royce, Peirce, James, and Dewey are—with their emphasis upon community, personal development, concrete history, and knowing as a mode of acting—in all of philosophical history among the philosophers most congenial to Christian theology, American theologians seemed to prefer German and Latin philosophical models. Even Reinhold Niebuhr spent years attacking Dewey, when he might have welcomed him as an ally in the beginning as, tacitly, he did at the end; certainly, pragmatism was to mean more to Niebuhr than the German idealism which so strongly nourished and still, unrecognized, nourishes Protestant theology.

Still, the fault was not only Tillich's; the parochialism was not one-sided. Professor Edwards, for example, accepts the framework of Hume's *Dialogues Concerning Natural Religion* without criticism.[18] Hume's Demea posed the problem in terms of a God whose attributes are "perfect, but incomprehensible." If God is perfect, man cannot know him; if man knows him, he is limited by man's mind and imperfect. Cleanthes calls thinkers like Demea "atheists without knowing it." Edwards then interprets Tillich as a Demea [19]—and it is not difficult to foretell how, in this framework, the analysis will go; a machine could perform it. Hume, and with him Edwards, imagines a God who is part of the world of our experience, among the rocks and trees and people and events of our lives. Consequently, they wish to be able to talk about him in language borrowed, as all language is, from this concrete world of experience; and they wish this language to lie still, to be tame, to be used literally and simply. If God cannot be spoken of in such a language, then of course one is not really speaking of anything at all.

But the theist who accepts the challenge of verbalizing his belief in God takes up a different point of view than Hume and Edwards: He recognizes from the outset that the Humean framework is too narrow. He knows from the beginning that the God in whom he believes is not an object among objects, nor a person among human persons. He knows, moreover, that there is no adequate name for God. It is impossible to speak of God adequately in human language. Consequently, all verbalizing of belief in God is, according to the ordinary rules of language, self-defeating. On his chosen ground, Hume has won the debate before it starts; but the main action lies elsewhere. The theist (if he knows what he is doing) is attempting to change the rules of ordinary language in systematic ways, so that what he is doing is plain to those who take up a fruitful framework from the beginning. In the most delicate of inquiries one expects initiative, self-criticism, and experimentation on the part of those who try to learn. If one method of proceeding fails, the teacher hopes the student will try a new framework for a moment. The difficulty with crying "unintelligible" is that one may be characterizing one's own intelligence or good will.

Tillich's way of pointing to the new, fruitful framework, it must be admitted, is misleading. To have chosen the suspect language of "being-itself" was a red flag to bulls in Tillich's china shop. But to have based his new framework for discussing the issue upon "metaphorical or symbolic" language was to make careful practitioners of linguistic analysis wince with pain. Tillich allows us to make one, and only one, statement "directly and properly" in our attempt to give utterance to what we mean by God. That statement makes plain that God is not a being among other beings, an object among objects, a person among persons. It is the statement that "God is being-itself." Edwards quotes one from among many relevant passages:

God as being-itself is the ground of the ontological structure of being without being subject to this structure himself. He *is* the structure; that is, he has the power of determining the structure of everything that has being. . . . If anything beyond this bare assertion is said about God, it no longer is a direct and proper statement.[20]

Such language is not likely to make the ordinary American Protestant utter a prayer; more likely, it will sound heretical to him, or scholastic, or—Edwards' word—meaningless. Still, the ordinary man does not think $a = \triangle v/t$ when he encounters instances of acceleration. One must allow a thinker his own language system; and to understand it, one must enter into it. That American philosophers should expend the effort required to master the language of "being" is too much to expect; to the extent that communication was important to Tillich, his choice of language failed.

Nevertheless, Tillich's point here—if the critic understands and accepts the rules of the language of "being"—is successful. The language by which we differentiate one object from another, one person from another, cannot properly and directly be used of God. Tillich is not a pantheist;[21] but he is saying that God is *more like* the structure of all things, or the force that in the green grass drives all things, than he is like any particular thing of our experience. God is not an object *within* reality, but "the ground of reality" or "the matrix of reality." [22] An exact notion of God, then, cannot be reached by the operations, or according to the methods, by which we reach other notions. God is not the object of our various operations of experiencing, nor can he be pointed to ostensively, nor can he be conceived of as a scientific hypothesis. Nor do we need God in those ordinary experiences which we can tend to ourselves. Nor, finally, do we need God to fill the "gaps" either in our science or in our ordinary experience.

If God were to be reached in any of these ways, Tillich's lifelong argument continued, such a God would be a function of man, an idol. We must look at the question the other way around. God does not make a difference *within* the universe of science or *within* the universe of ordinary experience; the fact that God is does not interrupt the probabilities and/or necessities of scientific laws, nor obtrude into our ordinary conscious experience. *Within* the world of our experience the actuality of being-itself is, as Edwards put it, "compatible with anything whatever." [23] Such a concession, Edwards argues, shows that the term "God" fails to have a referent; but to Tillich it shows that God is not an object in our experience but transcendent. The question that has arrested Tillich's attention, but not that of Edwards, is why anything should exist at all. The word "being-itself" does not refer to a power that is discovered by its interventions *within* the universe known to science or *within* the universe known to ordinary experience. It refers, rather, to a power [24] that has determined that the universes of science and ordinary experience, whatever their successive states of affairs, should *be* rather than *not be*. "Why should anything exist at all?" Wittgenstein sometimes felt obliged to ask.[25] Pitching his tent on the spot where that question perennially arises, Tillich answers: Because the ultimate point to which our minds can penetrate is that being-itself prevails; there could have been nothing at all, but there are things.

There are atheists and agnostics who search for God but do not find him. Tillich, in archaic language, tells them that God is not to be found *among* things; they are looking with the wrong focus. The fruitful focus is one that does not look for a God who is needed to manipulate the states of affairs within the world, but one who is present in any and all states of affairs, present wherever things, events, and per-

sons are, present by the fact that things are rather than by the characteristics that things have.

How is such a God found? If a man does not wonder why anything
exists at all, philosophical inquiry about God cannot in his case be
fruitful. Wonder is the beginning of adoration. For wonder about the
actuality of things—wonder at the sharp, clean taste of being alive,
and conscious, and related to real things, persons, and events—is the
only path whereby a God worthy of man's adoration can be conceived.
If God alters states of affairs, interferes, manipulates, makes things go,
then God is either a function of the world, inseparable from it, or a
meddler who may well be man's enemy. And, of course, scientific inquiry knows nothing of such a God; there is no such God. But if God
is conceived as present in all things, not by giving them their character
and motions, but by making them to be, his transcendence is preserved. All things depend upon him; but they have their own distinctive character, laws, and contingent relationships, which human
investigation can discern independently of theology. Tillich is implicitly defending the autonomy of science, as well as the dependence
in being of men upon God.

The power grasping us in the state of faith is not a being beside others,
not even the highest; it is not an object among objects, not even the
greatest; but it is a quality of all beings and objects, the quality of pointing beyond themselves and their finite existence to the infinite, inexhaustible, and unapproachable depth of their being and meaning.[26]

But perhaps man cannot know anything about "the structure of being,"
the "depth" of being.

It may be said that there is no approach for man to the structure and
meaning of being, that what being is, is revealed to us in the manifold-
ness of beings and in the world in which they all are united and interrelated to one another. It could be said: Look at minerals and flowers,
look at animals and men, look at history and the arts, and you will learn
what being is, but do not ask for being itself above all of them. To this
we must answer: You cannot prohibit man from asking the most human
question; no dictator can do so, even if he appears in the gown of humble
positivism or modest empiricism. Man is more than an apparatus for
registering so-called "facts" and their interdependence. He wants to *know*,

to know about himself as thrown into being, to know about the powers and structures controlling this being in himself and in his world. He wants to know the meaning of being because he is man and not only an epistemological subject. Therefore he transcends and always must transcend the "No trespassing" signs cautiously built by skepticism and dogmatically guarded by pragmatism. The meaning of being is his basic concern, it is the really human and philosophical question.[27]

It is from this vantage point that Tillich's famous definition of God as the name for our *ultimate* concern becomes relevant. Tillich chose the word "concern" because he wished to emphasize that the psychic drive in question is not merely rationalistic; it is intelligent, passionate, and willed: it is a "centered act" of the entire human personality.[28] But the word "concern" is misleading. Every man is concerned, and in some sense every man has an ultimate concern: in a vulgar phrase, every man can be bought at some price. As every novelist knows, a man's identity is clarified by his choices between conflicting concerns. Tillich argues, in effect, that an ultimate concern can be either creative or destructive. And Tillich has in the back of his mind a psychology and an anthropology: honesty, courage, compassion are creative; hatred, cowardice, hypocrisy are destructive. Given these criteria, a man can test his own ultimate concern. When the chips are down, what identity do his choices reveal? A man who is faithful to understanding, brave, compassionate, manifests the power of creativity— the power of being. But why should a man be honest, courageous, compassionate? Why should a man prefer to create rather than to destroy? Even an atheist or an agnostic must choose. Tillich would argue that atheists who are not nihilists and who opt for creativity are despite themselves testifying to their faith in the pre-eminence of being-itself; they side with being against destruction.

Thus Tillich reverses the claim of Hume's Cleanthes, who calls believers like Tillich "atheists despite themselves." Tillich calls atheists like Hume theists despite themselves. Atheists and theists dislike being mistaken for one another, but enjoy converting one another by definition. Perhaps the point is that the tyranny of names too easily overcomes even careful men. What differences does it make what we are called, so long as we support with all our power values like courage, compassion, and fidelity to understanding? Tillich finds in these inescapable values signs of a "depth" in human life; atheists and agnostics will see in them no such "depth." It is more important to practice such values than to interpret such values in the same way.

The argument between theist and nontheist, then, in America at least (where the temptation of nihilism has seldom been strong, and naturalism is benign), is a question of how to interpret the significance of the fact that human beings live by values like honesty, courage, and compassion. The issue is not whether men create these values for themselves and by themselves; for if this is the case, the fact that men can create such values indicates that human destiny is not as absurd as it sometimes appears. Theists are led by the power of such values to think that belief in being-itself (or the reality pointed to by some such name) is plausible, even compelling. Nontheists hesitate both to conceive of such a reality and to commit themselves to such an inference. The evidence—the existence of human values of certain kinds—is the same for both theists and nontheists.

What, then, is the main argument of the nontheist against Tillich? For Edwards, it is that Tillich's symbols and metaphors about being-itself are not "reducible." A symbol is "reducible" when "the truth-claims made by the sentence in which it occurs can be reproduced by one or more sentences all of whose components are used in literal senses." [29] "To say that a sentence is irreducible is to say in effect that no new referent can be supplied." [30] Edwards next goes on to show that Tillich's being-itself, like Locke's material substratum, "is, even in principle, inaccessible to anybody's observations." [31] Edwards then shows how even the one proper, direct statement about God which Tillich allows, that God is being-itself or the ground of being, is metaphorical. Never does Tillich offer us a literal sentence to which we might "reduce" the metaphors. His language is, even in principle, irreducible in Edwards' sense. For Edwards, Tillich's language therefore lacks cognitive content. But at this point, Edwards shows traces of docility. He notes that Tillich sometimes allows us to speak of God as "majestic," as "father," as "healer," and the like. He then goes on to suggest that, given Tillich's presuppositions, "God may no less appropriately be said to be a soprano, a slave, a street-cleaner, a daughter, or even a fascist and a hater than a father and a king." [32] This is a perceptive observation; for insofar as anything is, it participates in being-itself and stirs the contemplative mind. God, Edwards ought now to realize, is everywhere. "If God is the creative ground of everything that has being, everything insofar as it is must express something knowable about God." [33]

Edwards dislikes intensely the "bombastic descriptions of empirical facts" [34] to which existentialists like Tillich are prone. If Freud died in 1939, he died, he did not "migrate from being to nonbeing." If selfishness and other unadmirable motives are involved in even the best human actions, it does not follow that "Even in what he considers his best deed nonbeing is present and prevents it from being perfect. . . ." The literal, empirical mind wars with the symbolical, metaphysical mind; in our culture there is no question who will win.

But let us push the literal, empirical mind a bit. Edwards makes some effort to understand Tillich; he doggedly chases down references through two books. Let us assume that the inquiry was open, and could have gone in more than one direction, and reached other than one predetermined verdict. Edwards' drive to understand, in that case, is more fundamental than his decisions about criteria of relevance and evidence, his conceptual operations, and even his present range of information. The drive to understand is not limited by the given information; it may demand more. It is not restricted to the chosen conceptual operations; confronted with difficulties or chastened by criticism, it may try alternative operations before reaching a conclusion. It is not limited *a priori* to any one set of criteria of relevance and evidence; for arguments about presuppositions, point of view, and the weight to be assigned various factors are not only possible but common. The drive to understand, then, the relentless question-asking drive in man, is one of the elements in Edwards' actual argument. But Edwards nowhere draws attention to this drive. He is concerned with objects for experience, objects for conceptual operation.

Tillich, on the other hand, was concerned with objects of ultimate *concern,* and specifically with an object which is the appropriate response to the unrestricted human capacity for asking questions. He calls this response "being-itself," which he explicitly thinks of as an answer to a question. Being-itself is experienced by anticipation as (let us say) "everything that will be known when our drive to understand is wholly satisfied." Thus being-itself is known through reflection upon our drive to raise questions. We do not know being-itself directly, for we have not asked all possible questions, nor come to that unified vision in which all possible questions are related in one intelligible whole. But in proportion as we are aware of our own unlimited capacity for raising questions, we have a springboard for constructing, indirectly and as it were merely formally and without content, an anticipation of that full intelligence in whose light our partial inquiries cohere. Every act of inquiry presupposes the intelligibility of the relationship between knower and known, and between the things known. Tillich speaks the language of being rather than the language of knowing. But a careful reading shows that every sentence of his in which "being" occurs can be translated into a sentence employing a correlative act of knowing.[35]

In this sense, Tillich's "symbols" are all reducible. But the human experiences to which they are reducible are not sense experiences, nor are they concepts derived from scientific or ordinary commerce with things. They are the experiences of the inquiring subject, especially the experience of insight (Tillich leans to the Platonic side of the metaphysical tradition, and tends to rely heavily upon intuition); [36] and the experience of deciding upon which criteria of relevance and evidence to use in reaching reasonable judgments of fact. If the human spirit may be defined operationally as inquiry, these are the operations of spirit. It is these operations which suggest that man is different from other things in the world in which he lives, like trees and cats; that man is an end and not a means; that he does not live by bread alone; that the goods which constitute the profoundest levels of human community are truth and honesty and communication; and that the universe in which men live is not, finally, silent, mechanical, dead, but penetrated through and through with intelligence to which man's drive to understand is a progressive response.

Every being participates in the structure of being, but man alone is immediately aware of this structure. . . . Man occupies a pre-eminent position in ontology, not as an outstanding object among other objects, but as that being who asks the ontological question and in whose self-awareness the ontological answer can be found. . . . The point is that man is aware of the structures which make cognition possible. He lives in them and acts through them. They are immediately present to him. They are he himself. . . . The truth of all ontological concepts is their power of expressing that which makes the subject-object structure possible. They constitute this structure; they are not controlled by it.[37]

The prosaic, literal, empirical temper is correct so far as it goes. From Tillich's point of view, however, it fails to reflect sufficiently on those presuppositions by which it escapes nihilism and engenders, in America at any rate, so much hope in historical advancement. The will to act has beliefs implicit in it; Tillich argues that such beliefs include belief in the prevenience of being-itself over the absurd and the destructive. It is perhaps intellectual imperialism for him to argue that all humanism is implicitly theonomous; but it is easy to see why, from his point of view, that conviction is plausible. And until atheistic humanists tell us why they are not nihilistic, and spell out the implications of their liberalism in contrast to alternative and more pathetic conceptions of history, Tillich's case will continue to goad the uneasy conscience of many philosophers.

II. *Where Does Tillich Begin?*

Every resolution of the problem of theism vs. nontheism into a standoff of opposite points of view is unsatisfactory. We cannot rest content in the belief that there are two different kinds of men, such that for some, arbitrarily, "God" says something and for others not. Doubtlessly, the personal history in which each man has learned the use of the word "God" is here of critical importance. Sartre tells us in *The Words* how his childhood God was an all-seeing eye, an implacable bureaucratic ticket-collector at the end of the line.[38] How many are the men in our century whose experience of "God" led to bitter death at the hands of soldiers blessed by "God's" ministers? How many have heard the word "God" from those who speak, as Bernanos wrote, with lips like a hen's ass, mouthing the platitudes by which they re-enforce their bigotry, insecurity, and passion for violence? In the twentieth century, the chasteness of pragmatism and empiricism comes as welcome relief after the flatulence of religious speech. Few neutral observers are convinced that all ministers of God believe what they say.

"My whole theological work," Tillich said in 1964, "has been directed to the interpretation of religious symbols in such a way that the secular man—and we are all secular—can understand and be moved by them." [39] It seems certain, however, that although Tillich spoke clearly enough for a great many believers, he never broke down the difficulties which prevent nonbelievers from understanding him. The reason seems to be that in standing "on the boundary" Tillich in fact stood within the Christian community and barely placed one foot outwards; the questions he raised, and the symbols he employed, derived their meaningfulness from their source "within the theological circle." The inherent power in the Judaeo-Christian tradition, which has shaped all of us, assured that an original mind like Tillich's could stir chords which nearly everyone could at least take seriously. But at the crucial points, Tillich's argument failed.

To a nontheist, Tillich's being-itself appeared to be just as much an illusion as any other name for God. To say that a man has a genuine ultimate concern seems to say nothing whatever about an added reality like being-itself, but only about the way a man interprets his own identity; there may be no being-itself, no God, for him to relate to, except in his propensity for personification and projection. Tillich tried to meet this objection; but in so doing he was caught in the dilemma Freud pointed out in *The Future of an Illusion:* if the critical believer removes consolation and anthropomorphic images from his understanding of God, then he loses touch with the community of faith in which most ordinary people stand; and if he does not purify his understanding, the advance of science will do so for him.[40]

Tillich's view was that an historical community of faith supplies concrete symbols which "point to" God. These symbols are not adequate for all times or all purposes, but men cannot do without them; if churches do not supply them, political parties or other organs will. There is a tension between man's need for concrete symbols and his need for abstract, critical thinking.[41] The first involves his whole active personality; the second preserves him from understanding the concrete symbols to be more than "pointers." Tillich thought that it was necessary both to stand within a concrete historical community of faith and to deny through critical reflection that any concrete symbol is *identical* with genuine ultimate concern. The name "being-itself" warned that God is not a being like other things, and cannot be named like other things.

Tillich began, then, as one who already believed in God, in the Christian God, in the God of the Protestant tradition. He accepted

Gustave Weigel's observation that he had an "immediate awareness" of God, so strong that argument was neither necessary nor possible.[42] Thus Tillich interpreted the ontological argument, not as an argument, but as the most fundamental *expression* of this awareness.[43] The other traditional arguments, he thought, merely pointed to this same basic expression.[44] Tillich wrote as a man who has already experienced God in his conscious awareness; he urged others not to look for God as a reality to be added to other realities already known, but as one who was already present in their experience. Tillich viewed the matter as if every man is already in a conversation with God, in the very cognitive processes by which he inquires about anything at all. The fact that men do inquire shocked Tillich; he marveled at human inquiry. He claimed that empiricists give too shallow an account of inquiry. He himself did not so much point to new evidence, as ask us to look at the available evidence in a new way.

Tillich constantly warned his readers that no way can be found to God apart from the experience of a relationship already begun. "Man cannot speak of the gods in detachment. The moment he tries to do so, he has lost the gods and established just one more object within the world of objects. Man can speak of the gods only on the basis of his relation to them." [45] Moreover, men in the past have tried to understand this relationship with God: ". . . the idea of God has a history. . . . In order to understand the idea of God, the theologian must look into its history." [46] Increasingly in later years, Tillich looked to all historical religions for hints and analogues by which to discern the elements and the meaning of the experience of God which he had.[47]

It is the *experience* of ultimate concern which, for Tillich, is basic. He writes of "the openness of being-itself, which is given in the basic religious *experience*." [48] And again: "although essence and existence are philosophical terms, the *experience* and the vision behind them precede philosophy." [45] "God" is not an answer to a question about the existence of some *X* or other; "God" is the answer to the question which arises from the human awareness of finitude.[50] One must wonder why there is anything at all. One must recognize the contingency of the self and of all things besides. For Tillich, this intuition came rushing upon him in the contrast between nonbeing and being: the possibility that there might be nothing at all, and the apparently contingent fact that there are things. It does not matter whether things "began" at a point in time or "always were." It is not temporal origin which is in question, but the power to be at all.

When Tillich looked at the world, it was not only "empirical reality" [51] which preoccupied him—the discrimination between thing and thing, and the systematic classification of things. It was also a "dimension of depth." [52] Persons, things, and events evoked in Tillich a sense of mystery and reverence; more appeared to him to be happening in human life than meets the empiricist's eye. He wished with unrelenting hunger to know all that he could know. He recognized that he was finite, and yet in the very formulation of his awareness of his finitude he recognized by anticipation an infinite understanding of all that is to be understood. He argued that one did not "project" the infinite understanding. Rather, it was the screen, or background, or backdrop [53] of all finite acts of understanding; it was the matrix or ground which makes the sustained enterprise of understanding coherent and hopeful. Tillich recognized that he himself was in transition from limited, partial understanding toward fuller, complete understanding. Complete, full understanding was in some way part of his own being; he "participated" [54] in it; he was drawn by it and was ever on the move toward it. Yet he himself was not and could not be infinite. ("And a good thing too!" Professor John Herman Randall, Jr., used to chide Tillich at this point in their weekly conversations.)

Now if I am not mistaken, the empirical fact to which Tillich regularly pointed is the fundamental element in human inquiry which I have already called the unrelenting drive to ask questions. The drive to ask questions is unlimited in its range, in the search for further information, in the revision of presuppositions, and in the fundamental selection of criteria of relevance and evidence. We can turn this drive upon ourselves; it is the source of that self-questioning which discredits idols and uncovers self-deceits. Some call it conscience, or prophetic judgment, or even "the Protestant principle." [55] But we can also direct this drive in a scientific direction, inventing methods of inquiry designed to discount quirks of personality and accidents of time and place, in the search for self-consistent systems of general laws. Tillich has paused more than most thinkers in our century to reflect upon the significance for the human situation of the fact that man is possessed of such a drive. What does it tell us about ourselves if a basic drive of ours heads always beyond us, even to the extent of bringing us under its judgment? Tillich had a very strong sense of the fact that we do not possess truth; when we enunciate a true proposition, we are possessed by something greater than ourselves. We participate in an understanding in whose light our own hypocrisies or characteristic errors stand condemned. We pursue full understanding, trying to make our intelligence ever more faithful, accomplished, and docile.

Tillich translated the data of the drive to understand into the language of being. Total and complete understanding, fecund and creative and realized, is being-itself. Sense knowledge and concepts, by contrast, refer merely to beings and relations between beings. The human understanding *in via* is divided between understanding and not understanding; thence derives the experience of being and nonbeing. Ignorant, unable to dare the next steps, uncertain whether our efforts are assured success, we are anxious. To press onwards is to have the courage to be. Like man, moreover, reality is in progress.[56] The fundamental though usually implicit axiom of Tillich's thought is that being and knowing are correlative; that every statement of ontology may be translated into a statement about human psychology: specifically, about human ultimate concern.

Tillich did not choose to use the language of understanding; he preferred "concern." For in the wake of British empiricism, understanding has come to mean a relatively impersonal, dry, "merely" cognitive act. (Indeed, a dualism between cognitive and emotive is often deemed tenable.) To an empiricist, consequently, Tillich's language was bound to seem intolerably muddy; empiricists in general fear nothing so much as a draught of subjectivity. When Tillich combined two sentences such as the following, they shuddered: ". . . the gods are not objects within the context of the universe. They are expressions of the ultimate concern which transcends the cleavage between subjectivity and objectivity." [57]

Moreover, Tillich made a faulty step just at this point. He tells us: "It remains to be emphasized that an ultimate concern is not 'subjective.' " [58] Now there is a way of explaining ultimate concern so that it is clearly not "subjective." But Tillich has already effectively disguised that way:

"God" is the answer to the question implied in man's finitude; he is the name for that which concerns man ultimately. This does not mean that first there is a being called God and then the demand that man should be ultimately concerned about him. It means that whatever concerns a man ultimately becomes god for him, and, conversely, it means that a man can be concerned ultimately only about that which is god for him.[59]

In this passage, Tillich seemed to make "god" and "ultimate concern" analytical; wherever one term appears, the other may be supplied in its place.[60] As a phenomenological description, this device may be legitimate. But without warning Tillich began to use criteria by which to distinguish *genuine* ultimate concerns from spurious or even demonic ultimate concerns. "Only that which is holy," he wrote four pages later, "can give man ultimate concern." [61] But it is surely a misuse of words to claim that for the taxi driver whose ultimate concern is beer and television, the television room is "holy" or "sacred." Tillich himself seemed to fear the looseness of his thought here, and inserts a brief paragraph which offers at least one criterion: "Justice is the criterion which judges idolatrous holiness. . . . In the name of social justice, modern revolutionary movements challenge sacred institutions which protect social injustice." [62]

In short, Tillich had objective criteria for judging among the many candidates for ultimate concern which men in fact choose. He had a way of distinguishing the true God from false gods. But he was so anxious to counteract rationalistic-empirical prejudices that he did not wish to call this method "objective." For in an empirical, Anglo-American context, "objective" seems to connote the attitude of a scientific observer who, with impersonality and detachment, studies objects "out there" and their relationships. In eschewing this meaning for "objective," there is all the more reason for Tillich to work hard, in a prominent place in his system, to establish the necessary criteria and controls. Instead, Tillich's own language connotes dangerous attitudes which, in American philosophical circles, give rise to legitimate fears. He writes: "If the word 'existential' points to a participation which transcends both subjectivity and objectivity, then man's relation to the gods is rightly called 'existential.' " [63] But the word "existential" is as foggy as any in the language; it connotes passion, leap, uncritical commitment, true believing, adolescent identity crises, and highly unpragmatic and unproductive dramatic episodes. The verb "transcends" chills sensitive ears; while, since Plato, the word "participation" has made careful thinkers despair of finding a clear, obedient employment for it.

What can it mean, then, to "transcend both subjectivity and objectivity"? Perhaps the following translation of Tillich may be at least partly successful. It is naive to think that any human being can be objective *tout court*. In order to make judgments which will be given credence by other critical, questioning men, a man must submit himself to long discipline, arduous labor, and the demands of time, place, and situation relevant to his field of inquiry. In order to become "objective," a man must undergo many "subjective" changes. Lack of information, undue or aberrant emotional involvement, weak imagination, the absence of important kinds of experience, even the deficiency of a certain kind of sympathy—all such "subjective" deficiencies might disqualify a man as an "objective" judge in a given field of inquiry. There is no straight path to objectivity; the way lies through subjective growth, discipline, and socialization. "Objectivity" is itself a subjective state. The "cleavage" is overcome.

That Tillich must have meant something like this is shown by his analysis of the intellectual, volitional, and emotive components of "centered acts of the personality" in *Dynamics of Faith*.[64] In scientific inquiry as in ethical action, it is not the mind but the whole man that is implicated in judgment. A theory of scientific method or of ethical behavior which disregards the required development of the subject is lamentably deficient. This is precisely Tillich's criticism of Anglo-American empiricism. The philosopher dedicated to the methods of science is at one and the same time "subjective" and "objective" in his commitment. Such a commitment, like every other commitment, demands a justification. Tillich sows a further doubt: Is such a commitment, for a human being, a worthy ultimate commitment? What view of the relationship between human inquiry and reality does it presuppose? What does it take for granted about the human situation?

No doubt many interpretations of the significance of human life are possible. Moreover, it is part of the human situation that each person, faced with many possible interpretations of his own identity under these stars, must choose one of them. No one view imposes itself upon us. We must decide who we think we are. We do so by our actions if not by our theories; we do so by our style of life, our loves, our laughter, our fears, if not by explicit philosophizing or theologizing. As an argument compelling all men to change their view of themselves and to interpret their lives in a new way, Tillich's work could not hope to succeed. As one possible interpretation, his is not the least rich, the least fruitful, or the least discriminating. It would be well to live as Tillich lived; and, be it noted, he lived out his own theory.

Is not that, after all, the pragmatic test which at earlier points in such discussions eludes analysis? Theism and nontheism are ways of life; as interpretations of human identity, each is too comprehensive for ordinary pragmatic tests. The test comes in living. Most American atheists seem to live *as if* the "matrix of reality" is intelligible; as if fidelity to intelligence is a policy coherent with the world of our experience. To say that there is a God, for Tillich, means no more than that. God is not an extra, added being; he suffuses all things. He is the name for the effectiveness of our ultimate concern for honesty, modesty, compassion; he is not a being, but the power, bitterly contested, of intelligence, love, and creativity in ourselves and in our world. Communities of religious people continually project beings to put in his place. But even atheists "participate" in the power that makes things, where there could have been nothing, marvelously to be. Tillich seriously reduced the distance between critical theists and critical nontheists, by learning from the deepest currents of thought in Judaeo-Christian history that God is not an object among objects, or a person among persons, but must be thought of in a secular way. The critical theist is very like an atheist, in not thinking of God as a thing while yet giving ultimate and hopeful allegiance to the unrelenting drive to understand.

It is not of primary importance, then, for theist and nontheist, in America at least, to distinguish themselves from one another.[65] The real enemy, the enemy of both of them, is the crowd of idol-worshippers: the violent partisans of "the American way of life," of the white God of white men, of the God of the social and political status quo, of the God of tabu and conformity and inhibition. This God, this bitch, is so strong in American life that all available rebels, theistic and nontheistic, have urgent common cause.

III. *Paul Tillich and the Future*

Both Christians and secular thinkers, however, register sound objections against Tillich's attempt to stand "on the boundary." Ironically, the basic objection from both sides is the same: Tillich is not, after all, a Christian; it is impossible to see in Tillich's God the God of revelation. Here I think the critics are mistaken, although the difficulties involved must be sorted out and faced directly, and the fact that Tillich never quieted this doubt must count against him. Let us consider the argument of nontheists first.

An eminent American philosopher—"the high priest of positivism" he was called by the relator of this anecdote—was once obliged to hear Tillich preach at the funeral of an academic colleague. Tillich did not speak of hell or heaven, nor of the God of mercy and judgment; he spoke of anxiety, courage, ultimate concern, and being-itself. Descending the steps of the chapel, the philosopher grumped angrily: "Why, the man is not a Christian at all!"

Nontheists often play the role of defenders of orthodoxy. They often insist upon a literal interpretation of religious utterances and of religious tradition. With Freud, they opine that their own illusions are not, "like religious ones, incapable of correction." [66] Religion must be static; it cannot evolve. Entering upon religious terrain, they suddenly seem to lose their sense of discrimination and their sense of history; they sometimes lump all religious phenomena together and speak of Jesus, Lao-tse, Aquinas, Luther, and Billy Graham in one paragraph. They do not allow that the faith of a washerwoman and a theologian, a child and a grown man, a politician and a scientist, a third-century and a nineteenth-century philosopher might be significantly different as well as in some ways the same. Like the Russian astronaut who said after his long search through the heavens that, plainly, Our Father isn't there, they insist upon the literal sense or else accuse the religious man of cheating. Is there or is there not a hell? Where? Do you believe in Satan? Can God have a son, and would a good God wish his son to die (or bid Abraham to behead Isaac), or his flesh to be eaten in the Eucharist by human beings? Half the fun of being nonreligious appears to lie in the exercise of revulsion against literal interpretations, and in the exercise of suspicion against symbolical interpretations, of religious faith.

But there are more substantive reasons for this misunderstanding. Even when we grant that religious faith is for all men, in all eras of history, and that it does not require the educated to turn off their minds and become uncritical, the problems of relating critical, philosophical language to the ordinary language of the various religious traditions remain acute. There is, for example, an obvious gap between what Tillich says of God in the philosophical part of his work and what he says of him in the theological part. According to his famous "method of correlation," [67] Tillich argues that man is both a philosophical and a theological animal; there are not two separate truths about man. This point of view is a refreshing and an honest one, and I think Tillich has received too little credit for it.

What Tillich's conception implies is that Christianity presents itself as a full world view; it is a whole, rounded, although not yet complete, interpretation of human existence. It is, in brief, an hypothesis. It is to be tested according to how well it meets the facts of human experience. Tillich never states the matter quite so sharply; but surely when he says [68] that, from a philosophical point of view, human experience raises a question about the meaning of man and that, from a theological point of view, Christianity provides one answer to this question, he suggests that the logical status of Christian doctrine is that of an hypothesis. If the answer does not meet the requirements of the question, it must be rejected.

There have not been lacking critics who insist that Tillich has tailored the philosophical question to fit the theological answer, and other critics, like Karl Barth,[69] who insist that Tillich has violated the transcendence of Christianity by tailoring it to meet philosophical questions. Still, a Christian cannot, after all, lead a complacently divided life; Tillich's attempt to relate philosophy to theology must be judged both courageous and headed in a fruitful direction. Curiously, I find that many militantly secular students respond enthusiastically to Tillich's analysis of the questions which arise from human experience (as in *The Courage To Be*), even while they reject his theological answers; while some religious thinkers find his theology stimulating but dislike his ontology. This difference in estimation, it seems, points graphically to the mutual isolation in our society of secular philosophy and theological reflection. Other misunderstandings that Tillich risked arise both from the philosophical separation between Anglo-American analysts, who seldom examine publicly the arbitrariness of their own fundamental commitments to clarity and objectivity, and Continental existentialists, and from the theological separation between liberal and fundamentalist theologians.

What Tillich proposed to offer was an interpretation of language about God that could win the allegiance of critical philosophers, and also be employed as an instrument of prophetic criticism by ordinary people in ordinary theological discourse. Because human beings live in a concrete, historical world, Tillich had no fundamental objection to the employment of concrete, historical metaphors for God. After all, Moses spoke of God's extended right arm leading the people from Egypt, and Jesus spoke of his Father. What Tillich did object to was a literal understanding of such language. God has no right arm; he is not, biologically or anthropomorphically, a father. Neither is he a rock, a stream of running water, a tower, or any of the other things which the Bible employs in speaking of him. Moreover, the Bible itself provides criteria for interpreting its own symbols: Yahweh is the un-written, the ineffable, name, the name unlike any other name; no one should be allowed to think that it refers as other names do. In the Christian Testament, St. John tells us (1 Jn:4) quite clearly and re-peatedly: "No one has seen God."

Moreover, the Bible speaks of God both in an abstract, universal way and in a personal, anthropomorphic way; many of its symbols, particularly those derived from impersonal forces and those having to do with his power over "the heavens," operate as warnings that an-thropomorphic, personal symbols must be understood in an unusual way. In the Christian Testament, St. John's Gospel speaks of the Logos in whom and by whom and with whom all things were made. The early Greek church was especially fond of the more impersonal "Pantocrator," rather than the all-too-human "historical Jesus" of the early twentieth century. St. Augustine did not hesitate to find God within himself rather than in the cosmos, and thought of him not as some inner man but impersonally as "my love, my weight." Aquinas found in the unqualified energy and unceasing activity of *Actus Purus* a critical name for God, and in *caritas* or freely chosen love the most serviceable biblical category for speaking of his presence among men. Dante wrote of "the Love that moves the sun and all the stars."

Consequently, Tillich—I think rightly—felt himself to be part of a well-established tradition of religious discourse. Pascal gave warning that the "god of the philosophers" is not "the God of Abraham, Isaac, and Jacob," and he divided—accepting the Cartesian split of personality into the emotive and the cognitive—conceptions of the heart from conceptions of the mind. How after that can we repair Humpty Dumpty? Significantly, Tillich chose to define God in relation to that centered act of the person which Pascal seemed to intend by *"raisons du coeur."* Tillich thought of himself as continuing the tradition of Kierkegaard's "infinite passion and interest," [70] and perhaps also of the long section on subjectivity as the ground of objectivity in the *Concluding Unscientific Postscript.*

Some of the resistance to Tillich's effort, resistance which one encounters in students, at any rate, seems derived from the positive determination of many intelligent people not to be taken as religious. Such students resist any idea of God that is intelligible, all the more if it comes close to pointing to values that they already hold. Their nontheism is more easily defended if theists are constrained to uphold foolish, naive, anthropomorphic or objectified conceptions of God. Yet if in fact there is a God, it would be surprising if, of all men, he were not already present in the experience and profound presuppositions of intelligent, critical, honest, and compassionate men. It would be surprising if God could be found only in church buildings, spoken of only on the lips of a professional caste of clergymen and their phalanxes of stolid churchgoers, or described only in the categories of technical theological traditions. Tillich's instinct—that God, if there is a God, is already present in the experience of every human being, and most clearly in those with the most fully developed humanistic ultimate concerns—represents the most attractive and plausible, as well as the most traditional, hypothesis.

Tillich's execution of this point fails, however, because he does not face with sufficient clarity the problems of objectivity and historicity. By turning too quickly to the language of "symbol" and "myth," Tillich gave the impression of sleight-of-hand. It does not do to counter the objectifying, literal prejudices of most Anglo-American thinkers with a Germanic confidence in the "reality" of symbols (Tillich despised the locution "*mere* symbol"). In some sense, both Judaism and Christianity are historical religions; concrete, historical facts are important to them; they wish to assert that actions which occur in the space-time continuum bear, precisely as spatio-temporal, responsibility in the eyes of God. By interpreting the narratives of Scripture in a symbolical sense, Tillich at the very least (though not nearly so much as Bultmann) skirts too near the possibility of turning Christianity into a kind of gnosis: it is not the historical deed, in its empirical historicity, but its inward transtemporal significance that counts. "No historical criticism," Tillich writes in *Systematic Theology II,* "can question the immediate awareness of those who find themselves transformed into the state of faith. One is reminded of the Augustinian-Cartesian . . . immediacy of a self-consciousness which guaranteed itself by a participation in being. By analogy, one must say that participation, not historical argument, guarantees the reality of the event upon which Christianity is based." [71] There is truth in this: Christianity is verified by living it. But there is also the danger of surrendering concrete history to mystical inwardness.

These are the stickiest of all problems for the man who stands in an historical community of faith. The point of the biblical narratives is certainly not to provide us with "objective" information, of the sort useful to scientists, archeologists, demographers, historians, and the like. Clearly, their point is to induce a metanoia, to bring about self-criticism and a change of life. The point of the stories, then, is "real" enough: they call for concrete changes in concrete history—and they have, in fact, dramatically altered the course of civilization.

But in some sense the empirical historicity of the key biblical narratives must also be defended, or else we have the paradox that a faith which insists upon the capital importance of concrete historical deeds is not itself based on concrete historical deeds. Since no Christian theorist has yet given a satisfactory solution to this problem, Tillich, who wrestled manfully with it,[72] cannot be singled out for special blame. He did not wish faith to rest upon the vagaries of historical scholarship, although he gave such scholarship an indispensable role in checking superstition. Still, the empirically minded will urge, historical research cannot be merely a *removens prohibens* having nothing to do with the basis of faith. In some stronger way, Judaism and Christianity must allow themselves to be vulnerable to empirical research, at the price of forfeiting an important kind of historicity.

Consequently, the re-thinking of Jewish and Christian faith in the context of modern empirical sciences has yet to be accomplished. Tillich was right to see that the cosmic picture of the immediately preceding epoch has been dissolved; Judaism and Christianity can no longer receive support from what used to be called the Judaeo-Christian world view. It should not be presumed too easily, however, that the world view—or lack of one—presented by modern science is in fact less hospitable to Jewish and Christian faith than the neat, orderly cosmic structure taken for granted in the past. The Lord, if there is such a one, is no less Lord for being Lord of a bundle of loose ends, a changing, open, uncertain historical world, even an absurd world.[73] Despite Einstein God does, perhaps, play with dice. Tillich made a helpful move in locating the clue to God's presence in man's own dynamic striving to be creative in this baffling, contradictory world, rather than in God's supposed maintenance of an orderly cosmos.

The truly serious threat to Tillich's future relevance comes from the widespread indifference among the active and the intelligent to ultimate questions. Tillich himself seemed to sense this threat in his definition of indifference as the only true atheism.[74] A growing band of young religious thinkers believe that Tillich relied too much upon the inwardness, the romantic wonderment, the pervading religious experience of finitude, so natural to German romanticism but so foreign to American urban pragmatism. Nevertheless, the passionate search for ultimate values among the activists of the New Left is, however secular and even anti-theological its animus, a clear manifestation of what Tillich would call religious seriousness (just as its utopianism is related to the most simplistic theological traditions).

Thus one threat to Tillich's future relevance comes from a comfortable, visionless pragmatism, from a consensus concerned with social adjustment rather than with radical questioning. Wherever men are ultimately concerned with the most creative human values they can discover, they have in their experience, Tillich would say, pointers to the presence of God. And he would say that Judaism and Christianity—in his later years, he added Islam, Buddhism, and Hinduism —offer alternative historical languages for beginning to babble, however inadequately, about the mystery of human consciousness upon this earth.

But another threat comes from the passing of an era. Much that Tillich wrote will long be cherished, but when he died a mood, an age, died with him. Rabbi Richard L. Rubenstein learned of his former teacher's death while visiting the site of a Warsaw ghetto. He wrote:

Somehow, there was something appropriate in hearing the sad news in that place. An important part of Tillich's greatness was his ability to endow with theological meaning the universal dissolution in two world wars of the old certainties of European civilization. Tillich had known the stability which preceded the breakdown. He had the courage to confront the breakdown and discern within it possibilities of theological renewal.

My sadness was tempered by the knowledge that Tillich's work was, insofar as any man's can be, completed. He had spoken for and to his time, but we have moved beyond that time.[75]

NOTES

1. See, v.g., Hamilton, *The System and The Gospel* (Macmillan: New York, 1963), pp. 205-07; William F. Albright calls Tillich "a modern gnostic" and adds: "Tillich has grafted C. G. Jung on Schelling's pantheism . . . and produced a theological system which resembles traditional Christianity only in superficial aspects." Cited by Gustave Weigel in Leibrecht (ed.), *Religion and Culture* (Harper & Brothers: New York, 1959), p. 125.
2. *Mind*, vol. LXXIV, no. 294 (April, 1965), pp. 192-214.
3. See, v.g., Thomas J. J. Altizer and William Hamilton, *Radical Theology and the Death of God.* (Bobbs-Merrill: New York, 1966), pp. 160-07.
4. *Paul Tillich's Philosophy of Culture, Science, and Religion* (Harper & Row: New York, 1965), pp. 281-2.
5. See his extraordinary essay, "The Conquest of Intellectual Provincialism: Europe and America," in *Theology of Culture*, Robert C. Kimball (ed.), (Oxford University Press: New York, 1964), pp. 159-76.
6. In his autobiography, *On The Boundary*, which first appeared as an introduction to *The Interpretation of History* (Scribner's: New York, 1936) and was re-published just weeks after his death, Tillich describes twelve boundaries on which he felt he stood (Scribner's: New York, 1966). There are further autobiographical materials in Tillich's introduction to *The Protestant Era* (Phoenix Books, University of Chicago Press: Chicago, 1957), pp. v-xxvi, and to *The Theology of Paul Tillich*, Charles W. Kegley and Robert W. Bretall (eds.), (Macmillan: New York, 1952, 2nd paper

edition, 1964), pp. 3-21. See also the biographical tributes by Jerald C. Brauer, Wilhelm Pauck, and Mircea Eliade in *The Future of Religions* (Harper & Row: New York, 1966), pp. 15-36, and the essay by Walter Leibrecht, "The Life and Mind of Paul Tillich" in *Religion and Culture, op. cit.*, pp. 3-27.

7. Yale University Press: New Haven, 1952.

8. In *The Protestant Era*, pp. 161-81.

9. *Ibid.*, pp. 32-51.

10. *The Future of Religions, op. cit.*

11. Both these collections, together with *The Eternal Now* (1963), are published by paper editions, Scribner's: New York.

12. Harper & Row: New York, 1958, Torchbook edition (fourteenth printing, 1965).

13. *Systematic Theology I* (University of Chicago Press: Chicago, 1955), p. 163; and *Dynamics of Faith, op. cit.*, p. 1. Tillich varies his formulae slightly: " 'God' is the answer to the question implied in man's finitude; he is the name for that which concerns man ultimately." *Systematic Theology I*, p. 211.

14. *Op. cit.*, p. 195.

15. *Ibid.*, p. 194.

16. John Herman Randall, Jr., quotes a similar remark by G. E. Moore, "Now really, Mr. Tillich, I don't think I have been able to understand a single sentence of your paper. Won't you please try to state one sentence, or even one word, that I can understand?" "The Ontology of Paul Tillich," in *The Theology of Paul Tillich, op. cit.*, p. 133.

17. John Herman Randall, Jr., judges: ". . . it is (Tillich's) epistemology which seems the least adequate part of his thought, and raises the most questions. The one strand of the philosophical tradition which he does not take very seriously, and consequently fails to illuminate, is the empiricism stemming from Locke. This he is inclined to dismiss as the mere reflection of a transitory bourgeois culture . . ." "The Ontology of Paul Tillich," *op. cit.*, pp. 133-34.

18. *Loc. cit.*, pp. 192-93. The references to Hume are to the Kemp-Smith edition, pp. 156-59.

19. *Ibid.*

20. *Systematic Theology I* (University of Chicago Press: Chicago, 1951), p. 239. (Henceforth abbreviated: S.T.I).

21. But he does speak of "a 'pantheistic element' in every adequate doctrine of God." He invokes this element "against the half-deistic theism of much Protestant theology," which would remove God from the real world of our experience. He sharply denies calling God "the essence of all things," since this "dissolves God into the essence of the world and removes his qualitative transcendence. . . . But after this has been said, the so-called 'pantheistic element' must be used as a corrective . . ." "Appreciation and Reply," in Thomas A. O'Meara and Celestin D. Weisser (eds.), *Paul*

Tillich in Catholic Thought (The Priory Press: Dubuque, Iowa, 1964), p. 308.

22. *Ibid.,* p. 306. Tillich usually says "ground of being" rather than "ground of reality."

23. *Op. cit.,* pp. 195-97.

24. *S.T.I,* pp. 231-37. For Tillich's employment of various symbols see his "The Meaning and Justification of Religious Symbols" and a series of critiques by others in Sidney Hook (ed.), *Religious Experience and Truth* (New York University Press: New York, 1961).

25. Wittgenstein records a certain experience thus: "When I have it I wonder at the existence of the world. And I am then inclined to use such phrases as 'How extraordinary that anything should exist!' " See Norman Malcolm, *Ludwig Wittgenstein* (Oxford University Press: Oxford, 1959), p. 72. Tillich writes: "The ontological question, the question of being-itself, arises in something like a 'metaphysical shock' . . . This shock has often been expressed in the question 'why is there something; why not nothing?' . . . fundamentally (this question) is the expression of a state of existence rather than a formulated question." *S.T.I,* pp. 163-64.

26. *The Protestant Era,* p. 163.

27. *Ibid.,* pp. 86-7.

28. *Dynamics of Faith,* pp. 4-8.

29. *Op. cit.,* p. 199.

30. *Ibid.,* p. 200.

31. *Ibid.,* p. 201.

32. *Ibid.,* p. 206.

33. Letter to Gustave Weigel, S.J., published as "Professor Tillich Replies" in Weigel's "The Theological Significance of Paul Tillich," *Paul Tillich in Catholic Thought,* p. 23.

34. *Op. cit.,* pp. 206-09.

35. In my *Belief and Unbelief* (Macmillan: New York, 1965), I have tried to suggest that this is also true of Reinhold Niebuhr and of all religious thinkers.

36. ". . . Tillich stands broadly in the great Augustinian tradition, that is, in the central tradition of Christian Platonism. . . . he finds only the Platonic strain in Aristotle congenial." Randall, *loc. cit.,* p. 134.

37. *S.T.I,* pp. 168-69.

38. (George Braziller: New York, 1964), pp. 102-03; 110-11; 253.

39. See D. Mackenzie Brown (ed.), *Ultimate Concern: Paul Tillich in Dialogue* (Harper & Row: New York, 1965), p. 88. No better introduction to Tillich's thought is available than this transcript.

40. (Doubleday Anchor: New York, 1964), pp. 88-9.

41. *S.T.I,* pp. 211-13. On the role of the historical community, see *ibid.,* pp. 239-40, and "Faith and Community," *Dynamics of Faith, op. cit.,* pp. 22-29.

42. See "Appreciation and Reply," *Paul Tillich in Catholic Thought, op. cit.,*

p. 308. Also: "The question of God is possible because an awareness is present in the question of God. This awareness precedes the question. It is not the result of argument but its presupposition." *S.T.I*, p. 206.

43. *S.T.I*, pp. 204-08.

44. "The arguments for the existence of God neither are arguments nor are they proof for the existence of God. They are expressions of the *question* of God which is implied in human finitude. Their question is their truth; every answer they give is untrue." *Ibid.*, p. 205, see also pp. 208-10.

45. *Ibid.*, p. 214.

46. *Ibid.*, pp. 218-19.

47. See *The Future of Religions, op. cit.*

48. *S.T.I*, p. 235.

49. *Ibid.*, p. 204.

50. *Ibid.*, pp. 205-06 and 211.

51. *Ibid.*, p. 241.

52. *Ibid.*, p. 218, *passim.*

53. "The realm against which the divine image is projected is not itself a projection. It is the experienced ultimacy of being and meaning. It is the realm of ultimate concern." *Ibid.*, p. 212.

54. *Ibid.*, pp. 174-78.

55. See *The Protestant Era, op. cit.*, pp. 161-81; *S.T.I*, p. 227.

56. *S.T.I*, p. 181.

57. *Ibid.*, p. 214.

58. *Ibid.*, p. 214.

59. *Ibid.*, p. 211.

60. In *Ultimate Concern*, however, Tillich replies to an objection that ultimate concern merely "describes how we feel." "Of course we cannot replace 'God' by 'ultimate concern,' but we can and must understand that the term ultimate concern, like the German phrase of which it is a translation, is intentionally ambiguous. It indicates, on the one hand, *our* being ultimately concerned—the subjective side—and on the other hand, the *object* of our ultimate concern, for which of course there is no other word than 'ultimate.'" *Op. cit.*, p. 11.

61. *S.T.I*, p. 215.

62. *Ibid.*, p. 216.

63. *Ibid.*, p. 214.

64. *Op. cit.*, pp. 4-8.

65. Tillich writes: "As an individual I am strongly attached to the quasi-religion of liberal humanistic tradition. . . . The word liberal means here autonomous thought and action. . . . But I try to avoid, as I did as a religious socialist, falling into the process of emptying the liberal humanist ideas of their original religious content. I always go back to the religious source that underlies them, for there is no such thing as humanism in the abstract anywhere. Humanism is always based on a religious tradition. . . . In the Western world since the victory of Christianity, we have a humanism which is always Christian humanism, even if we act as much as

possible like anti-Christians. . . . Generally speaking, I would say that the danger of the quasi-religions tends more toward profanization, in the sense of emptiness. Whereas the danger of the religions proper is more that of demonization, in the sense of identifying the revelatory experiences on which they are based with the divine itself, and therefore usurping the 'throne of the divine' for themselves. Between these two dangers we have to grope our way." *Ultimate Concern, op. cit.,* pp. 36-39.

66. *Op. cit.,* p. 86.

67. *S.T.I,* pp. 30-34, 59-64. See also his spirited reply to his critics, *S.T.I,* pp. 13-16.

68. He adds: "Man cannot receive an answer to a question he has not asked." *S.T.I,* p. 13, also ff.

69. See, v.g., the doctrinal thesis done under Barth by Alexander J. McKelway, *The Systematic Theology of Paul Tillich* (John Knox Press: Richmond, Va., 1964) esp. pp. 261-67 and Barth's introduction.

70. *S.T.I,* p. 12, 215.

71. P. 114.

72. *S.T.II,* pp. 97-117. In Kegley and Bretall, *op. cit.,* A. T. Mollegen gives a crisp report on Tillich's solution, which Tillich praised for "a clarity which I have myself found it very difficult to achive." Pp. 230-45 and 348.

73. See Raymond Nogar, O.P., *The Lord of the Absurd* (Herder & Herder: New York, 1966).

74. "Or we may simply become cynical and have a good time, suppressing the ultimate questions so far as possible. And that is the only unproductive possibility." *Ultimate Concern, op. cit.,* p. 41; see also pp. 27-28 ff.

75. See Rubenstein's tribute to Tillich in "Cox's Vision of the Secular City" in *The Secular City Debate,* Daniel Callahan (ed.), (Macmillan: New York, 1966) pp. 129-44.

14

Dietrich Bonhoeffer

A new kind of Christianity and Judaism are taking shape today, and those whose theological sophistication reached its peak in Sabbath or Sunday school are due for a steady series of shocks. Serious Jews and Christians today are looking for a theory to account for an experience deeply felt by many, namely, that the empirical difference between belief and unbelief, between Christianity and contemporary atheism, is so slight as to be indiscernible. The atheist lives according to values—honesty, vision, resignation, compassion—that are indistinguishable in practice from Christian values. The Christian has no special "religious" experience, no special emotive advantages, no ascertainable security or peace that the unbeliever can empirically be said to lack.

Although both of them have become the major heroes of many young Christians, Dietrich Bonhoeffer (1906-1945) did not have so compelling and so authentic a personality as Albert Camus (1913-1960). Bonhoeffer was a man wholly consumed by what Tillich liked to call "ultimate concern." The ultimate concern of Dietrich Bonhoeffer was to testify to Jesus Christ. He was an intensely German witness to Jesus, even an intensely Lutheran witness. He had to struggle not to be contemptuous of less than total effort, less than total seriousness. He was critical of Germany, critical of the "leadership principle," critical of the aberrant and blind sense of duty, critical of the separation of religious inwardness from

266

the realities of political life. But he loved Germany to the hilt. It was like him to read an American writer (Reinhold Niebuhr, for example) and to remark in his diary (June, 1939) that Americans are fifteen years behind Germany, and that "it seems that Germany is still the land of spiritual discoveries."

Bonhoeffer could not have imagined how important for America were to be his own spiritual discoveries. His main accomplishments were two. First, he showed that the proper Christian question is not "Do men need God?" or "Of what use is God?" for this entrenched but despicable point of view makes God into a functionary in the service of man, a crutch, a security blanket. Rather, the orthodox question begins from a different viewpoint: "Having accepted Jesus as the revelation of God, what must Christians do in the world?" From this starting place, Bonhoeffer launched a scathing attack upon "religion" and turned Christians towards the social and political responsibilities of daily life. While Camus' Rieux the "secular saint" of The Plague, is saying of Father Paneloux, "He is one of us," Pastor Bonhoeffer is finding profound spiritual comradeship with the "secular saints" who share his imprisonment. The ethical differences between Christians and atheists, the crucible of modern experience reveals, do not appear where older theories said they should appear. "God" does not show himself to Christians any more than to atheists, and a God who could be "needed" is no God at all.

Secondly, Bonhoeffer combined the concern for politics, the arts, and culture manifested by liberal theologians (followers of Bultmann) with the firm and vigorous attachment to the figure of Jesus Christ manifested by neo-orthodox theologians (like Barth). The effect of this synthesis was to bypass as unworthy the liberals' appeal to existentialism, Angst, and the cult of inwardness, and to turn Barth's "obedience to Jesus" to practical employment in building up the concrete political and social structures of the city of man. It might not be too much to say that Bonhoeffer's American experiences (he spent a full year at Union Theological Seminary in 1930-1931, and returned eight years later for most of the summer of 1939) provided him with preliminary models for his theological thinking. The pervasive American conviction that "God's work must truly be our own" is itself a sample of "secular Christianity," and Rein-

hold Niebuhr's views on the relevance of Christianity to power politics offered mental support against a widespread German Christian view that the two "spheres" must be kept separate.

Such views did not lead Bonhoeffer to abandon Christianity, perhaps because he found no value pursued by atheists that his Christianity had not already taught him to cherish; and in the light of such actually lived values the interpretation of human life revealed in Jesus Christ does not lose, but gains, in plausibility. Men seeking to be men—to discover their own identity and, slowly, to create community—are at least very like what Jesus reveals them to be. One must in any case abandon churchiness and religious inwardness (i.e., religion as a distinct sentiment and a special sphere of human life, alongside other spheres) in order to become a genuine Christian. Thus Bonhoeffer, particularly in the last part of The Letters and Papers from Prison, *takes at least as many steps toward common ground in an ethic at once secular and Jewish-Christian as Camus does, from an opposite direction, in* The Fall. *It is not surprising that many Christians now love and admire both men equally.*

Yet the personality of Bonhoeffer remains Germanic, concentrated, disciplined, aloof. One wishes he had had a passionate love for a woman, or that he had written witty and possibly bawdy limericks to while away a few stray hours. As a "worldly" theologian, he is awfully monkish. Tillich was far better at worldliness. In fact, it seems as if in life each of them, Tillich and Bonhoeffer, were what the other's theory called for.

As early as 1937, as The Way to Freedom (Letters, Lectures and Notes, 1935–1959) *shows, Bonhoeffer was launching an attack upon "religion" and clarifying his meaning by references to piety in the United States. "Religion" as a special sphere of life, a distinctive sentiment, a matter for professional specialization, seems to have emerged in human consciousness in the seventeenth century. America was then to become almost a pure case of this new attitude. Some men became proficient in music, poetry, conversation, science, politics; others became specialists in religion. Handbooks and guides were written. Attempts were made to define the specifically religious emotions. Heretofore, all things in all their aspects had been related to God; everything had been at once both secular and religious. Now a special sphere of inwardness, duty, harmony, awe, dependence, and purity was separated from the concrete world of*

cities, economies, political parties, artistic ambitions. Christianity was re-
duced to a special feeling, a section of life like a section of Time *maga-*
zine. (Psychologists could ask: "Do you consider yourself to be religious?
hardly at all? moderately? usually so?") The effort now had to be made
to relate "religion" to "life," from which it had been sectioned off. The
pursuit of religion, Bonhoeffer saw, is anti-Christian. It is pagan.

"THERE is nothing at all comic," Soren Kierkegaard wrote in *Con-*
cluding Unscientific Postscript, "in the fact that a man teaches paganism instead of Christianity, but there is something comic in the fact
that an orthodox preacher when he uses all the registers on an occasion
of great solemnity, pulls out by mistake the stop of paganism without
noticing it." [1] Much of the Christianity preached in American churches
today is not Christianity but paganism. Law is taught instead of freedom. The person is subjected to the organization. Codes and rules
replace dangerous and authentic moral development. The true God is
replaced by the local deity, the patriot's god, the chancery's god. Men
are offered, not the risks of a dark faith, but peace of soul—as if God
were a security blanket, a protector of law and order, an all-seeing
inhibitor of experiment and risk. Paganism organizes God and makes
him functional to a human system.

In recent years, through the efforts of a growing band of revolutionaries, there is a more concerted effort than Christianity has long
experienced to restore Christianity to Christianity, to distinguish authentic faith from the easy, warm, inner glow of a "conscientious
religious sentiment." One man more than any other has come to
symbolize this reformation.

Not many years ago, in December 1943, that man was languish-
ing in a cold Nazi cell near Berlin. He was thirty-seven years old. He
had published several heavy, rather dull but respected books on traditional theological themes; his later, exciting works were still unpublished and unknown. He had been an active member of the select band
of conspirators that plotted the assassination of Hitler. The Gestapo
hanged him to death a few days before Allied troops reached his
camp. He was a Lutheran minister and his name was Dietrich Bonhoeffer.

I

The name Bonhoeffer is not as well known to the general public today as the names of other contemporary theologians, like Karl Barth, Rudolph Bultmann, and Karl Rahner in Europe, or Paul Tillich, Reinhold Niebuhr, and H. Richard Niebuhr in the United States. Yet no theologian more excites young, intelligent Christians today. Martin E. Marty has written in *The Place of Bonhoeffer:* "Younger European and American Christian thinkers often seem to be divided into two camps: those who acknowledge their debt to Bonhoeffer and those who are indebted but who obscure the traces to their source. Certainly in seminary halls, at student retreats, on college campuses, on the pages of ecumenical youth journals, in the fraternities of younger ministers few names must be conjured with so frequently as Bonhoeffer's." [2]

Perhaps the most talked-about Christian theologian writing in the United States today is Harvard's Harvey Cox, a Baptist. On nearly every page, his slender, provocative paperback of 1965, *The Secular City,*[3] is indebted to Bonhoeffer, and Cox closes a new volume, *The Secular City Debate,*[4] with an essay illustrating in detail how Bonhoeffer opened every major issue presently exercising American Christian theologians.

But "the Death of God" theologians make frequent references to Bonhoeffer, too. The phrases "religionless Christianity" and "worldly Christianity" derive from the fragmentary notes which Bonhoeffer sneaked out from prison. In *Radical Theology and the Death of God,* William Hamilton writes that "the most decisive theological influence on the younger generation of Protestants today is Dietrich Bonhoeffer." [5] And Professor Paul van Buren of Temple opens his seminal *The Secular Meaning of the Gospel* [6] with the poem "Friday's Child" by W. H. Auden, whose dedication reads: "In memory of Dietrich Bonhoeffer, martyred at Flossenburg, April 9, 1945."

Articles in the *Commonweal* and *The National Catholic Reporter* indicate that the issues raised by Bonhoeffer are not merely Protestant. Bonhoeffer posed the problems which, younger theologians believe, the whole of Christianity must answer if it is to survive the coming new civilization. The feast of December 25 was once a pagan festival.

If it is true that the day's significance is reverting more and more to its pagan origins, then unless the questions raised by Bonhoeffer are resolved there may not be many years of a Christian Christmas left.

Bonhoeffer, especially in his fragmentary notes collected posthumously under the title *Letters and Papers from Prison*,[7] is not an easy thinker to understand. Unavoidably, quoting him has become something of a fad, and words of his lifted out of context have become mere slogans. Some who knew him well accuse other writers of so gerrymandering Bonhoeffer's texts as to make him say things he never said.

Who was this man? What did he say? Why have his words shown such extraordinary fertility?

I I

Pastor Bonhoeffer was tall, broad-shouldered, handsome, reserved, brilliant. Almost everyone who knew him unites in praising him, and yet the impressions one gains of his character and style point to a kindness and spontaneity that were willed or permitted rather than born of impulse. Altogether, his friends and defenders work too hard at convincing us of his friendliness and naturalness.

Nevertheless, young Bonhoeffer manifested the kind of personality that others admired and trusted; and he had, apparently, an unusual capacity to listen to others with attention and accuracy. He sometimes made other people feel as though he knew them better than they knew themselves, and he spoke to them with rare calmness and concern. He knew his own mind and thrived on challenges to his courage. When the announcement of a German victory set the patrons of a *Gasthaus* to patriotic singing, Bonhoeffer, too, stood and waved his stein in song: he knew his own integrity well enough not to squander his protests on petty things.

Bonhoeffer had studied at Union Theological Seminary on a special fellowship in 1930. His friends Professors Paul Lehmann and Reinhold Niebuhr contrived to invite him to New York again in 1939. At the time, Pastor Bonhoeffer was laboring in clandestine seminaries and places of retreat, and maintaining contacts between important factions in Germany and in England. His own family tree was impeccable—the historian von Häse was counted among his relatives—and through the good offices of Admiral Canaris, Bonhoeffer was listed as a special agent of the government, so that he could avoid serving in the army.

Hardly had Bonhoeffer come to America in 1939 than he knew he must return immediately. He wrote, regretfully, to his American friends:

I will have no right to participate in the reconstruction of Christian life in Germany after the war if I do not share the trials of this time with my people . . . Christians in Germany will face the terrible alternative of either willing the defeat of their nation in order that Christian civilization may survive, or willing the victory of their nation and thereby destroying our civilization. I know which of these alternatives I must choose; but I cannot make that choice in security.[8]

In his homeland once more, Bonhoeffer labored with fierce resolve against his country's leaders. Many Christians shrank from the thought of assassination; like Camus, like Sartre, Bonhoeffer discovered that a morality for peace and prosperity does not cover all situations under conditions of tyranny, especially a tryanny whose oppressiveness is made weightier and more thorough by technology. Bonhoeffer did not shrink from the assassination for which the situation seemed to call.

In 1943, the Gestapo became suspicious of him. The inspectors could find nothing against him but his evasion of military service. They did not then recognize that on a trip to Sweden Bonhoeffer had engaged in secret negotiations with the Bishop of Chichester as an emissary of the conspiracy against Hitler. But they were sufficiently suspicious to keep him in jail. When, on July 20, 1944, the time bomb placed at Hitler's feet by Count Stauffenberg failed of its target, efforts to uncover the conspiracy became feverish. Certain papers clearly implicated Bonhoeffer and his friends. But when the conspiracy suddenly seemed to fan out in all directions, Hitler suspended his order of immediate death. The conspirators already in custody were moved about often, under heavy guard.

III

Bonhoeffer had published a modest book, much influenced by Barth, *The Communion of Saints* in 1930; Barth called it "a theological miracle." James Luther Adams said of Bonhoeffer's next book, *Act and Being* (1933), that it "would delight the mind and heart of a Milton or a Coleridge or a Jonathan Edwards." But it was with *The Cost of Discipleship* (1937) that the originality and special enthusiasm of Bonhoeffer began to manifest itself. By that time, Bonhoeffer was no longer allowed to speak publicly or to publish in Germany— as early as 1933 he had attacked the Nazis publicly on the radio. The opening words of his book, therefore, had concrete significance:

Cheap grace is the deadly enemy of our Church. We are fighting today for costly grace.[9]

By "cheap grace," Bonhoeffer meant the recurrent efforts of men to hide behind some principle, system, doctrine, or party in order to evade personal responsibility. By "costly grace," he meant a willingness to lose one's life, in order to live "the only true life." Bonhoeffer pointed out how perversions of the teaching of Luther allowed some Christians to hide behind "justification by grace" and go on living like the rest of the world, and how in the "christianizing" of the Roman world before the Reformation, grace had become the "common property" of all and "was to be had at low cost."

The same Bonhoeffer who was to spend the Christmases of 1943 and 1944 not in a monastic but in a prison cell, wrote in 1937 of the monks of old: "Here men still remembered that grace costs . . . monasticism became a living protest against the secularization of Christianity and the cheapening of grace." [10] From Tegel Prison on December 17, 1943, he wrote:

For a Christian there is nothing peculiarly difficult about Christmas in a prison cell. I daresay it will have more meaning and will be observed with greater sincerity here in this prison than in places where all that survives of the feast is its name. That misery, suffering, poverty, loneliness, helplessness, and guilt look very different to the eyes of God from what they do to man . . . a prisoner can understand better than anyone else.[11]

During the difficult years from 1940 through 1943, under constant surveillance, Bonhoeffer was working on what he hoped would be his masterpiece, his *Ethics.* He wrote sections for various parts of his shifting, projected outlines, burying them in hidden places. In time, many of the caches were recovered by his friend, confident and trusted editor, Pastor Eberhard Bethge. The Gestapo found and withheld some sections. Others were never written. Although a book of 330 pages has been assembled from Bonhoeffer's labors, the *Ethics* as it now stands is not the finished book he envisaged.

The main points of the *Ethics* were an orientation toward concrete worldly matters, concern for the future of human life on earth, and a plea for personal responsibility. Some possible titles Bonhoeffer had jotted down were: "The foundations and structure of a future world"; "The foundations and structure of a united west." He wrote:

Rarely perhaps has any generation shown so little interest as ours does in any kind of theoretical or systematic ethics. The academic question of a system of ethics seems to be of all questions the most superfluous. The reason for this is not to be sought in any supposed ethical indifference on the part of our period. On the contrary it arises from the fact that our period, more than any earlier period in the history of the west, is oppressed by a superabounding reality of concrete ethical problems.[12]

Bonhoeffer's chief contribution was to break down the separation between religion and real empirical life. He opposed all thinking which separates the religious and the secular into "two spheres." He did not think that men could encounter the reality of God except in and through the reality of the world. He did not think that men could discover the reality of the world except in and through the reality of God. For him, that was the meaning of the incarnation of God in human history.

In Christ we are offered the possibility of partaking in the reality of God and in the reality of the world, but not in the one without the other. The reality of God discloses itself only by setting me entirely in the reality of the world, and when I encounter the reality of the world it is always already sustained, accepted and reconciled in the reality of God.[13]

Bonhoeffer argued that Christians must look toward the future of civilization on earth and accept responsibility for it. Christians are called "to be men who share responsibility for the state of history." He pleaded with Christians to "dare to look into the future." The "final responsible question," he wrote, is "how a coming generation shall continue to live." He was particularly severe with those who solved ethical problems by relying upon authority or a sense of duty:

. . . in being limited to what accords with duty, one never comes to the boldness of a deed that leads to personal responsibility, [and] that alone can strike at the center of evil and overcome it. The man of duty will finally be obliged to fulfill his duty even to the devil.[14]

Bonhoeffer's ethic, then, was increasingly "secular" inasmuch as it turned Christians toward responsibility for this world, its social structures, and its political needs. But it was not "secular" in a way that those who do not believe in God would recognize to be their own:

Who stands firm? Only the one for whom the final standard is not his reason, his principles, his conscience, his freedom, his virtue, but who is ready to sacrifice all these, when in faith and sole allegiance to God he is called to obedient and responsible action, the responsible person, whose life will be nothing but an answer to God's question and call.[15]

However apt and concentrated, Bonhoeffer's *Ethics* is not a revolutionary book; it distills and focuses Christian ethical thinking in a direction which many others had already begun to take—which may in some measure be a traditional direction which has ever to be discovered afresh.

I V

After his arrest in April, 1943, Bonhoeffer's opportunity for sustained work was taken from him. He soon won the friendship of his prison guards, however, and sneaked letters, small packets of notes, and even some poems out of the prison. These papers, dutifully collected and arranged by Pastor Bethge and published in 1948, began to stir the Protestant world, first in Germany, then in England and the United States. To be more precise, the last 80 pages of its 240 pages provided the stimulus—the entries from April 30 until August 21, 1944. And even those entries might be considerably compressed if one had to select the basic startling paragraphs.

Living like a monk in his prison cell, Bonhoeffer began to see the Christianity he had inherited in a cold, clear light. There were many things he disliked about that form of Christianity, and he chose a paradoxical word to stand for them: "religion." Bonhoeffer meant by religion a human feeling, an inwardness, a special section of life and sentiment that men identify as godly. Bonhoeffer hated the efforts of Christian apologists to try to force people to see life in a special perspective, or to acquire certain precious sentiments, or to be broken or made anxious by certain "boundary situations" like guilt and death. In this view, Bonhoeffer could have found support by noting that "religion" entered Western thought as a category of specialized thought and sentiment only at the time of the Renaissance; before that, the religious and the secular were undifferentiated: everything was at once both sacred and profane.

Bonhoeffer thought that in depending upon "religion" in a specialized sense Christianity was basing itself upon improper, even pagan foundations. In the contemporary world, Bonhoeffer noted men no longer "need" God in any of the ancient ways; God is no longer, in science, medicine, economics, or politics, a *deus ex machina*. Bonhoeffer despised the efforts of "the existentialist philosophers and the psychotherapists, who demonstrate to secure, contented, happy mankind that it is really unhappy and desperate. . . ." He thought of the world of the twentieth century—the world, as he well knew, of Hitler, torture, and carnage—as a "world come of age," a world in its "adulthood." He did not like the effort of Christian theorists to point to a section of human experience which proves that man is weak and needs God. "The attack by Christian apologetic upon the adulthood of the world," he wrote, "I consider to be in the first place pointless, in the second ignoble, and in the third un-Christian." [16]

At this point, many a baffled reader wishes to interrogate the dead author further. If men do not need God, why bother? Shall we all become atheists? If *this* century marks an era of human maturity, to what kind of race do we belong?

"The thing that keeps coming back to me," Bonhoeffer wrote, "is, what *is* Christianity, and indeed what *is* Christ, for us today?" Something new has been added to human experience in our century. Bonhoeffer recognized that the revolution asked of Christianity in this century has never in its history had an equal. Heretofore, Christianity has asked men to behave in essentially pagan ways, to seek a kind of spiritual inwardness, to be of good conscience, to have a sentiment about the harmony of a cosmos presided over by a god. But the time of inwardness, conscience, and religion is past. "We are proceeding towards a time of no religion at all," Bonhoeffer observed. "Men as they are now simply cannot be religious any more." [17]

Bonhoeffer argues that a Christian is not a special kind of man; he is simply a man. It is enough to be a man. It is enough to labor, to love, to laugh, to suffer, to accomplish, to fail. Christianity adds nothing "extra" to these basic actions. Christianity does not offer a special sentiment to accompany them. Christianity is not an ornament over and above them. More emphatically still, Christianity is not a kind of fix-it, to repair human weaknesses, or to hold together parts of life that don't quite fit, or to fill in missing gaps. The apologist doesn't have to hover over human life "to make room for" Christianity wherever human life isn't adequate to itself. Human life is complete in its own right.

Bonhoeffer complained that "a Christian instinct" frequently drew him more to the religionless than to the religious:

While I often shrink with religious people from speaking of God by name—because that Name somehow seems to me here not to ring true, and I strike myself as rather dishonest (it is especially bad when others start talking in religious jargon: then I dry up completely and I feel somehow oppressed and ill at ease)—with people who have no religion I am able on occasion to speak of God quite openly and as it were naturally.

Bonhoeffer did not wish to be driven to God simply because human resources were at an end or because human efforts failed. He did not wish to use God as a crutch.

I should like to speak of God not on the borders of life but at its centre, not in weakness but in strength, not, therefore, in man's suffering and death but in his life and prosperity.[18]

There are, however, two major ambiguities in Bonhoeffer's fragmentary notes from prison. In the first place, he does not offer criteria by which to distinguish benign from vicious "religionlessness." It is true, as he discovered in prison, that many men who do not believe in God maintain higher human values, and maintain them more faithfully, than many Christians do. Contemporaneously with Bonhoeffer, Albert Camus was working out a conception of "the secular saint." But to infer from such evidence that every manifestation of our age represents progress and maturity is to be uncritical.

Secondly, Bonhoeffer does wish to speak of God, while many genuinely secular men do not. Bonhoeffer regularly commends Karl

Barth for being the first to recognize that Christians must not first "clear space for religion in the world or against the world," but simply "call the God of Jesus Christ into the lists against religion." Bonhoeffer rejects religion but clings to Christ. Is such a secular view truly secular? Could any atheist or agnostic, or Jew or Moslem, accept the following view of the human situation:

The world's coming of age is then no longer an occasion for polemics and apologetics, but it is really better understood than it understands itself, namely on the basis of the Gospel, and in the light of Christ.[19]

Bonhoeffer, then, is quite simply and purely a Christian: he is not a secular thinker. What, then is this "secular" Christianity of which he writes? For one thing, Bonhoeffer is certain that Christianity is not a salvation religion. Its purpose is not to save men from this world.

It is said that the distinctive feature of Christianity is its proclamation of the resurrection, hope, and that this means the establishment of a genuine religion of salvation, in the sense of release from this world. The emphasis falls upon the far side of the boundary drawn by death. But this seems to me to be just the mistake and the danger.[20]

Bonhoeffer is certain that salvation "from cares and need, from fears and longing, from sin and death into a better world beyond the grave" is *not* "the distinctive feature of Christianity as proclaimed in the Gospels and St. Paul." He is emphatic: "I am certain it is not." Christianity offers nothing to be seen but ordinary life in its ordinariness. "Christian hope sends a man back to his life on earth," Bonhoeffer writes. Christianity turns a man toward the earthly struggles of earthly life:

The Christian, unlike the devotees of the salvation myths, does not need a last refuge in the eternal from earthly tasks and difficulties. But like Christ himself ('My God, my God, why hast thou forsaken me?') he must drink the earthly cup to the lees. . . . This world must not be prematurely written off. In this the Old and New Testaments are at one.[21]

In the Middle Ages, perhaps because of the bitterness and hopelessness of life, Christians hoped for some ultimate escape from "this vale of tears." The Middle Ages built a Platonic interpretation of Christianity, full of mysticism, asceticism, and otherworldliness, a spiritual bent that through popular mysticism and pietism continued into the Christianity of the modern era. The Christian was pictured as a man of spiritual longing, a man enduring this early pilgrimage in the expectation of eternal release. It is just this Platonic vehicle of Christianity that Bonhoeffer was opposing. In the world of the present and the future, man is not merely passive before Providence. Man has in his hands the power either to build an international humane civilization or to destroy all civilization. Man has become responsible for his own destiny. Consequently, the old way of conceiving of God no longer carries conviction; perhaps inevitable once, now it is dishonest.

V

During the winter of 1944–1945, rapid hard journeys in rickety trucks characterized the lot of Bonhoeffer and his fellow prisoners. Frozen, bounced and jarred, ever in danger of a final summons, there was reason for men to grow jaded and disconsolate. At Buchenwald, one of his last stops, Bonhoeffer was described by Captain Payne Best of the British Secret Service:

Bonhoeffer . . . was all humility and sweetness; he always seemed to me to diffuse an atmosphere of happiness, of joy in every smallest event in life, and of deep gratitude for the mere fact that he was alive. . . . He was one of the very few men that I have ever met to whom his God was real and ever close to him.[22]

Finally, on April 8, 1945, two men in civilian clothes broke in upon the prisoners gathered for a Sunday service under Bonhoeffer's leadership. The dread formula was voiced: "Pastor Bonhoeffer, get ready to come with us." Bonhoeffer drew Best aside and gave him a message for the Bishop of Chichester. Of himself he said: "This is the end. For me the beginning of life." The next day he was seen praying in a schoolhouse in Schönberg in the Bavarian forest. Hours later, he was hanged to death.

During those last months he had described himself in remarkable verse:

Who am I? They often tell me
I stepped from my cell's confinement
Calmly, cheerfully, firmly,

Like a squire from his country-house.
Who am I? They often tell me
I used to speak to my warders
Freely and friendly and clearly,
As though it were mine to command.
Who am I? They also tell me
I bore the days of misfortune
Equably, smilingly, proudly,
Like one accustomed to win.

Am I then really all that which other men tell of?
Or am I only what I myself know of myself?
Restless and longing and sick, like a bird in a cage,
Struggling for breath, as though hands were compressing my throat,
Yearning for colours, for flowers, for the voices of birds,
Thirsty for words of kindness, for neighbourliness,
Tossing in expectation of great events,
Powerlessly trembling for friends at infinite distance,
Weary and empty at praying, at thinking, at making,
Faint, and ready to say farewell to it all?

Who am I? This or the other?
Am I one person to-day and to-morrow another?
Am I both at once? A hypocrite before others,
And before myself a contemptibly woebegone weakling?
Or is something within me still like a beaten army,
Fleeing in disorder from victory already achieved?

Who am I? They mock me, these lonely questions of mine.
Whoever I am, Thou knowest, O God, I am Thine! [23]

VI

There is no special secret to the impact and diffusion of Bonhoeffer's views. His much-trusted friend, Eberhard Bethge, published his texts, and the widespread dissatisfaction of Christians with current Christianity took the matter from there. Avant-garde Christians flocked to Bonhoeffer by instinct. He states what has been troubling them.

A more interesting question is, what will become of today's avant-garde Christians? It appears that many of them are headed for poignant disillusionment. For Bonhoeffer is not a strong enough thinker to support a reformation. His brain was fertile, his experience crucial, his witness compelling. But he was not, when all is said, a sufficiently "secular" thinker. He is Karl Barth with a concern for concrete historical responsibilities. He is a Bible-quoting Christian of great self-mastery, inwardness, and sensitivity. But, in the end, like many influenced by Barth, he is tempted to stand upon Olympus judging the maturity of the ages, and he attempts to speak "from God's viewpoint" or "from the viewpoint of the Gospels."

A genuinely secular thinker who reads Bonhoeffer will resent being told that only in the Gospels can he understand who he is. A genuine atheist will marvel at those who say they "live without God" only to be seen praying alone for hours before death. A genuine agnostic will observe that "religionless Christianity" assists him in making a decision no more than "religious Christianity" did. It will seem, in fact, as if Bonhoeffer and his followers are at last admitting what atheists and agnostics saw long ago: viz., that Christianity is no longer viable. It may, understandably, take committed Christians a little longer to make a clean break. But the best of Bonhoeffer sounds exactly like the best an atheistic humanist might perform.

Are avant-garde Christians presiding over—and assisting—the demise of Christianity? Are they so weakening the affirmations of Christianity that even atheists may now be inscribed on the rolls in good grace? There are two viewpoints from which to answer these questions. From one, Christianity is capitulating. From the other, Christianity has been so successful in inculcating its primary values in our civilization that even atheists and agnostics subscribe to them, and hence the Christian church is now free, like a good parent, to accept a new, less central position in the household.

The latter point of view seems to be more accurate. What Bonhoeffer admired in the religionless men he met was precisely their integrity, their love for human beings, their courage under suffering, their fidelity to intelligence. Such values do not suggest nihilism or absurdity. They suggest that what Christianity commends as the secret of human life is plausible. Dostoevsky had written: "If there is no God, everything is permitted." He might rather have said: "When everything is permitted, some men are faithful to intelligence, love, and honesty, exactly as if there were a God who revealed himself as truth, life, love."

Bonhoeffer's *Letters* reached the United States at a time when the giants of two generations—Tillich and the Niebuhrs—were growing old. It was a moment when the grip of German theology on the American Christian consciousness was weakening. For theological discourse was moving from seminaries to the universities and a new, American theological language had to be learned. Increasingly, theologians were no longer preaching from pulpits to already convinced Christians— and even there they were discovering through Nazism in Germany and racial hatred in the United States that presence in church does not Christian behavior make. On the contrary, young men taught by Tillich and the Niebuhrs were speaking to real political and social issues, and many in the Christian church hated—actually hated— them for it.

Again, whereas before theologians could take for granted that Americans who mattered were Protestant Christians and accepted a basic framework of religious beliefs and attitudes, all of a sudden after 1960 they began to discover Catholics, Jews, and nonbelievers. Desperately, they needed a "nonreligious" interpretation of Christianity. An enormous hunger and insecurity explain the eagerness with which Bonhoeffer's few-score fragmentary pages have been seized upon. And we now see Christians tumbling over one another to be religionless, atheistic, and secular—in the name of Jesus.

What, then, *is* Christianity? The enormous, laborious process of disengaging Christianity from Christendom, and Christianity from religion, has hardly yet been begun. It should not be surprising that scholars disagree, that the ordinary Christian is perplexed and even resentful, that prophets speak in riddles. But at least in turning toward men, Bonhoeffer was profoundly orthodox. The scandal of Christianity first began when (so it is claimed) God chose to reveal himself and speak his own name through a man, at a given place, in an appointed time, subject to all the ambiguities and probabilities of human history.

If Christianity has one meaning, then, it is a meaning Pastor Bonhoeffer discerned with the utmost clarity. Bonhoeffer refused to think of God as some distant magical figure, or someone waiting "beyond" death. On the contrary, "God is the 'beyond' in the midst of our life." God is found in ordinariness.

By contrast, many preachers (especially on festivals), in concert with Hollywood movies about Jesus, falsify Christianity at the central point. In their version, Jesus is always distinguishable from the crowd. He walks surrounded in a nimbus of light. He is always center-stage, a little higher than the others, singled out by a halo. In actual history, Jesus was a man like other men. Religion tries to escape from history; Christianity embraces its destiny within history.

The point of being a Christian is not to be different from other men; it is to become a man. Worship and prayer are not exercises in magic, but ways of penetrating through phantasy to reality, and gathering courage to act; in them, one identifies with the God of concrete, daily events. Christians err drastically in stressing their differences from other men, as if to boast of advantages. Bonhoeffer was faithful to the inner meaning of Christianity when he wrote:

God is teaching us that we must live as men who can get along very well without him. The God who is with us is the God who forsakes us (Mark 15:34). The God who makes us live in this world without using him as a working hypothesis is the God before whom we are ever standing. Before God and with him we live without God. . . . God is weak and powerless in the world, and that is exactly the way, the only way, in which he can be with us and help us. Matthew 8:17 makes it crystal clear that it is not by his omnipotence that Christ helps us but by his weakness and suffering.[24]

The mystery which Christianity preaches, the mystery which not every one can accept, is that God is God. God is not a function of man's needs. God does not show himself. God is silent, patient, still, and the surface of the world of ordinariness is unbroken. "Jesus does not call men to a new religion," Bonhoeffer writes, "but to life." The Christian tries to live his own life as well as Jesus lived his, with attention to each detail as it comes. That is enough for a lifetime. Whatever God plans to do with such modest accomplishments—even with a man's willingness to climb a hangman's scaffold, afraid but steady—is God's own surprise. The surprise, of course, may be nothing at all—in which case, to have lived as Jesus lived is joy enough.

NOTES

1. Princeton University Press (Princeton, New Jersey, 1941), p. 531.
2. Association Press (New York, 1962), p. 10.

3. Macmillan (New York).
4. Daniel Callahan (ed.), Macmillan (New York, 1966).
5. Bobbs-Merrill (New York, 1966), p. 113.
6. Macmillan (New York, 1963).
7. Macmillan Paperback (New York, 1962).
8. *The Way to Freedom*, Harper & Row (New York, 1966), p. 246.
9. Macmillan (New York, 1949).
10. *Ibid.*, pp. 35-38.
11. Quoted by Ved Mehta, *The New Theologian*, Harper & Row (New York, 1966) p. 168.
12. *Ethics*, Macmillan (New York, 1962), p. 3.
13. *Ibid.*, p. 161.
14. *I Loved This People*, John Knox Press (Richmond, Virginia, 1965), p. 20.
15. *Ibid.*, p. 21.
16. *Letters and Papers From Prison*, Macmillan (New York, 1962), p. 196.
17. *Ibid.*, p. 162.
18. *Ibid.*, pp. 165-66.
19. *Ibid.*, pp. 198-200.
20. *Ibid.*, p. 205.
21. *Ibid.*, pp. 205-06.
22. *The New Theologian*, p. 169.
23. *Letters*, pp. 221-22.
24. *Ibid.*, pp. 219-20.

15

The Emergence of Hope

Thinkers of the Free Church tradition characteristically imagine the Kingdom of God as a future transformation of the earth; their eschatology always has a biting socio-political edge. It is not that they expect heaven on earth; rather, they think it a Christian duty to help push the world into the new age ever glimmering upon the horizon. Sometimes they attempt to realize the Kingdom in small disciplined communities in retirement from the sinful world; at other times, they attempt—through public schools, separation of church and state, democracy, and a Social Gospel for the economic order—to help worldly society in its evolution toward a fuller realization of the Gospel in history. When the Free Church tradition takes the upper hand in American Christianity, hope and vision are born anew.

The more classical Protestant traditions are better suited to the mood of crisis and the deep conviction of abiding sinfulness than to the dreaming of hopeful dreams. Neo-orthodoxy seemed heresy to many in the Bible Belt. Moreover, when the revolt of the young theologians against the long unchallenged dominance of Reinhold Niebuhr and Paul Tillich finally arrived, it was led (in diverging directions) by two Baptist theologians, William Hamilton and Harvey Cox.

Hamilton and Cox are different in more ways than they are similar. But one theme they announce in common is the possibility of hope, the style of optimism, the sense of an unmade future yet to be built. Again, *they are both saddened by the present ineffectiveness of the institutional church, and they both urge greater emulation of the language methods, and ways of pragmatic, political, swiftly evolving American society. For both of them, that old-time religion has, like* Romanità, *seen its better days. The new style is secular.*

The sudden emergence of Harvey Cox as a theological hero was, for his friends, a challenge to their accustomed rhetorical strategies. It is one thing, imagining oneself one of the avant-garde, to argue against conservative or even reactionary companions in the Church; to argue with someone who overnight seizes the point of the caravan requires a different mode altogether. My main objection to The Secular City *was its unmitigated optimism; secondly, its more generous allowance for political problems in the city than for those in the Church. Otherwise, I share the sense of need for a theology of optimism. I do not agree with Cox's judgment about existentialism—that it marked the last decadence of a corrupt capitalist civilization; existentialism marks a movement of re-birth, and is one of the sources of our present hope. Nor do I think that Cox uses the word "metaphysics" with understanding, despite the fact that basic inquiries about human life are required for his own program. Finally, I felt he had protected himself too little against simple identification with the spirit of our own age; he did not seem to retain enough ground for the launching of prophecy and criticism against the urban, pragmatic, profane style we both admire. The strategic difficulty was how to agree with Cox, support his program, and yet voice large qualifications.*

With William Hamilton's assertions about the "Death of God" I again had mixed emotions. As a psychological description of what is happening to many people, Hamilton's writing is colorful, graceful, and accurate. Affluence and technology kill the sources of experience and insight from which awareness of God has usually come. When a man lives in a heated six-room house, drives an automobile to work, eats well enough to require dieting, lives softly enough to require Air Force exercises, and moves outside family and community patterns traditional for generations, he is apt to live outside the range of any but technical human experiences. The whole point of affluence and technology is to spare him experiences of inadequacy, fragility, commitment, risk, and earthy, complete love. He is never tied down. He can always move elsewhere. Nothing is crucial.

Bread and shelter will always be his. Urban man leads a trivial life. The city, not God, is the rock, the fortress, the treasure of middle-class life. Only the poor suffer from the city; but the middle classes use God's name in their own behalf, and that God cares little for the poor, who are dirty, lazy and lawless.

God, then, is dead. Why have white Anglo-Saxon Protestants in America become aware of it only lately? The God who brings Miss America her title, to whom her success is due, is stone-cold dead. The Beatles are more meaningful than Jesus.

On the constructive side, however, Professor Hamilton has had so far too little to say. *It is not enough to turn to Jesus as a mysteriously attractive model for ethical action. Unless Jesus is God, the mystery of his attractiveness reduces to personal whimsy, and there are certainly many historical figures closer to us who speak with greater relevance to our time. And if Jesus is God, those who confess his name must have at least rudimentary criteria for the correct use of the word "God." What are those criteria?* The constructive task still lies ahead of us. The easy dismissal of philosophy makes grace cheap.

If now is a time to build, the achievement of writers like Hamilton and Cox is to show us that we must build from the beginning. The theological revival of the '20s, '30s, and '40s, Langdon Gilkey has recently written, "sought boldly to speak to men of God in the old terms to a world of modern minds." In a time of crisis, middle-class illusions were shattered and many almost recovered an ancient Christian view of things. But now affluence and the pragmatic temper have taken over; the deep springs of human experience are dry. Hard philosophical questions about key theological words—the meaning of a phrase like "the mighty acts of God," or even the meaning of "God"—go unanswered and there is a growing suspicion that no one knows the answer. Five years ago, theologians seemed to think that all they had to do was comment upon Tillich, Niebuhr, Barth, Bultmann, Rahner and Häring; they saw themselves as "a generation of 'scholastics' whose function would be to work out in greater detail the firm theological principles already forged."

The renewal of Christianity has reached a new stage. The renewal is now so deep that many face the possibility that Christianity may have to be abandoned. For if it cannot be freely rejected as unworthy, neither

can it be freely chosen as worthy; examination is the requirement of re-
sponsible choice. "Our theological task," Gilkey writes, "is not that of
'scholastics' working out the implications of firm theological systems in-
herited from a more creative past. We must go back to the very begin-
ning, must defend the reality of God and the possibility of language about
him in a world in which no prior assumptions, metaphysical or religious,
can be taken for granted, and in which ordinary experience seems swept
clean of cosmic coherence and ultimate meaning alike. Our primary prob-
lem is to find where we can begin in this effort—however God may be
known, the knowledge of his reality is prior to all else; no revelation, no
Christ of faith, no ecclesiology is ultimately possible or intelligible if the
category of deity remains totally empty."

Professors Hamilton and Cox have brought us face to face with the
primary problem. No one yet knows how to give an answer; it is not,
then, invidious to say that Hamilton and Cox do not go deep enough.
The task is so huge that there is room for many laborers, each concen-
trating upon his own predilected pursuits. My preference is to press the
discussion closer to philosophical issues; one advantage in belonging to
an ecumenical community is that no one of us has to do alone all that
needs to be done.

I. *Where Is Theology Going?*

JOHN C. BENNETT wrote in 1933:

The realization that the human race has no such glorious future as we
had dreamed but that with our best efforts streaked with compromises we
are in for centuries of blundering and sin, with catastrophe never far
away, does something to our spirits. We may still believe that we can get
results. . . . *We will never again be even tempted to substitute humanity*
for God. We will look elsewhere than to enthusiasm for a social goal for
our dynamic. [Italics added.]

Whatever happened to Christian realism? And to neo-orthodoxy?
R. R. Niebuhr tells us in 1964 that Schleiermacher was wiser than we
have been led to believe. Harvey Cox celebrates the secular city.
William Hamilton tells us that current "radical theology is both de-

scribing and relating itself to a new feeling of hope and optimism in American life today, a conviction that substantive changes in the lives of men can and will be made."

How radical is a theology that changes when a mood, even a national mood, changes? What will happen to radical theology once the decisive moments of the Negro revolution have passed? Can Christian theology thrive only on crises, alternately optimistic and pessimistic in tune with events?

The "death of God" metaphor may represent a mood of nostalgia, and it may also characterize what is happening in the psyches of a particular group of modern Western Christians today. But the metaphor may also be a sham. In a sophisticated, highly critical and genuinely pluralistic age, the "Christian context" once supplied by the churches and the seminaries has been dissolved. In a hardheaded and pragmatic society the language of Scripture is bucolic and quaint; it is also an unneeded luxury. Consequently, the "biblical" part of "biblical realism" has brought increasing embarrassment. Many Christians, now truly involved in pluralistic living and thinking, have found that biblical language simply is not used by other people.

The crisis of the present generation is that it is looking forward to the birth of a new kind of culture whose shape nobody quite discerns. Having been brought up to distinguish the Greek mentality from the Hebrew mentality and to favor the latter, this generation of Christians has been embarrassed by the fact that the rest of the world does not think as the Hebrews thought. Consequently, this generation is now facing problems like those the Church of the twelfth and thirteenth centuries encountered when meditation on the Scriptures in repetitive patterns no longer sufficed. The excitement of those days was the Greek mentality; in our day it is the secular mentality. The task of the most sensitive and inquisitive Christians is now, as it was then, to work out a transcultural interpretation of their beliefs and attitudes, to turn with a sort of optimism to the new cultural horizon opening up before them.

Then as now there were many whose first concern was social: the Delta Ministry is to the local Mississippi clergy as the Friars Minor of Francis of Assisi were to their local clergy. The staff members of the various national church organizations are the "regular clergy," free of diocesan restrictions, of the Protestant church.

But the problems of the speculatively inclined do not arise from social mood or social need. When the horizon of a culture shifts, the ghosts of many dead questions rise from their tombs. In the polar night of contemporary agnosticism, in which all who live pluralistically are both obliged and privileged to live, the hidden God does not reveal himself; he remains hidden. The absent God is not also present, but merely absent. It is impossible to speak of God in the old ways— either those of a genial liberal theology or those of Hebraic neo-orthodoxy. Moreover, the exigent mind will not really be satisfied with "dropping the question altogether" or dodging the issue by immersing itself in the tasks, however noble, of building up the secular city.

The secular city must be built, and fashioned both with joy and chastened expectations. But the inaccessible God must also be given serious reflection. Agnosticism is exceedingly close to authentic belief. Should the death of God have come as a surprise? The "God" of the ordinary Christian context of our times, like the "God" of philosophical rationalism, was due to die. It has never been easy to speak well of God, and human language used of him is always systematically misleading. We are, and we have always been, in a great darkness. The feelings of belief we cherish, the images and habitual attitudes which occupy us when we pray or speak of him, are not God. To distinguish authentic belief, which has penetrated beyond all the created props of culture and personal conditioning and become silent in the darkness—to distinguish such belief from atheism has ever been a task for "the discernment of spirits." It exacts a maturity much labored for by those who would be proficient, and not merely children, in the Christian faith.

In theology it has always been exhilarating to follow moods around. But Christian theology is also pluralistic and needs some who follow moods and some who labor on the issues of the longer cycle. The Protestant churches are no longer young, traditionless, and institutions of one culture only. Protestant theologians must therefore begin to face those problems which emerge when one cultural horizon yields to another. How is it possible to maintain spiritual and intellectual continuity with a past that belongs to a very different cultural frame of reference? How can one be sure that the Christ of today is the same as the Christ of yesterday? If it is possible to express Christian faith in the language of two different cultures, can one also work out a language which is transcultural, for the longer cycle?

Langdon Gilkey was surely correct when he wrote in *Christianity and Crisis* last April that Anglo-American secularism had undercut the starting points of biblical religion. What now? William W. Bartley III spoke recently for the wholly secular man, pointing out that to say and to mean that God is dead and then to go on using the Bible or talking Christianity is, to say the least, a circuitous way of being secular. It seems much more economical simply not to believe.

Conventional language about God is dead, and some conventional religious institutions are useless where they are not harmful. But those who have daily eaten the bread of naked faith have not drawn their sustenance from "the religious age." Correspondingly, they are not frightened by its passing. Let those who wish to explore the meaning of the death of God in their own experience ask themselves whether they are simply coming to that boundary-line farewell to familiar images, feelings, and securities described so often in ascetical literature. In the ascent toward a purified faith, there are still further terrors to endure, a thicker darkness. Besides "God" and "conventional institutions" and "conventional pessimism," there are still other things to be brought into question. If we are to have a radical theology, and not merely a change in mood, let us also raise questions about ourselves. Perhaps we have lost the Christian faith. Perhaps we are atheists, under wraps. Perhaps in the darkness we are only just beginning to understand what it is to believe. Perhaps.

In any case, history is not a cup of tea and in the end we may expect to be as broken as other men have been. In the meantime the secular city deserves celebration, enthusiasm, and ardent hopes.

II. *Religion and Revolution*

In the main, the message of Harvey Cox is sound: our Christian faith must be related to that new culture which, everywhere, is rising up all around us. The new culture is rising on the rubble of the immediate past. For writers of thirty years ago, the image for our age was that of a great night, a tunnel, a passage through the depths of crisis and despair. Now that we stand blinking in a new daylight, their anguish should not be forgotten.

In *The Secular City* (pp. 114-23), Cox argues that we need a theology of revolution. In a recent article, he argues that we need an educational theory which stresses adaptability to change. What is striking about both arguments is that in each case Cox instinctively avoids questions about the *content* of theories of revolution and education, in order to stress the *dynamic factors of intelligence and imagination* in which such theories are to take root. In this sense, Cox is close in instinct to Bernard Lonergan. He is more interested in life than in lessons, in persons than in theories, in actual structures than in arguments. But for this reason his work reopens the desperately needed dialogue between thinkers and doers, between professors and the men who turn the heavy wheels of civilization: the one dialogue which ever revivifies the academy.

Still, the task that Cox has so successfully dramatized requires many hands and many types of talent and interest. I would like in this brief space to push his argument farther along in one of the many directions it opens up.

"Religion," in the pejorative sense in which Bonhoeffer uses the word, is largely a matter of unquestioning, uncritical acceptance of cultural feelings, pictures, beliefs, and practices. In general, these feelings and pictures tended to assure one that the world had a certain shape, and that the ecclesiastical is a special, privileged sector of that world, and that each human self needs to find its place in a vast but orderly "scheme of things." For most of human history, in fact, the world seemed to man to change slowly, if at all: there seemed to be pitifully little that, from age to age, was new under the sun. A premium was placed upon a man's obtaining a large view of things, and organizing his life according to the place he fitted within the scheme. It seems to have been difficult, in those days, for men to recall that they were finite; ironically, man's lack of power to change his world made him both acquiescent and complacent.

Just as ironically, now that in the late twentieth-century man has accumulated more knowledge and technical power than ever before, he also seems more humble. Men know that they are infinitesimal specks in the universe. They commonly recognize that even the best of their scientific theories are tentative, relative, and partial—in a sense, more like human projections or myths than what the ancients meant by a science of the real. Moreover, whereas the ancient Greeks and Romans could without apology imagine that foreigners were barbarians, today men grope toward a consciousness of a common humanity, requiring insight into and sympathy with the most diverse of peoples. Again, psychological sophistication has taught men how little they know about themselves, how vast and far-reaching is the power of the unconscious over them. The crisis of our age is not one of pride, as men of "religion" were wont to assert; it is rather one of too much diffidence. Men have lost confidence in themselves. They do not bestir themselves to act in a manner commensurate with their abilities and power; thus their power, because of a failure of nerve, threatens to destroy them. They *must* organize their common life. Their vocation is a new world politics.

In this perspective, the first task of a theology of revolution or a theory of Christian education is to teach men pride. Men must begin to be men; they must have vision, courage, and great-mindedness. Moreover, religion must be reconceived, and a neglected part of its inheritance drawn forth from its treasure house. For the root of religion is the same as the root of revolution: the unrestricted, detached, relentless drive to understand. It is because men raise hard questions about platitudes and the status quo that they revolt. It is because men raise ever further questions that no idol can, indefinitely, bear human scrutiny. Thus even "religion," which had domesticated God, has now been discredited, and those who seek the living God through the relentless drive to ask questions have moved off again into the night.

Ours is perhaps the first generation in human history to have to absorb the lesson of the transitoriness of human deeds and achievements in almost every aspect of our lives: that is what it means to live in a world of rapid change. Our household utensils, our entertainment, our travel—almost everything we use and do is different today from what it was ten years ago. Other generations found God, their rock and their foundation, through the achievement of a metaphysical or religious view of the stability of world order. We find him, our elusive, idol-resisting, inconceivable God, through our sense of complete responsibility for communal life on earth, and through our conviction of the tentativeness of theories, pictures, and world views. Openness, uncertainty, fragmentariness are our mode of life; boldness is the virtue we require most.

The true God will speak very clearly to modern men, but not where he spoke to our fathers. For nothing in the world is secular, just as nothing is "religious." Everything is at one both profane and sacred, both pragmatic and symbolic: a great jet 707 lunging into the gray overcast is both technical and sacramental, binding men together, ringing the entire community of men. The mystery of man's community—how in this absurd world can there be so much goodness?—is the mystery of God's presence. In the Middle Ages, men located God best in bits of bread; in our day, our Eucharist is the poor and the oppressed. Both ages celebrate community: *Ubi caritas et amor, ibi Christus est.*

Education of imagination, education for change: as for revolution, so for religion, the root of the matter is fidelity to the open-ended drive to ask questions. But one must question also the secular city. Our urban centers are not now, nor will they be, divine. Only sacraments, bearers of grace, to those who have faith.

III. *The God Who Will Be*

American Catholics down the years have committed grievous sins of rabid anti-communism. Consequently, one of the main imperatives of Catholics at present is to puncture the popular myths, biases, and prejudices about communism that distort American political debate. On the international scene, the time has come for Christians and Marxists, no longer merely to ignore or to destroy one another, but to learn from one another and to criticize one another. The shedding of one another's blood is useless, the ignoring of one another empty.

One of the main points at which the current dialogue between Christians and Marxists converges is the meaning of the future. Contrary to stereotype, Marxist philosophy is not materialistic in a Western sense; it hopes for a future in which men's capacities of imagination, decision and creative labor will be completely developed. Such a future may never, in fact, arrive; thus, the Marxist conception of the future might be open. In that case, the function of the concept of the future would be to provide leverage for criticism and reform of the present. *Secularia semper reformanda.*

At a recent conference of Catholics and Marxists in Austria, Karl Rahner defined Christianity in a perspective that might make sense to Marxists: "Christianity is the religion of the absolute future." Rahner's point is familiar to students of Reinhold Niebuhr; Christianity is eschatalogical; it refuses to call any present social arrangement final; within history, justice is never complete. Christianity refuses to idolize the present or the past, for its Lord is one who is ever to be awaited: "Come, Lord Jesus!" Christians are committed to building up the kingdom of God on earth, a kingdom of truth, liberty, justice, and love. Since we do not yet have an international social order characterized by such values, Christians cannot very well rest upon what has so far been achieved; the pilgrimage is not over; there are many painful miles yet to march. *Ecclesia semper reformanda.*

Marxist thinkers have always had a predilection for one of the rather neglected Christian traditions, that of Joachim of Flora, the Anabaptists, and the Free Churches. The more established Christian traditions—Catholic, Lutheran, and Calvinist—have preferred to work in continuity with the institutions of the Holy Roman Empire. They have found it possible to work out various arrangements with emperors, kings, princes, and later with parliaments and economic corporations. They have operated on the assumption that there is a natural, created base for Christianity—a set of pre-Christian or religious or human values on which Christianity can "build." They have been more or less protective of the "moral fiber" of society, of its educational system and its family mores. They are proud of an entity they call "western civilization," which they think of as "Christian."

By contrast, Joachim of Flora preached a coming "third age" of the Holy Spirit discontinuous with the pagan institutions, laws, and orders of the past. Anabaptists and Free Churchmen regarded the classical Lutheran and Calvinist reformations as "halfway reformations," much too limited in scope. For under Lutherans and Calvinists, as under Catholics, the establishment of religion remained intact; the social and economic institutions of the pagan past were still being "baptized." Free Churchmen desired a less institutionalized, more voluntary, more demanding church. Their desires were so exigent that the future became a crucial category in their thought. Some of them used the future as escape from the present; but still more of them used it as a weapon of criticism against the present. They demanded an authenticity, an integrity, and a commitment that empowered many poor and simple people to stand firm against feudal and monarchical institutions, and to generate much momentum for change in Western society.

In American theological thought, Harvey Cox stands more nearly than any other in this tradition. It is not surprising, then, that Cox is the Christian theologian most sensitively attuned to the Christian-Marxist dialogue and the importance of the category of the future. In his rejoinder in *The Secular City Debate,* in fact, he has promised us an approach to language about God through language about the future. Such an enterprise will be at the heart of the issue between Marxists and Christians. Since the basic notion seems sound, I would like to help the project along by voicing a few critical reflections.

In the first place, Marxist thought regards existentialism as a stage in the progressive decadence of the West. In the Marxist view, existentialism has not healed the split between thought and action which is the disease of Western philosophy. Western philosophy is too "intellectualist"; it does not give sufficient weight to the fact that the role of thought is not merely to reflect the world, but to *change* the world. Again, it does not give sufficient weight to the fact that thinking is highly conditioned by social, economic, and other circumstances. Harvey Cox is not especially interested in epistemological questions, but he has been convinced by the Marxist critique of existentialism as a mere emotional retreat, a philosophy of inaction and Hamlet-like reflection, a disease of inwardness. Moreover, he has joined the Marxist critique of inwardness to Bonhoeffer's complaint about still another kind of inwardness: the concern and anxiety which German and Scandinavian religious thought has cherished as "the religious dimension" of men's subjective life.

Nevertheless, both for Marxist thought and for Cox, the source of that thought which changes the world lies in the imagination, the projects, and the decisions of men. The future does not merely happen; men must invent it and take responsibility for it. For both, moreover, responsibility is not merely a factor of social conditioning; first one man must stand firm and then another—decision must well up from the strength of each individual. Otherwise there is no maturity, only docility, passivity, and conformity.

Existentialist emphasis on decision-making often seems to be too emotive and individualistic; even social relations are conceived on the model of eye-to-eye, deeply personal "encounters." With Marxist thinkers, Cox insists on the social dimensions and social realities of responsibility; much less than, say, Camus' Meursault in *The Stranger* will he allow a man to contemplate morosely his own emotional complexities. Does Cox at this point run the risk of evasion, promoting the reform of institutions because the reform of oneself is so difficult? There are some passages in *The Secular City*—particularly those on the "I-you relationship"—which read like the rationalization of a busy, harried man. But to criticize Cox in this way would be to acquiesce in a dualism that is untenable. The individual and the social are not, in reality, separate; our language and hence even our private thoughts and our personal values are social phenomena. Cox is right to insist that maturity arises through social and political commitment. An accurate criticism, perhaps, is that he has not yet told us very much about how to choose among or how to criticize alternative commitments; he has merely announced where he stands.

But even at this point Cox's rejoinder in *The Secular City Debate* offers promise. "In our time the metaphysicians," he writes, "instead of integrating our lives for us, will probably more often challenge the premature integrations and cultural foreclosures that constrict us. . . . Our task today is to transmute the answers of classical metaphysics into questions that will guard the openness of our symbol worlds today." I think Cox is wrong in his historical judgment that such thinkers as Aristotle and St. Thomas thought of their own work as "intellectual systems" which might "integrate whole cultural periods." Neither Aristotle or Aquinas had much success among their contemporaries, and their work presents to the serious student today a record of tentative, dialectical, constantly changing forays into uncharted areas. But the main point is that Cox now sees metaphysics as a critical enterprise, as the raising of further questions, as the dialectical exploding of presuppositions. The metaphysical impulse is the question-raising impulse.

Moreover, I would like to point out that the empirical ground which allows men to conceive of the "absolute future" or of an "open future" is precisely the human ability to ask questions without limit. The point of the expression "absolute future" or "open future" is that such a future cannot be conceived merely as a projection from present conditions; for a merely projected future is limited and does not represent the complete realization of historical possibility. Man is gifted with an imagination and a skeptical attitude which makes it possible for him to *alter* the conditions of the future, to *change* the world. Consequently, the human animal "transcends" even his own empirical projections: he calls them into question.

How, then, does a man know *now* that his authentic goal is the absolute future, not merely a projection? He cannot envisage an absolute future; all he can envisage is the projected future. He knows that his goal is the absolute future because he recognizes in himself a capacity on demand to change direction, to shift his presuppositions, to imagine no alternatives: in short, to raise limitless series of questions. Right now, this minute, a man can become aware, at least, indirectly, of the profundity and limitless resourcefulness of his drive to ask questions. There is no point in history at which he can imagine himself refusing to ask questions, surrendering his capacity to imagine, project, and break out anew. The ground of the conception of the absolute future is man's unrestricted drive to ask questions, his relentless openness.

This is the point of the question—a traditional one—put to the Marxists at the Salzburg Colloquy by J. B. Metz: "Will the realization of the total man give the final answer to man's questions, or will man when fully developed, be still more the questioner, more capable still of an ever-expanding future? Will the future be filled with questions which exceed and transcend our projects and our tentative notions of the future? This would in no way contradict the autonomy of the human race since it is this openness to the future which constitutes the very essence of man." [See R. Garaudy, *From Anathema to Dialogue* (New York, 1966), p. 60].

Without the drive to ask questions, revolution, reform, and progress are inconceivable. In order for a revolution to be launched, men must question the present and diagnose it; question other possible alternatives and imagine a new world; raise questions in others until a new community takes shape; and question alternative strategies and tactics for realizing the new against the inertia of the old. A theology of revolution depends at each step upon the relentlessness and the skills of the drive to ask questions. Of course, it is not enough to ask questions; one must also make decisions and, above all, act. But it is useful in the highest degree to notice the role of question-asking in intelligent social and political action.

Moreover, it seems to me that the drive to ask questions is at one and the same time the source of man's openness to God and the source of social and political change. In brief, there is a startling point of unity between language about God and language about social and political reforms; the human drive to ask questions constitutes the openness which allows men to transcend the present, and which gives rise to both languages. To think of the drive to understand as the generator of religious language is, of course, continuous with some strands of tradition; but it is mature to recognize one's continuity with the past.

What is new is the suddenly acquired power of men to change their environment, both natural and institutional. Whereas in earlier days the panorama of human life seemed to confirm that there is nothing new under the sun, nowadays the pace and scope of change are so obvious that someone might plausibly wonder whether there is anything stable. In a world now conceived as a bundle of loose ends, open to the most surprising, contingent, and unpredictable developments—a world of probabilities rather than of certainties—man's sense of responsibility for his values, his actions, and even his survival has become a sign much more cogent as an image of God than the ancient sense of dependence on the God of the ordered cosmos.

In short, theology grows out of reflection upon actual human experience in the world. The experience which captivates the imagination of our age is the experience of change, the move toward further frontiers, the hope of a human brotherly world civilization. In *every* human experience, the language of transcendence is available to men because the human drive to raise questions is present in every experience. It is not necessary to kick the faces of those who preceded us in order to speak of transcendence in our own way. When Heidegger used the language of anxiety and concern, he spoke to the experience of a dying civilization. The God spoken of as *will be* happens to speak more clearly to us, but we are not, except momentarily, at the apex of the human race.

Recognizing that fact, we do not think of God as one on whom we "depend" but rather as one who eludes our attempt to speak adequately of him, even as he eluded the clutches of our ancestors. Taking up our daily, concrete responsibilities, we cannot be sure that we hold God in our hands. Like the atheist, we work in darkness regarding God. But we accept the symbol of the community of truth, freedom, love, and justice bequeathed us in the Gospel of Jesus Christ and interpret our labors in its light. If we are correct, God is the one who is now with us without revealing himself magically, and the one who, in the absolute future, will be all in all.

16

The Philosophical Roots
of Religious Unity

The following paper was first read as a lecture at Brandeis University in the autumn of 1964. It later appeared in the Journal of Ecumenical Studies. *It represents an attempt to bring several philosophical traditions together—English and American language analysis, existentialism, phenomenology, and scholasticism. The fact of intentionality is felt in every one of these traditions, but is seldom conceptualized and brought into the center of discussion.*

WHEN Pope Paul VI traveled to Jerusalem in January, 1964, he addressed a prayer to the One God in which he hoped to be joined by other Christians, Jews, and Moslems. Yet surely there are differences among these different religious traditions about how to conceive of God. By what right, then, did the Pope utter such a prayer, and by what right do others join in it? In what way can those who believe in the One God be said to belong to one family?

The purpose of this short paper is to expose the philosophical roots of religious ecumenism. It is not a theological paper. It is philosophical. It is brief, and so it cannot be as detailed nor as technical as it might be.[1] My aim is to make a contribution toward settling two

301

related problems of religious language. The first problem can be stated in this way: How can men who conceive of God differently be said to be relating themselves to the same God? The second problem is: What is the relation between the sentences of a given religious tradition and the fundamental act of faith in God made by the individual believer within that tradition?

My answer to both these questions depends upon the same point: what is fundamental and of first importance in belief in God is neither the conception which one has of God, nor the sentences expressing the beliefs of the religious tradition in which one belongs, but rather one's response to the *intentionality* of one's own intelligence. This paper depends upon the distinction between the intentionality of intelligence and the conceptions of intelligence, or again between the intentionality of intelligence and the system of sentences by which the beliefs of intelligence are articulated. Most of our time must therefore be occupied with making clear what we mean by "intentionality."

I. *The Experience of Intentionality*

When most philosophers in the past have dealt with the question of God, they have been preoccupied with conceptions of God, or with the sentences of given religious traditions. They have, in the main, neglected to consider intentionality. For this reason, it appears, much philosophical theology is unsatisfying, even to believers; for it is often merely conceptual, and fails to touch genuine religion. And it is also for this reason that Catholic, Protestant, Jewish, and Moslem theologians, who heretofore have usually worked each within his own religious tradition, have been unable to find a method which would enable them to translate successfully from one tradition into another. They have sometimes been able to speak the language of sympathy and good will; they have not so often been able to speak the language of mutual intelligence and understanding. Attention to the factor of intentionality may help to remedy some of these difficulties.

The factor of intentionality is, furthermore, already available in our own experience; it requires only to be noticed. Why has it been overlooked for so long? My general argument is that our conscious attention is more easily taken up with the excitement and novelty of our ideas, our formulations, our conceptions, our words; [2] we easily neglect the restless, relentless drive of our intelligence which led us to discover or to fashion these instruments. We are prevented by the trinkets and the tools from reflecting upon the activity which produced them. In order to become conscious of our own intentionality, then, we must devise a way of going beyond the threshold at which we usually stop, of reflecting upon a part of our own activity which we customarily neglect. Each must join this effort, to become aware, each for himself, of a part of his intelligent activity he may have somewhat neglected.

No doubt the best way to enter upon this quest is to begin upon familiar ground. As we have noted, there has always been some dissatisfaction among philosophers, as among men in various religious traditions, concerning who or what it is that they are naming when they use the word "God." For some philosophers, "God" names a conception: that of the Supreme Being, the Being than whom no greater can be thought, the Omnipotent, the Eternal, etc. For them, the problem is to prove whether that conception "exists." For religious people, the name "God" is used according to the grammatical structure, forms of prayer and worship, and images from Holy Writ and daily action, which they have received in their own religious tradition. Each philosopher speaks of God according to the texture—logical, grammatical, and imaginative—of his own philosophical system. Each religious person speaks of him according to the texture of his own proper religious tradition. Out of the diversity of such textures, we have seen, arises the question: is there one God, or many Gods? Are we speaking of the same thing—Protestant, Catholic, Jew, Moslem, Buddhist; Anselmian, Thomist, Cartesian, Kantian, Spinozan, Humean, Whiteheadian—when we use the word "God"?

It is no doubt true that when different men use the word "God," they have different *conceptions* of God, or at least different rules for using the word. Moreover, so intimate is this word in our human vocabularies, it is probably true that no two men have exactly the same conception of "God," any more than any two have exactly the same idea in mind when they use the word "love." But a man's concept is not the same as his *intention*. It is entirely possible that men, when they speak of "God" in a babel of different ways, intend to name the same person or thing. They may be unable to understand each other's descriptions, or follow each other's methods, and, still, they may be speaking of the same person or thing.

Let us put it this way. God is unknown. No one has ever seen God. Our *conceptions* of him are like arrows which shoot in the direction of God, but do not reach him; or like moths which circle around the light without being able to penetrate it. On the other hand, it is possible that our aim exceeds the strength of our bows; that the attraction of the light is steadier than our giddy movements. Certain it is that "God" attracts some men. So much so that some would like to escape him; some would like to get away. They do not see him or know where he is. And yet when the word "God" comes to their lips, inadequate as they are in trying to describe what they mean, they know this much: what they mean by God is not to be caught by any description, nor by any conception.

It is here that an important fact comes to light. We can recognize the inadequacy of our conceptual powers. We can say: "God is not the Supreme Being, nor Prime Act, nor the Unconditioned, nor can he stretch forth his right hand, nor is he the sun, nor an impassive contemplator, nor any other description men have ever offered." In trying to speak of God, we grope to express what we mean. We feel inwardly a compulsion, or an invitation, which we cannot articulate. "Whereof one cannot speak, thereof one must be silent," Ludwig Wittgenstein has urged us.[3] But St. Augustine [4] notes the other side of our dilemma: recognizing that God is ineffable, we are yet driven to speak of him. We cannot speak well of God; nor yet can we be silent.

The grammatical reason for our difficulty is easy to spot. Our language is formed from metaphors taken from forests, stones, ocean waves, the movements of animals, the activities of commerce, the needs of the home. Our conceptions, no matter how purified, always have reference to things we can touch or taste or see, or to operations we can perform or observe. As a consequence, every conception of God confounds God with the other things of our experience; and something in us tells us: that cannot be God. We come then upon the crucial fact. *The root of our language about God lies in the discriminations we make about what is not God. The root of religion lies in our ability to criticize all our conceptions, to pass judgment upon them, and to say: none of them represent God.*[5]

Unlike every other noun in our language, therefore, "God" does not get its content from an image or an operation. "God" does not receive its content by the ordinary way. "God" is not, properly speaking, a concept—an understood word which enters our language system like other words. The ancient Hebrews did well to observe this fact by refusing to use the word for God, by putting in its place a series of letters to mark where the sacred name would go if it were like other names.

It is this anomaly which has ever caused trouble for rationally inclined inquirers who want to know where the content for the word "God" comes from, since it does not come in the ordinary way. If we can make no observable experiment to give the word a descriptive, conceptual content, how do we know whether we mean by it anything at all? [6]

Many solutions to this problem have been proposed. There are two main schools of thought, the rationalist and the irrationalist. For the latter, the solution is that there is no human solution: we know of God only through God's initiative, through grace, through a revelation. God first pursues men. Some he touches and others, apparently, he does not. God owes man nothing; moreover, life can in some circumstances be quite comfortable without him; why should he then call all men to know him? We cannot know God except through his touch upon our heart, his stealthy impulse in our minds; through a special grace.

This approach is quite attractive. Yet it does not answer one grievous objection: How can I tell whether the invitation in my heart is God or only an illusion? How do I know that my wishes are not encouraging my willingness to leap? The human heart is obscure·and thickly tangled. Who can trust the instincts of his heart?

Obviously, some men do trust these instincts, do believe in God, and seem to live as well as other men. Moreover, some of them would reverse the objection voiced to them by their rationalist friends. They retort, in defense of the instincts of the heart, why trust the instincts of the mind? In a statistical universe, in which unintelligent microbes and inanimate forces like storms and fire indiscriminately kill men, in which from a scientific point of view the survival of the species seems more valuable than the survival of the individual, in this world of inexplicable and unrequited consciousness, why should one prefer to

side with intelligence, rationality, and consciousness? In this absurd
world, the instinct of the heart has at least as much to commend it as
the instinct of the intelligence.[7]

But this debate between rationalists and irrationalists, which many
of us may feel in our own hearts, is based on a grievous and unnecessary misunderstanding. We are pulled, needlessly, in two directions.
For there are forms of intelligent activity of which our traditional
theories take too little note. We oppose "reason" to "heart," the cognitive to the emotive, nature to spirit, too easily in our Western tradition; our theories divide what is not divisible. We draw the line
between rational and irrational at a point where it cannot be drawn.

The most important decisions of our intellectual life are made according to a method, and rely upon a datum of experience, which our
theories seriously neglect. We may borrow a useful word to name
these elements so often overlooked: the *intentionality* [8] of human
knowing activity; the drive to understand; the impulse of further inquiry; the ability to move in a direction; the resources to criticize our
presuppositions, our methods, and even the criteria by which we
choose presuppositions and methods.

It is the intentionality of our intelligence which ties together the
presuppositions, aims, direction, inquiries, arguments, and conclusions of each of our knowing acts. We must not imagine that our
knowing is only what appears on the surface, in the words we speak
or commit to paper. Our activity of knowing is alive and vital, and it is
doubtful whether a man can ever articulate in detail all that he has
accomplished in order to be able to make even so simple an affirmation as "This is salt," not to mention, "Salt is soluble in water," or
"My chosen method of resolving problems is the scientific method." [9]
Our activity of knowing is spurred by something like a hunger; questions torment us like the pangs of appetite; and confirmed insights
satisfy us, for a time, as water slakes our thirst, or possession our
desire. There is an eros of the understanding, a dynamism, a drive,
and, in our activity of knowing, it is not so much mere words that
count, nor conceptions, nor going through the correct responses, as
whether that eros has been satisfied. Rote learning can fool an ex-
aminer, and a man can deceive even himself into thinking that he
knows what he does not know. The eros of the understanding, however, is restless until we know that we know.

II. *One Drive, Two Phases*

Our intelligence, in other words, operates in two phases,[10] like two lenses, and is not satisfied until the phases overlap. One phase is that of understanding, of cleverness, of glibness, of having all the right ideas and acceptable answers. The other phase is that of self-criticism, self-evaluation, and self-approval. Whiz kids and geniuses can operate successfully in phase one. Those who manage to synchronize both phases are those for whom we reserve our choicest praise: the wise. Human intelligence is restless until a man knows that he knows. To know that one knows—and that one does not know—is wisdom.

What we are calling "intentionality" is operative in both phases of human understanding. It is operative in the first phase, the seeking of insights, and it is operative in the second phase, self-approbation. It operates in the first phase by making us feel uncomfortable, or restless, or merely curious; that is to say, it drives us to attain peace and pleasure by laying our questions to rest with the insights they expect. Some of the readers of this article, no doubt, are eager to see more clearly what I am trying to express by "intentionality"; it is this eagerness that is felt until the point has been seen which I wish to bring to your attention.

Moreover, there are two things that I hope will be noticed about this eagerness to understand. One is that it represents a drive, an itch, an impulse. The other is that, at this phase, this drive is terminated by an insight. By "insight," of course, I refer to that act of "getting the point," "seeing the light," "getting the picture," which the intelligent experience frequently and the dull much more rarely.[11] It is important, incidentally, to note that this act of insight is pre-verbal, pre-conceptual. For it often happens in our experience that we get the idea before we can put it into words. We see the point, before we can express that point in those words which fit the systematic patterns by which we would explain it. This common experience of insight, together with recognition of the fact that insight of itself is pre-verbal and pre-conceptual, is of the utmost importance.

But what is of more importance to us here is rather to note in our own experience that we have a *drive* to attain to such insights, in all sorts of matters, whether from the telling of a joke, to the understanding of the situation in which we find ourselves; or to an understanding of our own behavior, past or present; or to an understanding of the subject matter set before us in the university or in the business world or government. The human animal, among his many other drives, has a drive to understand. There is no need for us to try to formalize that drive, to set limits upon it, or to say it points in this direction rather than in that. On the contrary, it is extremely important to note that this drive to understand, which is basic to the human animal, is of itself an open drive.[12] It aims to understand everything with which it is confronted. Of itself, it has no prejudices or preconceptions. Of itself, it is unlimited. There is no doubt that by our own personal history, each one of us is led to limit this drive to understand, to develop expectations that look for answers in this place rather than in that, to imagine our goals in this way rather than in that. But these limitations placed upon the drive to understand are not identical with that drive. The fact that they can be perceived as limitations show that the drive to understand is of itself critical of all the limitations put upon it. In its exercise, the drive cannot help being specific and limited. But a man can always ask himself what are my preconceptions, what are my prejudices. The fact that he can question such specifications of his drive to understand indicates that the drive is prior to those specifications. It is of course impossible for a man ever to argue his way back to the pure drive to understand, a position without preconceptions, a position without prejudices. For a man is always born in history, and he always begins to understand things gradually and one at a time. This means that before he is in a position to take an overview of everything, he has already had to take up a partial standpoint, he has already had to begin to be limited; and the lifetime given him to acquire information and to develop is very short.

In any case, we can gather still other testimonies from ordinary human experience about the fact of our drive to understand. Men have a hunger to hear the end of a story, and to get the point of a story. They look upon a joke which has no point as idle, and they heap ridicule on the man who tells too many such jokes. No man admits that he never understands. It would be proof of a closed mind to say that one does not ever wish to understand. It is a compliment to say of a man that he is a man of much insight. The hunger to understand, and the experience of insight in which it terminates, are two facts amply attested to in human experience.

But there is also the second phase in human understanding, in which we are not satisfied with mere questions and the insights which at first put them to rest. In this second phase, we wish to verify what we have discovered. "Yes, I see the point. But is it so?" "Am I warranted in claiming this to be true?" In this phase of understanding, our intelligence employs a method lately beginning to be noticed in philosophy.[13] This is the method of rational consciousness or the method of reflective subjectivity. The name of the method includes "subjectivity" because the method is not satisfied by a proof from rational consistency, nor by the amassing of empirical evidence. On the contrary, this method is satisfied only by a freely made decision. The method involves the entire human person, his experiences, imagination, insights, conceptions, skills, and "good judgment."

On the other hand, this method is called "rational," or "reflective," because the decision in which it terminates is not a blind decision. It is based upon reasons, most of which or many of which can be articulated. The method of rational subjectivity is the method of making a claim, of taking a stand, for which one can give compelling reasons.[14] Moreover, the method is called that of "rational consciousness," because the area of human life in which it is operative is that of reasonable discourse. Unless a man can to some degree articulate his reasons for his claims, he cannot claim to be making a rational decision.

III. *The Source of Objectivity*

This method of rational subjectivity, moreover, is basic to our intellectual life. All knowing begins in deciding. We must decide upon our criteria of evidence and relevance. We must decide upon our purposes. We must decide whether and how much we should change our point of view before making a claim to know. It is by the method of rational subjectivity, for example, that we decide to use scientific method for solving certain problems. It is by the method of rational subjectivity that we single out the criteria of relevance and evidence by which we justify our choice of scientific method as a useful tool for human purposes.

Now these two facts of experience which we have singled out, the experience of the drive to understand and the experience of the method of rational subjectivity, are the main factors in what we are calling intentionality. Intentionality is like a searchlight stabbing out in the darkness of our ignorance, this way and that. Intentionality is the drive in our intelligence that seeks understanding, and that finally justifies its seeking by means of the method of rational subjectivity. Now this searchlight is more demanding than any system of propositions, or any science, or any discipline, placed in front of it. This searchlight is more demanding, because it is the source of men's intellectual progress. It can always raise further questions about whatever putatively finished work is set in front of it. It can always question the presuppositions of a system presented to it. It can always raise questions about further facts or about overlooked facts, for any given system or putatively completed work of investigation is based upon a given set of facts and a given set of presuppositions, and the use of a given method of inquiry. But the drive to understand is of itself undetermined by such facts, such presuppositions, or such a method. The drive to understand is of itself the source of criticism by which these more specific matters are criticized. The drive to understand is the source of what we speak of as man's transcendence over all the things that he does, and all the specific activities of his knowing life. Man's capacity to be demanding of himself is greater than any of his temporal achievements exhaust just because his drive to understand is unlimited and undetermined.

At this point, a question arises about the source of this objectivity in man. For this capacity is certainly objective; it is the source of what we call objectivity. Of itself, it leads a man to criticize his own prejudices, his own preoccupations, his own presuppositions. Of itself, the drive to understand leads a man to put himself in suitable perspective, to discount as much as possible his own subjectivity.

The drive to understand, moreover, seeks objectivity in two directions: in moral judgments and in scientific judgments. It is becoming clear that there is such a thing as "scientific conscience," [15] by which a man learns to discount his own partial vision. It is also true that there is a moral conscience, by which a man learns to pass disinterested judgment upon his own actions and those of others. We are given ample witness to this objectivity of our drive to understand in our own experience, and also in the experience of philosophers and artists. In Mary McCarthy,[16] in Albert Camus, in Walter Kaufmann, we are constantly exhorted to the traditional values of living the examined life, of honesty, of truthfulness. So great and so strong is this drive for honesty, this drive to examine even our own best-loved illusions and habitual ways of erring, that we are able to picture our inner lives as a dialogue between two different parts of ourselves: a devil's advocate of honesty against our illusion-loving self. One part of us, as it were, speaks for honesty, one part for our convenience and our comfort. It is this first "part" which drives us forward towards honesty, which leads us to pass judgment upon ourselves, and which does not seem to have its origin wholly in ourselves. It is this part which we are referring to as our intentionality.

As Professor Stuart Hampshire makes clear in *Thought and Action*, intentionality is the center of our conscious life. At any moment, when you are conscious, it makes sense to ask: "What are you doing?" For to act consciously is to know what one is doing, even though one may not be able to put that knowledge immediately into words.[17] But Professor Hampshire's long analysis of "intention" is mainly concerned with ethics, and thus with action; whereas our main concern at present is more general. We are concerned with "intention" as it unifies inquiry, as it begins with questions raised by experience and concludes with claims of knowing supported by the method of rational subjectivity. Intentionality is not operative only in ethical action. It is also operative in speculative inquiry. When Professor Hampshire uses the word "intention," it is clear that he does not mean merely "good intentions," a wish, a velleity; he means the decision to try to do something. But we are trying to establish a still broader sense for intentionality, a sense which refers to that steady drive in us, that center of consciousness, which, when awakened, passes judgment both upon our intentions to do things and upon our efforts to come to know things.

By intentionality, then, I mean to call attention to certain facts of our experience of understanding, on both the practical and the theoretical side; to the facts, viz., of our drive to replace questions with answers, perplexities with insights, strands of narrative with a point, scattered efforts with a policy; and of our drive to criticize and to revise our gathering of facts, our insights, our behavior, our attitudes, our presuppositions, and our methods. By intentionality, I mean to call attention to the dynamic drive of our conscious life, the source of our transcendence of ourselves, the dynamism not only of our conscious doing but (if I may so speak) of our conscious being.[18]

I would like to suggest, then, that when the believer is naming God, he is naming God not according to some concept he has formed of God, nor any immediate experience of God; i.e., not by any ordinary method of naming. Rather, he names God according to the impulse of his own intentionality,[19] of his own drive for honesty. For any effort whatever to understand implies a context in which understanding is possible: "What prompts this hunger—self-critical and objective—which I experience in my heart and mind?" When a man names God, he is led toward this name by the undetermined, relentlessly honest light in his own conscious life. This light is the "spark of the divine" discovered in our own experience. This intentionality gives us a name to what we otherwise do not experience and cannot properly conceive.

Further reflection teaches us, of course, that God is not this light. It would be a mistake to identify God with our own conscience, scientific and moral. It would be self-defeating to make us part of God. But what the religious man does seem to want to express is that this light of conscience, this light of intelligence and of love, is somehow a sign of God, an invitation from God, a participation in God's life— in some way connected with God. This light of honesty and integrity is the thing most positively like God in human experience, the thing which some religious people are content to say most identifies what God is like. God, for them, is the source of light, that is to say, the source of conscious intelligence in men and of intelligibility in things. He binds together all the statistical spontaneity of things and events, and gives man the intelligence to begin to understand himself and the world in which he finds himself. The world is not meaningless. Men are not isolated, conscious objects which "strut and fret" their hour, and "then are heard no more." There is a conscious God present in all things, caring about all things.

My concern here is not, of course, to justify these last leaping steps from the facts of our conscious life to belief in God. Such justification is a pressing order of business, but here I will content myself with saying that attention to intentionality may carry us some little way along the road of this justification. For it is odd that men should have a drive to understand their destiny and to believe that the universe in which we live is such as to respond to men who seek understanding—by building universities, by developing sciences, and, indeed, by loving one another and having compassion on the weak. It is odd, because the universe could well be chaotic and loveless, as it sometimes seems. The world of our experience certainly seems to be *as if* there were a "God-ward trend" [20] in things. And even if we do not believe in God, we seem to act *as if* understanding and love were reliable enough factors in our experience to base our lives upon.

My point is that the drive of our conscious life—our intentionality —is such that it makes belief in God plausible. Indeed, in many ways it leads us to act *as if* there were a God. It seems more consistent to make explicit what is implicit in our conscious life. "Ah, *mon cher,*" wrote Albert Camus in *The Fall,* "for anyone who is alone, without God and without a master, the weight of days is dreadful. Hence one must choose a Master, God being out of style. . . . Take our moral philosophers, for instance, so serious, loving their neighbor and all the rest—nothing distinguishes them from [believers], except that they don't preach in churches. What, in your opinion, keeps them from being converted?" [21]

IV. *Autonomy and Community*

Our task, however, is not to justify the believer's belief in God. It is to suggest that the intentionality of human knowing gives us the most useful key to religious language. For by choosing the intentionality of human knowing as the best starting place for interpreting language about God, the religious man gains two advantages. One of these advantages is that he has thus chosen that very thing about God which allows all men, everywhere and at all times, to be related to God as to one self-same center. For, in proportion as all men are honest with themselves and faithful to their drive to understand, they are being faithful to the source of honesty and light: to one same source. All men are united in this inner light, however differently it is refracted in each individual in history. The second advantage is related to the first. Just as the approach to God which sees God as the source of man's objectivity about himself offers all men a point of unity in the one same God, so also the same approach allows us to emphasize the autonomy of each individual man. Far from a man's individuality being swallowed up in union with God, so conceived, the individual comes to God only by being faithful to himself, only by coming to grips with his own personality and uniqueness. Each man's way to God is personal, and that way must be traversed autonomously. Yet, at the end of that way, which each man pursues individually and on his own, is the one same God for all. A God conceived as the source of man's honesty and man's quest to understand the universe and his own destiny, defends at one and the same time the unity of all men in God and the autonomy and the uniqueness of every individual person.

Moreover, if we conceive of God as the source of honesty, integrity, light, we throw into relief the importance of prophecy and of fidelity to conscience in the life of the religious community. We also throw into relief the fact that man's moral life is mainly a *response* [22] to God who is already operating within his conscience. Our notion of *response*ibility, then, should be parsed not so much as a sense of duty, abstract and impersonal, but rather as a response to a drive in our own hearts, and, in religious terms, to a Person. Being faithful to himself, a man is faithful to the revelation God is making through him. In the same way, we are prepared to understand how God first pursues men, before men think of pursuing him. All our moral life, all our efforts to be faithful to conscience are a response to the God who is from the first present in this conscience.

Finally, we get a glimpse of why so much emphasis among theologians is placed upon charity or love. Love is the drive to enter into communion with the honest and approved good which conscience has already detected. Love is the effort of the human person to possess and to be possessed by what he has come to recognize as good for him. Love is thus intentionality become concrete and personal. It adds to the drive for honesty and understanding, the decisive involvement of the entire human person. It is easy to see, then, why Aquinas called charity the form of all the virtues. [23] If every individual life, like a tree, has a direction which each little act, each well-established habit, both expresses and reinforces, the man who responds "yes" to God says that same "yes" in every act of the day. When he sleeps, when he rises, when he works, when he feels enjoyment, in responding according to his best lights to other persons, to events, and to things, he is responding to God who reveals himself in persons, events, things. Once his spirit—his intelligence and love—are aimed towards God ("The Love which moves the sun and all the stars," as Dante saw) then every act of his spirit is open to the epiphanies of God in all things. Nothing is merely secular; nothing is profane. Everything that confronts his understanding is from God. The drive in him which impels him to understand and to love is identical with his religious spirit.

V. *Ecumenism*

The ecumenical application of this philosophical approach to God should be already clear. Every man—Protestant, Catholic, Jew, or nonbeliever—who pursues this light of conscience pursues one and the same thing. We are together, we are one, in choosing honesty as our ideal of life. Moreover, in the very light by which we choose this ideal each of us is able to see that his own tradition is finite, and does not contain the entire unlimited power of the drive to understand. For each of us, there are questions he does not ask, questions which do not hold his interest, questions which he has overlooked. Each of us, in our way, is unfaithful to the full range of our drive to understand. Yet each of us, finite, incomplete, and unfaithful, does what he can with what he has.[24]

Each of us is autonomous, must understand for himself, must choose for himself; no one can surrender these functions into the hands of another person to perform for him. We are each, then, worthy of dignity, and esteem, each deserving of the freedom necessary to fulfill his own destiny. At the same time, we are all brothers in the same quest. We each pursue, each in his own fashion and direction, the unlimited drive to understand, each one of us constantly questioning himself, pushing himself farther along. It is true that the believer thinks that this drive to understand and to love is itself a participation in the life of God, a sign of God, whereas the nonbeliever takes it simply as an inexplicable part of the life of man. It is true that the believer sees God or a participation in God's life, where the nonbeliever sees nothing but honesty, nothing but man. The reality is the same, the interpretation different. And who can say which is more important, the reality or the interpretation? For the fact is, believer and nonbeliever alike, each try to be faithful to conscience.

Finally, we come to the second problem we promised to treat: the relation of the sentences of a given religious tradition to the fundamental act of faith. We have tried to show in our preceding remarks that the fundamental act of faith is a "Yes" to God, perceived in one's own intentionality. The spirit pants for God as the deer for water, the Psalmist sings; our intelligence and capacity for love exceed all finite, impersonal objects. Either they are in vain or they are to be satisfied. Our life is absurd or our life is for God. Our unlimited hunger to understand may have no final satisfaction; our capacity to love may have no infinite response; our lives may be less meaningful than belief in God dares to suggest. But if one does believe in God, one says "Yes" to one's own intelligence and capacity to love; one says "Yes" to creation, and to the world as it is. Ivan Karamazov was inclined to say "No" either to God or to his creation; he could not accept both. But the believer says "Yes" both to creation, including himself, as he is, and to the source of intelligibility in creation and of intelligence in himself. This "Yes" is the font of his courage, his wisdom, his joy; and it is also the light by which he detects his own inadequacy, sins, and infidelities. The fundamental act of faith is a "Yes," a response to a question first heard in the depths of one's own intentionality.

On the other hand, the sentences by which one begins to articulate this "Yes," to follow out all of its manifestations, to form notions of sin and of hope, of dignity and of unworthiness, of individuality and of community, of interior life and of outward manifestations, of concern for human history and of detachment—all these things are susceptible of as many variations as there are human beings. No two human persons share exactly the same system of sentences about their religious beliefs. No given historical tradition can, even in principle, say all that is to be said about man's relationship to God, though one tradition, of course, may say some things more adequately than another.

Do such considerations lead us to religious indifferentism? I think not. We need not say that each religion is as good as any other (or as bad); or that all are equally true (or equally false). What we must say is that each of us is partly a product of his own history. Each of us begins from a unique historical point. What we must each do is be faithful to our conscience, to the community in which we live, to as much of the world as we can possibly experience; and we must talk, even argue, with one another. Our world is rapidly becoming a world in which it is impossible for us not to meet other men, other belief systems. In one sense, the many generic belief-systems—Catholicism, Protestantism, and Judaism, for example—are closer and more sympathetic to each other than ever before. In another sense, they are more competitive: each is exerting influence upon the other. As their members meet together, and begin to converse, they will learn from one another, and they will complement one another. Those who take a mathematical approach to human life will no doubt look forward to a kind of religious syncretism, when all differences will disappear, in favor of one formula. Those with a historical approach to human life will continue to rejoice, instead, in human diversity.

The advantage of distinguishing the intentionality of human intelligence from the conceptions and sentences by which its findings are expressed is to have prepared us to see that men can make fundamentally the same act of faith, in the same God, even though historically, imaginatively, personally, the way they have come to recognize that God, to reject him, or to pray to him, is proper to each.

NOTES

1. In *Belief and Unbelief* (Macmillan: New York, 1965) I offer a fuller statement.
2. For a glimpse of the way this distinction was adumbrated by Aristotle and transformed by Aquinas, cf. Bernard Lonergan, "The Concept of *Verbum* in the writings of St. Thomas Aquinas," *Theological Studies* 7 (1946), 349-92; 8 (1947), 35-79, 404-44; 10 (1949), 3-40, 359-93.
3. *Tractatus Logico-Philosophicus,* 7, 189 (Rutledge, Kegan Paul, London: 1960).

4. "Or what saith any man when he speaks of Thee? Yet woe to him that speaketh not. . . ." *Confessions,* Bk. I (Washington Square Press, New York: 1960), p. 8, and *passim.*

5. The tradition of "the unknown God" is basic. Aquinas is drawing on an already long tradition when he says, in *De Veritate,* q. 2, a. 1, ad 9m: "The highest knowledge we can have of God is to know that He is above and beyond whatever we might think of Him." And again, in 7 *Div. Nom.* 4, 731, "To know God is to know that we do not know of Him what He is."

6. Cf. John Wisdom's famous essay "Gods" in Flew (ed.), *Language and Logic,* First Series (Blackwell, Oxford: 1960), 187-206. For a general introduction to the contemporary debate, cf. *New Essays in Philosophical Theology,* ed. Flew and MacIntyre (SCM Press, London: 1958).

7. Cf. the long introductory argument of Albert Camus in *The Myth of Sisyphus* (Vintage Books, New York: 1960), 3-21.

8. Cf. Joseph Maréchal, *Point de Départ de la Metaphysique* V (Louvain: 1926), esp. for his confrontation with the Kantian Critique.

9. In *The Quest for Being* (St Martin's, New York: 1961), 216, Sidney Hook argues that "a certain decision is involved" in making the statement that all human knowledge is scientific knowledge; "but the decision is not arbitrary: one can give good reasons for it. . . ."

10. Cf. Bernard Lonergan, *Insight: A Study of Human Understanding* (Longmans, New York: 1958). His study is divided into two parts, according to these two phases.

11. *Ibid.,* x, xxii, 3-6, 333, etc.

12. Lonergan, *ibid.,* 220-22, 348-50, 599-600, etc. Lonergan speaks of the "detached, disinterested, pure, unrestricted desire to know."

13. Cf., v.g., Richard B. Brandt's "Qualified Attitude Method," in *Ethical Theory* (Prentice-Hall, New Jersey: 1959) 244-52; also Morton V. White's emphasis upon justification, basic to logic as to ethics, in *Toward Reunion in Philosophy* (Harvard University Press, Cambridge: 1956); similarly, John Henry Newman, in *Grammar of Assent* (Image Books, New York: 1958) 277 ff., tried to point out that Aristotle's notion of *phronesis,* or practical judgment, has a parallel in speculative reasoning.

14. Cf. J. L. Austin's notion of knowing as making a claim for which one has reasons, in his essay "Other Minds," in Flew, *Language and Logic,* Second Series (Blackwell, Oxford: 1959), 123-58, esp. 124-35.

15. Cf. White, 278.

16. Cf. the very revealing conclusion of *The Company She Keeps* (Dell, New York: 1963), 222-23.

17. (Viking Press, New York: 1959), ch. 2 "Intention and Action," 90-168, esp., v.g., 119 f.

18. Prof. Hampshire is eager to concentrate upon transitive action, and thus defines action as "making a change in the world." He does not pursue some of his own leads, about aesthetics, v.g., which suggest the other dynamism,

which we might call "immanent action," action which qualitatively changes the subject without a noticeable effect upon the external world. I should call this the dynamism of "being," signifying thereby the active growth and development of the conscious subject. This shift of attention, from action as transitive to action as transitive *and* immanent, probably accounts for the greater difference between Prof. Hampshire's philosophical theology and mine than our agreement in ethics would portend. Cf. also Josef Pieper's *Leisure, the Basis of Culture* (Pantheon, New York: 1959).

19. Cf. David Burrell in "Aquinas on Naming God," *Theological Studies* 24 (1963), 183-212, esp. 208-09.

20. The phrase is from J. N. Findlay, "Can God's Existence be Disproved?" Flew and MacIntyre, 74. He adds: ". . . certainly there are *some* facts in our experience which are (one might say) *as if* there were a God."

21. (Knopf, New York: 1961), 133.

22. Cf. Bernard Haring, C.SS.R., *The Law of Christ*, vol. I (Newman, Westminster, Md.: 1961), 42 ff.

23. Cf. Gerard Gillemann, S.J., *The Primacy of Charity* (Newman, Westminster, Md.: 1961), 35-45.

24. Emphasis on "intentionality" is not the same as emphasis upon "reason," as, for example, Reinhold Niebuhr understands "reason." Cf. his "Reply," *Library of Living Theology* II, ed. by Kegley and Bretall (Macmillan, New York: 1956, 432-36). Niebuhr rightly emphasizes that men easily deceive themselves, disguising their will-to-power and selfishness, and making "reason" an instrument of their unworthy purposes. Against "reason," Niebuhr regularly names "freedom" or "spirit" as more basic to man, the source of his self-transcendence. But the faculty by which he uncovers the deceptions of "reason," in himself and in others, seems to be the intentionality which we are here studying. We may, of course, and do allow our vigilance to slumber, tolerate self-deception, flee from understanding—in short, abdicate our intentionality. We sometimes even choose to "turn aside" from the direction our drive to understand and to love of themselves require. A good education and ample powers of intelligence do not suffice to make us faithful. "There are not four honest men in a century," Pascal said; nor ever.

Part Four

AN ETHIC

FOR A

NEW AGE

Four issues have dominated my lifelong interest: the intricate relationships of Christianity and secular culture; the renewal of Catholicism; the ecumenical movement; and, most important to me of all,
the quest for a viable human ethic. It is to this last issue that we turn.

Some of the following chapters are concrete and some are theoretical; it is impossible to construct a valid ethic which does not
share both strengths. For human action is concrete, even though the
judgments by which it is guided and justified require a sustained inquiry into alternative points of view and arguments.

The fragmentary nature of these chapters cannot be avoided. They
represent forays, into the past and into the present, searching expedi-
tions whose purpose is to try to look at certain matters in a new way.
Still, their aim is not novelty but fruitful understanding, for it is plain
that not every original idea is a sound idea. Not all of the judgments
expressed in them will be popular. Some will invite objection by their
newness, some by their antiquity; some by their liberal orientation,
some by their conservatism. An authentic ethic must be personal in
its synthesis, even if it is public and open to discussion in its quest
for objectivity.

17

The Traditional Pragmatism

What help do Christians find in Scripture for resolving the question whether Christians in Manhattan should support the bussing of children to eliminate de facto segregation? What light do they receive on whether the rhythm method and the use of a diaphragm are ethically permissible? How do Christians decide between alternative approaches to city planning? What guidance do they receive on whether to support the use of heavy fire power in the war in Vietnam? The concrete context of the advice given in Scripture is the rural context of an underdeveloped area of the world of two thousand years ago. How shall Christians in an urban society interpret that advice?

There are countless questions in modern life whose resolution requires acute political, technical, and pragmatic know-how. Christian ethics cannot rely wholly on Scripture, but must bring to bear upon ethical questions all the experience, insight, weighing of evidence, and technical mastery attainable. Christian ethics may be fundamentally—in its source and in its eschatology—based upon loving faith and faithful love. But the cutting edge of Christian ethics—in practice and in the concrete—is worldly. Christians need an ethic effective in the real world.

There are two conditions such a worldly ethic must meet. It must be sensitive to the variations and the dynamic unfolding of history, and cannot pretend to be static, immutable, abstract, or eternal. Secondly, it must be based on the metanoia *of the ethical agent. It must be based on authen-*

ticity, on fidelity to one's uniqueness, on the dialectic through which one discovers, gradually and in part, one's predilected self-deceptions. In this sense, a valid ethic must be at once supremely subjective and rigorously objective. It is objective, because it entails seeing oneself as others see one. It entails maintaining oneself under the scrutiny of God's burning judgment. It is objective because it applies to oneself the standards it applies to others. On the other hand, such an ethic is subjective, for its aim is to change the subject: to bring him to a greater fidelity to his own capacities for ethical development. It is subjective because its standard is not found outside the subject—in some set of laws or code of prohibitions—but in the subject's own growing awareness of the claims of others and of events upon him. Such an ethic finds its locus in an historical community, whose developing wisdom is communicated in many ways to the young. At a certain point each of the young must cease receiving this wisdom passively, and appropriate it in a personal, efficacious, and creative effort. Each man who thus grows up into a personal morality has fashioned a new creation. Grace ensures that more will be produced in this new creation than the individual put into it.

Evil is often portrayed as exciting, goodness as boring. Wherever goodness is boring, a new creation has not been achieved; mere conformity is in question. Nothing is more common or banal than egoism, dishonesty, dissimulation, laziness, escapism, selfishness; evil is insipid. To be good is to be creative, to do more than conventions insist, to risk one's present security, to exert oneself where without exertion nothing would be accomplished. To create is to make something which did not exist before. To destroy is to avoid becoming involved, to refuse to extend oneself, or to become distracted by trifles when needs cry out to be met.

The prior ethical question is not, "What should I do now?" but rather, "Five years from now what sort of person would I like to have become?" Moral growth, since it is creative, requires time and effort. Being follows from doing. To be a more free, more fully developed, more fully Christian personality in order to act effectively five years from now, one must begin to prepare oneself today. Paradoxically, the best preparation comes through learning to focus upon the needs of others rather than upon oneself. One finds fuller life by losing the life one has. To seek to develop oneself by concentrating upon the self—whether in pride or in contrition —is self-defeating.

Yet how can one learn to focus upon the needs of others? One would love the poor, except that they are so ignorant and uncivilized. One loves man, but finds those in one's environment petty and mean. It is necessary, then, to come to terms with one's own sympathies, repugnances, annoyances, delights. There is a difference between spontaneously disliking Jones and coming to understand what makes him as he is and oneself as one is. There is also a difference between both of these and the decision to act fairly and creatively toward Jones, whatever the state of one's feelings or insights. Moral action is not achieved primarily through the operation of spontaneous feelings, nor through the accuracy of one's understanding, but through the fairness and creativity of one's decisions. Pleasant feelings and brilliant insights often remain ineffectual; decisions alter the concrete flow of life. Yet decisions do not emerge from a vacuum; more often than not, and especially when they are educed by the pressures of the moment, they spring from our spontaneous feelings and our routine understandings. Feelings and understanding and willingness to decide require time and effort if they are to be sharpened and enlarged. For this reason, moral growth is slow and never complete.

Shall we call an ethic that concentrates upon the development of the operations of feeling, understanding, judging, and deciding a natural law ethic? I would like at least to call it a secular ethic. To live by the secular style of natural law is to develop one's own capacities for broad experience, accurate understanding, sound judgment and effective decision-making. Such an interpretation of natural law is open-ended; it does not dictate in advance what a given individual must do in a given situation. It is going to become increasingly attractive.

For the more theologians concentrate upon "holy worldliness" or a "secular style," the more surely what used to be called "natural law theory" is going to receive a new use and a new interpretation. In the medieval period, any ethical theory meant to account for the fact that even those who did not know Christ—Socrates, Plato, Aristotle, Virgil— could perform good actions, was bound to be drawn to the pre-conscious conviction that the universe is stable and its laws unchanging. Although

Aristotle and Aquinas (as the following essay attempts to show) did not share that conviction in the domain of ethics, the state of the physical sciences of that period made the conviction too entrenched to dislodge. In our time, physics has presented to us the spectacle of an evolving, open-ended, untamed world, a world not ruled by classical laws but developing in accord with schemes of probabilities in an indeterminable way. Consequently, we are free in ethics to employ the phrase "natural law" in a new context, free of the associations of necessity, immutability, and logical rationality that once clung to it. For "nature" today means what is known to physics; and what is known to physics is a dynamic complex of probabilities.

In the modern context, a secular ethic might well begin with a study of those key human operations by which men cope with the network of events in which they work out their lives. It may well be that there is a set of operations that must be performed before an action can count as moral at all. The material upon which the operations work, the viewpoint from which they are exercised, and the conclusions at which they arrive would obviously change from man to man, case to case. What is required is that the whole set of basic operations be performed. A judge who did not consider the evidence, or who lacked understanding, or who could not make up his mind, would not render a good judgment. From a study of how we disqualify actions for moral failure, we can single out at least four basic operations required for moral action: experiencing, understanding, judging, and deciding. A human action omitting one of these operations is not well enough formed to constitute mature, responsible moral behavior.

Such basic operations are the source *or* principles *of morality—"principles" in the sense of "empowering agents," not in the sense of "codes" or "prescriptions" or "commandments." The reason why Christian ethics must turn to them is that neither Scripture nor the Christian tradition shed light upon the novel and unheard-of configurations of circumstance with which history provides us. No two human actions are identical; no two situations are the same. Consequently, even from a theological point of view one must articulate a way of coping with such situations; one must at least point out the "light"—basic operations—by which men handle such situations.*

As Josef Fuchs points out in Natural Law: A Theological Investigation *(New York, 1965), natural law was, for Aquinas, a theological theory. It ment "light upon concrete ethical problems from non-Scriptural sources." It was not called "natural" in the sense that it expressed what men* would *have been like without the fall and the redemption. It was called "natural," rather, in the sense that it expressed what man is* in fact *called upon to do, even where revelation offers little or no guidance. From a Christian point of view, there is not now and there never was a purely natural man; "naturalism" is an abstraction. The real, concrete world is a world of evil and of redemption. Consequently, a realistic ethic must cope with a world in which men are often immoral. In such a world, the statistical frequency of the performance of all four basic operations is not nearly as high as the number of human acts in which one or all of the basic operations are not performed; people drift, or act routinely, by rote or habit or inertia. Through laws of probability, such frequencies can be fairly well predicted, and the character of the future actions of people projected.*

The point of this long introduction is that a contemporary, operational theory of secular morality is a promising avenue of reflection. The following essay shows that in the distant past Aristotle and Aquinas attempted to explore a similar if not identical avenue. The interpretation of Aristotle and Aquinas which I follow runs counter to conventional academic views in America, but there is ample scholarly evidence that this interpretation is that of the best-informed and is growing. In any case, whatever one's interpretation of Aristotle and Aquinas, the concrete actions of Christians today spring from both secular and Christian resources, and consequently an adequate Christian ethic today must be both secular and Christian.

"There is absolutely nothing new in the pragmatic method. Socrates was an adept of it. Aristotle used it methodically. . . . Not until in our time has it generalized itself, become conscious of a universal mission, pretended to a conquering destiny. I believe in that destiny, and I hope that I may end by inspiring you with my belief."

—William James, "What Pragmatism Means"

WHEN a Catholic enters upon serious studies in Protestant ethics, he is struck again and again by the serious misunderstandings which Protestant writers unblushingly entertain about the ethical thinking of Aristotle and Aquinas. This paper is an attempt to sow the seeds of a thorough re-examination of the historical texts of Aristotle and Aquinas on ethics which we have at our disposal. Nothing short of a revolution in the conventional interpretation is called for. The key to that revolution is the acquisition of a more historically accurate understanding of practical wisdom, as distinct from reason.

To be sure, an accurate view of notions important seven centuries ago will not solve the theoretical problems of today. But an ethic of practical wisdom, as distinct from an ethic of reason, is an alternative which Protestant writers have not so far considered.

I. *The State of Current Scholarship*

A view common among Protestants in facing the thought of Aristotle and Aquinas is reported by Douglas Sturm in an impressive article included in *New Theology No. 2*. In the perspective of the Greeks, he writes, "reality as a whole is basically inherently orderly, regular, uniform, systematic." [1] Thus:

Natural (moral) law seems to present itself as possessing the characteristics of permanence, immutability, universality, constancy, for it presumes to present a rule or canon of action that is the same for all men at all times and in all places. There is a tendency in a moral law that is founded in the common nature of the human species or in the nature of the cosmos to "leave out of account the variability of human desires and sensitivities in different times and climes," or to consider such variability unnatural, or of a lesser order of reality than the static and unvarying. . . . the tendency is for natural-law theorists to assume a non-historical or transhistorical stance." [2]

This view is such a parody of the actual texts of Aristotle and Aquinas that an explanation must be offered for why it has arisen. That explanation falls into two parts.

First, Protestant theology has probably been more deeply influenced by German rationalism than by any other philosophical tradition. Many Protestants seem to understand the words "reason" and even "practical reason" from the perspective of Kant. Even when they note that the subsequent Kantian doctrines are different from the Aristotelian, there is a tendency to assume that "reason" in Aristotle as in Kant is a faculty separate from experience, which forms concepts about the necessary structures, logical connections, or permanent forms which it discerns in reality. This tendency is basically Platonic. Few Protestant writers in ethics distinguish Platonic ethics radically from Aristotelian ethics; the distinction which seems to interest Protestants is that between the "Greek mind" and the "Hebrew mind," not that between Platonic *nous* and Aristotelian *phronesis*. To overlook this latter distinction is fatal to accurate historical understanding.

But, secondly, Catholic writers are not free of guilt for Protestant misunderstandings. For over a century, scholars of all faiths have applied new historical and literary techniques to the investigation of the texts of Holy Scripture. A proportionate amount of energy and talent has only begun to be applied to other texts of the Christian tradition, like those of Luther, Gabriel Biel, John Gerhard, and others. We are just now becoming accustomed to distinguishing the "pseudo-Luther" from "the real Luther," the penetrating historical interpretation from the conventional view. In our century, Catholic moral theology is thought to be tributary mainly to Aquinas; but this judgment is seriously in error. In 1878, the state of Catholic scholarship was so parlous—major Catholic theological schools in Europe had been confiscated in the revolutions subsequent to 1789 —that Leo XIII declared the need of an urgent and widespread revival; he turned to Aquinas as an exemplar of what needed to be done. John T. Noonan, Jr., has noted the extreme poverty of Catholic moral theology throughout the nineteenth century.[3] Cardinal Newman expressed his own dismay at the state of scholarship in ecclesiastical circles in Rome, particularly regarding historical studies.[4] In such a situation, the name of Aquinas might be bandied about; critical texts were not even available, and fundamental insights and methods were not at all in evidence. The revival of historical studies into the medieval context has only recently been bearing fruit, particularly since 1950.[5]

However, Catholic moral theology in the United States has not been oriented toward such studies; most such theology is directed toward the preparation of seminarians for the confessional or, more accurately, directed toward their mastery of canon law and papal statements. The textbook of Fathers Ford and Kelly, S. J., *Contemporary Moral Theology*,[6] is a case in point. Ironically, Fathers Ford and Kelly were regarded as "progressive" by the standard of American Catholicism before the Vatican Council; in many matters, such as alcoholism and the relationship of psychological disability to moral culpability, they were ahead of the field. Nevertheless, their volumes are structured around the deliverances of canon law and papal teaching; references to Aquinas are in the nature of proof-texts, and are almost wholly innocent of profound historical and philosophical understanding. In a different way, Vernon J. Bourke's widely used *Ethics*,[7] while it purports to offer a systematic and authoritative Thomism, in fact manifests a nonhistorical and abstract conventional interpretation which confirms Protestant expectations: classical rationalism with all its limitations. To be sure, Bourke's presentation is susceptible of a more flexible and contextualist employment than most Protestants would be inclined to see in it; there are certain terminological quirks in Protestant and Catholic dialogue about ethics which almost guarantee misunderstanding and unnecessary polarization.[8]

Finally, it should be added that the theology of the Roman congregations, and consequently of those papal statements which originate in that theology, are not distinguished by the advances in historical understanding which mark the work of Thomistic scholars in France, Belgium, and Germany. The scholasticism of some dominant groups in Rome is nonhistorical, and quite vulnerable to the criticisms Protestants and other Catholics bring against it, as the Second Vatican Council showed. Moreover, many leading Catholic thinkers have, for several reasons, been dissociating themselves from Aquinas. The Catholic Church is not a church of one author; biblical studies have made a great and welcome impact; the association of Thomism with Roman scholasticism is so prevalent that many despair of escaping serious misunderstandings; and, finally, many ardent spirits prefer to join the common intellectual battles of our age upon contemporary ground and with contemporary methods. Catholic moralists are, therefore, committed to three separate sorts of tasks, which no one of them can manage in its entirety, and a division of labors appears to be emerging. (1) Some few continue to believe that historical research to discover what the words of Aquinas meant in his historical context is of extraordinary utility. (2) Some turn for light primarily to modern biblical scholarship. (3) Some attempt to come to grips directly with contemporary philosophies and theologies. Any one of these tasks is forbidding; two just might be managed, in certain limited ways; but three are too many for one man.

Consequently, although the findings of historical research into the ethics of Aristotle and of Aquinas call for serious revision of conventional views, these findings are not widely known. Aristotle and Aquinas are part of the patrimony of every thinker in ethics; a change in conventional views affects everyone. In one short essay, of course, one cannot uproot a deeply implanted conventional interpretation. But the precise directions from which a serious revision can be achieved by joint efforts across denominational lines can, at least, be indicated. Recent statements by such leaders as Lehmann,[9] Gustafson,[10] Lindbeck,[11] and Reinhold Niebuhr[12] suggest that such efforts are already underway.

II. *The Aristotelian Revolution*

The Greek mind is not all of a piece. To illustrate this point, a close study of the text of the *Nichomachean Ethics* is in order. For it was the discovery of this text by his teacher, Albert the Great, that prompted Aquinas to his own original conception of the task of Christian ethics.[13] Until that time, the ethical teaching of the medieval schoolmen was almost wholly Scriptural in its categories; and the conceptual tools brought to the interpretation of Scripture were chiefly Platonic and Stoic.[14] Thus Aquinas found himself in an historical situation analogous to that of Aristotle; and he recognized in Aristotle's struggle against Platonism many of the features of his own struggle against Christian Platonism. Nowhere is this struggle so clear as in ethics. For the Platonist, reason (the Neo-Platonic and Stoic *logos*) is the guide, and objective principles "out there" reveal the unchangeable form of the good. The major ethical battle for the Platonist is between the "higher" faculties and the "lower." This present world is despised, and through *logos* and *eros* the moral man is exhorted to free himself from the flesh, the passions, and the concerns of earth.[15] Moreover, the "eternal law" is as unchangeable as the movements of the celestial bodies and needs only to be discerned by intuition to make its inexorable prescriptions known; concrete, singular action is merely an instance of unchanging universal law.

It still is not widely recognized in theological circles (nor in many Anglo-American philosophical circles), to what an extent Aristotle broke with this Platonic conception of ethics.[16] "[Plato] is dear to me," Aristotle wrote in the *Nichomachean Ethics,* "but truth more dear." [17] The tradition of Aristotle was that of Greek tragedy.[18] He was fascinated by the role of contingency, chance, and fortune in human affairs.[19] The Platonic *nous* could not serve him as a basic resource in ethical action. Convinced that each human action is singular and occurs in highly contingent circumstances, Aristotle warned that ethics could not be studied like mathematics.[20] Ethics does not concern the unchanging but the changing; not the necessary but the contingent.[21] Moreover, it does not consist of the grasp of abstract principles; though the young are brilliantly able to understand ideology, and the grammatical relationships of ethical propositions, they lack experience and therefore cannot even *understand* ethics.[22] Finally, insofar as ethical studies are obliged to employ generalizations which hold at best only "for the most part," such studies of themselves are ethically inefficacious; for the point of ethical reflection is action, and action is singular, not general.[23]

To cope with a universe of contingencies, Aristotle had to re-define the Platonic *nous*. Rackham points out, in a series of judicious notes to the Greek text, just how this transformation begins to occur in the *NE*.[24] But, in effect, Aristotle abandoned the attempt to re-define *nous* and placed the weight of his analysis instead upon the concept of *phronesis*. The force of this shift may perhaps be suggested by the shift in English from "reason" to "wisdom," or from "mathematical brilliance" to "practicality." Moreover, Aristotle refused to define *phronesis;* he described some of the characteristics it would involve, but he preferred to point to a concrete model of what he meant. He pointed to Pericles,[25] much as Reinhold Niebuhr in our day, when writing of "social wisdom," points to Churchill,[26] or as others of us might point to John F. Kennedy. The criterion for practical wisdom is not translatable into a list of abstract propositions, for each such list proves too limited to account for three factors: (1) the variety and contingency of historical situations; [27] (2) the uniqueness of each human agent (what is good for Jones may not be good for Brown); [28] and (3) the extent to which wisdom accumulated through experience cannot be set forth adequately in words or argument.[29] There is, for Aristotle, no abstract way of spelling out once for all a code for human conduct, or set of principles which invariably determine the character of *phronesis*.

It was to meet this extreme relativism that Aristotle developed his unfortunate theory of "the mean." With this ill-fated invention, he was struggling to find a way to meet two separate requirements. First, his ethical theory must respect the uniqueness of each agent and each situation. Secondly, it must provide some "general" guidance, or admit that ethical theory is simply impossible. However, as a systematic device, the attempt proved to be too artificial. (Superficial commentators confuse the Aristotelian "mean" with the Stoic *ne plus ultra,* a policy of moderation, the middle-of-the-road; the device fails, but *that* [30] is not its failing.) Nevertheless, even when he attempts to define what he means by "the mean," Aristotle is forced to fall back upon his basic ethical criterion, the man of practical wisdom.

Virtue then is a settled disposition of the mind determining the choice of actions and emotions, consisting essentially in the observance of the mean relative to us, this being determined by principle, that is, as the prudent man would determine it.[31]

Thus the Aristotelian criterion for the moral good runs as follows: That is good which the man of practical wisdom would say is good. Other men see their ethical decisions in a false light, because they are seeking what is merely pleasant, or useful to themselves.[32] The man of practical wisdom is distinguished because he tries to see things as they are, not as pleasure or utility would dictate. The man of practical wisdom has been tutored by experience; [33] learned through pleasure and pains; [34] observed consequences; [35] persuaded (rather than merely repressed) his desires, interests, and passions to support his desire to act intelligently; [36] lets his intelligence follow the lead [37] of his own trained dispositions of justice, courage, and steady acceptance of

pleasure and pain. In an important sense, appetite is prior to intelligence.[38]

For Aristotle, moreover, ethics is a part of politics.[39] It is the general civic community which sets the context for the development of the
individual. Unless the child is conditioned early to be steady under
the allurements of pleasure and the fear of pain, to enjoy acting cou-
rageously and to be ashamed of cowardice, to cherish justice and to
despise injustice, the child will never be able even to understand
ethics.[40] For *phronesis* is not a matter of abstract reasoning or grammatical analysis; [41] it is a matter of appetite and intelligence growing
together as one, in unison. *Phronesis* operates chiefly in choice
(*proairesis*)[42] and choice is for Aristotle "either desiring intelligence
or intelligent desire." [43] Intelligence and will [44] are two inseparable
operations of one same human spirit. For the intelligence to "master"
the appetites would be tyranny; [45] the appetites must be heard, because
in the immediate pressures of the concrete they lead the intelligence.
As Aquinas would comment: practical wisdom is *recta ratio,* rectified
or directed intelligence, and it is appetite which supplies the directing
force.[46]

I do not wish at this point to impose contemporary categories upon
Aristotelian analysis. But it seems to me that those who come to
Aristotle with the bias of classical rationalism seriously distort the
text we have at hand, and one device for exposing these distortions is
to try to classify the Aristotelian text in contemporary schemes and
types. Thus a full-dress study of the relationship of ethics to politics
in Aristotle might offer fresh grain for the stones of those interested in
the impact of the community upon the ethical development of the
individual. A study of Aristotle's emphasis upon contingency and
chance might offer support to those who see the contribution of concrete circumstances to the formulation of moral decisions. A serious
study of the compound of desire and intelligence in *phronesis* might
go a long way toward overthrowing the untenable dualism of the cognitive and the emotive, which is such a blight upon modern philosophical thought.

Finally, I would submit the following theses, of whose truth I am
convinced, to further scholarly investigation. (1) Aristotle cannot be
classified as a hedonist. For he clearly distinguishes between the
pleasant, the useful, and the moral (*kalon*), and consistently relegates

pleasure (a state of feeling) to a secondary place in his understanding of happiness (*eudaimonia*: excellence in operation). (2) Aristotle's ethics cannot be classified as purely teleological. For he recognizes instances, particularly those concerning courage, in which the final justification of moral action is not that it is effective but that it is beautiful or noble (*kalon*).[47] (3) Aristotle's ethics cannot be classified as deontological. For as a motive of action the sense of duty is hardly known to him, and "obligation" hardly figures in his ethical vocabulary.[48] (4) Aristotle's ethics cannot be classified as egoist. For the goal of his "self-realization" is not self-directed, but other-directed. A man realizes what is best in him, not through narcissism, but in excellence in action in the real world;[49] in friendship with other men;[50] in the service of the city;[51] and in attentive reflection upon "the divine."[52] Man is an animal whose ethical center is outside himself; he must act, reach out toward the real, become himself through relating self-critically to others. For the good for man is not a pleasant state of feeling, nor the clever manipulation of others to his own utility, but the concrete pursuit of excellence in real and effective action.

The ethics of Aristotle does not fit usual contemporary categories. That is the measure of what it has to teach us.

III. *Aquinas on Charity*

When the young Aquinas wrote out the lectures of St. Albert upon the *NE,* and still more when he obtained from William of Moerbeke the first Latin translation of the *NE* from the original Greek,[53] Christian ethical inquiry was so preoccupied with the categories of grace and charity that the emergent question was: What does *not* count as grace?[54] Peter Lombard had taught, following the conservative tradition established by Augustine, that without grace or charity there is no human excellence at all, and some thinkers added that human excellence without grace is sinful and evil.[55] Now Aquinas had in his hands what none of his predecessors had: perfectly clear evidence of a pagan thinker who both understood, and seemed to manifest, many kinds of human excellence, apart from grace and charity. Now how could this be? How could there be pagan excellences, unbelieving "saints"? Aquinas was unwilling to shut his eyes to what, quite clearly, was human excellence. On the other hand, he became increasingly convinced [56] that no such human excellence is salvific; it does not count for immortal life; man is not saved by his own excellence.

Thus, Aquinas found in Aristotle, first of all, a problem. For centuries, Church Fathers had called Aristotle a pagan, a materialist, an atheist. (Plato, incidentally, was "the divine Plato" in many writings of the tradition). Plato raised man's eyes to another world; Aristotle concentrated upon this one. Plato spoke of an "eternal law," and the Franciscans and many mystics delighted in his vision of *Eros* and his longing for dissolution in "The Highest Good." Moreover, even the Stoic conception of "natural law," so useful to the canonists of the heterogeneous Roman empire [57] just emerging from the melting pot of the Dark Ages, had been incorporated into Christian tradition through the Platonic category of "participation in the eternal law." [58] Finally, Peter Lombard had intensified the traditional view that charity is not only the form of all the human excellences, but is the only human excellence. He went one step further: charity *is* God, acting directly in and through men.[59] What was Aquinas going to do with pagan practical wisdom, justice, fortitude, steadiness under pleasure and pain, and the rest? [60]

To begin with, Aquinas made sure he understood Aristotle thoroughly. He commented at great length upon every sentence of the *NE*.[61] In the second place, Aquinas pushed Aristotle's emphasis upon history and contingency beyond the limits Aristotle had observed. For the God of Aristotle was still a part of the world; he was an "unmoved mover" who, at the end of the cosmic circles, imparted movement to the rest; he was, as it were, the immanent intelligence of the universe.[62] But the God of Aquinas was separate from the world; He was the Creator.[63] The world was thus one step more contingent than Aristotle could have supposed. Throughout the *Summa Contra Gentiles,* the most philosophical of his original and dialectical forays, Aquinas concentrated upon the various ways in which the world is contingent,[64] and upon the way in which God could be conceived accordingly. God is conceived, in fact, in the pattern, not of Platonic *nous,* but of Aristotelian *phronesis.* God is not Reason, but Providence.[65] The contingencies of human history do not surprise God, for he is contemporaneous with them. His knowing is not, properly, *fore*knowing but total and simultaneous knowing.[66] He understands each singular event, wills each, makes each possible.[67] He does not interfere with the creatures of his art; they are so consummately wrought that, in being themselves and acting with great complexity upon one another, they realize their own destinies, without his having like some *deus ex machina* to tinker with them.[68] Yet God is present in each event, in each thing, in every person, enabling them to be themselves.[69] He gives them existence, the ability to operate, a field of action in history—he is responsible for their freedom and contingency.[70] There is no extra "religious" dimension to his presence; everything is good, and everything speaks of him, just by being itself. Things owe their existence to him; to be is to be both dependent on God and a manifestation of God's power and presence.[71] The secular is sacred; the sacred is secular. Two aspects: one concrete world.

In turning his attention to the specific problems of human action, consequently, Aquinas does not need to conceive of "nature" and "grace" as two different "levels" of human life.[72] Nor does he conceive of God and man as rival agents; human actions are not fifty per cent man's and fifty per cent God's or sixty-forty. God and man do not act upon the same plane at all. Everything in human action is made possible by God and yet man's acts are man's own. Aquinas does not have to "make room for" grace and God, or for human freedom; they are not in conflict.[73] For even without grace nothing occurs without God's present, enabling action. Creation did not occur once, long ago; it is occurring at each moment.[74] God is "built into" creation, not as though he is a part of it, but because it is in every detail of its history contingent upon his knowing, his willing, and his loving. He is present everywhere, in everything, by his knowing, willing, loving.[75]

Nevertheless, men are not left to seek God merely in the events and objects and persons of history.[76] God has revealed Himself in Christ. Christ does not destroy the secular order, nor build a new order on top of it; he reveals what the God of this order is like, and what our destiny in this order is.[77] One of the things he reveals is that charity, not practical wisdom, is the secret of salvific, moral action. Charity enlarges [78] the fundamental moral tendency; and it is a gift of God, an excellence of operation which is at once ours (for love is, if anything, an act of free will)[79] and his (for it is a participation in his own loving).[80] That charity is the fundamental principle is not surprising to Aquinas. For he has already granted that, even for pagans, love for God above all things, *Amor Dei super omnia,* is the ultimate moral tendency.[81] The fact that men sometimes understand and sometimes love is a sign that the unseen God draws them through understanding and loving; all the moral tendencies they experience reduce to other-centered love.[82] The ten commandments, for example, reduce to such love.[83] What is astonishing about man's tendency to love the unseen God is only that God should reciprocate, and invite man into friendship with himself; nothing in human experience makes that invitation inevitable or necessary.[84] But given the centrality of ordinary love to human development, the form which God's grace takes—charity—is "fitting."

There are several features about this general overview of Aquinas' approach to the problem of a Christian ethic which deserve comment. In the first place, Aquinas always writes as a theologian, never solely as a philosopher.[85] Secondly, the theory of "natural law" figures only briefly in one of the four large volumes of the *Summa Theologica* (1:2.94); the whole third volume (2:2), which establishes the ethics of Aquinas, is structured around charity. Thirdly, the notion of "natural law" in Aquinas is surrounded with pitfalls for the unwary:

(1) The technical definition of "law" given by Aquinas at 1:2.90 does not apply to "natural law," but only to positive law.[86] So natural law is not, technically, a law.

(2) The definition of "natural law" does not apply to anything in nature except to man.[87] No other creature exhibits in its behavior what Aquinas calls "natural law." The implication is twofold: (a) there is a sharp distinction between man and the rest of nature (between nature and history?); (b) the natural law theory of Aquinas is not "natural" in the sense that the law of thermodynamics, or the principle of inverse squares, are laws of nature.

(3) Aristotle apparently never brought his early theory of scientific method, as expressed in his *Prior and Posterior Analytics,* into harmony with his later practice of scientific method.[88] His model for science was the deductive system of geometry. Consequently, having distinguished practical wisdom from art on the one hand, and now attempting to distinguish it from science on the other, Aristotle arrived at a theoretical impasse. The only method of argument in science which his theory (though not his working practice) countenanced was that of the deductive syllogism. (This theory was not exemplified, for

example, in his actual comparisons of political constitutions, his surveys of biological facts, or his inquiries into the actual ethics of Athenian moral praise and blame). When he wished to show that intelligence was operative not only in science but also in ethical deliberation, Aristotle thus erroneously but understandably attempted to carry through a comparison between speculative wisdom and practical wisdom, based upon the model of the deductive syllogism. The impasse was twofold: (a) The conclusion of ethical deliberation is not a proposition, as in a deductive syllogism, but an action.[89] (b) The relationship of ends to means in ethical deliberation is not parallel to the relationship of general law to particular instance in the deductive syllogism.[90] Consequently, the comparison is doomed from the start, and fraught with ambiguities.

Now Aquinas, in commenting faithfully upon Aristotle, was ensnared in the same ambiguities. In the most read and discussed section of the whole Aquinan *corpus* (often distorted by being studied out of context), the brief tract on law in the *Summa Theologica,* Aquinas likewise attempts to compare practical wisdom to speculative science. A speculative science has first principles or axioms; proceeds deductively; and ends with a conclusion discovered to have been implicit in the premises. A comparison between ethical deliberation and this deductive model cannot be satisfactory, even on his own principles; but Aquinas pushes ahead. In practical action, however, the "first principles" are not axioms but the ends aimed at.[91] The first principles of the speculative sciences—for example: One thing cannot in the same respect both be and not be at the same time; the whole is greater than its parts—are *known in themselves*; [92] that is, intellectual discourse cannot proceed without the employment of such logical rules. These principles are "known" even by the simple, who cannot articulate them. Forced to give an example of a similar "first principle" in practical action, Aquinas hesitates, then offers the following. (Recall that he must state a "first principle" *known in itself;* that is, such that ethical action cannot proceed without its employment.) He suggests: *"ut secundum rationem agatur*: that action be carried out with justifiable reasons." [93]

Aquinas has another, more common version of this basic "first principle" of ethics: "Good is to be done and pursued, evil is to be avoided." [94] But this version is a more general way of stating the former version. For Aquinas thinks of good as an end; *whatever* any-one or anything *tries to* attain, is *good*.[95] This generic notion of good is not the ethical good; it applies to everything in creation that changes, moves, or aspires. The *ethical* good is constituted by choosing one's ends intelligently, with justifiable reasons.[96] Only man can do this. Consequently, "Good is to be done, evil is to be avoided," may as an *ethical* principle be unpacked thus: "Ends chosen intelligently, with justifiable reasons, are to be pursued; ends chosen unjustifiably are to be avoided." In short: *"ut secundum rationem agatur."*

In this light, the practical syllogism is more different from than it is similar to the deductive syllogism. The "first principle" of the practical syllogism is not an axiom or a premise. It is best construed as a formal rule, or as a general prescription (Aquinas calls it a "first *precept*"), whose content is to be supplied by further empirical inquiry. This general rule runs: "When you have discovered the next step to a goal chosen justifiably, take it." Negatively: "If a proposed step leads away from that goal, or to a goal unjustifiable for a man in your position, avoid it." This interpretation of Aristotle and Aquinas explains: (a) why the practical syllogism properly terminates in a singular action, rather than in a descriptive statement; (b) why efforts to deduce *any* proximate ethical principles from the prescription, *"Bonum faci-endum; malum evitandum,"* prove barren; (c) why teleological and pragmatic considerations, rather than deductive logic, play a dominant role in the working practice of Aristotle and Aquinas. Moreover, by construing "good" as the object of intentional activity, that is, as an end, as any *X* that we try to attain or to do, Aristotle and Aquinas show that they think of man as a problem-solving, future-oriented, symbol-making, intentional animal: man is one who tries to do,[97] who seeks, who inquires, who plans, who invents. Whatever man seeks is, by definition, good (in a neutral, nonethical sense). But the *ethical* good is whatever man seeks *rationabiliter;* its criterion is whatever the man of practical wisdom would seek.

Moreover, Aquinas elaborates, the ethical good is present only when four conditions are met. If any one of them is missing, that lack is an evil; [98] the ethical good requires a total fourfold integrity. (1) The particular *object* of the action must be justifiably sought.[99] (2) The *intention* both of the agent and the action itself (the end toward which it leads) must be justifiable.[100] (3) The quality of the singular *action* itself must be commendable.[101] (4) The *circumstances* of the action, which often determine its object and its end, and always modify its quality, must be justifiably accounted for.[102] The ethic of Aquinas is not, therefore, merely teleological. It is also contextualist, but not contextualist merely. The action itself, its object, its intention, and its context must all be placed under judgment. *Malum ex quocumque defectu; bonum ex integra causa.*

The heart of the Aquinan analysis of "good" is thus how to *justify* a given object, end, action, and context. What he calls "natural law" arises for man and not for other creatures precisely because only man can, and attempts to, justify his actions. Man consciously chooses his own goals, and the means to them: *"proairesis* (deliberative choice) more than anything else *is* man." [103]

(4) For Aquinas, Providence is the practical wisdom of the universe, the free and conscious creative action of God in the singular, contingent events of history.[104] Aristotle had not conceived of God as *phronesis,* but rather as *nous,* the immanent intelligibility of the universe. Aquinas recognized that God is simply unknown to man,[105] but he did think of him rather as *phronesis* than as *nous.* Thus, there is no eternal law outside of God, by which God is bound.[106] On the contrary, God's understanding is free, undetermined,[107] and directed toward singular contingent events in history as well as toward general laws.[108] No event, no matter how unique, surprises Him. He "wills contingent things contingently." [109] Aristotle's "unmoved mover"— even where the words are retained—has become the Creator. The Creator is provident; and so is that creature of his to whom he has given intelligence and will.[110] Man participates in God's understanding and willing insofar as through his own understanding and willing man provides for himself and his own. History is a realm of contingency, accident, and change in this world. God is provident; man is provident. "Natural law is a participation in God's providence insofar as man provides for himself and his own." [111]

(5) Correspondingly, Aquinas thinks of conscience as man's participation in God's understanding. He regularly employs the classical metaphor of "light," and is fond of citing the Psalmist: "The light of thy face has been sealed upon us, O Lord." [112] In this way, he takes "natural law" out of the cosmos outside man, and makes it intrinsic and unique in each individual.[113] He argued strenuously against the

Averroists, who held that there was only one "light," one active intelligence, for all men; Aquinas insisted that each individual man has his own active intelligence; each man sometimes understands, on his own.[114] Thus he retained the consecrated phrase of the Platonic tradition, "the eternal law," but he reinterpreted it [115] in two ways: (1) he understood it now as free, undetermined Providence; (2) and he understood that it is present in man not as a passive impress (though he retained this classical metaphor),[116] but as man's own ability to provide for himself through his own understanding and willing. Man's employment of his own practical wisdom in the contingencies of human life *is* his participation in God's Providence. Thus "natural law" is realized in singular and unique events—in whatever man does *secundum rationem*—rather than in general laws. More forcefully still: as distinct from all other laws, natural law does not derive its force from its generality, so that individual actions are mere instances of a universal law. On the contrary, the entire ethical force of natural law is also present in singular, unique, contingent actions which fall outside ethical generalizations.[117] For the ethical force of natural law derives from the justification proffered for every individual case, on its own merits.[118] He who acts *rationabiliter* acts as a mature man ought to act, however unique or unusual his act may appear to others. Natural law is not a set of generalizations, but a set of individual intelligent actions.

(6) But conscience is theonomous. How do I know what God's will for me is? Nobody else can decide this question for me. God speaks to me through my own practical wisdom. All creatures participate in Providence, but we consciously and freely. When we understand, God understands in us. When we will, God wills in us. He created us men; gave us the abilities and operations of men; placed us in the field of action in which we find ourselves. In all these ways, He operates; we cooperate.[119] Add to this the fact that through Christ, who lives in us, God enlightens our understandings and whets our wills, and it is plain that whatever we do, God also does in us.[120]

(7) But in transposing the discussion of ethics from the Aristotelian criterion of practical wisdom to the Christian criterion of charity, grace, and revealed wisdom, Aquinas alters "the horizon" of ethics. For Aristotle, ethics is deliberative and autonomous. For Aquinas, it is relational and theonomous. Aristotle did not know that the Divine

is Providence rather than thought, nor that Providence is a Person who invites sinful men to be his friends; but Aquinas did. The transposition does not mean that the criterion of practical wisdom is to be wholly abandoned; but it is contradicted at some points and interpreted from a totally new and interpersonal viewpoint. The wisdom of men is often foolishness before God, and thus there are some things that charity demands which prudence would disavow. The rule and measure of divine wisdom is divine love.[121] But, when man acts *secundum rationem,* even as a pagan, he loves God above all things and his neighbor as himself; love is the goal of the entire human project.[122] Charity fulfills this goal in an undreamt-of and unmerited way. The source of charity is solely and totally God; we cannot by our own efforts win charity or increase it in ourselves.[123] Yet the tendency of our own nature is toward the fullest possible love. In Christ, what is possible to man has been expanded gratuitously beyond the expectations of nature. Thus Christ's grace does not destroy but adds to our practical wisdom. The human standard becomes a divine standard, and is thus contradicted, transformed, and fulfilled.

(8) The relationship of secular practical wisdom to Christian charity, according to Aquinas, is of the less to the more inclusive. Charity does not negate the role of secular wisdom; but divine wisdom exceeds human. Thus as Harvey Cox has recently written, the church is God's avant-garde.[124] The brotherhood established by God's free and unmerited charity blazes the trail for men *in via.* It continually establishes a new set of goals by which men are invited, if they will, to establish a community founded ever more thoroughly upon God's love.[125]

IV. *Conclusion*

The conjoined but mutually different ethics of Aristotle and Aquinas are wrongly understood if understood rationalistically, deductively, or legalistically. The point of an ethic of wisdom is that "Reason," above all mathematical, conceptual, deductive "Reason," is inadequate in ethics. The Aristotelian *phronesis* and the Aquinan *secundum rationem* are not the classical "Reason." Experience, conditioned feelings of pleasure and pain; an accurate sense of the concrete and the contingent; and, most important of all, the excellences of the appetitive faculty, count much more prominently than "Reason" in the constitution of wisdom. Even divine wisdom, given by grace, operates as a "taste" for divine things rather than as a conceptual articulation of them; the saint understands more adequately than the professor.[126] Moreover, God himself acts not through Reason, as the divine geometer, but through practical wisdom, as the one whose greatest glory is not that he moves everything in necessary, rigid patterns, but that he creates, loves, and respects contingent things in their contingency. Natural law is that style of life whereby a man participates in Providence.[127] It is, of itself, a pragmatic and profane style of life. But, in the eyes of faith and with a heart enflamed by charity, natural law is transformed into a relationship with the unseen but self-revealed God. The ethic of human wisdom thus becomes an ethic of divine wisdom. The style of natural law yields to the style of friendship with an unseen, hidden God, never perceived but adhered to in faith. The secular style is not thereby destroyed, but carried beyond its own modest expectations, and subjected to the withering judgment of the God of justice, mercy, and love.

NOTES

1. M. E. Marty and D. G. Peerman (eds.) (Macmillan: New York, 1965 paper) p. 80.
2. *Ibid.,* p. 88.
3. *Contraception* (Harvard University Press: Cambridge, Mass., 1965).
4. Cf. Louis Bouyer, *Newman* (Image Books: New York, 1960), p. 264.
5. Cf. Josef Pieper, *Scholasticism* (Pantheon: New York, 1960) pp. 126 f. Pieper points out the importance which has been assigned since about 1950 to the condemnation at Paris in 1277 of several principles of Aquinas.
6. Newman Press: Westminster, Md., 1958.
7. Macmillan: New York, 1951.
8. Eugene C. Bianchi, S.J., has isolated some of these quirks in *The Ecumenist,* vol. 3, no. 4 (1965), pp. 59-61.
9. *Ethics in a Christian Context,* (Harper & Row: New York, 1964).
10. "Dialogue on the Moral Life," *The Ecumenist,* vol. 3, no. 5 (1965), pp. 75-6.
11. "Revelation, Natural Law, and the Thought of Reinhold Niebuhr," *Natural Law Forum* 4 (1959), pp. 146-51.
12. *Man's Nature and His Communities* (Scribner's: New York, 1965).

13. Cf. F. Copleston, *A History of Philosophy,* vol. 2, pt. 1 (Image Books: New York, 1962) pp. 232-40, also J. Pieper, *A Guide to Thomas Aquinas* (Menter: New York, 1962), pp. 106-18.

14. For an unparalleled historical résumé, see Dom O. Lottin's *Morale Fondamentale,* (Desclée: Paris, 1954); and his monumental *Psychologie et Morale aux 12e et 13e siecles,* 7 vols., (Ducolot: Gembloux, Belgium 1946 f.)

15. Cf. H. Rommen, *The Natural Law* (B. Herder: St. Louis, 1959).

16. The classic text is W. Jaeger's *Aristotle: Fundamentals of the History of His Development* (Oxford: New York, 1962, paper). Jaeger's thesis has been much disputed—the literature evaluating it is enormous—but the central point seems to stand firm.

17. *N.E.,* I, vi, 1.

18. Cf. P. Aubenque, "La Source Tragique," *La Prudence d'Aristote* (Presses universitaires de France: Paris, 1963), pp. 155-77.

19. Cf. Pierre Aubenque, *op. cit.,* pp. 64-105, and "Etre et histoire," *Le Problem de l'être chez Aristote* (Presses universitaires de France: Paris, 1962), pp. 71-93. The role of fortune and chance in Aristotle's *Physics* is too seldom noted; also the fact that he defines "nature" not as what happens necessarily but only as what happens for the most part, i.e., with statistical regularity. Cf. *Physics,* II, chs. 1, 2, 5, 6.

20. *N.E.,* I, iii, 1-4. Again: ". . . the whole theory of conduct is bound to be an outline only and not an exact system. . . . Matters of conduct and expediency have nothing fixed or invariable about them, any more than have matters of health. And if this is true of the general theory of ethics, still less is exact precision possible in dealing with particular cases of conduct; for these come under no science or professional tradition, but the agents themselves have to consider what is suited to the circumstances on each occasion, just as is the case with the art of medicine or of navigation." II, ii, 3-4. Cf. also I, xi, 2; VI, v. 3, and *passim* (Loeb Library Trans. by H. Rackham, Harvard University Press, Cambridge, Mass., 1962).

21. "Moreover, it is not easy to see *how* knowing that same Ideal Good will help a weaver or carpenter in the practice of his own craft, or how anybody will be a better physician or general for having contemplated the absolute Idea. In fact it does not appear that the physician studies even health in the abstract; he studies the health of the human being—or rather of some particular human being, for it is individuals that he has to cure." *N.E.,* I, vi, 16.

22. "Hence the young are not fit to be students of Political Science. For they have no experience of life and conduct, and it is these that supply the premises and subject matter of this branch of philosophy." *N.E.,* I, iii, 5. Cf. also Erik Erikson, *Insight and Responsibility* (W. W. Norton: New York, 1967), pp. 90ff.

23. ". . . the end of this science is not knowledge but action." *N.E.,* I, iii, 6. ". . . our present study, unlike the other branches of philosophy, has a

practical aim (for we are not investigating the nature of virtue for the sake of knowing what it is, but in order that we may become good, without which result our investigation would be of no use) . . ." II, ii, 1.

24. Cf. his notes to VI, ii, 1; vi, 2; iii, 3; vii, 3-5; xi, 4. Cf. also P. Aubenque, *La Prudence d'Aristote, op. cit., passim.*

25. *N.E.,* VI, v, 5. Cf.: "We may arrive at a definition of Prudence by considering who are the persons whom we call prudent." VI, v, 1.

26. *The Self and the Dramas of History,* (Scribner's: New York, 1955), pp. 47-48. (See reference to Aristotle, pp. 48-9); p. 214.

27. "But no one deliberates about things that cannot vary, nor about things not within his power to do." *N.E.,* VI, v, 3. "Deliberation then is employed in matters which, though subject to rules which generally hold good, are uncertain in their issue; or where the issue is indeterminate . . ." III, iii, 10.

28. See *N.E.,* I, vi. 16. (Note 20 *supra*). The notion of the mean "relative to us" is also intended to account for differences from individual to individual: "Suppose that 10 lbs. of food is a large ration for anybody and 2 lbs. a small one: it does not follow that a trainer will prescribe 6 lbs., for perhaps even this will be a large ration, or a small one, for the particular athlete . . ." II, vi, 7-8. ". . . error is multiform . . . whereas success is possible in one way only (which is why it is easy to fail and difficult to succeed—easy to miss the target and difficult to hit it) . . ." *Ibid.,* 14.

29. "Nor is prudence a knowledge of general principles only: it must take account of particular facts, since it is concerned with action, and action deals with particular things. This is why men who are ignorant of general principles are sometimes more successful in action than others who know them . . .[often] men of experience are more successful than theorists." VI, vii, 7. "Consequently the unproved assertions and opinions of experienced and elderly people, or of prudent men, are as much deserving of attention as those which they support by proof; for experience has given them an eye for things, and so they see correctly." VI, xi, 6.

30. The image used by Aristotle is that of craftsmanship or skill in the arts. Excellence in the arts does not arise through compromise. A great professional football player today, for example, is not "moderate" in the way he blocks, tackles, or runs. The Stoic tried to avoid excitement or depression, to maintain an equilibrium. The Aristotelian is not afraid of great feelings of elation or of depression; but he hopes to feel them "at the right time; on the right occasion, towards the right people, for the right purpose, and in the right manner." (*N.E.,* II, vi, 11). Sandy Koufax does not aim at "moderation," but at using the right pitch, to the right man, at the right time, etc., and this is to aim at excellence, not the middle-of-the-road. The Aristotelian word for "good" is *kalon,* "beautiful," and excellence in sports provides the best approach to his theory of excellence in ethics.

31. *N.E.,* II, vi, 15.

32. "For the good man judges everything correctly; what things truly are, that they seem to him to be . . . and perhaps what chiefly distinguishes the good man is that he sees the truth in each kind, being himself as it were the standard and measure of the noble and pleasant. It appears to be pleasure that misleads the mass of mankind . . . they choose what is pleasant as good and shun pain as evil." *N.E.*, III, iv, 5-6. Any end which men seek is *good*. But neither the pleasant nor the utilitarian end is *ethically* good. The ethically good is the *kalon* or *honestum*. "There are three things that are the motives of choice . . . namely, the noble, the expedient, and the pleasant." *N.E.*, II, iii, 7. Pleasure (a state of feeling) is not sufficient; for Aristotle says the young, "who are led by their feelings," cannot understand ethics (I, ii, 5-6); and if he admits that "the generality of men and the most vulgar identify the good with pleasure," it is only to disagree (I, v, 1-3 ff.). See also I, viii, 10-14. Later, Aristotle clearly distinguishes practical wisdom from cleverness or calculation: the clever man chooses correct means acutely and successfully, but the man of practical wisdom is not only clever; he also sees things as they are, because "the eye of the soul" is purified and strengthened by other moral excellences. Cf. *N.E.*, VI, xii, 9-10.

33. See also VI, vii, 5-7; viii, 5-9; xi, 6; etc. "It is by the practical experience of life and conduct that the truth is really tested, since it is there that the final decision lies." *N.E.*, X, viii, 12.

34. ". . . the man who does not enjoy doing noble actions is not a good man at all . . ." *N.E.*, I, viii, 12. "Discourses on ethics" are not "sufficient in themselves to make men virtuous." Theories "are powerless to stimulate the mass of mankind to moral nobility. For it is the nature of the many to be amenable to fear but not to a sense of honour, and to abstain from evil not because of its baseness but because of the penalties it entails; since, living as they do by passion, they pursue the pleasures akin to their nature, and the things that will procure those pleasures, and avoid the opposite pains, but have not even a notion of what is noble and truly pleasant, having never tasted true pleasure. What theory then can reform the natures of men like these? To dislodge by argument habits long firmly rooted in their characters is difficult if not impossible. We may doubtless think ourselves fortunate if we attain some measure of virtue when all the things believed to make men virtuous are ours . . ." X, viii, 3-7. ". . . a man becomes just by doing just actions and temperate by doing temperate actions; and no one can have the remotest chance of becoming good without doing them. But the mass of mankind, instead of doing virtuous acts, have recourse to discussing virtue, and fancy that they are pursuing philosophy and that this will make them good men . . ." II, iv, 5-6.

35. "First then let us assert that wisdom and prudence, being as they are the excellences of the two parts of the intellect respectively, are necessarily desirable in themselves, even if neither produces any effect. Secondly, they do in fact produce an effect: Wisdom produces happiness, not in the

sense in which medicine produces health, but in the sense in which healthiness produces health . . ." *N.E.,* VI, xii, 4-5. (I have amended Rackham's translation slightly: substituting "excellences" for "virtues," and suppressing capital letters for prudence and wisdom. It seems Platonist to capitalize such words.

36. ". . . the seat of the appetites and of desire in general, does in a sense participate in principle, as being amenable and obedient to it (in the sense in fact in which we speak of 'paying heed' to one's father and friends . . .)." *N.E.,* I, xiii, 18. ". . . it is right to feel anger at some things, and also to feel desire for some things, for instance health, knowledge. . . . The irrational feelings are just as much a part of human nature as the reason . . ." III, i, 24-27.

37. ". . . Each man's conception of his end is determined by his character, whatever that may be." *N.E.,* III, v, 17. (But we help shape our own character by the things we choose and the things we do. *Ibid.,* 19-21.) "The attainment of truth is indeed the function of every part of the intellect, but that of the practical intelligence is the attainment of the truth corresponding to right desire." VI, ii, 3. ". . . if the choice is to be good, both the principle must be true and the desire right." *Ibid.,* 2. "Thought by itself however moves nothing, but only thought directed to an end, and dealing with action . . . man, as an originator of action, is a union of desire and intellect." *Ibid.,* 5. Excellence of the appetite "ensures the rightness of the end we aim at, prudence ensures the rightness of the means we adopt to gain that end." VI, xii, 6. But in ethics, the end is the "first principle;" hence, will is in a way prior.

38. Aquinas correspondingly defined practical wisdom as *"recta ratio agibilium,* rectified intelligence in action," but it is not usually noticed that it is the *appetite* (good will) which does the rectifying, guides the intelligence, and chooses the end.

39. *N.E.,* I, ii, 4. *Passim.*

40. "We must therefore by some means secure that the character shall have at the outset a natural affinity for virtue, loving what is noble and hating what is base. And it is difficult to obtain a right education in virtue from youth up without being brought up under right laws; for to live temperately and hardily is not pleasant to most men, especially when young . . ." *N.E.,* X, ix, 8. ". . . in order to be good a man must have been properly educated and trained . . ." See also I, iii, 5.

41. Politics "is practiced by the politicians, who would appear to rely more upon a sort of empirical skill than on the exercise of abstract intelligence." *N.E.,* X, ix, 18. Moreover, men of practical wisdom cannot communicate *phronesis* to their own sons or friends; each can acquire it only for himself, for it requires a change in the subject himself. Cf. *Ibid.,* ff. "We do not see men becoming expert physicians from a study of medical handbooks." *Ibid.,* 21.

42. *N.E.,* II, vi, 15.

43. *N.E.,* VI, ii, 5.

44. Aristotle, strictly speaking, has not clearly differentiated "will" from other desires, and this failure causes him serious difficulties in his theory of moral weakness or *akraisa*. See "The Aristotelian Prudent Man" in C. J. O'Neil, *Imprudence in St. Thomas Aquinas* (Marquette University Press: Milwaukee, 1955); and J. J. Walsh, *Aristotle's Conception of Moral Weakness* (Columbia University Press: New York, 1963).

45. Aquinas comments that the reason has only a "political" influence over the passions, not a "tyrannical" rule; it must persuade them as a father persuades his sons, or a democratic leader persuades free men.

46. See Note 38.

47. "On peut conclure que, de fait, l'ethique d'Aristote est beaucoup moins 'éloignée d'une éthique de devoir qu'on ne le croit d'habitude." C. J. Vogel in "Quelques Remarques à propos du Premier Chapitre de l'Ethique de Nicomaque." *Autour d'Aristote*, (Publications Universitaires: Louvain, Belgium, 1955), pp. 322-23.

48. See, v.g., Sidgwick, *Ethics*, (Beacon Press: Boston, 1964), pp. 51-68.

49. ". . . we become just by doing just acts, temperate by doing temperate acts, brave by doing brave acts. . . . It is by taking part in transactions with our fellowmen that some of us become just and others unjust; by acting in dangerous situations and forming a habit of fear or of confidence we become courageous or cowardly. . . . In a word, our moral dispositions are formed as a result of the corresponding activities." *N.E.*, II, i, 4-8.

50. "For friendship is a virtue, or involves virtue, and also it is one of the most indispensable requirements of life. For no one would choose to live without friends, but possessing all good things. . . . And if men are friends, there is no need of justice between them; whereas merely to be just is not enough—a feeling of friendship is also necessary. Indeed, the highest form of justice seems to have an element of friendly feeling in it." *N.E.*, VIII, i, 1-4.

51. "Yet probably as a matter of fact a man cannot pursue his own welfare without domestic economy and even politics." *N.E.*, VI, viii, 4. The politician Pericles is the model of the man of practical wisdom, and politics is the architectonic inquiry of which ethics is a part.

52. For Aristotle, intelligence is so great a gift to men that he speaks of it "either as being itself also actually divine, or as being relatively the divinest part of us." (*N.E.*, X, vi. 1). But to live by intelligence alone "will be higher than the human level: not in virtue of his humanity will man achieve it, but in virtue of something in him which is divine." (X, vii, 8). But the life of practical wisdom, though "happy only in a secondary degree," is a more "purely human life" and is more closely "related to our composite nature; now the virtues of our composite nature are purely human: so therefore also is the life that manifests these virtues and the happiness that belongs to it." (X, viii, 1-3). "Nor ought we to obey those who enjoin that a man should have man's thoughts and a mortal the thoughts of mortality, but we ought so far as possible to

achieve immortality, and do all that man may to live in accordance with the highest thing in him; for though this be small in bulk, in power and value it far surpasses all the rest." (X, vii, 8).

53. An older, faulty Latin translation was available; Moerbeke's became known as the *translatio nova*. See Copleston, *op. cit.*, pt. I, pp. 232-38.

54. See A. Landgraf, *Dogmengeschichte der Frühscholastik*, (Pustet: Regensburg, 1952), vol. I, pp. 20-29; 51-141.

55. See O. Lottin, *Morale fondamentale, op. cit.*, pp. 273-75; 382-434; 461-70.

56. See H. Bouillard, *Conversion et grâce chez S. Thomas d'Aquin*, (Aubier: Paris, 1944) and my "St. Thomas in Motion," *Downside Review* 78 (1960), 293-302.

57. See H. Rommen, *op. cit.*, pp. 21-30.

58. See Stanley S. Harakes, "The Natural Law Teaching of the Eastern Orthodox Church," in *New Theology No. 2, op. cit.*, pp. 122-33.

59. See O. Lottin, *Morale fondamentale, op. cit.*, pp. 388-462.

60. St. Ambrose was the first to call these virtues "the cardinal virtues." But in the conservative, Augustinian theory they were not true virtues unless they were refractions of charity. No pagan, lacking charity, could exhibit genuine moral excellence.

61. In a work highly critical of Aquinas, H. V. Jaffa writes: ". . . it is not unreasonable to assume that the Aristotelian teaching is more accessible in the pages of Thomas than in the original. Certainly no one in modern times, perhaps no one since Thomas, has possessed his mastery of the Aristotelian corpus, and his marvelous capacity for relating each point in that massive edifice to every other point. It is doubtful whether anyone today could possess his grasp of the whole of Aristotle's teaching, and it is almost certain that no one could attain his comprehensive knowledge." *Thomism and Aristotelianism* (University of Chicago Press: Chicago, 1952), pp. 6-7.

62. See Étienne Gilson, *The Spirit of Medieval Philosophy* (Scribners: New York, 1940), pp. 42-83.

63. Aquinas never forgot this, even if many interpreters fail to notice that he didn't.

64. See *SCG*, in Book I alone, chs. 53, 65, 67, 68, 71, 78, 79, 81, and above all 83 and 85.

65. Thus God knows singulars, and understands that the relationship between contingent events is not necessary nor deductive.

66. See *SCG*, chs. 64 and 67.

67. *Ibid.*, chs. 65, 78, 83.

68. *Ibid.*, ch. 85, "That the divine will does not remove contingency from things, nor does it impose absolute necessity upon them."

69. *Ibid.*, chs. 50, 75, 76, 77.

70. See the full but highly compressed study by B. Lonergan, "St. Thomas' Thought on *Gratia Operans*," *Theological Studies* 2 (1941), pp. 289-324; and 3 (1942), pp. 67-88, 376-402, 533-78.

71. "God is in all things, not as a part of their essence, nor as an addendum, but as an agent is present in that in which he acts." *S.T.*, 1.8.1. ad 3.

72. The metaphor implied in *"supernaturale"* requires demythologizing. The basic theorem of Aquinas is that operation follows from being; a new kind of operation (charity or agape), which is purely a gift of God, requires "a new being"; God's own operation in us makes it possible for us, sinners, to love with his own love. See *S.T.*, 1-2.109. and 2-2.24.

73. The key to the thought of Aquinas here lies in his notion of "action." (See Lonergan, *op. cit.*, esp. 3 (1942), pp. 375-402). He does not have in mind a physical model like pushing a book across a table, such that God would supply so much power and man the rest. For him, understanding and willing are the basic paradigms of action. If a man pushes a book across a desk, God understands that he does so, and wills that he do so; God's understanding and willing are simultaneous with the man's understanding and willing. Thus God is totally responsible for the action; and man is also totally responsible. The divine act and the human act are, in different ways, equally required if human acts are to occur. See, esp., *SCG*, I, 83.

74. *S.T.*, 1.104.1.

75. *S.T.*, 1.8.3.

76. Thus the utility of revelation. *S.T.*, 1.1.1.

77. This is the meaning of the phrase, *"Gratia non tollit naturam sed perficit eam."*

78. "Reason is not the regulator of charity as it is of the human virtues; charity is regulated by the wisdom of God and exceeds the role of human reason." *S.T.*, 2-2.24.1. ad 22.

79. See the argument of Aquinas against Peter Lombard in *De Caritate*, 1.1.; also *S.T.*, 2-2,23.2.

80. ". . . charity whereby we love our neighbor is a certain participation in divine charity," *S.T.*, 2-2.23.2. ad 1.

81. See *S.T.*, 1-2.109.3.

82. Aquinas has at least five words for love. The most general, *amor*, may be applied to the energies and tendencies even of inanimate things—thus Dante writes later of "the love that moves the sun and all the stars." But human love, *dilectio*, is based upon intelligent choice, and as *benevolentia* it respects the other as other, refusing to make of the other a means to the self's own pleasure or utility. See *S.T.*, 2-2.23.1 and 1-2.26.3.

83. *S.T.*, 1-2.100.3. ad 1 and 5. ad 1.

84. "Since charity, however, exceeds the proportion of human nature . . . it does not depend upon any natural virtue but solely upon the grace of the Holy Spirit infusing it . . . and giving His gifts where He wills." *S.T.*, 2-2.24.3. But Aquinas does not clearly express the way in which grace can "complete" nature, without seeming to say that man has a natural and exigent desire for such a completion. See *SCG*, III, 53, and the brief résumé of recent interpretations in Copleston, *op. cit.*, pt. 2, pp. 120-25.

85. See Copleston, *ibid.*, p. 123.
86. See Mortimer J. Adler, "A Question About Law," *Essays in Thomism* (Sheed & Ward: N.Y., 1942), pp. 207-36. It is a misuse of terms to say, for example, that natural law is "promulgated" in man's intelligence, "by one who has care of the community." Aquinas himself does not try to carry through such an analogy. Adler writes: *"The rules of positive law are laws. The propositions of natural law are not laws.* They are *only* principles, sources, or foundations *of law."* p. 234. (Italics his).
87. *S.T.,* 1-2.91.2. ad 3.
88. See articles by A. Mansion, G.E.L. Owen, and P. Aubenque in *Aristote et les problemes de methode* (Publications Universitaires: Louvain, 1961), pp. 57-81; 83-103; 3-19.
89. "No singular terms enter into scientific reasoning in its finished form. All action, on the other hand, is particular . . ." D. J. Allan, "The Practical Syllogism," *Autour d'Aristote, op. cit.,* p. 329.
90. *Ibid.,* pp. 326-31.
91. *S.T.,* 1-2.94.2.
92. *Ibid.*
93. *Ibid.,* 94.4.
94. *Ibid.,* 94.2.
95. Both Aristotle and Aquinas think of the world in dynamic, tendential terms; nature is defined as change and movement. Things in movement move toward ends, and so they think that when any X reaches its term, that is its good. See *N.E.,* I, 1: "What anything seeks is a good." This conception is too general for ethics; for man can seek many things, and not all of them are ethically good, though all are good in some respect.
96. ". . . as the man of practical wisdom would determine it." *N.E.,* II, vi. 15.
97. For an analysis of intention as "trying to do," see Stuart Hampshire, *Thought and Action* (Viking Press: New York, 1960), pp. 90 f.
98. *"Malum continget ex singularibus defectibus, bonum causatur ex integra causa."* See *S.T.,* 1-2.18.4 ad 3; 19.7. ad 3, etc.
99. *S.T.,* 1-2.18.2.
100. *Ibid.,* 4.
101. *Ibid.,* 1.
102. *Ibid.,* 3.
103. Aristotle says this of intelligence (*nous*), *N.E.,* X, vii, 9. But at VI, ii, 5, he notes that "choice may be called either thought related to desire or desire related to thought; and man, as an originator of action, is a union of desire and intellect." It is this union which leads man to seek to justify his choices.
104. *S.T.,* 1.22; also 1-2.94.1. And at *ibid.,* 93.5. ad 3: ". . . the eternal law is the intelligence (*ratio*) of divine Providence . . ."
105. "This is the extreme of human knowledge of God: to know that we do not know God." *S.T.,* 1.7.5. ad 14.
106. *S.T.,* 1-2.91.1. ad 3: ". . . the end of the divine governance is God

Himself . . . nor is His law something other than Himself . . ." See also 105.5.7. and 8.

107. *SCG.*, I, chs. 76, 85 and 88.

108. *Ibid.*, chs. 65-68.

109. The key to the Aquinan theory of a free Providence and the real contingency of things is his theory of supposition; *Ibid.*, chs. 83 and 85.

110. *S.T.*, 1-2.91.2 ad 3.

111. *Ibid.*, 94.3. And see *SCG.*, III, 78.

112. *S.T.*, 1-2.94.2.

113. See O. Lottin, "Raison naturelle, norme personelle et intrinseque," *Morale fondamentale, op. cit.*, pp. 126-28.

114. See Copleston, *op. cit.*, pt. 2, pp. 94-107; 144-63.

115. See O. Lottin, *Le Droit Naturel chez S. Thomas d'Aquin et ses Predecesseurs* (Beyaert: Bruges, 1931), pp. 54, 72-73, 100-03.

116. *S.T.*, 1-2.94.2: ". . . the light of natural intelligence . . . is nothing else but the impression of the divine light in us." On Aquinas' respect for traditional terminology, see M. D. Chenu, "The Procedure of Authority in the Middle Ages" and "The Technical Handling of Authorities," *Toward Understanding St. Thomas,* (Regnery: Chicago, 1964), pp. 126-48.

117. See K. Rahner, "On the Question of a Formal Existential Ethics," *Theological Investigations* (Helicon: Baltimore, 1963), vol. II, 217-34.

118. *S.T.*, 1-2.94.3: "Every act of the virtues is an act of natural law; his own intelligence tells each man . . . that he should act with excellence . . ." See also 93.5. ad 3.

119. See Lonergan, "St. Thomas' Thought on *Gratia Operans*," *op. cit.*, esp. 3 (1942), pp. 533 f. "The Freedom of the Will."

120. *S.T.*, 1-2.109.2; 110.3 and 4; 111.2.

121. "However, reason is not the regulator of charity as it is of the human excellences; charity is regulated by the wisdom of God and exceeds the rules of human reason." *S.T.*, 2-2.24.1.

122. *S.T.*, 1-2.100.3. ad 1.

123. *S.T.*, 1-2.109; 112.1; 2-2.24.

124. *The Secular City* (Macmillan: New York, 1965 paper).

125. "No terminus can be set for the growth of charity in this life." *S.T.*, 2-2.24.7.

126. ". . . The characteristic of reason is to order things to ends . . ." i.e., not to reduce concrete instances to general laws. *S.T.*, 1-2.90.1. Peter Hoeven describes how the Aquinan "first principles" are to be justified: *Reality and Judgment according to St. Thomas Aquinas* (Regnery: Chicago, 1952), pp. 164-82; p. 167.

127. *S.T.*, 2-2.45.2.

18

Moral Society and Immoral Man

Identity and community: these are the key realities which a viable human ethic must illuminate. It is concerning the second of these, community, that the Catholic tradition has something valuable to contribute. Catholic practice in the last few generations has sometimes done great harm to the sense of community; genuine community has too often been supplanted by more or less impersonal institutionalization. But the Catholic intellectual underground, more insistently than the Protestant or secular liberal traditions, has steadily emphasized the social texture of human experience. I have tried to reflect in this essay some of the things I have learned from Catholic liturgical life, as well as from writers of many viewpoints, and from the experience of daily living. The essay was first presented as a lecture at Duquesne University in the fall of 1965, and was printed in Church-State Relations in Ecumenical Perspective, *edited by Elwyn A. Smith in 1966.*

IN 1932, Reinhold Niebuhr published a book, *Moral Man and Immoral Society,*[1] which shocked the American Protestant world. The central thesis of that book was "that the Liberal Movement both religious and secular seemed to be unconscious of the basic difference between the morality of individuals and the morality of collectives, whether races, classes or nations." [2] The morality of individuals vs.

the morality of collectives: it is plain from Niebuhr's title that he favored the morality of individuals, and judged societies by the standards of individuals.[3] For Niebuhr, what is really real in Christian life is the "vertical relationship" between the individual and God; the ethic of Jesus, in his view, has almost nothing to say about the "horizontal relationships" between individuals in society.[4] For Niebuhr, the individual is the primary reality of Christianity; the community is secondary, instrumental, and inferior; it can never meet the purer standards of the individual.[5]

It will be the argument of this chapter, however, that the community, not the individual, furnishes the most accurate model for the discussion of social ethics. What is really real in Christian life is not the individual but the community. We are first baptized into a people, and only secondarily called upon to exercise our own unique individual witness among that people. Christian *agape* is primarily the love of God poured forth among men, calling into being and vivifying a chosen community, and only secondarily is it a personal, "vertical" relationship between an individual and God. What is really real in Christian ethics is a communal bond among men.[6] The community is the locus in which the individual learns *agape;* the community is the bearer of love, the teacher of love, the household of love. "How can you love God, whom you do not see, if you do not love your neighbor, whom you do see?" (I Jn. 4:20). We do not even know whether we have an authentic "vertical" relationship with God, except insofar as we know that we love our neighbor. Mutual love is the criterion by which we judge the authenticity of our love of God.[7]

In attempting to reverse the priorities between the ethic of individuals and the ethic of communities, we shall, moreover, be gaining a fresh vantage point for assessing the relationships between the church, the individual Christian, secular society, and the state. The conceptual apparatus for assessing these relationships may be governed (1) by the model of an individual's vertical relationship with God, or (2) by the model of an entire community's relationship with God. The choice of the first model has one set of consequences; the choice of the second model has another. Thus the issue of what is primary in Christianity, the individual or the community, plays the role of an important presupposition in considering many problems of church-state relations.

I. *The Meaning of Love*

A complete and fully grounded study of the question we have raised would require a study of the meaning of *agape* in the New Testament; such a study exceeds our competence.[8] Thus our present argument will not be based upon considerations drawn from a close study of Scripture. On the contrary, it will be drawn mainly from reflection upon certain human experiences. Nearly every man has sometimes loved others; nearly everyone has present in his experience the data out of which our problem arises. The difficulty lies in arranging this data properly, so as to come to terms with all the data and to overlook or to distort none of it. The problem is not to generate new experiences, but to understand correctly and fully experiences which are already at hand.

There are many theories of love, which attempt, some more and some less adequately, to tell us what is happening when we love. It may be useful to resume some of them here. One of the most famous and starkly drawn of the Protestant theories of love is that of the Swedish Bishop, Anders Nygren.[9] Nygren defines love in terms of the individual self: *agape* or Christian love is selfless, unselfish, disinterested, heedless, self-sacrificing. *Agape* is contrasted with *eros,* which is self-aggrandizing, self-fulfilling, self-realizing, acquisitive. Obviously, Nygren hopes to portray *agape* as unselfish, and *eros* as selfish. But in a subtle way, Nygren's view of *agape* is also self-centered. The self's attention is drawn to its own purity and selflessness. *Agape* is defined, not by the loveableness of the one loved, but by the purity of the lover; this situation is not changed because *agape* is a gift from God rather than a personal achievement.[10]

Reinhold Niebuhr disagrees with Nygren, because he thinks that Nygren creates too deep a gap between *agape* and human love; for Christ often used human love as a symbol of divine love.[11] George T. Thomas criticizes Nygren on several similar counts.[12] Still, both Niebuhr and Thomas think that the primary note in Christian *agape* is heedlessness of self, unselfishness, and self-sacrifice. Even Paul Ramsey, in criticizing Niebuhr's conception of love, decides that *agape* is primarily self-sacrificial rather than mutual.[13]

A quite different approach to *agape* is possible, however; we might define *agape,* not in terms of the purity of the self, but in terms of the attention, respect, affection, and effort which the self centers upon the *other.* In this case, the focus of *agape* shifts from what happens to the self to what happens to the other. Love is defined as willing and acting for the good of the other, as responding to the reality, dignity, and worthiness of the other. *Agape* is, then, not defined negatively as a matter of unselfishness, but positively as a response to the loveableness of the other. This difference is not merely a matter of emphasis; it is a matter of orientation and attitude.[14] The man who tries to be unselfish acts quite differently from the man who attempts to respond generously and realistically to others. The difference is one between an "inner-directed" and an "outer-directed" love though not in the sense which David Riesman delineates.[15] But it does suggest that one man might, quite lovelessly, be concerned with whether his love is sufficiently unselfish, while another may not worry at all about how selfish or unselfish he is but concentrate on responding to others with respect, affection, and service. *Agape,* in short, is not so much un-selfishness as it is other-centeredness. To love is to be concerned about the beauty, the dignity, the feelings, and the needs of others; and it is to respond not to what one would like others to be, but to others as they are.

II. *Where Is Love Learned?*

Thus two characteristics of *agape* can be pointed out: (1) *agape* is other-centered, and (2) *agape* is realistic: it responds to others as they are. In order to love, a man must be capable of attention to others, and he must be capable of coping with reality. However, it cannot be assumed that men are born able to love. On the contrary, it appears that infants are at first almost wholly ego-centered. Years may pass before a child is able to respond to others otherwise than as sources of its own security, warmth, clothing, cleanliness, nurture. Only gradu-ally does the child learn to distinguish between himself and others, learning that what pleases him does not necessarily please others, and that what he desires now may or may not be given him. Only grad-ually does the child learn to distinguish between appearance and reality, between a hot stove and a cold, between his images, desires, illusions, and the hard, stubborn, immovable world of reality. A child in a tantrum may attempt to lift a dresser and throw it at the object of his wrath; but the furniture will not yield just because he wants it to.

In short, children must learn to love. Nor is learning to love merely a matter of purring with contentment like a kitten, returning affection for affection, good behavior for a mother's loving praise. For the time comes in life [16] when playmates do not offer affection to the newcomer, when harsh and cynical outsiders replace the praising mother. What will the growing child do then: close his eyes and cry? To begin to take the steps out into the real world which lead to adulthood, the child must learn to meet others upon their own ground, to respond to the secret word which is the unique reality and identity of each of them. The child must become capable of attending to others; he must cease projecting a world which pivots wholly upon his own ego and its needs; he must place the center of his world not in his ego but in the search for what is real and other; he must become oriented toward reality, and above all to the reality of other men.

Again, man is a social animal. In discovering his own identity, each man discovers that the reality of his life is created by interaction with other lives.[17] There is no such thing as a human atom, no such thing as the pure individual. The human reality is not an "I" but a "we." The man who is psychologically isolated lives in a world of phantasy and unreality. The human consciousness turned inward upon itself does not find reality, not even the reality of the self; it begins totally to lose its bearings and to slip away. On the other hand, to become fully developed as a man, to gain one's own unique identity, one must become capable of reaching out to others, to others as they are in reality and not in phantasy.[18] The only road to personhood lies through community. In this sense, love is the law of human life. Who does not love, does not develop as a human being. Who does not love, is neither healthy, nor able to find himself. To find himself, a man must first find others. To discover who he is, a man must learn who others are.

Thus it is not by accident that in nearly all languages the verb "to know" has the same root as the verb for that fundamental symbol of human love and human realism, marital intercourse. To come to self-knowledge is to come to know oneself through knowing others. Love is creative, because by bestowing it upon one another realistically and truthfully we create persons of one another: we give each other new centers of life and meaning beyond ourselves, without losing our own identity and self-responsibility. There are, of course, some who regard love as ecstasy; some men are eager to escape from themselves. But before love is ecstatic, it is realistic; the lover is not eager to lose himself, he is eager to find the other. When he has found the other realistically and honestly, thus maintaining his own integrity and responsibility,[19] then the lover experiences joy and ecstasy. Such ecstasy is not that of flight from the self, but that of fulfillment of the self. The self is made for others; to find others is to taste reality, and such reality is sweet.[20]

Love, therefore, is learned not in isolation but in community. Love is not learned by pursuing unselfishness, but by pursuing reality and above all the reality of others. Progress in love is progress from phantasy and romance to fact and reality. Other people are real; they are not mere projections of ourselves. Their needs are real. Their wishes, aims, hopes, goodness, weaknesses are real. To learn to love is to learn to respect the real, not to escape from it.[21]

Moreover, it is chiefly living together in community that teaches us to be realistic. Alone, we dream and indulge in phantasy. We are lazy and do not push our inquiries hard enough. We accept as fact what may not be fact. Our criteria of relevance and evidence are slack. Our desires, wishes, and biases grow luxuriantly where critical intelligence seldom penetrates.[22] But forced to jostle against the standards, criteria, cynical inquiry, and contrary biases of other men, our laziness is challenged. The reality of other people rubs against us, pushes us, raises new and difficult questions for us. Community awakens us.

It is true, of course, that no community is infinite in its perspectives or totally alive. The horizon [23] of the individual community, like the horizon of the individual, has finite limits. Moreover, each community also has its biases, presuppositions, special spirit, laziness, particular enthusiasms, areas of apathy. Thus a dialectic [24] is established. At some points, the community prods all the individuals in its midst. At other points, some individuals are the gadflies of the community, exposing its biases and failings. No individual man and no human community exhausts everything that men can envisage, understand, or do;

progress depends upon the dialectic by which the community raises up in its own midst prophets who, in one respect or another, criticize the community and press it on toward further horizons.

The extent to which individual dissent is essential to this dialectic has been commonly recognized in Protestantism and in the Enlightenment. But the extent to which community nourishes even individual dissent has been commonly forgotten. Thus the theories of individualism common in our society are only partially adequate. For the individual does not develop outside of a community. Prophets are raised up in the midst of the people. The dissenter learns to speak, to distinguish reality from appearance, to prefer integrity to pharisaism, to love persons rather than codes, to differentiate living values from dead traditions, only in the midst of his community. A healthy community needs its own critics as love needs realism: phantasy is the disease of communities just as it is the disease of love.

III. *The Role of Society in Morals*

It is not true, then, that man is moral but society immoral. On the contrary, society is the matrix of ethical education; apart from society moral growth is inconceivable. Still, education is not communicated primarily through codes of law, conventions, textbooks, and sermons. Society educates primarily through those relationships between man and man, which it allows or encourages men to establish. In order to grow in honesty, perception, reconciliation, courage, hope, and responsiveness to one another, men must learn to prize such qualities; and they will learn even what such qualities are only with one another's help. Who am I? I will learn who I am only through interaction with others. Am I intelligent, honest, realistic, courageous, capable of love? How will I know unless I live with others? Others will tell me, through words or behavior, much that I could never learn through introspection. Moreover, the community with which I identify has formed my notion of what the words "intelligent," "honest," "realistic," "courageous," and "capable of love" mean. A dissenter may insist that the community no longer understands correctly its use of such key words; but to make himself understood at all (even by himself), the dissenter must use such words as derive from, or can now be incorporated into, the common inheritance of his community. A completely personal language is a contradiction in terms.

Several objections to the present line of thought leap to mind. Is not a human community often oppressive, mediocre, or even evil? Must not the individual be ready to stand against the herd? Isn't the differentiation of the individual from the society one of the great achievements of Western culture? Is not the thirst for community a disease which leads to goose-stepping, romantic fascism or a drab communism? These questions seem to show that the source of moral progress is not primarily in the community but in the individual. But the fallacy in the questions is that they seem to think of the community as a single total unit. There is no such "thing" as a society; there are, in fact, only millions of individual men, who live in certain relationships. "Society" is an abstraction, a way of speaking about the different ways in which men are related. We must exorcise from our minds the image of society as a great, gray "thing," standing menacingly behind the countless individuals we see, talk to, shake the hands of.

These individuals, however, are not isolated atoms. They speak, and speech is a communal phenomenon. All are children of other humans. Some of them love one another. Some teach, and others study with them. Some are in the employ of others. They have various ways of arranging for political decisions which concern the behavior of large numbers of them. It is these complex relationships that affect human consciousness that we speak of as *society*. And our thesis is that men become moral only through growing into these relationships; there is no possibility of growing moral in total isolation. One could not even love God if one had not learned how to love by discovering the reality of others; otherwise, there would be no way of defending oneself against illusions in a relationship with one who is unseen and who does not speak.[25]

Thus, while it is true that the organs of a particular church, nation, or social group in which one lives may suppress individual liberty, enforce complacent and apathetic conformity, or command racial injustices of the most flagrant sort, still, the remedy for these diseases does not lie in the attempt to escape from all social relationships. On the contrary, the love of liberty, the pursuit of excellence, and protestation against injustice are learned through social relationships. For such values spring from the acquired ability to distinguish reality from appearances, to discern alternatives, to make judgments based upon evidence, and to decide according to one's judgments. The individual learns these skills through living in a community. The requisite experiences, skills, and dispositions are more accessible in some societies than in others, of course; they are part of the tradition of a free society. But wherever men teach each other to speak, the basic tools of discrimination are accessible for further moral development. The culture in which one lives is the matrix in which the task of moral development is established, and the first steps in personal liberation begun.

Again, the individual could not stand against the herd unless he had learned the distinction between the self and the community, and learned enough from the community to judge when and how the community is betraying its own values or neglecting other values. When the prophet chastises the community, he stands upon the shoulders of the community.

Again, if the differentiation of the self from the society is one of the great achievements of Western culture, still, the view that the individual is independent of society and prior to society is one of the radical exaggerations which endanger the health of Western culture. Individual talent is nourished by the tradition, and tradition is revitalized by individual appropriation.[26] A man is not completely conditioned by his society, for he may criticize it; but neither is he independent of his society. A man is born into a community and, appropriating its values and acquired skills, criticizes it. He is not disloyal to his community for using on it the moral skills it has helped him develop.

Finally, there are two senses of community which it is important to distinguish. In a romantic sense, nostalgia for community may haunt the isolated individual; a man who experiences himself as an isolated atom hungers for identification with a group. In this sense, community totally absorbs the individual; the values, goals, and exigencies of the commune are uncritically devoured in exchange for comradeship. This is the sense of community which draws the insecure, the alienated, the threatened, and those incapable of realistic love. Millennial groups in Western history have long arisen out of this nostalgia.[27]

But the second sense of community is not romantic but realistic. The community is not perceived as an escape or refuge. Rather, community is already present because the individual experiences himself as related to others; he is not an "I" merely, but also a "we." He is not isolated, alienated, or unable to love. He has been nourished by a community of which he feels himself a part, and he is free to extend community to others. He is not uncritical; he does not accept all the values, goals, and exigencies of his community as equally valid. He feels a responsibility towards his community, a claim upon him to be intelligent, reflective, honest, and courageous. He does not feel that dissent is disloyalty, for the community of which he is a part does not demand his total submission but the total development of his humanity. Such a community has taught him to seek reality through intelligent and critical judgment, and to respond to others as they are, not as phantasy or pretense suggest. Such a community has maintained a tradition of at least some small measure of liberty, justice, truth, and love. In it a man is free to be himself: both an authentic person and a social animal. Such a community communicates the desire for a free, responsible, and critical life to as many of its members as are receptive to it.

IV. *The Open Society and the Open Church*

Love is mutual before it is selfless. It is other-centered rather than nonself-centered; its goal is community of life, rather than the purity of individuals. Man is a member of a community before he is an individual, and he develops as a genuine person through developing more creative, realistic, and profound relationships with others. The basic model for the understanding of human life and action, therefore, is not the atomic individual but the community of persons. Is this community the state? The church? Or neither one?

In the language of political science, the community is prior to the state; the state is an administrative, legal, and technical apparatus for securing certain purposes of the community. In the language of theology, God made his covenant with a people, an *ecclesia,* not with atomic individuals. A Christian is first a member of a people, secondarily an individual believer. The call is not first addressed to separate individuals, who then join together for their mutual protection; on the contrary, a church was first called into being, within which individuals might be nourished in a community of life, faith, and love. Likewise, the national community is not first a group of atomic individuals, who for self-protection create a government by contract; on the contrary, human communities are primordial, and various rules and institutions are from the first implicit in their ways of life.

Consequently, the problem of church and state is not the radical problem in the question of how to relate Christian life to secular life. The radical problem concerns the relationships which obtain between the many human communities which are prior to the two polities, church and state. Insofar as the community of believers has an historically articulated polity, a variety of offices, techniques of communal decision-making, and an unavoidable degree of bureaucratization, the meaning of the word "church" has a secondary, juridical sense. Primarily, the church is the people of God; [28] secondarily, it is an external, more or less bureaucratic polity. The two senses of the word are linked organically; no community can endure through the necessities of history without establishing an effective polity.[29] But the two senses must also be distinguished and their priorities observed, lest the church attempt to be purely "spiritual" and nonhistorical or, on the other hand, become a sepulchre of bureaucracy and legalism.

Similarly, insofar as a large community requires an articulated polity, it gives rise to a state. No national community can survive without government; but the ends of government do not encompass all the ends of the community.[30] In many areas of community concern, in the arts, the sciences, religion, and the like, the state has no competence, or only that marginal competence which restricts abuses against public order: forbidding religious practices, for example, which involve human sacrifice, the use of poisonous snakes, or polygamy. It is extremely difficult to mark off the limits which the state must observe in interfering with the broader life of the community. Criteria for deciding what constitutes an abuse against "public order" and what constitutes an illegitimate intervention of government in the liberty of the community are scarcely to be derived from abstract considerations; abstractions themselves cover too much ground and infringe upon liberty. Thus the history of the community and the concrete circumstances of each instance furnish more limited and less ideologically menacing criteria from case to case.

Nevertheless, a disproportionate amount of attention is usually given to the problems of church and state; for church and state are secondary realities. The church as polity is only an instrument of the church as community, and the state is but one instrument of the culture. When attention is focused upon the state rather than upon the culture, or upon the church as polity rather than upon the church as people, there is an overpowering temptation to construct a conceptual model with the atomic individual as their opposite pole. The state is taken to be a threat to the individual; individual conscience is brandished as a battlecry against the church. Moreover, the church is understood to be one separate collective, the state another; the dimensions of life in which the individual shares beliefs and attitudes which derive *at the same time* from both his church as community and his civic community are overlooked. Robert N. Bellah, from the Social Relations Department at Harvard, has described in a fascinating paper [31] the role and importance of "civic religion"—a shared body of ultimate assumptions and ways of action—in the life even of a religiously pluralistic society such as our own.

It may be fruitful, then, to concentrate our efforts for a while upon establishing a clearer notion of those communities which are prior to the polities of state or church. If, for example, we now list several ways in which beliefs, attitudes, and techniques of intellectual and moral growth are communicated among men, we may come to see (1) that a community is not merely a collective, and (2) that the morality of the community may not be directly opposed to the morality of the individual. For each man, it seems, benefits by the insights, loves, aims, hopes, and failures he shares with other men. It is in company with others than men acquire and develop what intellectual and moral abilities they have; even the solitude and intellectual or moral loneliness required for certain stages of personal growth have communal significance. For while the community provides the matrix of moral or intellectual growth, the individual must appropriate the basic values and orientations he learns from the community thoroughly and at his own pace.

Some examples from different types of communities may illustrate the role of community life in moral education. In marriage, husband and wife must learn a mode of life more thoroughly other-centered than they have known before. An ideal of unselfishness or of self-sacrifice is inadequate. For the primary reality of married life is not the personal purity or personal generosity of either party, but the degree to which the two persons can communicate in one life. The woman entering upon marriage with the goal of proving her spirit of self-sacrifice had best heed the poet's advice: "Get thee to a nunnery!" Even the act of intercourse between husband and wife teaches them that they are to be each concerned for the other; it is not a symbol of separate ecstasy but of mutual involvement.

Likewise, it is in the matrix of the family that children acquire their earliest moral experiences, begin to associate pleasures and pains with certain activities, develop tastes and skills, and otherwise acquire what Aristotle calls the indispensable starting-points of ethical judgment.[32] Again, it is in the scientific community that young men and women acquire the information, the series of insights, and the criteria of relevance and evidence that enable them to attain critical discrimination. Further, it is in the political community that those attitudes toward fairness,[33] liberty, law, and due process are nourished which make certain kinds of political techniques either practicable or unrealistic; for the same techniques do not work equally well in different communities. Finally, it is in the religious community that the word of God is heard, a context of interpretation acquired, and a tradition of reflection, prophecy, and reformation nourished or neglected.[34]

In each of these instances, the experience, understanding, reflective judgment and even personal decisions of the individual are nurtured and tutored by the community.[35] Rare is the large, historical community so limited that it is easy for the individual to outgrow it; ordinarily, only a few individuals bring to fruition a genuine strand of originality and thus contribute something new to their historical tradition. Thus, few individuals rise to the levels possible in their tradition; most seem to feed upon the community, like harmless parasites, deriving all their intellectual and moral nourishment from it and contributing to it perhaps not even an authenticity of their own. In many ways, therefore, the community may bear in itself moral resources superior to those realized by individuals within it.

The distinction between the state and the culture, and between the church as polity and the church as community, however, makes it possible for us in our time to heighten the dialectic between the community and its individual members. For these distinctions have become operational in recent times through that political wisdom which led to the conception of the open society and the open church. A closed or a total society is one in which all decisions are, in principle at least, subject to review by one authority. Leaders are separated from followers, officers from soldiers, superiors from subjects, staff from inmates. In such a society, the relationships among individuals are established by the attitudes and aims of the leaders; these leaders may be paternal or tyrannical, wise or restrictive. The total society is not, therefore, *ipso facto* an evil society. Nevertheless, our increasing differentiation of belief systems, professions, specialized sciences, economic opportunities, and political options has now rendered the total society obsolete and regressive as a model for the human community.

For the fact is that today there is not one human community; there are many human communities. It seems apparent that a human being may best reach his full potential if he belongs totally to no one community, but partially to many communities. An open society or an open church is designed precisely to accommodate a rich diversity, many voluntary associations, and freedom of choice.[36] But it would be a conceptual mistake to think that the model of an open society or an open church supposes that men are merely atomic individuals, and that individuals as such are the locus of moral power and fruitfulness. On the contrary, the open society and the open church are forms of polity which favor the multiplication of varied forms of community for various purposes. The community remains the locus of human exchange, conversation, stimulation, and development. The open society and the open church support the principle of diversity precisely to nourish as many different kinds of community as necessary or fruitful for human development. The atomic individual, the alienated man, is the man who has not learned how to live in the open society and the open church; since there is no closed society to take care of him, he withdraws into his own guts.

The authentic life of the human community, the lifeblood of moral and intellectual development, is civic conversation;[37] the criterion of a healthy culture is that men speak to one another, and listen to one another. Without speech and listening, there is no moral and intellectual development.[38] This is why segregation is so great a sin, why living in a ghetto is so stultifying, why denominational schools sometimes have an air of unreality about them, why the Iron Curtain is so politically dangerous, and the trivial "hot line" is yet so powerful a symbol.

Men are rapidly filling up this planet and yet they have created no one human community, but a congeries of partly isolated communities. Speaking and listening are not operational in many situations; thus labor unions resort to strikes, minority groups employ coercive pressures, governments engage in wars. If we are realists, we recognize that we do not have, neither at present nor in immediate prospect, a worldwide human community of discourse.[39] For community is organic. It grows by shared experiences, shared insights, shared criteria of relevance and evidence, and shared lives; it is not achieved by treaties, pacts, ordinances, or laws, though these sometimes spring from early steps in its acquisition and make further steps possible.

V. Conclusion

The pressures of world population and technical progress make imperative an ethical vision which all men can share. The argument of this paper is that an ethical ideal which conceives of *agape* in individualistic terms cannot supply that vision. For the primary reality of ethical life is not the atomic individual but the community of life in which the individual shares. *Agape,* whose source is in God, is precisely the highest and fullest form of community life. *Agape* is both other-centered and realistic. Thus those individuals who learn from their communities the experience and the meaning of the communal love which *agape* makes divine are in a position to reach out to others, and to do so not with illusions but realistically. They are in a position, not only to criticize themselves, but also to criticize their communities, and thus to extend, however gradually and modestly, the *agape* which they learned in their communities beyond the limits of their communities. In this way, men reach out toward one another across the gaps of silence that separate them. The conceptual model of the open society and the open church enables them to understand that to open civil conversation with one another they do not have to submerge their historical communities in one closed, total society. On the contrary, the whole point of the model of the open society and the open church is that the human community can be a community of conscience and reasonable discourse and mutual respect. In such a community, diversity prospers. Diversity contributes to the fundamental enterprise: that countless finite men in their variety may mirror back the infinite loveliness of God.

NOTES

1. Scribner's, 1932; paperback edition with new preface, 1960.
2. Preface, 1960 edition, p. ix.
3. In his introduction to *Man's Nature and His Communities*, Scribner's, 1965, Niebuhr cites the remark of a young friend who chided him that he should have called the book *The Not so Moral Man in His Less Moral Communities*.
4. See "The Ethic of Jesus" in *An Interpretation of Christian Ethics*, Meridian Books, New York, 1963, p. 45.
5. In his introduction to *Essays in Applied Christianity*, D. B. Robertsoɪ. writes: "It has been said by numerous people, speaking from a number of positions, that Reinhold Niebuhr has given little attention to the question of the church." Meridian Books, New York, 1959, p. 11. Prof. Robertson tries to redress this judgment; but Niebuhr's basic conceptual model is, until *Man's Nature and His Communities*, at any rate, the individual. But even in 1956, Niebuhr wrote that he "has increasingly recognized the value of the church as a community of grace", he spoke of this as "only a growing recognition." (*Reinhold Niebuhr*, The Library of Living Theology, vol. 2, Charles W. Kegley and Robert W. Bretall, eds., Macmillan: New York, p. 437). Thus Niebuhr's own underlying development appears to have been in the direction of a new conceptual model based upon community.
6. I am indebted to a stimulating discussion on this theme by Professors Robert N. Bellah and Krister Stendahl at a planning session for *Daedalus* Magazine, held at the home of the American Academy of Arts and Sciences in Brookline, Mass., on October 15-16, 1965. See note 31, *infra*.
7. Caught in a lifelong darkness of faith, St. Therese of Lisieux in 1895 described in a line of one of her poems her criterion for finding God:

Car je te vois dans les âmes, mes soeurs,
La charité, voilà ma seule étoile . . .

(*Histoire d'une ame*, Office Central de Lisieux, 51, rue du Carmel, 1946, p. 330). See also I John 4:12-13: "No man has ever seen God; but if we love one another, then we have God dwelling in us, and the love of God has reached its full growth in our lives. This is our proof that we are dwelling in him, and he in us; he has given us a share of his own Spirit."
8. See Ceslaus Spicq, O.P., *Agape in the New Testament*, Herder: St. Louis, 1963.

9. For a brief statement, see "Eros and Agape" in *A Handbook of Christian Theology*, M. Halverson and A. A. Cohen (eds.), Meridian Books: N.Y., 1958, pp. 96-101; the masterwork is *Agape and Eros*. Westminster Press: Philadelphia, 1953, esp. the "tabulation of contrasts," pp. 208-10.

10. In interpreting the "transvaluation" of pagan by Christian love, specifically as it was worked out by Aquinas, Nygren falls into a conceptual error made prominent among Thomists by a brilliant writer who died in his youth, Pierre Rousselot. Both Nygren and Rousselot interpret human love as a "higher" version of sensitive desire. But for Aquinas, the model of sensitive desire—acquisitive, self-aggrandizing—is not adequate for describing the love of human beings. The human spirit is capable of realistic judgment, and thus of relating itself to others, not as it would wish them to be, but as they are. Love is willing the real good of the other—it is not *amor,* nor even *benevolentia,* but *dilectio,* and not only *dilectio* but *amicitia.* Moreover, as *caritas* this love is wholly a gift from God and is not in man's power to attain, or to increase; and only God's wisdom, not human reason, is its rule. See *Summa Theologica,* 2.2., q.24.1. ad 4 and 24.10; q. 23.6. ad 1; q. 27.2 and 27.5, etc. See also P. Rousselot, *L'Intellectualisme de St. Thomas,* Beauchesne, France: 2nd edition, 1924, and *Pour L'histoire du problème de L'amour au moyen age,* Paris, 1933, and the critique by L. B. Geiger, *Le Problem de L'amour chez S. Thomas d'Aquin,* Montreal, 1952. Also, G. Gilleman, *The Primacy of Charity in Moral Theology,* Newman: Westminster, Md., 1961.

11. Contrast *An Interpretation of Christian Ethics,* p. 218 n., where Nygren is cited with approval, with *The Nature and Destiny of Man,* II, p. 84 n., where Niebuhr writes that Nygren "makes the contrast [between *eros* and *agape*] too absolute." In both cases, Niebuhr uses Mt. 7:11 as the basic text. See Niebuhr's fuller discussions of Nygren in *Christian Realism and Political Problems,* Scribner's, 1953, pp. 162-68, and *Faith and History,* Scribner's, 1949, pp. 178-79.

12. *Christian Ethics and Moral Philosophy,* Scribner's: N.Y., 1955, pp. 42-58, esp. 54.

13. Library of Living Theology, vol. 2. pp. 104-06.

14. Ramsey, *ibid.,* writes as though the point of mutual love were to secure the good of the self as well as the good of the other. More exactly, it is to make the aim of the self to become attentive to the good of the other. The concentration is upon the good of the other. Self-sacrifice may be required in the process, as a means or condition, not as a goal. Moreover, *agape* is a gift of God, a share in God's own life, and thus to say with Scripture "Let *agape* be among you" (Ramsey, *ibid.,* p. 106) is to say: "Let the mutual love you share among you be transformed by grace into God's own love." In this way, ordinary mutual love is kept under the judgment of a different standard (*agape*) than that of human intelligent love (*dilectio*), but the discriminate judgments of such ordinary healthy love are not simply abandoned.

15. Cf. *The Lonely Crowd,* Doubleday Anchor Books: New York, 1953, pp. 19-48.

16. See the discussion of *"variations in moral and ethical sensitivity"* in accordance with stages in the development of human conscience," in Erik H. Erikson, *Insight and Responsibility:* W. W. Norton, New York, 1964, p. 221.

17. "Yet to grow in the individual, ethics must be generated and regenerated in and by the sequence of generations. . . . The chosen unit of study must be the generation, not the individual." *Ibid.,* pp. 228-29.

18. "The failure of basic trust and mutuality has been recognized in psychiatry as the most far-reaching failure, undercutting all development." *Ibid.,* p. 231.

19. "I would call mutuality a relationship in which partners depend on each other for the development of their respective strengths." *Ibid.* Erikson's recognition of possible inequalities *to be taken account of* in a healthy relationship is a helpful modification of the Aristotelian notion that a genuine, uncorrupting friendship must be based upon a fundamental equality. But see *Nicomachean Ethics,* VIII, vi, on "The Friendships of Unequals."

20. Nygren's strategy is to by-pass human judgment in his attempt to glorify God. Like Peter Lombard, against whose theory Aquinas directed the first question of his Disputed Question on Charity, Nygren (cf. George T. Thomas, *op. cit.,* p. 54) tries to identify God himself with *agape,* so that the human self is displaced. The strategy of Aquinas is to allow the human self and its discriminating judgment full exercise in its attempt to reverence, respect, and respond to the reality of others; but then to say that the gift of *agape* gives man a created participation in God's own love, which exceeds the measure of even perfect human mutual love, by drawing it into the life of God's wisdom and God's love. Perfect human mutual love (which in actual history is impossible for man without grace to sustain; cf. *De Veritate* q.24, a.12) is not rejected nor demeaned, but placed under the judgment and necessity of a divine measure of love.

21. On the realism of love, see Erich Fromm, *The Art of Loving,* Harper's: N.Y., 1956; C. S. Lewis, *The Four Loves,* Harcourt, Brace, 1960;' and Jacques Maritain, "Some American Illusions" and "Marriage and Happiness," in *Reflections on America,* Scribner's: New York, 1958, pp. 131-45.

22. For a systematic account of various patterns and levels of such bias, see Bernard Lonergan, *Insight,* Longman's, Green: London, 1958, pp. 191-206; 217-44.

23. See Bernard Lonergan "Metaphysics as Horizon," *Gregorianum* 44 (1963), pp. 307-18.

24. For an analysis of philosophy as dialectic, and a theoretical construct of a fully developed community—"Cosmopolis"—see Bernard Lonergan, *Insight,* pp. 217; 225-41.

25. Cf. I Jn. 4:12-13.

26. See T. S. Eliot, "Tradition and the Individual Talent," *The Selected Essays of T. S. Eliot*, Harcourt, Brace: New York, 1950.

27. See Norman Cohn, *The Pursuit of the Millennium*, Harper Torchbooks: N.Y., 1961. Among Roman Catholics, Father Riccardo Lombardi's Better World Movement seems to be a contemporary version of dangerous and romantic millennialism.

28. Cf. Vatican II, *The Constitution on the Church*, ch. 2.

29. See, e.g., Yvres Simon, *Nature and Functions of Authority*, Marquette University Press: Milwaukee, 1940.

30. See, e.g., Jacques Maritain, *Man and the State*, University of Chicago Press: Chicago, 1956, ch. 1.

31. Working paper, for private circulation, for *Daedalus* Planning Session, Brookline, Mass., 1965. The finished version appeared as "Civil Religion in America," *Daedalus* (Winter, 1967), pp. 1-21.

32. *NE*, I, iii, 5-7; I, vi. 5-7; II, i, 8; etc.

33. See John Rawls, "The Sense of Justice," *Philosophical Review* 72 (1963), pp. 281-305.

34. See, e.g., Lehmann, *Ethics in a Christian Context*, Harper's: New York, 1965; G. Travard, *Holy Writ or Holy Church*, Harper's: New York, 1959.

35. For an excellent account of the many ways in which the church is a human community, see James M. Gustafson, *Treasure in Earthen Vessels*, Harper: New York, 1961.

36. See my "Diversity of Structures: Freedom within Structures," *Concilium*, I (1965), pp. 103-13, and "The Free Churches and the Roman Church," *Journal of Ecumenical Studies* 2 (1965), pp. 426-47, both *supra*.

37. Aquinas notes three fundamental inclinations or tendencies in man, of which the third is most specifically human: "that he might live in society." In following this inclination, he says, man learns "not to harm those with whom he dwells in conversation." *S.T.* 1-2.94.2.

38. On the need of civil discourse, see John Courtney Murray, "Natural Law and Public Consensus," in *Natural Law and Modern Society*, John Cogley (ed.), World Publishing Co.: New York, 1963, pp. 48-81; also Walter Lippmann, *The Public Philosophy*, Mentor Books: New York, 1956.

39. See R. Niebuhr, "The Illusion of World Government," *The World Crisis and American Responsibility*, Ernest W. Lefever (ed.), Association Press: New York, 1958, pp. 85-104. Contrast with Cardinal Ottaviani's impassioned plea for a "world republic" in the closing debates of the Second Vatican Council.

19

Reasons for Chastity

For popular American piety, religion is a matter of morality and morality is a matter of personal conduct; religion does not include social matters. Consequently, corporate business practices and political arrangements do not come under the rules of morality and the concern of religion. Morality means telling the truth, not accepting bribes, obeying the law. It does not mean creating new laws which end historical social injustices, or creating new institutions based on more equitable arrangements toward minority groups, or changing the sociological conditions under which Negroes and other nonwhite Americans live. "What does all that have to do with religion?" The pious churchgoer asks. "Those are political questions. The church should stay out of politics."

But the one moral issue that more than any other exercises white Christians in America (next to cleanliness) is premarital chastity. The most horrible of fates is a premature loss of virginity; the most loathsome of immoralities is the act leading to an illegitimate birth. Pious America does not seem self-assured concerning why premarital intercourse is evil; young people gain the impression that their parents cannot give specific advice and don't really care what happens, so long as a public scandal doesn't arise. Parents are generally not too anxious to learn what their sons and daughters are doing, lest perhaps they be shocked.

The following chapter results from an effort to state why premarital chastity is commendable. It is impossible, I recognize, to offer young peo-

ple conclusive reasons against doing what it seems so very natural and good to do. But sexual intercourse is one of those many matters on which the young must make a decision before they have had all the relevant experience. (One of the sources of tragedy in human life is that we must often commit ourselves to action before we understand fully what we have committed ourselves to.) The young have a right to hear from older persons a firm opinion on the subject and the reasons for it; if all adults are nondirective, it becomes impossible for the young to define themselves. Urban society is sufficiently open, pluralistic, and nonauthoritarian that one man's opinion cannot be imposed upon the young. They will listen to the many sources of counsel available to them and make up their own minds, thus creating their own identity. It is not only useless but self-defeating merely to tell them "Do" or "Don't" without supplying reasons.

It is important to present to ourselves imaginatively the stakes in what we are doing. Suppose that Christianity is mistaken. Suppose that human life is short. Then perhaps a policy of chastity deprives us of one of the great, creative, tender joys of human companionship. On the other hand, it may be that sexuality is more complicated than we sometimes think, and that the personal relation of which it is a part is enriched by honesty, chastity, and fidelity, and made into a lie by their absence. We have only one life to live. We cannot live according to both alternatives. We must choose. It is important, then, to consider the reasons on both sides.

The present chapter had two goals in mind. First, it was addressing itself to those conservative Catholic moralists who were arguing that, if the Church approved of contraceptives, then there would no longer be any way to prevent a mass outbreak of premarital intercourse. (One Catholic high-school girl in Massachusetts mirrored their emphasis on contraceptives. She was having relations with a college boy, but didn't use contraceptives because in her mind that was what was sinful. When she became pregnant, her parents sent her for an abortion). Secondly, the chapter was addressed to the question of premarital intercourse in its own right. I am far from arguing that every case of premarital intercourse is harmful and sinful; the inhibitions of a pious conditioning may possibly be more so. Here as elsewhere human beings must be unafraid of running risks, free in spirit, and as clear, wise, and respectful of others as possible. Nowhere more than here is fear an enemy. Intercourse should be long prepared for; it is the regular and happy expression of love for the longest period of one's life. It is an art, a discipline, a playfulness, a gift, that in our day of analysis and sophistication is overlaid with too much somberness. It may be God's wittiest joke on the human race, that in such clumsiness and glee human persons should be obliged to lose solemnity, and find each other.

DOES marital sexual love, apart from procreation, have an autonomy of its own? Does it also have a moral structure of its own? There appears to be a widespread fear among conservative moralists that if the Catholic prohibition against anovulants and contraceptives is removed, all moral restraint in sexual activity will be removed. This fear is groundless. But the discussion of the question of marital chastity has come so far that the issue of premarital intercourse is now the basic one.

Conjugal intercourse, both anthropologists and psychologists maintain, is an act symbolic of a permanent relationship between a man and a woman. The sexuality of the human species is distinguished from that of other animal species by two striking characteristics. In the first place, man and woman seek a permanent society together, for a lifetime. In the second, man and woman seek to express their union sexually, not only when procreation is possible, when the woman is "in heat," but regularly.

It is quite natural that man and wife should have regular intercourse, whether children are conceived or not; it is not original sin, not hedonism, which encourages regular intercourse. Childless couples, fertile couples at certain times, and older couples in the years after the wife's menopause are by healthy instinct led to have regular intercourse.

The burden of proof falls, then, on those who argue that intercourse is naturally and indissolubly tied to procreation. On the other hand, those who argue that marital sexuality has an autonomy of its own apart from procreation must supply the moral principles which rule out such immoralities as fornication, masturbation, and homosexuality. Young people out of high school (and, indeed, in high school), whether on college campuses or working, are asking *why* premarital intercourse is wrong. They are not satisfied with the reasons offered by the conservative theologians. It is incumbent, then, on those who disagree with the conservative theologians on marital sexuality, to offer reasons why they would declare the use of anovulants (or contraceptives) to be legitimate in marriage, but not out of marriage.

The moral problem of masturbation, of course, is easily resolved in theory. Even those psychiatrists who are not Christian and who do not look on masturbation as immoral regard it as a sign of immaturity and narcissism. If they do not lay down strict prohibitions against masturbation, it is not because they think it healthy or desire to see it practiced. It is because they do not wish to increase the probabilities of its continuance by heightening the insecurities on which it is based. Like the Catholic moralist, they ordinarily hope that the young man will soon outgrow his selfishness and introversion. The technique they use to help him is, however, not that of mere prohibition.

The reasoning that seems to be operating here is that the sexual orgasm is psychologically oriented toward another person. If a man (or woman) provokes the orgasm in solitude, he is acting counter to the dynamic of his own psyche. He or she has failed to grow from preoccupation with self to responsiveness to another. In this sense, even premarital intercourse is by nature preferable to masturbation; for selfishness, presumptively, is diminished by the responsibility of involvement with another person. Masturbation appears to be a childish way out. The dynamic of human sexuality leads beyond such immaturity—through which nearly all young men and many young women pass, with more or less turmoil—to openness and concern for another.

Why, then, is premarital intercourse immoral? In our society, the situation is only made more trying for healthy young people because of the sexual intimacy into which they are so early thrown, at the same time as their adolescence is prolonged for several years by our social traditions. From the time they are fourteen or fifteen, many American young people have dated, danced, kissed, and petted. Through a period of from five to ten years they are eligible for rides in cars and walks through the woods in which at least partial disrobement and intimacies are all but expected of them. It is not surprising that many of them come to think that straightforward intercourse is the more honest and the more human approach to sexuality. In the confined spaces of an automobile the aesthetics of petting and "all but" are not calculated to add to the dignity of their sexuality.

Why, then, no premarital intercourse? Fornication is a sin, not because it is ugly or beastly, but because the man and woman who indulge in it are not living according to the symbol they are using. By their sexual union they are saying something which by their un-united lives they are denying. The dynamic of human sexuality is not only interpersonal; it also seeks a permanent union. There are many persons, of course, in our age as in every age, who tell themselves that they are being "realistic" and that love between humans cannot be permanent. Temporary liaisons are more satisfactory, they say, than permanent ones; lovemaking is better in affairs than in marriage.

The conservative theologian meets their objection by tying sexuality to procreation. Outside a marital union in which children can be born, he says, intercourse is sinful. Such a reply appears to miss the point. For it is certainly clear in experience that intercourse is one thing, the having of children is another; the intention and the means are different, only the outward act is the same. Whether temporary liaisons are more satisfactory or not, taken in themselves, they fail to meet the conditions of human life, both socially and personally. They may be more "fun," and they surely bring romance and adventure for a while; but they are escapist.

Socially, it is plain that the human race gets along by marital relationships, not by fornication. The first and basic context for learning human relationships is in the home; this is as true for the relationship between the parents as man and woman, as it is for the relationship between children and parents. Where there is love and trust between husband and wife, children have a chance of learning how to love and how to trust, an opportunity which is denied the children of parents who are not so united. Moreover, the man or woman who moves from temporary liaison to temporary liaison, however advanced in other respects, forfeits any chance to learn such love and trust. Some heroines of Mary McCarthy's novels, for example, like Margaret Sargent in *The Company She Keeps,* are all but explicitly conscious of this forfeiture, and appear still to be seeking a stable relationship they can respect.

Thus even in the personal consciousness of the practitioners of temporary liaisons there seems to be testimony to the validity of the permanent relationship they do not share. So far is this true that psychologists are led to classify the Don Juans and nymphomaniacs of this world as abnormal types; and not only as abnormal, but as underdeveloped in their sexual life. From a biological point of view, of course—as from a conservative theological point of view—Don Juans have had a very active sexual life. From a fuller, human point of view, their sexuality is so undernourished that they are in need of a doctor's help.

It is noticeable, moreover, that those writers who appear to exalt the advantages of temporary loves are forced to construct elaborate pretenses. Lovers whose union is not permanent must "forget about tomorrow." The romantic poignancy of their situation, such as Western literature trades upon, derives from the fact that theirs is an escape from the real conditions of human life. Even when they try to be "realistic," like the heroines of Françoise Sagan, their effort to be cynical and "not to care" is plainly grueling.

Everything about a full personal relationship which terminates in sexual intercourse cries out for permanence. It takes a determined effort of will not to hear those cries, or to shrug them off.

There are, of course, many kinds of fornication and therefore many degrees of sinfulness. In each case, however, evil is present because of the untruthful use of the sexual symbol. In a house of prostitution or in the activities of the Don Juans and *femmes fatales* of either sex, the untruthfulness is most clearly marked. Among the prostitutes and their visitors, a studied effort is made "not to get involved" and to confine the human relationship to a minimum. The Don Juan is using other persons in acting out his own obscure compulsions. Those who commit fornication in either of these fashions do exactly as those do who argue against birth control from the biological structure of the act: they notice and respond to only the biological aspects of sex.

There is another kind of fornication, however, which is more difficult to analyze. This time it is not the conservative theologians but the moralists who stress "the personal relationship" who have most difficulty in saying why such fornication is a sin. When a man and woman truly love one another, but for some reason cannot marry, their relationship may manifest nearly every dimension of human union. The symbol of intercourse may seem to be all but perfectly truthful. Moreover, by comparison with the relationship between some married couples, two devoted lovers might conceivably believe their own relationship far more healthy and even more moral.

But it seems that even such perfect "affairs," even were they to endure for many years, fall short of the dynamic and symbolism of intercourse. The very reasons for which marriage is not possible tell against them. Lovers whose love is rich in many human dimensions cannot help seeking the permanence which marriage provides. The psychological structure of human sexual love appears to require that permanence, in fact or in imitation or in pretext. Only with a severe wrench of the affections can separation, or even the thought of separation, be accepted.

The protracted affair is an imitation of matrimony; the casual affair is an escape from human reality. In neither of them does intercourse tell the whole human truth.

This point is especially important in the education of young men and women of college age. There is a cult of "honesty" among American youths, and at present that honesty is making a parody of the idea that all that is important in premarital intercourse is "a personal relationship."

Those young people whose moral sensitivities are acute have come to see that their clumsy disrobing and petting in the backs of cars derive from prudishness and fear. Unlike their fathers and their fathers' fathers, they find the use of whorehouses crude—and, indeed, such houses do not seem to be as common as they once were. Since in our society some degree of sexual excitement seems unavoidable, these modern youths, despising masturbation and the bawdy house, are seeking out "meaningful relationships." The biological morality of the conservatives and the I-thou morality of the personalists, they believe, have nothing to tell them whose point they have not seen.

In their eyes, premarital intercourse is good for many reasons; and so far they are right. It is not good for man to be alone, and when two persons have respect for each other in their love, there is a certain goodness in their union no matter how wrong it is in other respects. Premarital sex is wrong, however, even when it expresses true "encounter," because it fails to fulfill the conditions of permanence implied in the symbol of intercourse. Whatever some girls from

Smith or Sarah Lawrence might think, intercourse is not a symbol of mere fellowship or good feeling; it signifies an enduring commitment, a commitment for life.

It is not necessary, of course, to interpret the symbol of intercourse in such a binding way; very many people don't, and there is such a thing as overdoing the mystique of intact virginity. But if the symbol is not interpreted as signifying a permanent commitment, certain consequences must also be accepted. It used to be that these consequences were understood solely as the risk of pregnancy; this was an inadequate understanding at any time, but all the more so now that contraceptives largely eliminate that risk. The serious consequence of premarital intercourse is that the symbol of commitment and trust is devalued. To use this symbol as lightly as another generation used the kiss is to forfeit its meaning and power, in advance of that time when what it has to say will be true.

The consequence of premarital intercourse, then, is to introduce into a symbol for trust and commitment an element of cynicism. Symbols have their own laws and their own criteria of use; those who cry "Wolf! Wolf!" when there is no wolf must pay for their lack of seriousness.

The honesty involved in sexual intercourse, then, is not only that of "a meaningful relationship"; it is also that of a permanent, day-to-day, realistic relationship. Sexual intercourse is so deeply rooted in the personality of each of us that in taking one another as sexual partners we are also accepting each other, hour-by-hour, for what we are. The symbol of intercourse is not of a sort to lead us to find escape, though that is its characteristic misuse, but to lead us to commit ourselves, just as we are, to one whom we accept, just as he or she is.

Where the symbol of sexual intercourse is not surrounded by trust, the bond between two persons cannot be firm. Premarital intercourse is not wrong because it is ugly or vicious. On the contrary, under certain conditions, abstracted from reality, it can be quite beautiful. But it can never be beautiful in the conditions of realistic human life, for it lacks the permanence, and the commitment to daily acceptance of the other person, which those conditions enjoin. In our culture, the prevalence of premarital intercourse is understandable; but it is, after all, an adolescent escape. And, in a context of a mature morality, that constitutes its serious evil.

Finally, we ought to add that the dynamic of human sexuality is not only interpersonal and expressive of a permanent relationship; it is also heterosexual. No doubt it is true that homosexuals can find "a meaningful relationship" with persons of the same sex; and no doubt this relationship can even be made permanent. It seems all too plain, however, that homosexuals are obliged to live out a parody of the heterosexual relationship. The more we learn about the homosexual tendency, the less we recoil in emotional horror from it. But, also, the more we learn about it, the more it appears to be psychologically abnormal, and rooted in the inability to relate to half of the human race.

The criterion for sexual morality, in short, is not a supposed "integrity of the physical act." The criterion is the integrity of the symbol of union. Like any other symbol, this symbol can be used lightly, or misused. There is no angelic, automatic way of avoiding the misuse of symbols, or of beginning to use them, all at once, perfectly. But a way of presenting chastity as truthfulness in the use of a most important human symbol would go far toward eliminating negative, prudish, fearful and even ugly approaches to marital love. At the same time, it manifests marital love as the crown of ordinary human love, of which masturbation, fornication, and homosexuality fall quite short.

20

Toward a Positive Sexual Morality

The Christian church has traditionally been preoccupied with premarital intercourse and infidelity in marriage; it has had very little to say about positive preparation for marital intercourse. Among Roman Catholics, the neglect is only more marked because marital intercourse plays no part in the daily life of the sister or the priest. Moreover, there are, as Anne Martin has written "too few sexy saints." Consequently, the faint odor of sin distorts the Catholic imagination when it turns toward—or away from —the subject of marital sexual love. Yet premarital chastity cannot be understood apart from its ordinary terminal point: intercourse in marriage. Intercourse is the central symbol of the ordinary human life; the most basic unit of society is founded upon it. The symbolic resources of intercourse have scarcely been noticed by the churches, and consequently their most successfully communicated word has been negative and inhibiting. The sins of the Christian Church in fostering destructive sexual attitudes are not minimal.

The following chapter was first written, in part, in 1961 and sent to various journals in the United States, England, and France. It was at that time difficult to question the stand of the Catholic Church publicly. The English journal Blackfriars, *at least, printed a short resumé of my argument, which was in the air at that time, without citing any source, and Father Thomas Gilby replied to it. His inconclusive response was one of the straws in the wind that indicated a change in theological thinking.*

The French journal Études *accepted the article on condition that certain arguments were strengthened; but a change of editors occurred, and my revised manuscript apparently was lost. Finally, in much longer form the article appeared as a chapter in* What Modern Catholics Think about Birth Control *(edited by William Birmingham, New York, 1964).*

WITHIN the Catholic Church the development of doctrine ordinarily proceeds by way of making a more delicate, more precise distinction than was made before. In this way an earlier position is partly contradicted by a later; the later takes more things into account than the earlier. The same desire to preserve the Christian faith motivates both positions. Christian faith remains consistent with itself.

Catholic teaching on marital sexuality seems to be on the threshold of such a development. In the last fifty years the moral situation of the layman has changed drastically. Actions that used to secure one effect now result in another. As a consequence there is often a discrepancy between what the formulas of the Christian tradition "say" and what they "mean." Unless more careful and more accurate distinctions are made in our generation, there is a grave danger that the authentic Christian tradition will be lost by indiscriminate respect for received words.

The heart of the development in Catholic moral teaching concerns a distinction to be made in the "essential subordination" of the "secondary end" of marriage to its "primary end," of the personal relationship to procreation. The reason for making a new discrimination is threefold.

In the first place it must be made clearer *why* the personal relationship of the married couple is held to be "essentially subordinate" to procreation. Fathers Ford and Kelly, who speak for the familiar Catholic tradition, write:

Reason itself can give us a clue as to what is more important, the personal purposes, or the purposes that serve the species. Undoubtedly procreation and rearing of children are of more importance to the species. Likewise it is of more importance to human society in general, and hence to the law, both civil and canon. . . . Since the *good of the species* is more important to nature than the good of individuals, procreation and rearing of children is a more important end of marriage than mutual help, conjugal love and the remedy [of concupiscence].[1]

Likewise, a long tradition that begins with St. Augustine and is resumed by St. Thomas puts the point succinctly: "As food is for the preservation of the body, so is sexual intercourse for the preservation of the race." [2] The good of the species takes precedence over the good of individuals. The preservation of the species is the first end of marital intercourse.

But in the second place it is necessary to see what has happened to the *good of the species* in the last two generations. There is no longer any fear that the species will become extinct through insufficient procreation. On the contrary, advances in medicine, the production and distribution of goods, and education have guaranteed that this primary end of marriage should be easily fulfilled. By using his intelligence, man has made the fulfillment of this first requirement of natural law almost a matter of course. Indeed, those concerned about the natural law insofar as it bears upon the preservation of the race are concerned, not about underpopulation, but about overpopulation. The human race has never faced this aspect of the natural law before. If virtue lies in the mean, we may say that human beings have for all of their previous history had to face only one extreme: famine, high death rate, high percentage of infant mortalities—in short, the dangers of extinction by insufficient procreation. Our own moral danger is at the other extreme.

In the third place we need to be clearer than we ever have been about the concept of "the marital act"—*actus per se aptus ad generationem,* the philosophers used to say, and "the penetration of the female by the male organ, and ejaculation," the canon lawyers specified, for their empirical, juridical purposes (in cases of *ratum non consummatum,* for example).[3] Now it is easy to see how philosophers who were preoccupied with physical nature, with biology, could have defined the marital act as they did. And it is also easy to see how canon lawyers could be satisfied with a definition that abstracted from almost the entire reality of the marital act. Further, it is easy to see how, at a time when the preservation of the species was an ever-present concern, the Church could avail herself of these definitions. But it is surely true that few are the Catholic married couples, howsoever philosophically trained or untrained, who believe that these definitions are sufficiently discriminating to match the reality. From a biological point of view, or from a legal point of view, they may be sufficient. From a human point of view they are philosophically inadequate.

Two important historical factors have arisen in recent years to require of us a deeper grasp of our own tradition of natural law. One of these is the discovery of the close interrelationship between sexuality and personality. The other is the fulfillment of those medical, economic, and social conditions which guarantee the fulfillment of the biological imperative of natural law, viz., the preservation of the race. We have already mentioned the latter factor, and will return to it. Now we must clarify the first.

It seems unlikely that the following statement can any longer be taken as representing accurately the nature of marital intimacy: "Mutual help and a total sharing of life can occur between two persons of opposite sex *outside* marriage, also, either as a mere matter of fact, as between brother and sister living together . . ." [4] Those who live the married life cannot believe, even for a moment, that their life, except for the fact that they perform acts *per se* apt for generation, is like the life of brother and sister, or even two good friends. Sexual intercourse is not a mere discrete, physical act, which fails to change the quality of one's life. Those who have intercourse together can never again be merely brother and sister, or good friends. The whole psychological tenor of their lives has been changed. Sexual intercourse involves the totality of their personal lives. It is a whole, of which the biological externals are only part.

Let us elaborate on this "totality principle." [5] Clearly, the act of intercourse is not, for married people, the mere placing of the male organ into the woman's vagina, together with ejaculation. The act of intercourse stretches out into all the moments of the day. The couple's present stage of emotional maturity, their love for one another, their casual contacts, their conflicts, their moods—all of these things, consciously perhaps, unconsciously surely, are motivating forces of and contributors to the act of intercourse. Moreover, each word, look, touch during the day is likely to influence the quality of the act. Not that passion is at stake, as between young lovers; rather, the two personalities constantly affect each other. At what precise moment does a given act of intercourse begin? From a merely biological view, only when the man begins to enter the woman. But the biological point of view hardly does justice to the human being.

Secondly, we must distinguish between the two levels of moral imperative in the sexual act. The first level is the biological; its end is the preservation of the species; its imperative is *do not allow the species to become extinct*. The second level is psychological; its end is the harmony and development of the human psyche, intelligence, will, emotions, and sentiments. Its imperative is *act toward one another as person to person; do not treat the other as an object or a means*.

Now we may argue in this fashion. In our generation the first moral imperative is easy to fulfill. If each couple has children according to its own reasonable possibilities, each couple fulfills the first imperative of the natural law. But the second moral imperative is much more difficult. Almost no guidance has been offered in teaching us how to fulfill it. On the contrary, the preoccupation of philosophers with the biological imperative and the preoccupation of canon lawyers with rights and contracts—with the "right to the other person with a view to acts which are *per se* apt for the generation of offspring" (can. 1081, #2)—could be easily mistaken as contributing to a morality for purely biological agents, or for persons who use one another as objects. How many women of the past have been led to feel like baby machines? How many men and women used one another for the "relief of concupiscence" with the impression that they were fulfilling the natural law?

We are concerned here with a development of the Catholic moral sense. It is *not* enough to use marital intercourse merely "to relieve concupiscence." It is *not* enough merely to produce babies. It is *not* enough merely to give each other pleasure, like two strangers playing on adjacent instruments. As in so many other areas, our generation is called to a higher degree of moral consciousness. The psychological imperatives of the natural law are beginning to make themselves heard all the more insistently, just as the biological imperatives of that law are receding because they are so easy to fulfill. Our generation is called, not to be less faithful to the natural law, but to be more consciously faithful to requirements of the natural law that have not been preached for centuries. The exchange of marital love is not merely the "rendering of a debt" or the "use of a right." Married persons are not strangers to each other or objects of trade. They are separate persons with full human dignity, and if they give themselves to each other, it is because their spirits do as their bodies symbolize: become two in one.

The crux of this newly understood moral imperative, however, is whether it can be obeyed without at the same time obeying the biological imperative. Here we are forced to admit that the philosophers who defined marital intercourse in terms of discrete, individual acts, each of whose end is *per se* the procreation of children, overshot the mark. *Intercourse* is for the preservation of the race. But not each act of intercourse. The precise point of difficulty lies in the definition of the marital act. If the received philosophical and canonical definitions are not sufficiently supple, we must attempt to formulate something better.

My own suggestion is the following. *The act of intercourse is that act of two persons which physically symbolizes the permanent union of their mutual good will, and which, when the biological imperative so commands, is apt for the generation of children.* As the good of the species is prior to the good of the individual, so is procreation prior to the symbolization of marital love. But when the biological imperative has been fulfilled, it no longer has force. The morality of sexual intercourse is then to be derived from psychological criteria. Chief among these criteria would be the victory of mutual consideration over lust, of friendship over concupiscence, of mutual concern over individual passion, hedonism, or egotism. The pre-eminence of lust, concupiscence, passion, indulgence, or egotism in marital sex cannot fail to harm one or both of the partners. The biological imperative alone does not guarantee the elimination of these evils. That is why the psychological imperative has such an important, though comparatively neglected role in the morality of marital sex.

Before going on, it may be well to show that our new definition effectively rules out certain basic evils. In the first place the permanence of the union rules out fornication and adultery. The symbolism of the act—described by the last clause, aptness for generation when required—rules out those varieties of the act which violate the dignity or intelligence of one or both parties. Masturbation, for example, offends the dignity and the mutuality of the act; even mutual masturbation is not union but separate giving of pleasure, and so the symbolism fails.

Again, the requirement of mutual good will guards against hedonism, lust, and indulgence. Sexual intercourse is so bound up with the whole range of psychic motivations and drives that where it is not performed in love and openness, the tensions of misuse begin to manifest themselves. If they do not show mutual love the partners cannot help but know that something is amiss. They need only reflect.

In fact, we may expand this consideration much further. It is precisely at this point that the "asceticism" of the psychological imperative makes itself felt. It is *difficult* to make love well. The husband's manhood is at stake; the woman's femininity is at stake. Emotional immaturity, inherited fear, unfounded feelings of guilt, misunderstood words or gestures, too much haste, too much apathy—any and all of these elements can make of intercourse a hell rather than a communion. Not by accident are many marriages wrecked by the difficulties of the marriage bed. A maximum of sensitivity, consideration, affection, trust, humility, humor, and playfulness are required. If we may believe psychiatrists, few men and women have achieved such emotional stature that they have nothing to learn. The marriage bed puts on trial every feeling, fear, and trait of the personalities of husband and wife. In making love they come to "know" each other and themselves in a way so profound that it has given to the verb "to know" its most radical meaning.

To conclude this section: the natural law remains the root of the Catholic morality of sex. In our generation the biological imperative of the natural law is easily fulfilled—and we must obey it. But the moral imperative that we have come to recognize is even more demanding than the biological imperative. The act of intercourse is not only defined by its biological externals; it reaches out into the total texture of our lives. This total texture is a "good of the whole," more important than the good of any part—i.e., the biological placement of the act. The part must sometimes yield to the good of the whole. We can no longer, in our marital love, merely "render the debt," or "relieve concupiscence": to do so would be to violate the psychological imperative that guides our marriages. We are obliged to overcome our fears, our pride, our lack of trust in one another, our roughness, our pettiness, our lust, so that our intercourse symbolizes our love truthfully. If we do so, we shall hardly be less Catholic than the generations that preceded us.

Under the pressures of experience, however, Catholic laymen will have to enunciate more exactly the criterion of morality in their marital love. Many misleading criteria have been proposed in the past. It will be useful for us to begin with a survey of recently expressed views, in order to get at the attitude of mind behind them. Then we may be in a position to propose a more adequate criterion.

The main effort among Catholics appears to be negative. Only one criterion of sexual morality is certain to be offered for the guidance of those about to be married: do not use contraceptives. If a couple is willing to risk a pregnancy in their lovemaking, this criterion seems to say, then they *must* love one another. The gravity of the possible consequences of their act will, it is argued, force the couple to a seriousness that ought to exclude mere lust or indulgence. The underlying assumption in this point of view seems to be that marital sexuality is not a good in its own order but needs some other reason to justify it. Moreover, it fails to notice that marital love and parenthood are usually two different, distinct goods, separately cherished, separately willed, even though both are part of the larger complex of a concrete marriage.

The invocation of this simple criterion, moreover, is inadequate in practice. Even if a couple observes the criterion, by not using anovulants or a contraceptive, one party may still use the other merely for the relief of concupiscence or merely "to render the marriage debt." And such intercourse would hardly be moral. The husband or the wife may still approach the act as something "to be gotten over with." This failure to appreciate the values proper to human sexuality appears to be quite widespread. Let us cite several examples, saving most of our comments until afterward.

The first example sounds like fiction but is fact. I remember a Catholic woman who said in conversation that if the Church ever permitted the use of anovulants, women would feel "like prostitutes." Surely, what she was saying is that in her acts of love she even now feels like a prostitute. The only way she can rationalize her submission to her husband is to concentrate (as she said) on the great good of "providing souls who would enjoy God through all eternity" and on showing her love for her husband by her "gift" of herself. In her mind sexuality is an occasion of self-sacrifice; it makes her a kind of martyr. Her husband, a quiet man, who was listening to the conversation, seemed to agree.

This woman and her husband seemed to consider marital sexuality as a necessary evil. They would have liked to do without it, if they could. Only by extraordinary concentration on "theological" motivations could they—the wife especially—bring themselves to go through with it. (The husband seemed to be dualistic: the urge of his body dominated the reluctance of his soul.) Less self-sacrificing women sometimes find in such an approach to marital love a powerful way of bribing their husbands. Using their own moods and tantrums to drive him away or to attract him, they use their assets in the marriage contract for purposes of barter. It is easy to see why in certain marriages, and especially among some national groups, the women become dominant and the men turn to drink and to explosions of temper. Both men and women accept a negative sexual code. The women capitalize upon it in the name of virtue.

Variations on this sexual code have received wide distribution in Catholic magazines. In one article the mother of five children argues against those who think "entirely in carnal terms." She wants to see everything in terms of "spirit." The reason for virginity, for example, is "spiritual motherhood." She goes on:

And conversely, *the end and meaning of carnal motherhood is virginity,* for the whole purpose of a mother's life should be total consecration to God in the married state. She must, like the virgin, belong to Him alone, to others only in Him. That she sacrifices her physical integrity to achieve this in her own way doesn't mean that true spiritual virginity can never be hers. How many saints pronounced "virgin and martyr" by the early Church were, we know now, brutally deflowered according to pagan custom before execution! The flesh, we must remember, profits nothing of itself; it is the spirit which gives life.[6]

A little reflection reveals this attitude toward sexuality as inhuman. Can a woman in love think of herself as "brutally deflowered" by her husband? Is the sexual union something she undergoes while she tries to keep her heart and her intention virginal? If so, guilt and horror will surely be generated in the heart of her husband and in her own heart, at the carnality into which their "state of life" forces them.

The contradiction between virginal ideals and sexual acts could hardly be more powerfully presented.

In another Catholic magazine an anonymous letter writer extends this attitude in order to make a tacit condemnation of those who use contraceptive devices.

After all, these devices so limit the physical contact that the intimate touch which *is* sexual union, is absent from the act. George Bernard Shaw called them, rather ungently, reciprocal masturbation; we must at least ask whether these things are ordered to that intimate conpenetration in which we join at the most responsive center of our being, or whether they simply permit the peripheral stimulation which is essentially a solitary sensual pleasure. Then it is the equivalent of kissing through a pane of glass.[7]

The Catholic columnist Donald McDonald adds to this point of view a quotation from Fr. Paul Quay, S.J.: "The act of love, to be complete, must be total; there must be no reservation as there is in the woman who, using a contraceptive, 'closes the depths of her spirit to her husband. She has accepted his affection but not his substance.' " Mr. McDonald adds that "the meaning of the marital act" is "total surrender, total self-donation." [8]

It is true, of course, that Catholics are conditioned to hold contraceptives in revulsion. This conditioning is reinforced by the idea that marital sexuality is not really a good for its own sake, anyway. But what is not noticed is that "total surrender" or "total self-donation" are not the language of ordinary human life. We learn to love only gradually. Perfect love is not attained so easily as the invocation of the simple criterion of the nonuse of contraceptives seems to imply. The language of "total surrender" concludes to a sense of moral superiority that perhaps has not been earned. Some who use contraceptives may love one another more than some who do not.

Frs. McHugh and Callan add another view in their *Moral Theology*:

The husband and wife who practice onanism and other similar vices cannot have the mutual respect they should have; the wife is deprived of the treasure of her modesty and is treated as a prostitute rather than as an honored wife and mother, and the husband is brutalized by the removal of the natural restraint to his sex passion—such self-indulgent persons would either selfishly neglect the one or two children they may have or spoil them for life by the luxury and laziness in which they are reared.[9]

Here again we meet the idea that sexuality is bestiality, unless restrained by procreation. Father Vincent M. Walsh records a further common American Catholic sentiment:

"What is the law of my nature? At one level it is to express affection toward my wife regardless of any consequence." Yes . . . and that level is the physical level. At this level the law of my nature says to do whatever pleases myself, whatever gratifies myself. We teach our children from birth not to live solely on this physical level.[10]

Again and again we hear the refrain that sexual expression in marriage is merely physical, self-indulgent, and in need of some justifying motive. We are invited to a "spiritual love" (whose criterion, however, is physical). We do not hear it said that marital sexuality is good for its own sake. We do not hear praise of its quiet, ordinary, but profound joys. We are not taught to look for the many subtle values that are inherent in its own structure.

One reason for this deficiency appears to be the failure to note that marital sexuality is primarily a psychological reality, like faith or charity or prayer. In all these things the expressive physical signs are important (at least in the Catholic tradition), but emphasis is wisely placed on the necessary interior dispositions. A wife who is resentful or a husband who is inconsiderate, for example, makes of the symbol of marital love a direct lie. But the problem here is that as soon as one makes a move to "spiritualize" sexuality, the temptation is to cross over into making men into angels. The only way to avoid this is to emphasize the importance of interior dispositions which are proper to incarnate men, not those proper to angels, nor those already trying to live according to an eschatological state.

Thus there is sometimes an effort to justify human sexuality by seeing it as a relational experience in which the couple can "even then" be rapt in union with God. Another way is to presuppose that virginal love is "a higher form of love" than sexual love, even in marriage. Louis Dupré, for example, in an otherwise excellent article,[11] ends by arguing that continence, periodic or prolonged, is the *ideal* solution for the married couple. No one seems to notice that married persons before their marriage have had many years of experience in the continent life. From a Christian point of view some of them, at least, believe that in marital love they have found something better; they do not wish to retrogress to an earlier and, in their experience, more self-centered emotional life. How, then, did the idea of virginal love as a higher form of love ever get started? Professor Dupré's article, for example, gives no justification for the superiority of virginal love. He begins by saying that "authentic human love cannot be attained without self-control." He then argues that the physical expression of love is not an absolute value to be isolated from the totality of existence. Of course not. But how do you get from that to calling continence "the highest level of spiritual love"?

In heaven, of course, there will be no marrying or giving in marriage. But neither will there be any hierarchy, institutional church, sacraments, or even faith and hope. This does not mean that men should begin to live as angels, seeking only an invisible, spiritual church of pure love. In becoming man Christ has indicated that Christians may wisely love and rejoice in the human situation as it is. As we love the church, so we may accept, respect, and love our human sexuality. Surely the days of our sexual power will pass, as all things human. But for as long as they are given us, they are given for our instruction and our joy.

Another way of "spiritualizing" the sexual relation is to insist on discipline, control, and abstinence. But the psychology implied in such insistence is dubious; it certainly is not, for example, the psychology of Aquinas. For its presupposition is that the "lower" passions rage and paw the ground like Plato's steeds and that rationality is the faculty of restraint and control. On the contrary, the sexual impulse is not only libidinal. Human sexuality is not animal; it is interpersonal. The desire to express one's love outwardly is proper to the human being, just as the desires to build churches and create a visible liturgy are proper to him. Man is a symbol-using, expressive creature. His lovemaking is a sign of his inner efforts to be unselfish, to find his center in another, however true it is that it can also be a disordered "lower impulse." The moral problem is not to eradicate or strictly limit this expressive impulse but to liberate it and to order it. But to "order" sexuality does not finally mean to control it, discipline it, and refrain from exercising it except when necessary; to order sexuality is to use it truthfully: to mean what it says. And that requires discipline of a type different from what has yet been articulated.

Because the Church lacks other criteria of just and wholesome marital relations (and because celibate theologians have naturally concentrated on the ideals and problems of virginity, not of sexuality), Catholics have generally heard of no other criterion for marital sexuality except the nonuse of contraceptives. This lack of other criteria appears to be the main reason why the Church has had to rest the main weight of its moral teaching about marital sexuality on the question of contraceptives and anovulants. An underlying fear seems to dominate the discussion: if *some* criterion for the good use of marital sexuality is not held onto, what will stem from the tide of indulgence, lust, and softness?

Toward what fuller criterion can Catholics turn if they are to derive the full moral benefit from their acts of marital love, and to avoid sin? Sexuality is not primarily indulgence, lust, or softness any more than authority is authoritarianism, or intelligence is rationalism. Moreover, the search for a simple, external criterion is surely misleading, here as elsewhere in human life. It would be nice to have a clear, simple test of what in a certain act is moral and what is not; but in most areas of human life such easy ways are not available; that is why the virtue of prudence is central in concrete moral life. The individual must weigh his actions in the light of conscience, in the presence of God and of the Church, and then act according to his prudential judgment. Rarely is there a rule of thumb that guarantees the correctness of his decision. He must assume responsibility for his own destiny; he will stand before God and account for his decisions. Usually the advice of past tradition or of the living Church may be assumed to offer the wise, correct course of action—but not always. Noncooperation with Hitler, for example, required a moral choice by individuals in which they received very little moral encouragement from tradition or the living Church.

In the question of marital sexuality the Church is presently embarrassed by the poverty of her teaching. In arguing for a more adequate, fuller, applicable criterion of morality in marital love, the individual Catholic must work out his atttude toward sexuality largely on his own. The negative discipline is plain enough: do not use contraceptives. Its adequacy is doubtful; the reasons for it are weak; more positive guidance is only beginning to be formulated. The present effort may not, finally, be acceptable, but it is at least an effort to open up a positive perspective on the moral possibilities latent in the sexual act.

I am aware that the standard Catholic objection to my argument will be that I am dividing the sexual act between its biological and psychological imperatives. I will be told that these imperatives form a unity—indeed, a *dynamic* unity. One cannot do anything to interfere with the biological mechanism of the act in order to exercise only the psychological upper reaches of the act. I am also well aware that many persons who use contraceptives or anovulants do so selfishly; that they, no more than others and even perhaps less so (though no one can prove such assertions), fail to achieve a truthful mutual love. My answer to the second objection would be that neither the use of contraceptives nor the nonuse of contraceptives guarantees the authenticity of the love between the couple. Mutual love is very difficult; it is so much easier just to "get used" to each other and find a mode of tolerable coexistence.

My answer to the first objection would be that the fundamental issue is how to define the marriage act. It seems that the marriage act has never been adequately defined—the definitions in scholastic theology and in canon law are historically conditioned and *ad hoc*. In the experience of married couples mutual love and parenthood are two separate moral intentions. Moreover, sexuality and fertility seem to be two separate orders. Again, the "act" of marital love is not easily compressed within the limits described by the definition that is useful for the purpose of canonical jurisprudence.[12] Its origins and its intentional duration extend throughout the day. The act of love is, in my judgment, a symbolic act. It receives its nature from what it symbolizes, and its morality is governed by the conformity of its performance to its intention: the outward expression of an inner, permanent bond. The correct moral analogy is with speech and its criterion of truthfulness.

To be sure, parenthood and the biological imperative are a part of the symbolism of the marriage act. But the moral responsibilities of parenthood are not quantitative but qualitative. The imperative is not to produce as many children as possible but to bring forth children and to *educate* them. This imperative is essential to marriage, but, granted the conditions of modern medicine, it is now much more easily fulfilled than formerly in its first part and, granted the conditions of modern society, much more demanding than formerly in its second part. Meanwhile, the exercise of marital sexuality continues to be a good for its own sake. It does not seem that we should encourage a race of Catholic people more virginal than ever before, but rather a race of Catholic people who draw more moral benefit from the use of sexuality than ever before. The ideal of marriage is not continence but wise, healthy exercise of sexuality.

But what are the criteria of "wise, healthy" sexuality? They are not merely external. I make no pretense of formulating them conclusively, but I offer the following reflections as a first step in their elucidation.

In their reaction against the inadequate, merely biological criterion, many Catholic theorists are beginning to appeal to "relational" criteria, and especially to the "I-thou" relation and a wordless, almost mystical "encounter." This appeal seems too grandiose and unreal. The first thing to be said about a wise understanding of sexuality, it seems, is that sexual acts are quite ordinary: misfiring often, fully satisfying physically and emotionally only sometimes, and full of insight or revelation only occasionally. There are two extremes to be avoided here. It seems unrealistic to pursue ecstasy and equally unrealistic to surrender to routine or boredom. It would surely be a misfortune if one's lovemaking were to be as regular and undistinguished as the rhythm of one's eating and sleeping; a bodily function, not much more, not much less. The rhythm of lovemaking is matter-of-fact: perhaps nightly, perhaps three times a week, perhaps—for many ordinary reasons not connected with purposive abstinence or fear of pregnancy— even less often. For single persons, sexuality may be romantic, exciting, mysterious, passionate; for the long-married, it is quite ordinary.

Yet there is a danger in deromanticizing sexuality. Sexuality is not only a reflexive function like eating and sleeping; it is an act of consciousness and communication, like speaking. When a couple ceases to "listen" to each other, their acts of love are in danger of becoming lies. Each will retreat into his or her private world, and the act of interpenetration—with or without contraceptives—will not be truthful. Sexual love is in the order of consciousness, not in the order of reflex, so we must stir our affections and our imaginations in approaching it.

The man's "substance" is not in his seed, nor is there a mystical "openness" or "total self-giving" available to those who do not use contraceptives as against those who do. The only significance I can detect in the nonuse of contraceptives is that the couple wishes also to have children as a fruit of this particular union, or at least to take the risk of having children. Contraceptives deprive the act of spontaneity, but almost any human act—wearing galoshes against the rain—involves care and forethought. In the total good of marriage anovulants or contraceptives seem at times to be a lesser of two evils. Would that life were purely spontaneous and simpler; but it isn't.

Our expectations have a habit of fulfilling themselves. If our theories expect our sexual acts in marriage to be ritualistic, routine, or even boring, no doubt they will soon become so. Could there be a clearer sign that the couple has ceased to communicate? Could anything more obviously be a misuse of another person (and of oneself) than to continue such a meaningless ritual? Surely this is why some couples soon find themselves moving to separate beds. Contrary to widespread opinion, many marriages do not need moralists to teach them restraint and abstinence; many need help in learning the ways to a more conscious, communicative sexuality.

The second point to make about the morality of sexual love is that in nearly all ancient languages the root meaning for a most important verb in human language, "to know," is taken from the act of marital love. Marital love is a way of knowing, and it is inimitable and inexhaustible if we are alert to its possibilities. Over the years, if we may believe older married persons, marital sexuality changes in its nature and in its demands; it changes many times; and it gets better, some say, as it goes along. This seems to make sense. As in all human things, we should expect to grow in sensitivity, in appreciation, in wisdom.

To be sure, the "insights" and "revelations" that come in sexual life are not often overwhelming, nor perhaps any more frequent than insights or revelations that come with other forms of daily life together. But married persons are not merely roommates. The quality of their lives is changed by their intercourse. For sexuality, as Freud showed and as our experience testifies, is at the root of human personality.

All of our emotions, attitudes, inhibitions, ambitions, fears, drives are affected by our sexuality. Our conscience is inevitably affected by the history of our sexual development. When two persons meet in intercourse, then, they are consciously or unconsciously affecting the core of each other's personalities. In their acts of love the couple's hidden and even repressed feelings toward each other either emerge or are more deeply buried. Resentments can gather and be nourished. Unsuspected selfishness can be exposed. Fear and trust, hatred and love, guilt and freedom, confusion and self-identity, all mingle and, sometimes, war. Marital sexuality is at once lovely and terrible. It is playful and light-hearted but it is also, almost without our noticing, full of responsibility. Moreover, its burden is not made lighter by never speaking of its ambiguities. Yet it is not surprising that for many couples sexuality becomes routine and automatic; its invitation toward conscious growth makes great demands on them. Sexuality is not an escape; it is the beginning of a new and sometimes frightening relationship.

Of course, understood in this way, marital sexuality must be defined in a larger rather than a narrower sense. It is not "going to bed" that constitutes marital sexuality. Where there is no courtesy, tenderness, concern in the countless actions of everyday, there can be little personal communion in the marriage bed. Where there is no friendship during the day, at night there is likely to be only the pleasant—or unpleasant—meeting of two separate bodies (whether contraceptives are in use or not). How many couples do not truly love one another? And how often has a couple's love been injured because early falsehood in their lovemaking destroyed their respect for and communication with one another? How many marriages have a merely legal union? And are not such marriages, whatever canon law might say, profoundly inhuman and immoral?

Communication in marriage is a subtle act. Successful marriages are those that maintain communication at one level or another. In some cases a couple living in the same house are bound by no other communication than that space. Other couples may have difficulty with words, and for them sexual intercourse may be the most important of their intimate ties. But surely that communication is best which is fullest: where conversation, interests, home, children, events, and all the elements of a life together give total truth to a couple's acts of love. Then the sexual symbolism is, of all human symbols, the one most apt for expressing their inner lives. Do not the Scriptures use it as a favorite symbol even for men's union with God?

A second criterion for the moral use of marital sexuality, therefore, may be articulated as follows: the symbol of sexual union must be truthful. It must be accompanied in the whole of daily life by efforts to be communicative. It must be grounded in mutuality, in the openness of each person to the reality of the other person: not as one would like the other to be, but as the other is. There is no rule of thumb complex enough to cover all the varieties of marriage relationships. Each marriage, each couple, is unique; a widow might marry happily twice, and yet each of her marriages would be different. But it is surely true that a failure in mutuality, a failure in the truth of the marriage act, is accompanied by clear signs. Resentment, impatience, short temper, nagging, jealousy—all the petty reactions to each other's shortcomings—reveal the degree to which the couple does not respond to each other. Their openness, honesty, and trust toward each other, and gradual peace with themselves, find a focal point in their attitudes, gestures, sympathies in the marriage bed. The symbol of the marriage act teaches them what is expected of them. The wordless gentleness required of them there gives them an ever-renewable starting place on the road to the mutuality they must learn in the whole range of their lives.

Truthful sexual acts must, therefore, be learned. One of the greatest helps in this matter is that of speech: the ability to speak to each other of their fears, insecurities, envies, resentments, as well as of their gladness. It is difficult for most persons to put these things into words. But the symbolism—and the risks—of the marital act encourage them to be frank and to take risks with words as they do with their unclothed, open bodies. The more things they can speak about (and often each new area of revelation requires an effort, requires trust), the more closely they can come to receiving and being received by each other. Words are often the channels of human unity. Of course, words are poor things at best, and each partner must be sensitive to silences, moods, hesitancies, gestures, too. Uneducated persons are sometimes more skillful at such communication than the sophisticated; but all persons need it.

Here an analogy may be helpful. The life of marital sexuality is in many ways like the life of prayer. Haste, routine, or distractions are in the one as in the other a token that the spirit is elsewhere, not with the other person. Words are sometimes useful; wordlessness is sometimes better. Prayer takes a long time to learn well; so does communication with another person. Prayer cannot be begun solely at the moment of dropping to one's knees, but requires preparation; marital love likewise reaches out in anticipation all through the day. Prayer is not a substitute for good living; marital sexuality is not an escape from mutual regard throughout the day. Prayer enlivens the whole range of one's religious life; marital sexuality refreshes the daily lives of the married couple.

In the daily strains of married life it is unlikely that selfishness, indulgence, or self-delusion in intercourse will go undetected. So closely is marital sexuality related to the rest of daily life that a failure in the former is bound to affect the latter, and vice versa. As we saw, it is for this reason that the nonuse of contraceptives is no criterion of a healthy marital sexuality. But the argument can be made stronger. If the couple has no control over pregnancy, intercourse may create anxieties that make marital love both a torture and a lie; it can create fear in the wife and guilt in the husband. In such cases intercourse is destructive, not moral.

Unless, therefore, one is ready to argue that continence is a universal ideal, of itself and without reference to the natural expressiveness of marital love, one must admit that at times and in the total context of a married life continence can be an evil. For at times either the biological or else the psychological imperative of married love must be violated. In actual experience there simply are some situations in which it is imperative *not* to have children *and yet* to express one's love according to its natural sign. The current dilemma of the Catholic couple is that these two imperatives cannot both be obeyed under the present discipline of the Church. I have tried to give reasons why the biological imperative, once fulfilled, may give way to the psychological imperative. And I have tried to suggest the moral controls by which this psychological imperative rules out indulgence, selfishness, and lust and instructs the couple according to the symbolism of marital sexuality itself. The criteria are two: marital sexuality is neither an escape through ecstasy nor a matter of routine and boredom, but an ordinary conscious act of communication; and marital sexuality is governed by the laws of truthfulness: the couple must be striving for the union their act symbolizes.

These criteria are not physical but psychological. But they are not unlike the criteria for faith or charity. The search for an external, simple physical criterion seems to me to be mistaken. My argument would perhaps be less alarming if I omitted all reference to contraceptives and spoke only of anovulants, or confined myself merely to elucidating the psychological imperative without reference to its supplanting of the biological. But such a strategy would have been dishonest, and done less than justice to the moral realities of marital sexuality. However incomplete these reflections may be, I hope they offer a beginning, and that others will come along to correct them, deepen them, and make them more precise. The Catholic people have need of a positive, creative morality of marital love.

NOTES

1. John C. Ford, S.J., and Gerald Kelly, S.J., *Contemporary Moral Theology,* Vol. II, *Marriage Questions* (Westminster, Maryland: Newman Press), 1963, p. 130.
2. *Summa Theologica,* II-II, q. 153, a.2. St. Augustine, *De Bono Conjug.,* 16.
3. Ford and Kelly, *op. cit.,* pp. 210, 311, *passim.*
4. *Ibid.,* p. 132.
5. There are, in fact, two "totality principles" in marriage. One covers the whole range of goods involved in the marriage of two persons: the preservation of the race; parenthood; the education of children; stable economic, physical, and psychical conditions; love for one another; sexual expression, etc. The other totality principle covers all the goods involved in the acts of sexual expression: biological, physiological, emotional, psychological, spiritual. One totality principle, in short, is more general in its scope than the other. The two are related; the second included in the first.
6. *Ave Maria,* February 29, 1964.
7. *Jubilee,* March, 1964.
8. *Kansas City Catholic Reporter,* March 20, 1964.
9. *Moral Theology,* Vol. II (New York: Joseph F. Wagner, 1929), p. 615.
10. *Jubilee,* March, 1964, p. 4.
11. Louis Dupré, "Toward a Re-examination of the Catholic Position on Birth Control." *Cross Currents* (Winter, 1964), pp. 63-85.
12. It is instructive to note, for example, that the entire structure of Ford and Kelly's view of marriage (*op. cit.*) rests on the concepts of canon law. They have legalized the reality of marriage. The key word in their analysis

is "essence": the essential ends of marriage, the essential character of the secondary end, the essential subordination of the secondary ends, etc. But they say in chapter three (p. 41): "We use 'essence' in the logical sense and mean by the essence of marriage all those things and only those things without which a true marriage cannot exist." They add in a crucial footnote: "This is the sense in which canonists speak of invalidating conditions . . . against the essence of marriage. . . . It is possible to speak consistently and pragmatically of the essence of marriage in this sense because centuries of canonical jurisprudence have established norms for determining the invalidity . . . " In a most important sense, Ford and Kelly have not given us a moral theology of marriage, but an essay in canon law. From a philosophical point of view, the essence of marriage needs to be determined according to a more philosophical, less legal, methodology. The radical debate here is a debate over methodology, not over conclusions.

21

Our Terrorism, Our Brutality

Both liberals and conservatives in our society are honorable men. Both are highly moral. Both are capable of playing maiden aunt. As a general rule one may distinguish liberal morality from conservative morality in the United States according to the following table: liberals abhor violence but are indulgent toward sexual behavior, whereas conservatives don't mind violence but are visibly upset by too much sexuality. Whence the precision of the (liberal) slogan: "MAKE LOVE NOT WAR." *And the fact that murder, fist fights, and military battles are approved (by conservatives) for family television shows, while a frank bedroom scene arouses intense moral indignation.*

Conservatives and liberals in our society do not so much debate or discuss as talk right past one another. They seldom listen, seldom respond directly, to one another.

Perhaps in the churches more than in any other place there is some slight hope of healing the breach between those divided by these two uncommunicating forms of life and thought in the United States. The churches are communities of reconciliation. The symbols of the churches transcend, or are supposed to transcend, less ultimate human attitudes and orientations. At the communion rail if nowhere else, liberal and conservative are one.

But even in the churches, liberals and conservatives seldom attain genuine human interchange. By and large, in Catholic circles at least, liberals

403

*read widely and love to theorize; conservatives seem to read compara-
tively little and seldom articulate their views, except when aroused by a
sudden change in favor of the liberals. Both groups are capable of
thinking in conspiratorial terms.*

*Conversation, Thomas Aquinas remarked, is the chief good of civiliza-
tion. Without civil conversation, the communication of ideas and values
must proceed by way of methods less worthy of men: by slogans, pressure, and violence. Nevertheless, dialogue has not characterized all human
communication in history. Many lessons men seem to learn only through
blood and destruction. Men may possibly be called to be, but they certainly are not, rational animals. Thus history often seems, to repeat
Hegel's phrase, a butcher's bench.*

In 1965 I wrote two short articles on the war in Vietnam for The
National Catholic Reporter. *My aim in writing those articles was to face
both the liberal and the conservative approaches to that war, and to reach
a modulated and open-ended judgment of my own. I gave tentative and
modified approval to the United States effort there, so long as political
aims took precedence over military ones. By late 1966, however, it was
apparent that military technology had grown to such proportions that the
war had changed in character. Consequently, in an article published in the
same weekly on January 13, 1967, I expressed a negative judgment on
the United States intervention and gave the reasons for my change of
mind.*

*It was at first my intention to reprint all three articles here, in order to
present a profile of the way in which, on an important matter, a sharp
change in moral judgment can occur. However, the more stringent demands of presentation in book form suggested an elaboration of the
argument at some places, both in the earlier and in the later judgment.
It seemed wiser, then, to prepare a new article moving upon a larger
theoretical base, while trying still to remain fair to the values cherished
by conservatives and to those cherished by liberals. The result, perhaps,
will please nobody fully. But the attempt to listen and to respond seems
needed now in our divided nation.*

I. *The Abstractions of National Interest*

MORAL judgment in international affairs is a slippery business, but it cannot be abdicated. The moralist who wishes to be a man, like the man who wishes to be moral, cannot escape messy decisions and merely concentrate on clear ones. How can power and ambiguity be embraced and enjoyed? Almost invariably, the exercise of power involves one in evils willed, half-willed, and unwilled. Yet power must be exercised; some measure of nobility must be wrung from ambiguity. It is hard to see how one can become a man without passing through the fires of exercising power and experiencing the partial evils, partial goods, that spring from such exercise.

Force is the rule, not the exception, in human relationships. One-upmanship is a domestic variety of force. Commonly in ordinary life men treat one another as objects rather than as persons; they employ others to serve their needs for recognition, praise, affection, security, domination. Camus remarks that the instinct to make others our slaves seems ineradicably embedded in our lives: we use the very beggars to whom we give alms for our gratification. We play games with one another; other persons are "it." Self-sacrifice is often a cover for subtle self-aggrandizement. In brief, force is the relegation of other men to the kingdom of means; we make them functional to our desires or our necessities. Force is both covert and overt. It almost always masquerades as altruism. The tyrant knows what is good for others better than they know for themselves; he announces himself (even in the chambers of his own conscience) as a benefactor of mankind.

In our society, the white middle-class Christian seldom recognizes the extent to which his existence rests upon the steady employment of violence. He is, by contrast, extraordinarily sensitive to the use of violence by others. The white middle-class Christian is the beneficiary of a "law and order" (maintained by armies, police forces, and even espionage agencies) which shape the world to his own interests. Since life on this planet is organized for his enrichment, comfort, and advancement, he scarcely needs to notice the coincidence between "law and order" and his own advantages. It is, he humbly recognizes, a benediction to have "law and order"—sanctioned by nature and by

God—operating to his own benefit. If other people wish a more just distribution of the world's goods, they have to resort to "violence," and in doing so to oppose both nature and God. Blessed are the white middle-class Christians!

The relations of men in different societies are necessarily based upon abstractions; the general form of such relations is "we" against "them," that is to say, bloc X against bloc Y. Those others over in the other bloc all seem to look alike; they are less fully human than we. They are abstractions, we are persons. Thrown into the scales of morality, our projects are bound to outweigh theirs. For we are seeking human dignity and civilization, but they are pursuing slogans and self-interests whose inadequacy we clearly recognize. Both Camus and Marcel have diagnosed the viciousness of the spirit of abstraction in our time: in judging others, we do not recognize the human variety, human complexity, human aspirations of concrete persons, but only the "aims" of bloc Y. On the other hand, in judging ourselves, we do not recognize that we appear to others as bloc X, but continue to think of ourselves as living, striving, aspiring concrete persons whose dignity must be respected. We see ourselves in the concrete, but others in abstractions.

But to see others as abstractions (under the impulse of passion, self-interest, competition, ignorance or indifference) is to see them as less than human persons. Here lie exposed the roots of all violence; here lies the initial and quintessential act of violence. Here, also, lies the source of international tragedy. For how can we recognize as persons those with whom we have no communion? Those who live far away, whose habits and manners and interests are different from our own, cannot be known to us in the concrete. We easily fall into abstractions in thinking of them, and the familiar experiences of friendship and argument which would shake us free from our abstractions, and reveal to us the variety and humanity of concrete persons, are lacking to us. Besides, the human mind is not infinite in its capacity to assimilate the complex and concrete panorama of human life. It is obliged, through weakness, to take the easy path of classification and abstraction. International affairs, consequently, inevitably begin in the spirit of violence. Hence the axiom: Politics is the science of power.

When men act as groups, they do not often succeed in treating one another as persons linked in concrete communities that share a larger human community. Most often, they perceive one another through abstractions. They voice the aims of their group in the symbols of their own national ideology. They give a benign interpretation to their own symbols, which they understand in the concrete contexts of daily life. "The American way of life" reminds Americans of all the joys, struggles, and familiar moments of their lives; it is redolent with childhood, adolescence, relaxation, love, family, friendship. It represents the concrete, humane, warm tissue of life. But men usually understand the symbols of other national groups abstractly, in their nakedness and inhumanity. In politics, abstractions clash with abstractions. The result is that the concrete, warm tissue of life is interrupted; and many persons lose the concrete life they value in order to die for abstractions, which other persons, also willing to die, do not understand, or fear, or despise.

Nevertheless, the human mind can organize the complex superabundance of concrete living only by means of abstractions. Each nation must define its own "national interest." Priorities must be established. Decisions must be taken and principles of selection exercised. Human tragedy arises because life is impossible without the employment of abstractions, yet the employment of abstractions constantly sets life against life, concrete good against concrete good. International relations, consequently, form a pattern of opposition and competition. They rest upon the principle of abstraction, the principle of violence. The only question is whether this violence will be manifested openly in war, or covertly in pacts, trades, and "peaceful" competition. Warfare breaks out when bloc X insists upon its own abstractions in their purity, against the claims of bloc Y. The concrete texture of human life and the full circle of aspirations of concrete persons are then sacrificed for "higher" values abstracted from the rest.

Violence, then, is the inevitable base of international life, and wars we seem to have always with us. For each nation must, inescapably, formulate its national interest. Yet the shared experience of international living is not yet so strong that nations readily understand and accept the national interest of other nations. Each takes its own concrete life into account, and is ignorant of or indifferent to the concrete experience of other nations.

Moreover, it is always possible for a nation to be mistaken in the formulation of its own national interest. We live increasingly in a world in which the concrete life of every people is interwined with that of others. The world's resources are not distributed equally, and in some respects every nation increasingly depends to at least some extent upon commerce with other nations. Furthermore, ideas and ideals are also shared. There has not yet been formulated an "international interest," sufficiently nuanced to take account of all the complex needs and aspirations of all peoples. But there are already shared elements of concrete living, shared necessities, shared aspirations. In the absence of international agreement upon how to order concrete living to the benefit of all concrete human persons, various schemes of national interest are in conflict and competition. We may be groping toward an international order, based on a community of international experience. But at present the peoples of the world do not share a sufficiently large fund of human experience for them to understand one another's symbols concerning how the world should be organized. The many nations still remain abstractions to one another. Overt violence and open warfare seem our lot for some time to come.

It is not premature, perhaps, to begin imagining a world order respectful of the varieties of the concrete experience and the concrete necessities of all the world's peoples. But it is certainly premature to expect a world order whose symbols can win the understanding and the acceptance of all the world's peoples. The negative symbol of nuclear destruction induces a community of fear; but fear does not provide a large enough base for a concrete community of life. It tempers the insistence upon national abstractions. It does not provide a positive sharing of concrete experience or induce mutual recognition between concrete living persons.

We must, then, continue working at the realistic formulation of national interests, in such a way as to be increasingly respectful of the national interests of others. No one nation shares this planet in isolation. There is sufficient technological power to destroy life upon this planet. Just as fear of God was inferior to love of God but perhaps more common, so also fear of other men is inferior to love of other men; yet we must begin with what we have and work toward better things. We in the United States must begin with as adequate a formulation as we can of the national interest of the United States in the real world of our time.

There is, unfortunately, no one who can tell a nation, cleanly and simply, what its national interest is. There is no set of absolutes written down somewhere which, by a kind of calculus, provides a clear and certain imperative. Out of the complexities of self-knowledge and a realistic appraisal of the world, a nation must decide that question for itself, through whatever institutional or voluntary agencies its national consciousness is articulated. In the United States these agencies are many and diverse: the press, the churches, business organizations, labor unions, universities, private associations, Congress, the courts, the President. More often than not, everyone has a different idea about what the national interest is. Who in fact knows what the *real* national interest is? There is no escape from uncertainty and the possibility of error. At a given moment, a national course of action (or inaction) passes the point of no return. The national interest in that particular matter, by whatever means, has thus been defined. Such a formulation may be well-conceived or tragically mistaken.

Thus any given definition of the national interest is subject to criticism after it has been made, just as its making (in our society at least) is subject to many rival pressures. No definition of the national interest is moral just because it has been made. Some such definitions are narrow, some stupid, some unjust, some positively cruel and evil, some treacherous, some avaricious. All, in other words, are abstractions. Some of these abstractions more adequately than others, and some less adequately, reflect the concrete situation of human persons in the given nation and in other nations.

Nevertheless, the basic question before a nation is to define as flexibly as it can, and as precisely as necessary, its national interest in the matters upon which national decisions must be made. Advocates of rival definitions are correct in pointing out the evils in other definitions than their own. Even after a definition has been made, opponents convinced that it is an evil definition are correct in dissenting from it. For every definition of the national interest is historically conditioned, has received only a limited amount of scrutiny and discussion, was made in ignorance of many facts and most consequences. A nation does well constantly to review its policies and to revise its judgments. Such revisions must, of course, take account of the long-range commitments and effects of past policies, the network of links with other nations' policies, and the problems of national credibility raised by casual or too-frequent changes. Revision must in any case be constant and evolutionary; in some situations, however, only boldness and sharp departures from the past suffice.

Moreover, the light in which such review and revision take place is not the light of "moral principles" stated in a list of propositions like the ten commandments (which have been used historically to justify almost everything, from slavery and the torture of prisoners to legalized prostitution and burning at the stake). The light in which such review and revision take place is, immediately, the light which concrete, informed, concerned citizens can throw upon them. Living persons, not dead codes, are the immediate source both of a moral judgment and of political judgment. On the other hand, the ultimate source of moral and political judgment is the faith, vision, and hope by which a people are guided. What kind of society are they trying to build? What kind of world are they trying to realize in history? A people's eschatology is the source of its moral and political judgment.

In the summer of 1965, Father Georges Tavard argued that a foreign government like ours, involved in a revolution like that in Vietnam, should be "guided first by respect for the collective personality of the country where the revolution takes place," and only secondly by considerations of national self-interest. Fr. Tavard is a careful theologian, and he was courageous to open this issue to discussion. However, it seems that he errs in his statement of priorities for the morality of political decision-making. The first consideration for a national politician is his country's self-interest. As Reinhold Niebuhr has made plain, the morality of national action is not the same as the morality of individual action. Individuals more readily encounter one another as human persons (though even that moral achievement is not statistically as frequent as it might be). But nations inevitably confront one another as abstractions. How, when I do not love my barber whom I do see, G. K. Chesterton once asked, can I love the Vietnamese whom I do not see? The

United States is in Vietnam because of a prevailing conception of the self-interest of the United States. Many critics argue that it is *not* in the self-interest of the United States to be in Vietnam. But here in any case is where the only argument of primary consequence is centered.

The phrase "national self-interest" is to be broadly rather than narrowly conceived. It is not true that "anything goes." But it is true that the best resources of a nation's mind and heart must be drawn upon in deciding what that nation ought to do in its own best interests. In our time, the interests of a nation are international in scope, and the fate of the poor involves the fate of the rich. A certain degree of what used to seem like altruism is required by the cold facts of realistic politics. But we should not be misled by political arguments which start from altruism or charity. It is beyond the moral power of national governments to practice charity. Their moral guide is much more modest: their own national self-interest broadly conceived.

In this light, the question in Vietnam is, What does the United States want in Vietnam? What are we trying to do? That is the basic and realistic question. Moreover, posing the question in this way ensures that one's answer begin with concrete reality and conclude in concrete reality. To be concerned primarily about the national interest of the United States is to refrain from presupposing that our problem is to act as God, or for the interest of the entire world. We don't know what God wants us to do in Vietnam, nor what the rest of the world is interested in there. We have no right to speak for God or for the rest of the world.

What is the national interest of the United States in Vietnam? The answer depends upon the realism and the vision, the modesty and the faith, the restraint and the courage, the experience and the insight, of our people and our institutions. Our definition of our national interest can be shortsighted or longsighted, intelligent or stupid, just or unjust, restrained or reckless, moral or immoral. As long as there are conscious men, alert to the demands of historical action, there will be men to pass moral judgment upon us and our definition. And the hidden God judges us also.

No matter what we decide, we are sure to make mistakes. We are certain to involve ourselves in a great deal of bloodshed and terror. We already have murdered civilians, scorched living children with napalm, caught pregnant women in machine gun fire, sent CIA and other agents behind enemy lines who must murder, lie, bribe, steal.

II. *Three Levels of Interpretation*

In the summer of 1965, I wrote in modified, reluctant support of the United States intervention in Vietnam. Many times since then, particularly on the occasion of the bombing of the oil fields in Hanoi and Haiphong in the spring of 1966, I regretted that public support and had almost been moved to retract it. Most of my friends abhor the war and oppose it vociferously, and I was almost converted by their arguments. Like them, I recognized the slender grounds on which the United States is operating—not to mention the violated accords of 1954. Like them, I recognized the senselessness of bombing which destroys a country in the guise of liberating it. Like them, I disliked the ideological anti-communism voiced by Dean Rusk and President Johnson, and the ugly war fever of patriots on every street of the land. Nevertheless, the arguments which I heard for and against the war seemed in the main too partisan, too one-sided, too self-certain. World order seems impossible without the use of force and the shedding of blood; yet the use of force and the shedding of blood are evil. If one expects to encounter unavoidable evils in human affairs, one feels sadness, not indignation, at the event.

Regarding Vietnam, perhaps others feel as I do: that one has never seen a moral issue so complicated, or encountered a statement about it that is not open to serious objection from other points of view. There are many levels of fact and interpretation which one must bring to a discussion of that war; at every level, there are partings of the ways, so that some agree up to one point, and others up to another.

The first level of fact and interpretation concerns the meaning of the Cold War. To some Americans, the following sentiment is obvious: "We are engaged in a struggle to the death with communism, and the sooner we recognize that the better." To others, among whom I count myself, the main struggle of our generation is against poverty, disease, and political, social, and economic underdevelopment. From this perspective, communism represents one family of responses by which heretofore underdeveloped nations can solve their grievous problems of reorganization. Both communist nations and nations like our own are battling the same enemy, but with different and rival strategies. The present internal structure of many nations of the world militates against the well-being of the peoples of those nations; consequently, ours is an age of many national revolutions. Revolutions must happen. The only question is, which strategies will these revolutions follow? The issue is further complicated because the United States, in the main, seems to prefer to work with existing governments, even if these are dictatorships or oligarchies of the wealthy, insensitive to the needs of their own people. The United States sometimes appears to favor the status quo at almost any cost, or in fact (as in Guatemala and in South Vietnam after 1954) to intervene on the side of whatever forces appear to be most strongly anti-communist. In other words, the policies of the United States appear to be governed more by the anti-communism of contending parties than by their readiness to promote the efforts needed to overcome poverty, starvation, ignorance, and long-standing political abuses.

Both liberal and conservative interpretations of the role of the United States in world affairs take for granted an important point, which needs to be made explicit. The United States is the greatest power among all the nations of the world and thus, willy-nilly, has been cast in the role of arbiter of a great many world affairs. Power abhors a vacuum; having power, one cannot avoid responsibility and complicity in evil for as far as that power extends. The power of the United States is international, and wherever the United States acts or decides not to act, world affairs are correspondingly affected. But if the power of our nation is international, the proper conclusion is not that the United States is either omnipotent or omniscient. The United States cannot become involved in every trouble in every nation on the earth; and there are a great many issues in world affairs which are impervious to the power of the United States and not in the least subject to our will. Selectivity, therefore, is required.

Something further, however, must be said about "the communist menace." Some years ago in *An End to Innocence* Leslie Fiedler suggested that liberals had to come to terms with their earlier failure to understand the forces which were to lead, after World War II, to the Cold War. They had been "innocent," and now it is time for innocence to come to an end. American society has become so polarized, however, that it is difficult to take up an intermediate position between the twin theses: "communism is our number one enemy," and "There is no such thing as 'communism' pure and simple, and in any case the many varieties of communism are not our major enemy." On the one hand, the enemy is clearly defined; on the other, anti-communism seems so simple-minded that one finds oneself always apologizing for the communists, sympathizing with their dilemmas, trying to see the world from their point of view. Nevertheless, the key to the difference between these two assertions does not lie in the assertion (a) that the communists are *not* our major enemy. The key to the difference lies in the assertion (b) that there are many different kinds of communism and that, therefore, other factors besides the influence of Marx and Engels and state control of political and economic life must be considered.

In brief, one may assert that nationalism is a more potent force in contemporary life than communist ideology. North Vietnam nourishes historical animosities against the Chinese, which outweigh the communism they are said to have in common. Russian communism is seriously different from Chinese communism. The communism of Yugoslavia differs from that of Poland. Albanian communists have a different view of the modern situation than do the communists of Italy. In order to act realistically in the contemporary world, one does well to attend to national character and history and to understand the meaning of the word "communist" differently as applied to various peoples.

Would one "communist" nation always support another "communist" nation in case of a struggle with other nations? Russia helps North Vietnam, but tries to end the war and also to keep China out of it. Many communists in East Europe wish closer ties with the United States, and hence hope the war ends speedily; others send at least token shipments of aid to their "comrades in world revolution." Certainly one must say that the *rhetoric* of communist nations obliges them to act, more or less, as a "united front." But one can detect also many concrete pressures which in fact lead them to act very little like nations of one single "orbit." The differences from nation to nation are important and, if they are accurately diagnosed, can also be exploited by those anxious for a less ideological, more concretely diverse and free world. The persistent use of one same word, "communist," to describe many varieties of nation oversimplifies the reality and flatters communist rhetoric by accepting it at face value.

But even if there is agreement at this level of discourse, there may not be at the next. Besides contrasting views of the Cold War in general, there are also contrasting views of the realities of Southeast Asia. Perhaps everyone can admit that the most explosive region for the next decade or so may well be Southeast Asia. The problems inherent in enormous and expanding populations and the problems inherent in rapid technological development represent sufficient sources of disorder. But there are also the racial and cultural scars of centuries of white colonialism; and there are ancient hatreds between the races of the East as well. Nevertheless, the overwhelming fact of Southeast Asia is the dynamism of Red China. If one interprets international affairs in terms of power, it seems obvious that the new power in China is the central factor not only in Southeast Asia but in virtually the whole Eastern hemisphere.

Moreover, the course of Chinese development is unpredictable. The severe internal dissensions (or at least a political style difficult for us to understand) which seem to grip a people almost wholly cut off from a real sense of the rest of the world—the paroxysms of the Red Guard in the fall of 1966 and the civil war of early 1967 are instances—almost guarantee that unrest in the Eastern hemisphere will have calculated support. As long as Red China is embroiled in vast internal problems, her leaders will be led to seek external enemies in order to enflame the patriotism and maintain the unity of her people. Minoru Omori, foreign editor of a major newspaper in Japan, wrote in *The New Republic* (January 28, 1967):

A showdown between Mao Tse-tung and Liu Shao-chi is therefore looming. This confrontation will touch off a series of bloody fights in major cities between Red Guards and workers. It is also possible that Mao's ally, Lin Piao, will seek to exacerbate tensions outside the country, so that he can show off his military power to the 700 million Chinese and demonstrate the unity of the whole country in face of external dangers.

While the concentration of Russian troops along the border between the Soviet Union and Manchuria is encouraging to Liu Shao-chi and his group in Peking, the escalation in Vietnam is equally encouraging to the Mao-Lin group, which welcomes trouble outside.

The military power of China may not yet, by Western standards, be impressive but the national interest defined by her leaders and her people is the first and basic fact of political life in Asia.

On the other hand, China comported herself in regard to the war in Vietnam with marked rationality and clarity. The limits she sets to U.S. intervention have been clearly stated: no invasion of North Vietnam and no attack upon China. (By contrast, the limits of escalation by the United States have never been clarified; major spokesmen —not in the administration—desire to bomb Hanoi and other cities of North Vietnam, and a few errant voices in the military have been heard to ask for war on China now, before her strength increases). Nevertheless, the limited sources of news about events within China allow the possibility of serious miscalculations about Chinese realities and Chinese intentions. For example, American hawks who are afraid of Chinese warlike aims argue with each fresh escalation of the war that the Chinese will not enter it; whereas the doves, who insist that the Chinese are basically peaceful, fear an imminent Sino-American war.

Thirdly, however, there is the further level of fact and interpretation which concerns the meaning of the struggle within Vietnam itself; and here, too, there is disagreement. It is clear, for example, that the Chinese early pointed to South Vietnam as one in a series of "wars of liberation" which they hoped to promote in various regions of the world; and they have also pointed at Cambodia, Thailand, and other nearby lands. On the other hand, the Chinese have everything to gain by talking tough, and in fact have committed themselves only in a cautious, guarded, and limited way. The deeper the United States sinks into the quagmire in Vietnam, the more freedom of action China has elsewhere and, above all, the greater spirit of self-sacrifice she achieves at home. However, the building of huge United States military bases in South Vietnam and Thailand cannot but threaten her safety. China can afford to act peacefully regarding Hong Kong and Macao (on whom China depends for foreign exchange), more peacefully even than the United States appears to act regarding Cuba and the Dominican Republic; while adventures in Tibet and on the borders of India, not to mention Korea, illustrate her willingness to act in her own interest.

Granted that China has restless energy to spare, it seemed to me in 1965 that the United States had no choice but to meet the internal crisis in South Vietnam with a firm show of force. A rebel victory in South Vietnam would only, it seemed to me, make China more confident than ever that she had only to talk tough—not even to become seriously involved—in order later to precipitate revolutions according to communist inspiration throughout Asia. I did not then argue, and I do not now believe, that the Chinese are "plotting" or "organizing" the overthrow of other nations or committing their own overt power in this direction. But I have a firm conviction that the main source of power in Southeast Asia is China, and that it is China whom men of international affairs must keep at the center of their calculations in that area. So great is that power, and so symbolic has it become, that China does not *have* to commit her own military or other resources openly; she merely has to make her will known in order to have others in Asia take note. With minimal actual exertion, she can achieve maximal effectiveness.

In one sense, then, the display of American seriousness and American military power in Asia has counterbalanced Chinese power and negated some of the possibilities of Chinese symbol and Chinese bluster. Events in Indonesia and elsewhere seem to show that China cannot now count upon easy or automatic influence upon the destiny of other Asian nations. Social, economic, technical, and political revolutions in other Asian countries are still necessary, but it is not now inevitable that these revolutions will take a communist direction; the range of possibilities is now wider. Much depends in this respect upon how Americans now promote the necessary revolutions. If they try to enforce the status quo, or stand with the traditional privileged classes over against the people, affairs may become only more bitter and, in the end, more bloody than anything yet seen. The men of the East seem to have awakened to new historical possibilities; Ho Chi Minh himself is said to have early taken George Washington and the American Revolution as a key ideal of his life. It is unlikely that such men will settle for less than the revolutions we in the West have experienced, even if in their eyes America seems now to have turned against the principle of revolution enunciated in her own Declaration of Independence.

At this point it is necessary to look more closely at the civil war in South Vietnam. The two Vietnams, South and North, are halves of one same nation artificially divided. Some members of the ruling Ky cabinet in the South, for example, are North Vietnamese. Cancellation of the elections following the Geneva accords of 1954 seems to indicate beyond a doubt that the United States intervened illegitimately in support of the Diem government. Consequently, the rebellion of many South Vietnamese against the Saigon government has motives quite separate from allegiance to communism or to the promotion of rebellion from the North. No one can doubt that communist inspiration is important to many in the guerilla army, and that the North Vietnamese, especially since the American buildup in 1965, are heavily supporting their fellow Vietnamese in the South. But the fact remains that there also exist other serious reasons for a civil war. The revolution which we are opposing is in many respects a just revolution. It is not fanciful to imagine that many Americans who share the ideals of their own revolution of 1776 find those principles enunciated much more adequately by some elements of the Vietnamese rebels than by the Saigon government. "I should like to be able," Albert Camus once said, "to love justice and still love my country." I find myself wondering whether, were I a Vietnamese but not a communist, I would wish to be supporting the Viet Cong rather than the Saigon government, in the name of the people of the land.

On the other hand, the civil war in Vietnam is not romantic. Guerilla warfare involves combatants of both sides in a new morality, a grisly and serious morality. The concept of such warfare was brought to technical sophistication by the Viet Minh in the war against the French (and in the minds of many the war against the Saigon government and the United States is only a continuation of that earlier war, necessiated by the betrayal of the elections of 1956). The concept of "total war" means that every person, every object, every event is to be made a means of political and military victory. Nothing is sacred. Nothing is neutral.

Where South Vietnamese village chiefs, teachers, or tax collectors are corrupt, the rebels single them out publicly, torture, and murder them as a way of showing the citizenry that their revolution believes in social justice. Where the village officials are just and respected, the rebels single them out for brutal assassination as a way of showing that the government cannot protect even its loyal officials. The human body, the human personality, are instruments of propaganda.

Such a war seems to be a great step backward for civilization. Civilized and sensitive people cannot take easily to the realities of "total war." They do not easily accept the fact that human persons can be so systematically used for merely partisan purposes. The "national interest" of the Viet Minh and their successors, the present rebels in South Vietnam, may require total war. A nation defines itself as totalitarian by such a national interest.

But how are other nations, involved with a foe that fights according to the rules of total war, to define their own "national interest" and so their own moral identity? Indignation does not suffice. A nation engaged against its will in total war must fight back, and fight back effectively. European Christians who fought for the underground of Belgium, Holland, France or Italy in World War II found themselves committing acts of terror, murder in cold blood, and violence which unavoidably took the lives of innocent persons. Before the war, they could not have justified what they did. During the war, they knew they had to do such things, with or without textbook rules. No doubt the Viet Cong see the Saigon government as a tyranny to be opposed as Hitler had to be opposed; no doubt the common reaction to atrocity is atrocity and the South Vietnamese and the Americans now obey rules they might not have approved before.

The depths of moral decision are very deep, and those who have moral rules upon their lips too easily are best regarded with suspicion: perhaps they understand what they are saying, and perhaps they do not. From the beginning it was apparent that United States intervention would involve the United States in many kinds of guilt. As President Johnson said in his State of the Union message in 1967, sometimes one must do evil in order to avert a greater evil. It is only honest, however, to catalog some of the evils in which the American people have become involved. Even in 1965, reporters listed such matters as the torturing of prisoners, practiced with much pleasure by the government troops; the beheadings; the dragging of prisoners behind armored cars until they are dead; the bombing and strafing of villages to kill a few "suspected" Viet Cong; the use of napalm on civilians; the mass resettlement of millions of people, with their hunger and disease; the use of artillery and aerial power which the rebels neither have nor need, and which kills much more indiscriminately than the rifle. Heavy armaments and technology are our substitutes for lack of rifle power and lack of help from the people.

Moreover, we are also guilty for the terror with which our government and the Saigon government are beginning to meet terror. In 1964, 50,000 emblems with a staring eye were printed on presses of U.S. agencies for use by squads of secret assassins who murdered rebel civilian leaders in their beds and posted emblems on their bodies and on the doors of victims next on the list. Terror is effective and common in this brutal war. What should not be forgotten is that the blood is upon our hands, too.

Many observers on the spot have said since at least 1964 that the main issue in any guerilla war is to win the political confidence of the people. For the people are the sea in which the guerillas must swim; if the people receive the guerillas—and assist them with enthusiasm and dedication in digging tunnels, storing food supplies, gathering information—the guerillas are virtually invincible. Only when the people refuse to help does the guerilla cause become hopeless. So far in Vietnam, the guerillas appear to have more people in their support, whether from fear or from dedication, than do the Saigon forces, and the war has been protracted accordingly. Thousands of hamlets in South Vietnam are secret fortifications for the rebels; vast networks of underground tunnels and hollow mud embankments have been dug with infinite labors by young and old alike—and by no means all of this work has been forced labor, for the countless villagers who know about it seldom reveal it to government forces. Moreover, the guerilla army grows steadily, and the men fight with much more ardor and dedication than the government forces marshal. The rebels frequently give their lives in human wave assaults; nearly every reporter on the scene finds it hard to disguise his disgust for the frequent cowardice of the government forces.

The best estimates publicly available in mid-1965 indicated that

more than eighty-five per cent of the rebel army was South Vietnamese. Until 1965, the larger part of all arms and equipment came
by capturing government outposts or ambushing government convoys
—which at that time usually traveled without scouts (who would
have had to risk venturing away from the main force.) Moreover,
the Saigon government has continued to conduct itself poorly from
almost every point of view, notwithstanding individual acts of hero-
ism and the sheer general endurance of so long a war. In 1965, the
government army was on the brink of total collapse. Press reports
do not encourage the belief that it has yet become an effective national force. Even when United States troops relieved the pressure
first in the central, and then in the northern, provinces of South
Vietnam, the government army made little significant progress in its
own restricted area, the Mekong Delta to the south. It was asked to
take over the task of securing inland villages and winning the support
of its countrymen; press reports suggest that it is failing at this
task, too.

The issue in South Vietnam, as the rebels have steadfastly seen,
is primarily a political issue. The task is to give security to, and
establish honest communication with, the Vietnamese people. The
military dilemma of the United States forces has been that man for
man, rifle for rifle, American troops are not numerous enough to
overcome the rebel forces or to deprive them of the support of the
people. Consequently, the Americans have made up for lack of
numbers with immense fire power. But the use of napalm, B-52 strato-
fortresses, and all the devices of mass destruction shown regularly on
television, is so out of proportion with the political problem to be
solved that it appears to be self-defeating. In Vietnam, there are no
front lines and few purely military targets. Consequently, not even
Viet Cong terror seems to be able to do more harm to the countryside or to kill more persons indiscriminately, than the employment
of our advanced technology. The rebel forces employ terror; but
we employ mechanized terror of our own.

With each passing month, the proportion of means to ends seems
more extravagantly violated. From an effort to sober possible Chinese
ambitions in Asia by a firm display of force on behalf of an internally
torn ally, and from an effort to keep political aims paramount, the
war seems to have passed into the hands of military professionals,

whose task is to search and destroy. Conceived at first as a means of providing the South Vietnamese army and officials with a breather, an umbrella of protection for the political task of reorganizing their national life, the intervention of the United States forces has become increasingly military in its aims, methods, and emphases. To be sure, token work is being done toward village "pacification." But foreign troops cannot win popular support for a national government; only the Vietnamese can do that.

But in early 1967 it seems increasingly plain that the Saigon government and the Saigon army do not particularly wish to give security to the people of their nation or to open up communication with them. Press reports convey rather the indolence and arrogance of the tired South Vietnamese soldier. By all reports, the South Vietnamese army, officials, and young people are content to let the United States troops fight the war and reform the political structure of the countryside. The United States cannot do what the South Vietnamese will not do for themselves. If the South Vietnamese are now too weary to retain responsibility for their own destiny, perhaps the United States had best let the civil war take its course, ensure the safety of its friends, and withdraw.

In short, in early 1967 it seems that the United States has done more than enough to honor whatever commitment it had to loyal friends in South Vietnam. It has shown courage and military strength. No one can doubt the firmness of the U.S. response. On the other hand, no one expects the United States to establish a colony or puppet state. The social and political structure of South Vietnam is apparently in a state of collapse. No foreign power can impose a stable structure from without, except by turning the southern half of the nation into a colony.

Many will no doubt disagree with some facts and interpretations presented at this third level of discussion. But I have noticed that disagreements at this third level depend a great deal upon prior decisions at the first or second levels. If one is convinced that "communism under whatever guise" is the number one enemy in the world today, and in Vietnam in particular, then one will be inclined to read all the evidence in such a way that it always comes to one conclusion: a United States victory at any cost. If one is convinced that the major enemy of the United States in the world today is not the many varieties of communism but the urgency of the problems of hunger, ignorance, ancient injustice, and the need for rapid political development, then the war in Vietnam is only increasing these problems and not contributing to their solution. Depending on one's picture of the world—depending, then, on one's conception of the national interest of the United States—one is for or against the war in Vietnam, with whatever qualifications and reservations.

But whatever one's judgment on the war, honesty compels one to face the terror and the brutality in which it has involved the American people. We are not innocent. The war in Vietnam is a nasty, brutish war. It is now our war. We should be very clear about what we are doing, and be able to stomach what our men are doing in our name. War is never pleasant. But twenty years from now we do not want to be like those German citizens who said they never realized what their government was doing. No one of us likes this war, and we all wish it to be over as soon as possible. For, clearly, moral choices like this one do not allow us to pretend that we are innocent. Even if one believes that we are acting morally, one must agree that we are by no means pure.

III. *The Plague Is in Us, Too*

The morality of the war in Vietnam, however, cannot be judged only by what the war is doing to Vietnam. One must also study its effect upon the United States. The people of the United States, once aroused, demand the blood of enemies. We are impatient of the efforts required to seek organic political solutions. We would rather kill the enemy wholesale, to "teach him a lesson," in the hopes of ending a war speedily, than mount the large-scale effort that would be required to do the job less crudely. Americans seem to think the blood of Americans is more precious, more pure, than the blood of foreigners. Without hesitation, many would bomb cities and harbors, heedless of the cost in the life of other peoples, if the lives of a comparatively few Americans could be saved. Thus we are faced with the expenditure of vast and historically unequaled fire power— from strategic bombers, ships off shore, artillery, fighter planes, and nightmarish devices invented by military technology—for the killing of a few hundred of the enemy each week. Huge tracts of jungle are bombed in patterns; napalm is dropped prodigally.

To be honest with ourselves, Americans ought to be willing to send sufficient manpower to lower the threshold of destruction. Americans wish to defend the stability of Southeast Asia without disturbing our own stability. We are buying domestic comfort at the expense of lives and property in South Vietnam. We are using heavy fire power in lieu of personnel. We want to buy victory as cheaply as possible, and it is this unwillingness to face the immense cost of the task we have undertaken that constitutes our lack of realism and our immorality.

The main premise on which the war seemed supportable in 1965 was that it was to be a limited war, waged protectively for political rather than military purposes. The chances of success were slight, since the political tissue of Vietnam had virtually disintegrated. Perhaps the United States should never have become so deeply committed to South Vietnam in the first place. But almost certainly the then imminent Viet Cong victory in South Vietnam would not have brought peace to Southeast Asia, but on the contrary heightened pressures for "wars of liberation" throughout the region. By a series of small steps, the United States had become increasingly committed to the defense of South Vietnam; each rise in the threshold of assistance made the next rise more probable. The magnitude of the task was consistently underestimated. The character of the United States intervention has changed drastically, step by step, until it has become the greatest military involvement since World War II and the fourth largest in our entire history.

The effect of the changed character of the war upon the quality of life in the United States has been tragic in almost every respect. Since the fall of 1965, we have seen a growing fever in this nation; we have heard public figures urging the mass bombing of cities in North Vietnam and even in China. We have seen important moral issues in the United States—the elimination of civic injustice, poverty, and urban degradation—increasingly neglected. With civil strife of huge proportions pressing upon us at home, it seems invidious to pretend to solve someone else's civil war abroad. Charity, in such cases, begins at home; there is a huge beam in our own eye.

The increased concentration of American troops in South Vietnam

—now approaching 400,000 men—has raised the expense of the war beyond what this nation is spending to eliminate poverty, disease, and hunger in the world. By early 1967 our command had lost the astonishing number 1750 airplanes. Our main enemy in the twentieth century is not some alien ideology; it is world poverty. Here again there is an immoral disproportion in our present set of values. According to our actual deeds and expenses, will we be known to history as killers or as creators?

Moreover, the war has heightened the paranoid anti-communist sentiment which afflicts many good people in the United States. The underestimation of the difficulties to be encountered by the war, furthermore, has led the Johnson Administration to equivocate, disguise the realities and alternate between warlike threats and peacelike overtures. Honesty and trust have broken down, both at home and abroad. Many citizens no longer trust the government; the government appears to distrust the American people. Soldiers in the field—particularly airmen—complain that official reports from battle scenes do not tell the truth of American losses.

We are told that "victory" (now conceived in military terms) is as far off as ever. We are warned to expect as much as a twenty-year war. That means that boys born in this nation during this year may well die in South Vietnam, eighteen years from now.

What alternatives to the present line of action can be proposed? It seems that in the light of the altered situation, the United States must recognize that the lesser of two evils is negotiation rather than a continued or an enlarged war. Such negotiation must include the rebel forces in South Vietnam as well as their kinsmen and countrymen from North Vietnam. The bombing and the shooting must stop. But friends of the United States and opponents of communism must be guaranteed their safety. If necessary, some United States troops should remain to protect certain areas for a well-defined period. Attempts at a compromise government for South Vietnam must be begun, a government including representatives of the strong and numerous rebel elements.

We are told that the United States government is willing to negotiate, but that the "other side" is not. But there is a serious discrepancy in our notion and theirs about who the "other side" is. We wish to negotiate with Hanoi, but Hanoi points out correctly that native rebel forces in South Vietnam constitute one of the chief interested parties and must be included in the negotiations. It is difficult to see how the United States can be in good faith in announcing its willingness to negotiate while denying a voice to one of the key parties to such negotiations. Nor does the United States government appear to recognize that its own record in dealing with the Vietnamese, both North and South, does not lend its statements the limpid trustworthiness of the innocent. Moreover, United States offers of "unconditional" negotiations reveals a steadily growing number of conditions, humiliating to the opposition and demanding little of us.

Why does the United States find it so difficult to be modest, so hard to accept compromise and ambiguity? One of the great disappointments of this entire episode in our history has been the performance of the intellectual community. When the green wood produces no fruit, what is to be expected from the dry? In the beginning, the peace movement had an enormous advantage. The war was remote, and seldom had the people of the United States been called upon to face a situation so unclear and difficult to dramatize. In mid-1965, the people were confused, divided, and uncertain in their support of the war.

In such a context the academic community, in particular, could have exploited the complexities and ambiguities of the situation so as to make people even more reluctant. But, on the one hand, so many of the professors were political "realists" (I include myself) that they were inclined to accept the war as another in a series of necessary Cold War evils. The early peace demonstrators, on the other hand, perceiving the illegality and ultimate logic of the war more clearly, nevertheless, attempted to simplify, and the necessity of simple slogans led them to shout "Gestapo," "Stormtroopers," and "murderers" at confused young recruits on their way to a war they hardly understood. The predictable outcome occurred: American opinion crystallized in favor of "our boys," the flag, and the Commander-in-chief. Many members of the academic community thus abandoned the tool which is uniquely theirs and which promised most thorough success—exposure through reasonable discourse of the contradictions in government policy and execution—and chose instead the tools of Madison Avenue and political ideologies. They sloganeered, when an awareness of historical complexity was required.

Opponents of the war, however, soon recognized that tactics which were successful in the early stages of the civil rights struggle were counterproductive in the moral struggle for peace. The tactic of mass demonstrations and parades depends upon the clarity and precise definition of a concrete issue. Their role is to polarize public opinion on a specific point. A parade in favor of "Peace in Vietnam" is too abstract and will polarize public opinion—but that is precisely the effect which is not desired in time of war. Yet the inability of the Johnson Administration even to understand the critics of the war, much less to give them a hearing, made parliamentary protest almost impossible. There was nowhere to go but the streets.

The community of educated Americans in particular has an obligation not to oversimplify, and to point out to all who can be made to hear that the issue in Vietnam is complex and confused. In such a situation, the appropriate response is not a military crusade against communism, but negotiation, adjustment and moderation. We must accept the possibilities of the situation as they are; we cannot make them what we would like them to be. We may well have to accept a divided government in South Vietnam, and the possibility that that government will become, one day, a nationalistic communist regime. We might work to prevent that eventuality by putting as much of our resources into peaceful assistance as we now put into war.

IV. *Conclusion*

In attempting this long and difficult analysis, I recognize that the issues are forbiddingly complex, and that in the long perspective of history many judgments which today appear to be moral or immoral will later appear otherwise. It is impossible for human beings to make judgments which are absolute. We must judge as best we can, and act according to our convictions. I am prepared to admit that my judgment may be wrong and that those who favor a more militant and violent stand, may in the long run, prove to be correct. But it seems to me that in a situation as confused and complex as that of Vietnam, the use of great force is immoral precisely because of the lack of clarity. Once destruction and death have been wrought, one cannot bring the dead back to life. The proneness of Americans to pursue absolutes—especially an absolute war against communism—seems to me our gravest moral weakness, and the main ingredient in war fever.

For the characteristic flaw in United States public opinion is its simplicity, its abstractness, its desire for absolutes. The only hope for a change in our policy lies in the growing sophistication of Americans, so that the American people will respect the complexity and confusion of present political realities. Then they will be able to act with modesty, humility, and a sense of their own weaknesses, rather than attempt to play moralistic maiden aunt to all the world. It is our misfortune that even our pacifists play maiden aunt.

2 2

The New Nuns

Moral revolutions are sparked by men and women in action, not by words on the pages of books. One of the most instructive models of the revolution required of religious people in our time is supplied by many among American religious sisters. The symbol of sisters in picket lines disturbs many people. Many people, even very pious people, have life divided up into categories: so much is religious, so much is worldly. They are comforted by the oddness of the sisters' dress, the unusualness of their hours, the seeming unreasonableness of their rule of life. For if that is what religion pure and concentrated is, they may be excused from practicing it. The irrelevance of convent life is a consolation to the worldly. When sisters begin to change their patterns of behavior, such people understandably feel threatened.

Even in the convent, there is much resistance to change. The education of many sisters has been so poor that they respond to stereotypes; they are not discerning. At conferences, some sisters appear to applaud antagonistic positions with equal enthusiasm. On the other hand, an increasing number of sisters are receiving the best education available in America; more sisters than priests have already been educated in secular universities. Shortly, sisters will constitute the best-educated, concentrated group in American Catholicism, if not in American Christianity.

I undertook the following study for the Saturday Evening Post three months after first refusing it. I had already written one short article on *sisters, and did not particularly wish to become a chronicler of convent life. But a series of coincidences occurred in October, 1965, during which four separate persons (two of them sisters) urged me to reconsider. In the middle of the fourth conversation, the telephone rang; it was the editor of the* Post. *I asked him if he had assigned a new writer for the article. He said he was about to query someone the next week. I asked him to wait for an outline from me. Thus began nine months of interviews, hundreds of letters, and several rewritings of the article. At least twenty sisters criticized the manuscript at each major stage. Afterwards, the* Post *received over a hundred letters from sisters and I received about thirty. Almost sixty per cent were enthusiastic, twenty-five per cent opposed, and the others voted approval* juxta modum—*that is, in the language of the Second Vatican Council, with reservations. At least three letters came from girls who had long postponed entering a sisterhood and now wanted the address of a group of "new nuns." These letters pleased me most.*

Because of its extraordinary length, the Post *could not print my original report in full—as it was, the editor printed twice the number of words they had asked me for. I am glad to be able to present the complete study here, as a concrete example of how Christianity is beginning to build anew.*

"THERE they are! There's three of them!" a spindly ten-year-old girl shouted. Three Roman Catholic sisters were just closing the side door of their unusual home in a sprawling Midwestern slum. Two little girls, poorly sweatered against the cold, ran across the pavement. "My mommy wants you," the ten-year-old blurted out, then with her shy friend led the way to a basement apartment several streets away.

Inside, dozens of empty soda bottles were left in disarray; footprints were visible in the dust on the floor. From a bed in the darkness a woman, not completely sober, began to complain. She told the sisters her oldest daughter, aged fourteen, was being "dated" by a man of sixty-two. The same ·daughter was being drawn into a teen-age "sex gang" at the local school.

The three sisters were new to the neighborhood. Instead of living in a conventional convent, they had, together with several other sisters from various parts of the country, rented a small apartment house for the duration of their graduate studies at the nearby university. The sisters soon found a place for the troubled girl in a private academy not far from her home. One of the sisters returned regularly to help out in the home, and to direct the deserted mother to other sources of assistance.

The same sisters, led to another apartment, discovered an aged, crippled woman who was unable to care for herself—couldn't even read the numbers on the telephone. One of the sisters cleaned out the accumulated dirt and refuse, scrubbed the floors, and, despite her upcoming doctoral examinations, returned at least every three days to prepare a good meal and to chat.

Such charity from the Roman Catholic sisters is not, of itself, newsworthy. But the striking part of this episode has not yet been stated. *There were two other permanent Roman Catholic convents in that same neighborhood,* one for the sisters who ran the parish elementary school, and one for the sisters who taught at the private academy; *and the sisters from these ordinary convents did not get out into the streets to share the lives of the people of the neighborhood. They were separated from the suffering around them.*

"The Sisters of Mercy were founded to help the poor, the sick, the suffering," one of the student sisters explained. "So were many of the other communities. But then we became institutionalized. We became separated from the poor our foundresses wanted to help. Now some of us want to serve again. We think that sisters belong with the poor."

Another Roman Catholic sister, one of several score parochial school teachers who have begun to give their weekends and their summers to tasks before neglected, stepped tentatively into a hallway in a Harlem tenement. The door of the room she had been assigned to visit, on the fourth floor, was ajar; the air was stale, rancid, and compressed. Garbage was rotting through a paper bag. The bathtub in the kitchen was dirty, and the tiny sink was full of rust. The refrigerator didn't work, and beside it the toilet bowl had no seat. The other room of the apartment was jammed with six ugly wooden cots upon which rested dirty mattresses.

The sister stepped inside and called weakly, "Mrs. Howard?"

"What you want here?" a surly man asked. Five or six small children, seeking air at the gritty window sills, turned to stare at the strangely dressed woman.

"They told me Mrs. Howard wanted to talk to someone."

"She ain't here."

The sister was afraid. "They said she'd be here. Will you tell her I came? I can stop again next week."

"She don't need no help."

The sister studied the young faces a moment, and took a quick inventory of the room. "Tell her I'll be back next week," she said.

In still another city, Sister Maura Sullivan searched for her size among the ladies' suits in a department store; her sister companion sullenly looked the other way. In twenty-four hours, Sister Maura would once again be Miss Dorothy Sullivan (to protect her privacy, I have used pseudonyms). She had taught junior high school for thirteen years; she was now thirty-six, having lived in a convent for almost half her life—sixteen years. For many years, she had argued with herself that convent life was supposed to be "accepted on faith" or "under obedience," just as it was, uncritically. But the Vatican Council had led her to see the importance of creative thinking, personal responsibility, and the need for experiment. At first she was excited by new possibilities, but her enthusiasm earned her much opposition and several rebukes. For three years, she had worked for "gradual change." But it was now plain that her community would not move very far during her lifetime. Minor adjustments were being made, but many, many sisters resisted change.

Sister Maura had only one life to give to God: and she had become convinced that she could spend herself more effectively as Miss Dorothy Sullivan. She planned to join three other ex-sisters she had met, who were continuing to live their life of consecrated virginity. They earned their living by teaching in public schools, and they used their free hours to help organize Negro freedom schools, rent strikes, and community services. They had abandoned the convent rule and monastic notions of obedience. Sister Maura tried on the suit she liked, and asked to have it wrapped. She emerged smiling from the dressing room, re-adjusting her nun's veil for the last time; a dour look from her companion, an older woman, warned her to hide her smile. It was no easy thing to ask for a formal dispensation from one's vows. But after four years of anguished doubts, Sister Maura had decided and now she was content, and not even her companion's distress could chill her joy.

On a windy street in front of the Lewis Towers in Chicago, in 1963, Sister Angelica Seng, a Franciscan from Alvernia High School, led a group of pickets in protest against a racially segregated pool used by the Illinois Club for Catholic Women. Repercussions were swift: thousands of dollars pledged to the support of various Catholic girls' schools in Chicago were withdrawn. Sister Mary Ignatia Griffin, B.V.M., Dean of Mundelein College in Chicago, later told a national audience that this protest "dramatized for all of us what had happened to nuns." She explained: "The fact that there was such shock in the Catholic community told me, at least, that we had become, as it were, stylized, costumed dolls who should be kept inside a convent, but who had no right to be out there where there was social injustice or discrimination or where there should be Christian witness."

In the summer of 1965, a Ford station wagon edged off the highway across a dusty driveway and stopped in front of a motel office. Five sisters drew themselves wearily from the vehicle. Each wore a different style of dress: a Franciscan in brown, a Dominican in white, a Maryknoller in gray, and in black a School Sister of Notre Dame and a Sister of the Holy Names. Each had a doctorate in a different subject: history, economics, psychology, sociology, and social work. Their station wagon was equipped with a library, films, and tapes on the cultures of American ethnic groups, and the speedometer showed that they had driven 11,000 of the 12,000 miles on their schedule. They had tried to help conventions of sisters and lay people in the Northeast, South, and Midwest to understand the frustrations of the poor and dispossessed.

One of their number, Sister Mary Audrey Kopp, a sociologist from Oregon, reported: "One can't help but discover on such a safari·that one's fellow sister in her eighteenth-century dress is often struggling with nineteenth-century means to attain twentieth-century ends and prepare students for the problems of the twenty-first. We have met sisters frustrated or fearful, some rigidly cemented to impractical cultural patterns of the past, others struggling to meet the challenges of the day and forging forward."

Evidence of the forging forward is everywhere. Even one of the eldest, most conservative bishops of the United States, who does not like the quiet revolution of the new sisters, described the changes in a sermon: "Some people are shocked by the manner of dress of the

[new] nuns: some [sisters] can hardly be distinguished from the laity
—knee-length dresses, a lot of color, almost no headdress. The reason
their superiors give for such is that it brings them closer to the laity.
Is this desirable? If they dress like lay-people, will they not be treated
like lay-people? The sister's habit not only protects her, but is a source
of inspiration and veneration to the people."

The bishop added: "What is more alarming: we find nuns more and
more out of the convent and appearing in public. They appear at
evening meetings with the laity; give lectures to the public; eat in
public restaurants; march in picket lines and demonstrations for social
justice; travel alone from one end of the nation to the other, and live
alone on the campuses of universities, because they have been offered
a scholarship or grant." He concluded plaintively: "One sometimes
wonders, 'Why did they go to the convent?'"

But the new sisters are not afraid of laymen, the world, or themselves; they didn't enter the convent to escape from the world. Recently, Sister Mary Consolata Delaney, a doctoral candidate in Russian literature at Harvard, returned from an extended visit to Russia,
during which she gathered research materials; in Russia she dressed in
lay clothing. Sister Francetta Barberis now works as assistant to the di-
rector of the Women's Job Corps in Washington, and she dresses as
other women. The Sisters of Charity of the Blessed Virgin Mary have
sent thirty-two sisters for doctorates, forty-one for masters degrees,
fourteen for post-doctoral research—to such universities as Harvard,
Yale, Stanford, Chicago, California (Berkeley), The Sorbonne, Oxford, London, Munich, Venice, and Loyola in Rome. They say this is
"just a beginning." A California sister has been a visiting professor in
chemistry at Brown; sisters have accepted teaching posts at Berkeley,
the University of Rochester, and Notre Dame. At Selma, Alabama,
more than two score sisters marched with Martin Luther King.

Perhaps the most publicly visible of the American sisters is the
vivacious, clear-thinking, outspoken Sister Jacqueline Grennan, President of Webster College in St. Louis and member of President Kennedy's Panel for Research and Development in Education. Through
her service on the panel, Sister Jacqueline has come to know some of
the most sensitive and learned scientists and thinkers in America; several of them confided to her, as they came to trust her, that they had
long thought of religion "as a sinking ship." None of the sisters is as

aware as she is of the gap between the world of belief and the world of unbelief in America. At Webster, Sister Jacqueline and her community are trying to create a new type of Catholic women's college, open, ecumenical, pluralistic, critical and free.

Standards are constantly being raised, experiments in interfaculty communication and conversation between the sciences and the humanities are continual, and the resources of nearby non-Catholic colleges are drawn upon. A few of the Webster girls live in downtown St. Louis among the Negro poor. All the girls are expected to take their Catholic faith apart creatively, and critically to work out their basic values. Some of them are afraid of the freedom Webster offers; they want more answers, fewer questions. Others shed complacencies like cocoons and emerge with fresh, resilient spirits.

In June, the sisters of the community at Webster ceased living in one huge convent, and moved in small groups to residential homes in the neighborhood, where they will manage their own finances and live a less institutionalized, more community-centered life. One of the sisters recently sought release from her vows and left the sisterhood, but stayed on at the college in her old post because her role in many of the new developments made her services critical; she changed clothes and place of residence, and stayed on the job. The sisterhood was mature enough to absorb her change of life without shock. Some young sisters from another community who are studying at Webster do not like the new spirit; after graduation, they retreat to their own more highly institutionalized convent routine with relief.

The decision of the sisters of Loretto to make Webster a secular college under the management of a lay board of trustees is a pioneering move in the tradition of that community. Sister Jacqueline's decision to request a dispensation from her vows in order to serve both the Church and the world as a lay woman may also point the way which other Catholic women will take in the future.

There are 175,000 sisters in the United States. For years they have been, as it were, hidden away in the Catholic "ghetto," teaching in parochial schools, administering huge and successful hospitals. Few educated non-Catholics have ever in their lives had a conversation with a sister. Newspapers were fond of running pictures of sisters on roller-coasters, sisters on skateboards, sisters swinging softball bats, sisters on motorcyles: "Look, ma, they're human!" The new American sisters are weary of such stereotypes; they long to be taken for what they are: women, Americans, Christians, professionally skilled workers. They are beginning to break out of the old stereotypes, and out of the past and out of the "convent in the Catholic ghetto" as well. "The sisters are moving," says one sister sociologist, "they are moving outside the cloister and the classroom. They are beginning to appear wherever there is tension and conflict and need."

The new sisters wish to be the avant-garde of the American Catholic Church. In the process, they may well become pioneers of a new style of American religious life. For almost twenty years, they have been sinking their roots deeply into the Bible, into the new theology which emerged at the Second Vatican Council, and into their own traditions. They are beginning to discover the poor of America, the sorrows and joys of modern urban life, the responsibilities of citizenship in an international, secular, political, ecumenical world. The sisters are stepping from past centuries into the twentieth century.

Sister Mary Luke Tobin, chairman of the conference of women in charge of all the American sisters, has legitimized the new attitude succinctly: "The sisters have a place in the front lines of any movement that is working for the betterment of humanity." In a speech to the executive officers of the sisters at Denver in the summer of 1965, Sister Mary William Kelley of Los Angeles stated the alternative sharply: "Either the American sister . . . becomes the avant-garde of the Church or she will quietly fade from the American scene. . . . She may say more, but she will be heard less, unless and until she is willing to put her body where her words are."

The new sisters are not satisfied with the position in society into which they have allowed themselves to lapse. They are proud of the sacrifices made by their predecessors, and of the immense contribution made by sisters during past generations. But many now feel that they have been trapped by a hardening of their possibilities; they are treated as "nice little things," "the good sisters," of no consequence to real adult life in America. They are challenging American society, and they are challenging Roman Catholic canon law. "Too often," Sister Mary Peter Traxler of Chicago says, "sisters are considered a money-saving device for a middle-class society with middle-class values. And people want them to keep their middle-class status." She adds: "Sisters have often been isolated from the suffering of the poor, but it is not entirely their fault. The canon law of the Church looks upon them as minors and defines their conduct as though they were Victorian ladies designed for Victorian drawing rooms. Even the structure of the Church in the United States has frozen them in the economics of running hospitals and schools."

The revolution sought by sisters is full of poignancy and pain. Many sisters, old and young, are opposed to the new way of life. Many others, especially the young, find the changes much too gradual. In some communities, a few of the conservative sisters are leaving the convent because the new style is not what they had entered for; in others, a few of the restless and imaginative ones are leaving because the old style blocks them from doing what they had entered to do. The mothers general of the sisters' communities are divided, some closed to change and others open; many others seem anxious and afraid. "The mothers general are scared," one sister comments. "They don't understand how deep the changes will be. Some of the older communities are not changing at all. Some of the more ethnically mixed ones —especially those founded in the United States and located in the Midwest—are changing very rapidly. But only a very few sisters have broken through to a theory about what is happening."

In a sense, the Roman Catholic sisters are making an experiment on behalf of the rest of us. With the avant-garde of all religiously oriented people in America—Baptists, Lutherans, Presbyterians, Jews, Catholics, and others—they are testing out the proposition that a new society is being born in America, and that religious people must enter into it as fully and enthusiastically as they entered into the rural, more placid society of old-fashioned America. As one of the new sister sociologists says, "There are *two* cultures co-existing side-by-side in American life." One of these cultures, the one in which the sisters had been happily and effectively living until the end of the Second World War, is "family-centered, traditional, stable, sheltered, relatively changeless, often rural, proud." The second culture, in whose anxieties the sisters have increasingly found themselves involved, is "technical, swift, mobile, faceless, pragmatic, restless, pluralistic, urban." The question the sisters ask is: "Can our life retain its values in the new culture? Can we swim in that sort of sea?"

No religious group in America can avoid facing the risks, confusions, and powerful solvents of the oncoming culture. Nor is it certain that American religion can survive the vast cultural shift it is power-less to postpone. Must religious people cling to the old comforts and the old ways? Dare they reinterpret their values and practices in new ways? Many of the Roman Catholic sisters are ready to accept that dare. They are a test case, and countless other Americans are watch-ing them with fascination.

II

To understand the changes taking place in American convents, one must recall what convents were like twenty-five years ago—what some are still like today. Most American sisterhoods were founded in Eu-rope and received their inspiration there (though some of them are now more conservative than their European counterparts). Conse-quently, the description given sisters by Cardinal Suenens of Belgium in *The Nun in the World* (1962), while it annoyed some American sisters, struck others forcibly: "Religious too often seem to be living in a closed world, turned in on themselves and having but tenuous contact with the world outside. A community of nuns often enough gives the impression of being a fortress whose drawbridge is only furtively and fearfully lowered." He continued: "It has been said of certain congregations of nuns that they are the last strongholds of the very studied manners of the middle-class woman of the nineteenth century."

What does it mean to become a sister? Girls who become sisters take three vows: poverty (not to own or to use property without the permission of their superiors), celibacy, and obedience. Through these vows, the sisters establish a common life, and undertake together a common work: teaching, nursing, domestic tasks, and the like. Prayer is very important to their lives; they often spend two to four hours in prayer every day. Sisters, like sectarian Protestants, are constantly starting new groups. There are more than 750 different Roman Catho-lic religious communities of women in the United States; only about a half-dozen of these have more than 5,000 members; a great many have fewer than 100 members. A few communities are distinctive, but most list their requirements in the *Guide to the Catholic Sisterhoods in the United States* in some such fashion as this:

SPIRITUAL LIFE: The sisters spend nearly four hours each day in spiritual exercises which include the Holy Sacrifice of the Mass, a half-hour of adoration of the Blessed Sacrament, vocal prayers in English, mental prayer, spiritual reading, and private acts of devotions.

TRAINING PROGRAM: The postulancy of six months is followed by the two years of novitiate. At the conclusion of the novitiate, the novice takes temporary vows for five years and then pronounces her perpetual vows. Monthly spiritual conferences, days of recollection, and a period of tertianship strengthen the dedicated zeal of the sister while her professional education is continued by post-graduate studies and in-service training.

QUALIFICATIONS:
- Age: 17 to 30.
- An earnest desire to serve God faithfully in the religious life.
- Average intelligence.
- Entrance date, September 8.

Until even five years ago, the clothing that sisters wore usually dated from the century in which their community had been founded—the thirteenth, or more often the eighteenth or nineteenth. Sister Mary Ignatia Griffin explains what happened to her own community: "When we were founded in 1833, the dress that was adopted was the dress of the time. The purpose of wearing the dress was to disappear into the public so you wouldn't be noticed. What happened was that what our founders wore in 1833, which was not too unlike in length and color and so forth from what we're wearing now, was discarded by women within four or five years, but we kept it. So, in a way we have achieved just the opposite effect of what we really wanted. We wanted to disappear into the public, and instead we have the highest visibility of almost any group in America."

The hourly schedule—or as the sisters call it, the *horarium*—which the young girl followed in the convent twenty-five years ago was also established in earlier centuries—before the invention of electric lights. Rising was at 5 a.m. At 5:30, a half-hour of mental prayer would be followed by Mass and communion, and then by a plain breakfast usually eaten in silence or to the sound of one of the sisters reading from *The Imitation of Christ* or another similar pious work. Afterwards, there would barely be time to wash the dishes, dust the chapel and hallways, make one's bed, and be ready for the classrooms of the parochial school or the wards of the Catholic hospital. After work, more prayers, supper and brief recreation—conversation or knitting or singing in the community room—then more prayers, an hour or so of work, and then retiring.

The demands of modern professional life have made great incursions into this daily schedule. Important lectures in the city are scheduled in the evenings; studying at a major university requires late hours; hospitals demand availability around the clock. One sister comments wryly: "We try to live modern nights and medieval mornings."

By about 1950, many convents were beginning to make at least minor adjustments. Fewer prayers were to be recited together; greater flexibility was allowed for individual necessities; later retiring was permitted and sometimes later rising; in some communities, the hours were left to individual discretion.

One older sister describes what even these minor changes meant to her, after thirty years under the older regimen:

We used to answer the Chapel bell at four o'clock each afternoon after school. We had a full forty-five minutes of vocal prayer, litanies and novenas, followed by a half-hour of meditation. Most of us were so dead tired after forty-five minutes of vocal prayer that we slept during meditation, or sat there dazed, unable to drum up a single reflection or affection. This was changed in 1953 to just a half-hour of mental prayer with all vocal prayer eliminated, and now it's a joy to answer the bell for Chapel —I come out feeling like a new person.

But this same sister recognized that even these small adjustments in her community had not gone nearly far enough:

If only we'd go the whole way on *aggiornamento!* In the morning I drag myself out of bed too tired to think. I get down to the Chapel where we say Matins and Lauds, followed by a half-hour of mental prayer and twenty minutes of vocal prayers for the church, the community and benefactors, and then Mass starts. By Communion time I'm lost in frustration because I can feel no fervor—only fatigue. Sometimes I kneel at the Communion railing wondering if I can possibly please God feeling as I do. Then we go to breakfast and are served in rank. Since I'm near the end of my particular table, I'm served near the last, and I practically choke with smoldering resentment—and yes, let me be honest—with scruples because I'm in such a bad humor every morning. Yet, I love to pray. What a joy and peace it would be if we just had meditation as a preparation for Mass. I could sing aloud with the best of them or join in hearty dialogue at Mass in all the glory of the new liturgy. And if we didn't waste so much time in the refectory serving by rank, life would be perfect. . . . But it's still a wonderful life, and thank God I can still laugh out loud at myself.

Until recently, all changes had to wait upon the good will of higher superiors. No idea was more exaggerated in American convents twenty-five years ago than the concept of "religious obedience." Recently, in front of the television cameras of David Susskind's "Open End," Sister Mary Ignatia Griffin described the fundamental change in the theory and the practice of obedience from the time when she first entered. She recalled: "When I began to live a life of religious obedience, I was expected to expect specific direction. In fact very specific direction. And I was expected, if I possibly could, to bring my mind to see that the direction that was being given to me by my higher superiors was the best. I was supposed to get a sort of intellectual agreement with them, if I could do this. However, it was recognized that I couldn't always, but at least this was the ideal." She flashed a smile. "Well, this concept of obedience, I think, is doomed. It's dead. It's gone and thank God that it is gone, because really today I think that obedience means to young people, not mere following, but responsible freedom. Young people coming into religious communities today realize that they have a major share in making the congregation what it is."

The old ideal that governed convent life, in fact, was that of the monastery of the medieval period. The sisters were supposed to be totally involved in one institution. "Each time I go outside my cell," the writer of *The Imitation of Christ* wrote in the fifteenth century, "I return less a man." The convent represented safety, shelter, *real* Christianity; the outside world was distracting, worldly, and artificial. "It would take a very high degree of spiritual strength and concentration to remain in the hurly-burly of the world and maintain any kind of recollection [spiritual calm]," a priest recently admonished a group of sisters. A bishop repeated the warning: "The spirit of the world will dominate instead of the spirit of Christ." Thus the girl entering the convent had to learn a new "spiritual" point of view. She had to accept sharp distinction between "superiors" or staff members and "subjects." The convent would become geographically and psychologically the center of all major, and even many minor, decisions. The staff made these decisions; subjects obeyed. Even the letters which a sister received from her family were opened by her superiors. Perfection was to be reached through obedience and self-effacement. God spoke through superiors. Even the convent bell summoning the silently moving sisters to prayer or meals or classes was "the voice of God."

Ordinarily, the young girl entered the convent knowingly and generously. Twenty-five years ago, she would probably have entered upon September 8, the day of Our Lady's Nativity, or some other feast day of Our Lady. She would have been to a great farewell party thrown by her former girl friends and tearful parents: a lovely dinner, group singing, dancing the jitterbug—a "last fling." In the night, after everyone had gone home, the future nun would think long thoughts, and end by "placing herself in the hands of God." On the average, such a girl was nineteen years old.

At the convent, she would change from her bright clothes to black skirts and sweaters and long black stockings. For six months to a year, the future nun would live the life of a "postulant," by her studies and her performance of duties asking for the favor of being admitted afterwards to the novitiate. On Sundays there would be walks, or perhaps lawn sports. Prayer, silence, and constant, steady acclimatization to rules marked this period: Walk slowly, Speak softly, Waste nothing, Wax floors and Sweep halls as if for the King of Glory, All for Jesus through Mary, Peace, etc. Sister Charles Borromeo Muckenhirn, one of the most balanced and perceptive of the new nuns, describes the orientation: "The old system was to depersonalize persons and to upgrade things. Anything run by sisters was to be cleaner and—" she deliberately coined a word—"waxeder than anybody else's. You had to be a person on the sly."

The old system believed that "perfection" was reached by discipline —discipline which emptied out all traces of self-will, self-assertion, personal idiosyncrasy, "rebelliousness." Accepted with great warmth and love, such discipline could, of course, become a daily school of self-knowledge and richer sensitivities. At the same time, it sometimes merely drove self-will and self-assertion underground. No system can guarantee growth in selflessness; and sometimes sisters who thought they were being unselfish because they were letter-perfect in their observance of the rule developed hard shells of egoism, irritable tempers, smoldering inner resentment. The psychological roots of these suppressed feelings were not commonly recognized twenty-five years ago, and some sisters interpreted their feelings merely as further signs of their "fallen nature" and "constant imperfection," and threw themselves only more seriously into minute observance of the convent rule.

In the novitiate, a special house often situated in a country place, the future sister began "living the life of the rule" in earnest. With anywhere from six to a hundred other novices, depending on the size of the community, the future sister would receive approximately the same dress as the full-fledged members of the community, except that maybe the veil would be white instead of black, or shorter, or of a slightly different style. The novitiate was to be a period of the utmost fervor. "Remember," one group of sisters was cautioned by the reader at the beginning of breakfast every morning. "What you are in the novitiate, that you shall be for the rest of your lives." It was commonly assumed that in religious life as in marriage, fervor, romance, and enthusiasm would only wane in the years ahead; the novice had to build soundly.

Throughout the novitiate, the young sisters would live in silence for most of the day, except for carefully specified times of recreation or for when their work made speech indispensable. They tried to learn to pray even as they worked, at the very least by "offering" their work to God, or by beginning it and ending it consciously "in His presence." They were taught, in the spirit of poverty, not to waste even scraps of paper; in some communities, the rule prescribed that a small piece of formica or a piece of paper be slipped underneath the thumb as one used one's prayer-books, so that the thin pages would be preserved from soiling. "You can tell a perfect sister," one nun once told a young novice, "by whether she always has a piece of formica under her thumb." To a young novice, such advice was often just sufficiently practical to mask its pharasaism.

But many sisters were too busy and too eager to get on with their service of God to be troubled by such advice, even though it was often voiced, not by random nuns, but by highly regarded books recommended for spiritual reading. (St. Thérèse of Lisieux, a French

Carmelite nun who died in 1897, once complained that such books gave her headaches; she could find nourishment only in the Gospels.) During the novitiate, the sisters sometimes carried a relatively light load of class work, toward a college degree. Putting together the classes they took as postulants and as novices, they often had completed two years of college work by the time they took their first vows.

These vows, usually taken for a one-year period and then renewed year by year for six years, until the moment for perpetual vows, theoretically marked the great step into the religious life. Twenty-five years ago, some American novitiates treated profession day like a wedding day. By her vows of poverty, celibacy, and obedience, the young girl would become a "Bride of Christ." For the last time, she would wear a long white gown, a "bridal" gown, and carry flowers. Then, or else on the occasion of her final profession six years later, she would accept a gold "wedding" ring. Most of the new nuns are embarrassed by this symbolism now, and one points out—with marked emotion—that it was based on "incredibly bad theology." (Theologically, only the Church is the bride of Christ, the whole Church, lay people included.) But twenty-five years ago, most of the theology of the religious life was sadly underdeveloped.

The romantic, feminine overtones of the profession ceremony were, moreover, only a prelude to the de-feminization subtly required of the sisters. All the rules made for religious women are made by men. The conference of all the major superiors of women's communities meeting in Denver in 1965, addressed a rather sharp request to the Vatican asking that some women religious be represented, at least as consultors, upon the Congregation of Religious in Rome. That bureau, which has so much legal jurisdiction over their lives, is at present entirely masculine.

A view encountered very often among sisters is that, in the words of one of them: "Bishops and priests are afraid of women. That's why they have tried to make us neuters." Sister Charles Borromeo, in this connection, pointed to her heavy dress, her heavy men's shoes, even her large-sized men's handkerchief. "It's as if being a woman were being evil."

According to canon law, made entirely by men, the status of sisters in the Church is that of "minors"; they are not treated as adults, but as women were everywhere treated two centuries ago. From the Roman congregations to the local bishop and even the parish priest, men legally and effectively have the last word about convent life. Many educational, liturgical, or administrative reforms which competent women have wished to institute in the parish school or in the schools of a diocese have been thwarted by a word from a pastor or bishop who knew less about the matter than the sisters. Many sisters noted the fact that not a single woman took part in the deliberations of the Second Vatican Council, until a few token "auditresses" were appointed in the third session; only one of them was an American sister.

Twenty-five years ago, the fact of male dominance was almost disastrous for the sisters' communities in the United States. Unrelenting demands made upon the sisters in the name of the Catholic school system rarely took account of the welfare of the sisters and in 1887, there were in the United States 2,697 elementary schools taught by sisters. For the next 43 years an average of 9 new schools were under construction each month, until by 1930 there were 7,293 such schools. By 1964 this number had almost doubled. Most of the bishops of the period were builders; in his first 25 years as Archbishop of New York, from 1939–1964, Cardinal Spellman built 299 schools, for 104,325 new pupils. Where would the sisters come from to staff these schools? Who would pay for their education? Cardinal Spellman's new schools alone required 3,249 new teachers. From all over the country requests for more sisters flooded in from harried bishops. The sister superiors had learned badly the meaning of obedience, and often a sister superior would accede to a request for more sisters without pointing out strenuously to the bishop how much harm was being done the young sisters by the work placed prematurely upon their shoulders.

For the new schools devoured young sisters. Fresh from the novitiate they would come, two years or so of college work in their heads, to cope with elementary school classrooms whose average student enrollment was 38. Some harassed pastors loaded 80 to 100 children in a classroom, rather than turn applicants away. "In many regions of the country after World War II," one sister comments, "state legislators granted emergency certificates to almost anyone who would help alleviate the shortage of teachers. Standards in parochial schools were sometimes higher, sometimes lower, than standards in nearby public schools." But the sisters, unlike public school teachers, were still trying to live according to medieval monastic standards, as well as to acquire professional competence, as well as to answer all requests made upon them. At night, they had no home, no family circle, to retire to; they lived in the institution where they worked, or with the same people they worked with all day long. Even though they could take their cares to the dark, silent chapel, the pace was inhuman, and something had to give.

III

The renewal of the sisterhoods has proceeded in cycles, with each cycle spiraling further and higher than its predecessors foresaw. The leaders of one cycle have often come to seem quite conservative to those of the next. Thus the first wave of the present renewal began in 1941 with the publication of Sister Bertrande Meyer's doctoral dissertation, *The Education of the Sisters.* Sister Bertrande critically assessed the deplorable schedules the sisters were trying to meet, and reported upon hundreds of interviews with sisters. "Neither bishops nor priests," Sister Bertrande now recalls, "could quite grasp the necessity of holding the young sister back until she was fully formed, academically and spiritually, to enter the professions of teaching and nursing." Many a sister struggled to earn an A.B. and then an M.A. solely by attending summer sessions. Even this year, one sister from Oregon told a friend proudly: "I will be sixty-two, and it's taken me twenty years, but this spring I'll be awarded my master's degree."

During and after the Second World War, little came of Sister Bertrande's investigations. But in 1949, Sister Madeleva Wolff, a refined, highly cultivated poetess, and later President of St. Mary's College at Notre Dame, delivered a sharp, pungent paper to the National Catholic Educational Association, which was later published as *The Education of Sister Lucy.* Sisters, she argued, could no longer be treated as mere cogs in a vast machine. "Lucy and her companions are our most priceless and irreplaceable materials in the whole world of education. Let us treat them with much more than the care and caution bestowed on centers of atomic energy. Let us keep them out of the categories of vacuum cleaners and Bendix washers."

The first cycle of reform, in short, insisted that the sisters must be educated; they must be professionally prepared; their own sense of dignity must be respected. The opposition to this first reform was threefold. Many bishops and pastors didn't see why fifth-grade teachers needed university degrees. Secondly, many sisterhoods had a tradition of pietism and anti-intellectualism. "I would rather feel compunction than know how to define it," was an accepted maxim. Many more convent gardens had a white statue of the almost illiterate but pious St. Bernadette of Lourdes, than featured the brilliant St. Teresa of Avila, whose writings were to become classics for all ages.

But, thirdly, and least admirably, many of the conservatives of that period were afraid because the young student sisters were precisely the ones who had not yet committed themselves by lifelong vows; Lucy might get her Ph.D. and leave. To this Sister Madeleva replied: "Nothing can possibly do more to undermine her vocation than to send her out to try to teach without adequate, often without any, preparation. Nothing can so disillusion her in her community as the dishonesty of assigning her to do in the name of holy obedience what professionally she is unqualified to do."

By 1953, the second cycle of reform had begun. Its leaders were a triumvirate of especially equipped and powerful personalities. Sister Mary Emil Penet, like Sister Madeleva before her, argued brilliantly in a brief public lecture to the National Catholic Educational Association for the absolute necessity of a special training program for sisters. The NCEA subsequently established a new committee, the Sister Formation Conference, and Sister Mary Emil was elected its head. Cardinal Spellman offered her a temporary office in New York. And then, unlike Sister Madeleva, Sister Mary Emil received funds to *do* something: $50,000 from the Ford Foundation to study the actual conditions of sisters' education. One of her first acts with Ford money was to purchase a car—a Chevrolet—and to set off with a companion upon a trip of 25,000 miles to study the education of sisters in all parts of the country.

Sister Mary Emil (today the President of Marygrove College in Detroit) is a thin, dynamic, restless person, with a firm, icy will, whose professional training was in philosophy. She soon inspired scores of other sisters with confidence that she had thought things through, and that, once her mind was made up, she would not waver. Almost overnight, 150 Sister Formation Centers sprang up in the U.S.; for the first time the various sisterhoods were cooperating in a systematic way to discuss mutual problems. Despite her own strong will and clear ideas, Sister Mary Emil was deferential to bishops and respectful to the executive officers of the sisterhoods with whom she had to deal; and in group discussions among "the new breed" of Sister Formation personnel she edified everyone by the free speech and critical inquiry she promoted. Gradually, the sisters' communities succeeded in convincing bishops that a three-year hiatus in the supply of new personnel was necessary while young sisters completed their education. "Sometimes," Sister Mary Emil recalls now, "you had to promise that after three years you wouldn't forget the bishops who had agreed to wait. You couldn't blame them for being worried. They had countless demands to meet."

"Renovation and adaptation" were the key words among sisters at this period—almost ten years before the Second Vatican Council. No sisters were better equipped to explore the meanings of these words than Sister Annette Walters, a trained psychologist from St. Paul, and Sister Ritamary Bradley, a bright young writer and college teacher from Ottumwa. The former was named executive secretary of the Sister Formation Conference, and the latter became editor of the Conference *Bulletin*. Together with Sister Mary Emil, these two sisters traveled many thousands of miles and gave hundreds of lectures, established a vast and orderly network of communication, and offered American Catholicism more stimulating philosophical and theological reflection than any other institution of the decade. The *Bulletin,* printed on blue paper, regularly carried translations of major articles from the "new theology" of Europe often unavailable elsewhere in the United States. It grew to 7,000 subscribers, and was far more avant-garde than any journal for American priests.

The key idea of these three sisters was centered in the word "formation"—a word which they understood in the sense of "development," "growth," "integration of personality." The sister performs a unique kind of service in the Church, they thought, and so she needs a unique kind of education. The values of piety must be integrated with the values of intellectual inquiry and professional competence. This basic philosophy received its clearest expression in the creation in 1956 of an ideal curriculum for the education of sisters, which because it was articulated at a summer-long brain session at Everett, Washington, came to be called "The Everett curriculum." Six special colleges for sisters were built, in different parts of the country, in at least partial accordance with this curriculum. The basic assumption of the curriculum was that "the spiritual and the intellectual life reinforce each other," and that a solid philosophical-theological synthesis of high interest to the special work of sisters should form the base of sisters' education.

For more than ten years, the programs of the SFC have prospered, even though the three pioneering leaders have resumed work in their own proper communities. An intensely human drama was enacted four years ago, through the changing relationships of these three strong personalities. Although all three still speak most appreciatively of one another, and though all three have the basic interests of the Conference at heart, severe personality conflicts arose during the last few years. Misunderstandings multiplied; unfounded accusations were made; during more than one organizational meeting emotions got out of hand, someone banged fists on the table, feelings were deeply hurt, groups silently formed behind the scenes, and rumors flew. Letters, and then counterletters, were written to all the bishops of the United States. All of which is to say, more poignantly than pictures of nuns on roller-coasters, sisters are like the rest of mankind.

The *Bulletin* is still being published; Sister Formation is still doing indispensable and immeasurably fruitful work. But already a third cycle of reform has developed. The young sisters who have benefited by the programs SFC established ten years ago take it for granted. "I would like to see you ignore it," urged Sister Suzanne Kelly, the first sister to hold a teaching position at the University of Notre Dame. "Sister Formation Colleges have aided the upgrading of sisters' education but have at the same time often kept the young sisters in an all-sister environment for several years. Do we want to continue this? Communities have large sums of money invested in these colleges and so I doubt that it would be wise to question their existence now. At least, you can avoid mentioning them as centers of renewal."

One sister who has come to symbolize this third cycle of development is Sister Charles Borromeo Muckenhirn, head of the theology department at St. Mary's College, Notre Dame. Ever since the weekly *National Catholic Reporter* has run a monthly supplement called "Sisters' Forum," Sister Charles Borromeo (her friends call her "Charlie B.") has been its imaginative and courageous editor. In

1965, she assembled a set of essays by nine sister scholars called *The Changing Sister,* which brilliantly illuminate the sociological and theological revolution occurring in the lives of sisters; it has already been translated into seven languages.

I spoke to Sister Charles Borromeo in the newly decorated seminar room of the St. Mary's theology department. Upon the wall hung a pennant on which bright lettering proclaims joyously: *"WISDOM hath built herself a house . . . a house, a house, a beautiful house!"* Speaking rapidly, in a colorful, colloquial style, Sister Charles Borromeo describes the problems faced by many communities. "In some places when you mention renewal, some people still turn their eyeballs and see pea green. Really. In others, it's 'O.K. now, let's crawl into our little telephone booths and have our renewal.' They don't see that we have to get out of ourselves, otherwise we can sit forever and listen to our arteries harden. Renewal—it's not magic. We have to get out of our little nunny world."

It is possible to distinguish the present wave of reform from the preceding: "There are the excellence people and the people-who-want-to-live-the-Gospel-in-the-world." The latter take intellectual excellence for granted; the former are "utterly and sincerely dedicated to improving every sister so that she will be a better cog in a bigger machine." For Sister Charles Borromeo, "The renewal is a welling up of the Christian life in sisters who want to live in genuine communities." Earlier reforms established new committees, conferences, institutions. "Fine, this has to be done. It would be a glaring mistake if people think that the new sisters are against the organizational structures. Organization is necessary, but the new sisters want more than organization. They are totally committed to personal prayer, thought, dialog across all lines, in order to become witnesses for the Spirit. And witness does not mean carrying a sandwich board. It means living a free and genuine life, from inside out. Prayer is primary for a sister, like marital intimacy for the married. But all Christians are responsible for acting in the world!"

"Education" and "formation" were the key words in the third cycle. "I think the sisters interested in renewal want two things and would like to be pictured as wanting these two things," says Sister Suzanne Kelly: "a more meaningful community life, and a noninstitutional way of serving the Church." Pressed, she specifies that she wants "smaller, less regimented groups" where personal relationships are warm and genuine, and "the freedom to be responsible Christians rather than to go on being mere position-fillers." In her soft Oklahoma accent, Sister Suzanne adds: "Exactly what this new community life will be, few of us are willing to say. We don't pretend to have *the* answer; most of us doubt that there is one answer, but we certainly would like the chance to try."

The new sisters have tried more experiments in the last two years than sisters had tried for centuries. A Belgian priest, Father Jean Lefevre, who worked for some time with Cardinal Suenens on the renewal of convent life in Belgium, told one group of American sisters: "It took religious communities of women five hundred years after Christ to be invented, a thousand years in monastaries to ponder God's gifts to them, and four hundred years more to win the liberty to take their proper place in the adult, secular world." The new sisters feel that they are just beginning to enter the secular world on its own terms. It is not so much that convent rules have been changed to allow them to go out on the streets alone instead of in pairs. (Occasionally, as happened recently in downtown Los Angeles, a protective layman accosts a sister on a busy sidewalk and lectures her severely for being "out" alone; in New York, a ticket salesman refused to issue a ticket to a sister who wanted to see "Who's Afraid of Virginia Woolf?" on the grounds that it wasn't "her kind of play.") It is rather that wherever there is suffering and need, there the sisters are beginning to be able to go, without red tape.

There are, points out Sister Roseanne Murphy, a sociologist from Belmont, California, three basic types of sisters' communities, and some of them are experiencing the new adulthood more quickly than others. The first type is rule-oriented; the whole purpose of the community seems to be to preserve a certain set of rules, traditions, or "spirit." Such communities are in serious difficulties in a rapidly changing world. The second type is task-oriented; their purpose is to perform certain services: to teach, or to run hospitals. Such communities have a struggle in revising their inherited rules, so as to meet the professional standards required by their present duties. The third type is person-oriented; their purpose is to prepare free and deeply committed persons, who will be able to take on whatever tasks are required, and to meet any conditions that arise. Such communities—the

Glenmary Sisters and the Sisters of Loretto are perhaps the best examples—can change quite rapidly.

For example, the young postulants of the Sisters of Loretto do not change into any special black dress to set them off from the other girls with whom they go to college in Denver. One postulant confided that she was at first a little disappointed: "We had looked forward to looking like postulants. But, you know, once I got here and thought about it awhile, I realized that my commitment must be internal—I can't depend on clothes." This comment was favorably received by her mistress of novices.

In a rule-oriented community, by contrast, young girls of eighteen or nineteen, or twenty-two or twenty-three, learn to become anonymous and to submit. "They come with their guitars," a sister in one such community sadly reports. "They are full of joy and vivacity. The only Church they know is the Church of the Second Vatican Council, Pope John's Church: critical, questioning, free. But in our community, the women training these girls have no psychological training. They are a good administrative personnel—a perfect 'staff.' But they are very rigid personalities and the new girls strike deathly fear into their hearts—they'll *never* fit into slots. These girls are reading Sartre and don't know if they still have faith, but the novice mistress makes fifty of them sit in a classroom for an hour after Mass because on the way to church one girl almost stepped on a worm and those behind her giggled. Another girl is told she doesn't have a vocation because she tidied up her room in five minutes, when the rule said fifteen, and sat reading Albert Camus for the extra time."

In a community like the Sisters of Notre Dame of Namur in Belmont, California, the younger sisters were able to schedule a pizza party for me, in order to discuss this article for the *Post*. "The last week before I entered the convent," one junior sister reminisced, "I had my last hamburger, my last milkshake, my last pizza, my last everything. Then at our first dinner in the convent they served us ice cream. The record collection we had was just like my collection at home. I was so surprised. When I came, they could have done anything to me. There were far more connections with home than I expected." The young sisters talked with uninhibited gestures, fingers moving as fast as their speech.

"Why are you writing this article anyway?" one sister asked

directly. "What do you think we are doing here? Who do you think we are?"

"The problem is, who do you think you are?"

The discussion lasted a long time. "Christians," they finally answered, "trying to learn to live as a community."

"What is the essential thing?" I asked.

"We told you. Community."

Like these junior sisters, the new sisters have discovered that living together under one roof, taking meals together, even conversing charitably together, does not make a community. In the old days, sisters were warned to beware of forming affective friendships with one another; their relations were to be governed by controlled, willed "charity." Many of the sisters found that the old system made them afraid to get close to people, afraid to open themselves even to one another. Many sisters, however, prefer institutional living, precisely for its solitariness—they are close to no one. But the new sisters find institutional living less than Christian, and they are not afraid to love.

Upon the walls of the rooms of many new sisters are serigraphs by Sister Mary Corita Kent, the artist of renewal, whose colorful work pleased so many at the Vatican Pavilion of the World's Fair, and the Fifth Avenue offices of the IBM Corporation. One such print reads: "To understand is to stand under which is to look up to which is a good way to understand." Reality, risk, trust, joy, love, these are the themes by which Sister Corita speaks of the sources of genuine community. Her own convent, Immaculate Heart College in Los Angeles, lives by the spirit of Sister Corita's prints. When the Immaculate Heart sisters speak of "our community," they do not mean only their sisters but all the people with whom they come in contact: students, lay faculty, workmen, visitors. It would be difficult to find a more thoroughly free and joyful household in the United States. Only the arch-conservatism of Cardinal McIntyre blinds him to the most brilliant Christian presence in his archdiocese.

Constantly spied upon (even conversations over dinner are reported by telephone), criticized, and obstructed by archdiocesan officials, the Sisters of the Immaculate Heart are one of the most highly educated, open, imaginative, and rapidly developing sisterhoods in the country. Several of the sisters have taken salaried positions at clinics and other institutions, returning to the convent community in the evenings just as other adults return to their homes. Even the grammar school teachers make a point of taking meals in the children's homes on occasion, recognizing that a teacher must understand children's home life if education is to be realistic. When the program of home visiting first began, one older sister said nervously to their host: "I'm so glad to be having dinner with you. After being with children all day, it's a pleasure to be with adults." "Just like my wife!" the man of the household laughed.

The Sisters of the Immaculate Heart are convinced that the problems of American sisters are the problems of American women in general. Last fall, at their retreat house, they sponsored a small conference of sisters, married women, and single women, to discuss such themes as celebration, anger, love, aging and death, faith, the self. About 1880, the role of women in the United States and the role of sisters was about the same: second-class citizenship, almost total dependence upon men, minimal professional competence. Since then, both in the convent and outside, the life of women has become more adult, responsible, and free. The sisters are still obstructed by nineteenth-century rules, rapidly disappearing, which treat them as children; lay women have difficulty balancing the claims of their families against the demands of civic and professional responsibility.

The bitter conservative resistance to renewal imagines that the new sisters want childish things like freedom to eat in public, colorful dresses, total freedom from discipline and rules, an ordinary lay life: why did they enter the convent at all? To this, one of the older new sisters, sixty-two, retorts: "Do we want to have the privileged sanctuary of the convent and yet be able to do the things normal adults do in normal adult society? I wonder if anyone would think that Benedictine, Carmelite, Dominican, Franciscan or other priests are reprehensibly eating their cake and having it by playing golf, swimming at public or semi-public beaches, going to the theater, to concerts, to restaurants, having regular vacations, visiting and dining with their friends in homes?"

To the new nuns, these things are not serious. They are embarrassed that in attending professional conventions they cannot, according to the rules of some sisterhoods, take their meals with "seculars." Sometimes a sister who is working among the poor in the slums cannot, without a companion, respond to a call from a family in immediate need. But such matters are mere nuisances, to be ended speedily. The new sisters are thinking about far more basic Christian issues: how to live a mature, prayerful, free Christian life among people who are in need. Their motivation is what one of them calls "Biblical conscience," and which ten sisters summed up at a conference last spring as "prayerfulness; responsible freedom; community; service to the Church and the world, especially to the poor; and openness to new possibilities of thought, ways of life, and action."

I V

What the new sisters have in mind is, in a striking way, coherent with the whole history of religious sisterhoods. This history begins with those devout women who regularly ministered to Jesus and his disciples, and who stood by at his crucifixion when the Apostles had fled. For four centuries, women served in an official capacity as "deaconesses" in the early Church. They tended the sick, fed the poor, instructed new believers, comforted the sorrowing.

The first great revolution in the role of women in the church occurred in the sixth century: the Church approved of public communities of consecrated virgins. About 540, at Subiaco, St. Benedict established the first monastery in the Western world, gathering together in one community those choice spirits who, heretofore, had lived as isolated hermits in the deserts of the East. Near his monastery—which Pope Paul VI recently called "the cradle of modern Europe"—St. Benedict also built a convent, which still stands today, for St. Scholastica and the first community of nuns. In those days, every woman needed to be protected by "either a man or a wall." The Church insisted upon strict enclosure of its consecrated virgins behind convent walls. This insistence stood firm—a solid wall itself—for a thousand years.

Six centuries after St. Benedict, a second revolution in the life of sisters was launched—or almost launched. In 1215, St. Dominic founded his Order of Preachers, and in 1209, St. Francis of Asissi established the Friars Minor: two mendicant orders whose members lived among the people, preaching the Good News, and begging for their daily necessities. But the Dominican and Franciscan women were not allowed the freedom of movement allowed the men. Thus the second revolution aborted; the men religious preached the Gospel in the world, but the sisters were kept behind walls. In 1544, St. Angela Merici sent a new sisterhood, the Ursulines, outside the medieval cloisters to meet the enormous needs of the people. But again male traditionalists put an end to this brave attempt; the Ursulines were cloistered. A century later, however, St. Vincent de Paul and the saintly Louise de Marillac, with "patience and pious cunning," circumvented conservative resistance. They dropped the name "religious" and spoke merely of "good girls of the parish"—nothing formal, simply women who wished to live the Gospels, together, in a common life. St. Vincent and Louise envisioned prophetically a group of women: "Whose only cloister would be the streets of the city; their only chapel the parish church; their veil, holy modesty; and their only enclosure, holy obedience."

The Daughters of Charity, as these "good girls of the parish" were called, dressed as other women dressed, went where other women went. But they did not escape from monastic patterns as thoroughly as St. Vincent had hoped. Conservatives in the Church insisted upon precautions to safeguard sisters from the "contamination" of the world. There were to be regular hours of prayer. There were to be superiors and subjects, rules and regulations. The sisters went outside for certain explicitly permitted tasks; then they returned. Thus, they could not really belong to the poor of the streets, to the active world of men, except part-time.

Today the Daughters of Charity of St. Vincent de Paul operate Marillac House in Chicago, a settlement house in East Garfield Park, an area with the highest crime rate, the highest rate for venereal disease and illegitimate children, the highest illiteracy, and the highest degree of desperation in the city. The sisters have worked at Marillac House for more than twenty years, and are slightly amused when other sisters discover their work and take it as something new. "Read St. Vincent de Paul," Sister Winifred Kilday smiles. "It's all in his conferences. 'The poor are anyone who needs us.' We've been here through the frustrated 'forties and the desperate 'fifties. Now others are on the brotherhood kick and the inner city bandwagon. But it isn't new, sir, it isn't new."

The immediate problem in East Garfield Park is hunger. "Another baby dies of malnutrition," Sister Winifred says evenly. She is a tall professional, with a dry wit and an intense devotion to her community's work. "Children are always being bitten by rats. Then there is the 'sin of referral.' The poor are referred from one bureaucratic agency to another. What do we do here?" She sat in a neatly waxed and painted office on the ground floor of a public housing project, several blocks away from the much larger Marillac House. "There are 28,000 people in our fifty-block area. We have trained three direct service workers to tend to immediate emergencies. We keep no records: it's either care for people or keep records, and we prefer people. The people here have started twenty-six block clubs; we give them some leadership training, bring in speakers, offer them our center. The work is slow. The poor have no one to speak for them, sir. They need a voice. They need someone to speak for them." She looked for the thread of her account. "The work is slow. This month the project is 'a garbage can for every family.' Garbage is collected only once a week in this area. Next month the project will be, 'Put the garbage *in* the can.' The work is slow. The people need secondary leadership, their own leadership, their own sense of community."

Phone calls often interrupt Sister Winifred. "Gotta see ya, sistah," one caller recently told her, a thirty-year-old woman with five children, whose husband had been in prison for three months. Sister Winifred went immediately, climbing to the fifth floor three buildings from her office. Shasta lay on the bed treading her sheets. "Gotta have sex, Sistah," Shasta told her. "Don't let me cheat. Don't let me cheat." Sister Winifred said later that in that neighborhood "anyone can get a lay for fifty cents." She sat on the bed and took Shasta's hand on her lap, caressing her hair until she grew quiet. "Every woman goes through what Shasta goes through," Sister Winifred said later. "In her I saw the beautiful purity of our people. I learned what my own vow of celibacy means. 'Don't let me cheat, sistah. Don't let me cheat.'"

From her office in Rendu House, Sister Winifred retreats when the bell rings at 12:45 (unless an emergency has arisen) to return to Marillac House for lunch and an hour of common prayer. The people know what the bell means. "Sistah, you know that bell's gonna ring. Now ya better git there." "You can't cheat on the common life," Sister Winifred says. "I wouldn't want those hours of prayer changed." She returns to Rendu House from 2:30 until 5:45. After dinner, recreation (including the news on television) and a brief period of common prayer, she returns to the office from 7:15 until 10:00, sometimes until 11:30, or as late as necessary. "Sisters must specialize," she says. "Some must teach the wealthy to care for the poor, and some must help the poor. For us, the poor are our masters. They teach us the meaning of the Gospel. Christ is really present in them, not only in the tabernacle."

The Daughters of Charity represent a transition from the past into the present. They have kept, at least in a few places like Marillac House, their three-century-old commitment to the poor (in the United States they also teach in many schools). They retain, however, a heavy, ankle-length dress, and a set of strict convent rules. Many of the new sisters admire their work at Marillac House, but feel that the commitment of the sisters to the poor must break still further from the idea of enclosure and common life.

In vivid contrast to Sister Winifred's defense of a strict common life, Sisters Evelyn Eaton, Marie Cirillo, and Gerald Peterson of the Glenmary Sisters are proud of the fact that "going to a convent is outside our experience." The Glenmary Sisters were founded twenty years ago in Cincinnati, to serve the poor of Appalachia. They number at present just over a hundred sisters; sixty-six girls are in school getting their A.B.'s or M.A.'s; about fifty new girls apply for admission each year, thirty actually come for an orientation week in June, twenty are accepted for the postulancy in September, and of these almost fifteen go on to become sisters. Typically American, the sisters wear a simple gray dress cut according to fashion and blouses of various colors—a fitting symbol of their openness to change, tentativeness, experimentation, and flexibility.

Sisters Evelyn, Marie, and Gerald live temporarily in "uptown" Chicago, in the Irving Park, Bryn Mawr district where thousands of Appalachians have migrated. They are blessed with having as their advisor a bishop a man who understands the ambiguities and complexities of their work with the poor, Bishop Joseph H. Hodges of Wheeling. He has told them they "have his permission" to make mistakes, as they try to understand the vast social forces which are unsettling

Appalachia. The sisters have come to Chicago "to be present and available," and to study the needs of migrants in the city. Rents on the block where the sisters have taken an apartment run as high as $130 a month for three rooms. Most of the migrants arrive penniless, but are expected to pay rent in advance. Even when they find jobs, pay day does not come for at least a week, if not a month. What do they do in the meantime? "Who knows?" says Sister Evelyn. "Survive," says Sister Marie.

Sister Marie, a trained sociologist, has a small grant to make a community study of the once elegant middle-class neighborhood, now a crowded, teeming wasteland. In the streets, children greet each sister by name, calling joyfully from overhead windows, from the tiny asphalt playground where broken glass shines in the sun, or running down the sidewalks. No one knows everyone in the neighborhood, but almost everyone knows the sisters. Only a tiny percentage of the people are Catholic. They do not perceive the sisters as Catholics, or as sisters, but as distinct persons, Evelyn, Marie, and Gerald, whom they trust.

A pregnant nineteen-year-old whose husband is in jail comes by for lunch. An eighteen-year-old boy who has already been in Korea ("five months, twenty-nine days, and three hours") before the army discovered his true age, and arrested in Mississippi for having no money in his pockets, and "in prison" (as he tells it) in a federal Job Corps camp, comes to ask them for $30.00 to pay a week's rent, until his first pay check arrives. (He woke up one morning recently to find that the seventeen-year-old girl he was sleeping with had marriage papers, with his signature, which he could not remember signing; the girl's mother, a prostitute, had encouraged their relationship.)

The Appalachians do not understand northern bureaucracy. They are charged 15–30 per cent interest by salesmen who sell them "installment purchases." They do not know that they have rights regarding their landlords and the city government. They are shunted from office to office, distrusted, accused of lying and other immoralities on the merest assumption. They perceive immediate human relationships more clearly than anything else—family, a few friends. The skills of living in an impersonal urban center elude them. Yet hundreds of thousands of Appalachians will be moving into cities in the next decade. The Glenmary Sisters are trying to invent techniques for helping them: block clubs, clean-up campaigns, block parties, choral groups, folk singing, job hunting. The sisters try to become links between the migrants and the rest of the city.

On the opposite side of the block from the Glenmary's three-room apartment is a huge yellow-brick convent, in which six sisters—never seen in the streets—are living. In a building that size, at least ninety Appalachians would be crowded. From the street, one can see a gleaming silver service on a white linen tablecloth at the huge three-story priest's house on the next corner. Four priests live there. The solid school building—once that of an upper middle-class Irish parish—stands locked and unused after school hours.

One of the Glenmary Sisters—they maintain two apartments, a block apart—teaches at Mundelein College; her salary helps to support the others. Some of the girls from Mundelein come down to help and make friends, tutor, and organize parties in the neighborhood. Between the wealthy high-rise apartments on the lakefront and Clark Street, as in a valley between their native mountains, the Appalachians are born, suffer, return South in battered jalopies, and come back again.

The Glenmary Sisters are discovering among the Appalachians what genuine community is. Sister Evelyn confesses that she joined Glenmary because she didn't like "the institutional kind of nuns." The sisters poke fun at the traditional nun's title of "mother general": "Does she wear five stars on her shoulder or something?"

Even the student sisters of the Glenmary's are different. Eight of them live in an apartment together in Milwaukee, where they are studying for degrees in history, sociology, English, painting, and other fields. Sister Germaine Habjan composes folk songs, which the entire community sings. In November, 1965, two graduate students from Marquette were married in the living-room chapel of the sisters, and the whole group sang two of Sister Germaine's songs: "Love One Another" and "All of My Life, I Will Sing Praise to My God." Recently, the sisters were saddened because the use of folk music in the liturgy was forbidden by the Archbishop of Milwaukee, as "unsuited" for worship. On Sunday mornings, nevertheless, Marquette students crowd into the dining room and living room of the Glenmary apartment for the Eucharist, and for coffee and rolls afterwards. The eight lovely, talented sisters are not afraid to "mix with seculars," but instead are strengthened thereby in their service of God's people.

It does not seem fanciful to see in the Glenmary Sisters,* and in other new sisters who are trying to revolutionize convent life in a similar pattern, a return to the original practice of dedicated women in the Church. They dress like other women; they move about in the adult, lay world without fear; they are sustained by the strength of their own inner freedom, love, and desire to serve God's people; they are unhampered by the medieval institutionalization, modern impersonality, rules, regulations, and nineteenth-century practices which inhibit so many sisterhoods.

V I

Why do women become sisters?

In the South Pacific during the Second World War, an American sergeant watched an American missionary sister tend a family stricken with advanced leprosy. He said loud enough for her to hear: "I wouldn't do that for a million dollars." She replied: "Neither would I."

The sociologist points out that for countless daughters of Irish (and other) immigrants, the Roman Catholic sisterhoods have offered status, security, and acceptance in the educated middle class. The psychologist points out that some girls who are afraid of their sexuality, uncertain of their own worth, or unable to make independent decisions, find in the sisterhoods a perfect excuse for avoiding contact with men, and a guaranteed route to official sanctity, honor, and prestige.

But, in the daily life of the sister, only love for a hidden, often seemingly distant, God provides the sustenance of spirit that makes their life worth its sacrifices. The sister lives by faith. Praying in the dark chapel, while the benches creak, she directs her will, her

* Whose experiments, nevertheless, were set back seriously by regulations imposed on them by Archbishop Alter of Cincinnati late in 1966.

thoughts, her affections to one she does not see, but in whom she has the utmost confidence. Prayer, to a sister, is like water to fish or fresh air to healthy lungs. It is a constant "yes" to God's will. It is a frequently renewed awareness that she is always in his presence. Sisters deplore every discussion of their way of life which overlooks their love for God. "Without faith," a New York sister says, "my life would be absurd."

The new sisters share deeply in this faith. But what distinguishes them is that they are bursting with the desire not to let their faith be hidden, "like a candle under a basket." They became sisters in order to live as closely in the presence of God as they could, and in order to serve God's needy people. It is their ardor to seek God wherever he is, and to serve his people according to real present needs, that leads them to criticize the present convent system. The conservative sisters, on the other hand, moved by the same love of God, fear the risks and dangers of too much mingling with the secular world. Whereas sisters of the old school find God in quiet, retirement, obedience, peace, the new sisters find God in people, in the city, in initiative, in conflict, as well as in prolonged periods of silent prayer. Thus the theological orientation of the new sisters differs from that of the old. But the fundamental love for God, the fundamental spirit of faith, is the same.

"I've watched the young sisters for the last five years," reports an older sister, for many years a highly ranked superior in her community. "At first I was suspicious. But I have watched them at prayer, and I have seen their charity for one another, and also for sisters who don't approve of them. They are not like we were in my generation. But they are beautiful religious. We can be proud of them."

For the sisters, holiness is to be found through their daily work. A tiny minority of American sisters, some two thousand, belong to fully cloistered, contemplative sisterhoods; their entire lives are spent in silence, prayer, and whatever limited work they can do within the cloister. The Poor Clares in Chicago, for example, print lovely bookmarks—one card cites the novelist Léon Bloy in red letters upon a golden ball: "Joy is the most infallible sign of the Presence of God." Another cites Teilhard de Chardin: "May the Lord only preserve in me a burning love for the world and a great gentleness;

and may he help me persevere to the end in the fullness of humanity."
The contemplative sisters, like the active ones, are in great turmoil;
new vocations have dropped off alarmingly. Many contemplatives are
coming to be inspired by the new theology, and wish to develop their
intellectual and artistic gifts to the utmost, making their contribution
even from behind the walls of their enclosure to the present renewal
of the human spirit.

Most of the sisters find that holiness lies in serving men—in nursing, orphanages, homes for the elderly; thus most sisters join the
"active" communities. Of the 175,000 American sisters, an estimated
105,000 teach—most of them in elementary and secondary schools,
the rest in the 140 sisters' colleges (and 26 junior colleges) around
the country. Many of the sisters' colleges are small, having 500 or
fewer students; often they are more or less isolated out in the countryside. On every level, the sisters have been making strides, especially
through the S.F.C., to improve their own professional competence
and to raise the standards of their schools. In some sections of the
country, students in Catholic schools rank lower on standard achievement tests than students in other schools; but often they rank higher—
Catholic schools can be selective in whom they accept. Over all, the
sisters are justly proud of their performance, although their own
self-criticism is growing healthily.

A more profound question often arises among them: Are Catholic
schools worth the effort? Couldn't the sisters do better as professional
public school teachers, or even better by setting up youth centers in
each parish district for after-school hours? Studies seem to show that,
in observable moral and religious behavior and reported attitudes,
Catholic school children do not differ appreciably from public school
children. In religious terms, then, is the vast expenditure of money
upon the Catholic school system worth the effort? Some sisters answer
a ringing Yes! Others are not so sure.

One community of sisters is already carrying out what Defense
Secretary McNamara might call a "cost accounting" of an alternative
to their commitment to the Catholic schools. They are trying to figure
out whether they could support themselves as a community—care
for their aged and their sick—if they abandoned their present school
assignments, and asked their sisters to seek salaried jobs in the public

schools, Operation Headstart, social services, and the rest. How much do they presently depend upon their earnings from their girls' colleges and salaries from the Catholic schools (usually $125.00 per sister per month, plus upkeep of the convent building)? Could they successfully finance ventures in other directions?

One new educational field that attracts the new sisters is teaching and counseling at secular colleges and universities. In 1965, at least two dozen sisters accepted positions as assistants to the Newman center chaplains at various universities; more are scheduled to enter the work next year. Many students find it easier to bring their problems to a sister than to a priest; the priest seems to play a more judgmental role in their eyes. Five out of eight Catholics in college are on secular campuses; they have been largely neglected by the Church in the past. Some new sisters feel they can serve more effectively on a secular campus than through teaching (say) mathematics in a Catholic college; and even courses in theology seem to be more exciting, more controversial, in a secular atmosphere.

On the elementary and secondary school level, some sisters argue that the sisters should cut back on the number of their schools, and aim for quality. The Catholic schools are freer from political pressure than the public schools and could attempt educational experiments of a very high order, both among the poor and among the upper classes. The Sisters of Loretto in Kansas City are experimenting in their Loretto Academy with a nongraded school in which the students proceed at their own pace, as one subject after another catches their developing curiosity. Students have responded well to the initiative placed in their own hands; parents are delighted.

"One of the things we greatly admire in Loretto," says Mrs. John Hodes III, "is the way the teacher tries to stimulate the greatest amount of imagination in the student." Mrs. A. W. Kaufmann points out that Loretto helps to overcome educational blocks: "The greatest thing that ever happened to our child was to transfer from a school where she was convinced that she was too stupid to learn to Loretto where incentive, reprimand and approval made her eager to work. After receiving a good report she said, 'I guess I have some brains after all.' "

VII

What then are the prospects for the future? Sisterhoods vary in hopefulness. Many sisters resist serious renewal; many who passionately desire change are blocked by tokenism, insecurity, fear, the vast network of real estate, schools and hospitals, and unmodernized canon law. But the two factors that inhibit renewal most are the political naiveté of sisters and certain emotional barriers.

"We study too much canon law, pious literature and scholastic philosophy," says the astute Mother Patricia Barrett of St. Louis, author of an often quoted study of voting patterns in the presidential election of 1960, "and not enough politics. The sisters don't know enough pragmatism, so they don't know how to benefit by the democratic structures in their own communities." In her study of the organizational dynamics of three representative American sisterhoods, Sister Roseanne Murphy discovered that some sisters merely go through the motions of voting for officers: they vote for what they think their present officers want. Other sisters think of authority as a reward for long and faithful service; they don't so much seek good leadership as give a vote of commendation. In other communities what one sister calls "government by dynasty" emerges: outgoing officers point out their successors. In short, although the structures of convent life are highly democratic, calling for the election of major officers and representative bodies (called chapters) at six-year intervals, obedience to existing authority often outweighs critical personal responsibility.

A favorite word of the new sisters is "dialog." The reason for this is that communication between officers and members of religious communities is sometimes rudimentary. In *Asylums,* Professor Erving Goffman has shocked many of the new sisters by his study of "total institutions" like mental hospitals, the army, prisons—and convents. Goffman's references show that he has not made a first-hand study of convents, but taken his material from books like Monica Baldwin's *I Leapt Over the Wall* and Kathryn Hulme's *The Nun's Story.* Still, his book has been eagerly studied by the new sisters and was favorably reviewed by Sister Aloysius Schaldenbrand in the *National Catholic Reporter.* In a total institution, the "staff" exercises control over the decisions and attitudes of their "subjects." The staff trains the inmates to treat authority figures as separate, aloof, and sacred. The sense of outside values is broken; the world of the inmates is deliberately narrowed. Communication between staff and members cannot be frank, because it is not between equals. In the name of loyalty and "their own good," the critical faculties of inmates are put to sleep.

In sisterhoods which most resemble "total institutions," superiors are most likely to warn against grumbling and criticism in the ranks; but since the staff is so elevated above the other sisters, the "criticism" is in fact no more than futile griping. In such situations, the new sisters cry out for "dialog" with a passion. One of the greatest fruits of Vatican II was the introduction, in nearly all sisterhoods, of regular self-study projects, discussion committees, and both written and open airing of suggestions for renewal and reform.

In brief, the first factor which retards renewal among some sisterhoods is the lack of an acute, critical, democratic sense in the election of good officers. Concomitantly, clear avenues of frank criticism and warm communication are not kept open. "A Christian sisterhood should not be run like an army, let alone an asylum," one sister exclaims. "Why can't sisters treat one another like adults, trust one another, help one another with criticism? We should call no one 'mother' [as in mother superior], for none of us are children. We can find unity of wills without putting anyone up on a pedestal and waiting for orders. Other Americans do it all the time."

The second factor which inhibits renewal is the feeling of dependency which has come to characterize many sisters, particularly the older ones. In the old system, sisters did not handle money, or buy their own clothing, food, or toilet articles. Their unusual dress effectively removed them from being treated like other adults, with candor and directness; it also gave them, over and beyond their personal talents, status and authority. Moreover, by its large numbers and its regularity, the older system gave the illusion, but often not the reality, of community; the sister knew that she would be fed and housed, and cared for when old, even if she did not have a single close friend who knew her secret thoughts and her hidden emotions. She could feel part of a great institution, whose praises she would uninterruptedly hear sung. The new sisters, however, are a threat to this whole pattern of life. Personal responsibility, new clothes, money, critical freedom, love, meeting people, irregular hours—many a sister can hardly suppress a shudder of insecurity.

Besides, many of the older sisters have become so focused upon the trivia of institutional life, upon questions of rank (in some convents, every community action is done according to the seniority established by the date on which one entered the convent), upon literal fidelity to rules, and upon issues of nunlike propriety, that the indifference of the new sisters to such matters is held to be proof of moral turpitude. After watching four thoughtful and sensitive sisters answer questions for two hours on David Susskind's "Open End," one older sister was asked her opinion. She frowned: "Sister Jacqueline had her legs crossed all during the show. All four of them laughed too loud." The irony is that the most conservative sisters are often the very ones who in the past manipulated community rules to secure exceptional treatment for themselves; one such sister spent three weeks of every summer at her family's beach house; another traveled to Ireland every other summer.

Sister Claire Marie Sawyer, sociologist from Milwaukee, calls attention to another factor to be considered; in many communities the older sisters seriously outnumber the younger. In one community of 3000, 250 sisters are already retired, and sixty per cent are older than forty. Moreover, sisters have so long thought of themselves in terms of usefulness that there is a subtle linking of ability to work with personal value: "If I can work, then I am worth something."

Again, in many communities it is somehow taken to be a disgrace for a superior to become a subject again; thus over the years a class system emerges, particularly among the higher echelons of the community. Since in almost all communities, the decision-making power rests with officers and councillors of an advanced age, and since it is sometimes only the younger sisters who are trained in the new theology, insecurity and tension mount wherever the major officers lack understanding. The recent trend toward the election of younger and more vigorous mothers general should help to alleviate such tensions. The mothers general face some sisters terrified by the rapidity of change and others appalled by its slowness.

Father Elio Gambari of the Roman Congregation for Religious said in 1963: "We have seen more changes in the last decade and a

half than the Church has seen since the Council of Trent [1546–64]."
Almost simultaneously, a survey of 360 superiors from fifty-five
American sisterhoods showed that 95 per cent expected many further changes in the role and image of the sister within the next twenty
years, and 34 per cent expected the changes to be radical. Still,
some sisters do not see much hope for serious changes in their communities during their lifetime. "What good is it to change our dress
from circa 1820 to circa 1920?" one sister asks. "The changes in
our community deal only with trifles—things that all American adults
take for granted."

Paradoxically, at the very moment when the Second Vatican
Council has promoted a wave of renewal and reform in the entire
Church, perhaps more sisters than ever before are asking to be dis-
pensed from their vows and leaving the convent. No hard statistics
are available, but competent sisters estimate that in 1965 about 3,300
sisters left, or almost two per cent. In some communities, fewer
girls are entering now, too, and fewer go on to final profession. But
other communities have so far experienced no more "defections"
than hitherto—"Not more than 2 in 300 sisters in the last ten years,"
one sister writes.

A Sister of Mercy says: "In our community, the younger sisters
live a 'hothouse' formation for seven or eight years, in a world composed entirely of sisters. When they accept their first professional
duties, they are in their middle or late twenties, sometimes highly
intelligent, well-trained in their fields. In the next five years comes
the crisis." An older, Midwestern sister adds: "It sometimes happens
that superiors, less well-trained, may have an inferiority complex
and quite unconsciously set out to crush a bright young girl. Or other
older sisters, who resist the young one's new ideas, may launch cruel
calumnies about what a poor religious she is. Or she herself may
become depressed with the general comfortable mediocrity." An
Eastern sister writes: "When a well-trained sister sees a beloved
school or project or organization, a worthwhile, beneficial thing,
falling to pieces because of an inefficient superior, then, despite all
the blithe talk about obeying superiors, it is only the terribly holy
or the terribly foolish who can remain cool and uninvolved."

Ironically, it is sometimes the more open and advanced communities that seem to be losing the highest number of sisters. Some sister

observers think that it is often the most intelligent and most sensitive
who leave. But a good number of those who leave the convent are
now establishing new types of communities on their own, or teaching
as lay women in other parochial or public schools, or taking a more
direct part in the work of the inner city, like one former sister from
Webster College who has taken charge of a special racially integrated
school in Boston. Should such women count among those who leave?
Who *are* the women who leave the convent? Why do they leave?
What becomes of them? A national survey is being launched by several sisters to answer such questions.

In outline, a tentative opinion seems to be that in the last few
years the expectations of the new sisters have jumped enormously,
far beyond what the more conservative sisters are prepared to allow.
Some women, with only one life to spend for the Church, can no
longer spend it conscientiously in institutions which of necessity must
change with "deliberate speed." Other women, more conservative,
are oppressed by the sudden uncertainties of convent life; their sense
of stability has evaporated. Still others have suddenly become critically awake, after years of devoted, unquestioning service.

One such girl was Alice Watson, a registered nurse who entered
one of the most inflexible of American sisterhoods, a nursing and
missionary community, in 1950. She spent three years in the Congo,
and until the Vatican Council was so intent upon becoming "a good
religious" and "doing her duty" that, in conversation with other
sisters, she always defended authority, even when she disagreed with
its decisions. She received reprimands for not immediately answering
the bell for community exercises when a patient needed help; or for
pausing to congratulate one of her students after his confirmation,
when she was supposed to be keeping silence. She suddenly realized
she was being treated as a child; her superior used to inspect each
private room, and snoop into every drawer, leaving pink slips of
paper wherever things were untidy. When questionnaires concerning
reform were sent to each house, her superior filled them out herself,
without telling the sisters. A clique of eight or ten women controlled
the politics of the community.

When Miss Watson finally left her community, hoping then to
establish a small group of her own based on more evangelical and
flexible principles, she was sent away without money; and the last

words from her superior were, when Miss Watson at last signed her papal dispensation and asked when she might leave: "The sooner the better."

Miss Watson soon was earning a good income for herself as a nurse in the West, until she had the opportunity to enroll in a Montessori school. "I've never been happier," she says a year later, though she admits that the first year was difficult. "The surprising thing is that I'm not lonely any longer. I have forty wonderful children in my class, and good people, really good people, to work with. When I get home to my room at night, I feel free and just . . . just very good." She has not entirely forgotten her dream of opening a new kind of evangelical community; but she had one disillusioning experience last summer with several restless, insecure sisters who wished to join her on a special project. She is now, for the first time, beginning to think of marriage as a Christian way of life open to her; the sheer Christianity of her married friends has taught her a new perspective. In her convent, all nonclerics were called "seculars" or "worldlings," and sisters were forbidden to mix with them unduly.

Not all stories of ex-nuns are filled with such vivid contrasts. But it is one of the scandals of convent practices which the new sisters wish to correct that those who decide to leave are treated so poorly and cut off from their former companions like dead limbs, forbidden sometimes to write to their friends. "Is this what we mean by Christian community?" a Midwestern sister asks. Moreover, the new sisters recognize that a religious vocation is not a mysterious "call" from God, which arrives in some magical manner; God does not speak as someone outside them but through the free and reflective decisions of their own conscience. When they conscientiously decide what they wish to become, then *that* is God speaking in them. Consequently, to leave the convent is not to "turn one's back on God," but to follow him where self-critical, reflective judgment leads. "For myself," says Sister Claire Marie Sawyer, "I think it would be throwing away a tremendous grace to leave the convent in this transitional period; but I understand how others are led differently. We each serve the Church; we are all Christians."

No doubt, every one of the new sisters has thought of leaving the convent; a decision to remain a sister, they argue, should be made anew every day. It is not that their commitment is temporary; not at all. It is rather that they wish their commitment to be realistic, meaningful, conscious, reflective; for them a vocation is not a matter of drifting. Besides they are fully aware that, whereas twenty years ago the only outlet by which women could give dedicated service to the Church was the sisterhood, today the possibilities and responsibilities of the lay woman in the world are much more fully recognized. The new sister sees herself as serving in one role among many; she is glad to be where she is, but she does not think the world begins and ends with the convent.

VIII

The move toward renewal in the convents has not been merely organizational; it has been a grass roots movement. Often older sisters take part in it with as much zest as younger sisters, and often they prove to be more flexible. The older sisters came to see during the Vatican Council that canon law was not the absolute they had thought it was, and all the conclusions contrary to canon law which they had long been tempted to by common sense now gained a legitimacy in their minds. There is hardly a sister who has not had to obey some rule which she thought was un-Christian: forbidden to attend a brother's wedding, forbidden to visit her parents' home even if she was stationed only a few blocks away, etc. The roots of the renewal lie in common sense, and in a more biblical, freer conscience. The new sisters wish to free themselves from outmoded institutional structures in order to be effective, committed Christians in the world.

But what, then, is to distinguish a sister from an ordinary lay woman? What is the essence of the sister's life? The new sisters argue such questions incessantly. Poverty, celibacy, obedience—it is plain that in the slums of our cities there is a biting poverty which sisters do not experience. As for the "spirit" of poverty, many of their brothers and sisters struggling to raise a family must practice more detachment from worldly goods than sisters. Obedience? In modern society, does not everyone work with others in such a way that the common good and common purposes of all must be respected? As for celibacy, some of the new sisters question whether even that is truly biblical. They see that celibacy is supposed to free them for a full-time dedication to the service of men which their married sisters who have children can hardly attain; but if institutional living takes such freedom away from them again, what meaning does celibacy have? They do not think that loving a human being takes away from one's love of God. The new sisters are not afraid of their femininity, nor are they reluctant to accept a meaningful celibacy. But they do not admire celibacy for celibacy's sake.

The other pillar of religious life, besides the three vows, is "the common life." From the urban poor, however, the new sisters are learning that living in the same building with other people, sharing the same lot, does not of itself create community. The poor in the inner city are often doing more for the sisters who come on weekends or free evenings to help them than the sisters are able to do for the poor. "What's the mattah, ya tired today, sistah? Ya have ta take care of yor'self, sistah. I worry about ya."

Entering into the real lives and sufferings of the poor, many sisters are discovering what it means to care for others, and to be cared about. As they try to build up pride and community in block clubs in the Pruitt-Igoe complex of public housing in St. Louis, or in East Garfield Park in Chicago, they learn the unimportance of the proprieties by which they have tried to live in the convents. Cleanliness, grammar, the appearance of things, politeness, reserve, emotional distance, the traditional role of teacher to children—all such barriers to reality collapse the first time they are asked by the strangers they are trying to help: "Where do y'all live, sistah? Where is yo' family?"

Consequently, the attraction which the inner city is exercising upon the imagination of thousands of American sisters, even those who never go to the inner city, is not shallow. They are learning there the meaning of genuine human community, genuine human sharing. Moreover, as Sister Angelica Seng of the Cabrini project in mid-Chicago notes, "They are also learning the importance of the twentieth-century struggle against the authoritarian structures in all our lives." Sister Angelica, like so many of the new sisters, is a trained sociologist. From her office in a partially abandoned parochial school, which has been turned into a community center for the tens of thousands of people living in new housing projects, she can look across at the Jenner Street Public School, scene of a bitter argument in Chicago. Negro families want equal attention from the school board for their children in that school; they have a list of grievances.

In the ensuing dispute, the sisters of the Cabrini project were not allowed by the archdiocese to join the picketing. "The sisters came to see, that they, too, are part of a system," Sister Angelica says. "And all the systems interlock." At first bitter towards the sisters, Negro leaders came to see that the sisters, too, were trapped by the system; a sense of common identity was established. "The real leaders are courteous to us, but they don't think the sisters can understand. To be honest, I'm not sure we always can."

The new sisters have discovered in the inner city an image of the sisters' own lack of community, an image of the lack of communication in their own community structures, and a sense of how far removed they have been from the hard struggles of millions of human beings. "I can never go back to my beautiful Lake Michigan campus and be comfortable again," Sister Mary Gabriel of Racine reported after a summer stint in such projects.

Thus, the heart of the renewal does not consist of changing into a knee-length dress, or of eating dinner in public with "seculars," or even of calling a sister's bedroom a bedroom instead of a monastic "cell," or even of allowing the sisters to decorate their bedrooms as brightly as they please (though all these changes are being made in some communities). It lies in returning sisters as women to the world for which God had so much love he sent his son. The new sisters wish to be committed Christians, not in sheltered institutions, but in the midst of ordinary men and women. Of what use are large institutions, they ask, when they have lost their savor?

I X

Experiments already undertaken provide a look at how the sisterhoods of the future might develop. While the Sisters of Loretto, the Immaculate Heart Sisters, the Sisters of the Blessed Virgin Mary, and the Glenmary Sisters are, each in their different way, leading the other sisterhoods into the future, some imaginative women have skipped ahead several steps. They have founded small associations in which they live out a new form of religious life.

One such group is made up of six women, formerly sisters in the midwest, who left their sisterhoods to look for a more flexible mode of dedicated service. By chance, they made contact with Bishop Walter W. Curtis of Bridgeport, Connecticut, who offered to rent them living quarters and to hire them to teach in a new, lay Catholic college in his diocese. The six women, aged thirty to forty-five, have tried to avoid publicity. Emphatically, they do not wish to become a refuge or jumping-off place for ex-nuns, although already dozens of applications have piled up, unanswered, in their hall. For want of a better name, they are known as "the Christian Institute."

They dress as other women their age dress—on Sunday afternoon, a visitor at the door finds one of them in slacks and a University of Texas sweatshirt, the others in assorted dresses, slacks, sweaters. They live now on a small suburban farm, though they would like to find a place in the city slums. Four of them teach in college. One, a professional social worker, is hired by the federal Office of Economic Opportunity to help the Negro and Puerto Rican teen-agers of the Bridgeport slums to learn the skills of competitive white society. The other is a secretary. Putting their salaries together, these women have been able to help one another further their studies: one has spent a year in Florence, Italy, studying painting; a second will go to Europe next year for advanced studies in theology.

"The Christian Institute's only rule is: 'Love one another as I have loved you,'" says Sylvia Tackowiak, their leader. "Our aim is to witness to Christ through a life of evangelical perfection." The members assume that each of them is adult, mature, and has the interests of the whole group at heart; such persons need few rules. They will accept newcomers to their group only if they have sufficient professional competence to support themselves, wish to live a celibate life, and choose to give meaning to their professional occupations through living in a Christian household. The women make whatever vows they choose, in the privacy of their own conscience, although they do renew their dedication to the Institute annually during the liturgical services of the Easter vigil. Any member is free to walk out at any time.

The experiment is only three years old, but the six are happy with one another and with their new life. They delight in the freedom and flexibility they have, all the more because all of them experienced the struggles of renewal within traditional sisterhoods. They live, in the words of St. Vincent de Paul, as "good girls of the parish," sharing in all ways the life of the nearest Catholic parish community. They have no formal link to the bishop; they reserve the right to accept, or to refuse, any task that he proposes to them. Above all, they are richly feminine: in appearance, in manner of living, in style. Their living room is simple, bright, relaxed, warm.

Meanwhile, five other attractive young women have launched the Association for Christian Development in Oklahoma City. They are not nuns, but dedicated Christian women living in community. They too dress in bright, cheerful dresses; each needs and has a car; each works at a different task, though all but one of them are on the diocesan payroll of Bishop Victor Reed, one of the most balanced and progressive of the United States bishops. Elizabeth McMahon and Connie Scott came to Oklahoma after their graduation from Manhattanville College in New York, to work as lay volunteers in what was then an understaffed, needy diocese. They loved the free and open climate of the Church in Oklahoma, and the opportunities they found for their own professional development. By 1962, they had met Mary Chrystie, another New Yorker, and Sharlene Shoemaker, a Nebraskan; in 1964, a young registered nurse from Illinois, Betty Jacober, joined them.

The five hate to be thought of as "nuns." To them the word has associations of institutionalization, rules, regulations, formalities. They wish to live a celibate, dedicated life, nourished by common life in a Christian household. Connie Scott says simply: "I want my life to speak to people of more than just me—of Christ. Not in words, but by something in myself. I want to speak as a healthy woman, as someone happy, fulfilled. I'm single, I've chosen to be so. For me the Association is a chosen way of life, the way I choose to love and to grow in love, to love Christ."

Connie runs a highly successful Montessori school for disadvantaged Negro children, and has trained several of the children's mothers to help her. Elizabeth McMahon and Mary Chrystie try to teach the Catholic parents of the entire State of Oklahoma how to educate their children in religion; Sharlene works for the statewide diocesan Youth Department. Betty Jacober works among the poor Negro children of the Walnut Grove area of Oklahoma City.

The five girls have a remarkable friend, Sister Nativity Heiliger, formerly a Sister of Mercy, who now lives, on her own, in a tiny abandoned convent in a Negro neighborhood. Sister Nativity was educated in public schools and so never experienced, she says, the "mystification" with which many Catholics surround nuns. Throughout her seventeen years in the convent, her own attitudes were common sensical; she always manifested a courageous independence. "Having been reared in a Protestant country town," she says, "where the title of brother and sister are frequently used between Christians in the community, I learned to love these titles, and to think of them as meaning availability and service." Sister Nativity maintains close ties with her friends in the Sisters of Mercy, and retains the name by which she was known for so many years. She has shortened her black skirt to normal length, and has designed a new veil for her hair; more clearly than the girls of the Institute her dress is still that of a sister, though it does not hide her femininity. "When I wear slacks or something casual for picnics and the like," she says, "I'm still Sister Nativity."

Sister Nativity has become the center of countless activities on behalf of the poor in Oklahoma City. She joins civic and neighborhood associations, and draws other sisters into them. She sponsors lectures and classes on the problems of the city. It is not surprising that the girls of the association often meet at her house. Like them, she drives her own beat-up car. Her program is simple. "The Church should go to the people instead of waiting for the people to come to it. My role here is to be a link between people who want to help and people who need help. I'm willing to stay here a long time before I see any results."

Asked, What is a sister? Sister Nativity answers: "A sister is simply a person who has chosen to make herself available as sister instead of as wife and mother. She is certainly not different from other women except as people are naturally different. She should not be set 'apart' or 'above' but simply take her place wherever people gather to communicate. She should live among friends, for she needs the human support of loving exchange. I think she should be poor, chaste, and obedient—but then I think all Christians should be that. . . . I agree with St. Irenaeus that 'The glory of God is man fully alive' and that whatever promotes life or growth is good."

X

The new sisters, still working within the institutional structures Sister Nativity has left behind, surely agree with her. They have chosen to struggle, to reform, to remake their institutions from within. I see them, in retrospect, 250-strong in the halls of St. Bridget's Church and School in the slums of St. Louis on a Sunday afternoon, each one patiently tutoring a Negro boy or girl, man or woman, in English and arithmetic. I climb behind Mother Patricia Barrett, (some eighty pounds of dynamite, she tells me she is learning ju-jitsu for self-protection) as she winds through the darkness and stench of the cement stairway to the eleventh-floor of a tenement. She has helped find a room for a mother of eight whose husband has deserted her—a room her husband could not share anyway, without forfeiting their right according to Missouri law to public assistance. I remember Sisters Judith Mary, David Maureen and Madeleva of Kansas City telling me of their new inner city quarters in an abandoned hotel on Twelfth Street: "Every morning one of us will have to get up and empty the rat traps. . . . But all these young kids in the neighborhood do it." I hear the calm, ebullient, hopeful voice of Sister Mary Luke, mother general of the Sisters of Loretto and chairman of the conference of major superiors of women, as she says: "We must experiment, that's the most important thing, experiment. Who knows what sisters will be like twenty years from now?"

As the new sisters set about creating a new style of religious life, they become the vanguard of all Americans who believe in God and who trust that "the glory of God is man fully alive." The sisters come from farther back than most other groups; their rules and traditions date from long ago. But if they can maintain their integrity, their love, their passion for justice, in the world of computers, super-markets, and slums, there is hope for all of us.

INDEX

Index

Abbot, Walter M., 210
Absurdity, 17, 40, 65, 94, 260, 295, 306, 316, 462
Action, 55–57, 68, 83, 93, 253, 318n, 337, 349n, 351n
Activism, 33, 189, 260
Adams, James Luther, 192, 235, 273
Adler, Mortimer J., 338, 352n
Africa, 2, 7, 104
Agape, 54, 355–57, 368, 370n11,14, 371n
Aggiornamente, 34, 72, 74, 109, 119, 143–44, 159, 440
Agnosticism 23, 62–63, 122, 142, 241, 243, 281, 290; *see also* Atheism
Aiken, Henry David, 55, 83–86, 94, 95n
Albright, William F., 234, 261n
Albritten, Roger, 168, 183n1,4
Allan, D. J., 339, 352n
Allport, Gordon, 22
Altizer, Thomas J. J., 48n, 234–35, 261n
Ambrose, St., 350n
Anabaptists, analogous to Catholic religious communities, 197–204; and baptism, 198, 200–3, 206; community discipline of, 204–7; and Marxist thinkers, 295; obedience and discipleship of, 199–204, 213n
Anglican Church, 19, 26, 223
Anglo-American philosophy, 89, 94, 109, 238, 251–53, 257

Anscombe, G. E. M., 168, 183n
Aquinas, Thomas, 93, 211n, 218, 231, 257, 297, 314, 317n, 327–29, 331, 370n, 371n, 384, 404; on action, 337, 351n; on active intelligence, 342; and Aristotle, 29, 336, 344, 350n; on contingency, 336–37, 342, 344, 350n; on ethical deliberation, 339–41, 346n; on ethical good, 340–41; on eucharist, 166; on first principle, 337–40, 348n; on hidden God, 318n; on practical wisdom, 340–41, 348n; on *proairesis*, 334, 341; on Providence, 336, 343–44, 353n; psychology of, 393; on reason and appetite, 344, 349n; on self-awareness, 219; on society, 372n; starting place of, 81; on substance, 165–66; on will, 341–42; world view of, 29
Aristotle, 93, 184n, 216, 230–31, 235, 263n, 297, 317n, 318n, 326–29, 348n, 366, 371n; on action, 349n; on appetite, 334, 348n; and Aquinas, 29, 336, 340–41, 344, 350n; on being, 171, 185n, 187n; on cause, 169, 175, 185n35,38; on contingency, 332, 334, 336–37 344, 350n; on deductive syllogism, 338–39; on deliberation, 346n; process of discovery, 177; as empiricist, 170–74; on essence, 168–72, 175, 177, 180, 183n, 187n59,60; ethic of,

Aristotle (*continued*)
331–35, 346*n*; on First Mover, 182, 187*n*; on formal unity, 177–78; on *kalon*, 334, 335, 346*n*, 347*n*; on knowledge, 169, 173, 184–85*n*, 186*n*, 349*n*; on "mean," 333, 346*n*, 347*n*, 384; and modern philosophy, 182, 183*n*, 185*n*, 186*n*; on pleasure and pain, 333–35, 347*n*, 366; on practical wisdom, 52, 333, 340–44; on *recta ratio*, 334, 348*n*; on substance, 165–82, 183*n*, 185*n*38,43, 186*n*, 187*n*59,61,65, 188*n*; starting place of, 81

Asia, 2, 7, 222, 233, 415, 417

Association for Christian Development, 475

Atheism, 3, 10, 20–24, 28, 33, 37–38, 44, 53, 61–62, 65, 67–69, 114, 122, 142, 237, 241, 243, 247, 254–55, 260, 281, 290, 315

Aubenque, P. 345*n*, 346*n*, 352*n*

Auden, W. H., 270

Augustine, St., 257, 304, 335; tradition of, 259, 263*n*, 350*n*

Austin, J. L., 90–91, 309, 318*n*

Authenticity, 12, 52, 296, 321, 324, 363, 393, 395

Autonomy, 98, 314–15, 342

Awareness, 85, 219, 249

Ayer, A. J., 237

Bainton, Roland H., 198, 212*n*

Baptists, 189, 191, 221, 223

Barrett, William, 25

Barth, Karl, 19–20, 32, 189, 207, 217, 222, 265*n*, 272, 281

Bartley, William W., 20–21, 291

Bax, Belford, 195

Belief, 101, 141, 201, 219, 266, 290, 302; and believers, 44–46, 62, 121, 206, 248, 315, 363; and drive to understand, 315; motive for, 160; and unbelief, 62, 121, 142, 315; *see also* God

Belief and Unbelief, 37, 50*n*, 246*n*, 263, 317*n*

Bellah, Robert N., 365, 369*n*

Bellow, Saul, 20, 48*n*

Bender, Harold S., 199

Bennett, John C., 288

Berkeley, George, 89

Bianchi, Eugene C., 330, 344*n*

Birmingham, William, 383

Birth control, 116, 122, 128–30, 148, 153, 157–58

Bishops, 5, 71, 99, 101, 110, 117–30, 146–47, 210, 441, 444–48, 475; college of, 118, 151; *see also* Catholic Church

Blackfriars, 382

Blamires, Harry, 18

Blondel, Maurice, 79–80

Bonhoeffer, Dietrich, 48*n*, 189, 232–34; on "cheap grace," 273; on meaning of Christianity, 283; his concept of God, 283; personality of, 271; reaction to, 19–21; starting place of, 267; differs from Tillich, 232

Bouillard, H., 350*n*

Bourke, Vernon J., 330

Bouyer, Louis, 329

Brandt, Richard B., 95, 309, 318*n*

Brotherhood, 48, 167, 456; among Anabaptists, 197–202

Brown, Mackenzie D., 247, 252, 263*n*, 264*n*

Bultmann, R., 20, 32, 259

Burrell, David, 312, 319*n*

Callahan, Daniel, 34, 37, 50*n*, 261*n*, 265*n*

Calvin, John, 191, 194, 195

Calvinists, 189, 191, 195, 295

Camus, Albert, 1, 3, 5, 24, 35, 45, 52–53, 55, 64, 66–67, 70, 216, 266–68, 277, 297, 311, 312, 406, 418, 452

Canon law, 116–17, 126, 330, 383–84, 395, 401*n*, 436–37, 444, 465, 471

Capitalism, 4, 118, 222, 223

Caritas, 132, 231, 257, 370*n*; *see also* Charity

Carmichael, Stokely, 13

Cartesian philosophy, 169, 185*n*, 218, 258

Categories, The, 165, 168–76, 183*n*, 187*n*54,59

Catholic Church, 5, 32, 43, 144, 165, 221, 224, 317; and Anabaptists, 197–204; reasons for belief in, 62; Celtic heresy in, 70, 117; community life of, 98, 100, 110, 124, 140–47, 475 (*see also* Dioceses,

Parishes); criticism in, 100, 122, 127, 129, 131, 144, 227–28, 257–58; hierarchy of, 99–100, 108, 110, 115, 117, 121–22, 162, 205, 210, 223 (*see also* Bishops); intellectual life in, 79–80, 108–9, 114–15, 124, 133, 143, 329, 354, 447; in Italy, 79, 100, 108, 115; moral theology of, 70, 329, 383, 388–89; nature of, 106–7, 115; and Protestants, 42, 160, 190, 193–95, 198, 220, 224, 330; relevance of, 72–74, 229; religious liberty in, 101, 196; renewal of, 34, 42, 97–98, 159, 190, 227, 321; traditional view of, 106–10, 115, 139, 159, 295, 354, 383; in United States, 23, 70, 74, 97, 100, 112–33, 329, 392, 448–49

Celibacy, 125, 199, 394, 444, 457, 471–72, 474–76

Charity, 343, 350n, 351n, 453, 462

Chenu, M. D., 353n

Christian Institute, The, 474

Christian Realism and Political Problems, 356, 370n

Christianity, 54, 256, 287, 374, 383, 419, 441; and atheism, 7, 20–21, 37–45, 50, 58–59, 266–67; and community, 34–35, 75–77, 168; contemporary, 7–8, 38–39, 168; and ethics, 53, 267, 288; future of, 5, 7–8, 13, 18, 22, 28, 30–34; historical, 6, 29, 31, 34, 253, 259, 455; intellectual tradition of, 18, 32, 218; and Judaism, 109, 266; and Marxism, 294–96; meaning of, 58–59, 77, 283; medieval, 166–67; nature of, 29, 31, 33, 47, 200–1, 276, 282–83; and philosophy, 25, 239; Platonic, 29, 263n, 278–79; and politics, 2, 20, 222, 268; relevance of, 20, 33–36, 168, 222, 268; "religionless," 19–21, 31–37, 46, 282; and secular culture, 321, 364; symbols of, 25, 31–32, 38–39, 42, 46; structures in, 192; and theology, 25, 61, 239; world view of, 23–24

Christianity and Crisis, 241

Christianity and Encounter with World Religions, 39

Church, 13, 14, 25, 34, 221, 222, 373; checks and balances in, 50, 111,

117, 126, 146, 151, 159; as community, 365–66, 403; problems of institutional, 13, 20, 34, 42, 74–76, 100, 105, 120–21, 124–27, 139–44, 149, 204–5, 411; meaning of, 363–64; nature of, 106, 129, 199, 213n, 364; distinguished from sect, 197, 213n; and state, 364; *see also* Catholic Church, Christianity

Clergy, 65, 100, 105, 109, 115, 140, 145, 147, 206, 258, 289

Cogley, John, 71, 103, 367, 372n

Cognition, 57, 82, 86–94, 246, 251, 258, 306, 334

Cohn, Norman, 195, 362, 373n

Cold War, 412, 414–15

Commentary, 43, 181

Commitment, 64, 253, 296, 452, 470–71; to critical intelligence, 81–82, 91; voluntary, 198, 203

Commonweal, 270

Communism, 4, 130, 222–23, 294, 361, 412–15, 418, 422–23, 425, 427–28

Community, Anabaptist compared to Catholic religious, 197–204; of conscience, 369; ethics of, 354–69; of faith, 66, 76–77, 157, 164, 166–68 206, 210, 248, 259, 363–64; historical, 98, 324; and identity, 354, 358–59; sense of, 136; structures of, 135–38; theonomous, 159

Compassion, 45, 74, 243, 254, 258, 266, 313

Concilium, 372n

Concluding Unscientific Postscript, 258, 269

Concupiscence, 384, 386–87

Congar, Yves, 104, 190

Conscience, 73, 75, 77, 101, 106, 126, 131, 156–57, 206, 220–23, 250, 275, 312, 365, 369, 394, 405, 455, 470–71, 474; Aquinas on, 341–42; of church, 119, 150; fidelity to, 314; informed, 158; sovereignty of personal, 111; personal vs. public, 130

Consciousness, 86, 110, 183–84n, 305–6; Christian, 206, 218, 223, 225; empirical, 89, 92; intellectual, 89, 92, 95; mythic, 84; national, 409; rational, 89, 92, 95; self-, 259

Consensus, 143, 205–10

Conservatism, in church, 19, 79, 110, 154, 203, 433, 447, 454, 456; of moral code, 403-4; in politics, 413
Constantinian order, 192, 195, 196, 204-5, 208-10
Contemporary Moral Theology, 330, 383n, 384n, 401n
Contingency, 36, 80-81, 108, 132, 332-36, 341, 344
Contraception, 154, 344n, 374, 376, 389, 391, 394-95, 397, 400
Contraception, 116
Copi, Irving, 168, 183n
Copleston, Frederick, 331, 345n
Coreth, Emerich, 83, 85, 87, 91, 93, 95n
Courage To Be, The, 232, 236, 256
Covenant, 205-8, 210
Cox, Harvey, 33, 48n, 270, 284n, 286, 288, 291, 292, 296, 297, 343
"Crisis theology," 20, 48n, 233
Cross Currents, 401n
Crowe, F. E., 90

Daedalus, 372n
Daughters of Charity, 456, 458
Dawson, Christopher, 24, 30
"Death of God" theology, 2, 3, 19, 32, 33, 44, 48n, 49n, 70, 270, 286-91
Decision, 82-83, 297, 309, 325, 366
Descartes, René, 79, 92, 108, 168, 169, 183n, 218
Dewart, Leslie, 37, 50n
Dewey, John, 88, 238, 239
Dioceses, 100, 110, 140, 445
Disciples of Christ, 191
Discipline, 115, 202, 204-9, 211, 253, 375, 454
Dissent, 12, 117, 123, 360, 427
Docility, 127, 243, 297
Doctrine, 227, 262n; of Assumption, 101, 112; development of, 152-53, 164, 383
Dominicans, 433, 455-56
Dostoevsky, Fyodor, 23, 53, 281
Downside Review, 336, 350n
Drive to ask questions, 37-40, 46, 68, 79, 82, 85, 92, 167, 245, 250, 293-94, 298; see also Inquiry
Drive to understand, 86-87, 90-94, 122, 138, 142, 218, 245, 251, 293, 306-8, 313, 315, 319n

Dunne, John S., 12
Dupré, Louis, 392, 393
Dynamics of Faith, 236, 253, 262n, 263n28,41

Ecclesiam Suam, 109
Ecumenism, 42, 44, 110, 115, 119, 128, 148-9, 159, 164, 191, 220, 223, 230, 301, 321
Ecumenist, The, 330, 344n8,10
Edwards, Paul, 234, 238, 239, 241, 243, 245
Eliot, T. S., 30, 103, 362, 372n
Emerson, Ralph Waldo, 64
Emotive component, 57, 251, 253, 258, 306, 334
Empiricism, 81, 170-72, 174, 238, 242, 245, 247, 249, 251-53, 262n
England, religion in, 25-26, 108, 110, 194, 205; see also Anglo-American philosophy
Enlightenment, The, 24, 25, 360
Epistemology, 57, 80, 185n, 219, 262n
Erikson, Erik, 332, 345n, 358, 371n
Eros, 87, 90, 332, 336, 356, 370n
Eschatology, 202, 222-23, 284, 295, 322, 392, 410
Essays in Applied Christianity, 216, 220, 228, 229, 338, 352n, 369
Ethical judgment, 21, 24, 33, 52-53, 89, 95, 136, 181, 201, 366, 410-11
Ethical Theory, 95, 309, 318
Ethics, 44, 230, 311, 323, 334, 343, 360, 368, 371n, 373; Christian, 201, 330, 355; ethical good, 340; particularity of, 345; situation, 51; social and individual, 355; and the young, 332, 345n
Eucharist, 13, 101, 112-13, 144, 165-68, 294, 439, 440, 461
Evidence, criteria of, 95, 245, 250, 359, 366, 368
Evil, 2, 122, 323, 367, 387, 405, 412, 426
Existentialism, 25, 32, 33, 91, 131, 201, 245, 252, 257, 267, 276, 296
Experience, 21, 56, 166, 201, 217, 238, 240, 249, 306-7, 332, 356, 368; cognitional, 40, 82, 84, 86, 88-94, 171, 176, 246, 311, 317, 333; faithful to, 317; no language for, 64; and practical wisdom, 333;

religious, 38, 249, 266; sense, 170, 172, 179, 182, 187*n*, 188*n*; subjective, 193, 200

Fackenheim, Emil L., 38, 39, 46, 50*n*
Faith, 146, 218, 242, 383; of Anabaptists, 204, 208; of Catholics, 101, 113–14, 116, 139, 142, 152–53, 163; crisis of, 70, 140–41, darkness of, 36–37, 291, 369*n*; in God, 18, 62, 63, 67, 236, 239, 313; justification by, 149, 273; and obedience, 123; personal, 140, 461; philosophic, 81, 322; religious, 35, 42, 44–46, 66, 120, 131, 168, 209, 256, 259; secular, 62; and tradition, 302; understanding of, 21, 25; see also Belief
Fall, The, 24, 31, 268, 317
Fiedler, Leslie, 413
Findlay, T. N., 313, 319*n*
Fontinell, Eugene, 37, 50*n*
Ford, John C., 330, 383–84, 401*n*3,4
Fornication, 375, 377–78, 381, 387
France, 79, 104, 108
Franciscans, 197–98, 336, 433, 456
Franck, Sebastian, 205
Free Church tradition, 191-92, 208, 284; see also Anabaptists
Freedom, in the Catholic Church, 98, 123, 126, 205, 228; new nuns on, 441, 448, 451, 454, 455, 461, 467, 472; Péguy on, 159; in society, 138, 221, 367; and theology, 161, 223, 300, 315, 319*n*, 337
Freud, Sigmund, 21, 22, 24, 35, 40, 45, 248, 255
Friedmann, Robert, 197, 198, 199, 212*n*12,23
Fromm, Erich, 371*n*
Fuchs, Josef, 327
Furfey, Paul Hanly, 1
Future, Christian-Marxist meaning of the, 294–300
Future of an Illusion, The, 21, 22, 24, 248
Future of Religions, The, 39, 262*n*

Garaudy, R. 298
Germany, 25, 233, 266, 277; Catholics in, 73, 108; philosophical tradition of, 219, 228, 236, 239, 260; religious tradition of, 194, 232

Gilby, Thomas, 382
Gilkey, Langdon, 233, 234, 287, 291
Gillemann, Gerard, 314, 319*n*, 356, 370*n*
Gilson, Étienne, 79, 93, 350*n*
Glenmary Sisters, 452, 458–61, 473
Gnosis, 234, 259, 261*n*
Gnosticism, 83, 84, 90
God, 3, 167, 219, 232, 305, 315, 351*n*, 353*n*, 370*n*, 371*n*, 406; Aquinas' concept of, 336–39; awareness of, 264*n*, 286; belief in, 18, 62–63, 67, 236, 239, 313; as deus ex machina, 19, 61, 65, 67, 246, 247, 337; experience of, 19, 57, 239, 258, 312–13; hidden, 6, 36, 45, 60–61, 68, 290–91, 300, 304, 344, 369*n*, 411, 461; in Judaeo-Christian history, 5–6, 46, 56, 61, 66, 254, 255; love of, 58, 338, 369*n*, 408; nature of, 23–24, 57, 240, 283, 303–4, 314, 337, 341, 350*n*; need for, 73, 233, 267, 269; in philosophy, 23–24, 239, 258, 262*n*, 264*n*; service of, 201, 293, 442–43, 462; Tillich's definition of, 240–41; 243, 254, 264; transcendence of, 19–20, 221; see also "death of God" theology
Goffman, Erving, 465
Gospel, 6, 11, 143, 151, 224, 278, 284, 300, 329, 444, 458; in Anabaptism, 111, 194, 199, 202, 204; spirit of, 74–78, 208, 213*n*
Grace, 7, 53, 57–59, 67, 146, 198, 305, 324, 335, 343; justification by, 273
Grammar of Assent, 181, 309, 318*n*
Grennan, Jacqueline, 434, 467
Griffin, Sister Mary, 433, 439, 441
Guardini, Romano, 190
Gustafson, James M., 331, 366, 372*n*

Haecceitas, 52
Hamilton, Kenneth, 33, 48, 234–35, 261*n*, 270, 284, 286–89
Hamilton, William, 33, 48*n*, 261*n*, 270
Hampshire, Stuart, 311, 318*n*, 352*n*
Häring, Bernard, 314, 319*n*
Häring, E. S., 168
Hechinger, Fred M., 43, 44
Hegel, G. W. F., 2, 94, 404

Heidegger, Martin, 32, 80, 299
Herder Correspondence, 116, 133n
Hersch, John, 196, 211n
Heuristics, 166–67, 171, 175, 179–80, 185n
Hitler, Adolf, 2, 4, 65, 73, 235, 272, 276, 394, 419
Ho Chi Minh, 417
Hoenen, Peter, 344, 353n
Holy Spirit, The, 164, 189, 205–8, 210, 226–27, 295, 351n
Homosexuality, 375, 381
Honest To God, 19–20
Honesty, 73–74, 129, 132, 142–43, 243, 246, 254, 258, 281, 311–15, 319n, 360, 374, 379
Hook, Sidney, 40, 50n, 86, 88–89, 91, 181, 241, 263n, 318n; starting place, 81–82
Hope, 3–4, 13, 81, 231, 278, 284, 289, 410
Hopkins, Gerard Manly, 52
Horizon, 56–59, 87–88, 90–91, 359
Hughes, H. Stuart, 34, 115
Humani Generis, 226
Humanism, 12, 26, 29, 62, 67, 97, 121, 230, 247, 264n
Hume, David, 66, 92, 172, 174, 182, 186n, 239, 243
Humility, 73, 100, 111, 160, 202, 227–28, 428
Husserl, Edmund, 57, 80
Hutterite Studies, 197
Hyneman, Charles E., 22

Idealism, 91, 129, 223–24; German, 218, 236, 239
Identity, 11–12, 64, 109, 219, 354, 358, 419
Imitation of Christ, The, 439, 441
Immaculate Heart Sisters, 453, 473
Individual, the, 12, 28, 98, 136, 140, 367–68, 371n; conscience of, 143, 206, 365–66; faith of, 110, 355, 363
Individualism, 137–39, 141, 180, 186n, 201, 209, 222, 225, 230–31, 314, 324, 360
Infallibility, 116–17, 151–52, 160–62, 164
Inquiry, 83, 162, 182, 245, 249–50;

intelligent, 171–73, 175, 179, 188n, 448; process of, 90–92; scientific, 253
Insight, 56, 81, 89, 138, 246, 307, 309, 366, 368; Aristotle on, 172, 174, 176, 186n, 188n; Ryle on, 187n
Insight: A Study of Human Understanding, 83, 86–88, 92, 138, 170, 172–73, 181, 183–84n, 186n, 188n, 318
Insight and Responsibility, 332, 345n, 358, 371n
Intelligence, 7, 24, 41, 45, 58, 132, 231, 292, 302, 306, 312, 315–17, 334, 352n; Aristotle on, 171, 178, 180–82, 188n; and the community, 352n; critical, 81–83, 85–86, 91, 94, 359; and God, 352n, 353n; fidelity to, 254; two phases of, 307
Intelligibility, 38, 40, 180, 246, 312; of God, 258
Intentionality, 79–80, 161, 302–3, 306–7, 310–13, 317, 319n, 340, 352n
International Relations, 405–8, 411, 415
Intuition, 80-81, 92, 95n, 173, 181, 185n, 187n, 246
Irrational, the, 6, 138, 305–6, 348n

Jaeger, W., 332, 345n
Jaffa, H. V., 336, 350n
James, William, 327
Jesus Christ, 5–7, 19, 54, 58–59, 101, 107, 155, 166, 199–200, 206, 218, 224–25, 278. 355–56, 475; divinity of, 6, 287, 337; ethic of, 355; in Eucharist, 166–67; revelation of, 6–7, 192, 337; witness to, 474
Joachim of Flora, 295
John XXIII, Pope, 34, 42, 72, 74. 106, 109, 115, 220
Johnson Administration, 22, 419, 425, 427
Journal of Ecumenical Studies, 192, 301, 372n
Journal of Philosophy, 168, 183n
Journet, Msgr., 226
Jubilee, 401n
Judaeo-Christian faith, 42, 46, 61, 248, 259–60; and culture, 18, 39; and

nontheists, 62, 67–68; world view of, 28–30, 36–39, 67, 260; *see also* Christianity, Judaism
Judaism, 46, 61, 67, 115, 315, 317; and ecumenism, 42; need for reform, 7–8, 30, 33, 35–36; and secular culture, 18, 32, 38–39, 46, 62, 67–68; world view of, 24
Judgment, 56, 87, 100, 162, 253, 311, 325, 370–71*n*, 427; act of, 171–73, 177; critical, 179–81, 185*n*, 187*n*, 188*n*, 366, 470
Jung, C. G., 261*n*
Justification, 253, 313; ethical, 21, 24, 33, 40, 53, 181, 201; by faith, 149, 273

Kalon, 347*n*
Kant, Immanuel, 83, 90–94, 98, 171, 329
Kaufmann, Walter, 24, 53, 311
Kegley, Charles H., 261, 265*n*, 369*n*
Kelley, Sister Mary, 436
Kelly, Sister Suzanne, 450
Kelly, Gerald, 40*n*, 330, 383–84, 401*n*
Kennan, George, 229
Kennedy, John F., 22, 42, 229, 333; assassination of, 48, 65; style of life of, 32, 42, 51
Kent, Sister Corita, 453
Kierkegaard, Søren, 28, 32, 94, 236, 269
Kilday, Sister Winifred, 456–58
Kimball, Robert C., 235, 261*n*
Kingdom of God, 197, 201–2, 284, 295
Knowledge, 92, 173, 176, 181; pragmatic, 82; scientific, 88–91, 184*n*, 318*n*, sense, 170, 182, 185*n*26,41, of singulars, 350*n*
Knox, Ronald, 193
Küng, Hans, 6–7, 38, 50*n*

Landgraf, A., 335, 350*n*
Language, 110, 162–63, 165–66, 169–71, 239, 361; analysis, 32–33, 51, 91, 301; difficulties, 112–13, 122; about God, 246–47, 257, 299, 304–5; and intentionality, 302; of knowing, 246, official of Church, 107, ordinary, 81, 84, 93, 113; of philosophy, 131, 303, political, 299; rationalistic, 161; religious, 299,

302, 313; symbolic, 240; and logic, 305, 318*n*
Laski, Marghanita, 20
Law, 6, 100, 110, 339, 352*n*, 364, 366; definition of, 338; and ethics, 52; and freedom, 115, 269; of God, 353*n*; and order, 2, 405; public, 130
Lawler, Justus George, 37, 50*n*
Laymen, 43, 73, 76, 99, 104, 109–10, 117, 122–27, 134, 139–46, 202–3, 383, 389, 433, 451; Anabaptist, 199; and Bishops, 143, 145; intelligence of, 142, responsibility of, 147; synod of, 145; and Vatican, 210; women, 454, 469, 471
Lefever, Ernest W., 368, 372*n*
Lefevre, Jean, 451
Lehmann, Paul, 331, 366, 372*n*
Leisure, 47, 132
Leo XIII, Pope, 118, 211*n*, 329
Letters and Papers From Prison, 19, 48, 232, 268, 271, 282
Lewis, C. S., 359, 371*n*
Liberalism, 38, 40, 231, 247, 404
Lindbeck, George, 331
Lippmann, Walter, 367, 372*n*
Littell, Franklin H., 199, 204–6, 211*n*, 213*n*39, 40, 41
Liturgical Conference, National, 71
Liturgy, 14, 47, 70, 75–78, 100, 105, 139, 203, 221–23, 354, 393, 439, 441; reform of, 64, 74, 77, 124, 226–27, 445
Locke, John, 92, 182, 243, 262*n*
Logic, 90, 92, 95, 110, 130, 154, 169, 177, 320, 340, 402*n*
Logos, 6, 41, 83, 257, 331–32; *see also* Word and Gospel
Lombard, Peter, 335–37, 351*n*, 371*n*
Lonergan, Bernard, 79–95, 174, 219, 292, 317*n*, 318*n*, 350*n*, 353*n*, 371*n* 22,23,24; horizon in, 85, 87–88, 91; *Insight*, 83, 86–88, 92, 138, 173; on substance, 170, 172, 181, 183–84*n*, 186*n*, 188*n*
Loretto, Sisters of, 435, 452, 464, 473, 477
Lottin, Dom O., 331, 335–36, 341–42*n*, 345*n*, 350*n*55,59, 353*n*
Love, 7, 66, 159, 314, 351*n*, 358, 363, 370*n*10, 14, 371*n*20,21, 375, 391,

Love (*continued*)
393, 397, 462; defined, 357, goal of,
343, 363; as intentionality, 314;
marital, 393, 395
Loyalty, 100, 115, 117, 129
Luther, Martin, 191, 195–96, 199,
212n, 273, 329
Lutherans, 19, 189, 191, 195, 232,
295

MacIntyre, Alasdair, 20, 26, 35
McCarthy, Mary, 311, 377
McHugh, Father, 391
McKelway, Alexander J., 256, 265n
McNeill, John T., 198, 212n

Malcolm, Norman, 263n
Mansion, A., 338, 352n
Marcel, Gabriel, 406
Maréchal, Joseph, 79
Marhenke, P., 170 184n
Marillac House, 456–58
Maritain, Jacques, 79–81, 359, 364,
371n, 372n
Marriage, 365, 470; ends of, 383–87,
401n, 402n; love in, 393, 397; sexu-
ality in, 345, 382–91, 399–400
Marty, Martin E., 270, 344n
Martyrdom, 204, 206, 225; and Ana-
baptists, 194–96, 199–200
Marx, Karl, 414
Marxists, 6, 12, 195; and Christians,
294–96; and existentialism, 51, 296–
97; on the future, 298
Mascall, E. L., 19, 48n
Mass, 76, 137, 439, 441; *see also*
Liturgy and Eucharist
Mass media, 117, 136; *see also*, Press
Masturbation, 375–76, 379, 381, 389
Mauriac, François, 108
Mediator Dei, 221, 226
Mehta, Ved, 273, 279, 284n
Mennonites, 196, 198, 203
Metaphysics, 57, 83–93, 141, 238,
245–46, 286, 297
Methodists, 189, 191, 221
Metz, J. B., 298
Middle Ages, 23–24, 72, 79, 166–67,
183, 197, 211n, 278, 440, 445, 461
Middle-class, 8, 26, 46, 287, 406
Missionaries, 39, 107, 117, 194
Modernists, 110

Moerbeke, William, 335, 350n
Mohler, Johann, 115
Mollegen, A. T., 265
Monasteries, 191, 441, 455
Monasticism, 197–99, 201–2, 456
Montessori school, 470, 475
Moore, G. E. 262n
Morale Fondamentale, 331, 335–36,
345n, 350n, 353n
Morality, 326, 365, 367, 374–75, 403,
406, 410, 418, 423; code of, 70, 130,
328; of individual action, 355, 361,
410; and judgment, 95, 310, 404;
and theology, 116, 391
Muckenhirn, Sister Charles Borromeo,
442, 444, 449–50
Münzer, Thomas, 205, 213n
Murray, John Courtney, 372n
Mussolini, Benito, 226
Mystery, 31, 36, 46, 166, 283, 294
Mystici Corporis, 226
Myths, 8, 11, 65, 278, 293

National Catholic Reporter, 270,
404, 449, 465
National interests, 408–9, 419; *see
also*, United States
Nationalism, 29, 414
Natural law, 228, 325–28, 331, 336,
341–42, 344, 352n, 353n, 367,
384–86
Nature, 27, 53, 57, 177–79, 326, 352n,
392, 405; and grace, 337, 351n
Nazis, 24–25, 166, 222–23, 226, 269;
and Christianity, 282
Negroes, 32, 115, 289, 373, 432, 472–
73, 476
Neo-orthodoxy, 33, 215–17, 232, 267,
284, 288, 290
New Generation, A, 102
New Republic, The, 43
New Testament, 110, 206, 257, 356
"New Theology," 124, 127, 190, 448,
463
New York Times, The, 43, 100
Newman, John Henry, Cardinal, 181,
230, 318n, 329; on real and notional
assent, 100–1, 219
Nichomachean Ethics, 331–32, 335–
36, 345–46n, 348–49n, 352n, 371–
72n

Niebuhr, H. Richard, 198
Niebuhr, Reinhold, 20, 32, 216, 219–23, 226–31, 239, 263n, 268, 295, 319n, 331–32, 355–56, 359, 368, 369–70n, 372n, 410
Niebuhr, Richard R., 216–20, 288
Nietzsche, Friedrich, 32, 64, 234
Nihilism, 3, 4, 9, 23, 121, 243, 247
Nogar, Raymond, 37, 50n, 260, 265
Nonbelievers, 73–78, 109, 121, 142, 248, 315
Noonan, John T., 116, 329
Nostalgia, 114, 136–37, 289, 362
Nous, 329, 332, 336, 341
Novak, Michael, 37, 50n, 133, 199
Novitiate, 439, 442, 444
Nuns, 125–27, 434–35, 438, 443, 446, 455, 473–77; community life of, 431–32, 441, 445–52, 455, 459–60, 462–69, 472–73; contemplative, 462–63; dress of, 458, 461, 466, 474–76; and education, 448; and Free Churches, 191–92; renewal of, 436, 439–40; work of, 454–55, 462
Nygren, Anders, 370–71n

Obedience, 100, 122, 201, 223, 432, 441–42, 444–45, 447, 462, 465, 468, 471, 476; in Anabaptism, 200
Objectivity, 12, 40, 87, 89, 92, 95, 157, 181, 218, 251–53, 310–11, 314, 321
O'Meara, Thomas, 260, 262–63n
Omori, Minoru, 415
On the Boundary, 232, 236–37, 248, 255, 261
On the Church, 110, 226, 372n
On the Church and the Modern World, 111
On the Sacred Liturgy, 77
O'Neil, C. J., 344
Ontology, 32–33, 171, 177, 185n, 187n, 236, 240–41, 246, 251, 263
Open Church, The, 102, 119, 133, 214n
Orthodoxy, 64, 110, 223–24
Ottaviani, Alfredo, Cardinal, 372n
Owen, G. E. L., 338, 352n
Owens, J., 172, 185n

Pacem in Terris, 109

Pacifism, 195
Pain, 343, 366; see also Suffering
Pantheism, 240, 261n, 262n
Pantokrator, 6, 257
Papacy, 109, 116, 150, 164, 207; see also Pope
Parish, 99–100, 123, 126, 140
Parsons, Talcott, 35–36
Pascal, Blaise, 65, 258, 319n
Pastor, 100, 106, 109, 123–24, 147, 205, 210, 219
Paternalism, 98, 156, 159
Paterson, Gerald, 458
Pauck, Wilhelm, 29
Paul VI, Pope, 75, 100, 103, 106, 109, 301, 455
Paul, St., 218, 227
Peerman, Dean, 344n
Péguy, Charles, 159
Penet, Mary Emil, 447
People of God, 116, 192, 210, 218, 226, 363
Pepper, S. C., 170
Periodization, 135, 138
Personalism, 32
Phillips, J. B., 31, 49n
Philosophers, 82, 84, 95, 234, 237
Philosophical Review, 168, 183n, 372n
Philosophy, 79, 83, 90–91, 93, 115, 121, 130, 224, 242, 256, 465; critical, 93, 170, 224; existentialist, 257, 276; modern, 80, 109; rationalist, 93, western, 83, 296
Philosophy and Phenomenological Research, 168
Phronesis, 132, 230–31, 318n, 328–29, 332–33, 336, 341, 343
Physics, 332, 345n
Pieper, Josef, 312, 319n, 329, 331, 344n, 345n
Pietism, 197, 206, 222, 232, 447
Piety, 110, 204, 222, 225, 373, 448
Pius XI, 118
Pius XII, 221
Plato, 171, 188n, 329, 332, 336
Platonism, 28, 57, 172, 174, 182, 184n, 329, 342; and Christianity, 278–79
Pleasure, 343, 366, 388
Pluralism, 70, 111, 117, 122, 131, 195, 230, 289–90, 374; and the Christian Community, 34–35

Podhoretz, Norman, 18, 112
Politics, 22, 73, 84, 111, 127, 129–31, 143, 146, 293, 348n, 349n, 366–67, 465; and Anabaptists, 195; and the Church, 149, 222, 286, 373; and democracy, 131, 155; and ethics, 334; and power, 130, 268, 406; realistic, 411, 422–23, 426
Pope, 5, 71, 99, 109, 116–18, 151, 224; and birth control, 158; as servant, 150; teaching office of, 158, 162–63; see also Papacy
Positivism, 22, 223–24, 233, 238, 242, 255
"Post-religious age," 215
Postulancy, 439, 442, 444, 451, 458
Poverty, 2, 111, 124, 413, 424–25, 436, 443–44, 454, 458–60, 471, 476
Power, 8, 74, 129, 405, 408, 413, 416–17, 421; of Curia, 100; ecclesiastical, 126; moral, 411; political, 268; and responsibility, 413
Practical wisdom, 52, 338–43, 347n; definition of, 348n
Pragmatism, 5, 32, 44, 54–56, 58, 66, 68, 81–82, 91, 121, 131, 143, 172, 230, 233, 243, 247, 254, 260, 323, 465; method of, 327; naturalistic, 57, 238; and political action, 42; and society, 289; temper of, 287; traditional, 329
Prayer, 53, 163, 232, 283, 438–42, 455, 461–62; personal, 450; public, 127, 457; tradition of, 132
Presbyterians, 43, 207
Press, 100, 104, 112, 117, 122, 129, 143, 422
Priests, 5, 71–73, 76, 99, 113, 117–18, 127, 130, 140, 146, 382, 441, 444, 454, 464
Primacy of Charity in Moral Theology, The, 314, 319n, 356, 370n
Probabilities, 241, 299, 326–27
Procreation, 375, 377, 383, 387, 392
Prophecy, 6, 100, 125, 230, 257, 286, 314, 360, 366; as judgment, 250
"Protestant principle, The," 43, 236, 250
Protestantism, 20, 32, 51, 74, 109, 189–91, 197–98, 217, 220–22, 230, 317, 328, 354, 356, 360; and Catholicism, 160, 224, 328, 330; and the ecumenical movement, 42, 222

Prudence, 129, 132, 346n25,29, 348n, 394
Psychiatrists, 376, 388
Psychoanalysis, 236
Psychologists, 98, 378, 393
Psychotherapists, 276

Quakers, 198, 223
Question-asking, see Drive to ask questions
Quine, W. V., 170, 187n

Racial justice, 2, 8, 54, 72–73, 122, 128–29, 146, 427, 433, 472–74
Radical theology, 20, 53, 288–89, 291; see also Death of God
Rahner, Karl, 190, 295, 342, 353n
Ramsey, Paul, 365, 370n
Randall, John H. 262n16,17
Rationalism, 90, 93, 153, 160–61, 228, 290, 300, 305, 309, 334, 343, 394; classical, 57; German, 328
Rationality, 23, 176, 300; of God, 23–24
Rawls, John, 366, 372n
Realism, 54, 91, 132, 327, 360, 363, 424, 428; of John F. Kennedy, 42; of Niebuhr, 221, 230; in Vietnam, 411
Reality, 12, 169–71, 179, 182, 187n, 254, 328, 354, 358–59, 367–68, 371n, 379, 411; empirical, 249; and God, 241
Reason, 21, 83, 231, 319n, 328–29, 336, 343–44, 349, 353, 370n; classical, 343; and experience, 40; and laws, 353n; and sexuality, 383
Rebellion, 65, 98
Reconciliation, 48, 167
Reed, Bishop Victor, 475
Reflection, 90, 95, 185, 245, 309–10, 332, 366, 440, 448
Reform, 44, 118, 201, 297–98, 447, 449–50, 477; and renewal 34, 42, 74, 101, 109–10, 115, 119–20, 123–24, 190, 203, 209, 228, 450, 463, 465–66, 468, 471, 473–74
Reformation, 73, 191, 194–96, 200, 205, 208, 229, 295, 366
Relativism, 12, 138, 165, 188n, 333

Relevance, criteria of, 95, 245, 250, 359, 368
Religion, 25–26, 73, 106, 268, 276–77, 292–93, 365; as an academic discipline, 43; basis of, 219, 293, 304; an faith, 131, 312, 316; ignorance of, 46; influence of, 53
"Religionless Christianity," 19–20, 232, 277, 281
Religious liberty, 100–1, 109, 129, 154–55, 194–96, 198–99, 205, 210, 213n
Religious life, 201, 204, 314, 364, 366, 436, 438, 444, 451; experiments in, 473–77; see also Nuns, community life of
Renewal, see Reform
Rerum Novarum, 222
Resignation, 45, 65, 230
Responsibility, 61, 68, 77, 158, 296, 314, 363, 394–95; personal, 159, 275, 432, 467; social, 144, 274
Revelation, 5–7, 56, 59, 192, 220, 223, 305, 351n
Revolution, 38, 42, 61, 84, 195–96, 205, 252, 298, 410, 413–14, 417–19; in biblical studies, 124; moral, 429; Negro, 289; and religion, 167; of sisters, 433, 437, 455; social, 80, 232; of women's role in the Church, 455
Riesman, David, 357
Ritschl, Albrecht, 197–98
Robertson, D. B., 212
Robinson, John A. T., 19
Rome, 105, 108, 113–14, 444; during the Council, 100–5
Rommen, H., 332, 336, 345n, 350n
Ross, W. D., 175, 184n, 187n
Rousselot, P., 356, 370n
Rubenstein, Rabbi Richard L., 261
Rules, 444, 454, 456, 471
Russell, Bertrand, 24, 35, 40, 53, 88, 170
Ryle, Gilbert, 171, 187n
Rynne, Xavier, 119, 133n

Sacraments, 13, 53, 76, 130, 294
Sagan, Françoise, 378
Salvation, 110, 159, 162, 200, 203, 278
Sartre, Jean-Paul, 23, 25, 52, 70, 247, 272, 452

Sattler, Michael, 195, 199
Scharlemann, Robert B., 219
Schelling, F. W., 32, 236, 261
Schleiermacher, Friedrich, 32, 190, 215, 217–20, 288
Schlesinger, Arthur, 229
Scholasticism, 81, 93, 113, 128–32, 218, 230–31, 301, 329–30, 344n, 395
Schools, parochial, 123, 126–27, 129, 431, 435, 440, 445, 469, 472; public, 127
Schwenckfeld, Casper, 198, 205
Science, 3, 23, 25, 29–30, 40–41, 44, 61, 82, 113, 174–81, 185n, 186n, 242, 260, 293, 310, 326, 337, 366; and Aristotle, 166, 168, 170–73, 338; and God, 240, 242; method of, 40, 82, 129, 306, 309, 338; point of view of, 66, 121; questioning of, 68, 87; speculative, 339
Scripture, 5, 6, 206, 223, 226, 228, 356; and ethics, 323, 331; language of, 289; revival of, 225, 227; symbolic sense of, 259; and tradition, 110, and Vatican II, 109
Sects, 197–98, 213n, 221–23
"Secular Christianity," 19, 267, 278
Secular City, The, 33, 48n, 270, 288, 290–94, 297, 353n
Secular City Debate, The, 261, 265n, 270, 296–97
Secular saints, 66–67, 143, 267, 277
Secular world, the, 5, 8, 28, 34, 67–68, 106, 120–21, 131, 140–43, 150, 221, 224, 232, 247, 275, 289, 343, 451, 461, 470; Church in, 114; ethic of, 325–26; and faith, 62; philosophy in, 131; and the sacred, 337; standards of, 81; style of, 286, 325, 344; universities in, 73, 132, 429, 464
Secularism, 22, 122, 131–32, 146; Roman, 114
Secularization, 26, 32, 131, 145; of Christianity, 273
Self-knowledge, 66, 219, 358, 409
Sellars, Wilfred, 168, 183n1,4
Seminaries, 99, 103–4, 113, 271; Anabaptist, 209; manuals of, 116; theology of, 119
Sermon on the Mount, 197–98
Sermons, 70, 123, 129, 131

Sevareid, Eric, 9

Sexuality, 11, 22, 52, 156, 374, 378, 381, 392, 395, 397–98, 401; and conscience, 397; and intercourse, 148, 373–82, 384–85, 387–88, 399; and love, 156, 377, 379; in marriage, 154, 376, 383–92, 400; and personality, 385

Sidgwick, Henry, 335, 349n

Simon, Yves, 364, 372n

Sin, 138, 200, 202, 206, 211, 221, 226, 230, 284, 351n, 367, 382

Sister Formation Conference, 447–48, 450, 463

Sisters, see Nuns

Social action, 111, 129–30, 136, 143

Social Gospel, The, 222, 284–85

Social justice, 23, 252; Protestant concern for, 189; Jewish tradition of, 230; see also Racial justice

Socialism, 29, 118, 195

Socrates, 58, 66, 327

Spain, 79, 108, 194, 210, 227

Spellman, Cardinal, 115, 445

Spicq, Ceslaus, 369n

Spirituality, 224, 439; Anabaptist, 198; monastic, 199, 201

Standpoints, 12, 165–66

Starting place, 79, 81–82, 171, 179

Stendahl, Krister, 369n

Stoic, 331, 333, 346n

Structures of the Catholic Church, 127, 143–46

Sturm, Douglas, 328

Sturzo, Don, 226

"Subjectivism," 51, 218

Subjectivity, 41, 87, 90, 92, 162, 181, 194, 251–53

Substance, 112, 165–82, 186n

Suenens, Leo Cardinal, 104, 111, 210, 438

Suffering, 6, 45, 233; see also Pain

Suhard, Emmanuel Cardinal, 18

Susskind, David, 441, 467

Symbolism, 60, 68, 245, 444; ethical, 53; of intercourse, 378–79, 387, 395

Symbols, 8, 27, 30, 34, 41–42, 46, 55–56, 67–69, 80, 167, 243, 247, 259, 297, 368, 393, 403, 407–8; of Bible, 257; of community, 300; of Judaism, 46; "point to" God, 248; Tillich's, 246

Synods, 47, 146, 207

Systematic Theology, 236, 259, 262n, 263n

Tavard, George, 366, 372n, 410

Technology, 7, 24, 26, 28–29, 65, 120–21, 368, 420–23; and art, 232; and development, 415; and primitivism, 209

Television, 117, 136; see also Mass media

Theism, 3, 23, 61–69, 237, 243; and Judaism, 61; and nontheism, 247, 254; see also Belief and Faith

Theologians, 134, 143, 210, 219, 270; celibate, 394; conservatives and liberals, 257, 376–78

Theological Studies, 302–3, 317, 319n, 350n

Theology, 43, 115, 121, 123, 130, 149, 160, 163, 282, 284, 329; of the Church, 225; critical, 257, 286, 296; liberal, 215, 218, 290; logic of, 153; new, 124, 463; of optimism, 286; papal, 117; and philosophy, 93, 182, 236, 319n; Protestant, 328; radical, 20, 53, 288–91; of revolution, 292–93, 299; in seminaries, 119; task of, 218, 288

Theology and Culture, 32, 39, 49, 235, 261n

Thérèse of Lisieux, St., 229, 369n, 444

Thomas, St., see Aquinas

Thomism, 70, 79, 330, 370n; objectivity of, 12

Tillich, Paul, 22, 32, 39, 49, 190, 232, 237–38, 242–43, 261n, 263n, 264n, 282; and atheists, 241; and "being-itself," 245, 248–49; and Bonhoeffer, 20, 232; "boundary situations" in, 233, 248, 255, 276; on Catholic Thought, 240, 262n, 263$n33,42$; and empiricism, 253; epistemology of, 262n; on God, 237, 251, 262n; ground of being in, 241, 262–63; language of, 32, 252; and logical positivism, 262n; ontology of, 240, 242; pantheism of, 262n; vs. young theologians, 284

Tobin, Sister Mary Luke, 477

Traditions, 5–6, 31, 61, 84, 116, 136, 394; philosophical, 219, 301

Transalienation, 168; *see also* Eucharist
Transcendence, 19–20, 39–40, 221, 238, 242, 253, 256, 312, 319n
Transubstantiation, 165–68
Troeltsch, Ernst, 190, 196–97, 211, 213n

Ultimate concern, 84, 234, 237, 243–48, 251–54, 263–65n
Unbelief, 45, 68, 101, 146, 266; *see also* Nonbelievers
Underground, 124; intellectual, 114–15, 118; theologians, 119
Understand, drive to, *see* Drive to understand
Understanding, 58–59, 66, 83, 88–92, 161–62, 172, 251, 310, 366; acts of, 250; experience of, 311; and feelings, 325; fidelity to, 68, 162; flights from, 91; of God, 67; logic of, 153
United States, 8, 13, 17, 24, 27, 408; "American way of life, the," 254, 407; Bible Belt in, 191, 284–85; capitalism in, 222; Catholicism in (*see* Catholic Church); conservatives and liberals in, 403; culture in, 32–33, 64, 240; generation gap in, 8–11; national interest of, 409–11; poverty in, 412; religion in, 7, 17–18, 202–8, 203–8, 239, 282; and Vietnam, 404, 411–12, 422–26; violence in, 2, 4, 65
Unity, 138, 148, 150; *see also* Ecumenism
Updike, John, 20, 27–28, 64
Urban society, 122, 287, 294, 374, 436; degradation in, 424; poor in, 472, 474, 477; renewal of, 131
Utopianism, 26, 223

Vahanian, Gabriel, 33, 49n
Van Buren, Paul, 33, 270
Vatican Council, First, 106, 164
Vatican Council, Second, 24, 72, 99, 110–11, 211, 220, 226, 330, 372n-28,39, 432, 436, 444–45, 448, 452, 466, 468–71; and Eastern churches, 109; and educated Americans, 74; and Free Churches, 193; and liturgical reforms, 71; main concern of, 106; pastoral task of, 106; reform, 101, and religious liberty, 210; and secular press, 43; and sisters, 445
Viet Cong, 419–21
Vietnam, 4, 229, 410–13, 418–23, 427; escalation of war in, 416; moral issue of, 412; premise of war in, 424; religious aspect of, 22; U.S. intervention in, 404, 411–12, 422–26
Violence, 1, 2, 4, 24, 65, 72, 81, 120, 233, 323, 403–7, 417, 419, 421
Virginity, 380, 390–95, 432, 455
Vogel, C. J., 335, 349n
Vows, 438–39, 444, 447, 474

Walsh, J. J. 344, 349n
Walsh, Vincent M., 392
War, 131, 423; *see also* Violence, Vietnam
Waugh, Evelyn, 193
Weigel, Gustave, 104, 261, 263n
White, Morton V., 95, 96n, 170, 181, 318n
Whitehead, Alfred North, 23–24, 53, 174
Williams, D. C., 168, 183n
Williams, George H., 194, 196, 211n
Wilson, N. L., 68, 183n
Wisdom, 84, 132, 307, 324; and experience, 333; of God, 353n, 370n, 371n; political, 367; practical, 333, 340, 343, 347, 352n; and prudence, 347n; of Tillich, 234
Wisdom, John, 305, 318n
Wittgenstein, Ludwig, 94, 241, 263n, 304
Word of God, 5–6, 75–77, 200, 207, 219–20, 366; *see also* Gospel
World Council of Churches, 222
World religions, 6, 50n, 236, 260, 301–2
World view, 11, 23, 31, 36, 53; Judaeo-Christian, 44, 66; scientific, 66
World War II, 18, 414, 424, 437, 445–46, 461
Worship, 53, 283; *see also* Liturgy

Youth, 10, 111, 123, 130, 137, 332, 345n

Date Due

JUN 18 '71			
NOV 24 '71			
DEC 7 '71			
JAN 11 '71			